The Federal Reserve

The
Federal
Reserve

A NEW HISTORY

Robert L. Hetzel

THE UNIVERSITY OF CHICAGO PRESS
CHICAGO AND LONDON

The University of Chicago Press, Chicago 60637
The University of Chicago Press, Ltd., London
© 2022 by The University of Chicago
Published 2022
Printed in the United States of America

31 30 29 28 27 26 25 24 23 22   1 2 3 4 5

ISBN-13: 978-0-226-82165-8 (cloth)
ISBN-13: 978-0-226-82166-5 (e-book)
DOI: https://doi.org/10.7208/chicago/9780226821665.001.0001

Library of Congress Cataloging-in-Publication Data
Names: Hetzel, Robert L., author.
Title: The Federal Reserve : a new history / Robert L. Hetzel.
Description: Chicago : University of Chicago Press, 2022. | Includes
bibliographical references and index.
Identifiers: LCCN 2022006676 | ISBN 9780226821658 (cloth) |
ISBN 9780226821665 (ebook)
Subjects: LCSH: United States. Federal Reserve Board—History. |
Board of Governors of the Federal Reserve System (U.S.)—
History. | Monetary policy—United States—History—20th century. |
United States—Economic policy—20th century.
Classification: LCC HG2563 .H48 2022 | DDC 332.1/10973—dc23/
eng/20220304
LC record available at https://lccn.loc.gov/2022006676

♾ This paper meets the requirements of ANSI/NISO Z39.48-1992
(Permanence of Paper).

Marvin Goodfriend was an intellectual soulmate who
talked me through the ideas in the book until close to his death
in December 2019. His thirst for ideas was unquenchable, and his
contributions to an understanding of central banks are enduring.

Contents

Figures and Tables

TABLES

CHAPTER 1

In Search of the Monetary Standard

Summary: Central banks create the monetary standard. Standard Federal Reserve System (Fed) rhetoric is that the Federal Open Market Committee (FOMC) pursues the dual mandate legislated by Congress. Over some appropriately long time horizon, the FOMC assures the public that it conducts policy in a way that achieves "maximum employment" and "price stability." But how? In a market economy, there is no central planning. There are no wartime price controls that dictate how firms set prices. There is no wartime rationing to control the spending of households. The financial system is free to allocate credit. What then is the monetary standard?

As a central bank, the Fed has the unique responsibility to give money a well-defined value, that is, to determine the behavior of the price level. A perennial empirical regularity is the joint occurrence of monetary (price level) instability and real instability (cyclical fluctuations in output and employment). What accounts for fluctuations in the value of money over long periods of time, and what accounts for the joint interaction of the value of money with the cyclical fluctuations in the real economy?

An answer not only to the question "What is the monetary standard" but also to the question "What is the optimal monetary standard" requires a model. The model will explain how the behavior of the Fed in setting its instrument interacts with the price system to influence the behavior of households and firms. That model should bring coherence to the monetary history of the United States. It should do so by organizing a summary of the evolution of the monetary standard and by informing when the standard has stabilized the economy and when it has destabilized the economy.

Knut Wicksell (1935 [1978], 3) said a hundred years ago in his *Lectures on Political Economy*:[1]

---

1. Wicksell first published his lectures in 1906. The reference here is to a 1935 translation.

With regard to money, everything is determined by human beings themselves, i.e. the statesmen, and (so far as they are consulted) the economists; the choice of a measure of value, of a monetary system, of currency and credit legislation—all are in the hands of society.

Wicksell followed up by noting:

The establishment of a greater, and if possible absolute, stability in the
value of money has thus become one of the most important practical objectives of political economy. But, unfortunately, little progress towards
the solution of this problem has, so far, been made.

The Federal Reserve System operates under a "dual mandate" from
Congress to provide for stability in prices and in employment. Because the
mandate is so general, it provides no guidance as to the actual monetary
standard that policy makers (Wicksell's "statesmen") have "determined."
Without explicit articulation by Fed policy makers and without thorough
debate and examination by academic economists, the monetary standard
will always be fragile and subject to political pressures. The accident of per-
sonality of who becomes a policy maker can cause the monetary standard
to become destabilizing.

Wicksell (1935 [1978], 4) also wrote: "Monetary history reveals the fact
that that folly has frequently been paramount; for it describes many fateful
mistakes. On the other hand, it would be too much to say that mankind
has learned nothing from these mistakes." How does one know what the
Fed has learned? Learning requires admission that policy makers can make
"fateful mistakes." What model captures those mistakes and the lessons
learned?

Economists have long asked the Fed for a model and for a characterization of the consistency in its behavior (a rule). James Tobin (1977 [1980],
41) wrote:

There is really no substitute for making policy backwards, from the desired feasible paths of the objective variables that really matter to the
mixture of policy instruments that can bring them about. . . . The procedure requires a model—there is no getting away from that. Models are
highly imperfect, but they are indispensable. The model used for policy-
making need not be any of the well-known forecasting models. It should
represent the policymakers' beliefs about the way the world works, and
it should be explicit. Any policymaker or advisor who thinks he is not
using a model is kidding both himself and us. He would be well advised

to make explicit both his objectives for the economy and the model that expresses his view of the links of the economic variables of ultimate social concern to his policy instruments.

The most famous proponent of an explicit rule was Milton Friedman (1988), who wrote:

> Every now and then a reporter asks my opinion about "current monetary policy." My standard reply has become that I would be glad to answer if he would first tell me what "current monetary policy" is. I know, or can find out, what monetary actions have been: open-market purchases and sales and discount rates at Federal Reserve Banks. I know also the federal funds rate and rates of growth of various monetary aggregates that have accompanied these actions. What I do not know is the policy that produced these actions. . . . The closest I can come to an official specification of current monetary policy is that it is to take those actions that the monetary authorities, in light of all evidence available, judge will best promote price stability and full employment—i.e., to do the right thing at the right time. But that surely is not a "policy." It is simply an expression of good intentions and an injunction to "trust us."

A characterization of the monetary standard requires a structural model of the economy and a rule that summarizes the behavior of the Fed, that is, a summary of how the Fed responds to incoming information on the economy given its objectives. In modern monetary models, households and firms ("agents") base their behavior on how the Fed's rule determines the monetary standard ("the stochastic environment agents believe themselves to be operating in"): Robert Lucas (1980 [1981], 255) wrote,

> Our ability as economists to predict the responses of agents rests, in situations where expectations about the future matter, on our understanding of the stochastic environment agents believe themselves to be operating in. In practice, this limits the class of policies the consequences of which we can hope to assess in advance to policies generated by fixed, well understood, relatively permanent rules (or functions relating policy actions taken to the state of the economy). . . . Analysis of policy which utilizes economics in a scientific way necessarily involves choice among alternative stable, predictable policy rules, infrequently changed and then only after extensive professional and general discussion, minimizing (though, of course, never entirely eliminating) the role of discretionary economic management.

Lucas (1980 [1981], 255) also noted, "I have been impressed with how non-controversial it [the above argument for rules] seems to be at a general level and with how widely ignored it continues to be at what some view as a 'practical' level."

An answer to the pleas of these economists for articulation by the Fed of the consistency in its behavior (the rule it follows) and of the structure of the economy that constrains its behavior requires a model that elucidates the nature of the monetary standard. Discovering the nature of the monetary standard, how it has evolved over time, and what constitutes the optimal monetary standard is an exercise in "identification." The reason is that the Fed functions as part of the macroeconomy in which all variables are correlated. "Identification" of the monetary standard requires a model that allows separation of how the Fed influences the behavior of the economy and how the behavior of the economy influences the Fed. That is, it requires separation of causation from correlation.

The strategy pursued here is to use historical narrative based on contemporaneous documentary evidence and the state of knowledge among policy makers and economists to understand how the Fed has responded to the state of the economy. How has monetary policy in the sense of the consistency in its response to the behavior of the economy (its rule or reaction function) evolved over time? This evolution comprises the semicontrolled experiments that provide evidence on the optimal monetary standard. A conclusion is that absent monetary disorder produced by money creation that causes the price level to evolve unpredictably the price system works well to maintain macroeconomic stability.

The hypothesis tested here is that the monetary standard provides for macroeconomic stability if the Fed follows a rule that provides for a stable nominal anchor (price stability) and that allows the price system an unfettered ability to determine real variables like output and employment. Failure to follow the rule creates the correlation in the data between monetary and real disorder. This rule emerges from the Goodfriend and King (1997) basic version of the New Keynesian model in which a policy of price stability is optimal. With price stability, the central bank turns over to the price system (the real business cycle core of the economy) the unfettered determination of real variables like output and employment.

CHAPTER 2

The Organization of the Book

There is a need for another Fed history to work out a methodology for identifying causation in the correlation between nominal and real instability. In
attributing the business cycle to instability in money, Milton Friedman and
Anna Schwartz focused on the procyclicality of money and on the observation that peaks in money growth preceded peaks in the business cycle. A
methodology relevant for the period after 1980 when real money demand
became interest sensitive and unstable needs to work for the entire history
of the Fed. The book focuses on the way that the Fed maintained short-
term interest rates at cyclically high levels well past cyclical peaks. For the
pre-1981 period, this attribution of real instability to monetary causes also
accords with the Friedman-Schwartz identification in terms of the behavior
of money.

**Chapter 3, "What Causes the Monetary Disorder That Produces Real
Disorder?"** FOMC procedures are stabilizing when they cause the funds
rate to track the natural rate of interest and destabilizing when they do
not. This chapter provides an empirical generalization for recessions that
flags destabilizing procedures: the monetary contraction marker. In the
period before 1981 when real money demand was stable, the monetary
contraction marker highlights the behavior of the FOMC that accounts
for the Friedman-Schwartz generalization that monetary decelerations
precede business cycle peaks. Afterward, it replaces observed monetary
decelerations. Briefly, the monetary contraction marker captures behavior in which the FOMC prevents a decline in the funds rate when economic weakness develops so that the real rate of interest remains high
well past cyclical peaks. In the stop-go era this situation evolved when
the FOMC allowed inflation to develop during economic recoveries out
of a reluctance to raise interest rates and "abort the recovery."

Chapter 4, "The Creation of the Fed." Prior to the creation of the Fed, the
United States was on the gold standard. Under that standard, market

forces determined the interest rate, money, and the price level. All that changed with the creation of the Fed. Because the Fed did not follow gold standard rules, the monetary standard changed to one of fiat money creation. The great disasters of the pre–World War II period followed from the failure to understand the change in the monetary standard and the new responsibilities entailed in the control of money and prices.

Nothing in the background of policy makers prepared them to understand the kind of monetary regime they had created. Just as important, the economics profession lacked the body of knowledge required to understand monetary policy. The systematic development of monetary economics within the discipline of macroeconomics was a post–World War II phenomenon. There were pre–World War II quantity theorists, but they lacked a comprehensive theory capable of explaining both the operation of the pre–World War I gold standard and a fiat money regime.

Chapter 5, "Why the Fed Failed in the Depression: The 1920s Antecedents." The founders of the Fed wanted to end financial panics, which cut off borrowers in the interior of the country from credit. To that end, they designed the Federal Reserve based on real bills principles.[1] A core principle of real bills was that the collapse of episodes of speculative excess caused recession and deflation. In the 1920s, the original intention proved illusory, namely, that the regional Reserve Banks would prevent speculative excess by allocating credit to legitimate uses only. They would do so by lending only on real bills (short-term commercial paper). In response, the New York Fed developed a policy of economic stabilization based on the control of credit. However, because the guiding principle remained the need to squelch incipient signs of speculative excess, the Fed became an engine of economic disaster.

Chapter 6, "A Fiat Money Standard: Free Reserves Operating Procedures and Gold." Real bills operating procedures meant that collectively member banks always had to obtain significant amounts of reserves through discounting eligible paper at the discount window. As a result, the level at which the regional Reserve Banks set the discount rate plus the nonpecuniary costs to borrowing from the window determined the marginal cost of bank reserves. In turn, through arbitrage, the marginal cost of reserves (today's analogue of the funds rate) determined the interest rate in the money market. The interaction of the money market interest rate with the price system (the natural rate of interest) determined money

---

1. Lloyd Mints (1945) first used the term "real bills doctrine." Before Mints, the term used was "the commercial loan theory."

creation and in the Great Contraction (1929 to 1933), with the real rate of interest held above the natural rate of interest, money destruction.[2]

No one understood the consequences of these procedures, later, in the 1950s, called "free reserves" procedures, where the term refers to the difference between excess reserves and borrowed reserves. In part the ignorance derived from the lack of concepts developed only later as part of macroeconomics. In part, policy makers associated the idea of the Fed as a central bank controlling fiat money creation with populist movements and the advocacy of a government-run printing press.

Chapter 7, "A Narrative Account of the 1920s." As soon as the Fed gained its independence following World War I and following the Treasury's last Victory Drive to issue bonds, it set off the major recession of 1920–21, a recession that could have become the Great Depression. However, during the following years, gold inflows and a concern by the New York Fed for reestablishment of the international gold standard kept monetary policy from becoming contractionary. Nevertheless, given the real bills views of policy makers, the prosperity of the 1920s made it inevitable that the Fed would again set off a major recession through contractionary monetary policy. That happened when the Fed began in 1928 to force a contraction of the banking system to limit the "excess" credit creation it believed had spilled over into speculation in the stock market.

Chapter 8, "Attacking Speculative Mania." In the 1920s, the idea emerged of a central bank charged with the task of macroeconomic stabilization. However, its intellectual underpinnings were those of real bills. Maintenance of stability presumably required the suppression of the speculative excess that furnished the precondition for recession and deflation. In response to the dramatic rise in the stock market starting in 1927, the Fed raised the cost of reserves to banks through open market sales and increases in the discount rate.

Commercial banks in the interior had adjusted their reserve positions through the call loan market in New York using deposits at their correspondent banks. They also used the discount window. The Fed shut down the first and significantly limited the second through the policy of "direct pressure." High discount rates and the stigma attached to discount window borrowing as evidence of weakness caused banks to try to restore their liquidity through building up excess reserves. The banking system could do so only through contraction of loans and deposits.

---

2. "The Great Contraction" refers to the period from August 1929 to March 1933. "The Great Depression" refers to the period from August 1929 until the end of the decade of the 1930s.

Throughout the entire Great Contraction (August 1929 to March 1933), monetary policy remained contractionary because of the incessant pressure on the banking system to contract.

Chapter 9, "The Great Contraction: 1929–33." In 1930, the Fed failed to follow through on the open market purchases and reductions in the discount rate following the 1929 stock market crash for fear of reviving the speculation whose collapse presumably led to the recession. The combination of a stock market collapse followed by a profound depression only perpetuated the quicksand foundation for Fed policy that associated speculative excess with an inevitable collapse followed by the liquidation of firms and deflation. Because of the stigma associated with borrowing from the discount window, the banking system adjusted to the bank runs that began toward the end of 1930 and continued into 1931 by contracting rather than by borrowing.

In fall 1931, in response to the gold outflows that followed Britain's abandonment of the gold standard, the Fed raised discount rates to restore the confidence of the business community in maintenance of the gold standard. In 1932, the association of deflation and the contraction of bank credit caused the New York Fed to coordinate open market purchases by the regional Fed banks. However, the Fed abandoned the program when the regional Reserve Banks backed out after seeing the reserves created flow to New York. In early 1933, a cascade of statewide closure of banks created a nationwide closure of the banking system.

Chapter 10, "The Roosevelt Era." With the Bank Holiday of March 1933, the bank panics ceased. As banks accumulated excess reserves, they no longer had to borrow from the discount window. With the resulting end of the free reserves operating procedures, Fed control over interest rates ended. The monetary standard changed to one in which the Fed controlled the reserves of the banking system through its open market purchases first of securities and then of gold and with the marketplace setting the interest rate. After the United States devalued the dollar and pegged the price of gold on January 31, 1934, the country ran a commodity stabilization scheme for gold financed by the monetization of the purchases by the Fed.

Government policies and the Fed's attempt to return to free reserves procedures, which gave the Fed control over bank borrowed reserves and presumably control over the speculative extension of credit, ended the recovery. There were two major supply shocks, one in summer 1933 with the National Industrial Recovery Act and one in 1935 with the Wagner Act, which produced an exogenous rise in wages. In 1936 and 1937, to

eliminate excess reserves, the Board of Governors raised reserve requirements and induced a sharp contraction in growth of the money stock.

Chapter 11, "The Guiding Role of Governor Harrison and the NY Fed."
George Leslie Harrison was governor, then president, of the Federal Reserve Bank of New York from November 1928 to December 1940. During
the Great Contraction, like his predecessor, Benjamin Strong, he dominated the conduct of monetary policy. Because Harrison worked behind
the scenes, that fact is obscured. The record he kept allows an understanding of the views of early policy makers. It was a world of real bills,
a gold standard mentality, and fear of the populist movements to create
paper money.

Chapter 12, "Contemporary Critics in the Depression." A summary of the
views of leading economists in the Depression makes clear that many
ideas assumed self-evident today did not exist then. No one had the concept of a banking system with nominal liabilities resting on a reserves
base maintained through the bookkeeping operations of the central
bank. No one understood the Fed as a central bank with the power to
create fiat money, that is, as a "creator of money." The populist reform
movements wanted the Fed to issue paper money by monetizing government debt, but that was not the same as an understanding that the Fed
already created money through a bookkeeping operation when it lent
through the discount window or purchased government securities. The
gold backing for note issue, the high level of the gold reserve ratio, and
the convertibility of note issue into gold obscured the reality of a fiat
money standard.

Chapter 13, "From World War II to the 1953 Recession." After World War
II, the Treasury continued its dominance over the Fed by requiring it
to maintain a ceiling on the interest paid on long-term bonds. Treasury
dominance ended with the 1951 Treasury-Fed Accord when the Fed
refused to monetize the bonds being unloaded by banks. That experience ended real bills views. Inflation arose not from speculative excess
but rather from the failure of the Fed to control the reserves creation of
banks. The two recessions with cycle peaks in November 1948 and in July
1953 originated in the way in which expectations of the behavior of the
price level formed in the gold standard era interacted with the nominal
interest rate to determine the real interest rate. Namely, the expectation
that a fall in the price level would follow a rise raised the real interest rate
and made monetary policy contractionary.

**Chapter 14, "LAW (Lean-against-the-Wind) and Long and Variable
Lags."** When the Fed regained its independence with the March 1951

Treasury-Fed Accord, it had to reinvent monetary policy. FOMC chairman William McChesney Martin did so with "lean-against-the-wind" (LAW) procedures, which possessed the modern characteristic of a re-action function. However, the Fed stumbled over how to both stabilize the real economy and maintain price stability. Milton Friedman's "long and variable lags" critique highlighted the issues. This chapter provides a framework for thinking about post-Accord monetary policy as a choice between alternative LAW strategies, termed "LAW with credibility" and "LAW with trade-offs."

Chapter 15, "The Early Martin Fed." William McChesney Martin created the modern central bank. With procedures he termed "lean-against-the-wind" (LAW), the FOMC began to move short-term interest rates procyclically (to counter strength or weakness in the economy associated with sustained changes in the rate of resource utilization) with the goal of controlling the quantity of bank credit rather than its allocation to presumed productive uses. "Bills only" confined open market operations to Treasury bills to encourage the "depth, breadth, and resilience" of the government bond market. The market determined bond yields, which could then offer evidence of inflationary expectations. With LAW, concern for inflationary expectations replaced the real bills concern for speculative excess.

Chapter 16, "From Price Stability to Inflation." In the Johnson administration, Martin found himself isolated. In an environment of guns and butter due to the Vietnam War and Great Society programs, the political system demanded that the economy grow flat out. In an environment of urban riots, it demanded a low unemployment rate with 4 percent a provisional target. Keynesian aggregate-demand management promised all this. With an increasingly Keynesian Board and staff, if Martin had challenged the political system, he would have done so with his own house divided. He entered a bargain with the administration and the Congress: pass an income tax increase to eliminate the government deficit, and the Fed would hold off on interest-rate increases. If Martin could not control the fires of inflation with higher rates, he would turn down the fire by limiting credit creation. The bargain was a Faustian one, and Martin lost.

Chapter 17, "The Burns Fed." Arthur Burns epitomized the "measurement without theory" tradition of the National Bureau of Economic Research (NBER). He understood monetary policy through the eyes of businessmen, whose psychology, he believed, drove the business cycle. Burns also believed that the country needed him to reconcile the low unemployment required for social stability with the low inflation required for business confidence and investment. For Burns, inflationary expectations were crucial. However, they were the expectations of the business-man, and the businessman was concerned about wage inflation. Burns believed that the country could lower inflation and stimulate economic activity by assuaging these expectations through use of incomes policies and evidence of fiscal discipline in the form of a budget surplus. In prac-tice, Burns traded monetary policy for influence over incomes and fiscal policy.

Chapter 18, "Stop-Go and the Collapse of a Stable Nominal Anchor." In the 1970s, the social, political, and economic consensus held that infla-tion was driven by powerful cost-push shocks. To limit inflation through monetary policy, it followed that the Fed would have had to create sig-nificant (and socially unacceptable) unemployment. Cost-push infla-tion, as opposed to aggregate-demand inflation, required intervention in the particular markets that created it. G. William Miller, who succeeded Burns as FOMC chairman, was unprepared for the need to raise interest rates dramatically to prevent a rise in expected inflation from depress-ing the real interest rate. By summer 1979, the country had lost a stable nominal anchor. Expected inflation rose in line with actual inflation.

Chapter 19, "The Volcker Fed and Birth of a New Monetary Standard." In the 1960s while at the Treasury, Paul Volcker had been the manda-rin of the Bretton Woods system. He believed that a stable dollar was a bulwark of the free world against communism. For Volcker, a strong dollar was a moral imperative and a patriotic duty. As a product of the Open Market Desk of the New York Fed, he understood the crucial role of expectations. Volcker also understood that the Fed was the only alter-native for confronting inflationary expectations. Volcker's acceptance of responsibility for inflationary expectations rendered irrelevant the end-less discussions about the causes of inflation as cost-push or demand-pull and about tailoring the remedy accordingly. Whatever the cause of those inflationary expectations, the Fed had to get them under control, or they would pass quickly into negotiated wage settlements and lock in high inflation.

Chapter 20, "The Greenspan FOMC." The effort by the Volcker-Green-span FOMC to reestablish the nominal expectational stability lost dur-ing the prior stop-go period finally succeeded in 1995. With the sharp in-creases in the funds rate in 1994 and early 1995, the Fed at last succeeded in allaying the fears of the bond market vigilantes, who had pushed up bond rates in response to above-trend real growth and inflation shocks. Expected inflation ceased being a function of above-trend real growth and of actual inflation.

Chapter 21, "The Great Recession." The Great Recession followed the general pattern of recessions. During economic recoveries, the FOMC raises the funds rate in a measured but persistent fashion until the economy weakens. If at that point the FOMC is concerned about inflation, it limits reductions in the funds rate. Short-term real interest rates remain at cyclical highs. The FOMC allows a negative output gap to develop to lower inflation. The difference in the Great Recession was that high headline inflation emerged from a worldwide commodity price inflation shock rather than prior unduly expansionary monetary policy.

Chapter 22, "The 2008 Financial Crisis." Through decades of a policy of too-indebted-to-fail, regulators created a financial safety net that made moral hazard the foundation of a shadow banking system (financial institutions with the characteristics of banks but not regulated as banks). Various money funds relied on the willingness of short-term cash investors to fund portfolios of hard-to-value, illiquid, long-term assets like mortgage-backed securities. The cash investors assumed that any significant financial institution would be protected. With the Lehman bankruptcy in September 2008, the apparent retraction of the financial safety net caused the cash investors to jump to the safe side of the financial safety net: the too-big-to-fail banks and government money funds. Regulators spent the rest of the year trying to undo their flight.

Chapter 23, "The Eurozone Crisis." Both the European Central Bank (ECB) and the Fed followed the same monetary policy intended to prevent the high headline inflation caused by the world commodity price inflation from raising inflationary expectations and thus passing permanently into a higher inflation rate. Like the United States, given the public expectation of price stability, the resulting contractionary monetary policy initiated by an inflation shock caused a sharp fall in output.

Chapter 24, "Recovery from the Great Recession." The recovery from the Great Recession was a period of significant stability of prices and output. That stability demonstrated that the Fed is not "out of ammunition" at the zero lower bound for interest rates. Quantitative easing (QE) works. The public's expectation of inflation did not become unanchored to the downside but remained anchored at near price stability. The FOMC was wrong to conclude that the preemptive increases in the funds rate that began in December 2015 limited reductions in unemployment. The resulting long period of price stability allowed labor markets to work to lower unemployment.

Chapter 25, "Covid-19 and the Fed's Credit Policy." Traditionally, central banks have separated monetary policy from financial intermediation, which is credit policy. Credit policy is fiscal policy in that it allocates credit in a way that supersedes the market allocation. In the Covid-19 crisis, however, the Fed took private credit risk onto its own balance sheet. The Fed should avoid credit programs, which allocate credit, and concentrate on its traditional monetary policy responsibilities.

Chapter 26, "Covid-19 and the Fed's Monetary Policy: Flexible-Average-Inflation Targeting." With a revision to the FOMC's Statement on Longer-Run Goals and Monetary Policy Strategy termed "flexible-average-inflation targeting" (FAIT), the FOMC made the trade-offs of the Phillips curve the center of monetary policy. The new strategy was to pursue an expansionary monetary policy to cause the economy to grow rapidly to restore the low prepandemic unemployment rate. The FOMC believed that there would be no conflict with the objective of price stability because of the existence of a flat Phillips curve. That is, the unemployment rate could decline to a level consistent with a new inclusive definition of maximum employment. A revival of inflation would flag the lowest unemployment rate consistent with price stability. Moreover, with the new strategy, a persistent overshoot in inflation was considered desirable to offset earlier undershoots.

Chapter 27, "How Can the Fed Control Inflation?" In 2020, the monetary aggregate M2 rose by 25 percent. Experience, most recently the inflation of the 1970s, associates high rates of money growth with high inflation. The bulge in money represented an accumulation of liquid assets ready to be spent on services when they again become available with the end of the pandemic. That purchasing power will be unwound through inflation if the Fed does not raise interest rates preemptively and sell debt to undo the bookkeeping operations of the banks that created the bulge in money.

Chapter 28, "Making the Monetary Standard Explicit." The goal in this chapter is to formulate a rule based on the consistent behavior of the FOMC in the Volcker-Greenspan era, known as the Great Moderation. The formulation of policy by the FOMC rests on forecasts of the behavior of the economy. A rule should discipline this forecasting effort so that the FOMC communicates a consensus forecast to financial markets consistent with maintenance of price stability and output growing at potential. The spirit of the general rule is that it should guarantee a stable nominal anchor and allow the price system an unfettered ability to determine real variables. Such a rule precludes any attempt to trade off unemployment and inflation objectives as embodied in Phillips curves.

Chapter 29, "What Is the Optimal Monetary Standard?" The optimal rule derives from a concept of the optimal monetary standard. The exposition here assumes the desirability of the goal of rules in the tradition of the quantity theory to isolate the real economy from monetary instability through a monetary policy of price stability. In the Goodfriend and King (1997) version of the New Keynesian model, a policy of price stability is optimal. The exposition relates a policy of price stability to the procedures pioneered by William McChesney Martin termed here "lean against the wind with credibility." With these procedures, the FOMC moves the funds rate preemptively to maintain price stability by preventing the emergence of inflation.

Chapter 30, "Why Is Learning So Hard?" Despite the accumulation of episodes of monetary instability (real and nominal) over time, there is little consensus over the optimal monetary standard and the associated rule the central bank should follow. What is required is identification of these episodes combined with information specific to those episodes relevant to the direction of causation between real and nominal instability. The economist must then generalize over all these episodes. This book attempts that task.

CHAPTER 3

What Causes the Monetary Disorder
That Produces Real Disorder?

Summary: Monetary policy is stabilizing when it employs a rule that causes the funds rate to track the natural rate of interest. In the post-Accord 1951 era, monetary policy developed the principle of a reaction function in which the FOMC moves the funds rate in a systematic way in response to the behavior of the economy. Properly implemented, monetary policy could stabilize rather than destabilize the economy.

Milton Friedman and Anna Schwartz (1963a) documented the empirical generalizations that large, sustained increases in money preceded and accompanied inflation and that monetary decelerations preceded cyclical peaks in the business cycle. The use of money to summarize the behavior of monetary policy lapsed after 1980 when deregulation made real money demand interest sensitive, and money ceased being a useful predictor of nominal expenditure. There is then a need for an empirical generalization that can explain the behavior of money before 1981 and that can also replace money after 1981 as an indicator of when monetary policy is stabilizing or destabilizing.

In the period before the Treasury-Fed Accord, monetary policy was rarely stabilizing. For the subsequent period, there exist alternating periods of stability and instability. One can use this alternation to generalize about the optimal monetary rule. The identification of such a rule must start with the lean-against-the-wind (LAW) procedures developed under the FOMC chairmanship of William McChesney Martin. With LAW, the FOMC raises the funds rate above its prevailing level in a measured, persistent way in response to sustained growth above potential indicated by increased rates of resource utilization (declines in the unemployment rate), and conversely for sustained weakness. LAW works because growth above potential indicates a natural rate of interest above the real rate of interest and thus the need to raise the real rate, and conversely for growth below potential.

In the decade of the 1950s, LAW procedures evolved toward "LAW with credibility." The FOMC monitored bond markets for evidence of

its credibility to control inflation. Monetary policy moved toward being preemptive in that the intention was to prevent the emergence of
inflation rather than to respond only after it emerged. The emphasis was
on maintaining an environment of nominal expectational stability (price
stability) rather than on responding directly to realized inflation.

With the Great Inflation of the 1970s, during economic expansions, a
concern for "not aborting the recovery" led to hesitant increases in the
funds rate until inflation emerged. The FOMC then raised the funds rate
significantly and limited reductions while the economy went into recession. The Great Moderation succeeded the Great Inflation when FOMC
chairmen Paul Volcker and Alan Greenspan returned to LAW with credibility through a policy aimed at preempting the emergence of inflation
and establishing an environment of nominal expectational stability.

The impediment to the Volcker-Greenspan policy lies with preemptive funds-rate increases. Inevitably, such increases incur populist and
Keynesian criticism that the FOMC is limiting growth and raising the
unemployment rate to control a nonexistent inflation.

Before deregulation rendered money demand unstable starting in 1981,
economists benefited from the ideal monetarist laboratory in that stability
in real money demand made large, sustained changes in nominal money a
sufficient statistic for capturing the stance of monetary policy. Using step
functions fitted to growth rates in the monetary aggregate M2, Friedman
and Schwartz (1963b) documented that monetary contraction (reductions
in the steps fitted to M2) preceded cyclical peaks in the business cycle. After 1981, however, identifying instances of monetary instability must focus
on Fed procedures that do not ensure monetary control. That failure arises
from a failure to cause the short-term interest rate (the funds rate) to track
the natural rate of interest, where the latter is the real interest rate that
maintains aggregate demand equal to potential output.

The equilibrating power of the price system appears in the Fed's LAW
procedures in that sustained growth above potential is a signal that the real
rate of interest lies below its natural counterpart. (A converse statement
holds for weakness in growth.) When implemented in a stabilizing way,
LAW works as a search procedure for the natural rate of interest. In that
respect, the empirical investigation here classifies LAW procedures into
two classes. With LAW with credibility, the FOMC raises the funds rate
sufficiently during economic recoveries to preempt the emergence of inflation as characterized by policy in the Volcker-Greenspan era. The spirit is
to maintain price stability. With LAW with trade-offs, the FOMC raises the
funds rate only hesitantly during economic recoveries until the emergence

of inflation as characterized by policy in the Burns-Miller era. The spirit of policy then becomes balancing off inflation and unemployment using a Phillips curve, which relates unemployment (slack in the economy) to inflation.

The empirical generalization summarized below in tables for recessions since 1919, the "monetary contraction marker," shows the following Fed behavior associated with recessions. In recovery periods, the Fed raises the funds rate in a persistent fashion until the economy weakens. Recessions occur when the Fed (concerned about inflation, speculation, or the external value of the dollar) maintains short-term interest rates at cyclical highs past the cycle peak. The Friedman-Schwartz identification of monetary instability causing real instability documented the reduction in an M2 step function prior to cyclical peaks. The method of identification employed here generates that same identification for the period prior to 1981 when money demand was stable. It also applies equally well to the subsequent period of instability in real money demand.

APPENDIX: TABLES OF THE MONETARY CONTRACTION MARKER BY RECESSION

Nominal and real GNP are from Balke and Gordon (1986). Commercial paper rate on four-to-six-month maturities from "Short-Term Open Market Rates in New York City," in Board of Governors (1943), *Banking and Monetary Statistics*. M1 is from Friedman and Schwartz (1970), table 1. Real M1 is M1 divided by the CPI. Industrial production and funds rate are from St. Louis FRED. For construction of real funds rate, see chapter 18 appendix, "Real Rate of Interest." P and T designate peaks and troughs of the business cycle. Shaded rows indicate recessions.

Table 3.1. Series Values Relative to NBER Cycle Peak—1920: Q1 Peak

Time	Commercial Paper Rate	Real GNP	Industrial Production	M1	Real M1	Nominal GNP	CPI (NSA)	Dates
$t-8$	5.90	19.8	0.0	13.2	−1.1	15.3	14.5	1918Q1
$t-7$	6.08	36.7	0.0	−29.8	−37.8	57.9	12.9	1918Q2
$t-6$	6.11	10.1	0.0	74.3	35.7	38.9	28.4	1918Q3 P
$t-5$	6.00	−15.2	0.0	18.5	−4.8	0.0	24.5	1918Q4
$t-4$	5.29	−22.8	0.0	10.1	7.4	−17.5	2.5	1919Q1 T
$t-3$	5.34	−1.8	3.1	15.4	3.1	18.9	11.9	1919Q2
$t-2$	5.38	2.7	52.0	17.7	−2.2	32.1	20.4	1919Q3
$t-1$	5.46	−0.2	−9.2	20.2	−0.8	15.2	21.2	1919Q4
$t=0$	6.42	−3.3	42.7	8.7	−11.9	26.9	23.4	1920Q1 P
$t+1$	7.38	−18.6	−17.4	2.0	−18.1	−0.1	24.5	1920Q2
$t+2$	8.13	−6.6	−7.2	−2.8	1.7	−8.5	−4.5	1920Q3
$t+3$	8.09	−20.1	−43.3	−6.8	6.4	−46.1	−12.5	1920Q4
$t+4$	7.71	−17.0	−45.9	−15.6	7.0	−43.3	−21.1	1921Q1
$t+5$	7.09	10.7	−3.6	−15.5	0.1	−6.9	−15.5	1921Q2
$t+6$	6.17	12.3	9.6	−10.2	−6.7	4.8	−3.7	1921Q3 T
$t+7$	5.50	13.7	29.1	−0.1	5.3	6.0	−5.2	1921Q4
$t+8$	4.88	14.1	35.5	−1.4	12.6	−4.0	−12.4	1922Q1

Table 3.2. Series Values Relative to NBER Cycle Peak—1923: Q2 Peak

Time	Commercial Paper Rate	Real GNP	Industrial Production	M1	Real M1	Nominal GNP	CPI (NSA)	Dates
$t-8$	7.09	10.7	−3.6	−15.5	0.1	−6.9	−15.5	1921Q2
$t-7$	6.17	12.3	9.6	−10.2	−6.7	4.8	−3.7	1921Q3 T
$t-6$	5.50	13.7	29.1	−0.1	5.3	6.0	−5.2	1921Q4
$t-5$	4.88	14.1	35.5	−1.4	12.6	−4.0	−12.4	1922Q1
$t-4$	4.42	20.8	29.7	16.8	20.6	17.0	−3.1	1922Q2
$t-3$	4.13	12.8	23.3	8.0	8.9	17.9	−0.8	1922Q3
$t-2$	4.67	16.1	62.1	9.6	6.2	20.4	3.2	1922Q4
$t-1$	4.75	16.2	12.4	5.1	5.1	31.7	0.0	1923Q1
$t=0$	5.13	10.3	23.6	1.5	−1.6	12.1	3.2	1923Q2 P
$t+1$	5.21	−6.6	−11.0	−1.1	−6.4	−10.9	5.6	1923Q3
$t+2$	5.17	0.5	−12.4	4.0	0.9	1.2	3.1	1923Q4
$t+3$	4.88	11.4	5.6	−2.6	−0.3	11.6	−2.3	1924Q1
$t+4$	4.42	−12.0	−27.8	5.6	10.7	−18.8	−4.6	1924Q2
$t+5$	3.29	−4.1	−9.4	14.6	12.8	−4.1	1.6	1924Q3 T
$t+6$	3.34	22.0	37.9	9.9	5.7	28.8	4.0	1924Q4
$t+7$	3.75	9.6	24.9	6.8	5.9	18.2	0.8	1925Q1
$t+8$	3.92	4.9	1.2	5.3	3.7	0.8	1.6	1925Q2

Table 3.3. Series Values Relative to NBER Cycle Peak—1926: Q3 Peak

Time	Commercial Paper Rate	Real GNP	Industrial Production	M1	Real M1	Nominal GNP	CPI (NSA)	Dates
$t-8$	3.29	−4.1	−9.4	14.6	12.8	−4.1	1.6	1924Q3 T
$t-7$	3.34	22.0	37.9	9.9	5.7	28.8	4.0	1924Q4
$t-6$	3.75	9.6	24.9	6.8	5.9	18.2	0.8	1925Q1
$t-5$	3.92	4.9	1.2	5.3	3.7	0.8	1.6	1925Q2
$t-4$	4.04	10.7	1.2	12.1	3.1	14.5	8.7	1925Q3
$t-3$	4.38	8.6	18.6	4.3	0.4	8.9	3.8	1925Q4
$t-2$	4.34	3.7	1.1	−0.2	−0.2	0.7	0.0	1926Q1
$t-1$	4.13	1.2	2.8	−1.7	−0.2	−1.9	−1.5	1926Q2
$t=0$	4.34	9.8	9.7	−1.9	5.8	7.6	−7.3	1926Q3 P
$t+1$	4.54	2.3	4.4	−4.3	−8.5	0.2	4.7	1926Q4
$t+2$	4.17	−1.4	0.5	1.0	7.4	−8.1	−5.9	1927Q1
$t+3$	4.17	2.4	−3.7	3.4	2.6	−2.1	0.8	1927Q2
$t+4$	4.08	−6.1	−6.8	−0.3	3.7	−2.8	−3.8	1927Q3
$t+5$	4.00	−7.4	−11.5	2.2	0.6	−3.7	1.6	1927Q4 T
$t+6$	4.04	3.1	13.6	2.5	6.6	1.8	−3.8	1928Q1
$t+7$	4.54	5.0	6.1	0.8	1.6	8.2	−0.8	1928Q2
$t+8$	5.38	9.5	15.9	−4.6	−5.3	12.3	0.8	1928Q3

Table 3.4. Series Values Relative to NBER Cycle Peak—1929: Q3 Peak

Time	Commercial Paper Rate	Real GNP	Industrial Production	M1	Real M1	Nominal GNP	CPI (NSA)	Dates
$t-8$	4.08	−6.1	−6.8	−0.3	3.7	−2.8	−3.8	1927Q3
$t-7$	4.00	−7.4	−11.5	2.2	0.6	−3.7	1.6	1927Q4 T
$t-6$	4.04	3.1	13.6	2.5	6.6	1.8	−3.8	1928Q1
$t-5$	4.54	5.0	6.1	0.8	1.6	8.2	−0.8	1928Q2
$t-4$	5.38	9.5	15.9	−4.6	−5.3	12.3	0.8	1928Q3
$t-3$	5.42	4.2	21.8	6.4	6.4	0.6	0.0	1928Q4
$t-2$	5.59	8.4	13.5	−2.1	0.2	7.8	−2.3	1929Q1
$t-1$	6.00	17.5	14.1	−0.3	1.3	16.8	−1.6	1929Q2
$t=0$	6.13	2.6	6.2	5.1	−2.0	6.6	7.2	1929Q3 P
$t+1$	5.67	−17.5	−25.4	3.4	4.2	−20.0	−0.8	1929Q4
$t+2$	4.63	−13.7	−19.9	−10.3	−4.6	−16.3	−6.0	1930Q1
$t+3$	3.71	−2.3	−14.7	−6.7	−4.5	−5.2	−2.3	1930Q2
$t+4$	3.08	−18.2	−30.7	−4.9	3.0	−26.0	−7.7	1930Q3
$t+5$	2.92	−17.3	−24.6	−2.6	3.0	−23.0	−5.5	1930Q4
$t+6$	2.67	0.8	−7.4	−4.3	11.2	−9.8	−13.9	1931Q1
$t+7$	2.21	7.2	0.6	−10.0	0.6	−4.5	−10.6	1931Q2
$t+8$	2.00	−14.8	−26.1	−7.2	−1.4	−21.8	−6.0	1931Q3

Table 3.5. Series Values Relative to NBER Cycle Peak—1937: Q2 Peak

Time	Commercial Paper Rate	Real GNP	Industrial Production	M1	Real M1	Nominal GNP	CPI (NSA)	Dates
$t-8$	0.75	1.3	−4.2	13.1	9.9	1.5	3.0	1935Q2
$t-7$	0.75	11.5	18.4	23.2	25.6	10.7	−1.9	1935Q3
$t-6$	0.75	24.1	36.0	12.6	10.4	25.0	2.0	1935Q4
$t-5$	0.75	1.9	−5.4	5.8	5.8	1.2	0.0	1936Q1
$t-4$	0.75	27.5	37.7	23.7	24.9	24.5	−1.0	1936Q2
$t-3$	0.75	11.9	23.9	14.0	6.6	18.8	7.0	1936Q3
$t-2$	0.75	13.9	27.2	7.7	6.7	19.1	1.0	1936Q4
$t-1$	0.75	−1.3	18.6	4.9	1.0	9.9	3.9	1937Q1
$t=0$	1.00	10.5	7.2	−1.7	−7.9	14.6	6.8	1937Q2 P
$t+1$	1.00	−1.5	−6.3	−4.9	−9.1	0.8	4.7	1937Q3
$t+2$	1.00	−25.7	−54.7	−12.2	−11.4	−32.0	−0.9	1937Q4
$t+3$	0.96	−15.9	−40.1	2.1	13.1	−18.4	−9.7	1938Q1
$t+4$	0.88	6.5	−12.7	−3.2	−3.2	4.4	0.0	1938Q2 T
$t+5$	0.73	25.5	48.3	12.6	13.7	27.1	−0.9	1938Q3
$t+6$	0.67	17.0	43.9	18.7	22.1	15.0	−2.8	1938Q4
$t+7$	0.56	−3.8	11.4	4.7	6.8	−6.7	−1.9	1939Q1
$t+8$	0.56	−5.7	2.6	9.5	13.8	−8.0	−3.8	1939Q2

Table 3.6. Series Values Relative to NBER Cycle Peak—1945: Q1 Peak

Time	Commercial Paper Rate	Real GNP	Industrial Production	M1	Real M1	Nominal GNP	CPI (NSA)	Dates
$t-8$	0.69	15.6	23.3	41.4	34.9	24.3	4.8	1943Q1
$t-7$	0.69	9.0	12.3	20.1	7.7	15.0	11.4	1943Q2
$t-6$	0.69	13.9	22.7	35.1	38.2	15.4	−2.3	1943Q3
$t-5$	0.69	11.8	18.6	4.4	3.6	14.5	0.8	1943Q4
$t-4$	0.69	3.3	4.9	16.2	16.2	7.0	0.0	1944Q1
$t-3$	0.74	2.4	−1.5	20.9	17.3	5.0	3.1	1944Q2
$t-2$	0.75	6.7	0.2	14.8	10.6	7.1	3.9	1944Q3
$t-1$	0.75	8.8	−1.3	26.5	25.5	9.2	0.8	1944Q4
$t=0$	0.75	8.4	−7.4	17.5	15.8	8.3	1.5	1945Q1 P
$t+1$	0.75	−4.4	−18.0	11.5	8.2	−0.3	3.0	1945Q2
$t+2$	0.75	−25.6	−44.9	9.8	5.8	−21.6	3.8	1945Q3
$t+3$	0.75	−24.8	−37.5	9.5	8.7	−16.2	0.7	1945Q4 T
$t+4$	0.75	−15.7	−15.6	0.1	−1.4	−1.3	1.5	1946Q1
$t+5$	0.75	−12.7	10.8	13.9	5.9	0.5	7.5	1946Q2
$t+6$	0.80	6.9	43.9	5.7	−24.1	43.3	39.3	1946Q3
$t+7$	0.94	−4.9	21.5	1.4	−17.5	17.0	22.9	1946Q4
$t+8$	1.00	−6.3	10.0	4.7	−3.4	−1.3	8.4	1947Q1

Table 3.7. Series Values Relative to NBER Peak—1948: Q4 Peak

Time	Commercial Paper Rate	Real GDP	Industrial Production	M1	Real M1	Nominal GDP	CPI (NSA)	Dates
$t-8$	0.94	−4.9	21.5	1.4	−17.5	17.0	22.9	1946Q4
$t-7$	1.00	−6.3	10.0	4.7	−3.4	−1.3	8.4	1947Q1
$t-6$	1.00	−0.5	0.3	6.7	1.0	5.7	5.7	1947Q2
$t-5$	1.01	−0.2	0.8	3.5	−7.6	7.0	12.1	1947Q3
$t-4$	1.13	6.0	11.4	1.8	−8.4	17.0	11.1	1947Q4
$t-3$	1.35	6.5	4.1	−0.1	−6.2	9.8	6.5	1948Q1
$t-2$	1.38	7.2	4.3	−3.3	−9.6	11.0	7.0	1948Q2
$t-1$	1.46	2.3	3.8	0.4	−8.1	10.2	9.2	1948Q3
$t=0$	1.56	0.9	−4.1	−1.5	2.3	1.9	−3.8	1948Q4 P
$t+1$	1.56	−5.9	−12.3	−2.1	4.0	−7.3	−5.9	1949Q1
$t+2$	1.56	−1.2	−12.0	0.6	0.6	−5.5	0.0	1949Q2
$t+3$	1.46	4.6	0.8	−1.2	−0.1	2.3	−1.1	1949Q3
$t+4$	1.36	−4.0	−1.8	0.0	1.7	−3.7	−1.7	1949Q4 T
$t+5$	1.31	17.5	22.7	3.7	6.6	16.0	−2.8	1950Q1
$t+6$	1.31	12.4	38.1	6.0	3.0	14.4	2.9	1950Q2
$t+7$	1.46	16.6	36.2	4.5	−4.9	26.8	9.9	1950Q3
$t+8$	1.71	7.5	7.1	3.5	−4.6	16.0	8.5	1950Q4

Table 3.8. Series Values Relative to NBER Peak—1953: Q2 Peak

Time	Commercial Paper Rate	Real GDP	Industrial Production	M1	Real M1	Nominal GDP	CPI	Dates
$t-8$	2.19	7.0	1.3	3.7	0.0	9.7	3.9	1951Q2
$t-7$	2.25	8.2	−9.2	5.2	3.6	8.5	−0.2	1951Q3
$t-6$	2.26	0.7	2.8	7.6	1.2	5.2	6.0	1951Q4
$t-5$	2.38	4.2	9.6	5.4	5.4	3.8	1.5	1952Q1
$t-4$	2.32	0.3	−5.6	3.4	2.3	1.0	1.1	1952Q2
$t-3$	2.31	2.6	12.2	4.1	0.0	7.3	2.7	1952Q3
$t-2$	2.31	13.8	31.9	4.1	4.1	15.2	0.5	1952Q4
$t-1$	2.33	7.8	8.2	1.6	3.6	7.8	−1.1	1953Q1
$t=0$	2.62	3.1	5.7	2.7	0.7	3.9	1.5	1953Q2 P
$t+1$	2.75	−2.4	0.4	0.6	−1.8	−0.9	1.9	1953Q3
$t+2$	2.37	−6.2	−17.6	0.3	−0.7	−5.3	0.7	1953Q4
$t+3$	2.04	−2.0	−12.1	1.1	1.6	−0.6	0.9	1954Q1
$t+4$	1.63	0.4	−1.6	0.9	1.4	0.7	−0.6	1954Q2 T
$t+5$	1.36	4.5	2.0	3.9	3.9	5.2	−1.0	1954Q3
$t+6$	1.31	8.2	11.6	4.1	5.7	9.5	−1.2	1954Q4
$t+7$	1.61	12.0	23.4	4.7	5.8	14.1	0.5	1955Q1
$t+8$	1.97	6.7	18.5	2.4	2.4	8.5	−0.5	1955Q2

Table 3.9. Series Values Relative to NBER Peak—1957: Q3 Peak

Time	Commercial Paper Rate	Real GDP	Industrial Production	M1	Real M1	Nominal GDP	CPI	Dates
$t-8$	2.33	5.4	6.3	1.7	−0.3	8.6	0.3	1955Q3
$t-7$	2.83	2.1	9.8	0.7	0.2	6.3	1.2	1955Q4
$t-6$	3.00	−1.9	1.5	1.4	2.4	2.2	0.0	1956Q1
$t-5$	3.26	3.2	−1.7	1.1	−2.4	5.6	2.7	1956Q2
$t-4$	3.35	−0.5	−2.2	0.1	−4.7	4.8	4.2	1956Q3
$t-3$	3.63	6.7	15.4	1.9	−0.6	8.3	3.5	1956Q4
$t-2$	3.63	2.4	3.8	0.8	−1.6	8.4	3.3	1957Q1
$t-1$	3.68	−1.0	−4.9	0.2	−4.0	1.8	3.5	1957Q2
$t=0$	3.95	4.0	1.5	0.1	−4.1	6.4	3.6	1957Q3 P
$t+1$	3.99	−4.2	−15.8	−2.1	−3.0	−4.1	1.9	1957Q4
$t+2$	2.82	−10.4	−20.7	−0.5	−4.6	−6.3	4.8	1958Q1
$t+3$	1.72	2.4	−6.5	4.7	1.3	3.7	2.7	1958Q2 T
$t+4$	2.13	9.6	22.9	4.0	3.6	12.4	−0.2	1958Q3
$t+5$	3.21	9.5	19.3	5.0	5.0	11.8	0.4	1958Q4
$t+6$	3.30	7.9	18.8	−3.8	−3.8	8.9	0.7	1959Q1
$t+7$	3.60	10.9	20.9	3.4	2.0	10.9	0.7	1959Q2
$t+8$	4.19	−0.3	−15.4	2.9	0.2	0.7	2.1	1959Q3

Table 3.10. Series Values Relative to NBER Peak—1960: Q2 Peak

Time	Commercial Paper Rate	Real GDP	Industrial Production	M1	Real M1	Nominal GDP	CPI	Dates
$t-8$	1.72	2.4	−6.5	4.7	1.3	3.7	2.7	1958Q2
$t-7$	2.13	9.6	22.9	4.0	3.6	12.4	−0.2	1958Q3
$t-6$	3.21	9.5	19.3	5.0	5.0	11.8	0.4	1958Q4
$t-5$	3.30	7.9	18.8	−3.8	−3.8	8.9	0.7	1959Q1
$t-4$	3.60	10.9	20.9	3.4	2.0	10.9	0.7	1959Q2
$t-3$	4.19	−0.3	−15.4	2.9	0.2	0.7	2.1	1959Q3
$t-2$	4.76	1.4	1.9	−3.5	−5.7	3.1	2.4	1959Q4
$t-1$	4.69	9.2	26.4	−1.1	−0.7	11.1	0.4	1960Q1
$t=0$	4.07	−2.0	−8.4	−0.8	−3.0	−0.6	2.4	1960Q2 P
$t+1$	3.37	0.6	−6.4	3.8	2.9	2.1	0.2	1960Q3
$t+2$	3.27	−5.1	−9.3	−0.2	−2.8	−3.9	2.6	1960Q4
$t+3$	3.01	2.4	−5.9	2.0	2.0	3.3	0.8	1961Q1 T
$t+4$	2.86	7.7	16.8	3.0	3.0	8.7	−0.1	1961Q2
$t+5$	2.90	6.6	13.4	2.4	0.1	7.9	1.6	1961Q3
$t+6$	3.06	8.4	14.8	3.7	3.2	9.9	0.6	1961Q4
$t+7$	3.24	7.4	6.1	2.6	1.7	10.0	1.6	1962Q1
$t+8$	3.20	4.4	3.9	2.7	0.9	5.1	1.5	1962Q2

Table 3.11. Series Values Relative to NBER Cycle Peak—1969: Q4 Peak

Time	Funds Rate	Real Funds Rate	Real GDP	Industrial Production	M1	Real M1	Nominal GDP	CPI	Core PCE	Dates
$t-8$	4.17	0.42	3.0	11.1	6.7	3.0	7.7	4.5	4.1	1967Q4
$t-7$	4.79	1.11	8.4	5.8	5.1	0.3	13.3	4.0	4.6	1968Q1
$t-6$	5.98	1.92	6.9	5.5	7.3	3.2	11.5	4.0	4.7	1968Q2
$t-5$	5.94	2.07	3.1	3.1	8.1	2.4	6.9	5.5	4.5	1968Q3
$t-4$	5.92	2.32	1.6	6.2	8.9	4.1	7.6	5.0	4.8	1968Q4
$t-3$	6.57	2.92	6.4	8.0	7.4	2.3	11.0	5.0	4.4	1969Q1
$t-2$	8.33	3.69	1.2	1.8	3.2	−3.4	6.5	6.5	4.9	1969Q2
$t-1$	8.98	4.76	2.7	4.9	1.8	−3.9	8.5	5.6	4.7	1969Q3
$t=0$	8.94	5.18	−1.9	−2.5	3.2	−2.5	3.3	6.3	4.8	1969Q4 P
$t+1$	8.57	4.62	−0.6	−9.3	4.5	−0.9	5.2	6.6	4.4	1970Q1
$t+2$	7.88	3.6	0.6	−2.2	2.8	−3.8	6.4	5.7	4.6	1970Q2
$t+3$	6.7	3.03	3.7	−1.4	5.4	0.8	6.9	4.2	4.5	1970Q3
$t+4$	5.4	0.97	−4.2	−8.4	7.3	1.6	0.8	5.9	5.7	1970Q4 T
$t+5$	3.83	−0.25	11.3	7.9	7.1	3.9	18.4	3.4	5.2	1971Q1
$t+6$	4.56	0.27	2.2	3.7	8.5	3.9	7.8	3.7	4.7	1971Q2
$t+7$	5.58	2.24	3.3	1.2	7.1	2.6	7.4	4.0	3.8	1971Q3
$t+8$	4.77	1.71	0.9	9.6	3.8	1.8	4.4	3.0	2.3	1971Q4

Table 3.12. Series Values Relative to NBER Cycle Peak—1973: Q4 Peak

Time	Funds Rate	Real Funds Rate	Real GDP	Industrial Production	M1	Real M1	Nominal GDP	CPI	Core PCE	Dates
$t-8$	4.77	1.71	0.9	9.6	3.8	1.8	4.4	3.0	2.3	1971Q4
$t-7$	3.58	0.13	7.6	18.1	8.2	5.1	14.2	3.3	3.9	1972Q1
$t-6$	4.33	0.86	9.4	7.8	6.5	3.1	12.4	2.6	2.7	1972Q2
$t-5$	4.79	1.61	3.8	5.2	8.6	4.5	8.0	3.2	3.0	1972Q3
$t-4$	5.17	3.22	6.9	14.7	10.2	6.1	12.5	4.2	2.5	1972Q4
$t-3$	6.31	2.28	10.3	11.8	8.3	3.0	15.9	6.4	2.8	1973Q1
$t-2$	7.67	3.15	4.4	3.4	4.7	−4.2	11.4	8.6	5.6	1973Q2
$t-1$	10.33	4.24	−2.1	3.5	4.8	−3.9	5.7	8.1	5.4	1973Q3
$t=0$	10	3.63	3.8	6.1	5.1	−4.0	12.4	10.5	5.7	1973Q4 P
$t+1$	9.5	2.10	−3.4	−3.5	6.9	−4.4	4.2	12.4	7.0	1974Q1
$t+2$	11.08	3.50	1.0	0.2	3.6	−7.3	11.0	11.1	10.3	1974Q2
$t+3$	12.17	3.22	−3.7	−1.6	3.7	−7.9	8.0	11.7	11.9	1974Q3
$t+4$	9.17	−1.93	−1.5	−15.0	4.9	−6.8	10.8	12.9	10.1	1974Q4
$t+5$	6.08	−0.84	−4.8	−23.9	2.4	−4.7	4.3	8.8	8.1	1975Q1 T
$t+6$	5.33	−0.86	2.9	−5.3	6.1	−0.1	9.4	4.9	6.2	1975Q2
$t+7$	6.19	−0.79	7.0	10.2	7.9	−0.8	15.1	8.3	6.2	1975Q3
$t+8$	5.38	−0.77	5.5	9.0	3.2	−3.1	13.0	7.6	6.7	1975Q4

Table 3.13. Series Values Relative to NBER Cycle Peak—1980: Q1 Peak

Time	Funds Rate	Real Funds Rate	Real GDP	Industrial Production	M1	Real M1	Nominal GDP	CPI	Core PCE	Dates
$t-8$	6.75	0.17	1.3	−1.1	8.1	1.0	7.5	7.1	6.4	1978Q1
$t-7$	7.33	0.14	16.4	17.1	9.2	−1.2	25.5	9.4	7.1	1978Q2
$t-6$	8.04	1.18	4.1	3.5	8.2	−1.5	11.1	9.6	7.1	1978Q3
$t-5$	9.63	1.84	5.5	7.4	7.2	−1.0	14.6	9.6	7.4	1978Q4
$t-4$	10	1.07	0.7	1.7	4.9	−4.9	8.1	10.5	5.6	1979Q1
$t-3$	10.13	1.16	0.4	−0.9	10.4	−3.7	10.7	13.3	9.1	1979Q2
$t-2$	10.63	0.83	3.0	−1.1	10.3	−3.2	12.1	13.5	7.6	1979Q3
$t-1$	12.5	3.37	1.0	1.5	3.6	−7.4	9.5	13.3	8.6	1979Q4
$t=0$	15.14	7.09	1.3	1.6	6.7	−8.6	10.1	16.7	10.2	1980Q1 P
$t+1$	12.29	3.57	−8.0	−15.9	−3.3	−16.3	0.6	14.2	9.3	1980Q2
$t+2$	9.73	1.75	−0.5	−6.4	15.9	7.8	8.7	7.7	9.2	1980Q3 T
$t+3$	16.68	7.93	7.7	16.3	11.5	0.5	20.1	11.7	10.1	1980Q4
$t+4$	15.97	7.59	8.1	1.0	−1.3	−11.1	20.0	11.5	9.2	1981Q1
$t+5$	20	11.35	−2.9	1.2	6.5	−2.8	4.4	8.6	7.8	1981Q2
$t+6$	18.09	8.92	4.9	3.9	1.1	−9.5	12.6	11.6	7.6	1981Q3 P
$t+7$	13.49	5.53	−4.3	−8.5	4.0	−1.8	2.2	6.7	7.3	1981Q4
$t+8$	14.25	7.44	−6.1	−8.0	0.0	0.0	−1.2	3.6	6.0	1982Q1

Table 3.14. Series Values Relative to NBER Cycle Peak—1981: Q3 Peak

Time	Funds Rate	Real Funds Rate	Real GDP	Industrial Production	M1	Real M1	Nominal GDP	CPI	Core PCE	Dates
$t-8$	10.63	0.83	3.0	−1.1	10.3	−3.2	12.1	13.5	7.6	1979Q3
$t-7$	12.5	3.37	1.0	1.5	3.6	−7.4	9.5	13.3	8.6	1979Q4
$t-6$	15.14	7.09	1.3	1.6	6.7	−8.6	10.1	16.7	10.2	1980Q1
$t-5$	12.29	3.57	−8.0	−15.9	−3.3	−16.3	0.6	14.2	9.3	1980Q2
$t-4$	9.73	1.75	−0.5	−6.4	15.9	7.8	8.7	7.7	9.2	1980Q3 T
$t-3$	16.68	7.93	7.7	16.3	11.5	0.5	20.1	11.7	10.1	1980Q4
$t-2$	15.97	7.59	8.1	1.0	−1.3	−11.1	20.0	11.5	9.2	1981Q1
$t-1$	20	11.35	−2.9	1.2	6.5	−2.8	4.4	8.6	7.8	1981Q2
$t=0$	18.09	8.92	4.9	3.9	1.1	−9.5	12.6	11.6	7.6	1981Q3 P
$t+1$	13.49	5.53	−4.3	−8.5	4.0	−1.8	2.2	6.7	7.3	1981Q4
$t+2$	14.25	7.44	−6.1	−8.0	0.0	0.0	−1.2	3.6	6.0	1982Q1
$t+3$	13.75	7.72	1.8	−5.0	0.0	0.0	7.2	5.9	5.5	1982Q2
$t+4$	9.5	4.23	−1.5	−5.6	0.0	0.0	4.2	7.1	6.6	1982Q3
$t+5$	9	3.90	0.2	−7.3	0.0	0.0	4.7	1.2	5.7	1982Q4 T
$t+6$	8.5	3.74	5.4	4.7	0.0	0.0	8.5	0.3	5.4	1983Q1
$t+7$	8.75	4.46	9.4	9.2	0.0	0.0	12.5	4.7	3.1	1983Q2
$t+8$	9.44	5.08	8.2	14.4	0.0	0.0	12.6	4.0	6.2	1983Q3

Table 3.15. Series Values Relative to NBER Cycle Peak—1990: Q3 Peak

Time	Funds Rate	Real Funds Rate	Real GDP	Industrial Production	Nominal GDP	CPI	Core PCE	Dates
$t-8$	8.13	3.04	2.2	2.1	6.8	5.0	4.7	1988Q3
$t-7$	8.47	3.63	5.4	3.2	8.6	4.4	4.5	1988Q4
$t-6$	9.53	4.41	4.1	1.5	8.9	4.6	4.4	1989Q1
$t-5$	9.81	4.74	2.7	−1.8	6.6	6.6	3.7	1989Q2
$t-4$	9.16	4.55	2.9	−2.5	5.8	3.2	3.0	1989Q3
$t-3$	8.58	4.30	1.0	1.8	3.8	4.1	3.7	1989Q4
$t-2$	8.25	3.84	4.7	3.2	9.8	7.1	4.7	1990Q1
$t-1$	8.25	3.62	1.0	2.8	5.8	4.0	4.5	1990Q2
$t=0$	8.13	2.99	0.0	1.4	3.6	7.1	4.1	1990Q3 P
$t+1$	7.5	1.91	−3.0	−6.0	0.0	7.0	3.4	1990Q4
$t+2$	6.13	1.62	−2.0	−7.5	2.7	3.0	3.6	1991Q1 T
$t+3$	5.75	1.81	2.6	2.6	5.3	2.4	3.1	1991Q2
$t+4$	5.63	1.47	1.9	5.5	4.9	3.1	3.7	1991Q3
$t+5$	4.67	0.43	1.9	0.7	4.0	3.4	3.2	1991Q4
$t+6$	4	0.26	4.2	−0.3	6.7	2.7	3.1	1992Q1
$t+7$	3.75	0.06	3.9	7.3	6.2	3.1	2.9	1992Q2
$t+8$	3.5	−0.33	4.0	2.9	5.9	3.1	2.4	1992Q3

Table 3.16. Series Values Relative to NBER Cycle Peak—2001: Q1 Peak

Time	Funds Rate	Real Funds Rate	Real GDP	Industrial Production	Nominal GDP	CPI	Core PCE	Dates
$t-8$	4.75	2.59	3.4	4.3	5.1	1.5	1.3	1999Q1
$t-7$	4.88	2.79	3.4	3.8	4.8	3.0	1.3	1999Q2
$t-6$	5.25	2.83	4.7	4.0	6.2	3.0	1.4	1999Q3
$t-5$	5.42	3.23	7.3	8.0	9.1	3.0	1.8	1999Q4
$t-4$	5.88	3.79	1.0	4.9	4.7	4.0	2.2	2000Q1
$t-3$	6.5	4.32	6.4	5.0	8.3	3.2	1.3	2000Q2
$t-2$	6.5	4.58	−0.5	−0.3	1.6	3.7	1.8	2000Q3
$t-1$	6.5	4.43	2.1	−1.3	3.8	2.9	1.9	2000Q4
$t=0$	5.25	3.39	−0.5	−5.5	2.8	3.9	2.3	2001Q1 P
$t+1$	3.88	2.08	1.2	−5.2	4.4	2.8	1.5	2001Q2
$t+2$	3.5	1.10	−1.4	−5.9	0.2	1.1	1.1	2001Q3
$t+3$	2.08	−0.14	1.6	−5.2	3.6	−0.3	2.0	2001Q4 T
$t+4$	1.75	0.28	2.7	2.3	4.3	1.3	1.2	2002Q1
$t+5$	1.75	0.36	2.2	6.3	3.7	3.2	2.3	2002Q2
$t+6$	1.75	0.27	2.4	2.3	3.9	2.2	2.0	2002Q3
$t+7$	1.25	−0.30	0.2	−0.5	2.4	2.4	1.4	2002Q4
$t+8$	1.25	−0.13	1.2	2.7	4.4	4.2	1.0	2003Q1

Table 3.17. Series Values Relative to NBER Cycle Peak—2007: Q4 Peak

Time	Funds Rate	Real Funds Rate	Real GDP	Industrial Production	Nominal GDP	CPI	Core PCE	Dates
$t-8$	4.13	1.84	2.6	3.9	5.9	3.8	2.6	2005Q4
$t-7$	4.63	2.40	5.4	3.8	8.4	2.1	2.3	2006Q1
$t-6$	5.13	2.78	0.9	2.4	4.4	3.7	2.9	2006Q2
$t-5$	5.25	2.77	0.6	1.5	3.5	3.8	2.2	2006Q3
$t-4$	5.25	2.83	3.5	0.9	5.0	-1.6	1.7	2006Q4
$t-3$	5.25	3.05	0.9	3.6	5.0	4.0	2.9	2007Q1
$t-2$	5.25	3.07	2.3	5.0	5.0	4.6	1.5	2007Q2
$t-1$	5	2.89	2.2	1.1	4.3	2.6	2.0	2007Q3
$t=0$	4.38	2.35	2.5	1.2	4.1	5.0	2.6	2007Q4 P
$t+1$	2.63	0.33	-2.3	-1.5	-0.8	4.4	2.2	2008Q1
$t+2$	2	-0.40	2.1	-5.8	4.3	5.3	1.9	2008Q2
$t+3$	2	-0.63	-2.1	-12.5	0.8	6.3	1.9	2008Q3
$t+4$	0.56	-1.20	-8.4	-16.0	-7.2	-8.9	0.2	2008Q4
$t+5$	0.125	-1.16	-4.4	-20.6	-4.5	-2.7	0.4	2009Q1
$t+6$	0.125	-1.09	-0.6	-10.9	-1.2	2.1	1.8	2009Q2 T
$t+7$	0.125	-1.10	1.5	6.1	1.9	3.5	1.4	2009Q3
$t+8$	0.125	-1.10	4.5	6.4	5.9	3.2	2.5	2009Q4

CHAPTER 4

The Creation of the Fed

Summary: In the pre–World War II period, the preeminent question is what responsibility the Fed bore for the Great Depression. To answer that question, one must address several questions. What monetary standard did the Fed create? What responsibilities did that standard impose on policy makers? If policy makers caused the Great Depression by failing to fulfill those responsibilities, why did they fail? How did they understand the monetary standard, and why was learning about the actual standard seemingly impossible?

A brief answer to these complex questions is that the monetary standard was one of fiat money creation. Although policy makers had responsibility for money creation and the price level, they did not understand that responsibility. Their operating procedures entailed the setting of the marginal cost of reserves to banks and, as a result, the economy's short-term interest rate. The interaction of that interest rate with the operation of the price system, specifically, the natural rate of interest, determined money creation or, in the Depression, money destruction. However, policy makers understood the regional Reserve Banks as one influence on the cost and availability of funds to banks, not as creators of money.

Any monetary standard must answer the question of what endows money with a well-defined value, that is, what makes the price level determinate. With a fiat money standard as opposed to a classical gold standard, the central bank must take responsibility for the behavior of the price level. Nothing prepared early policy makers to go from the automatic operation of the late nineteenth-century gold standard to a monetary regime that thrust on them responsibility to control money creation and prices.

The motivation for the creation of the Fed with the Federal Reserve Act passed in December 1913 came from the desire to end the financial panics that had occurred periodically and most recently in 1907. The act created twelve Federal Reserve Banks thought of as reserve depositories of the banks in their Federal Reserve districts. Such a regional concentration of reserves would not only make reserves available in a bank panic but, presumably, remove them from the Wall Street banks, which could deny access in a panic. Moreover, elimination of the concentration of reserves in New York would prevent the New York banks from using them for speculation—the collapse of which policy makers believed led to recession and deflation.

Allyn A. Young (1927), a Harvard professor, wrote:

> Those who planned the Federal Reserve system confidently expected that the system would operate so as to do away with the "artificial" concentration of banking power in New York. . . . The Federal Reserve Bank of New York was to be merely one of a number of regional banks. . . . Dr. H. P. Willis, who at the time was expert to the House Banking and Currency Committee, explained in 1913 in a memorandum prepared for President Wilson that the presumed effect of the new plan would be "to end the placing of reserves with Central Reserve city banks for use in stock market operations, to keep reserves . . . at home." . . . The new reserve system has not been an effective obstacle to the use of banking funds in financing Stock Exchange speculation.

Lauchlin Currie (1934b, 34) wrote that "the primary reason for the establishment of the Federal Reserve System was probably the desire to curb stock market speculation, which, it was believed, led to the successive suspensions of payments under the National Banking System." The regional Reserve Banks would assure the extension of credit exclusively to legitimate uses by basing that credit on the discounting of "real bills," short-term self-liquidating commercial paper. These erroneous ideas made the Federal Reserve System into a source of recurrent, enormous instability in the pre–World War II era.

In congressional testimony on a price-stabilization bill, Western Starr (US Congress 1926, April 1, 1926, 233), representing the National Committee of the Farmer-Labor Party, talked of the panic of 1857:

> I can remember the financial panic of 1857 and I remember what happened to the people in the town in which I lived out on the Mississippi River. It was a steamboat town, a lumber and saw mill town. The town was, at that time, of perhaps 5,000 or 6,000 people, and the whole town went broke. Every mill shut down and the steamboats quit running. There was absolutely nothing they could do to earn a living. They were down and out. That was only one of them. But I remember every one since, and I remember that every last one of them has been caused by precisely the same cause, brought about by precisely the same cause—

restriction of credit and the cutting down of the ability to utilize opportunities that lie all around us.

The solution to such panics was to remove the concentration of reserves from New York by decentralizing them in regional reserve depositories. These regional Reserve Banks would always provide credit with no more suspensions. As stated in the Federal Reserve Act, the Reserve Banks would purchase "bills of exchange arising out of commercial transactions . . . with a view of accommodating commerce and business." Credit would expand and contract in response to the legitimate needs of business. There would be an "elastic currency."

The creation of the Federal Reserve reflected the consensus that the United States needed an "elastic currency." An elasticity based on the discounting of real bills at the regional Reserve Banks would provide for seasonal needs for currency in moving crops to market. Such a system would end the speculative excess whose collapse led to recession and deflation. It would do so for two reasons. First, it would assure that credit expanded and contracted to meet the legitimate needs of commerce—no more and no less. Second, the availability of the discount window at the regional Reserve Banks would end the concentration of reserves in New York. Not only would the New York banks no longer exercise life and death control over the extension of credit in a panic to banks; they would no longer have the funds of those banks to use for speculation.

Currie (1934b, 35) traced the real bills doctrine to proponents of the Banking School in Britain, who

> wished to secure elasticity of note issue while guarding against the danger of over-issue. They thought this could be accomplished if notes were issued only on loans to business men for the provision of working capital. In this way, they argued, an increase in notes could only occur if there were an increase in production. A falling off in production would automatically result in retirement of notes. Notes issued to long term borrowers disturbed this automatic adjustment, since they would remain outstanding after goods had been purchased.

4.1. POPULIST OPPOSITION TO A CENTRAL BANK

The United States had not had a central bank between the expiration in 1836 of the charter of the Second Bank of the United States and the creation of the Fed in 1913. That fact reflected populist animosity toward the centralization of power in the eastern financial establishment. It also reflected the opposition to the establishment of a central bank with the power to create fiat money. These fears appeared in the farewell address of Andrew Jackson in 1837 (American Presidency Project):

> In reviewing the conflicts which have taken place between different in-terests in the United States and the policy pursued since the adoption of our present form of Government, we find nothing that has produced such deep-seated evil as the course of legislation in relation to the cur-rency. The Constitution of the United States unquestionably intended to secure to the people a circulating medium of gold and silver. But the establishment of a national bank by Congress, with the privilege of is-suing paper money receivable in the payment of the public dues, and the unfortunate course of legislation in the several States upon the same subject, drove from general circulation the constitutional currency and substituted one of paper in its place. . . . But experience has now proved the mischiefs and dangers of a paper currency. . . .
>
> The paper system being founded on public confidence and having of itself no intrinsic value, it is liable to great and sudden fluctuations, thereby rendering property insecure and the wages of labor unsteady and uncertain. The corporations which create the paper money cannot be relied upon to keep the circulating medium uniform in amount. In times of prosperity, when confidence is high, they are tempted by the prospect of gain or by the influence of those who hope to profit by it to extend their issues of paper beyond the bounds of discretion and the rea-sonable demands of business; and when these issues have been pushed on from day to day, until public confidence is at length shaken, then a re-action takes place, and they immediately withdraw the credits they have given, suddenly curtail their issues, and produce an unexpected and ru-inous contraction of the circulating medium, which is felt by the whole community. . . . The ruthless and unsparing temper with which whole cities and communities were oppressed, individuals impoverished and ruined, and a scene of cheerful prosperity suddenly changed into one of gloom and despondency ought to be indelibly impressed on the memory of the people of the United States.[1]

1. The charter of the First Bank of the United States had expired in 1811. When the United States entered the War of 1812, it lacked the resources to finance the war. The Treasury issued Treasury notes, which served as money. A rise in the price level forced the United States off the gold standard. Congress chartered the Second Bank of the United States in 1816, and it began operation in 1817. The last sentence of the Jackson speech refers to the way in which the Second Bank of the United States helped to enforce

Given the Jacksonian populist tradition of opposition to the creation on a central bank, one must explain what happened in 1913 that led to the Federal Reserve Act. Financial panics had been a recurrent feature in the United States but had not heretofore led to a reform of the monetary system (Wicker 2000). The explanation is that Woodrow Wilson brought the populists on board through the promise of a monetary system that would remove control of money from New York.

Consider again comments of Western Starr (US Congress 1926, April 1, 226):

> With respect to the Federal reserve act, we were told this was something that would save us from the economic domination that we are confronted with all the time; that it would prevent panics and lockouts and stabilize currency and give us a flexible currency that would meet all the demands of commerce; that it was the one thing that the world had been looking for and we must have it, and they even got William Jennings Bryan, who had been fighting the principle involved in the Federal reserve bank bill all of his life, to go personally and dragoon Members of Congress and the Senate of the United States in his party to support the bill; and if it had not been done it could not have been passed; and he said, before he died, it was the one thing he had done in his public life that he regretted having done.

William Jennings Bryan (D-NE) had organized the discontent of farmers over the deflation that had followed the end of the Civil War. As shown in figure 4.1, the decline in the price level lasted until 1897. As debtors through mortgages on their farms, farmers considered the effect of deflation in increasing the real value of debt to be exploitation by the "moneyed power" (Andrew Jackson's term). Bryan formed a new populist coalition comprising rural interests and the free silver western interests, which wanted the free coinage of silver.

With the deflation that took hold in the last quarter of the nineteenth century, populism moved away from its hard-money, antibank stand in favor of fiat money creation. Reeve (1943, 3) sketched the populist American tradition:

> The presence of a large and geographically unified debtor class has given solid political incentives for many "representatives of the people" to

---

the deflation required to return to the gold standard. See Timberlake (1993) and Hetzel (2014a).

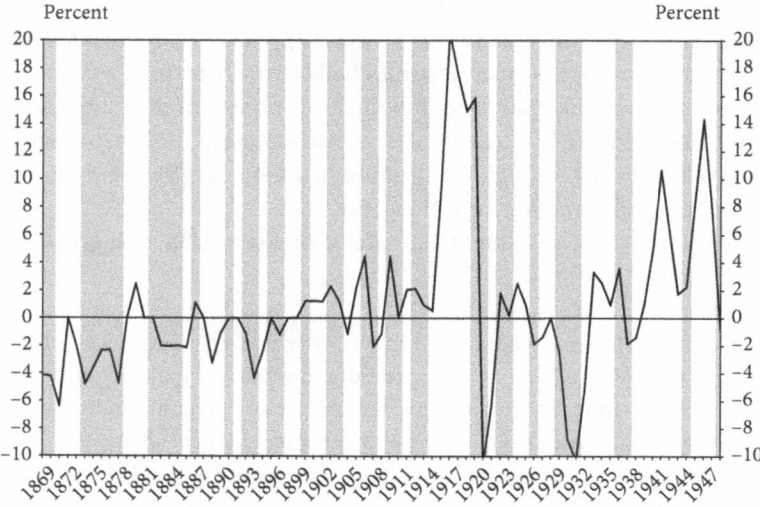

Figure 4.1. Inflation: 1869–1949
Annual percentage changes in the CPI. Shaded areas represent NBER recessions.
Source: Officer and Williamson (2012)

espouse such [paper money] causes. The rapid expansion westward and the later developments behind the frontier were financed in large part with credit from the eastern seaboard and from across the Atlantic, coupled with liberal loans from "wildcat banks" or their successors. When the inevitable speculative reactions led to economic distress, the debtors were ready to welcome almost any kind of monetary expansion which would lighten the incubus of debt and thus foil the machinations of Wall Street and its English overlords. Cheap money dogmas thus became an essential part of the traditional beliefs of the common people.

Bryan promised to end the deflation by abandoning the gold standard in favor of bimetallism. The promise of a bimetallic standard with a sixteen-to-one silver-to-gold mint ratio would have effectively put the country on a silver standard. The reason was that with a market price of silver relative to gold in excess of sixteen to one, the public would have drained the Treasury of its gold by asking for gold in return for silver. The resulting silver standard would have produced inflation.

Bryan was the Democratic nominee in the 1896 presidential election. The most famous line in his 1896 speech at the Democratic national convention was its ending (Wikipedia 2021):

Having behind us the commercial interests and the laboring interests and all the toiling masses, we shall answer their demands for a gold standard by saying to them, you shall not press down upon the brow of labor this crown of thorns. You shall not crucify mankind upon a cross of gold.

Bryan lost to the Republican William McKinley. The populist movement temporarily retreated when deflation turned into inflation after 1897 and World War I buoyed commodity prices. However, after the 1920–21 deflation, it would return as the bugaboo of the eastern financial establishment with its proposals for paper money creation.

Reeve (1943, 189) wrote:

> Paper money schemes probably excite more widespread and violent opposition among the more conservative sections of the public than any other important type of monetary heresy. For this, historical reasons seem largely responsible. . . . The disastrous inflationary experiences in postwar Europe reinforce this aversion, until the very suggestion of "printing press money" excited derision, rather than serious consideration, among the great majority of the responsible leaders of public opinion.

In the Depression, the association of populism with paper money and the gold standard with financial orthodoxy made it impossible for policy makers to comprehend that the Federal Reserve really had created a paper (fiat) money standard despite continued convertibility of gold.

4.2. REFORM OF THE NATIONAL BANKING SYSTEM AND THE NATIONAL MONETARY COMMISSION

The bank panic of 1907 and the associated recession revived the reform movement that had lapsed after the 1893 panic in which central reserve city banks (New York, Chicago, and St. Louis) had suspended payments on their deposits held by interior banks.[2] There was universal assent on the need for an "elastic currency." During the Civil War, in order to help to finance its debt, the North had passed the National Banking Act, which created a national bank charter. Although nationally chartered banks gained the exclusive right to issue banknotes, those notes had to be collateralized

2. On the Panic of 1907, see Bruner and Carr (2007) and Tallman and Moen (2012). On early reform movements, see Wicker (2005).

by Treasury bonds. The fixed supply of those bonds meant that the supply of banknotes and credit could not expand to meet the seasonal demands that arose in moving crops to market nor could they expand during bank panics.

The immediate result of the 1907 panic was the 1908 Aldrich-Vreeland Act, which created the National Monetary Commission, with Nelson Aldrich (R-RI, and chairman of the Senate Finance Committee) as chairman. The resulting Aldrich bill proposed creation of a National Reserve Association with headquarters in Washington and fifteen branches that would discount the bills of exchange of member banks in their district. Critics of the Aldrich proposal considered the National Reserve Association, which would have the power to set a uniform rate of discount throughout the United States, to be a central bank with regional branches. The 1912 Democratic Platform opposed "the so-called Aldrich bill or the establishment of a central bank" and demanded "protection from control of . . . the money trust" (Woolley and Peters 1999–2015).

Nevertheless, the Aldrich bill became the blueprint for the Federal Reserve Act. The report of the National Monetary Commission had highlighted that the National Reserve Association with its decentralized branch structure would prevent the flow of funds to New York with the resulting encouragement to speculation. The discounting of member bank paper disciplined by real bills principles would ensure that the National Reserve Association would not be a central bank with the power to create money. The report of the National Monetary Commission (1912, 8, 27, 37, and 39) stated:

> The narrow character of our discount market . . . results in sending the surplus money of all sections . . . to New York, where it is usually loaned out on call on Stock Exchange securities, tending to promote dangerous speculation. . . .
>
> An advance in bank rates is used to curb speculation and prevent overexpansion of credit. We give the Reserve Association effective means to check speculation and to prevent undue expansion through the power to advance its discount rate. We can not suppose that the directors of a local association would be likely to indorse the paper of an individual bank to promote speculation or when dangerous expansion would be likely to follow.

In summer 2012, Woodrow Wilson acted decisively to push the Federal Reserve Act through Congress (Link 1956). In 1924, the year Wilson died, Josephus Daniels, secretary of the Navy, wrote a Wilson biography, which included a chapter on the genesis of the Fed. Daniels (1924, 166) wrote:

On June 23, 1913, President Wilson . . . read his message. . . . "We must have a currency, not rigid as now, but readily, elastically responsive to sound credit. . . . Our banking laws must mobilize reserves; must not permit the concentration anywhere in a few hands of the monetary resources of the country or their use for speculative purposes in such volume as to hinder or impede or stand in the way of more legitimate, fruitful uses."

The unintended and long-misunderstood result was to create a central bank with the ability to create and destroy money.

4.3. THE REAL BILLS FOUNDATION OF THE EARLY FED

As conceived in the Federal Reserve Act, the Reserve Banks would regulate financial intermediation within their districts.[3] Lending only on real bills would proportion the extension of credit to the demands of legitimate business. In the National Banking era, banknotes, which had to be collateralized by government bonds, were supplied inelastically because of the fixed availability of government bonds. A rationale for the Federal Reserve was the assumption that in times of slack business demand the inelastic supply of banknotes meant that an excess supply of credit would spill over into speculative excess, laying the groundwork for the next cyclical boom and bust. Lending on real bills would also assure a supply of funds to banks in financial panics when correspondent banks had suspended redemption of their respondent balances (Hetzel 2014a).

Alvin Hansen (1941, 75 and 71), a Harvard professor and the chief prose-lytizer for Keynesianism in America, summarized real bills views (the commercial loan theory of banking):

The Reserve System had been established on the commercial banking theory. The member banks ideally were to extend credit only on the basis

3. Jacob Viner (1937, 148) summarized real bills views, which were held by the Bank of England and were criticized by the Bullionists in their celebrated *Report on the High Price of Bullion* (1810) (quoted in Cannan 1969, 48–49). The Bank of England "claimed that as long as currency was issued only by banks, and was issued by them only in the discount of genuine and sound short-term commercial paper, it could not be issued in excess of the needs of business, since no one would borrow at interest funds which he did not need." John Wood (2005, 14) reproduced some of the testimony before the Bullionist Committee by Governor Whitmore of the Bank of England: "We never forced a Bank note into circulation, and the criterion by which I judge of the exact proportion to be maintained is by avoiding as much as possible to discount what does not appear to be legitimate mercantile paper."

of self-liquidating loans. They were to "monetize" the credit of producing and marketing units. Bank loans work to refinance goods during the process of production or marketing. And when the process was completed, the sale of the goods would supply the funds to repay the loans. Thus, the process of production would be facilitated by bank credit accommodation.

The central basis of stabilization policy rested upon the firm belief that the boom was the progenitor of the depression and, if it could be controlled, stability would result. It would not do to wait until depression was already upon us to introduce control measures. The time for action was in the preceding phase of the cycle. Once the boom had been allowed to run its course, depression was regarded as inevitable and it, in turn, would perforce have to be permitted to run its course. Preventive, not remedial, measures were required.

Paul Warburg (1910, 37) wrote:[4]

Elasticity [of the note issue] does not mean expansion, but expansion and contraction. . . . The additional benefit of contraction is that it prevents inflation [of asset prices], with all its dangerous consequences. . . . Notes issued against discounts mean elasticity based on the changing demands of commerce and trade of the nation, while notes based on government bonds mean constant expansion without contraction, inflation based on the requirements of the government without connection to any kind with the temporary needs of the toiling nation.

Carter Glass (1927, 61) wrote in his book *An Adventure in Constructive Finance*:[5]

The national currency was inelastic because it was based on the bonded indebtedness of the United States. The ability of the banks to meet the currency needs of commerce and industry was largely measured by the

4. Paul Warburg was an original member of the Federal Reserve Board. He had been a partner in the New York firm of Kuhn, Loeb, and Company. Warburg had campaigned for a bank modeled after the German Reichsbank or Bank of England. By making a liquid market for discounted paper, New York would become a rival to London as a financial center. See also Roberts (1998).
5. Carter Glass was elected to the House of Representatives as a Democrat in 1902. Glass became chairman of the House Committee on Banking and Currency in 1913. He and his assistant H. Parker Willis helped to pass the Federal Reserve Act, which is known as the Glass-Owen Act. Robert Latham Owen had been elected as a senator in 1907 from Oklahoma. In 1913, he became chairman of the Senate Banking Committee.

volume of bonds available. . . . For half a century we banked on the absurd theory that the country always needed a volume of currency equal to the nation's bonded indebtedness and at no time ever required less, whereas we frequently did not need as much as was outstanding and quite often required more than it was possible to obtain. So, when more was needed than could be gotten, stringencies resulted and panics would be precipitated. . . . When currency was redundant, when the volume was more than required for actual currency transactions, instead of taking it through the expensive process of retirement, it was sent by interior banks to the great money centres to be loaned on call for stock and commodity gambling. . . .

In seasons of depression, with moderate demands for credits and currency for local commercial transactions, the country banks would bundle off their surplus funds to the money centres, to be loaned, on call, for speculation. At periods with stock gambling in full blast, trading in business would revive, demands for credit and currency would ensue, and, with speculative loans extended beyond all capacity to pay, the call for funds from "the street" would create consternation. Interest charges would quickly jump higher and higher, panic would seize gambler and banker alike, and prevailing prosperity would be superseded by distress everywhere.

Real bills ideas filled an intellectual vacuum that could be satisfactorily filled only by the post–World War II creation of modern macroeconomics. Mass psychology rather than the price system produced economy-wide movements in output and prices. The hallmark of real bills was that the alternation of periods of boom and bust occurred through the contagious optimism of speculative excess followed by an inevitable reaction in the form of the collapse of speculative excess accompanied by excessive pessimism.

The desire to understand the Great Depression and to prevent a recurrence provided the impetus to the creation of macroeconomics. Modern macroeconomics explains the behavior of aggregate variables like employment and output in models in which the price system coordinates their behavior. No such conception existed in the Depression. The monumental intellectual effort required to construct models of the economy based on the operation of the price system lay in the future. Universally, before modern macroeconomics, the belief prevailed that the coordination of individual actions that led to fluctuations in aggregate economic activity occurred through mass psychology.

Washington Irving (2008, 4) offered an early example inspired by the 1819–20 recession:

Every now and then the world is visited by one of these delusive seasons, when the "credit system" ... expands to full luxuriance: everybody trusts everybody; a bad debt is a thing unheard of; the broad way to certain and sudden wealth lies plain and open.... Banks ... become so many mints to coin words into cash; and as the supply of words is inexhaustible, it may readily be supposed that a vast amount of promissory capital is soon in circulation.... Nothing is heard but gigantic operations in trade; great purchases and sales of real property, and immense sums made at every transfer. All, to be sure, as yet exists in promise; but the believer in promises calculates the aggregate as solid capital....

Now is the time for speculative and dreaming of designing men. They relate their dreams and projects to the ignorant and credulous, [and] dazzle them with golden visions.... The example of one stimulates another; speculation rises on speculation; bubble rises on bubble.... No "operation" is thought worthy of attention, that does not double or treble the investment.... Could this delusion always last, the life of a merchant would indeed be a golden dream; but it is as short as it is brilliant.

These foundational real bills views formed the lens through which policy makers understood the world throughout the Great Depression. Eugene Meyer (US Congress 1932b, May 18, 178 and 179), governor of the Federal Reserve Board, recast these beliefs in terms of the real bills views of the time.

I feel that more thought has to be given to the quality of the credit. If the amount of building that had been done in the United States had been done on a sound credit basis, instead of an unsound credit basis, the picture of the financial condition of the building industry and the present depression, I believe, would have an entirely different aspect. Now, it is not only the quantity that has to be thought of, it is the quality, and it is a warning to the banking authorities when they see obviously dangerous speculative activities in larger areas.

A whole lot of these maladjustments come from neither one standard nor another, but from the conduct and behavior of people; and sometimes a large number of people, en masse, get optimistic together, and overdo things; then they get pessimistic and overdo things on the other side. I think that all you can safely do is to try to restrain and limit the extremities of the expansion and contraction of credit by the mechanism of the banking systems.

4.4. A GOLD STANDARD MENTALITY IN A
REGIME OF FIAT MONEY CREATION

How did the Fed reconcile real bills views with the operation of the gold standard? Policy makers understood the gold standard as maintaining convertibility of the dollar with gold. The Reserve Banks would have to raise their discount rates, if necessary, to maintain the legal gold cover for their liabilities (35 percent against member bank deposits and 40 percent against the issue of Federal Reserve notes). If the gold cover was ample, the "gold standard" was secure. The Fed did not follow the rules of the classical gold standard. The dollar presumably had value because it could be exchanged for gold, but there was never any sense among policy makers of a price level determined by the parity price of the dollar with gold and changes in the real value of gold. Raising the discount rate in response to gold outflows would prevent recessions by preventing the easy money conditions that spurred unsustainable speculation, the collapse of which led to recession.

The Fed dealt with gold flows in the context of its real bills views. Starting in 1922, gold flows into the United States raised the gold cover well above its legal minimum. Following the gold standard rules of the game by lowering discount rates would have, based on real bills principles, created an excessive amount of credit, which would spill over into speculation. The Fed then sterilized the inflows. Ample gold reserves allowed the Fed to maintain convertibility. In fall 1931, in response to gold outflows following Britain's departure from the gold standard, the Reserve Banks raised their discount rates. The primary motivation was to maintain the confidence of businessmen in maintenance of gold convertibility. Recessions originated in the collapse of speculative excess. Recovery would begin when businessmen once again regained confidence in the future.

With the Fed, the monetary standard changed to one of fiat money creation. Nevertheless, the gold standard mentality carried over from pre-Fed days and blinded policy makers to the actual nature of the standard. With the pre-Fed gold standard, the banking system operated with a given supply of gold as the base for supporting its assets and liabilities. For the banking system, gold could increase only through internal currency inflows or through an external inflow produced by a balance of payment surplus. With the creation of the Fed, the regional Federal Reserve Banks centralized the gold reserves of their member banks. By discounting real bills (commercial paper), they could provide an elasticity to the credit base not possible under the pre-Fed gold standard.

Under the pre-Fed gold standard, the interior banks held their reserves with their correspondent banks in the central reserve cities. Neither class of banks held any significant amount of excess reserves. As a result, during the fall season of moving crops to market, heightened demands for credit and currency caused stringency in credit markets and spikes in short-term interest rates. An elastic currency would eliminate the occasional panics and bank runs that arose during these periods. That would represent standard central bank practice as represented by the Bank of England, which would judge whether a gold outflow was transitory before raising the discount rate.

No one understood that this "elasticity" endowed the Fed with the ability to create and to destroy the deposits of commercial banks through a bookkeeping operation. The continued convertibility of Federal Reserve notes into gold and the legally mandated gold cover for notes and discounting obscured that fact. Policy makers kept the psychology of the gold standard of thinking of their own gold-based reserves as a reservoir of funds limited by the constraints of the gold standard. In fact, they were living in a different world with new and uncomprehended responsibilities.

In the pre–World War I gold standard, the discipline imposed on the Bank of England of keeping its banknotes proportioned to its gold reserve meant that the international gold standard working through the international balance of payments determined the interest rate, the money stock, and the internal price level. With that discipline, real bills views did not lead to a breakdown of the standard. There was then no challenge to the prevailing view that speculative excess led to a subsequent collapse of asset values and banking panics. The Bank of England presumably had a responsibility to raise the discount rate to forestall speculative excess. Hardy (1932, 12) wrote:

> If it appeared that a gold outflow was due to a mere seasonal strain which carried no threat of future trouble, or to a financial crisis abroad, the central bank would put credit into the market by purchasing bills or government securities to offset the loss of gold, and withdraw it again when the strain was past. On the other hand, in cases where the pressure appeared to be due to speculative expansion of credit on the part of commercial banks which threatened to grow cumulatively greater, sound policy required the central bank to tighten the market without waiting for the movement to deplete the reserves and thereby compel contraction.

In the United States in the early 1920s, with the world off the gold standard, gold flowed in from the rest of the world. The Fed abandoned the gold reserve ratio (the ratio of its gold holdings to its note and discount liabilities) as a guide to adjustment of the discount rate. With member banks borrowing from the Reserve Banks, the Fed was determining the interest rate, the money stock, and the internal price level. Now, when the Fed followed the dictum to forestall speculative excess summarized in the Hardy quote above, the results were disastrous.

4.5. CONCLUDING COMMENT

Why did the Fed did not learn to respond similarly to a modern central bank with a reaction function that causes its instrument to move in a way that offsets destabilizing movements in output and prices? Early policy makers understood the Fed as comprising independent reservoirs of funds available to member banks. The funds in those reservoirs were presumed finite given a legally mandated ratio for the gold cover. Within that discipline, the Reserve Banks could extend credit to their member banks that allowed bank credit to contract and to expand in a way that limited the extension of credit to productive uses instead of speculative uses.

The combination of a real bills and gold standard mentality prevented policy makers from understanding that they had left the discipline of the gold standard for a regime of fiat money creation. The classical gold standard provided for monetary control with a nominal anchor and the market determination of the interest rate. A fiat money regime did not. With a money policy undisciplined by a reaction function that allowed the price system to work, the unlimited power to create and, also, to destroy commercial bank deposits led to the monetary pathology of recurrent recession. Under the prewar gold standard, the price system operated automatically to determine the real rate of interest. With the establishment of the Fed, the price system operated only if the Fed allowed it to operate, something the Fed failed to allow.

CHAPTER 5

Why the Fed Failed in the Depression

The 1920s Antecedents

Summary: Milton Friedman (1982, 103) wrote:

> In our book on US monetary history, Anna Schwartz and I found it possible to use one sentence to describe the central principle followed by the Federal Reserve System from the time it began operations in 1914 to 1952. That principle, to quote from our book, is: "If the 'money market' is properly managed so as to avoid the unproductive use of credit and to assure the availability of credit for productive use, then the money stock will take care of itself."

Given the enormous economic disruptions in the 1920s and 1930s, why did not early policy makers question these real bills beliefs? Why did the quantity theory fail to offer an alternative to real bills views that would allow policy makers to understand the disastrous fallacies of real bills views?

Even today, economists differ over the causes of the Depression. Does an explanation of the Depression require an eclectic combination of real and monetary forces? How do monetary explanations account for positive money growth in fall 1929 at the start of the Depression? Why did the Depression last so long rather than ending after about a year and a half like other recessions? Would the Depression have been short-lived if Benjamin Strong, governor of the New York Fed, had lived? What role did the gold standard play in the US recession?

Even among scholars who attribute the Great Depression to contractionary monetary policy, there remains a debate over the reasons for that policy. The debate remains important because it highlights the issue of whether central bankers learn. Why do they make mistakes, and can one have confidence that over time they learn from those mistakes?

Friedman and Schwartz (1963a, 411) argued that in the 1920s the Fed understood its responsibilities under the existing monetary standard but then ignored them in the Depression:

Neither the climate of opinion nor external financial pressures nor lack of power explains why the Federal Reserve System acted as it did. None of them can explain why an active, vigorous, self-confident policy in the 1920's was followed by a passive, defensive, hesitant policy from 1929 to 1933, least of all why the System failed to meet an internal drain in the way intended by its founders.

They argued that the Fed in the 1930s failed to fulfill the responsibilities of a central bank because of a shift in power away from the New York Fed to the Federal Reserve Board.

Brunner and Meltzer (1968) challenged this view. They argued that in the 1920s and 1930s the Fed used a faulty indicator: borrowed reserves. A low level of borrowed reserves led policy makers to conclude that policy was easy. Wheelock (1991, 117) also argued that "Federal Reserve behavior during the depression was . . . largely consistent with earlier policies. . . . There was no fundamental alteration of Fed strategy." He referred to the Brunner-Meltzer hypothesis and to the discount-rate increases in fall 1931 "in defense of the gold standard, an even more traditional pillar of monetary policy."

The view argued here is that in the 1920s, led by the New York Fed, the Fed believed it was following a policy that would prevent recessions. The intellectual foundation of that strategy was the real bills view that the prevention of recession required prompt stifling of the prior speculative excess. Left unchecked, that excess would ultimately collapse and require a period of recession to eliminate imbalances between wages and prices and to purge enterprises built on excessive credit. The foundation of the strategy of monetary policy rested on a pile of tinder, and the match that lit it was the forced contraction of bank credit by the Fed to "liquidate" the New York Stock Exchange. The Fed's strategy in the 1920s of preventing recessions by preventing financial excess followed from the real bills views of the founders of the Fed. Those views continued in the 1930s.

The 1920s and 1930s exhibited enormous instability. There were three major economic downturns. In the first, real GNP fell 11 percent from the cycle peak in 1920Q1 to the cycle trough in 1921Q3 (13.6 percent through 1921Q2). The GNP deflator fell 18.8 percent. In the second, real GNP fell 36.2 percent from the 1929Q3 peak to the 1933Q1 trough. The GNP deflator fell 26.9 percent. In the third, real GNP fell 10.0 percent from the 1937Q2 peak to the 1938Q2 trough (11.4 percent through 1938Q1). The GNP deflator fell 2.8 percent. There were also periods of inflation. From 1933Q1 through

1937Q2, the GNP deflator rose 22.1 percent.[1] Why did early policy makers learn nothing from these episodes?

Friedman and Schwartz argued that learning was not necessary to have avoided the mistakes of the Great Depression. All those policy makers had to do was to make use of central bank practice for dealing with bank panics as codified in Bagehot's (1873) *Lombard Street*, that is, lend freely at a high rate of interest (Friedman and Schwartz 1963a, 395). Friedman and Schwartz, however, vastly understated the extent to which policy makers failed to understand the actual monetary standard and the extent to which an understanding had to await their own work. The reality was that policy makers could always rationalize episodes of economic instability with their existing beliefs. Given the premise that instability is inherent in a market economy, there are always plausible reasons ex post to rationalize recession.

Refutation of the real bills beliefs would have to wait until Milton Friedman had put the quantity theory into a form that could not only offer an alternative but yield superior forecasts of alternative policies. Refutation would also have to wait for the evidence assembled by Friedman that instability is not inherent to a market economy but instead arises from the absence of monetary control, or, equivalently, interference by the central bank with the operation of the price system.

5.1. THE REAL BILLS ETHOS OF THE 1920S

The intention in creating the Federal Reserve was to eliminate financial panics and the associated restriction of credit and consequent recessions. The presumed driving force behind these phenomena was the collapse of an unsustainable level of economic activity inflated by speculative excess. That speculative excess in turn was made possible by the diversion of credit from productive to speculative uses.

Adolph Miller, member of the Federal Reserve Board, was the most articulate of the proponents of real bills (see Humphrey and Timberlake 2019). Miller (US Congress 1926–27, April 30, 1926, 854) testified:

> If we can keep its credit sealed up to its proper self-liquidating uses, you are not going to get any disturbances in price levels through maladjustment in the volume of reserve credit to the total volume of current credit needs as they proceed from industry, trade, and agriculture. So I am very definitely of the view that if we can restrain Federal reserve credit from any speculative uses—and by that I mean not only in the securities mar-

1. Figures from Balke and Gordon (1986).

kets but in commodity markets and in other forms of speculation, such as land and building speculation—we have got what must always be a goal in good, sound banking administration. We have gotten about as far as we possibly can get toward economic stability, and toward price stability as one of its accompanying features.

Later, Miller (US Congress 1931, January 23, 128, 147, 149, and 150) would blame sources that allowed for the expansion of bank credit independently of real bills for a speculative excess whose collapse he held responsible for the Depression:

> Taking the movement of credit since 1922, the main basis of expansion was provided by gold imports and it probably will be the verdict of economic history that the volume of those imports was in excessive amounts; that is, in excess of what the credit system of the country could absorb without producing disturbances; in other words, without producing inflationary developments.
>
> You must not leave it too easy for the Federal reserve system to inflate. We have had too much inflation in the Federal reserve system, and its favorite instrument is the open market purchase of Government securities. We have had something of an obsession for easy money in the system, a feeling that it makes the atmosphere of business; that it can stop a recession of business and turn a period of depression into one of recovery.
>
> The inflation which caused bad banking came largely through gold imports and the open-market operations of the Federal reserve system. . . . Where the reserve system puts money into the market by open market purchases, the money goes eventually to the highest bidder, and inasmuch as the open money market of the country is first and foremost in New York where the great call market is, that is the market to which the Federal reserve money tends to go.
>
> I believe that our troubles will be enormously minimized—in fact I think we will pretty nearly get rid of most of them—if the Federal reserve banks are operated as institutions of rediscount.

Earlier, Charles Hamlin, another original member of the Federal Reserve Board, expressed these real bills views. Friedman and Schwartz (1963a, 266) cited Hamlin's views as recorded in a 1923 entry in his diary:

> There was a fundamental difference between putting money into circulation by a) Buying government securities and b) Bills. . . . Money put out

for b) went primarily to aid a genuine business transaction, while in the case of a) no one could tell where it might go, e.g., to be loaned on Wall Street, etc.

Hamlin (US Congress 1931, January 23, 165) also added security loans as an additional source of the circumvention of real bills principles that led to the stock market collapse and the Depression.

There was, in my opinion, an undue expansion as between security loans and commercial loans covering the period of 1922 to 1927. In that period security loans increased three and nine-tenths billions for the reporting member banks, or over 100 per cent. Commercial loans in the same period increased one and three-tenths billions, or merely 18 per cent.

The regional Reserve Bank governors were bankers who understood their world from their assigned task. As described by Burgess (US Congress 1926–27, May 4, 1926, 1019) of the New York Fed, "Every day the Federal reserve banks are receiving millions of dollars worth of commercial paper from the member banks for rediscount or as collateral against member bank borrowings. The reserve banks, under the law, must submit this paper to critical examination." The individual banker did not control the quantity of his deposits. There was no framework that would allow him to imagine a banking system with which the Reserve Banks controlled the quantity of deposits.

5.2. STOPPING SPECULATION WITHOUT THE DISCIPLINE OF REAL BILLS AND THE INTERNATIONAL GOLD STANDARD

The founders of the Fed thought of the Reserve Banks as reservoirs of funds whose flow of funds to commercial banks would be automatically adjusted to the needs of commerce through the discount of real bills. Money policy worked by directing intermediation to productive (legitimate) uses and away from speculative uses. The whole system would be self-regulating if the Reserve Banks discounted only the short-term, self-liquidating debt ("real bills") that arose in the process of transferring goods from producers to consumers and of bringing crops to market.

Because of the issuance of large amounts of government debt in World War I and because of the inflow of gold and the emergence of a securities market, in the 1920s, however, the credit structure of the country came to rest only to a limited extent on real bills. The Fed struggled with how to reconcile traditional real bills views with this new reality. Moreover, the intentions of the founders of the Fed had been frustrated in another major way. They had failed to remove New York from its central role in allocating credit by dividing the country into segmented credit markets demarcated by the twelve Federal Reserve districts. It became evident in the early 1920s that there continued to be a national money market. That fact became evident when the open market purchases of securities of any of the regional Reserve Banks influenced the New York money market.

These tensions appeared in the 1926 congressional testimony of Adolph Miller (US Congress 1926–27, April 30, 1926, 853), one on the original members of the Federal Reserve Board:

> The view practically universally entertained at the time that the Federal reserve banks were organized was that no part of the credit coming from those banks would get into speculative loans or even security loans. . . . The Federal reserve banks were to keep their operations entirely distinct from any contact, not only direct but indirect, with the securities markets and the securities loans of the country. . . . I think it is also fair to say that the expectation has not been fully realized, and that the full realization of it presents a problem of considerable administrative difficulty; and I am doubtful whether any method could ever be worked out that would completely insure that credit coming from the Federal reserve should not leak into the stock market by way of security loans.

Policy makers believed that money (Federal Reserve banknotes) had value because it was convertible into a commodity, gold, that possessed intrinsic value. There was no understanding that the working of the international gold standard in the pre-Fed era had determined the price level. In setting up the Federal Reserve System, the assumption had been that the continued operation of that standard would limit the speculative extension of credit through the threat of gold outflows.[2] Convertibility of the currency to gold and a real bills criterion for discounting would act in tandem to prevent the evil twins of the speculative extension of credit and the printing of paper money.

The views of Benjamin Strong, governor of the New York Fed from the inception of the Federal Reserve System until his death in 1928, were representative. Strong's views reflected the pervasive ethos of the gold stan-

2. In terms of the modern understanding of the operation of the international gold standard, the combination of a real bills guide to monetary policy and the gold standard is incoherent (Bordo, Edelstein, and Rockoff 1999). However, early policy makers understood the world without the benefit of an understanding of the price system.

dard as the foundation of monetary and financial stability. Restoration of the international gold standard, whose operation ceased with the start of World War I, would eliminate the Fed discretion required in the 1920s to prevent "credit inflation." The control of price inflation would follow as a by-product of balance of supply and demand in individual markets.

The congressional testimony by Strong presented the operation of the gold standard not as the Humean price-specie flow mechanism but rather as an automatic system for the control of speculative excess. Strong (US Congress 1928, March 19, 19–21) testified:

> The creation of a great volume of credit, in excess of what the business of the country requires, immediately has certain reactions. Interest rates go down. . . . Gold would leave the country. . . . It would be an apparently short time . . . before the reserves of the country would become so impaired that we would be facing a suspension of specie payment. I do not know of anything that would bring the country to its senses any quicker. . . . The gold standard is a much more automatic check upon excesses in credit and currency than is a system . . . left to the human judgment of men. . . . Where you are speaking of efforts simply to stabilize commerce, industry, agriculture, and employment, and so on, without the penalties of violation of the gold standard, you are talking about human judgment and the management of prices which I do not believe in at all.

Strong's views attested to the priority he attached in the 1920s to reestablishment of the international gold standard. They also explain the aversion of the eastern financial establishment to the idea of fiat paper money. In a 1913 letter, Strong wrote (cited in Chandler 1958, 35):

> Paramount in importance to any defect is the provision that the note issues [Federal Reserve notes] provided by the bill are to bear the obligation of the United States Government. This is a provisional return to the heresies of Greenbackism and fiat money. . . . The theory has been rejected not only upon the basis of the theories of sound economists, but upon the disastrous practices and experiments of the past in this country and every other civilized country.

5.3. THE CONTROVERSY OVER STABILIZING THE PRICE LEVEL

Opposition by the Fed to legislation to require it to stabilize the price level illustrated the level of ignorance of early policy makers over the nature of the monetary standard. Along with the contention that the Fed lacked the ability to control the price level, the chief argument against a price-stability mandate was that at times when the price level was falling the credit creation required by a mandate for price stability would exacerbate speculation, which would set up an even greater decline in prices in the future.

Adolph Miller (US Congress 1932b, May 18, 247) testified on a bill to require the Fed to stabilize the price level of T. Alan Goldsborough (D-MD):

> It is the view of the Federal Reserve Board that the price situation and the credit situation, while sometimes closely related, are nevertheless not related to one another as simple cause and effect; they are rather both to be regarded as the outcome of common causes that work in the economic and business situation. The same conditions which predispose to a rise in prices also predispose to an increased demand for credit. . . . The demand for credit is conditioned upon the business outlook. Credit is created in increasing volume only as the community wishes to use more credit—when the opportunity for the employment of credit appears more profitable.

Governor Eugene Meyer (US Congress 1932b, May 18, 214) reinforced Miller's testimony.

> We have no power to determine a price level or to restore any given price level. . . . We are exercising a power which is designed to make funds available to the member banks more freely and therefore help to improve business conditions. . . . Passage of the [Goldsborough] bill through the house was very disturbing.

W. R. Burgess (US Congress, 1926–27, May 4, 1926, 914, 918, 923) testified on a bill requiring the Fed to stabilize the price level of James F. Strong (R-KS):

> There does not seem to me to be any close causal relationship or perhaps very little causal relationship between wholesale commodity prices and the bank discount rate, certainly no more than between the cost of living and wages. The discount rate affects credit, the volume of credit. The volume of credit is one influence on wholesale commodity prices. That is, before the discount rate affects prices it goes through a number of different steps, at any one of which other factors come in and modify the picture.
> The price index is not a good indication of the amount of credit required. . . . It is a very serious problem as to what can be done to restrain

a serious speculative orgy. There is no doubt but what last fall, in the latter part of the year, there was a very large extension of credit for stock-exchange uses. . . . Commodity prices were moving downward rather steadily at that time, and if we had had Congressman Strong's bill as our guiding star, our course would not have been to raise the rate, but reduce it.

Representatives Goldsborough and Strong spearheaded the stable-price movement. However, they failed to understand how the Fed was determining the behavior of prices. Like the quantity theorists including Irving Fisher, they had no theory abstracting from financial intermediation of how the Fed controlled bank deposits and money. Lacking in addition a theory of recession organized around a Fed failure to maintain the money stock, quantity theorists could offer no convincing alternative to real bills views. Not until the post–World War II experiences of inflation did quantity theorists like Friedman have available convincing empirical evidence to rebut the embedded speculative-excess/subsequent-collapse view of recession and deflation.

Lacking a theory of monetary control independent of Fed control of bank credit, proposals to have the Fed control prices ran into the argument that such control would require giving up on the control of credit and speculation. Even the congressmen advocating for price stabilization viewed inflation as arising from speculative excess. The following exchange occurred between Representative Goldsborough and Walter W. Stewart (US Congress 1926–27, April 22, 1926, 770–71), director of the Division of Research and Statistics at the Federal Reserve Board from September 1922 until January 1926:

MR. GOLDSBOROUGH: I have always felt that the primary benefit to be accomplished by stabilization [of prices] was to halt periods of unhealthy inflation, which, of course, of necessity would interfere with the demoralizing deflation which follows. . . .

MR. STEWART: To what extent, by an addition to credits at a time when prices are declining, not as an aftermath of war inflation but of maladjustments in business, can you cure the causes which lay back of declining prices? My point is that in such circumstances you take a chance of aggravating the very causes which are responsible for the declining prices. If stocks are accumulating and the mood in the community is speculative, then an attempt to use credit for the purpose of stabilizing prices is more likely to aggravate the causes responsible for the movement in prices. . . . To use the price index as a guide would tend to make credit conditions increasingly unsound. . . . To assume that declining prices, which are, after all, largely a readjustment to take care of the mistakes made previously, can be overcome by an additional extension of credit is more likely to add to the difficulties in the situation rather than to cure it.

Stewart considered deflation to be a consequence of a "maladjustment of prices." Adding credit during deflation in response to a rule to stabilize the price level could then exacerbate the imbalance that caused the price decline in the first place. Especially in 1930, these views impeded an aggressive response to recession and deflation.

In 1932, Representative Goldsborough resuscitated the effort made in the 1920s to require the Fed to stabilize the price level (see Hetzel 1985 and 2012a, chap. 3). On May 2, 1932, the House of Representatives passed the Goldsborough bill, which legislated that "the average purchasing power of the dollar . . . for the years 1921 to 1929 . . . shall be restored and maintained by the control of the volume of credit and currency." It also authorized revaluation of the price of gold if gold reserve ratios became binding. In 1932, New York Fed governor George Harrison was willing to experiment with open market purchases in an attempt to stimulate the economy but never with a commitment to control the price level. Harrison always anticipated the day in which the Fed might have to withdraw the credit forced on banks if it were not productively employed but instead spilled over into speculative excess.

Harrison (US Congress 1932a, April 13, 485) testified:

Suppose . . . the price level is going down, and the Federal reserve system begins to buy government securities, hoping to check the decline, and that inspires a measure of confidence, and a speculation is revived in securities, which may in turn consume so much credit as to require our sales of Governments. There was that difficulty in 1928 and 1929.

Miller (US Congress 1932b, May 18, 250) repeated this view:

The average of commodity prices does not mean anything. . . . The price level is wholly metaphysical. It is a statistical summation of the movements of an infinite variety of commodities in a vast number of markets scattered over the face of the world. . . . The commodity price level, with the stability it showed during those years [the 1920s], was a cover for one of the most vicious and costly, disastrous and destructive inflations this country or any country in a state of solvency had ever experienced. . . .

The thing to be expected in this country if we operated under a stabilization philosophy would be inflations.

H. Parker Willis (1933, 233, 245–46), who had advised Carter Glass in the writing of the Federal Reserve Act, expressed real bills views:

> The root evil, as is now apparent in our whole programme of "recovery," whether under the Hoover or the Roosevelt Administration, is that of seeking to restore something that should never have existed—the price and business situation of pre-panic days, say, of 1926 or 1929. . . . Banking can never be safe or solvent under an artificial price level, and that the effort of assumed necessity to control or maintain prices is always the deadly foe of wise and safe credit extension. A prerequisite to the restoration of banking soundness is, in short, the total abandonment of any and all attempts to direct prices through what is termed "credit control."

5.4. REGULATING THE FLOW OF CREDIT: THE "TENTH ANNUAL REPORT"

In the 1920s, with the inoperability of the gold reserve ratio as a guide to policy and with political pressure for expansionary monetary policy created by a ratio well in excess of the legally required value, the Fed needed new guidelines for policy. The response was the "Tenth Annual Report of the Federal Reserve Board Covering Operations for the Year 1923," published in 1924. Gold flows would not serve as the basis for the expansion and contraction of credit. That responsibility would rest with the Fed. Without a self-regulating system, the Fed would need new guidelines.

As conceived in the Federal Reserve Act, the Reserve Banks would extend whatever credit was demanded for legitimate uses. Confined to this productive use, the quantity of credit would be self-regulating. The report (Federal Reserve Board 1924a, 33–34) stated:

> The Federal reserve system is a system of productive credit. It is not a system of credit for either investment or speculative purposes. . . . It is the belief of the Board that there will be little danger that the credit created and contributed by the Federal reserve banks will be in excessive volume if restricted to productive uses.

The report then attempted to formulate guides. The prevention of speculative excess would require more than the restriction of discount window lending to real bills. The Federal Reserve System would have to control the quantity of credit extended to prevent an excess from spilling over into speculative uses. Friedman and Schwartz (1963a, 253) summarized the new guides in terms of the warning that "the danger is that credit will be used to finance the speculative accumulation of commodity stocks, which will in turn produce a disequilibrium between production and consumption and subsequently a contraction in prices and economic activity." The report was a "marriage of the traditional real bills doctrine and an inventory theory of the business cycle . . . doubtless inspired by the 1920–21 episode."

Given this perspective, deflation would come too late to signal the speculative excess that caused it. Goldenweiser (1925, 31), director of research at the Federal Reserve Board, with reference to the 1920–21 recession and deflation, explained:

> The liquidation, which began in the late fall of 1920, . . . was brought about by the inevitable work of economic forces which, when a period of inflation reaches its peak, brings about a reversal, and after the turn comes accelerates the decline until the pendulum once more swings in the opposite direction. During the period of advancing prices business accumulates a large number of weak concerns which are kept afloat merely by the fact that the value of their inventories advances continuously. . . . When confidence was once shaken and prices began to decline these accumulated stocks began to be thrown on the market, thereby accelerating the price declines.

The report (Federal Reserve Board 1924a, 30) rejected the price level as a guide to policy:

> Particular prominence has been given in discussions of new proposals to the suggestion frequently made that the credit issuing from the Federal reserve banks should be regulated with immediate reference to the price level, particularly in such manner as to avoid fluctuations of general prices. . . . But it must not be overlooked that price fluctuations proceed from a great variety of causes, most of which lie outside the range of influence of the credit system. No credit system could undertake to perform the function of regulating credit by reference to prices without failing in the endeavor.

According to early policy makers, what drove the booms and busts of the business cycle with its associated inflations and deflations was the mood of the business community. Good credit administration would read that mood and react early to avoid speculative excess. The report (Federal Reserve Board 1924a, 32) stated:

> When the business outlook is inviting business men are apt to adventure and new business commitments are made in increasing volume. . . . Credit administration must be cognizant of what is under way or in process in the movement of business before it is registered in the price index. The price index records an accomplished fact. . . . The problem of efficient credit administration is, therefore, largely a question of timeliness of action. . . . No statistical mechanism alone, however carefully contrived, can furnish an adequate guide to credit administration. Credit is an intensely human institution and as such reflects the moods and impulses of the community—its hopes, its fears, its expectations.

5.5. CONTROVERSY OVER THE MONETARY STANDARD: THE EASTERN ESTABLISHMENT VERSUS THE POPULISTS

There was a quantity theory alternative to Fed policy. That alternative, however, lay on the William Jennings Bryan populist side of the split in American society. Acceptance of the purposeful money creation entailed by the quantity theory was the antithesis of real bills. From the experience with the assignats in the French Revolution to the still-fresh experience of hyperinflation in the early 1920s in Germany, Hungary, and Austria, fiat money creation had led to social disorder. The quantity theory and paper (fiat) money were indissolubly identified with each other in the spirit of the time. All the historical episodes of a paper money standard had ended in inflation, most recently, the post–World War I hyperinflations.

The *New York Times* reported, "No one doubts that the outright issue of illimitable and irredeemable government fiat money would do more even than to restore the prices of 1929. Germany's experiment in that direction brought the average price level in the Autumn of 1923 . . . three million times as high as that of 1914" (January 30, 1933, 19, cited in Sumner 2015, 177). The belief prevailed that the value of a dollar derived from convertibility to the ultimate source of value: gold. The fact that the United States maintained convertibility of the dollar into gold, even though the Fed never followed the rules of the gold standard, blinded policy makers to the fact that they had in fact created a fiat money standard.

Edwin Kemmerer (1944, 109), a professor at Princeton, known as the "money doctor" for advising foreign central banks, wrote:

The paper-money standards of the war and early postwar period were terrible failures. In the field of economics, the war probably left no conviction stronger with the masses of the people of Europe than that *never again* did they want to suffer the evils of such an orgy of inflated paper money. Everywhere there was a popular longing to get back to a "solid" monetary standard, to something in which the people had confidence; and in the distracted world of that time there was no other commodity in which they had so much confidence as gold. (italics in original)

The challenge to the conservative eastern financial establishment by the southern and western populists appeared to present a stark choice between the current system or a runaway printing press. The anti-Fed populist spirit appeared in the following exchange between Irving Fisher and Congressman Otis Wingo (D-AR). Representative Wingo started by complaining that the purpose of creating the Fed was to make credit available to banks during financial crises when the large New York banks refused to provide credit. However, in 1919–20, the Fed had used its power to restrict credit and forced farmers to dump their crops on the market at depressed prices. Fisher argued that his proposal to stabilize the price level would remove that power from the Fed (US Congress 1923, December 19, 52):

MR. WINGO: I will tell you about the people who are back of what you characterize as the spirit of populism in the West. . . . They say, "Somehow this great Federal Reserve system that we thought was going to liberate us from dictatorial, autocratic control that refused to let us have money and credits when we needed them is undertaking to bawl us out. . . . You have no right to hold cotton and wheat." Have they any right to tell me that that I must close down my factory if I want to keep on producing. . . .

PROFESSOR FISHER: This is not controlling the price of an article. It is controlling the rate of interest. They do it now; they do it badly. I propose that they do it well, so as to stabilize business and the price level.

MR. WINGO: That is what every autocrat says, whenever you give him autocratic control.

PROFESSOR FISHER: They have it now. We want to take it away from them; this will take it away from them.

No one understood the monetary regime that the Fed had created as one of fiat money creation. No one knew how to translate the universal understanding of the Fed as a reservoir of funds used to influence the cost and availability of credit to member banks into an understanding of a central bank responsible for money creation and destruction. As O. M. W. Sprague (US Congress 1935b, May 3, 225), a Harvard professor and expert on money and banking, said: "The major function of a central banking organization is to influence the supply and cost of credit."

In one of the great ironies of monetary history, policy makers, whose views represented the conservative eastern financial establishment, viewed the populist proposals to print paper money as destroying the monetary system. In fact, Fed policy makers had exactly that power, but they used it in the Depression not to control money creation but to destroy bank reserves, the banking system, and the paper money (deposits) created by banks. In the 1920s and 1930s, the route to understanding the monetary standard lay through development of the quantity theory to explain that the Fed was in fact controlling bank deposits through the way in which it controlled reserves creation (monetary base creation). Along with the quantity theory, that understanding languished. In its place, the economics profession wandered lost in a Keynesian desert for decades.

5.6. CONCLUDING COMMENT

Policy makers had no comprehension of the responsibility to set a nominal anchor (give money a well-defined value) under the regime of fiat money creation they had created but could not comprehend. Such a regime, a regime of "managed money," would have represented, they believed, the triumph of the populist, agrarian forces that threatened the conservative, eastern financial establishment. Nothing prepared policy makers for the transition from a gold standard in which a world market determined money and interest rates to a monetary standard that thrust those responsibilities on them.

CHAPTER 6

A Fiat Money Standard

Free Reserves Operating Procedures and Gold

Summary: The creation of the Federal Reserve System led to creation of a new kind of monetary standard. Under the metallic monetary standard that existed prior to World War I, market forces determined the interest rate, the money stock (nominal and real), and the price level. The Fed's primitive free reserves operating procedures determined the interest rate on bank reserves (the marginal cost of obtaining reserves from the Fed). Arbitrage spread that rate to money market rates of interest. The interest rate then was determined endogenously in the market for bank reserves through a Fed reserves supply schedule and a banking system reserves demand schedule. There was nothing in early Fed procedures in the form of a reaction function to cause the resulting interest rate to track the economy's natural rate of interest. No one understood that the interest rate operated as part of the price system to maintain the economy growing at potential. No one understood that Fed interference with that role would create destabilizing monetary emissions and absorptions.

Monetary disorder led to real disorder. The fact that the Fed maintained convertibility between gold and Federal Reserve notes obscured the reality that the Fed had created a fiat money regime. No policy maker understood the Fed's responsibility for the behavior of the price level in the new regime. Sorting out the sources of ignorance of early policy makers about the monetary standard they had created usefully starts from an understanding of the Fed's operating procedures. Understanding of the responsibilities of the central bank in a regime of fiat money would occur only slowly in the post–World War II period.

In short, early policy makers failed to understand that the monetary regime they had created after the Federal Reserve Act of 1913 made the short-term interest rate their instrument. In reality, monetary policy worked through the interaction of the interest rate set in the market for reserves with the working of the price system. Those procedures kept the real rate of interest from playing its equilibrating role. Unlike in the gold standard, market forces could not work to determine the Wicksell-ian natural rate of interest.

"There is probably little need to insist upon the necessity of a correct under-standing of the monetary mechanism in the years immediately preceding the Great Depression." Lauchlin Currie (1934b, 145) wrote these words in 1934. The goal here is to enhance that understanding for the decade of the 1920s. Like other works in the quantity theory tradition, this work empha-sizes the failure of the Federal Reserve System to provide for the monetary control required to prevent deflation. What is missing in the existing litera-ture, however, is an explanation of how the Fed's procedures determined market interest rates. With this summary of Fed procedures, one can ex-plain monetary contraction as a consequence of maintenance by the Fed of the real rate of interest (the marginal cost of reserves to banks) above the Wicksellian natural rate of interest.

One can then ask why in the Depression the Fed did not respond simi-larly to a modern central bank with a reaction function that causes the central bank's instrument to move regularly in response to the behavior of output and prices. What beliefs caused policy makers to implement policy within their free reserves framework without aggressive reductions in dis-count rates and open market purchases to counter recession and deflation? Answers to these questions highlight the vast gulf separating policy makers' understanding of the Fed's role and the role played by a modern central bank. In the event, three decades elapsed after the Treasury-Fed Accord of 1951 before the modern concept of a central bank became established.

6.1. CHANGING THE MONETARY STANDARD WITH NO UNDERSTANDING OF THE CONSEQUENCES

When the Fed was created in December 1913, the developed world was on a gold standard. When the Fed first gained its independence in 1919, the world had left the gold standard. When gold flowed into the United States in 1921, the Fed found itself with large amounts of free gold above the amount legally required to back its liabilities (Federal Reserve notes and member bank reserves). It then ignored the reserve ratio and effectively abandoned the gold standard. As summarized by Bopp et al. (1947, 24):

> The exceptional character and volume of international gold movements demonstrated that the reserve ratio is an unreliable guide to central banking policy. . . . [In the 1920s] the ratio ceased to be used as a guide to policy.

In the absence of the international gold standard and with the gold reserves ratio no longer an operable guide to changes in the discount rate, the Fed had to invent new guides for the conduct of policy. The original real bills guide of rediscounting real bills (commercial paper) offered no guidance for how to set the discount rate or how to handle the newly discovered tool of open market operations.

Policymakers understood their new procedures as influencing the cost and availability of loanable funds to banks. To replace the reserves extinguished by open market sales of government securities, banks borrowed from the discount window. Because the regional Reserve Banks applied administrative pressure on banks in the discount window for other than brief periods, a significant amount of borrowed reserves for the banking system created pressure on the banking system to contract assets. If the Fed wanted to tighten, the Reserve Banks would engage in open market sales, which increased borrowed reserves and market interest rates. They would then "follow" the increase in market rates by raising the discount rate.

Brunner and Meltzer (1964) and Meltzer (2003) invented the term "the Riefler-Burgess doctrine," using the names of the early Fed economists who documented the relationship between money market rates and the new operating procedures. Brunner and Meltzer attributed the contractionary monetary policy of the Great Contraction to the mistaken belief that policy was easy if the borrowed reserves of the banking system were at low levels. Governor Strong of the New York Fed explained the use of borrowed reserves as an indicator of the degree of pressure the Fed was exerting on banks to adjust their loan portfolios.

In a statement to the Governors Conference in March 1926, Strong commented on how the Reserve Banks could affect business conditions (reproduced in Chandler 1958, 239–40):

> Experience in the past has indicated that member banks when indebted to the Federal Reserve Bank of New York and in less degree at the other money centers constantly endeavor to free themselves from the indebtedness, and as a consequence such pressure as arises is in the direction of curtailing loans. As a guide to the timing and extent of any purchases which might appear desirable, one of our best guides would be the amount of borrowing by member banks in principal centers, and particularly in New York and Chicago. Our experience has shown that when New York City banks are borrowing in the neighborhood of 100 million dollars or more, there is then some real pressure for reducing loans, and money rates tend to be markedly higher than the discount rate. On the other hand, when borrowings of these banks are negligible,

as in 1924, the money situation tends to be less elastic and if gold imports take place, there is liable to be some credit inflation, with money rates dropping below our discount rates. When member banks are owing us about 50 million dollars or less the situation appears to be comfortable, with no marked pressure for liquidation and with the requisite elasticity. Under these circumstances no single bank tends to be in debt for any extended period and borrowings are passed around among the different banks. Call and time money rates tend to be but slightly above our discount rate. . . . In the event of business liquidation now appearing, it would seem advisable to keep the New York City banks out of debt beyond something in the neighborhood of 50 million dollars. It would probably be well if some similar rule could be applied to the Chicago banks, although the amount would, of course, be smaller and the difficulties greater because of the influence of the New York market.

The Brunner-Meltzer insight is essential to understanding Fed behavior. By itself, however, it does not explain why early policy makers were so ignorant about the monetary standard they had created. Early policy makers lacked the analytical apparatus required to understand the consequences of their actions. They had no sense of the operation of the price system and how their procedures interacted with it. As pioneers of a fiat money standard, they lacked the rich set of episodes of monetary disorders required to test the validity of alternative analytical frameworks for understanding the monetary standard. All that lay in the future.

6.2. THE FED'S PRIMITIVE FREE RESERVES OPERATING PROCEDURES

In the 1920s, the Fed developed a dimly understood and erratically implemented form of free reserves procedures. The term "free reserves" refers to the excess reserves minus the borrowed reserves of the banking system. Policy makers held the belief that free reserves measured the degree of pressure on banks to expand or to contract their assets. Before 1932, banks held small amounts of excess reserves (reserves in excess of the legally required minimum). Within the loanable-funds framework used at the time, a low level of borrowed reserves meant that the Fed was supplying ample reserves. Banks then had an incentive to expand their lending. However, lack of demand for loans could frustrate that incentive.

With such procedures, the Fed determined the marginal cost of bank reserves. It did so by forcing banks collectively to borrow from the discount window through setting nonborrowed reserves at a value less than the reserves demanded by banks. The marginal cost of reserves then was de-

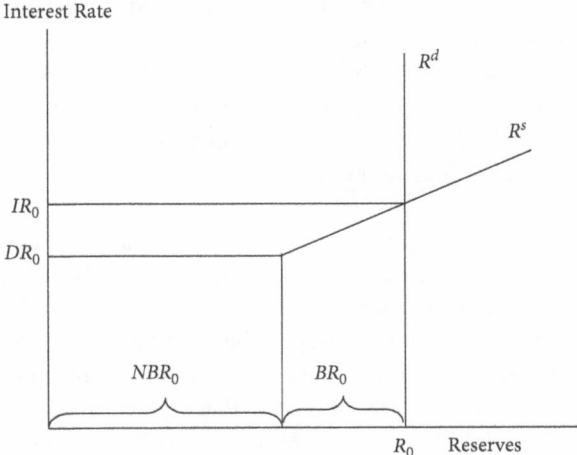

Figure 6.1. Market for Bank Reserves

R is bank reserves. R^d is the reserves demand schedule of the banking system and R^s the reserves supply schedule of the Fed. IR is the interest rate on bank reserves. DR is the discount rate. NBR and BR are nonborrowed and borrowed reserves, respectively. The 0's denote particular values.

termined by the sum of the discount rate and a nonpecuniary cost imposed by the regional Federal Reserve Banks for use of the window. Those costs took the form of being called on the carpet and being subject to increased supervisory oversight for extended use (Wheelock 1991, chap. 3).

Figure 6.1 shows free reserves procedures graphically. It displays the reserves demand and reserves supply schedules under these procedures. The reserves demand schedule measures required reserves plus desired excess reserves. At any given time, reserves demand is completely inelastic because banks must adjust loans and investments to adjust deposits and required reserves. The reserves supply schedule comprises two parts. The vertical part measures the nonborrowed reserves of banks, NBR_0. Gold outflows, increases in both currency in circulation and Treasury deposits with the Fed, all factors beyond the Fed's immediate control, shift the nonborrowed reserves schedule leftward, and conversely for flows in the other direction. The Fed could shift the nonborrowed reserves schedule rightward through open market purchases of government securities or through purchases of bankers' acceptances, and conversely for sales.

The Fed set total nonborrowed reserves below reserves demand. Collectively, banks had to borrow from the discount window. The marginal cost of reserves, that is, the interest rate paid for obtaining the marginal dollar of reserves, IR_0, is then the sum of the discount rate, DR_0, plus a nonpecuniary cost of borrowing from the window that varies positively with the amount of funds obtained from the discount window. Based on real bills principles of self-liquidating loans, use of the window was presumed incompatible with continuous borrowing and was associated with speculative purposes and capital investments. The regional Reserve Banks applied stringent supervisory oversight if a member bank borrowed continuously.

Keynes (1930, 240 and 243) wrote:

> In the first place, pressure is put on the Member Banks to restrain their use of re-discounting facilities with the Federal Reserve Banks by criticizing them, asking inconvenient questions, and creating a public opinion to the effect that it is not quite respectable for a Member Bank, or good for its credit, to be using the resources of the Reserve Bank more than its neighbor. . . . Since 1925 the convention that Member Banks should not re-discount except for very short periods has been gaining ground.

Early on, the New York Fed realized that to cause money market rates to increase when it raised the discount rate, it would have to maintain nonborrowed reserves below total reserves demand and thus keep banks in the window. The first instance in which the commercial paper rate fell below the discount rate occurred in 1922, and the Reserve Banks sold Treasury securities "to regain their influence on the money market" (Hayek 1925 [1999], 124). That practice would keep the paper rate above the discount rate until summer 1932.

With minimal total borrowing by member banks (a low value of BR_0 in figure 6.1), individual member banks were in the window because of reserves deficiencies for only brief periods, and borrowing did not incur nonpecuniary costs. Figure 6.2 shows this situation with a horizontal section (the dashed line) of the reserve supply schedule, R_S. In contrast, with a significant amount of total borrowing (a relatively large value of BR_0 and a relatively small value of NBR_0, some individual banks were forced into the window for long enough periods to incur significant costs.

In figure 6.2, the reserves supply schedule slopes upward after the initial horizontal section, that is, when borrowed reserves, BR_0, become relatively important. When the Fed wanted to raise the cost of funds to member banks, it would first sell government securities (decrease nonborrowed reserves) to move the reserves supply schedule leftward and push member banks onto the upward sloping segment of the R_S schedule. Governor Strong (US Congress 1926, April 8, 332) testified:

> If speculation arises, prices are rising, and possibly other considerations move the Reserve banks to tighten up a bit on the use of their credit, and

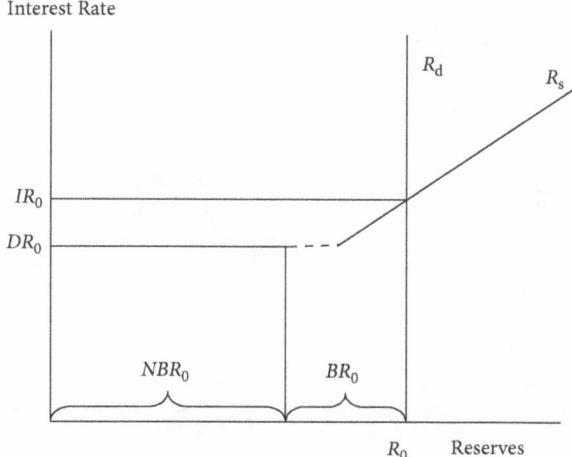

Figure 6.2. Market for Bank Reserves: Horizontal Section Reserves Supply
R is bank reserves. R_d is the reserves demand schedule of the banking system and R_s the reserves supply schedule of the Fed. IR is the interest rate on bank reserves. DR is the discount rate. NBR and BR are nonborrowed and borrowed reserves, respectively. The o's denote particular values.

we own a large amount of Government securities, it is a more effective program, we find by actual experience, to begin to sell our Government securities. It lays a foundation for an advance in our discount rate. If the reverse condition appears . . . then the purchase of securities eases the money market and permits the reduction of our discount rate.

Through arbitrage, the marginal cost of bank reserves, IR_0 in figure 6.1, determined money market rates of interest. Figure 6.3 shows how the commercial paper rate stayed above the New York Fed discount rate. W. Randolph Burgess (US Congress 1926–27, May 4, 1926, 1021) of the New York Fed, stated:

There is a very close relationship between the money rates in New York and the amount of money which the member banks owe us, and that is the entire secret of the effectiveness of our open-market operations. . . . As a matter of fact, it is my personal opinion that the amount the member banks owe us is more important in determining conditions than the rediscount rate.

Two facets of these procedures would become important in the contractionary monetary policy that characterized the Great Contraction. First,

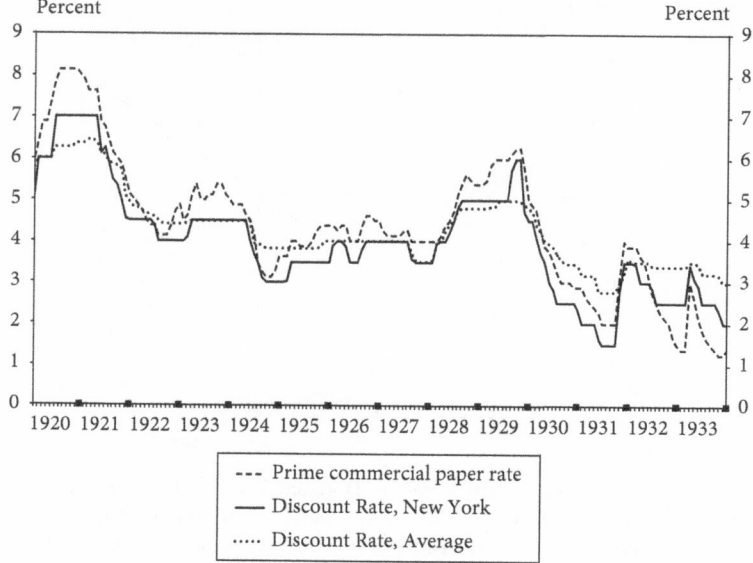

Figure 6.3. Money Market Interest Rates and Regional Fed Bank Discount Rates
Monthly observations of the prime commercial paper rate, the New York Fed discount
rate, and the average of the discount rates set by all other regional Reserve Banks.
Heavy tick marks indicate fourth quarter.
Source: Board of Governors (1943, tables 115 and 120)

when the Board announced its policy of "direct pressure" warning banks
against securities loans if they were borrowing from the discount window,
any borrowing initiated administrative oversight. The horizontal section of
the reserves supply section shown in figure 6.2 disappeared. Second, the
Reserve Banks worried that significant open market purchases of government securities would eliminate discount window borrowing and their discount rates would then no longer affect money market rates. They would,
consequently, it was supposed, lose their ability to control the reemergence
of speculative lending.

Walter W. Stewart (US Congress 1926–27, April 22, 1926, 769), who had
been director of research at the Federal Reserve Board testified:

It is also clear to me that with a continued and considerable price decline month by month, that as the recession took place currency would
come in from circulation, member banks would have smaller demands
for credit, and the reserve banks would be out of touch with the situation
and have a diminishing control as prices declined.

Stewart did not allow for a reduction in the discount rate that would shift downward the R^S schedule, lower the interest rate, IR_0, stimulate economic activity, shift the R^d schedule rightward, and thus increase borrowed reserves. The modern concept of a reaction function with a two-way interaction between Fed behavior and that of the economy did not exist.

6.3. RESERVES ADJUSTMENT AND THE CALL LOAN MARKET

Until the Great Contraction, banks carried minimal excess reserves. Hardy (1932, 21) noted, "In normal times member banks carry practically no surplus reserves for seasonal needs or emergency use. Instead they rely on their secondary reserves—call loans, deposits with correspondents, salable securities—and on the facilities of the Reserve Banks."

W. Randolph Burgess (US Congress 1926–27, May 5, 1926, 1010–11) explained the reserves management of banks:

This black line is the call-loan closing rate. The interesting thing about this chart is that when the [bank] reserves are below [reserve] requirements the call-loan rate goes up, and when the reserves are above [reserve] requirements the call-loan rate tends to go down. There is almost an exact inverse relationship there and, of course, that is a perfectly reasonable thing to expect. Each one of these banks has an officer whose business it is to study the reserve position of that bank, to judge their money position, if you will. It is his business to bring reserves out at the end of the week, just as near the requirements as possible. He does not want to bring out reserves beyond the requirements, because then he is losing money. He wants to invest all the money he possibly can and keep it working. He does not want to bring them out below the requirements, because then the bank has to pay a penalty. His business is to make his reserves average for the week to just hit the requirements, and he usually hits it with a very small amount over.

Burgess (US Congress 1926–27, May 4, 1926, 929) explained the central role of the call loan market ("stock exchange money market") in bank reserves adjustment:

New York is a center for surplus funds from all over the country. Anybody having some money left that he does not know what to do with sends it to New York, either directly or through a correspondent bank in New York. The amount of funds involved in the bill market is $600,000,000 to $800,000,000; Government securities, about $2,000,000,000, including short-term Government securities, certificates, and notes; commercial paper, around $700,000,000; stock exchange money market at the present time about $2,800,000,000.

However, policy makers viewed the call loan market as a source of funds feeding speculation on the New York Stock Exchange (NYSE). In the following exchange with Adolph Miller of the Federal Reserve Board, Congressman James Strong (US Congress 1926–27, April 30, 1926, 881–82) observed that stock market speculation was being fed by funds channeled to New York from all over the country.

> MR. STRONG: In other words, these country banks that had raised objections to stock-market operations were feeding the market and furnishing the sinews of war?
>
> DOCTOR MILLER: I think that during the year 1925, or at the end of the year, roughly speaking, about one-half of the money loaned on so-called broker's loans in New York was contributed by the New York banks and about one-half by the out-of-town banks. . . . And it is not to be understood that these were only big banks. Many of the smaller banks were maintaining, in proportion to their total resources, very considerable balances in New York, either with their correspondents or invested by the correspondents on their behalf in call loans.

Miller (US Congress 1931, January 23, 150–51) recognized the role played by the call loan market in reserves adjustment but the presumed speculative excess on the NYSE indicated an excess of funds beyond what was required for legitimate commercial use:

> It will be noticed that funds, as witness 1927, pour into the call-loan market from all over the country, whenever there is an accumulation of banking reserves beyond what the banks can find good use for at home. The banks usually send the most considerable part of their surplus money to New York—usually for investment in call loans, especially when the rate on call loans is attractive. Bankers still use the phrase that was current in pre–Federal reserve days and describe the call loan as "secondary reserve." Among the interior banks it is so treated and used. The advantage of a good secondary reserve is that you can get it when you want it and in the meantime get a return on it. In other words, when you call your loan, you must be sure that you will get the money, otherwise it is a poor reliance as a secondary reserve.

6.4. THE PRAGMATIC DEVELOPMENT
OF THE NEW PROCEDURES

In the last part of 1921 and early 1922, the individual Reserve Banks bought Treasury securities to replace their earning assets, which were being depleted as gold inflows caused member banks to reduce discount window borrowing. The Treasury complained that the purchases made it difficult to price their issues. Strong organized a committee of governors to coordinate purchases. In March 1923, when Strong was on leave because of illness, the Board dismissed the original committee and formed the Open Market Investment Committee (OMIC), which made purchases for a Federal Reserve System account.

When the regional Reserve Banks made open market purchases of government securities to increase their earnings assets, it became evident that open market operations by the Reserve Banks along with the discount rate of the New York Fed influenced interest rates in the New York money market. Strong offered the following description at the November 1923 Governors Conference (reproduced in Chandler 1958, 239):

It has been disclosed by the figures in the past that the first result of buying by Reserve Banks, no matter which Reserve Banks buy, is to bring about a very sharp reduction in the borrowings of member banks from the Reserve Banks in New York, first, and in Philadelphia, Boston and Cleveland. The proceeds of the purchases will drift at once to the money centers, and as discounts are repaid, it eases money in the three or four principal money markets. . . . It reduces the rate on bills, and the effect of easier money at the money center spreads throughout the whole country, and the banks in the money centers have a surplus to loan.

Burgess (1964, 220) wrote:

First, as fast as the Reserve banks bought government securities in the market, member banks paid off more of their borrowings; and, as a result, earning assets and earnings of the Reserve bank remained unchanged. Second, they [the Reserve Banks] discovered that the country's pool of credit is all one pool and money flows like water throughout the country. . . . These funds coming into the hands of banks enabled them to pay off their borrowings and feel able to lend more freely.

Governor Strong shaped the operating procedures of the Fed in the early 1920s. There were three instruments for influencing the cost and availabil-

ity of credit: the discount rate, open market operations in government securities, and purchases of bankers' acceptances. Open market purchases
reduced member bank borrowing while sales increased borrowing. Along
with the level of the discount rates of the member banks, the extent of member bank borrowing influenced interest rates in the New York money market. The relative importance assigned to these instruments reflected a hier-
archy according to Strong in which the discount rate was the most potent.
Next came open market operations. Finally, adjustment of acceptances,
which also furnished reserves, was used to make short-lived adjustments to
bank reserves, especially in response to seasonal demands.

Strong (US Congress 1926, April 8, 333) described the psychological impact of raising the discount rate in congressional testimony:[1]

> It seems to me that the foundation for rate changes can be more safely
> and better laid by preliminary operations in the open market than would
> be possible otherwise, and the effect is less dramatic and less alarming
> to the country if it is done in that way than if we just make advances and
> reductions in our discount rate.

The psychological impact that Strong attributed to changes in the discount rate appeared in an exchange between him and Walter Stewart, a
Board economist, at a meeting of the Open Market Investment Committee
for the Federal Reserve System, December 19, 1924. Strong opposed an increase in the discount rate. Strong (Federal Reserve Board 1924c, 19) commented "You must remember that we can kill business in this country very
easily," and Stewart asked, "Do you think an increase to 3½ percent would
kill business?" Strong responded:

> I think at the moment it would have a very chilling effect. . . . The way to
> get the rate advanced is just as Dr. Stewart has described—to liquidate
> the securities and establish a higher market rate and prepare the minds
> of the people for an increase in the discount rate. . . . The thing that con-
> trols in this country is the mood of the people and it can be changed in
> a flash.

1. These procedures also had political economy advantages. The criticism of the Fed
for raising the discount rate to engineer the deflation of the 1920–21 recession could be
diffused by procedures that caused an increase in the discount rate to follow an increase
in market rates. That is, the New York Fed sold government securities to cause an initial
rise in money market rates by shifting the reserves supply schedule leftward (figure 6.1).
It then subsequently raised its discount rate. According to the Fed, it was simply "following" market rates.

Both Burgess (1927 and 1936) and Winfield W. Riefler (1930) at the Federal Reserve Board examined the relationship between the interest rate in the New York money market and the discount rate set by the New York Fed and the open market operations of the Federal Reserve Banks. Riefler offered two explanations for why banks borrowed from the discount window: One explanation is that banks found it profitable to borrow with the discount rate below market rates. The other was that banks borrow only when forced to by a reserves deficiency and get out of the window as soon as possible. The discussion is confused because neither explanation distinguished between banks collectively, which had to borrow, and the individual bank, which chose the least-cost alternative to meeting its reserves needs.

To wit, Riefler (1930, 19–20, cited in Meltzer 2003, 162) wrote:

> The most obvious theory is that member banks, on the whole, borrow at the reserve banks when it is profitable to do so and repay their indebtedness as soon as the operation proves costly. The cost of borrowing at the reserve banks, accordingly, is held to be the determining factor in the relation between the reserve bank operations to money rates, and the discount policy adopted by the reserve banks to be the most important factor in making reserve bank policy effective in the money markets. At the other extreme, there is the theory that member banks borrow at reserve banks only in case of necessity and endeavor to repay their borrowing as soon as possible. According to this theory the fact of borrowing in and of itself—the necessity imposed by circumstances on member banks for resorting to the resources of the reserve banks—is a more important factor in the money market than the discount rate. . . . Open market operations . . . contribute more directly to the effectiveness of the reserve bank credit policy than changes in the discount rate.

The deficiencies in the Fed's understanding of its operating procedures became a central reason for the contractionary monetary policy of the Great Contraction in 1929 when the Fed was trying to restrict the flow of credit for margin lending on the NYSE. Policy makers interpreted increases in the discount rate in 1928 that left borrowed reserves unchanged while increasing the money market interest rate and leaving the difference between it and the discount rate unchanged as meaning that banks still had an incentive to borrow from the discount window and lend the funds for securities speculation. (In figure 6.1, the vertical segment of the R_S schedule, which rises above NBR_0, lengthened leaving borrowed reserves unchanged but raising IR_0, the interest rate in the money market.) As discussed in chapter 8, the result was the Board policy of "direct pressure" aimed at keeping banks out of the discount window if they had loans on their books to brokers or loans collateralized by securities.

Using real bills views, policy makers understood their operating procedures within a loanable-funds framework rather than within a reserves market framework. The regional Reserve Banks were reservoirs of funds that could add to the supply of funds to aid in the financing of productive activity. Just as important was to limit the supply of funds when necessary to prevent speculative excess. The task of augmenting or of restricting credit required assessing the speculative temper of markets.

This loanable-funds, real bills understanding of the Fed's role appeared in the testimony of Adolph Miller (US Congress 1926–27, April 21, 1926, 708), member of the Federal Reserve Board, in his repetition of a claim made in the "Tenth Annual Report" (Federal Reserve Board 1924a, 13) that an open market sale of a security, which reduced reserves and was met by an offsetting increase in reserves borrowed through the discount window, demonstrated that the credit was needed:

> It gave a fair indication that, in the judgment of the member banks, it was needed, because as cash was taken out of the market by the reserve banks the member banks came right back to the Federal reserve banks and rediscounted in substantially the same amount. We thus threw upon the member banks of the country the responsibility of exercising their judgment as to whether or not they should continue in use the existing volume of credit extended to their customers.

The Fed's failure to understand its responsibility to set a price for bank reserves that made the quantity demanded consistent with maintenance of bank deposits and credit as opposed to being the regulator of a flow of credit proportioned to the need for credit for productive uses had tragic consequences in the Great Contraction. In a way almost incomprehensible to modern economists, the Fed did not understand that the credit and deposits of the banking system rested on a base of reserves that the Fed itself controlled. Ultimately, that ignorance derived from the failure to realize the nature of the monetary standard as one of fiat money creation. With no realization of the consequences of its actions, the Fed allowed the superstructure of credit and deposits resting on that reserves base to collapse.

With no conception that it was responsible for the money stock, the Fed could have no conception that it was responsible for the price level. The failure of the Fed to understand its responsibility to maintain money and prices appeared in Miller's 1928 congressional testimony. Miller (US Congress

1928, April 30 and May 17, 109, 348, and 180) commented on Congressman Strong's bill to stabilize prices:

> One of those assumptions [of the Strong bill] is that changes in the level of prices are caused by changes in the volume of credit and currency; the other is that changes in volume of credit are caused by Federal reserve policy. Neither of those assumptions is true of the facts or the realities. They are both in some degree figments—figments of scholastic invention—that have never found any very substantial foundation in economic reality, and less to-day in the United States than at other times. . . .
>
> Undertaking to regulate the flow of Federal reserve credit by the price index is a good deal like trying to regulate the weather by the barometer. The barometer does not make the weather; it indicates what is in process.
>
> The total volume of money in circulation is determined by the community. The Federal reserve system has no appreciable control over that and no disposition to interfere with it.

6.5. GOLD CONVERTIBILITY AND FREE GOLD: FROZEN INTO A GOLD STANDARD MENTALITY

Until April 1933, the United States maintained convertibility between the dollar and gold. Contemporaneous observers assumed that the United States was on the gold standard not a fiat money standard. As Edwin Kemmerer (US Congress 1935b, May 13, 350) said, "The gold standard exists in any country when the monetary unit in which exchanges are made, in which debts are contracted, carried, and paid, consists of the value of a fixed quantity of gold in a free gold market." This gold standard mentality prevented policy makers from comprehending that their free reserves operating procedures had changed the monetary standard to a fiat money standard. They never understood that they were responsible for money creation and destruction and thus the behavior of the price level.

The classical gold standard operated in the United States in the last quarter of the nineteenth century and in the pre–World War I period. For the United States, which lacked a central bank, its operation was automatic. The price level was an equilibrating variable that adjusted to provide the terms of trade required for balance in international payments. For example, if the United States experienced good harvests while the rest of the world experienced crop failures, an excess of US exports would result in an inflow of gold. That inflow would make US prices more expensive relative to prices in other countries thus restoring balance to international payments.

Under the classical gold standard, there was no central control of the quantity of bank reserves. Gold flows, which were determined by the international balance of payments, controlled bank reserves. After the creation of the Fed, the carryover of a gold standard psychology obscured the fact that the Fed was responsible for the behavior of bank reserves, money, and prices. Policy makers instead believed that they worked with a limited supply of reserves. The legally mandated gold reserve requirements imposed on its liabilities (note issue and member bank deposits) to maintain convertibility between gold and the dollar and the Fed's limited gold reserves made it appear to policy makers that their sphere of action was limited by their free gold.

A positive level of free gold assured convertibility of dollars into gold. As policy makers understood their world, without convertibility, the United States would be on a paper money standard. Money would soon become worthless, and confidence would collapse. At the time, there was no sense of giving money value by controlling its quantity. Convertibility and concern for free gold promoted the gold standard psychology of a Fed with limited resources. In reality, however, the Fed was on a fiat money regime with an unlimited power to create and destroy money.

When the Federal Reserve Banks regained the ability to set their discount rates in 1919, they did not adopt the classical gold standard rule practiced by the Bank of England. They did not alter their discount rates to maintain the monetary gold stock of the United States in fixed proportion to their note issue. Monetary gold and thus the monetary base in turn did not move systematically with the balance of payments. As a result, the domestic price level did not work to determine the real terms of trade required to equilibrate the balance of payments. There was no understanding that the gold standard as operated by the Bank of England provided for both a nominal anchor and a level of interest rates set in a world market by countries on the gold standard. Lionel Edie (1932 [1983], 120) wrote, "True, we have the trappings, earmarks, and accessories of the gold standard, but we do not have the essential economic service of that standard because gold has been divorced from credit."

Burgess (1927, 187) wrote:[2]

---

2. Friedman and Schwartz (1963a, 399ff.) argued that at no time did a lack of free gold force policy makers to adopt a policy they otherwise would not have followed. That contention is consistent with the view here that the regional Reserve Bank governors viewed an ample cushion as providing them with resources to lend in an economic recovery and, by assuring convertibility, as protection against the overissue of currency, that is, managed money. Friedman (1960, 79) wrote that apart from the special cases of

Historically, banks of issue the world over have watched their reserve ratios and . . . have raised their discount rates when the reserve ratio went down and, and lowered discount rates when it went up. . . . As gold poured into the country in 1921 and 1922 the reserve ratio rose by leaps and bounds and lost its significance as a guide to credit policy. Since then discount rates have been increased or decreased without any necessary relation to the movement of the reserve ratio.

Similarly, Keynes (1930, 258) wrote, "The successful management of the dollar by the Federal Reserve Board from 1923 to 1928 was a triumph— mitigated, however, by the events of 1929–30—for the view that currency management is feasible, in conditions which are virtually independent of the movements of gold."[3]

Gold flows were, nevertheless, an important part of why monetary policy was contractionary in the Great Contraction (Eichengreen 1995; Sumner 2015). On three occasions, fall 1919, fall 1931, and February 1933, the Fed engineered drastically tight policy in response to gold outflows. As explained later, these episodes did not reflect a symmetric response to gold flows. In the first case, it reflected an asymmetric response to the gold cover of the regional Reserve Banks, raising discount rates in response to outflows but not lowering them in response to inflows. In the second and third cases, it reflected the desire to maintain the confidence of the conservative business and financial community.

Gold was part of the monetary base, and international gold flows affected the nonborrowed reserves of banks. However, there was no direct relationship with the money stock. Money was determined by the overall operation of the operating procedures as summarized in figure 6.1. The reserves supply schedule was a function of factors supplying and absorbing reserves other than just gold as well as the discount rate and administration of the discount window. The reserves supply schedule interacted with the reserves demand schedule to determine the marginal cost of bank reserves. The ultimate determination of the money stock emerged out of the way in which the marginal cost of reserves interacted with the price system, especially the natural rate of interest.

1919–20 and fall 1931, "it is hard to see any close connection between the internal behavior of the money supply and the needs of external equilibrium."

3. However, Keynes continued by stating that the Fed's policy aimed at internal economic stability had been possible only because gold inflows in the early 1920s had been absorbed by significant increases in the demand for currency. Never did Keynes consider floating exchange rates as a desirable and necessary condition for a monetary policy directed toward domestic stability.

The prevailing belief was that convertibility of the dollar into gold at a fixed parity gave the dollar value. In fall 1931, the Reserve Banks had sufficient free gold to offset the external drain without raising interest rates. However, the existing gold psychology made that impractical. Hardy (1932, 238) wrote:

> Public opinion still regards gold movements as so important a symptom of soundness of the policies pursued, that the Reserve system can only temporarily ignore them. The events of the winter of 1931–32 showed clearly that long before the gold flow becomes technically a necessary factor in the credit policy it becomes a psychological factor.

In sum, convertibility of gold did not mean that the United States was on the classical gold standard in which market forces determined the price level, money stock, and market interest rates. In the case of England, which had a central bank, the market also dictated the behavior of its discount rate. For the United States to have been on this classical gold standard after the creation of the Fed, the Fed would have had to move market rates in response to the balance of payments. Balance of payments surpluses and gold inflows would require reductions in discount rates while deficits and gold outflows would require increases in discount rates. Such behavior would be organized around maintenance of the gold cover (the ratio of monetary gold to Fed liabilities) around a steady value. Instead, the United States was on a fiat money standard. The Fed moved the discount rate primarily in response to concerns about the domestic economy and speculation and only sporadically and infrequently in response to gold outflows. It tolerated large, sustained variations in its gold cover.

6.6. THE FED'S INCOMPREHENSION OF THE CONSEQUENCES OF ITS OPERATING PROCEDURES

Policy makers saw all the correlations represented in figure 6.1 between the variables shown. However, they did not interpret those correlations in terms of figure 6.1, that is, in the quantity theory sense of a market for reserves used in effecting finality of payment. They understood what they were doing through their assumed influence on financial intermediation. The idea that the Fed was setting the interest rate in the New York money market through arbitrage of the discount rate and the marginal cost of reserves would have been anathema. Member banks were not to borrow to relend at a profit.

The underlying assumption in creating the Federal Reserve System was that the twelve Federal Reserve Banks would represent twelve independent reservoirs of funds derived from removing the concentration of reserves in the New York banks and dispersing them throughout the country.[4] These reservoirs of funds were limited by the legally imposed gold reserve ratios imposed on note circulation and discount window lending. For example, in explaining the increase in the discount rate in 1920, the Board (Federal Reserve Board 1921, 12) associated the need to maintain the gold cover with the "strength" of the Reserve Banks: "The Board's purpose was to maintain the strength of the Federal Reserve Banks, which are the custodians of the lawful reserves of the member banks." The "Tenth Annual Report" (Federal Reserve Board 1924a, 9) noted:

> The Federal reserve supplies the needed additions to credit in times of business expansion and takes up the slack in times of business recession. It is its responsibility to regulate the flow of new and additional credit from its *reservoirs* in accordance with solid indications of the economic needs of trade and industry. (italics added)

The role of the Federal Reserve Banks was to add and to subtract to the credit offered by banks to their customers in a way proportioned to the need for legitimate, that is, nonspeculative, credit. The Board's (Federal Reserve Board 1922, 5) report on the year 1921 stated:

> Normally, the Federal Reserve System is called into activity when the supply of ordinary credit facilities is inadequate. It supplements, temporarily, the resources of its members. It is the extent of the deficiency in the lending power of the member banks, as measured by their ability to meet credit requirements, that is reflected in the upward or downward movement of the Federal Reserve loan account. When business is speeding up beyond their normal credit capacity, commercial banks must resort to the Federal Reserve Banks for accommodation. When business is receding and liquidating in a period of economic reaction, slackening of

---

4. In the library of the Philadelphia Fed, there are posters from the 1920s showing the individual Fed banks as giant reservoirs of funds available to member banks in time of need. Louis T. McFadden (US Congress 1926, April 8, 274), chairman of the House Committee on Banking and Currency in reference to participation of the Federal Reserve System in a loan to Great Britain, commented: "If this Federal reserve system is the sacred reservoir for the maintenance of the liquid reserves of the banks of this country for use in emergency, is it proper that those reserves shall be invested in a foreign credit of this kind?"

credit requirements will result in a marked reduction of borrowings from
Federal Reserve Banks.

Through the exercise of judgment, the Reserve Banks were supposed to
set their discount rates at a level that achieved a balance between being too
low so as to "stimulate speculation in securities, commodities, or real estate" and being too high so as to "be detrimental to commerce and industry"
(Federal Reserve Board 1929, 9). Debate centered on the availability of the
funds supplied to banks rather than on the level of the discount rate. Especially, should the Reserve Banks supply only the funds demanded by banks,
that is, funds supplied through the discount window? Alternatively, should
they supply them with "unwanted" funds through open market purchases
of government securities?

Those questions seemed relevant because of a fundamental misconception of the nature of the banking system and its relationship to the Fed. As
understood contemporaneously, banks with their assets and liabilities existed side by side with the Fed. There was no sense that the Fed controlled
the reserves of a "banking system" and had a responsibility to support the
reserve base banks used to clear payments among themselves. The Fed did
not understand the interaction shown in figure 6.1 between Fed supply and
bank demand for reserves as the fundamental building block of the transmission of monetary policy.

In figure 6.1, the reserves demand schedule represents the demand of
banks for reserves for clearing payments. As a central bank, the Fed had a
responsibility to maintain reserves demand at a level commensurate with
a level of deposits that did not require deflation or inflation. To fulfill that
responsibility, it had to maintain a level of short-term interest rates that
kept monetary policy from being contractionary or expansionary. Such understanding developed only slowly after the Treasury-Fed Accord of 1951.
Though the following sentiment is articulated by T. Alan Goldsborough
(R-MD), it could have come from any of his contemporaries and reflected
Irving Fisher's debt-deflation theory (chap. 12). Goldsborough is interesting because he worked tirelessly for two decades with Irving Fisher to pass
legislation that would require the Fed to stabilize the price level. However,
neither explained how the Fed should accomplish that task through the
control of bank deposits.

Goldsborough (US Congress 1935a, March 15, 324) stated:

> You cannot control deflation under our system, and you cannot do it for
> this reason: That the creation of money amounts simply to the extension
> of credit, and whenever the banks start—when the banking system starts

to collect its debts, it immediately decreases the circulation medium, it immediately causes a fall in all values, and it immediately causes the calling in of other debts. You just cannot stop it when you once start it under our system of fractional reserves.

This flawed understanding of the monetary transmission process created the belief in the impotence of monetary policy in the 1930s that formed one of the building blocks of Keynesian economics. Governor Eccles explained that the Fed could supply banks with funds to lend. However, as Eccles (US Congress 1935a, March 15, 331) explained, "There is no action that the Board itself can take that will induce people to borrow, induce corporations to borrow, the excess funds which the banks may have as a result of the Board's action in creating excess funds."

This presumed asymmetry in the effectiveness of monetary policy emphasized the importance of forestalling the emergence of speculative excess. Eccles (US Congress 1935a, March 18, 377, cited in Orphanides 2004b, 105) testified:

GOVERNOR ECCLES: Under present circumstances there is very little, if anything, that can be done.

MR. GOLDSBOROUGH: You mean you cannot push a string.

GOVERNOR ECCLES: That is a good way to put it, one cannot push a string. We are in the depths of a depression and, as I have said several times before this committee, beyond creating an easy money situation through reduction of discount rates and through the creation of excess reserves, there is very little, if anything that the reserve organization can do toward bringing about recovery. I believe that in a condition of great business activity that is developing to a point of credit inflation monetary action can very effectively curb undue expansion.

The concept did not exist that monetary policy worked through the way in which the Fed controlled the quantity of bank reserves in a market for reserves. Necessarily, the concept did not exist that the Fed had a choice of either setting the quantity of reserves and letting the market determine the marginal cost of reserves (the funds rate) or setting the marginal cost of reserves and supplying the reserves demanded. It is a modern idea that either way the transmission of monetary policy takes place through the way in which this monetary control in a centralized market for bank reserves propagates to market interest rates through arbitrage. Similarly, it is a modern idea that the extent of real intermediation that takes place through the banking system is something determined by the marketplace and is determined independently of monetary control.

In sum, there was no theory of monetary control by the Fed independent of the control of credit. Contemporary policy makers could not conceptualize a world in which a central bank could control money without a monetary regime of the government issue of fiat money. Moreover, the conservative eastern financial establishment believed such a regime was the populist road to perdition.

6.7. CONCLUDING COMMENT

There was a national market for bank reserves in the form of the call loan market and commercial paper market in New York. The Fed could have added and subtracted to the reserves of banks to control the interest rate in this money market and thus set a single marginal cost of reserves for the banking system. The interest rate in the Fed funds market that existed among New York City banks (Goodfriend and Whelpley 1993) would have reflected this cost of reserves and would have, through arbitrage, set the interest rate in the money market.

This counterfactual exercise shows how hopelessly far policy makers were from understanding the monetary regime they had created. One of the major objectives in creating the Fed had been to limit use of the call loan market, which concentrated reserves in New York. That concentration, it was presumed, would allow reserves to spill over into speculation in the stock market. Policy makers understood policy through the lens of the Fed's influence on financial intermediation.[5] The guiding principle was to provide just enough credit to finance productive activities but not so much that credit spilled over into speculative activities.

Figure 6.4 shows the market for bank reserves with exogenously determined supply. It became the relevant market in the United States after March 1933, but for the period between 1919 and March 1933 the relevant market was that of figure 6.1. With their rudimentary free reserves operat-

---

5. For example, at the July 16, 1924, OMIC meeting, Governor Strong (Federal Reserve Board 1924b, 3) recommended and the other governors concurred that

> the situation in the New York money market was now such that it would be more advantageous to have purchases made as largely as possible in Federal reserve cities other than New York for the reason that the New York banks are discounting practically nothing and purchases at this time in New York would have a tendency to increase the volume of loanable funds in New York, whereas purchases made in other districts would have a tendency to increase the volume of loanable funds in other sections of the country.

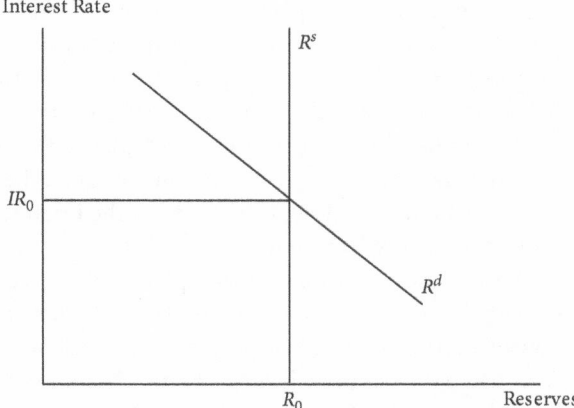

Figure 6.4. Market for Bank Reserves with Exogenous Reserves Supply
See notes to figure 6.1. The market for bank reserves with exogenous reserves supply, R^s, and reserves demand, R^d, shown over a long enough period for banks to adjust their loans and deposits.

ing procedures, the interest rate in the market for reserves and, through arbitrage, in the money market was endogenously determined through the interaction of the reserves supply schedule and the banking system's reserves demand schedule. In the Great Contraction, validating the interest rate set in the market for reserves required destruction of reserves and bank deposits.

Nothing in the prior gold standard era prepared policy makers to understand the consequences of their procedures. There was never any sense of using the interest rate in the money market as the policy instrument and then moving that interest rate based on a reaction function capturing the behavior of the economy. The confusion over these procedures appeared in Governor Strong's comments to the Governors Conference in November 1925 (cited in Chandler 1958, 237):

> It is practically impossible to have it [the discount rate] above the market rate. As the discount rate advances the market rate advances. Which is the cause and which is the effect I am not competent to say.

The statement seems odd as the Reserve Banks set the discount rate. However, as market rates rose, they raised the discount rate so as not to be "out of touch" with the market.

Numerous concepts would have been required in the 1920s for policy makers to have understood the consequences of their operating procedures: (1) the concept of a market for bank reserves as well as the understanding that bank reserves constituted money (the media of exchange for effecting finality of payment); (2) the idea of bank deposits (broad money) resting on the reserves base; (3) the concept that the creation by the Fed of reserves through bookkeeping operations had replaced the gold inflows of the classical gold standard as the determining factor in the size of the reserves base; (4) the influence though arbitrage of the interest rate determined in the market for reserves on money market interest rates; (5) the importance of the interest rate given the role it plays in the price system and the need to respect the central role of the natural rate of interest; (6) the relationship between money creation and the price level; (7) the real-nominal distinction that changes in the price level discipline the ability of the Fed to determine the real interest rate and other real variables.

Application of the gold standard rules required an understanding of none of these concepts. There was no sense of exercising monetary control, that is, control over bank deposits and the money stock, independently of the control of credit required to prevent speculative excess. Indeed, there was no concept of a banking system whose nominal liabilities rested on a reserves base subject to control through the bookkeeping operations of the Fed. "Because member banks had originally transferred cash to Federal Reserve Banks, member bank reserves were considered balances deposited by the banks rather than a creation of the System" (Friedman and Schwartz 1963a, 195–96). In the words of the Federal Reserve Board's "Eighth Annual Report" for 1921, "The Federal Reserve Banks are made the sole custodians of the legal reserves of all member banks" (Federal Reserve Board 1922, 93–94, cited in Friedman and Schwartz 1963a, 250). The failure to understand the Fed as a creator of money through its bookkeeping operations meant that no one could fully grasp the role played by the Fed in the Great Depression. An understanding of the money creating powers of the Fed would have to await the crisis precipitated by the Korean War for the bond pegging program carried over from World War II.

No one understood that the convertibility of gold into money without following the traditional gold standard rules did not in itself give money value. Without an operational quantity theory, there was no way to challenge the prevailing view of the price level as an average of dollar prices without significance as a concept separate from relative prices. For Fed policy makers, the "price level" was just the average of dollar prices, and that average could change for all kinds of nonmonetary reasons. An understanding of all these concepts would emerge only much later.

CHAPTER 7

A Narrative Account of the 1920s

Summary: The May 1923 issue of the *Federal Reserve Bulletin* reinforced the idea that the Fed was engaged in economic stabilization through the regulation of credit. It did so by stating that "the time, manner, character, and volume of" open market operations would be governed by not only the "accommodation of business and commerce" but also "the general credit situation" (cited in Hayek 1925 [1999]). Despite its modern sound, however, in the background of credit policy aimed at cyclical stabilization was always the understanding of recession and deflation as the collapse of speculative excess. The perceived need to preempt such excess caused policy to turn contractionary in 1928 in response to the dramatic rise in the NYSE. The 1929 stock market crash followed by economic contraction seemed to validate the speculative-excess/inevitable-collapse explanation of recession and deflation. The incipient development of countercyclical monetary policy in the 1920s disappeared. The perception that a policy of credit management in the 1920s had failed would cause Keynes to abandon monetary policy for fiscal policy to combat the Depression.

The narrative here interprets the events of the 1920s and 1930s as understood contemporaneously by policy makers in the Federal Reserve System. One difficult question is why they failed to learn from their mistakes. The answer here is they could always rationalize bad outcomes in terms of their preexisting framework. Subsequent narrative histories written from the perspective of the quantity theory pointed out that there was a quantity theory tradition that offered an alternative. However, debating the validity of real bills views of policy makers and quantity theory views was like debating two opinions. Not until the post–World War II development of macroeconomics was there a framework for seriously challenging early Fed views.

7.1. (MIS)UNDERSTANDING A PAPER MONEY STANDARD

At the time of its creation, the monetary standard created by the Federal Reserve Act was unique. It was a regime of fiat money creation with an independent central bank (after 1919). Fiat money regimes had existed in the past but always organized around the use of the printing press to finance government deficits. No one conceived of the Fed in those terms. In its regional banks, the intention had been to decentralize the holdings of the reserves of member banks away from New York. Using those limited reservoirs of funds, the regional Reserve Banks would augment the lending of member banks to "accommodate business and commerce" and would provide funds in response to seasonal demands for credit and bank runs.

At the time of the Fed's creation, the fiduciary money of banks (their banknotes and deposits) all required convertibility to a commodity money—gold or silver. In the past, only such monetary regimes had solved the problems highlighted by François Velde. Velde (2020, 413 and 427) wrote:

> Using paper instead of precious metal was a way to economize on resources but also allowed governments to finance their deficits. The experiments surveyed show how issuance of paper by a central bank, coexisting with coins made of precious metal, came to be the dominant model in the nineteenth century. . . . Paper money's advantage, its low cost of production relative to its potential value in exchange, is also its weakness, leaving it exposed to the twin threats of counterfeiting and overissue.

The only successful models of paper (fiat) money available in the early twentieth century all provided for a nominal anchor through conversion to a commodity—gold or silver. Pure fiat money regimes always ended disastrously in high inflation.

The Federal Reserve Act provided for gold convertibility, which lasted until April 1933. Despite convertibility and despite the fact that at times gold inflows and outflows from abroad influenced the monetary base, that influence was not direct and automatic as occurred under the classical gold standard. As explained in chapter 6, the influence of gold flows worked through their impact on the nonborrowed reserves of banks, which in turn determined the marginal cost of reserves to banks and through arbitrage money market interest rates. Other factors, especially the discretionary actions of the Fed, generally dominated the behavior of the cost of reserves and money market rates (the funds rate in modern terms). Through interaction with the natural rate of interest (the interest rate required by the price system to maintain economic output at potential), the interest rate determined by the Fed controlled money creation and destruction.

No contemporaneous observers in the twenties and thirties understood the role of the Fed in controlling money creation and destruction. Similarly, no one explained the behavior of prices in terms of the Fed's control of bank deposits and money. Although quantity theory reformers wanted the Fed to assume responsibility for the control of prices, that desire did not stem from an understanding that the Fed had itself caused deflation.

7.2. BENJAMIN STRONG

The views of Benjamin Strong, governor of the Federal Reserve Bank of New York from 1913 until 1928, are especially important in understanding monetary policy in the Great Depression. Even though he died in October 1928, before the start of the Great Contraction, he determined the culture of the New York Fed. That culture embodied the views of the conservative eastern financial establishment and Strong's reworking of the real bills views incorporated in the Federal Reserve Act.

The real bills doctrine assumed that the Reserve Banks would prevent the speculative excess whose inevitable collapse led to recession and deflation. They would do so by restricting rediscounts at the discount window by member banks to real bills—self-liquidating debt instruments that financed the movement of goods from producers to consumers and crops to market. As originally conceived, this version of real bills never took root. With World War I and the inflow of gold in the early 1920s, the reserves of member banks (their deposits at the Fed) supported a credit superstructure that did not rest primarily on discounted real bills. To a significant degree, it rested on gold and on discount window loans collateralized by government securities. Moreover, the discovery of open market operations and the associated realization of the existence of a national money market centered in New York made evident the impossibility of segmenting the country into twelve regional credit markets dominated by their respective regional Reserve Banks. However, the speculative-excess/inevitable-collapse view of recession and deflation grew in vitality with the interpretation of the 1920–21 recession. As understood contemporaneously, the recession grew out of the inability of the Fed to deal with prior speculative excess due to the imperative of "cheap money" to finance the war effort and the placement of Liberty bonds after the War.

Gold flows and open market operations meant that the regulation of the credit extended by member banks would not happen through limiting discount window borrowing to loans collateralized by real bills. Strong emphasized the fungibility of credit. Funds obtained through the discount window, even if collateralized by a "real bill," could be used for any purpose. At the same time, Strong retained the central assumption of real bills that economic stability required the early suppression of the financial excess that led to an artificial level of activity, the inevitable collapse of which led to recession and deflation. Achievement of the presumed required balance between accommodating the needs of business and preventing speculative excess therefore required regulation of the total flow of credit.

Reliance on the allocation of credit to productive uses through restricting discounting at the window to real bills would be ineffective in controlling speculation. Strong was willing to manage credit in recession by supplying credit through open market purchases to help revive business. But he was willing to do so only provided there was no evidence of speculative activity. That was the case in 1927. At the same time, he would restrict credit in a boom to squelch speculation.

There is no way to know whether Strong would have been more assertive in the Depression in advocating open market purchases. In any event, Strong's real bills views fed into the nearly universal assumption that attributed the Great Depression to the speculative excess and subsequent collapse evidenced in the stock market boom and crash. Those views crowded out any argument that the cause of the Depression was contractionary monetary policy. That interpretation also undercut any influence from the price-level-stabilization movement pushed by Congressmen James Strong and T. Alan Goldsborough.

Insight into Strong's views can be gained from his commentary on initial versions of the Federal Reserve Act. Like other bankers, Strong feared government involvement in the control of the banking system. Link (1956, 225) wrote that in the summer of 1913, "the evidence was overwhelming that the great majority of bankers, whether from Wall Street or Main Street or from the North or the South, regarded the Federal Reserve bill with repugnance ranging from merely strong to violent hostility." Strong especially feared that the replacement of the banknotes of the nationally chartered banks by Federal Reserve notes partially guaranteed by the credit of the government could lead to a regime of paper money.

Chandler (1958, 34) noted that Strong "provided Senator Elihu Root with materials for a speech warning against inflationary consequences of the proposed legislation." Root, a Republican senator from New York and earlier secretary of war under McKinley and secretary of state under Roosevelt, declaimed in 1913 (cited in Grant 1992, 143):

With the exhaustless reservoir of the government of the United States furnishing easy money, the sales increase, the businesses enlarge, more new enterprises are started, the spirit of optimism pervades the community. Bankers are not free from it. They are human. The members of the Federal Reserve Board will not be free of it. They are human. All the world moves along upon a growing tide of optimism. Everyone is making money. Everyone is growing rich. It goes up and up, the margin between costs and sales continually growing smaller as a result of the operation of inevitable laws, until finally someone whose judgment was bad, someone whose capacity for business was small, breaks; and as he falls he hits the next brick in the row, and then another, and then another, and down comes the whole structure.

That, sir, is no dream. That is the history of every movement of inflation since the world's business began, and it is the history of many a period in our own country. That is what happened to greater or less degree before the panic of 1837, of 1857, of 1873, of 1893, and of 1907. The precise formula which the students of economic movements have evolved to describe the reason for the crash following this universal process is that when credit exceeds the legitimate demands of the country the currency becomes suspected and gold leaves the country.

Strong attributed the inflation that emerged in 1919 to the creation of an excessive amount of credit that spilled over into speculation. On November 3, 1919, Strong wrote in a memo (cited in Chandler 1958, 150): "The Government's [wartime] requirements for loans were, and would continue to be during a large part of the war, in excess of the amount of credit created by savings." Given that banks expanded credit as a multiple of the reserves furnished by the Fed, the loans of commercial banks would have to decline by a multiple of the decline in discount window lending. On February 5, 1919, Strong wrote Montagu Norman, governor of the Bank of England (cited in Chandler 1958, 137), "Our problem is really confined to the liquidation of possibly four or five billions of bank expansion, which I believe would be completely accomplished if the Reserve Banks were able to liquidate about a billion dollars of their advances."

Strong believed that the liquidation of the excess credit would be painful but necessary. On February 6, 1919, Strong wrote the following to Russell Leffingwell, assistant secretary at the Treasury (cited in Chandler 1958, 139):

The day of deflation approaches. The process of deflation is a painful one, involving loss, unemployment, bankruptcy and social and political disorders. . . . WE MUST DEFLATE: Not withstanding the hardships and losses resulting, I believe you will agree that it is inevitably necessary that our banking position must be gradually deflated. (capitals in original)

The prerequisite for economic stability was the prevention of a speculative mentality. Economic and price stability would follow. The lesson from the 1920–21 deflation was not that the Fed should use the price level as its target but rather that it should prevent speculative excess from developing in the first place and thus forestall a cycle of speculative collapse and deflation. Strong (US Congress 1926, April 9, 375) testified:

GOVERNOR STRONG: One definition of inflation that is common enough as applied to credit is an amount of credit furnished to the country in excess of what the country needs for conducting a given volume of business at a given level of prices; and that, if you please, relates directly to the volume of credit rather than to the level of prices. . . .

MR. GOLDSBOROUGH. Before you finish your answer, would not a reasonably stable price level for four years be a very strong indication that there was neither serious inflation or deflation of any kind?

GOVERNOR STRONG. It would be as to commodity prices, but you might not be able to say that there has been no inflation whatever if you had a big real estate speculation and a building speculation and possibly a stock speculation at the same time. . . . I rather doubt that this real estate speculation that people have been talking about has had much effect on prices. It has a considerable effect on the state of mind of people about speculation generally.

Strong's discussion with Norman, governor of the Bank of England, about Britain's return to gold at the prewar parity revealed the doubt in Strong's mind about whether the Fed could control the price level. Both understood that a return to the prewar parity would require a decline in prices in Britain to make British exports competitive. The issue was whether the Bank of England could force deflation as a prior condition for a return to convertibility or whether the deflation would have to occur as a consequence of a return to convertibility by raising unemployment in the export industries.

In a letter to the Bank of England's Cecil Lubbock written September 10, 1924, Strong questioned "whether a change in relative price levels in your country and ours must be relied upon as the major cause of a return to sterling at parity; or whether we may not have cause and effect reversed." In a letter to Norman dated July 9, 1924, Strong noted the decline in British prices but questioned whether the decline came from purposeful policy by the Bank of England (letters cited in Chandler 1958, 302–3):

> I cannot see that you have gained anything as yet, nor in fact have I ever believed that general prices are or could be so strongly influenced by Bank Rate under present conditions as to give you any power or control to be effective toward the objects which you outlined to me in London. The changes are too slow, and arise from too great a variety of causes.

7.3. ADOLPH MILLER—THE NEMESIS OF BENJAMIN STRONG

The 1920s featured a contest for control between two strong personalities: Benjamin Strong, governor of the New York Fed, and Adolph C. Miller, member of the Federal Reserve Board. Strong and Miller both shared the view that recession and deflation originated in the collapse of an artificially elevated level of economic activity made possible by prior speculative excess. Strong argued that the Reserve Banks could not control the final use of credit. Consequently, to deal with speculative excess, the Federal Reserve System would at times have to limit the total amount of bank credit. Miller believed that, in contrast, the Reserve Banks had a responsibility to allocate credit toward legitimate uses and away from speculative uses.

In his congressional testimony, Miller (US Congress 1926–27, April 20, 1926, 671) likely referred to the unwillingness of the New York Fed to become directly involved in the allocation of credit to productive as opposed to speculative uses:

> The whole intent and implication of the act is that credit of the Federal reserve system is to be restricted to productive uses in commerce, agriculture, trade, and industry. But I think possibly there are some who take a different view. . . . They might at times perhaps regret that there is evidence of some seepage of Federal reserve credit into speculative channels, nevertheless, they feel that it is not their responsibility to try, by all means, direct and indirect, to stop it. . . . To me the most simple formula of operating the Federal reserve system to give the country stability . . . is to stop and absolutely foreclose the diversion of any Federal reserve credit to speculative purposes.

Strong disliked the discretion entailed by the 1920s policy of reading the psychology of markets to limit speculative excess. He believed that a return to the international gold standard would provide the required discipline.

Miller felt comfortable with exercising the required discretion. As reported in the Federal Reserve Board's "Tenth Annual Report" (Federal Reserve Board 1924a, 31):

> No statistical mechanism alone, however carefully contrived, can furnish an adequate guide to credit administration. Credit is an intensely human institution and as such reflects the moods and impulses of the community—its hopes, its fears, its expectations. The business and credit situation at any particular time is weighted and charged with these invisible factors. They are elusive and can not be fitted into any mechanical formula, but the fact that they are refractory to methods of the statistical laboratory makes them neither nonexistent nor nonimportant. They are factors which must always patiently and skillfully be evaluated as best they may and dealt with in any banking administration that is animated by a desire to secure to the community the results of an efficient credit system. In its ultimate analysis credit administration is not a matter of mechanical rules, but is and must be a matter of judgment—of judgment concerning each specific credit situation at the particular moment of time when it is has arisen or is developing.

In the 1928 hearings over legislation to stabilize the price level, Miller opposed the legislation and the idea of a rule. The following exchange occurred between Congressman James Strong and Miller (US Congress 1928, May 3, 193).

> MR. STRONG. You think the law, then, could be changed so that it would read for the accommodation of commerce and business or at the will of the Federal Reserve Board?
>
> DOCTOR MILLER: It is the same thing.

Like his colleagues, including Governor Strong, Miller believed that instability of the price level was the result of some prior speculative disturbance. Targeting the price level could do nothing to correct that prior disturbance (Miller, in US Congress 1928, May 17, 348).

Although Miller and Strong were rivals for control of the Fed, they were united in their belief in the core of the real bills doctrine—prevention of recession and deflation required prevention of the prior speculative excess whose collapse led to those twin evils. In the absence of the automatic check to speculation formerly provided by the gold standard, that task was the Fed's. On December 13, 1922, Strong addressed the American Farm Bureau Federation (cited in Chandler 1958, 199):

> There should be no such excessive or artificial supplies of money and credit as will simply permit the marking up of prices when there is no increase in business or production to warrant an increase. . . . We should aim to keep the credit volume equal to the country's needs, and not in excess of its needs. . . . We could indulge in a riot of speculation in this country which would put prices to very high levels, and with few exceptions, hardly any nation in the world would be in a position to withdraw large amounts of our gold. . . . There is every possible inducement for the Federal Reserve System to adopt . . . a policy of stabilization in every direction; to avoid encouragement of unhealthy speculation, on the one hand, and to encourage the return of stable values on the other.

7.4. THE 1920–21 RECESSION

After the end of World War I in November 1918, inflation surged. Consumer prices rose at an annualized rate of 15 percent from January 1919 through June 1920.[1] The Treasury retained the control over the Fed that it had exercised during the war. For most of 1919, the Fed chafed at its inability to curb the speculation believed responsible for the inflation. In a June 10, 1919, letter from the Federal Reserve Board to the Reserve Banks, the Board wrote (cited in Hardy 1932, 120):

> The Federal Reserve Board is concerned over the existing tendency towards excessive speculation, and while ordinarily this could be corrected by an advance in discount rates at the Federal Reserve Banks, it is not practicable to apply this check at this time because of government financing.

Finally, in November 1919, the Treasury relented and allowed the Reserve Banks to raise their discount rates. From November 1919 to June 1920, the New York Fed raised its discount rate from 4 percent to 7 percent. Measured by the NBER, there was a cyclical peak in January 1920 and trough in July 1921. Friedman (1960, 16) wrote, "The result was a collapse in prices by nearly 50%, one of the most rapid if not the most rapid on record,

---

1. "Index of the General Price Level for United States," NBER Macrohistory Data Base, St. Louis FRED.

and a decline in the stock of money that is the sharpest in our record up to this date."

Representative Goldsborough (US Congress 1935a, March 15, 325) later recounted an anecdote that illustrated the importance the Fed assigned to reducing speculative activity:

> In 1920 a very distinguished Member of this House, who is now on one of the boards down town, came to speak to me in my district. He said he had just had a talk with Mr. W. P. G. Harding, who was then Governor of the Federal Reserve Board. Cotton was then 30 cents a pound. He said Harding had told him they were going to bring the price of cotton down to 25 cents and stabilize it. I said, "My God! If you ever start that, you can't stop it." And cotton did not stop until it got down to 5 cents a pound.

When the New York Fed raised its discount rate, it made clear that it intended that there be a reduction in the total of bank credit (*Report on Business Conditions*, Second Federal Reserve District, November 20, 1919, cited in Hardy 1932, 120):

> The reason for the advance in rates announced today by the Federal Reserve Bank of New York is the evidence that some part of the great volume of credit, resulting from both government and private borrowing which war finance required, as it is released from time to time from government needs, is being diverted to speculative employment rather than to reduction of bank loans. As the total volume of the government's loans is now in course of reduction, corresponding reductions in bank loans and deposits should be made in order to insure an orderly return of normal credit conditions.

One reason for the short lag between the initial tightening in November 1919 and the cyclical peak in January 1920 may have been the practice of enforced credit rationing that accompanied the discount-rate increase. Similarly, while the July 1921 trough occurred with still relatively high market rates, an end to that rationing would have been stimulative (figure 6.3).

Fisher (1934, 221–22) used the term "moral suasion" to characterize how the Reserve Banks intervened directly to limit the extension of credit by banks. He referenced the statement of Congressman Harry C. Canfield (D-IN), who recounted a speech by Congressman Swing (R-CA) made in the House on May 22, 1922 (reported in US Congress 1926–27, June 10, 1926, 1111):

I was present at a meeting of the bankers of southern California held in my district in the middle of November, 1920, when W. A. Day, then deputy governor of the Federal Reserve Bank of San Francisco, spoke for the Federal reserve bank. . . . He told the bankers . . . they were not to loan any farmers any money for the purpose of enabling the farmer to hold any of his crop beyond harvest time. If they did, he said, the Federal reserve bank would refuse to rediscount a single piece of paper taken on such a transaction. He declared that all the farmers should sell all their crops at the harvest time unless they had money of their own to finance them, as the Federal reserve bank would do nothing toward helping the farmers hold back any part of their crop, no matter what the condition of the market.

Fisher (1934, 219) also cited Governor W. P. G. Harding (1925, 177), who in reference to the 1919–20 restriction quoted John Skelton Williams, comptroller of the currency and ex officio member of the Federal Reserve Board, "It is tremendously important that every individual bank . . . should bring about a proper and reasonable degree of contraction." In a prelude to the 1929 policy of "direct pressure," Harding explained the Fed's club, namely, the threat to exclude member banks from the discount window: "There is nothing in the Federal Reserve Act which requires a Federal Reserve bank to make any investment or to rediscount any particular paper or class of paper" (cited in Fisher 1934, 219).

The organizing principle behind the Federal Reserve Act, the real bills doctrine, embodied the belief that panics derived from the collapse of speculative excess. In the spirit of real bills, the 1920 "Seventh Annual Report of the Federal Reserve Board" provided a roadmap for the behavior of the Fed in the 1920s and 1930s. It did so through its analysis of the recession and deflation of 1920–21. The report began with a statement of the speculative-excess explanation for recession: unrestrained "inflationary" booms beget deflation and recession in the form of a purging of the prior excess. The report (Federal Reserve Board 1921, 1–2) absolved the Fed from responsibility for the recession but only by placing responsibility on the credit expansion forced on it by the war.

The past year has been essentially a period of reaction. The year immediately preceding was characterized by an unprecedented orgy of extravagance, a mania for speculation, overextended business in nearly all lines and in every section of the country, and general demoralization of the agencies of production and distribution. Beginning with abnormally large importations of gold in 1915, the course of world events forced upon this country during a period of five years the greatest expansion it has ever known. It was universally realized that there would be sooner or later reaction and readjustments. . . . The process necessarily has been painful, but it was inevitable and unavoidable, and . . . could not have been long deferred in this country by any artificial means or temporary expedients. . . . The precautionary steps which were taken during the year [1920] did not produce deflation, but they checked the expansion which had been proceeding at a dangerous rate and prevented a larger measure of distress than has actually occurred.

Although not stated in the report, the Fed aided in financing the wartime deficits by taking the interest rate on Treasury debt as given. As mandated by the Treasury, it then set a lower discount rate so that banks could borrow profitably to hold government securities and lend on them as collateral. As soon as the Fed was relieved of financing the government's debt issue, it returned to real bills principles. The report (Federal Reserve Board 1921, 11–12) stated:

The system was looked upon by many as an engine of inflation and doubts of its ability to restrain undue expansion at the proper time were frequently expressed. . . . From the outset, it recognized its duty to cooperate unreservedly with the Government to provide funds needed for the war and freely conceded that the great national emergency made it necessary to suspend the application of well-recognized principles of economics and finance which usually govern banking operations in times of peace. But, as soon as the armistice put an end to the war, the Board made a new survey of the situation in order to determine what could and should be done to check undue and unnecessary expansion of credit. In the situation which existed ordinary prudence dictated plainly that not only should speculation in corporate stocks and securities be restricted but that further expansion of banking credits made against goods and commodities in storage should be checked. The loans and advances of a Federal Reserve Bank should be as nearly as possible of a self-liquidating character. . . . Toward the end of May, in order to discourage applications for rediscounts for nonessential purposes, the Board deemed it expedient to approve an advance in the discount rates of some of the Federal Reserve Banks to 7 percent.

The lesson learned was that in the future an independent Fed should act preemptively to prevent "credit inflation." That is, it would prevent boom-bust cycles by acting to stifle the boom cycle in its infancy by preventing an expansion of credit in excess of the legitimate needs of productive activity. Economic stability required raising the discount rate to squelch a speculative mentality before it got out of control.[2] That belief would trigger contractionary monetary policy repeatedly in the pre–World War II period.

George Harrison, who became governor of the New York Fed after Strong's death in 1928, made the same argument for the Depression. In his testimony before the Committee on Banking and Currency, Harrison (US Congress 1931, January 20, 66) stated, "When I look back on 1928, I feel that we made two particular mistakes—first, we raised our rate the first time too late, and, second, we did not raise it enough." The point is that in neither instance did policy makers attribute recession to contractionary monetary policy but rather to failure to prevent prior speculative excess.

Fed policy makers attempted to develop guidelines to implement these real bills ideas. The Board's 1921 "Eighth Annual Report" (Federal Reserve Board 1922, 10) stated:

> Thus there was unavoidably a more and more serious lack of adjustment between the activities of producers and the demand of consumers as exhibited in the use of their buying power. "Overproduction" in the sense of badly adjusted production—excess production . . . was consequently characteristic of the industrial situation.

At the October 1922 Governors Conference, the governors unanimously adopted the following policy statement: "Open market operations should be administered in each district in such manner as to assist the system in discharging, as far as it may be able, its national responsibility to prevent credit expansion from developing into credit inflation" (cited in Meltzer 2003, 148).

The incentive for such preemptive action was not only economic but also political. Farm groups especially blamed the Fed for the deflation that followed the 1919–20 increases in discount rates. Not only did the prices of commodities fall sharply, but also the debt owed on farm mortgages rose in real terms. On April 13, 1921, members of the American Farm Bureau Federation met with the Board and governors of the Reserve Banks and asked, "Who decided that deflation was necessary?" In a letter of July 25, 1921, Governor Harding of the Board wrote, "I do not know whether you appreciate how violent the attacks are which are now being made upon the Board and the system" (cited in Meltzer 2003, 114 and 115).

William Jennings Bryan, who had led the populist assault on the gold

2. See also W. P. G. Harding (1925, 157) and Harris (1933, 1:224).

standard and the eastern financial establishment in the 1896 presidential election, attacked the Fed (the excerpt is from the testimony of Western Starr representing the National Committee of the Farmer-Labor Party, in US Congress 1926, April 6, 226). Starr quoted from Bryan (1923), "My Forecast on Next Year's Election":

> The Federal reserve bank that should have been the farmer's greatest protection has become his greatest foe. The deflation of the farmer was a crime deliberately committed, not out of enmity to the farmer but out of indifference to him. Inflation of prices had encouraged him to buy, and then deflation delivered him into the hands of the money lender. The Federal bank can be a blessing or a curse, according to its management. If the Wall Street speculators are in control of it they can drain the agricultural districts and keep up a fictitious prosperity among the members of the Plunderbund. While the Federal reserve bank law is the greatest economic reform achieved in the last half century, if not in our national history, it would be better to repeal it, go back to old conditions, and take our chances with individual financiers than to turn the Federal reserve bank over to Wall Street and allow its tremendous power to be used for the carrying out of the plans of the Money Trust.

The populist forces in Congress challenged the Fed and its independence over the recession and especially over the drastic decline in commodity prices. Those forces introduced legislation requiring the Fed to stabilize prices (Hetzel 1985). As William T. Foster (US Congress 1926, March 24, 190), director of the Pollak Foundation, testified, "Then [early 1923], as at all times, the board was under pressure from the 'foes of the money monopoly'—from those whose cure-all for economic ills is always easy money." Robert Owen (Democratic senator from Oklahoma) criticized the Fed for the 1920–21 recession and the deflation that followed. In a written reply to Owen, the Board (Federal Reserve Board 1920, 8, 10) responded that the regional Reserve Banks had raised the discount rate "with the object of bringing about more moderation in the use of credits, which a year ago were being diverted into all kinds of speculative and non-essential channels." The Board letter went on to argue that the decline in prices came from factors affecting individual prices. "Sugar was advanced by speculative manipulation until it reached a price which checked domestic consumption. . . . Then followed a drastic decline in the price of sugar."

Owen (1935, cited in Wilkerson 2013, 113) later wrote:

> It should be obvious that when the records of our government disclose that the value of the dollar can be doubled or cut in half in the course of

two or three years, there is something radically wrong with our monetary structure, and our laws which permit such a violent variation in the purchasing power of money. Such fluctuations make it impossible for the most prudent of businessmen to make dependable contracts extending over a period of time, and leave the people defenseless against depressions.

The Fed never accepted, however, the price level as a guide to policy. At the May 28, 1921, Governors Conference, Strong told the other governors, "It is not the business, the duty, or the function of the Federal Reserve System, or of central banks generally, to deal with prices" (cited in Meltzer 2003, 125). The price level was presumed to be an amalgam of relative prices whose individual behaviors reflected booms and busts.

An implication of the need to preempt speculation was the need to refrain from a cheap money policy in recession before the required liquidation of excess credit had occurred. Although the NBER cycle peak occurred in January 1920, not until April 1921 did the New York Fed lower its discount rate to 6 percent from the 7 percent set in June 1920. After April 1921, it steadily lowered its rate until it reached 4 percent in June 1922. Although the NBER trough is dated July 1921, using the Balke and Gordon (1986) data on real GNP, Meltzer (2003, 117) argued that economic expansion did not take hold until 1922Q2.

Wicker (1966, 54) documented real bills reasons for the reluctance to lower the discount rate. (Coordinated open market purchases had not yet been discovered as a tool.) In a December 1920 letter to the Board, John Skelton Williams argued for a reduction in the discount rate. In a letter dated January 13, 1921, the Board responded that the effect "would be to induce a temporary and artificial ease in the money market . . . which might result in a temporary revival of the speculative spirit which was so strongly in evidence fourteen months ago and which had such an unhappy effect upon the commerce of the country."

At a Board meeting in February 1921, Charles Hamlin reported that "officials of the New York Bank said that the reduction would encourage 'wild speculation.'" When Boston requested permission to lower its discount rate, Strong opposed it arguing that "public opinion would force the New York Reserve Bank to do the same and this would cause a violent speculative boom in stocks" (Wicker 1966, 55).

The 1920–21 recession illustrated the characteristics of recessions under the Fed. (Chapter 3 labels those characteristics "the monetary contraction marker.") Namely, the Fed, concerned about inflation, maintained short-term interest rates at cyclical highs past the cyclical turning point in output while growth of output declined. In the era before 1981 when real money demand was stable and relatively interest insensitive, the money stock declined. As shown in table 3.1, at the NBER cyclical peak of 1920Q1, the commercial paper rate was 6.42 percent but climbed above 8 percent in quarters 1920Q3 and 1920Q4. Annualized M1 growth, which reached 20.2 percent in 1919Q4, declined steadily reaching −15.6 percent in 1921Q1 (−15.5 percent in 1921Q2). Growth rates of real GNP and industrial production declined rapidly after the cyclical peak in 1920Q1. In 1920Q3, growth in the CPI turned negative.

The figures show these cyclical relationships graphically. Figure 7.1 shows the Treasury bill rate and the commercial paper rate. Figure 7.2 shows growth rates of nominal and real GNP. Figure 7.3 shows step functions fitted to monthly growth rates of money as done originally in Friedman and Schwartz (1963b). Figure 7.4 shows growth of M1 and nominal GNP.[3] Figure 7.5 shows the price level (consumer price index, CPI).

7.5. FREE GOLD

Free gold expressed the excess of the ratio of the Fed's monetary gold to its liabilities over the ratio required by the Federal Reserve Act. By law, the individual Reserve Banks had to back their note issues by a 40 percent gold reserve and their deposits due to member banks by a 35 percent gold reserve. The importance of the free gold position appeared in the construction of the balance sheet statement "Condition of Federal Reserve Banks" issued weekly. This statement highlighted the line "Ratio of total reserves to net deposit and F. R. note liabilities combined." The next line reported "ratio of gold reserves to F. R. notes in circulation after setting aside 35% against net deposit liabilities."

On three occasions, when the actual ratio fell toward its legal limit, the Reserve Banks raised their discount rates. The first instance occurred in fall 1919. (The other two were October 1931 and February 1933.) After the United States lifted its gold embargo on June 9, 1919, gold flowed out of the country. On August 3, 1919, the gold reserve against notes was 61.4 percent. By September 5, 1920, it had fallen to 46.6 percent. Partly in response to that decline as well as to rising inflation, the Fed banks raised their discount rates sharply. Gold then returned to the United States. On March 6, 1921, the ratio had risen to 59.3 percent. Figure 7.6, reproduced from the congres-

3. One dissimilarity with other recessions is that the commercial paper rate at the cyclical trough while below the cyclical high is still somewhat above the rate at the prior cyclical peak. Monetary policy was likely easier at the cyclical trough because of the end of Reserve Bank coercion of the member banks to contract their lending. Real M1 growth turned positive in 1920Q3 well before the cyclical trough in 1921Q3.

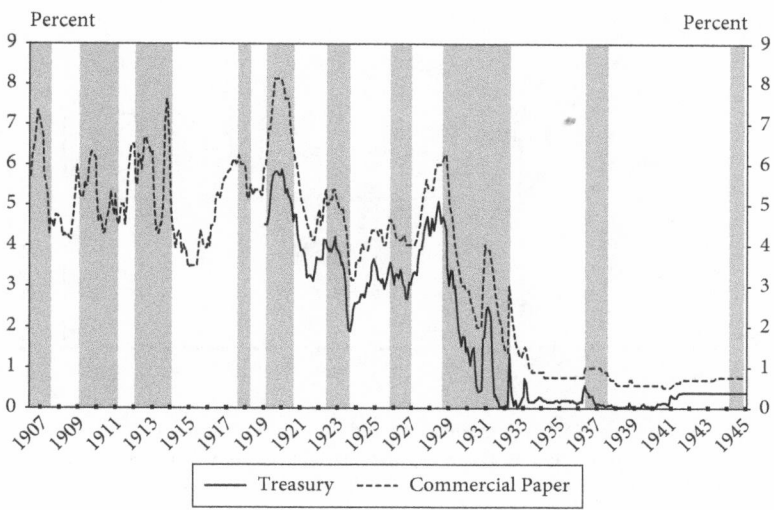

Figure 7.1. Money Market Rates: 1907–45
Treasury yields on three-month Treasury bills (from Board of Governors 1943 and
1976, tables 122 and 12.9, respectively). Commercial paper rate on four- to six-month
maturities from Board of Governors (1943 and 1976, tables 120 and 12.5, respectively).
Shaded areas indicate NBER recessions. Heavy tick marks indicate December.

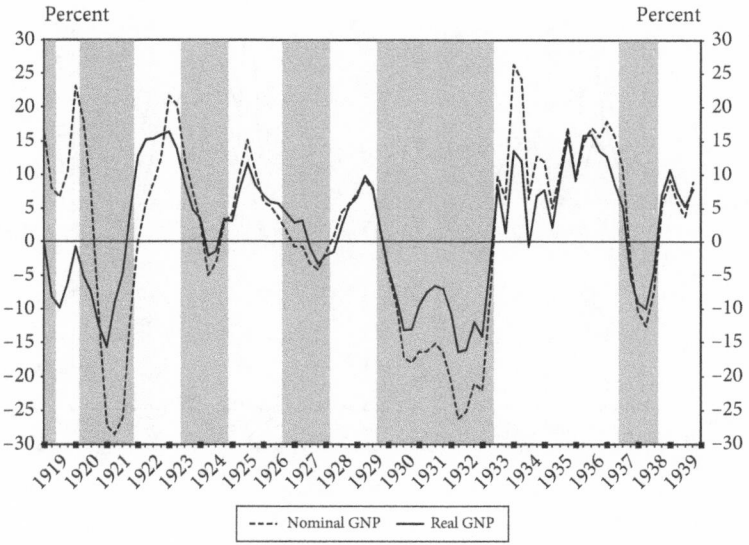

Figure 7.2. Real and Nominal GNP Growth Rates
Quarterly observations of four-quarter percentage changes in real and nominal GNP
growth. Data from Balke and Gordon (1986). Shaded areas represent NBER recessions.
Heavy tick marks indicate fourth quarter.

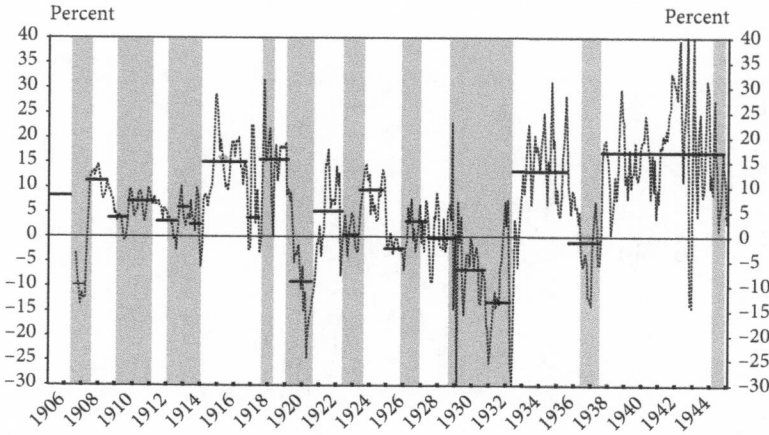

Figure 7.3. M1 Step Function and Recessions: 1906–45

Series are a three-month moving average of the annualized monthly money growth rates and a step function fitted to monthly annualized growth rates of money. Step function before May 1907 uses annual growth rates based on June observations of M2 from 1900 to 1907. Observations for money from June 1900 to May 1914 are for M2; observations from June 1914 to December 1945 are for M1. Data are from Friedman and Schwartz (1970). Shaded areas indicate NBER recessions. Heavy tick marks indicate December.

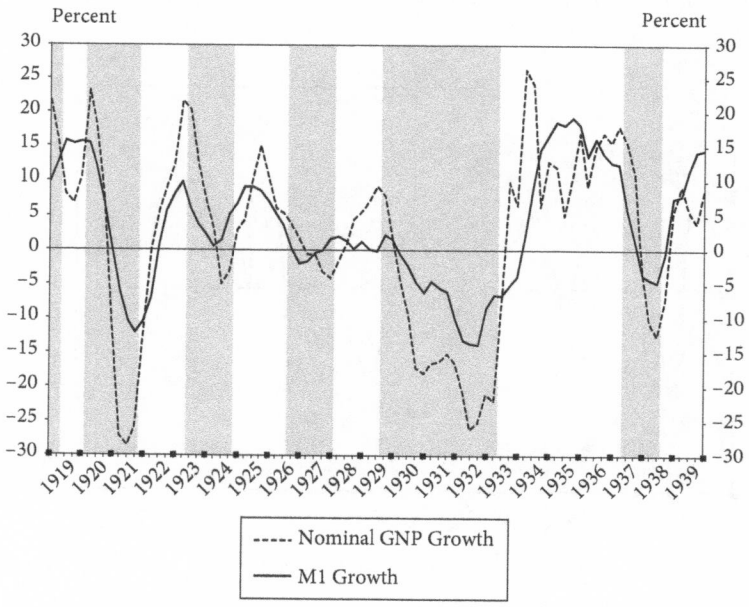

----- Nominal GNP Growth

— M1 Growth

Figure 7.4. M1 and Nominal GNP Growth

Quarterly observations of four-quarter percentage changes in nominal GNP and M1 growth. Data for GNP are from Balke and Gordon (1986). M1 is from Friedman and Schwartz (1970). Shaded areas represent NBER recessions. Heavy tick marks indicate fourth quarter.

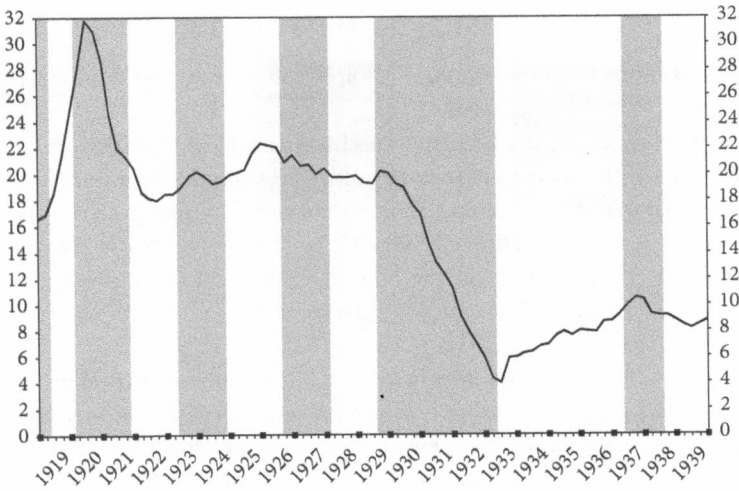

Figure 7.5. CPI

Quarterly observations of the CPI. Shaded areas represent recessions. Heavy tick marks indicate fourth quarter.

Source: NBER Macroeconomic Database, St. Louis FRED

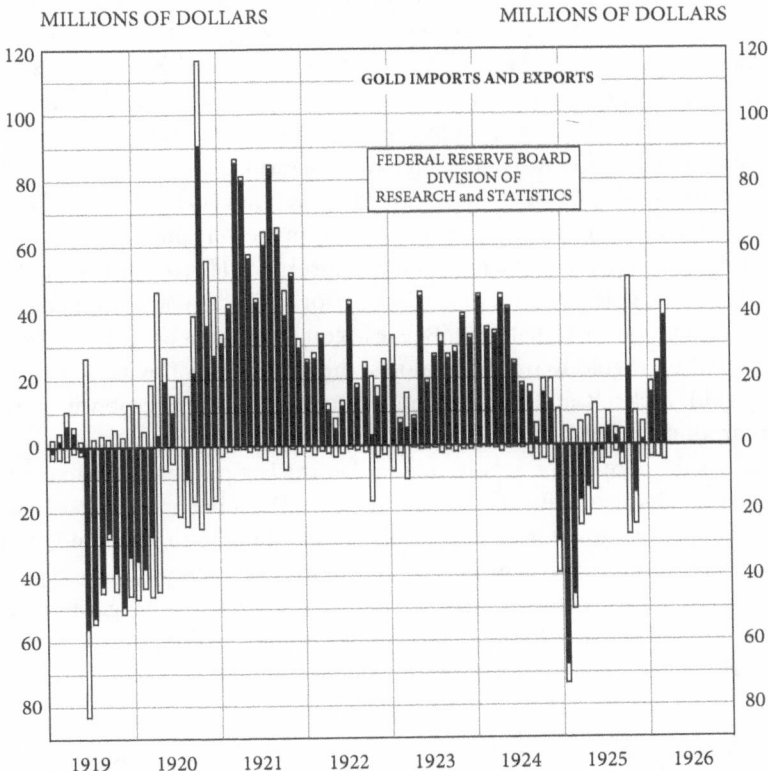

Figure 7.6. Gold Imports and Exports

Bars above base line represent imports; those below represent exports. Black portions represent excess imports or exports.

Source: US Congress 1926–27, April 20, 1926, 670

sional testimony of Board member Adolph Miller, shows gold imports and exports.

By the early 1920s, the United States had come to hold a disproportionate amount of the world's monetary gold. The United States was the only country that maintained convertibility of its currency into gold during the war and thereafter. Gold flowed to the United States because that convertibility made the dollar into the medium of exchange that financed international trade. Hayek (1925 [1999], 72–73) wrote:

> Its total monetary gold reserves before the war had amounted to about 1.9 billion dollars, that is, nearly one fourth (23 per cent) of the entire world's gold stock. . . . As a result of new imports between September 1920 and November 1924 . . . American monetary gold stocks reached nearly 4.6 billion, almost half the known world reserves. . . . The 1834 million dollars in gold that had been in circulation in Europe in 1913 were almost completely drained off (mainly in the direction of the United States).

Gold flowed into the United States after summer 1920 when the gold reserve ratio had fallen to about 41 percent. In summer 1924, it had risen to about 83 percent. To mitigate the rise, the Fed issued gold certificates, which were backed 100 percent by gold. Federal Reserve notes, in contrast, were backed by only 40 percent in gold.[4] The intention was to limit popular pressure for easy money due to a high reserve ratio.

In *The Economic Consequences of the Peace*, Keynes (1920) predicted how the onerous reparations required of Germany in the Versailles Treaty would destabilize Europe. In an analogous way, Cassel and Hawtrey predicted that a return to the gold standard as it existed prior to World War I would destabilize Europe through deflation. Because countries went off gold in World War I and used gold to pay for imports, the demand for the world's monetary gold stock fell, and its real (commodity) value fell. In response, world gold production fell (Batchelder and Glasner 1991).

Just as the spread of the gold standard in the last part of the nineteenth century had increased the demand for the world's monetary gold stock and forced deflation, going back to the gold standard in the 1920s would force deflation if countries returned at the old parities (Hawtrey 1919 [1923]). In the 1920s, countries returning to gold adopted the gold exchange standard in that central banks held their reserves in sterling and dollars as well as in gold. However, they did not adopt the bullion standard recommended by

---

4. Board of Governors 1943, table 93, "Deposits, Note Circulation, Reserves, and Reserve Percentages of Federal Reserve Banks, Monthly, November 1914 to December 1941."

Ricardo when Britain returned to the gold standard after the Napoleonic wars. That is, they did not economize on gold by using only paper money as the circulating medium of exchange. France returned to the gold standard in 1928. Legislation required the Banque de France to back its note issue with a 40 percent gold reserve. France then absorbed monetary gold stocks from other central banks by selling dollars and sterling.

With its surplus gold reserves, the Fed could have prevented deflation in the gold standard countries by allowing its gold stock to flow abroad. Governor Strong initiated such an effort in 1927 by coordinating a reduction in the discount rates of the regional Reserve Banks to a level somewhat below the discount rate set by the Bank of England. However, the reduction in the New York Fed's discount rate from 4 to 3.5 percent coincided with a bull market in US equities. The New York Fed then came to be blamed both internally and externally for the stock market speculation, the collapse of which in October 1929 was presumed to have caused the Great Depression. Along with that assignment of blame came the discrediting of the hope of economists like Keynes that the nascent efforts in the 1920s of Governor Strong would successfully achieve economic stabilization through the regulation of credit. Any possibility of an enlightened monetary policy disappeared, and the Great Depression prevailed until the Roosevelt Treasury took control away from the Fed.

Policy makers should have drawn the conclusion that the inoperability of the international gold standard transferred responsibility to them for the domestic price level. They did not. The belief was too ingrained that the value of currency derived from its convertibility into the ultimate source of value: gold. Continued convertibility of the dollar into gold would render it impossible for early policy makers to understand that they had moved to a monetary regime of fiat money creation. The alternative as they understood it was "managed money," in which the government issued paper money without backing. All such monetary experiments had in the past ended with inflation and a worthless currency. The gold reserve ratio would in fact continue to exercise an influence on money creation but in an asymmetrically contractionary way. As in October 1931, regional Reserve Bank governors would raise the discount rate in response to gold outflows and declines in the gold cover. They would not lower the discount rate, however, in response to gold inflows and increases in the gold cover.

7.6. MONETARY POLICY IN RECESSION: 1923–24 AND 1926–27

Given that early policy makers feared incipient signs of speculative excess, one can ask why it took so long before the Fed set off the Great Depression.

The obvious answer is that it required the stock market boom to set off a fiercely contractionary monetary policy. Luck also played a role. There was no settled monetary policy in the 1920s before 1928. That unsettled state appeared in the absence of a consistent policy for dealing with gold inflows, which supplied bank reserves. Walter W. Stewart (US Congress 1926–27, April 22, 1926, 757), who had been director of research at the Federal Reserve Board, testified:

> The effect of the importing of gold upon the credit situation depends upon the conditions prevailing at the time. During the period from 1922 to 1926 we had such a variation of conditions prevailing that to almost every one of the various uses to which gold can be put it has actually been put. No one can estimate in advance what the effect of a gold import will be on our credit situation. It always is conditioned upon what the credit situation is at the time.

The steady inflow of gold from 1921 through 1924 was a factor due to luck that militated in favor of an expansionary monetary policy. Stewart observed that in 1923, if gold had not flowed in, banks would have had to borrow at the discount window to meet additional demand for currency. That is, in the absence of the gold inflows, monetary policy would have been tighter and probably contractionary. Stewart (US Congress 1926–27, April 22, 1926, 752–53) testified:

> In 1921 six hundred and sixty millions came in, and was all used to pay indebtedness at reserve banks. In 1922, $238,000,000 came in. Part of that was used for the same purpose, and the remaining portion was added to the reserves of the member banks, increasing their lending power, which was used in the purchase of investments. In 1923, $298,000,000 came in, and practically all of it was used by member banks to meet the increased currency requirements. In 1924, $258,000,000 came in, and a portion was used to repay indebtedness and the remaining portion was added to reserve balances of member banks at the reserve banks. If the gold had not come in 1923, the member banks would have had to borrow from the reserve bank to get currency to meet the increased demands. In view of the fact that the gold came in just about the same amount as the increased demand for currency the requirements for currency were made up out of the inflow of gold.

As Stewart (US Congress 1926–27, April 22, 1926, 753) noted, "In 1925, $134,000, 000 of gold was exported, and the member banks borrowed at the reserve banks to obtain the gold." Figure 7.5 shows that after 1925 the price level, which had been rising, declined.

The individual Reserve Banks began to purchase government securities in 1921 with especially heavy purchases in early 1922. Although the economy was in recession, those purchases had nothing to do with countercyclical stabilization of the economy.[5] The gold inflows that began in earnest in 1921 had reduced the discount window lending of the Reserve Banks and the rediscounted bills that furnished income to cover expenses and the dividend paid to member banks. The Reserve Banks purchased government securities to provide income. Complaints by the Treasury that such purchases were interfering with debt management led to formation of the Open Market Investment Committee (OMIC) to coordinate purchases.

The newly formed committee allowed government security holdings to largely run off at the Reserve Banks in the first half of 1923, and the New York Fed raised its discount rate early in the year. Underhill (1941, cited in Wilkerson 2013, 113) wrote that in 1923, "with inflation tendencies abroad and gold flowing into the United States from Europe, it was felt on this side of the Atlantic that business was recovering too rapidly. An increase in discount rates and open market sales of government securities by Reserve banks was recommended by the Federal Reserve Board as a means to counteract the situation."

Representative Goldsborough (US Congress 1928, May 17, 327), who sponsored legislation to enact Irving Fisher's compensated-dollar plan, commented on 1923 monetary policy:

> In 1923 we were cautious, not because we are habitually wise enough to be cautious, but because and only because we had just had our lesson. Various banks in their monthly letters during 1923 gave reminders of the disasters of 1920; the monthly letters of the National City Bank of New York, for example, . . . warned its readers that every upward movement is in danger of running away. In April it again called attention to the danger of inflation. "The industries of the country," it declared, "are already working practically at capacity or to the limit of the labor supply. Under this condition they can not use more credit to advantage." . . . In February and March, 1923, the reserve banks of New York, Boston, and San Francisco raised their rediscount rates. Due in part to this action, interest rates of commercial banks rose in February and again in March, rates on call loans on 60 to 90 day paper and on 4 to 6 months

5. The NBER cycle troughs and peaks are as follows: July 1921 (T), May 1923 (P), July 1924 (T), October 1926 (P), November 1927 (T).

paper being all higher in March than in any month of the previous year. Raising of money rates was followed promptly by curbing of the upward movement of prices and overproduction. Not so generally understood is the fact that the open-market operations of the Federal reserve banks in the first half of 1923 tended to curb the involuntary movement. . . . Early in January the Federal reserve banks held open-market acceptances and United States securities to the value of $734,000,000. These they reduced steadily throughout the period of incipient business boom.

Carl Snyder (1940, 227), chief statistician at the New York Fed, described an accidental start to Fed policy in the 1920s:

> Towards the end of 1921 several Reserve banks . . . began considerable purchases of government securities. Within six months the fall in prices had stopped, business began to recover and confidence returned. . . . Then through 1922 and into 1923 there was a sharp rise in several types of price and a corresponding expansion of bank credit, with a renewed outbreak of speculation. Because of this the Reserve Banks again intervened by raising discount rates. Again a sharp check to the rise in prices, and likewise to trade. So, in 1924, . . . Governor Strong proposed that the Federal Reserve Banks again lower their rates and buy heavily of government securities. . . . The recession in business was soon over.

As part of congressional hearings held in early 1931, the Reserve Banks submitted answers to a questionnaire. The New York Fed submitted a memorandum written by Strong on December 26, 1924. It described the early implementation of Fed procedures. Figures 7.7 and 7.8 are reproduced from congressional testimony by Governor Strong. Figure 7.7 shows how open market sales increased discount window borrowing while open market purchases reduced borrowing. Figure 7.8 displays an index of industrial production from 1922 through 1930. It shows the relationship between cyclical weakness and easing actions (open market purchases and discount-rate reductions) and cyclical strength and tightening actions (open market sales and discount-rate increases).

Strong (US Congress 1931, "Federal Reserve Questionnaires," 804–7) described a countercyclical response to the 1923–24 recession:

> By the fall of 1923 . . . there was developing some recession in business. . . . Notwithstanding imports of gold, there was continued pressure by member banks to liquidate their indebtedness to the reserve banks, causing, in turn, pressure by member banks upon their borrowers to

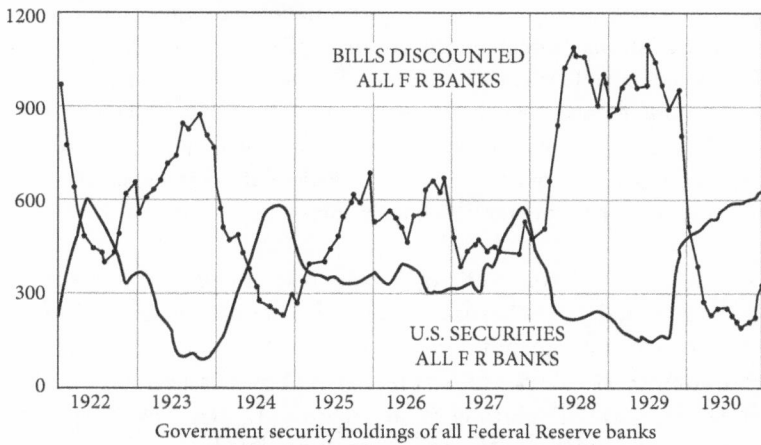

MILLIONS OF DOLLARS

BILLS DISCOUNTED
ALL F R BANKS

U.S. SECURITIES
ALL F R BANKS

Government security holdings of all Federal Reserve banks
and member bank borrowings at reserve banks
(monthly averages of daily figures)

Figure 7.7. Open Market Operations and Discount Window Borrowing
Government security holdings of all Federal Reserve Banks and member bank
borrowings at Reserve Banks (monthly averages of daily figures)
(US Congress 1931, part 6, 804).

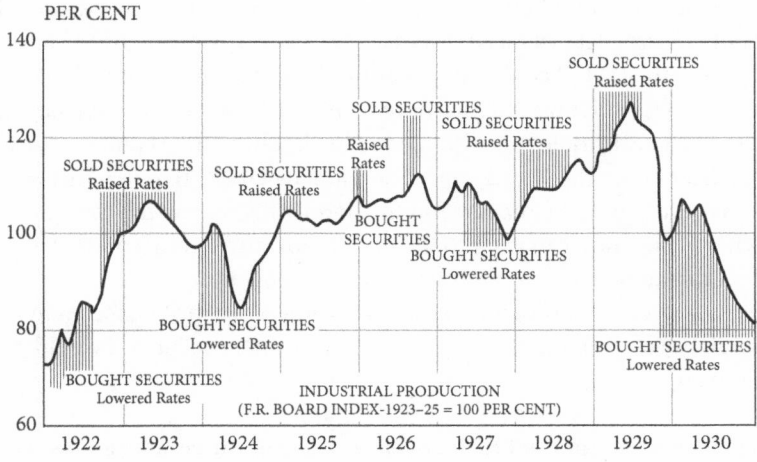

PER CENT

SOLD SECURITIES
Raised Rates

SOLD SECURITIES
SOLD SECURITIES
Raised Rates

SOLD SECURITIES
Raised
Rates

SOLD SECURITIES
Raised Rates

SOLD SECURITIES
Raised Rates

BOUGHT
SECURITIES

BOUGHT SECURITIES
Lowered Rates

BOUGHT SECURITIES
Lowered Rates

BOUGHT SECURITIES
Lowered Rates

BOUGHT SECURITIES
Lowered Rates

INDUSTRIAL PRODUCTION
(F.R. BOARD INDEX-1923–25 = 100 PER CENT)

Figure 7.8. Industrial Production, Discount Rate, and Open Market Purchases
US Congress 1931, part 6, 803.

repay loans. . . . The conditions of the farming community, including the cattle industry, became perilously near a national disaster, and feeling became so strong throughout the West that all sorts of radical proposals for legislation and other Government relief were being urged. . . . It was under these conditions that the Federal Reserve Banks undertook the gradual repurchase of short-term Government obligations . . . to accelerate the process of debt repayment to the Federal Reserve Banks, so as to relieve this . . . pressure for loan liquidation.

The accounts of Strong and Snyder sound as though the New York Fed had a modern understanding of countercyclical monetary policy. However, the memo Strong wrote for his private files on December 26, 1924, offered a more complex set of reasons for open market purchases in 1924 (cited in Chandler 1958, 242–43). Strong wanted to lower rates in New York relative to London "to render what assistance was possible by our market policy toward . . . the resumption of gold payments by Great Britain." Until 1928, Strong's desire to aid Europe to reestablish the gold standard imparted a bias toward ease. "The desire of the Federal Reserve Bank of New York to establish a rate spread between New York and London to encourage capital outflows and reduce gold imports was indeed the chief determinant of policy" (Wicker 1966, 77). That would change with the stock market boom.

The second factor working to impart a countercyclical aspect to policy was the desire to build up a portfolio of government securities that could be sold at a later date when advances in business displayed signs of speculative fever. The OMIC could buy securities in recession when there was no evidence of speculation and then have them to sell in a boom when the sales laid the groundwork for an advance in the discount rate. Hamlin recorded in his diary about the May 29, 1924, decision by OMIC to purchase securities that they could be made without "unduly disturbing the market, but that it was imperative to get into the market now to exercise control later in case of threatened inflation" (cited in Wicker 1966, 89).

Strong wrote Treasury undersecretary Gilbert on April 18, 1922 (cited in Chandler 1958, 211) that the purchase of government securities would give the Fed an

investment account sufficient at a later date when it became necessary to prevent dangerously low interest rates in the market, and check unwholesome speculation. . . . If we relinquish our hold on the market now, . . . we will later deliver the situation to the speculator without any means of checking it. . . . The fact is that the shelves are getting dangerously bare, and, with this demand springing up all over the country, the first thing we will know we will suddenly break into a run-away market such as occurred in 1919, with no means of checking it.

The reasoning seems odd that the OMIC desired to purchase securities (increase reserves) so that it could later sell them (decrease reserves).[6] However, as noted, the purchases changed the composition of the Federal Reserve System's assets to put them in a form that could more easily be contracted.

Another factor worked to impart a fortuitous countercyclical aspect to monetary policy. As shown in figure 6.1, strength in the economy would induce a rightward shift in the reserves demand schedule through the increased demand for reserves coming from increased deposits. Market rates would then rise. At the same time, "the attitude of the governors of the individual Federal Reserve Banks seemed to be that [discount] rates should follow, rather than lead, the market" (Wicker 1966, 84). The Reserve Banks would then raise their discount rates at times of cyclical strength. The converse held for cyclical weakness.

The governors had to confront the contradiction between using open market operations countercyclically and real bills principles. At the Governors Conference of May 1924 (pp. 17–19), Governor Calkins of San Francisco expressed concern about buying government securities to bolster earning assets. During recessions, because discount window lending would have declined, earnings would be low. However, purchasing securities at this time would supply funds when they were not needed, "exactly the reverse of what is desired" (cited in Meltzer 2003, 159).

Real bills adherents unsheathed their long knives at signs of countercyclical monetary policy. Benjamin Anderson (1924, 3), an economist at Chase National Bank, wrote:

> Since November 21, 1923, the Federal Reserve Banks have increased their holdings of Government securities from $73,000,000 to $477,000,000, while the rediscounts and commercial paper holdings of the Federal Reserve Banks have declined with the falling off of commercial demand for money. In the present state of declining trade, both incoming gold and

6. One can find the logic in Douglas (1935, 114):

> The ability of the Federal Reserve System to sell government securities is strictly limited by the amount of such securities which they have previously accumulated. As Keynes puts it, "The Reserve Banks can only fire off against an incipient boom such ammunition as they have been able to pick up whilst resisting the slump." The reference is to Keynes 1930, 259.

Federal Reserve Bank investments are reflected almost entirely in an increase of member bank balances, with immediate and even violent effect upon the money market. The situation is abnormal and dangerous. . . . Commodity prices have fallen pretty steadily for over a year. . . . But even if we have not blown up a price bubble, we have been blowing up a credit bubble, especially in the form of long-term debts. . . . A great volume of short-time money market funds has been diverted to capital uses.

The economy reached a cyclical trough in July 1924. "From the end of 1923 to the autumn of 1924 the policy of the Federal Reserve system was directed toward monetary ease with more vigor than at any other period in the history of the System prior to 1930" (Hardy 1932, 43). The Fed bought Treasury securities, and the New York Fed lowered its discount rate from 4½ percent in April 1924 to 3 percent in August 1924 (see again figure 6.3).

In summer 1924, the culmination of strong gold imports and weak demand for credit due to the recession produced a near elimination of discount window borrowing. As seen by the Fed, if banks were out of the window, that would eliminate its ability to control the expansion of bank credit. Such concern would become paramount in the Depression when the Fed wrestled with whether to conduct open market purchases of government securities. In a review of Fed operations in 1931, Senator Carter Glass (US Congress 1931, January 23, 153) observed:

I am satisfied that if the reserve system has its hands tied against too easy a yielding to the seductive expedient of inflation through open market purchase operations, we need not worry so much about speculative abuses and excesses. The only nullifying influences against a prudent Federal reserve attitude that might happen would be uncontrollable imports of gold, which would put the member banks in an independent position. That, as you know, has been a large factor since the war.

The economic expansion after the July 1924 cycle trough continued until the cycle peak in October 1926. What would become most notable afterward was the rise in the stock market by 50 percent from mid-1924 to the end of 1925 combined with "the very rapid increase of investments in securities and of loans on securities" (Hardy 1932, 44). W. Randolph Burgess (US Congress 1926–27, May 4, 1926, 921), assistant Federal Reserve agent for the New York Fed, testified:

It is a very serious problem as to what can be done to restrain a serious speculative orgy. There is no doubt but what last fall [1925], in the latter part of the year, there was a very large extension of credit for stock-exchange uses. The question is, what can be done about it.

Tables 3.2 and 3.3 for the 1923 and 1926 recessions, respectively, show the same patterns as table 3.1 for the 1920–21 recession. Short-term market interest rates stay at cyclical highs past the cyclical peak while M1 growth and economic activity decline. Figure 7.3 shows the declines in the M1 step functions associated with cyclical peaks. The underlying Fed behavior reflected concern for speculation. On November 20, 1925, Strong wrote a letter to Governor Norman of the Bank of England presaging the increase in the discount rate and open market sales in August 1926 (cited in Chandler 1958, 329):

> We have had a dangerous speculation develop in the stock market, with some evidence that it is extending into commodities. There has been a rampaging real estate speculation in some spots. . . . You must prepare your mind for our advancing the discount rate in New York before the end of the year.

7.7. 1927

A cyclical peak occurred in October 1926 followed by a moderate recession with a trough in November 1927. Throughout the year 1927, the stock market continued to climb. Gold flowed in during the first half of the year. On August 5, 1927, the New York Fed reduced its discount rate by ½ a percentage point to 3½ percent followed by the other Reserve Banks except for Chicago. Departing from convention, the Federal Reserve Board ordered an unwilling Chicago Fed to also lower its discount rate. The Fed purchased government securities in the summer.

Although consistent with a policy of economic stabilization, Strong's primary motivation was "more to obtain a rate differential between New York and London than to stimulate economic activity" (Wicker 1966, 107). The reduction in the New York bank's discount rate occurred after a meeting of Governor Strong with Bank of England governor Montagu Norman, Reichsbank president Hjalmar Schacht, and Bank of France deputy governor Charles Rist. Wicker (1966, 112) quoted from a letter written later by Rist to E. A. Goldenweiser: "You probably know that the decision to lower the discount rate was taken directly in a conversation between Montagu Norman and Benjamin Strong." The concern was that the imminent return of France to the gold standard would produce an increased demand for gold and would require a restrictive policy on the part of European central banks. Norman did not want the New York Fed to allow rates to rise in the United States in response to gold outflows.

When the Fed began raising discount rates, led by New York in February 1928, the outflow of gold of about $250 million in 1927 completely reversed between June 1928 and October 1929. However, Strong had forewarned Norman that concern for speculation would trump concern for foreign economic stability. In a memo written January 11, 1925, summarizing his conversation with Norman, Strong had written (cited in Chandler 1958, 311):

> There must be a plain recognition of the fact that in a new country such as ours, with an enthusiastic, energetic, and optimistic population, where enterprise at times was highly stimulated and the returns upon capital much greater than in other countries, there would be times when speculative tendencies would make it necessary for the Federal Reserve Banks to exercise restraint by increased discount rates, and possibly rather high money rates in the market. Should such times arise, domestic considerations would likely outweigh foreign sympathies, and the protection of our own economics situation, forcing us to higher rates, might force them to maintain still higher rates, with some resulting hardship to business, etc.

The timing of events appeared to offer conclusive confirmation of the view that speculative excess was the progenitor of boom-bust cycles. Despite a surging stock market, in 1927, the Reserve Banks reduced their discount rates and undertook open market purchases. The market continued to climb but collapsed in fall 1929. The Great Depression ensued. Later, Board member Adolph Miller would blame the Great Depression on the New York Fed. He was only the conductor of a chorus.

A near-universal consensus developed that the Fed had nourished a speculative fever through its "cheap" money policy in 1927. Originally, Miller had supported efforts to restore the international gold standard (Fisher 1934, 237). However, as the NYSE rose, he turned on Governor Strong and accused the New York Fed of fomenting the speculative fever. Miller testified (US Congress 1928, May 2, 172):[7]

> The money that was released by the Federal reserve banks to the open market through its policy of open-market purchases had to go some-

---

7. Miller comes across as inconsistent if not hypocritical. Meltzer (2003, 193) cited interviews from the Committee on the History of the Federal Reserve System. Charles J. Rhoads, who was the first governor of the Philadelphia Fed, described him as "didactic" and "quite sure he knew the answer to every question." Governor Harrison, who had worked as a Board lawyer before going to New York, said that Miller was unwilling "to admit that he was ever wrong." Also, he listened little to others.

where.... The low money rates that resulted from Federal reserve policy, in light of subsequent developments, appear to have been particularly effective in stimulating the absorption of credit in stock speculation.... I would say that cheap and easy money in the New York market the last autumn must be recognized to-day as having been a distinctly provocative factor in the remarkable speculative movement that has been in process now for several months.

7.8. ELIMINATING CREDIT DIVERSION
INTO SECURITIES SPECULATION

By the end of 1927, the Fed had become concerned about the diversion of lending for speculation on the NYSE and more generally for lending collateralized by securities. The diversion of credit into speculative uses through circumvention of real bills principles also concerned previous years. The "Fifteenth Annual Report" of the Federal Reserve Board (1929, 2, 8) stated: "Growth of security loans in 1928 accompanied an extraordinary growth in activity in the securities market and a rapid advance in security values.... In recent years the most rapid expansion of bank credit has been in the direction of increasing use of bank funds in investments and in loans on securities." The report then cited the increase from the middle of 1925 to the middle of 1928 in member bank holdings of investments and loans on securities and noted that of "the volume of nearly $37,700,000,000 of loans and investments of member banks, more than 57 percent are either in investments or in loans on securities."

The presumed long-run culprit was gold imports with the issuance of Treasury silver certificates an accomplice. The increase in bank reserves due to gold imports increased the ability of banks to lend without recourse to borrowing from the discount window. Banks then escaped the discipline imposed by the restriction on continuous borrowing that assured that loans were short-term and self-liquidating. The "Seventeenth Annual Report" of the Federal Reserve Board (1931, 5–6) explained: "This inflow of gold ... provided a basis for credit expansion by member banks without increasing their requirements for reserve-bank credit.... The entire period from 1922 to 1927 was consequently characterized by a relatively low level of money rates and an abundance of funds." As a result, banks engaged in "a continuous growth of loans on securities."

Later, Board member Adolph Miller attacked the New York Fed publicly in Senate hearings. The text merits review because Miller attacked the open market purchases and reduction in the funds rate that occurred in 1927, which was a year of recession. Undertaking these actions in the Depression required repetition of the very actions widely understood as having created the speculative bubble whose bursting produced the Depression. Miller (US Congress 1931, January 23, 134, 135, 136, and 144) told the senators:

> In the year 1927 . . . you will note the pronounced increase in these holdings [of United States securities] in the second half of the year. Coupled with the heavy purchases of acceptances it was the greatest and boldest operation ever undertaken by the Federal reserve system, and, in my judgment, resulted in one of the most costly errors committed by it or any other banking system in the last 75 years. . . . There followed immediately an increase in the reserve balances of the member banks. . . . That was a time of business recession. Business could not use and was not asking for increased money at that time.
>
> "What then," one asks, "was the use made of the reserves which, so to speak, were handed to the banks by the Federal reserve banks, through open market purchases of securities"? Well, they bought investments in increasing amounts.
>
> A not inconsiderable part of the funds that came into the call-loan market, from 1927 on, as loans for account of others, loans of corporations, firms and individuals, also traces back to the impulse that the great creation of cheap credit in 1927 gave to company financing and refinancing. By issues of stock as well as bonds companies obtained funds in excess of immediate requirements which became available for loans in the call-loan market.
>
> I had no misgivings as to the ultimate consequences of the speculative expansion at that time. It was clear to me . . . that it would end in some sort of violent revulsion.

Miller (US Congress 1931, January 23, 140) restated the view that the New York Fed had contravened real bills principles by acting like a central bank in creating reserves on its own initiative. "You strip your regional banks of their separate control of credit in their several districts when you operate with their resources in the central money market of the country." Senator Bulkley asked, "Was the 1927 adventure in the nature of a central bank operation?" Miller replied, "Distinctly. It could hardly have been more so if we had but one bank."

Had Strong lived, he might have agreed with Miller. Strong had written Emile Moreau, governor of the Banque de France, on August 30, 1927 (cited in Chandler 1958, 451):

> Our rate reduction seems for the present to have accomplished the results desired. We were anxious to avoid further large shipments of gold to this country and, even more, to postpone or possibly to completely

avoid the need for any general advance of bank rates in Europe this fall. . . . Fortunately, we have so far escaped anything like an outburst of stock speculation because of this rate reduction and the cheaper money which has accompanied it, but one cannot promise as to the future.

Similarly, on July 14, 1928, Strong wrote Parker Gilbert, agent general for reparations (cited in Chandler 1958, 458):

Our policy for the last four years . . . has enabled monetary reorganiza-tion to be completed in Europe, which otherwise would have been im-possible. It was undertaken with the well recognized hazard that we were liable to encounter a big speculation. . . . Speculation has not occurred in commodities, but almost wholly in stocks. . . . Our course was perfectly obvious. We had to undertake it. . . . In view of this we have had advances in our discount rate with member banks borrowing over a billion dollars from us and absolutely in our grip.

Walter Stewart, who had become an adviser to the Bank of England, wrote Strong in early August 1928, "Pressure on New York Banks is now ap-proaching the breaking point" (cited in Chandler 1958, 45). Strong replied on August 3, 1928, that "it is really a problem of psychology. The country's state of mind has been highly speculative. . . . The growth in the volume of member bank credit had become too rapid and was largely the outcome of speculation. . . . The problem now is to avoid a calamitous break in the stock market, a panicky feeling about money, a setback to business because of the change in psychology" (cited in Chandler 1958, 460–61).

In his reply to Stewart, Strong recognized the danger of high rates caus-ing "a chill to domestic business" but was confident that in the event of "a ca-lamity growing out of money rates" the Fed would have "the power to deal with such an emergency instantly by flooding the street with money. . . . In former days the psychology was different because the facts of the banking situation were different. Mob panic, and consequently mob disaster, is less likely to arise" (cited in Chandler 1958, 462). On October 16, 1928, after an operation arising out of complications due to diverticulitis, Strong died of a hemorrhage at age fifty-five.

7.9. WERE THE 1920S THE "HIGH TIDE" OF FEDERAL RESERVE MONETARY POLICY?

The period between the 1920–21 recession and the start of the Depression in 1929 was one of price stability and relative economic stability. Did policy makers exhibit an understanding of the world in this period, which, if maintained, would have avoided the Depression? In their term "high tide," Friedman and Schwartz (1963a, chap. 6) answered affirmatively. They attributed the Fed's contractionary monetary policy in the Depression to a shift of power from the New York Fed to the Federal Reserve Board, home of real bills ideas, following the death of Benjamin Strong in 1928 (Friedman and Schwartz 1963a, 415).

Friedman and Schwartz (1963a, 411) asked why

an active, vigorous self-confident policy in the 1920s was followed by a passive, defensive, hesitant policy from 1929 to 1933 . . . [and] why the System failed to meet an internal drain in the way intended by its founders. . . . The explanation for the contrast between Federal Reserve policy before 1929 and after, and hence for the inept policy after 1929 . . . is the shift of power within the System and the lack of understanding and experience of the individuals to whom the power shifted.

Wicker (1966, xi) challenged the Friedman-Schwartz assertion, as he described it, that "the administration of monetary policy somehow changed from good to bad between the two periods (from 1922 through 1927 and thereafter), mainly as a result of the death of Benjamin Strong." Instead, Wicker (1966, xi) argued that "historical evidence revealing neither a sharp break in the logic nor in the interpretation of Federal Reserve monetary policy is used to demonstrate that the behavior of System officials was consistent throughout the entire period."[8] Brunner and Meltzer (1968) and Meltzer (2003) agreed and highlighted what they term "the Riefler-Burgess doctrine." Namely, Fed policy makers considered the policy "easy" as long as there was little borrowing from the discount window and money market interest rates were "low." Their insight underscores that fact the policy makers in the spirit of real bills thought in terms of influencing financial intermediation rather than the control of money creation.

David Wheelock (1991) estimated a reaction function for the Fed for its holdings of government securities over the interval January 1924 to September 1929. He then extrapolated the results for the interval September 1929 through February 1933. Wheelock (1991, 39) found that "relative to the decline in economic activity, the purchases were small compared with

8. Wicker was the first scholar to obtain unfettered access to Board records. Like Friedman and Schwartz, he had access to the George Leslie Harrison papers at Columbia University and to the detailed diary of Charles S. Hamlin, member of the Federal Reserve Board. He also obtained access to the papers of E. A. Goldenweiser, director of the Board's Division of Research and Statistics from 1927 through 1945. Finally, he had access to Federal Reserve Board correspondence.

those made during the recessions of 1924 and 1927." He conducted a similar exercise for the New York Fed's discount rate with similar results. Starting in mid-1931, the discount rate should have been zero, whereas it reached 3½ percent on October 17, 1931. Wheelock, however, attributed these results to a consistency over the entire period in the real bills views of policy makers.

In the 1920s and 1930s, policy makers did not understand the transmission of monetary policy through a national money market and did not understand how their operating procedures could, if allowed, move the interest rate in the money market in a way designed to stabilize the economy. Wheelock (1991, 43) noted:

> The reductions in the Federal Reserve Bank of New York's discount and bill buying rates in 1930 and 1931 were made simply to keep them in line with market rates, as had been done during the 1920s. This explanation suggests that there was no change in Federal Reserve strategy with the onset of the Depression.

The ignorance of early policy makers came from the absence of a macroeconomics that explained the operation of the price system. Interfering with the market determination of interest rates constituted price fixing, which created the monetary destruction that powered recession and deflation.

The answer given here to why monetary policy was relentlessly contractionary during the Great Contraction is that no one understood the nature of the monetary standard created by the Federal Reserve Act. The newly created standard was one of fiat money creation with an independent central bank. As Friedman and Schwartz (1963a, 411) noted, it is true that the Fed undertook open market purchases in the 1923–24 and 1926–27 recessions and also after the 1929 stock market crash. It is also true that at least the New York Fed and the Board believed they had a responsibility to stabilize the economy.

However, the Fed operated with the real bills premise that recession and deflation originated in a collapse of speculative excess. Economic stabilization required the Fed to repress incipient speculative excess as evidenced by increases in asset prices and business inventories. Those phenomena are normal signs of prosperity. The early Fed was an economic doomsday machine. The reason that the Great Depression did not begin earlier was the timing of the stock market boom. The boom, which triggered contractionary monetary policy, gained real strength in 1928 and early 1929.

The fundamental insights of Friedman and Schwartz are correct. They understood the monetary standard as one of fiat money creation with the Fed responsible for the reserves base on which nominal bank liabilities rested. The Fed allowed the collapse of the banking system by not maintaining that reserves base. The Fed remained ignorant of its responsibility to maintain price stability under a regime of fiat money creation. The Depression was a failure of monetary policy not an inherent defect in the working of the price system that caused it to fail to maintain aggregate demand at a level sufficient to assure full employment.

7.10. CONCLUDING COMMENT

The intellectual foundation of the countercyclical monetary policy of the 1920s was built on quicksand. The spirit was to prevent the development of speculative excess. Based on that foundation, in 1928–29, the Fed initiated a contractionary monetary policy to squelch the speculative excess presumed raging as evidenced by the stock market boom.

The real bills guidelines of the Board's "Tenth Annual Report" (Federal Reserve Board 1924a) could have been consistently stabilizing if they had prompted policy makers to concentrate on the behavior of the economy as occurred after the 1951 Treasury-Fed Accord. However, policy makers looked through the behavior of the economy for signs of speculative excess. Currie (1934b, 43) wrote:

> It may be objected that even though the reserve administration conceives that the primary function of a central bank is to enable member banks to supply at all times and at reasonable rates the needs of their commercial borrowers, there is no great harm in this theory so long as it is so interpreted to call for an easy money policy in the downswing of business and a restrictive policy in the upswing. It is, however, dangerous to expect adherence to a wrong theory to lead to adoption of correct policies.

CHAPTER 8

Attacking Speculative Mania

Summary: Starting in 1928 and continuing into 1929, the Fed tightened the monetary screws. In 1928 and the first half of 1929, the economy grew strongly. At the same time, monetary restriction prevented an expansion of the banking system. In 1928 and 1929, the combination of increases in the discount rates of the Reserve Banks and "direct pressure" that created a stigma for borrowing at the discount window if a bank was making "speculative" security loans effectively closed the markets that banks used to adjust their reserve positions: the discount window and the call money market. The resulting effort by banks to increase liquidity by increasing excess reserves required a contraction of the credit and deposits of the banking system. The stress on the banking system appeared in the spike in the call loan rate in the call money market.

Expressed in terms of the reserves supply schedule (figure 6.1), open market sales shifted the reserve supply schedule leftward; increases in the discount rate raised the reserves supply schedule; and the policy of "direct pressure" caused the upward sloping segment of the reserve supply schedule to rotate upward. With these actions, the Fed pushed the marginal cost of reserves above the economy's natural rate of interest. Only in March 1933 did monetary policy cease to be contractionary.

A Wicksellian framework modified to incorporate a central bank creating fiat money offers a coherent view of contractionary monetary in the Great Depression. The Fed kept the real rate of interest high relative to its "natural" counterpart. The resulting excess of the real rate of interest over the natural rate of interest required contraction in the money stock. The weakening of the economy caused by monetary contraction weakened the banking system and made it susceptible to runs. A currency outflow from banks precipitated by bank panics forced banks into the discount window. Because borrowing from the discount window was a sign weakness, banks tried to obtain the reserves required to repay discount window borrowing by liquidating loans. Because of the fractional-reserves character of the banking system, the decline in bank loans and deposits required to increase excess reserves was a multiple of the increase in excess reserves.

8.1. LIQUIDATING SPECULATIVE CREDIT
BY LIQUIDATING TOTAL CREDIT

In 1928, Fed policy makers began the campaign to extinguish what they perceived to be an excess of credit that supported a speculative rise in the NYSE. Initially, the Board and New York agreed that this liquidation had to occur through a reduction in the total amount of credit extended by banks. As stated by Federal Reserve Board member Charles S. Hamlin, the intention was to liquidate the excess of credit before "this mad speculative mania" produced an inevitable collapse (US Congress 1931, January 23, 174).

In its "Annual Report" for 1928, the Board made clear that, because of the fungibility of credit, policy had to aim for a reduction in total bank credit. The example used was that of a member bank having "recourse to the discount window using legitimate collateral" but then lending to customers who were making "security loans." To limit speculative lending, the Fed had to resort to "credit policy" by raising the "cost of bank credit" in general. The "Annual Report" for the year 1928 (Federal Reserve Board 1929, 8–9) noted:

> Every class of loan or investment . . . rests in the final analysis upon reserve bank credit, which is the base of the entire credit structure. . . . The Federal reserve system's responsibility is not limited to the control of funds obtained directly from the Federal reserve banks. There is no way of earmarking for special purposes the credit extended by the Federal reserve banks, and even if that were possible, it would still be true, under existing law, that the entire credit structure rests upon Federal reserve credit as a base.

The presumed excessive extension of credit by banks had allowed credit to spill over into speculative securities lending. The required reduction in credit necessitated a reduction not only in commercial bank credit but also in total credit. Currie (1934b, 56) quoted E. A. Goldenweiser, who was director of research at the Federal Reserve Board. "Take, for instance, 1929. Bank credit was not growing. . . . But, as everyone knows, it was a year of extraordinary expansion of credit and speculative activity. Credit policy of necessity was one of restraint."

Currie (1934a, 157) also offered an excellent overview of the resulting monetary policy:

> There is a widespread impression that the primary cause of the System's failure to check speculation lay in the mildness of its restraining mea-

sures in the first six months of 1928. Available statistical evidence appears to afford little support to this view. The Reserve banks' average daily holdings of acceptances and government securities declined 409 million dollars from January to June. In addition the average daily monetary gold stock declined by 258 million dollars in the same period. As a result, member banks were forced into debt to the Reserve banks to an amount exceeding one billion dollars—the highest level since 1921. Due to the repugnance of member banks to continuous indebtedness at the Reserve banks, a repugnance reinforced by a rise in the rediscount rate to 5 percent, net demand deposits declined 914 million dollars from December 31, 1927, to June 30, 1928. . . . This restrictive policy was the most drastic ever consciously pursued by the Reserve banks.

Although New York and the Board would differ starting in 1929 over how to rein in speculation, they both agreed on the need to deflate the NYSE. Initially, they both agreed on the need to restrict the total volume of credit. Hamlin (US Congress 1931, January 23, 173, 177) had the following exchange with Carter Glass, member of the Senate Committee on Banking and Currency:

HAMLIN: The position of the New York Bank was that, beginning at 6 per cent, we should start in on an affirmative rate policy of repeated increases of discount rates until the situation should be corrected.

GLASS: What situation?

HAMLIN: I have been asked that a great many times. I think it meant until the stock market was liquidated. . . . When people have gone mad, in a wild, hysterical craze, I feel that it is the duty of a banker to the depositors to repress even his best customers.

Benjamin Anderson, economist at Chase National Bank, answered affirmatively to the question "Should the Reserve Board Control Speculation?" Anderson rebutted critics who argued that the Fed could not control the "outside money" financing stock market speculation. Anderson (1929, 735) pointed out that "since December 26, [1928], brokers' loans for account of others have increased half a billion dollars, but since that same date collateral loans against securities for these 600 odd banks [for which the Fed had data] alone have also increased approximately $500,000,000." That is, by making loans using securities as collateral, banks were financing the loans made to brokers by the general public. Anderson (1929, 733, 735) argued that "if the Federal Reserve banks can control the volume of bank credit, they can control the volume of credit available for security speculation."

Anderson continued that the Fed could indeed control total bank credit if it were willing to "curtail the total of Federal Reserve bank credit."

8.2. NEW YORK: RAISE THE DISCOUNT RATE AND BANKS WILL CUT BACK ON SPECULATIVE LOANS

One reason why the Great Depression lasted so long in contrast to the severe but shorter recession of 1920–21 is that in the former the Fed shut down the markets that member banks used to meet routine reserves deficiencies. The resulting need to be liquid by building up excess reserves forced a contraction of loans and deposits. First, banks could no longer use the call loan market to adjust their reserves position. Second, discount window borrowing, initially because of the Fed oversight that it incurred and later because of the stigma from being perceived as a weak bank, limited its use for adjusting reserves positions. For the individual bank, avoiding recourse to the call loan market and to the discount window required contracting assets to accumulate excess reserves. The Great Depression and the contraction of the banking system ground on powered by the desire of banks to build up excess reserves as an alternative to avoiding the traditional avenues of reserves adjustment.

Governor Harrison of the New York Fed viewed credit as fungible. The New York Fed could identify banks "in the window" that were also making broker loans and pressure them to reduce those loans. However, the result would be to cause the security lending to move to some other bank not in the window. Alternatively, a corporation borrowing from a bank for legitimate purposes could make broker loans. The only realistic way to limit the credit flowing into stock market speculation was to pressure all member banks to restrict total credit. Harrison (HPNY, Confidential Files, February 11, 1929, 4) recorded in his personal notes of a conversation with Governor Young of the Board not only the New York Fed objective of restricting total credit to end its speculative use but also the dangers high interest rates posed to other countries on the gold standard:[1]

> So long as the total volume of credit in the country, that is the total volume of bank credit plus the credit represented by corporation and individual loans to brokers, continued to expand at its present rate, it would be difficult, if not impossible, for us to go into "reverse" [buy government securities and reduce the discount rate]. . . . An expansion of 4½ billions of dollars, representing an expansion of about 8 percent in the total volume of credit in the country contrasted with an expansion of

1. "HPNY" indicates Harrison papers in the New York Fed archives.

3 per cent in business, was an exorbitant use of credit. . . . If the present situation [high interest rates causing imports of gold from abroad] should continue too long, it would not only have a directly detrimental effect on our domestic business and commerce, but would force penalty rates of discount abroad and a possible consequent depression. . . . The chief question of the System is to determine whether we want to let the present situation go along until it corrects itself or whether we should increase discount rates and through sharp incisive action quickly control the long continued expansion in the total volume of credit.

Based on the observation that banks used the call loan market to adjust their reserve positions and to make short-term liquid investments, Harrison assumed that a "high" discount rate would cause banks first to restrict their loans to brokers while leaving intact their commercial loans. The hope was to break the back of stock market speculation before hurting commercial lending and the economy.

Harrison (US Congress 1931, January 20, 59–60) testified:

I do not think it is possible, through any action on the part of the reserve system or any other central banking authority to make money cheap for business and expensive for speculation. The credit pool is too big and fluid a pool for any group of men, whoever they may be, to dictate the rates for funds that are to be put to different purposes.

   If, on the other hand, you can advance the rate quickly enough without regard to any temporary effect on the business rate, you can probably accomplish what you want to accomplish without too severe pressure on business because the higher discount rate will, in the first instance, put pressure on the banks to liquidate their call loans and not their customers' business loans. It has always been that way.

Harrison was just continuing the philosophy put into place by his predecessor Benjamin Strong. Strong (US Congress 1926, April 8, 340) had earlier testified "that the most that the system can do is to exercise influence as to the quantity of the whole volume of credit, what the total sum of it shall be, and what it shall cost. That is the influence we exert."

Open market sales combined with higher discount rates would put banks under pressure to repay their discount window loans and thus limit the flow of funds to the New York call loan market. Burgess (US Congress 1926–27, May 4, 1926, 923) testified:

Banks do not like to be in debt to us for long periods. They want to pay us off. . . . Increases in the discount rate increase that pressure and have a tendency to check the flow of funds toward New York. . . . You can not walk directly into a speculative situation and grapple it with your hands. You have to do it by some indirect method.

Later, in the 1950s, when Winfield Riefler was an adviser to William McChesney Martin and the Fed attempted to revive the free reserves procedures of the 1920s, Riefler recalled how those procedures could pressure banks to restrict lending. Earlier, Riefler (1930, 28) had written, "Member banks are in general reluctant to borrow from the reserve banks, [and] when they do borrow they are in most cases motivated by necessity rather than profit." Restrictive policy started with open market sales sufficient in size to force member banks into the window for more than a brief period of a few days. Reserve Banks then increased their discount rates. An increase in the discount rate not only caused an increase in market rates of interest but also signaled to member banks that they should liquidate assets to repay the borrowing. Riefler (1954) wrote:

> Changes in the discount rate were extremely important as a means of establishing a general level around which market rates of interest fluctuated. They also acted as a sort of discipline that maintained an attitude among member banks where borrowing would be used for short adjustments but continuous or heavy borrowing was avoided.

Harrison expressed dismay that credit restriction had failed to limit speculation before it got to the point that a collapse would cause a recession. (The reference below to "inflation" refers to stock market speculation.) Harrison (US Congress 1931, January 20, 65–66) blamed himself for a failure to act quickly and aggressively enough to stop speculation in its early stages.

> Beginning in 1928 we raised our discount rate three times. We sold over four hundred millions of Government securities. We lost $500,000,000 in gold. Had anybody said two years before that it was possible to raise the discount rate three times and sell $400,000,000 of Government securities and export $500,000,000 of gold without checking inflation, it would have been thought impossible, but that is just what happened.
>
>   When I look back on 1928, I feel that we made two particular mistakes—first, we raised our rate the first time too late, and, second, we did not raise it enough. I mean that had we had at that time the light of the experience we have since had, it would have been better perhaps to have raised the rate 1 per cent in December of 1927. . . . Instead of that we waited until January, after the turn or the year, when we raised it only

one-half of 1 per cent. I think that more prompt, vigorous rate action at that time would have been more helpful.

Harrison (US Congress 1931, January 20, 66) also blamed "bootleg" lending, that is, loans to brokers by corporations, for the failure to control speculation early on.

At one time over half the total volume of money borrowed by brokers and dealers was money advanced . . . wholly outside of the control of the banking system. . . . When we raised our rate and put pressure upon the bank reserves, instead of putting a grind, as we call it, on the judgment and the freedom of the lending officers of a member bank, instead of putting a pressure upon them to contract, in a way which might be effective in reducing loans, the higher rates resulted importantly in attracting other lenders quite outside of the banking system to come in and lend their funds to speculators.

Figure 8.1 shows brokers' loans by lender. Starting in 1928, much of the growth in loans came from corporations (the excess of total lending over the lending made by banks for their own account). The excess is shown by the difference between the "Total" line and the lower line "for Domestic Banks." Board member Adolph Miller (US Congress 1931, January 20, 136) blamed "the impulse that the great creation of cheap credit in 1927 gave to company financing and refinancing. By issues of stock as well as bonds companies obtained funds in excess of immediate requirements which became available for loans in the call-loan market."

Policy makers also believed that intermediation in the 1920s through the capital markets rather than through bank lending based on the discounting of real bills with the Fed encouraged speculation. Harrison (US Congress 1931, January 20, 68–69) testified:

Business expanded very rapidly during those periods, not by borrowing on commercial paper, not by borrowing on direct loans from banks, but by issuing their securities which subsequently became an object of speculation. They got their accommodations through the security markets rather than through commercial loans and used their new capital for expansion, which, perhaps, was unduly rapid, merely because they thought speculative paper profits were going to sustain their business at an increased rate.

The Federal Reserve Board believed that the New York Fed wanted to raise the discount rate relentlessly until it broke the back of specula-

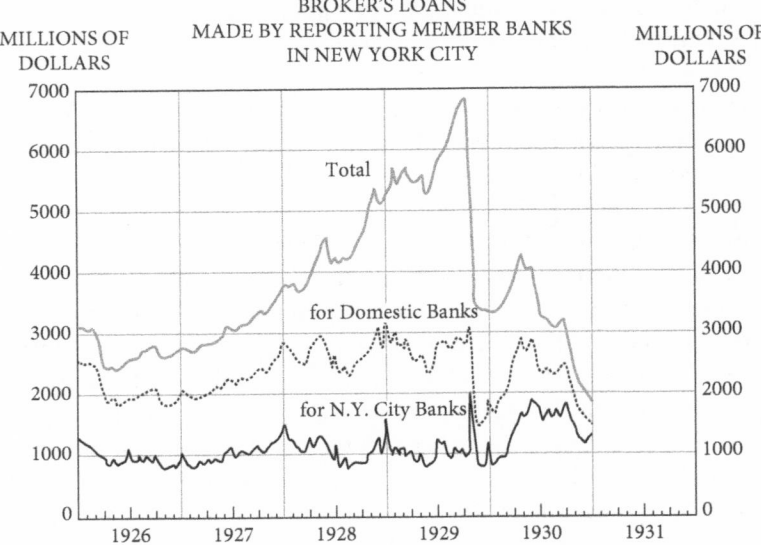

Figure 8.1. Brokers' Loans

US Congress 1931, January 23, 136.

tion. Board member Charles Hamlin (US Congress 1931, January 23, 174) testified:

> Governor Harrison, in an official letter dated April 9, 1929, to Governor Young, among other things, stated . . . [that] public realization that the discount rate would be employed incisively and repeatedly, if necessary, would greatly strengthen the effectiveness of the system's policy, and in itself hasten the time when the system might lend its influence towards easier money conditions. . . . As a matter of fact, rates as high as 7, 8, and 9 per cent were discussed at conferences in the board as being possible under such a drastic increased rate policy.

The failure of policy makers to understand how their operating procedures set money market rates above the discount rate contributed to this view. Chandler (1958, 466) wrote: "By February 1929, every interest rate in the open market was appreciably above the discount rate. This, the officers and directors of the New York Bank believed, was an open invitation to borrowing and further credit expansion."

In quoting a respected newspaper, Hamlin (US Congress 1931, January 23, 175) recognized support for the New York position.

This paper [the *Manchester Guardian*] did not approve our wish to keep the discount rate down to 5 per cent. I quote from its edition of March 4, 1929: There appeared to be some slender hope that the Federal reserve authorities were meditating action drastic enough to precipitate the crisis in Wall Street, which, in the opinion of most monetary students, must come sooner or later.

The Board's alternative to increases in the discount rate was "direct pressure."

8.3. THE BOARD: USE "DIRECT PRESSURE" TO MAKE BANKS CUT BACK ON SPECULATIVE LOANS

"Moral suasion," in the parlance of the time, had been a facet of monetary policy since 1919. When the Reserve Banks raised their discount rates, they also exhorted banks to restrict credit. Hardy (1932, 19) included, as a "channel of influence," "the issuance of warnings and propaganda directed to securing voluntary co-operation of member banks, and of the financial community." In 1929, the Board policy of "direct pressure" ratcheted up the intensity of the policy of liquidation of credit and of the stock market.

Hamlin traced the failure to eliminate stock market speculation to summer 1928 when the Fed decided to accommodate the normal increased seasonal demand for credit. By early 1929, presumably, the past increases in the discount rate no longer deterred speculation. Hamlin (US Congress 1931, January 23, 166–67) testified:

> In the middle of August, August 13, 1928, authority was given by the board to buy acceptances in the New York market, to take up any seasonal credit demand which might arise. And it is a surprising fact that while under this authority the seasonal credit was taken care of it was, in fact, much more than taken care of, by buying acceptances. About $286,000,000 of acceptances were in fact bought, so that the Federal reserve banks finally held two-thirds of all the acceptances outstanding. So many were bought that the banks were able to take down $193,000,000 of discounts with the proceeds. This was all during a time, as we supposed, of a steady, firming policy. These purchases, however, turned our policy from a policy of strict firmness into a policy of ease. . . . I believe that at that moment, January 1, 1929, the discount rate had ceased to be an effective instrument for curbing speculation which had developed into a perfect mania. While I would have been willing, looking back, to

have voted for a 6 per cent rate in the middle of 1928, thinking that then it might have proved a curb, I felt that in January, 1929, it had absolutely gone by the board, and the discount rate would have been of no help to us whatsoever.

Board member Miller (US Congress 1931, January 23, 143–44) reiterated Hamlin's account of the initiation of direct pressure.

> It was our belief that an increase to 6 per cent in February, 1929, would have been nothing but a futile gesture; that it would have been a practical declaration to the speculative markets of the country that the doors of the Federal reserve system were open to all comers with paper of the kinds eligible for rediscount provided they paid 6 per cent. With call rates mounting to 8, 9, 10, 15, and 20 per cent, a 6 per cent discount rate would have been an admission of defeat and given great relief to the speculating public.
>
> I had no misgivings as to the ultimate consequences of the speculative expansion at that time. It was clear to me that it had already gone beyond all the ordinary forms of control; that it would end in some sort of violent revulsion.

In early 1929, the Board issued a letter to banks warning them to restrict use of the discount window. Hamlin (US Congress 1931, January 31, 167) testified: "The board, on February 7, issued a public warning that Federal reserve money had been going into use as the basis of speculative transactions, and calling on the banks to conserve, to cut down their unnecessary borrowings, and bring back the Federal reserve credit and put it back in its proper channels." The letter sent to the Reserve Banks, reproduced in Miller's (US Congress 1931, January 23, 142–43) testimony, read:

> The extraordinary absorption of funds in speculative security loans which has characterized the credit movement during the past year or more, in the judgment of the Federal Reserve Board, deserves particular attention. . . . It has . . . a grave responsibility whenever there is evidence that member banks are maintaining speculative security loans with the aid of Federal reserve credit. . . . The board would like to have from them [the directors of the Reserve Banks] an expression as to (a) how they keep themselves fully informed of the use made of borrowings by their member banks, (b) what methods they employ to protect their institution against the improper use of its credit facilities by member banks.

The letter mentioned a variant of the phrase "speculative security loans" seven times.

It is important to understand how sweeping the injunction in the public letter was interpreted to be. The letter used the phrase "speculative security loans." Banks made loans to brokers who were carrying inventories of stocks purchased by their clients on margin. They also made loans to individuals and businesses collateralized by securities. The published recommendation of the Federal Advisory Council, the group of banks that advise the Board as legislated in the Federal Reserve Act, clarified that banks were on notice that the Fed wanted to restrict both kinds of loans. Miller (US Congress 1931, January 23, 145) testified: "The council approved it [the letter] and even went further than the board in its own recommendation. The board, in its statement always referred to 'speculative security loans.' The council, in its approval, referred to 'security loans,' which was much broader."

Initially, the policy of direct pressure aimed at reducing all borrowing and the total credit extended by banks. Hamlin (US Congress 1931, January 23, 170) testified, "We simply in the first instance, at least, brought pressure to bear on the total amount of borrowings they [the banks] were making, no matter how they were produced, by speculation, or by other loans which could be cut down, or by investments which could be reduced." As 1929 unfolded, the policy of direct pressure focused increasingly on threatening banks making security loans with elimination of access to the discount window. That meant any use of the discount window invited Fed scrutiny. In figure 6.1, the upward sloping section of the reserves supply schedule rotated upward. Without any increase in the discount rate, the marginal cost of reserves to banks increased. The elusive goal by banks of becoming more liquid by restricting loans and building up excess reserves would force a multiyear contraction of the banking system.

Harris (1933, 440–41) explained the events that led to the policy of direct pressure.[2] The assumption in 1928 was that sales of government securities by the Fed and the gold outflows that forced banks into the discount window would cause them to restrict their holding of securities and street loans to brokers and dealers on the NYSE. Although the street loans of New York banks declined, security loans (loans collateralized by securities) increased. Harris (1933, 447, 529) wrote:

---

2. Seymour Harris (1897–1975) became an instructor at Harvard in 1922 and remained there until 1964. He became one of the foremost exponents of Keynesian ideas. His two-volume book (*Twenty Years of Federal Reserve Policy*) is invaluable for capturing the understanding of policy makers in the Great Depression. In writing the book, Harris had free access to internal documents at the Federal Reserve Board.

Loans on the stock market by New York member banks for others and outside banks increased. . . . [In early 1929] security loans declined, but all other loans, the proceeds of which were probably in part used for speculative purposes, tended to increase. . . . The spectacular increase in call money rates had not effectively checked the demand for funds on the security market.

The policy of direct pressure then was a response to the failure of the New York Fed's policy of forcing a general contraction of bank credit through forcing banks into the discount window combined with raising the cost of that borrowing with higher discount rates. It had not stopped the flow of funds to the stock exchange and the continued rise in stock prices. Although the Board vetoed the requests of the New York directors to raise the discount rate in the first half of 1929, the New York Fed still practiced direct pressure (Harrison called it "direct action.") Harrison (HPNY, Confidential Files, February 11, 1929, 7) recorded in his notes a conversation with Governor Young about this:

A bank might be borrowing the equivalent of capital funds from us as a result of a deliberate investment. . . . In such a case we consider we have the right to check the borrowings of such member bank whether the purpose is to invest in government bonds, corporation bonds, call loans or any other sort of investment not resulting from a demand from the community which they serve.

The practical effect of direct pressure was to cause member banks to attempt to limit the use of the discount window as a means of reserves adjustment. What made monetary policy in the Great Contraction so restrictive then was the way in which direct pressure forced contraction of the banking system. Restricting the call loan market and the discount window for reserves adjustment caused banks to want to avoid recourse to them. For that to happen, they had to become more liquid by building up excess reserves. And, for that to happen, the banking system had to contract.

In the 1920s, the national market for bank reserves centered on the call loan market in which loans to brokers and dealers in New York financed lending on margin to purchase stocks. It was liquid, allowed overnight lending, and was collateralized. Banks outside New York could access it through their correspondent banks. Policy makers, however, viewed the call loan market as a conduit for speculative lending and actively discouraged it with the policy of direct pressure. The discouragement of the call loan market as a market for reserves adjustment forced banks to use the discount window more extensively despite the increased cost of doing so. That cost also came from the policy of direct pressure, which subjected banks using the window to scrutiny by regulators for having security loans on their books.

In early 1929, renewed open market sales again forced banks into the discount window. Once in the window, they faced intensified regulatory scrutiny over their lending practices. Hamlin (US Congress 1931, January 23, 169) testified later that Gates W. McGarrah, who was chairman of the New York Board of Directors, wrote the Board a letter in May 1929 stating that

> our direct pressure had affected the banks so that they did not dare to come to borrow at all, that there was going to arise a demand for more credit and that this might reach nearly a hundred million, and they said they did not want our board to keep that pressure on the member banks all the time to reduce their total borrowings when they have got to increase them to a certain extent.

In response to the request of the New York Fed to allow accommodation of coming seasonal needs, as Hamlin (US Congress 1931, January 23, 170) testified, "We simply told the New York bank that on those banks, as they had to borrow for commercial purposes, we would not continue our pressure to reduce total borrowings." That concession did nothing to remove the onus on borrowing from the window created by direct pressure as any borrowing could trigger increased scrutiny for security loans and possible exclusion from the window.

The October 1929 stock market crash was significant because it closed the call loan market for reserves adjustment. It was a liquidity shock.[3] Although the large New York City banks took over many of the loans to brokers while the underlying collateral was liquidated, banks could no longer use the call loan market as the market for reserves adjustment.[4] The forced contraction of the banking system appeared first in New York. As Harris (1933, 540–43) noted:

3. This paragraph benefited from discussion with Ben Chabot. The recent analogous event was the the way in which the failure of Lehman Brothers on September 15, 2008, disrupted the RP (repurchase) market (Gorton 2010). Overnight RPs, which provided funding from cash investors to investment companies and brokers and dealers in the government securities market, became problematic because of uncertainties associated with the haircuts (discounts) required to render the collateral safe.

4. Another more recent analogy would be the Fed's response to the Penn Central crisis in May 1970. When the commercial paper market shut down with the failure of Penn Central, the Fed made clear that banks would have free recourse to the discount window to accommodate any increased loan and associated reserves demand. In 1929 and 1930, that did not happen. Recourse to the window continued to carry stigma.

The first effects of the application of moral suasion apparently were liquidation by the New York banks of security loans. . . . New York banks were cooperating (or perhaps were ordered to cooperate), as is especially evident in a reduction of their [reserve] balances [at the Fed] by 56 millions from February to May [1929]. . . . A reduction of indebtedness for New York City was now a symptom of increasing stringency rather than ease. The popular doctrine is that an increase in indebtedness brings higher rates; but a failure to rediscount and a reduction of [reserve] balances that make liquidation necessary may well be more restraining than an increase in rediscounts.

8.4. MARCHING TOWARD THE GREAT DEPRESSION

On February 14, 1929, the New York Fed requested permission from the Board to raise its discount rate from 5 to 6 percent, but the Board refused to approve it. The New York Fed, nevertheless, tightened monetary policy in the first half of 1929 by restricting the supply of reserves to banks. As Hawtrey (1932 [1962], 76) explained, "As acceptances are bought in the open market, credit is created without any of the deterrent effects of rediscounting for member banks, which are reluctant to be indebted to the Reserve Bank." That source of reserves, however, ceased in early 1929 when the New York Fed raised the rate at which it purchased acceptances from below to above the discount rate. The market then stopped offering acceptances to the Fed, and bank reserves declined accordingly, along with the declines produced by open market sales of securities.

The New York Fed continued to push the Board to allow it to increase its discount rate. Harrison (HPNY, Confidential Files, April 11, 1929, 1) told Edmund Platt, member of the Board, "that the longer we delayed in making this rate adjustment the longer we delay the ultimate correction." New York also argued that with a higher discount rate banks could limit credit collateralized by securities to customers without losing the deposits of their customers because rival banks would find it more costly to finance new loans transferred to them. Harrison (HPNY, Confidential Files, May 14, 1929, 2–3) noted in a summary of a conversation with Governor Young of the Federal Reserve Board:

Banks are getting in less liquid condition all the time and having more difficulty getting out of debt. . . . Government bonds . . . were almost impossible to sell . . . without further pressure on the market. . . . The more these bonds are being sold the less liquid is the condition of the banks. . . . They had much better liquidate their collateral loan account which they cannot do now without risking the deposit of the customer whom they deny. . . . An increase in the [discount] rate, which would be equally applicable to all banks, would make it possible for individual banks to put the screws on to customers borrowing on collateral, without the fear of their going to some other less cooperative bank who would take over the account and make the loan.

On August 9, 1929, the New York Fed raised its discount rate to 6 percent while lowering the buying rate for acceptances to 5⅛ percent. The intention was for banks to obtain their seasonal financing needs through the acceptance market while keeping credit in general expensive to reduce credit overall to attack speculation. Although Hamlin (US Congress 1931, January 23, 173) later characterized the combined moves as "part of an easing policy," monetary policy was extremely restrictive as the marginal cost of obtaining reserves rose with the increase in the discount rate. Table 3.4 in chapter 3 shows the "monetary contraction marker" for the 1929–33 recession with cyclical peak in August 1929. From 4.04 percent in 1928Q1, the commercial paper rate rose to 6.13 percent in 1929Q3. The real economy (real GNP and industrial production) weakened in 1929Q2 while the commercial paper rate continued to rise.

Although M1 grew at the annualized rate of 5.1 percent in 1929Q3 and 3.4 percent in 1929Q4, monetary policy nevertheless remained contractionary. That growth reflected increased money demand. Money demand increased in 1929Q3 and 1929Q4 initially because of the intense speculative activity on the NYSE and subsequently because of the liquidation of margin accounts after the October crash. With respect to the first factor, money demand increased because of the transactions due to the stock market boom. In 1927, debits to bank accounts in the New York Federal Reserve Bank District grew by 15 percent, in 1928 by 27 percent, and in 1929 by 20 percent.[5] With respect to the second factor, after the crash, money demand increased when the New York city banks put onto their books the loans to New York brokers that had come from nonbank sources. Given the Fed's free reserves procedures, which were determining short-term interest rates, the Fed accommodated the increased money demand. From September 1929 to November 1929, the net demand deposits of the weekly reporting banks in New York City grew by 21 percent (not annualized).[6] In October 1929, the

5. Data from Federal Reserve Board, "C.5 Bank Debits and Demand Deposits, 1920–1977, Debits to Individual Accounts," from St. Louis Fraser.

6. From Board of Governors 1943, table 49, "Weekly Reporting Banks in New York City—Principal Assets and Liabilities," 174.

month of the stock market crash, M1 grew at an annualized rate of about 7 percent.

Benjamin Anderson (US Congress 1935b, May 16, 443), an economist at Chase National Bank of the City of New York, testified:

> When the crisis came there was a sudden panicky withdrawal of these loans [brokers' loans] "for account of others," with the result that there had to be an immense expansion of bank credit, loans, and deposits, to take care of it. In the panic week of 1929, the total of loans for the reporting member banks in New York City increased by $1,281,000, while the demand deposits of these same banks showed an increase of $1,565,000,000. Of this increase in loans, 374 millions, or over 29 percent, was in the Chase National Bank alone.

While real money demand was increasing, the Fed was forcing a contraction of the banking system. Over time, the reduction in money supply due to contractionary monetary policy overcame the transitory increases in money due to increased real money demand, and nominal money declined. With currency holdings of the public stable in this period, M2 offers a good measure of the liabilities of the banking system. From 1928Q2 through 1930Q1, M2 (and the banking system) basically stopped growing with a quarterly average for the period of 0.17 percent (figure 8.2). Even with the positive M1 growth in 1929Q3 and 1929Q4, M1 growth weakened starting in 1929Q1 (figures 7.3 and 7.4).

In quantity theory terms, a reduction in the expenditures of the public began with the interaction of an increased demand for real money (M1) balances and Fed pressure on the banking system to contract.[7] Because the Fed was setting short-term interest rates, nominal money was endogenously determined, with the behavior of M1 buffeted by these two conflicting forces. As shown in table 3.4 and figure 7.4, money growth blipped up in fall 1929. Over the months December 1928 through September 1929, however, monthly growth rates of M1 averaged zero.

In *A Monetary History*, Friedman and Schwartz (1963a) explained the behavior of money through a reserves-money multiplier framework. They argued for causation running from money to nominal output based on bank

7. The equation of exchange is $M = k(py)$, with M money, k the fraction of nominal expenditure the public desires to hold in the form of cash balances, p the price level, y real income, and (py) nominal expenditure. An increase in k in fall 1929 increased M but only transitorily as contractionary monetary policy over the longer run forced a reduction in M. Although contractionary monetary policy was the dominant factor, both factors forced a decline in nominal expenditure, (py).

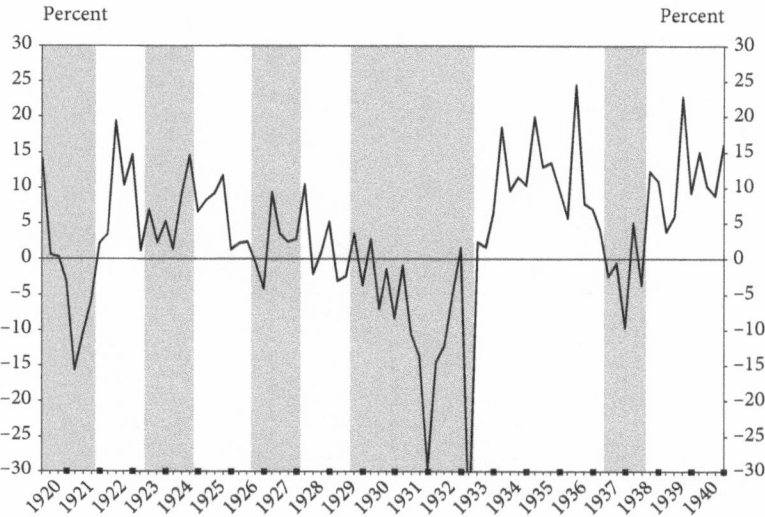

Figure 8.2. M2 Growth Rates
Quarterly observations of annualized percentage changes in M2. Data from Friedman and Schwartz (1970). Shaded areas indicate recessions. Heavy tick marks indicate fourth quarter.

runs that raised the currency-deposit ratio. Chapter 9 explains how bank runs exacerbated contractionary monetary policy. However, the Friedman-Schwartz argument is incomplete for the period before late 1930. Not until summer 1931 did bank reserves begin to decline. The deposits-currency ratio began to decline starting only in November 1930. The deposits-reserves ratio began to decline earlier but still only after March 1930. The argument here is that monetary policy became contractionary in 1928 through the way in which the Fed maintained the marginal cost of funds to banks above the natural rate of interest. It took time for contractionary policy to produce the contraction of the banking system that produced the sharp, sustained declines in M1 starting in 1930Q1.

8.5. A GRAPHICAL OVERVIEW OF THE TRANSMISSION OF CONTRACTIONARY MONETARY POLICY

The exposition of the contractionary policy that began in 1928 uses the free reserves framework exposited in chapter 6 (see also Hamilton 1987). Figure 8.3 illustrates the tightening. Tightening began with open market sales of government securities, which shifted the reserves supply schedule, R_0^S, leftward owing to the decline in the nonborrowed reserves of the banking

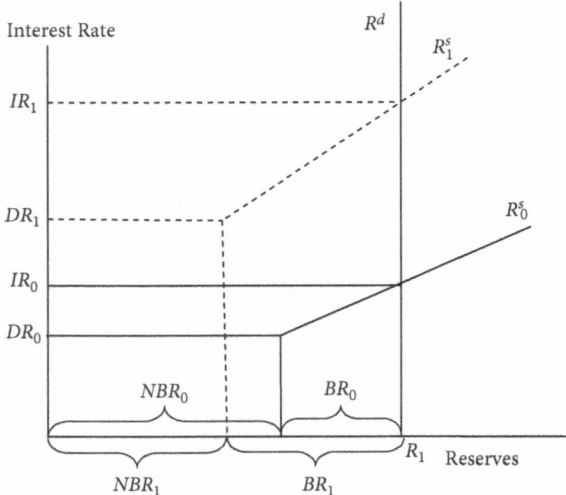

Figure 8.3. Market for Bank Reserves after Fed Tightening
See notes to figure 6.1. The 0's denote the initial values and the 1's the values after tightening (lowering NBRs, raising the discount rate, and increasing Fed oversight of the discount window).

system from NBR_0 to NBR_1. Because the reserves demand schedule, R^d, is fixed in the short run, borrowed reserves increased from BR_0 to BR_1. With banks forced into the discount window, the Reserve Banks then raised their discount rates from DR_0 to DR_1, shifting the reserves supply schedule upward. The combined effect of the open market sales and the increases in the discount rate shifted the reserves supply schedule to the left and upward from the solid line to the dashed line. At the same time, the Fed raised the nonpecuniary costs of being in the window through increased supervisory oversight. In figure 8.3, the upward sloping segment of the reserves supply schedule rotated upward from the kink. The marginal cost of bank reserves rose from IR_0 to IR_1.

Open market sales of government securities reduced bank reserves and forced banks into the discount window. Pressure to get out of the window forced a contraction of bank assets and deposits. As stated in the "Fifteenth Annual Report" of the Federal Reserve Board (1929, 5–6, 8):

This heavy indebtedness caused member banks to reduce their holdings of investments and of loans on securities, and . . . was thus an important factor during the larger part of 1928 in restraining the growth of member bank credit. . . . Continuous indebtedness at the reserve banks . . . is an abuse of reserve bank facilities. In cases where individual banks have been guilty of such abuse, the Federal reserve authorities have taken up the matter with officers of the offending banks and have made clear to them that their reserve position should be adjusted by liquidating a part of their loan or investment account rather than through borrowing.

Evidenced by the decline in output, monetary policy in the Great Contraction (1929Q3 through 1933Q1) remained continuously contractionary with the Fed holding the real rate of interest above the natural rate of interest. Figure 8.4 shows that with the real rate held above the natural rate the reserves demand schedule shifts leftward, from R_0^d to R_1^d. Although the interest rate declined from IR_0 to IR_1, the Fed maintained the real rate above the natural rate by holding the discount rate above the natural rate (NR).

There was a self-reinforcing character to this policy. As the economy weakened and banks sold securities, banks' nonperforming loans increased, and their securities (chiefly railroad bonds) declined in value. As the cash flow and liquidity of banks suffered, they had to go into the window more often. An increased desire to avoid the scrutiny entailed by borrowing increased the desire for excess reserves to protect against reserves outflows. An individual bank increasing its excess reserves, however, would force other banks into the window. Collectively, banks could increase excess reserves only by contracting loans and deposits, thereby contracting required

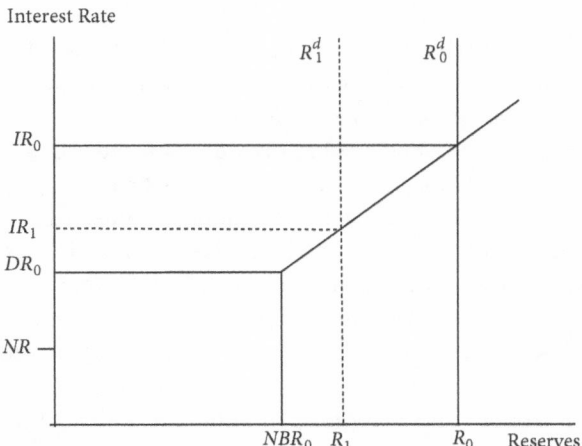

Figure 8.4. Market for Bank Reserves, Real Rate above the Natural Rate
See notes to figure 6.1. Contraction of the banking system and declining reserves demand with the real rate (IR_0 and IR_1) in excess of the natural rate (NR). The 0's denote initial values and the 1's the values after the contraction in bank loans and deposits.

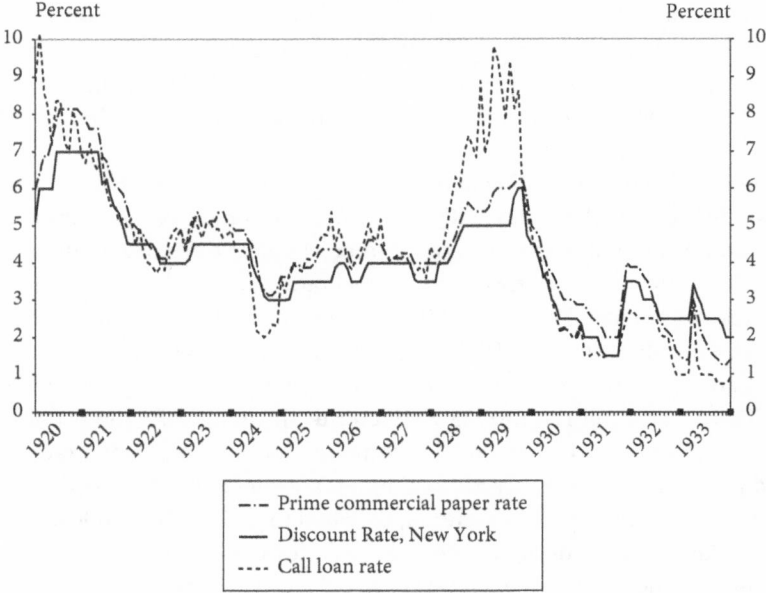

Figure 8.5. Money Market Interest Rates and New York Fed Discount Rate
Monthly observations of the prime commercial paper rate, four to six months; the
New York Fed discount rate; and the rate on new stock exchange call loans. Heavy tick
marks indicate fourth quarter.
Source: Board of Governors (1943, tables 115 and 120)

reserves and shifting the reserves demand schedule leftward—a contractionary process without an end in a regime in which the central bank could
keep the real rate of interest above the natural rate.

Figure 8.5 shows the New York Fed discount rate, the prime commercial
paper rate, and the call loan rate. The stress on the banking system appears
in the spike in the call loan rate in the call money market. The call loan rate
shows the high cost to banks of obtaining the marginal dollar of reserves
required to meet reserves demand. Just as in the pre-Fed era, seasonal stringency in the fall of 1929 helped to precipitate a financial panic, this time in
the form of a stock market crash. Hawtrey (1932 [1962], 77) commented
about the United States: "The dear money policy accomplished its purpose
in the end. It stopped speculation by stopping prosperity." Keynes (1930,
196) commented similarly:

The high market-rate of interest which, prior to the collapse, the Federal
Reserve System, in their effort to control the enthusiasm of the speculative crowd, caused to be enforced in the United States—and, as a result

of sympathetic self-protective action, in the rest of the world—played an essential part in bringing about the rapid collapse. . . . Thus I attribute the slump of 1930 primarily to the deterrent effects on investment of the long period of dear money which preceded the stock market collapse, and only secondarily to the collapse itself.

8.6. IDENTIFYING THE CAUSE OF THE DEPRESSION AS CONTRACTIONARY MONETARY POLICY

The narrative here uses the monetarist counterfactual of the optimal monetary standard to identify episodes of monetary disturbances. Namely, the price system works well to maintain output at potential as long as the central bank follows a rule that provides a stable nominal anchor and allows the price an unfettered ability to determine real variables like output and employment. In the two major recessions that began in the 1920s, the 1920–21 recession and the Great Depression, the Fed's concentration on quashing speculation prevented the price system from working to stabilize economic activity.

In the 1920s, the Fed considered domestic stability and the quashing of speculative excess to be identical objectives, but only if it acted aggressively to forestall incipient speculative activity. If speculation got out of control, the country would have to endure a period of liquidation. In a letter to Norman on November 20, 1925, Strong explained the reason why the Reserve Banks were raising their discount rates (cited in Chandler 1958, 329): "We have had a dangerous speculation develop in the stock market, with some evidence that it is extending into commodities. There has been a rampaging real estate speculation in some spots."

One reason it was impossible for policy makers to learn in the Depression was that events had unfolded as foreseen in the event that speculation was not curtailed in a timely manner. Moreover, policy makers and the markets assigned responsibility for high rates of interest to the speculative demand for credit not to the Fed. Oliver M. W. Sprague (1929, 724–25), head of the economics department at Harvard and adviser to the New York Fed, commented on the "disastrous effect of reduction of discount rates":

At times of speculative optimism [speculators] seem . . . impervious to any moderate or ordinary advance in discount rates. . . . If the Reserve banks are going to do anything at all about the security situation they must act, and should act, before security prices become too high. . . . We have . . . in the state of mind of the public, a readiness to make a demand upon the supply of credit for this particular use at rates which are seriously disturbing to the functioning of the credit mechanism and threaten in some measure the maintenance of the gold standard in many countries. . . . When the business recession comes, it would unquestionably be accompanied by a very catastrophic collapse of stock exchange prices, which in turn would have a repercussion accentuating the business recession. . . . Very few people . . . are in favor of an easy money policy.

The two major recessions of the 1920s illustrate the stark contrast between the pre–Treasury-Fed Accord "money policy" and the post-Accord "monetary policy," with the latter's emphasis on moving the funds rate in a systematic way to keep output growing around potential. With regard to the 1920–21 recession, as shown in figure 7.2, the Fed's contractionary policy began with real GNP still recovering from the March 1919 cycle trough. Out of concern for speculative activity, the New York Fed raised its discount rate from 4 percent to 4¾ percent in November 1919, to 6 percent in January 1920, and to 7 percent in June 1920 (figure 8.5).

Similarly, with the Great Depression, Lauchlin Currie (1934a, 160–61) made the point that the Fed raised rates not in response to cyclical strength in the economy but rather to quash speculative excess supposedly exhibited by the NYSE.

The general impression appears to be that not only was there a "speculation boom" in 1928–29 but that this was, in addition, accompanied by what is now referred to as a "business boom." Whether or not a business boom prevailed in 1928–29 is an extremely important question in appraising central banking in its wider aspects. . . .

I think it is correct to say that the term ["boom"], in its standard usage, connotes a condition in which monetary incomes, for a considerable period, are increasing more rapidly than goods are produced. This results in rising commodity prices, abnormal profits, overtime work, growing inefficiency, speculation in commodities leading to increased hoarding of goods. Such a condition is obviously undesirable and extremely difficult to translate into a period of healthy prosperity without a depression first intervening. On the other hand, a period in which the increase in production is being taken off by consumers at steady prices; in which, although most of the factors of production are fully utilized, there is still some slack; and in which firms are enabled to make profits due to efficiency in production rather than because costs are lagging behind selling prices—such a period would appear to be eminently desirable. It would seem that business conditions in 1928–29 approximated more closely the latter condition of desirable prosperity than that of an undesirable boom.

Throughout the Great Contraction monetary policy was unrelentingly contractionary. Policy errors were errors of commission. There is no need for an eclectic explanation of the Depression that emphasizes real and monetary factors. In contrast, the eclectic analysis of Allan Meltzer emphasized errors of omission on the part of the Fed. Meltzer (2003, 389–90) wrote:

> The extreme positions—that monetary policy was the only cause or that monetary policy played no role—are difficult to sustain. A more plausible explanation is that the depth and severity of the Great Depression were the consequence of a series of shocks that the Federal Reserve neglected or failed to offset completely. The shocks include French gold policy, banking panics, increased demand for currency, departure of Britain from the gold standard, the stock market decline, failure of banks in Austria and Germany, collapse of United States exports markets in Latin America, the effects of tariffs and retaliation on prices and thus on gold movements, and other events. Some of these events are both the effect of prior changes and the proximate cause of subsequent changes. We are unlikely to develop a complete list of "true" causes that operated independently of other events.

The analysis here stresses a more fundamental cause. The Fed lacked procedures for letting the price system work by causing the real rate of interest to track its natural rate counterpart. Throughout the Great Contraction, the Fed kept short-term interest rates above the natural rate of interest.

Meltzer (2003, 407) also contended that Fed policy makers ignored established central banking practice:

> The severity of the crisis would have been lessened if the governors had allowed the monetary base to rise by the full amount of their estimate of the increased demand for currency. . . . Indeed, if the System had done no more than follow the principles established in the nineteenth century, it would have prevented the internal drain and the greater part of the monetary crisis. There can be no doubt that most of these principles were known at the time.

When the internal drain of currency began in spring 1931, the Reserve Banks continued to discount the paper of the member banks. They did not see themselves as violating Bagehot's principle of lending freely in a financial panic. The problem was that at the time everyone, not just the Fed, failed to understand that the deposits and credit of the banking system rested on a base of reserves created and destroyed by the Fed through the stroke of a pen. Of course, early policy makers understood the nature of a fractional-reserves system. What they did not understand was how their operating procedures caused the destruction of the reserves base that supported the fractional-reserves system.

Meltzer attributed the Fed's inaction at critical moments to what he termed "the Riefler-Burgess doctrine." Its central assumption was that if discount window borrowing was low monetary policy was easy. Meltzer (2003, 245) wrote, "Under Riefler-Burgess, the volume of discounts replaced the gold reserve ratio as the principal signal for expansive or contractive action." Again, Meltzer (2003, 398) wrote:

> The real bills or Riefler-Burgess doctrine is the main reason for the Federal Reserve response, or lack of response, to the depression. . . . They [Fed governors] believed that a low level of member bank borrowing and low nominal interest rates suggested there was no reason to make additional purchases. Additional purchases of government securities would expand credit based on speculative assets, which was inconsistent with the real bills doctrine and the gold standard.

Those criticisms are valid and insightful. At the same time, Meltzer failed to recognize that with member banks borrowing from the discount window, the Fed was determining the marginal cost of reserves and through arbitrage short-term interest rates. It is true that borrowed reserves were an unsatisfactory indicator for monetary policy. However, the more fundamental failure was the absence of a reaction function that would allow the Fed to set short-term interest rates in a way that responded to the economy and tracked the natural rate of interest.

Meltzer (2003, 281) criticized Fed officials for not having read Henry Thornton (1802 [1939]). However, Meltzer does not mention obviously applicable passages. Thornton was explaining inflation. According to Thornton, as long as the Bank of England's discount rate lay below the rate of interest obtainable in capital markets, the Bank of England would extend credit and create banknotes.[8] Thornton (1802 [1939], 255–56) also ex-

---

8. H. Thornton (1802 [1939], 227 and 253–54, cited in Hetzel 2016, 289) wrote:

Every additional loan obtained from the Bank . . . implies an encreased issue of paper. In order to ascertain how far the desire of obtaining loans at the Bank may be expected at any time to be carried, we must enquire into the subject of the quantum of profit likely to be derived from borrowing thereunder the existing circumstances. This is to be judged of by considering two points: the amount, first, of interest to be paid on the sum borrowed; and, secondly, of the mercantile or other gain to be obtained by the employment of the borrowed capital. . . . Any

plained that the "mercantile gain" from borrowing was the rate of return on capital. Because capital is a real variable, nothing in the emission of bank-notes by the Bank of England would affect its return and make it less profit-able to borrow. The Bank of England's real bills criterion would not limit money creation.

In the Depression, Thornton's analysis would entail a marginal cost of re-serves above the return to lending and consequently money destruction. In the Depression, no one, policy makers or quantity theorists, thought in this way. The assumed lack of demand for borrowing from banks was the rel-evant factor limiting credit and money creation. Most important, Thornton understood that England was on a fiat money standard. In the Depression, no one understood that reality.

8.7. CONCLUDING COMMENT

Banks developed markets in which they could adjust their reserves posi-tions by moving reserves around between surplus and deficit banks. In the pre-Fed era and continuing into the 1920s, banks traded through the call loan market in New York. Banks outside New York would maintain depos-its with their New York correspondent banks. Banks with surpluses would draw down their deposits to make loans in the call market, and banks with deficits would rebuild their deposits by letting such loans run off.[9] Signifi-cant reserves adjustment also took place through the discount window. A bank with a surplus could repay discount window borrowing, and a bank with a deficit could borrow from the window.

In 1929, the Fed severely limited bank access to the two sources that banks used for reserves adjustment: the call loan market and the discount window. As a result, banks desired to build up excess reserves to deal with reserves deficiencies. The Fed could have accommodated that demand through supplying reserves with open market purchases but did not. Banks then had to liquidate loans and investments. Indirectly, that would decrease their deposits and reduce required reserves, but doing so required a con-traction of the banking system because of its fractional-reserves character. Together with sales of government securities by the Fed and increases in the discount rate, monetary policy remained highly contractionary throughout the Great Contraction.

---

supposition that it would be safe to permit the Bank paper to limit itself, because this would be to take the more natural course, is, therefore, altogether erroneous.

9. In the 1920s, banks in New York traded reserves in a federal funds market (Good-friend and Whelpley 1993).

CHAPTER 9

The Great Contraction

1929–33

Summary: The consequences of the failure of early policy makers to understand the monetary regime they had created and how through the gold standard contractionary monetary policy in the United States spread to all the major industrial countries remain unimaginable even today. In 1933, the unemployment rate reached 25.2 percent, and even in 1938 it was 19.1 percent. In a later foreword to his book *A Century of Bank Rate*, the English economist Ralph Hawtrey (1938 [1962], xiii) wrote:

> The great depression of the nineteen-thirties has passed into history as a unique period of misery and distress. The helplessness of successive Governments in Germany, faced with six million unemployed, led directly to the accession of Hitler to power, and so to the second World War.

Hawtrey (1938 [1962], xxi, xi) also wrote, "When we look back on the monetary experience we have had . . . surely the moral to be drawn from it is above all the vital importance of maintaining the stability of the value of the money unit." In the Depression, however, Hawtrey continued, "it was little use urging a stabilization policy on the monetary authorities of the world so long as they were completely skeptical of their power to carry it out." Today, there remains enormous uncertainty over when the Fed is a source of stability and when it is a source of instability. There remains much to learn from "the monetary experience."

During the Depression, policy makers paid little or no attention to the cost of credit. The discount rates of the Reserve Banks were at historically low levels. They assumed that "low" interest rates could do little to stimulate loan demand as long as a lack of confidence in the economy translated into a lack of demand for loans. Debate turned on how to manage the availability of credit. Open market purchases that increased bank reserves would lower member bank borrowing. Banks could then increase loans starting from a lower level of indebtedness at the discount window. But with minimal loan demand, it was supposed, open market purchases of government securities would force unwanted credit into securities markets and potentially reignite the "credit inflation" that had created the original "credit debauch."

The Great Depression was the outstanding economic disaster of the twentieth century. From 1918 through 2009, the nineteen recessions lasted on average thirteen months. The Great Depression lasted forty-three months. Why was it an outlier? Was it a pathological case? The answer offered here is that monetary policy was unrelievedly contractionary from 1929 through March 1933 because the Fed did not have the framework required to understand how the implementation of its operating procedures kept the real rate of interest above the natural rate of interest required to maintain output at potential.

In the Great Contraction, from August 1929 to March 1933, debate turned on whether and how to make additional funds available to banks for lending. Within the real bills framework, the Reserve Banks should wait for the demand for loans to revive. Given the near-universal view that in 1929 an "inflationary" credit structure had collapsed and along with it an artificially created level of production, there was little policy could do until the economy reorganized itself in a way that would allow once again productive investment.

George Harrison, governor of the New York Fed, thought of "money policy" in terms of "reserves availability," that is, the amount of funds made available to member banks by the operation of the Reserve Banks. Just as important as the Fed's supply of loanable funds was that there had to be a demand to use the funds. Creating that demand required implementing the conservative policies of the time to revive the confidence of the business community. They included balancing the budget and raising rates in response to gold outflows that threatened the Fed's gold reserve. Confidence also required that the radical populist programs of paper money creation not come to pass.

The following excerpt from Herbert Hoover's State of the Union address delivered on December 8, 1931, captured much of the contemporaneous understanding of the Depression and the way out. Recovery required restoration of a sense of confidence, which would revive loan demand and end the hoarding of money.[1] Hoover (cited in H. Stein 1969, 33–34; and Lindert 1981, 130) spoke:

1. Later, after his inauguration, Franklin Roosevelt would restore that confidence but, ironically, by standing on its head the assumption that the maintenance of the gold standard was a bedrock of the required confidence.

Whatever the causes may be, the vast liquidation and readjustments which have taken place have left us with a large degree of credit paralysis, which together with the situation in our railroads and the conditions abroad, are now the outstanding obstacles to recovery. . . . Many of our bankers, in order to prepare themselves to meet possible withdrawals, have felt compelled to call in loans, to refuse new credits, and to realize upon securities, which in turn has demoralized the markets. . . .

Our first step toward recovery is to reestablish confidence and thus restore the flow of credit which is the very basis of our economic life. The first requirement of economic recovery is financial stability of the United States Government. Even with increased taxation, the government will reach the utmost safe limit of its borrowing capacity by the expenditures for which we are already obligated and the recommendations here proposed.

With the correspondent banking system and call money market in New York, there was a banking system with a common market for reserves. However, there was no understanding that the deposits of the banking system rested on a reserves base with the Fed responsible for maintenance of that base to prevent a monetary collapse. As Currie (1938b, 7) explained, "The primary function of banks was believed to be that of making local loans and this has colored our national attitude toward banks. . . . Our banking system has remained localized. . . . This has been due in large part to the deep-seated American distrust of financial concentration." Without a sense of a national banking system that maintains a level of deposits that rests on a common reserves base and without a sense of the Fed having responsibility to maintain that reserves base in a fiat money standard, there was no basis for understanding the responsibility of the Fed to control money creation. Currie (1938b, 8) wanted policy makers "to secure a removal of the defects of the American banking system" by viewing it "as a medium through which monetary control must be exercised" and by stressing "the money-supplying function of banks." That simply could not happen given the aversion to the idea of a central bank creating fiat money.

9.1. AN OVERVIEW OF THE GREAT CONTRACTION

What turned a "regular" recession like 1920–21, which lasted a year and a half, into the prolonged recession termed the Great Contraction by Friedman and Schwartz? An answer to that question requires dividing monetary policy into the period before and after March 1933. The answer given here for the earlier period is that from early 1929 through March 1933 (the Great

Contraction) monetary policy imposed a relentless pressure on the banking system to contract. Collectively, member banks remained in the discount window in the earlier period, and the imperative to avoid recourse to the window forced them into liquidating their loan and securities portfolio to acquire excess reserves.

Because the Fed maintained the level of nonborrowed reserves below the level required by reserve requirements and desired excess reserves, banks had to obtain the marginal dollar of reserves through recourse to the discount window. The cost of obtaining the marginal dollar of reserves remained at a level that forced contraction of the banking system for two reasons. First, the regional Reserve Banks apart from the New York Fed maintained relatively high discount rates in their districts throughout the Great Contraction. Second, the combination of direct pressure and the stigma of being a weak bank associated with borrowing meant that banks wanted to become liquid enough to avoid the need to use the window. In a letter of July 1930 to the other Fed governors, Governor Harrison wrote, "An even small amount of borrowing under present conditions is as effective a restraint as substantially a greater amount was a year ago" (cited in Friedman and Schwartz 1963a, 370). In reference to the bank runs in June 1932, Currie (1934b, 147) wrote, "The extremely abnormal loss of confidence in 1932 led to a greater decline in new borrowings than had probably ever occurred in a previous depression." That is, in response to runs, banks chose to liquidate assets rather than to borrow from their regional Fed banks. To use a modern analogy, the Fed kept the funds rate (the marginal cost of obtaining reserves) above the natural rate of interest.

The year 1930 was one of anticipatory waiting. Liquidation of the economic excesses presumed to have resulted from the speculative excesses manifested most obviously in the bull market in equities should have led to a strong, healthy economic recovery as had occurred following the 1920–21 recession. That recovery failed to occur. Policy makers believed that the recession had nothing to do with monetary policy and that in turn monetary policy could do nothing to alleviate it. Those beliefs came from entrenched real bills views. Earlier, Wilbur Aldrich (1903, iv, 96–97, cited in J. Wood 2006, 6) had expressed the impossibility of rectifying the collapse of speculation with what would today be considered stimulative monetary policy: It was not possible

> to find a way by which . . . over-speculation and conversion of liquid capital into fixed capital can be made to go on forever, by legislation or intervention of government. . . . When over-production and inflation of credit have brought on a crisis, no currency juggle can prevent losses. . . .

Any permanent plan of extending credit in face of crises would simply be discounted and used up before the pinch of the succeeding crisis. . . . The true time for banks to begin to prepare for a panic and provide for their reserves, is before a careless extension of credit in the mad industrial race which invariably precedes a panic.

One striking fact is the almost complete absence of any discussion of lowering discount rates. The average of the discount rates for the Reserve Banks apart from New York declined only to 2¾ percent in the short period from May 1931 to September 1931 (figure 6.3). Harrison (HPNY, Confidential Files, June 3, 1930, "Conversations with Members of Open Market Policy Conference and Governor Young," 4–6) summarized the comments of Governor Norris of the Philadelphia Fed:

The feeling is . . . that the Depression is due principally to reduced prices in commodities[,] and an analysis of commodities in which the reductions in price have been most marked disclosed in almost every case a specific reason, which has nothing to do with credit. . . . The trouble is . . . not with an over-production of goods but over production of the capacity to produce. . . . Governor Norris then stated that the other members of the Executive Committee of the Open Market Policy Conference can not bring themselves to believe that a further purchase of Government securities would help, but feel that such purchases would be an interference with the natural effect at this time and would not be productive of any good.

The year 1931 was devoted to maintaining the confidence of markets that policy makers believed was a prerequisite to economic recovery. In 1931, an impetus to renewed contraction came from currency outflows as depositors withdrew their deposits from banks. Because of the stigma associated with recourse to the discount window, to offset the reserve drain, banks chose to contract their asset portfolios rather than to borrow at the window. A bank experiencing a run, which would require extended borrowing, would not only contravene real bills principles but also advertise its weakness by the fact of borrowing.

When Britain went off gold in September 1931, the Reserve Banks raised their discount rates. Given the conservatism of policy makers, maintaining confidence meant maintaining confidence in the maintenance of the gold standard. That confidence required monetary stringency in order to counteract the external drain of gold. The regional Reserve Bank governors also viewed the outflow of gold as threatening the gold reserves that constituted the basis of their ability to supply funds to the market when it came time to accommodate economic recovery.

The year 1932 became one of an aborted attempt to supply funds to start an economic recovery. If successful, that attempt might have changed the perceived character of the monetary regime from one of passive accommodation of credit demands in response to "legitimate" demands for credit to one of purposeful "credit inflation." For policy makers, it was terra incognita. Sustained open market purchases would have forced member banks out of the discount window. In the minds of the regional Reserve Bank governors, that meant fiat money creation. The reason is that it would have breached the gold cover requirements and would have required backing the issue of currency with government securities. In the first two months of 1933, a massive bank panic occurred while the Fed withdrew from supporting the banking system.

Output declined throughout the Great Contraction (figure 7.2), and the price level declined relentlessly (figure 7.5) along with the money stock (figures 7.3 and 7.4). A decline in nominal money confronting an increased demand for real money balances forced deflation. That deflation was largely unanticipated and created the pathology of the Great Contraction. Monetary disorder was the consequence of Fed actions and inactions. A forced contraction of the banking system contracted bank deposits and money. At the same time, the increased uncertainty caused an increased demand by the public for real money balances. Figures 9.1 and 9.2 show the velocity of M1 and M2. Velocity declined (real money demand increased) in the Great Contraction. The fact that velocity increased with the end of the Great Contraction while interest rates remained low implies that the earlier decline in velocity was due to uncertainty.

9.2. THE GREAT CONTRACTION AND UNRELIEVEDLY CONTRACTIONARY MONETARY POLICY

Monetary policy moved in the direction of contraction when the New York Fed raised its discount rate from 3½ percent to 4 percent in February 1928, to 4½ percent in May 1928, and 5 percent in July 1928. The other Reserve Banks followed. Figure 8.2, which shows quarterly annualized growth rates of M2, can serve as a measure of changes in the size of the banking system. With the currency of the public stable until early 1931, M2 was a good measure of bank deposits. From 1927Q1 through 1928Q1, M2 growth averaged 5.7 percent. Monetary policy became contractionary over the period 1928Q2 through 1930Q1, when the banking system stopped growing with M2 growth averaging 0.17 percent. With M2 growth averaging −4.4 percent

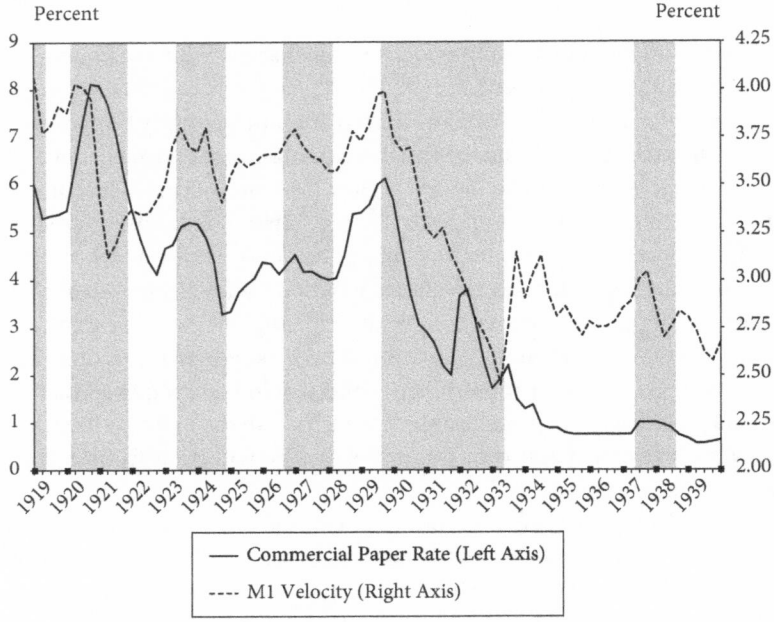

Figure 9.1. M1 Velocity and Commercial Paper Rate
Quarterly observations of M1 velocity: GNP divided by M1. Data for GNP are from
Balke and Gordon (1986). M1 is from Friedman and Schwartz (1970). Shaded areas
represent recessions. Heavy tick marks indicate fourth quarter.

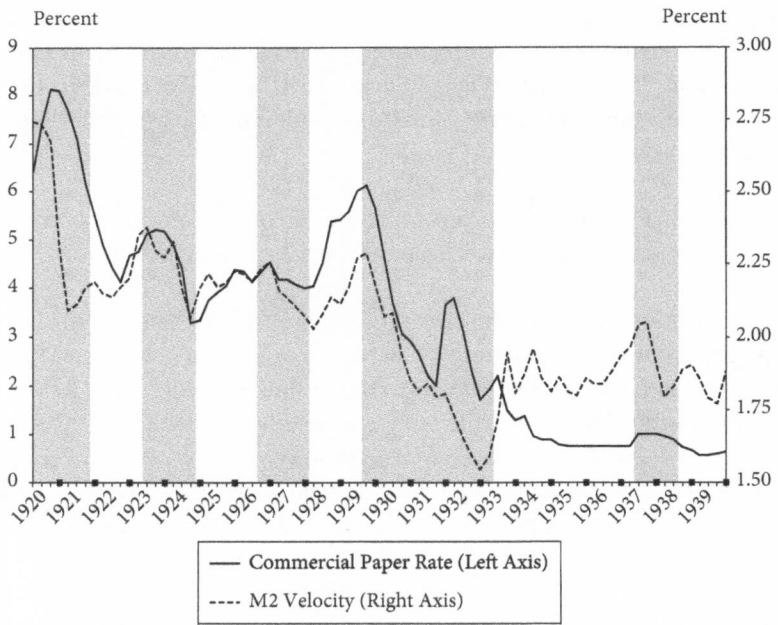

Figure 9.2. M2 Velocity and Commercial Paper Rate
Quarterly observations of M2 velocity: GNP divided by M2. Data for GNP are from
Balke and Gordon (1986). M2 is from Friedman and Schwartz (1970). Shaded areas
represent recessions. Heavy tick marks indicate fourth quarter.

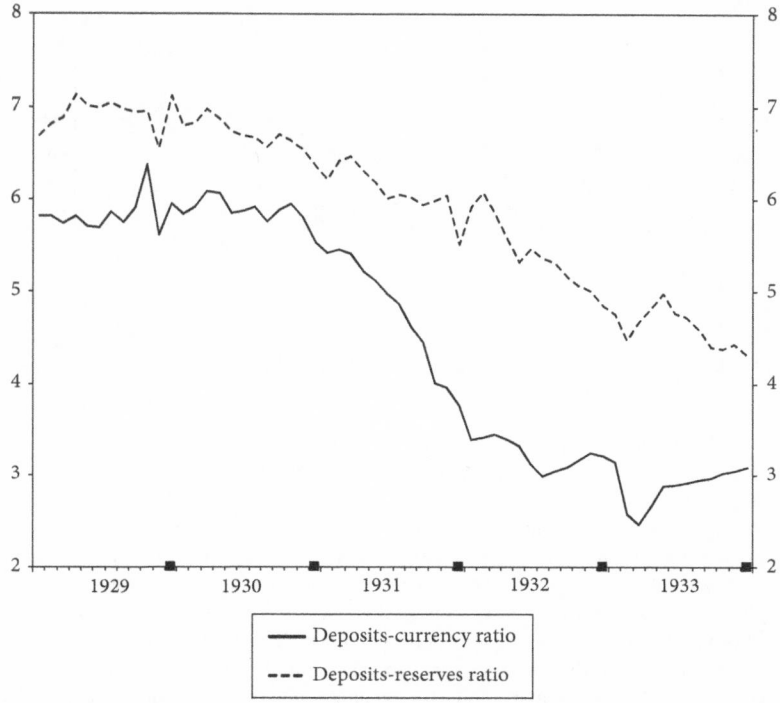

Figure 9.3. Deposits-Currency and Deposits-Reserves Ratios
Heavy tick marks indicate December.
Source: Friedman and Schwartz (1970)

from 1930Q2 through 1931Q1, monetary policy became significantly contractionary for the first time since the 1920–21 recession.

As shown in figure 9.3, the deposits-currency ratio of banks was steady
in 1929 through November 1930 at about 5.9. However, consistent with a desire by banks to build up excess reserves, the deposits-reserves ratio started
a steady decline in January 1930. Starting in 1930Q1, annualized monthly M1
growth dropped sharply and steadily (figure 7.3).

Two sources of reserves supply interacted to determine the nonborrowed reserves of banks. "External" reserves supply equaled the gold stock
minus currency in circulation and Treasury deposits with the Fed. "Active"
reserves supply equaled bills (acceptances) plus US government securities
held by the Fed. Figure 9.4 shows cumulative changes in these series after
December 1927. (If a series touches the x-axis, it equals the December 1927
value.) As shown, over the years 1928 and 1929, with little change in external
reserves supply, the reduction in active reserves supply dominated banks'
nonborrowed reserves.

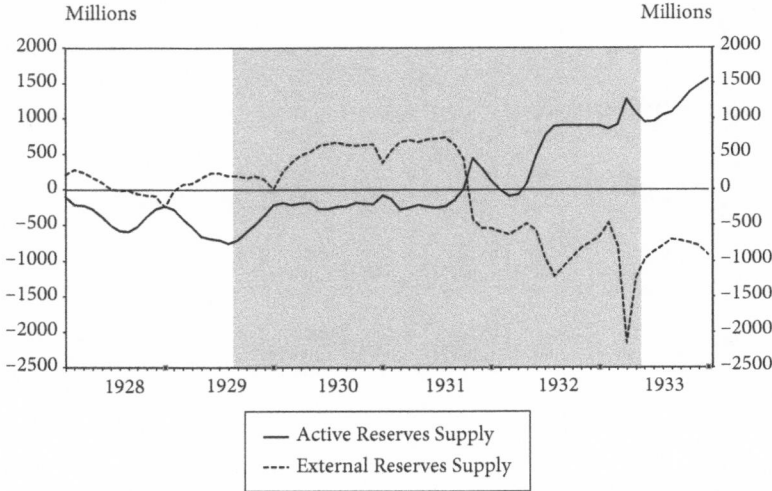

Figure 9.4. Active and External Reserves Supply, Cumulative Changes
Observations are monthly averages of daily figures. "Active Reserves Supply" equals
"bills bought" plus "US government securities" held by Fed. "External Reserves
Supply" equals "gold stock" minus "money (currency) in circulation" minus "Treasury
deposits with Federal Reserve Banks." Series are normalized by subtracting their
December 1927 value. All series therefore represent cumulative changes from
December 1927. Heavy tick marks indicate December. Shaded area indicates recession.
Source: Board of Governors (1943, table 101)

Figure 9.5 shows cumulative changes in "net" reserves, which is the difference between active and external reserves supply. As shown, in the first
half of 1928, open market sales reduced net reserves supply and shifted the
reserves supply schedule leftward (figure 8.3). The reduction in nonborrowed reserves forced banks into the discount window (figures 9.5 and 9.6)
while increases in discount rates increased the marginal cost of borrowing
(figure 8.3). In fall 1928, the Fed relaxed somewhat the pressure on banks'
nonborrowed reserves in order to allow for the seasonal increase in the
demand for credit. The New York Fed bought acceptances, and the active
reserves supply increased in the second half of 1928 (figure 9.4). Borrowed
reserves declined moderately.

However, in 1928, security loans continued to increase, the stock market rose appreciably, and by mid-1929 net reserves supply had fallen again
to its mid-1928 low. With the seasonal demand for loans and currency and
then with the stock market crash in October 1929, the Fed caused active
reserves supply to increase (figure 9.4). That is, the Fed bought Treasury
securities (figure 9.7). Net reserves supply increased, although it did not

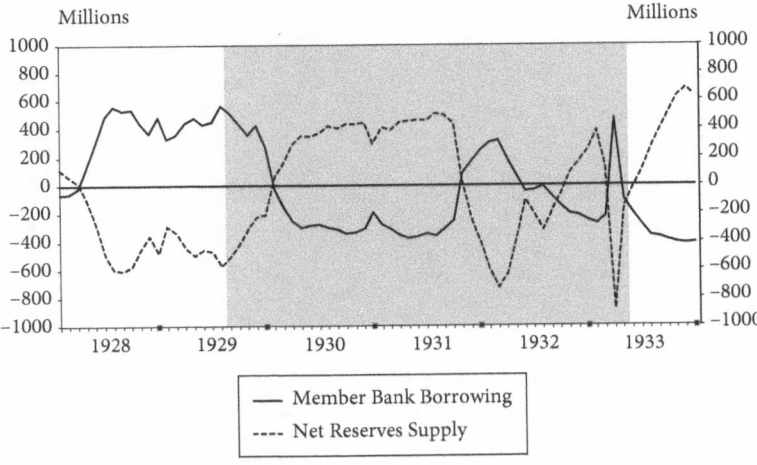

Figure 9.5. Member Bank Borrowing and Net Reserves Supply, Cumulative Changes
Observations are monthly observations of daily figures. "Net Reserves Supply" equals
"Active Reserves Supply," that is, bills bought plus government securities held by the
Fed minus "External Reserves Supply," that is, the gold stock minus money (currency)
in circulation minus Treasury deposits with Federal Reserve Banks. "Member Bank
Borrowing" is "bills discounted." Series are normalized by subtracting their December
1927 value. All series therefore represent cumulative changes from December 1927.
Shaded area indicates recession. Heavy tick marks indicate December.
Source: Board of Governors (1943, table 101)

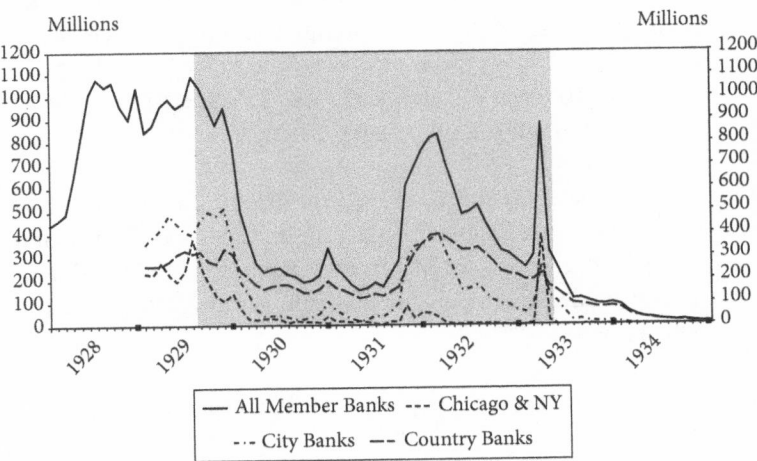

Figure 9.6. Member Bank Borrowing: Total and by Class of Member Bank
For 1929 onward, monthly averages of daily figures. For 1928, monthly averages of
weekly figures. Shaded area indicates recession. Heavy tick marks indicate December.
Source: Board of Governors (1943, table 105 and table 106 for 1928)

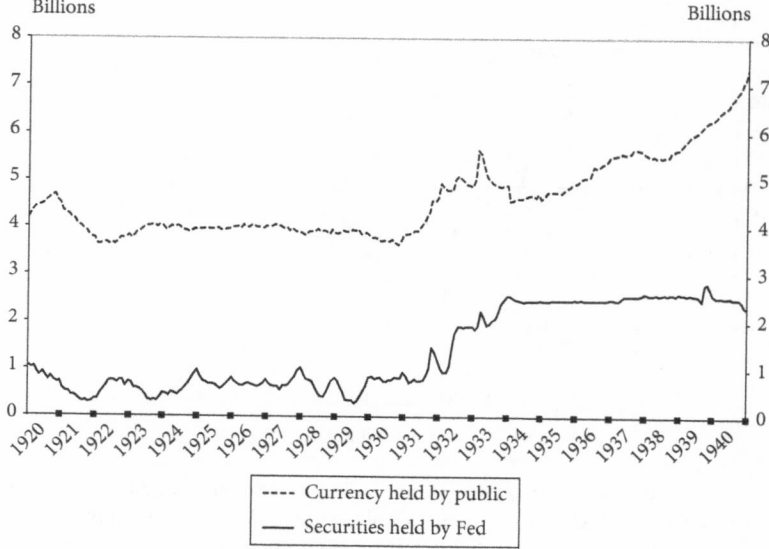

Figure 9.7. Securities Held by Fed and Currency Held by Public
Observations are monthly. Securities held by Fed is Reserve Bank credit outstanding
minus discount window borrowing, from Board of Governors (1943, table 102).
Currency held by the public is from Friedman and Schwartz (1970). Heavy tick marks
indicate December.

reach its December 1927 value until January 1930. Because of gold inflows,
net reserves supply increased through September 1930 (figure 9.5).

9.3. 1930: WHY DID THE FED BACK OFF
BEFORE RECOVERY BEGAN?

Why did not the economy recover in 1930 after suffering a relatively short
recession? There were three aborted recoveries in the Great Contraction,
which lasted from August 1929 to March 1933. Each time, contractionary
monetary policy snuffed them out. Mitchell and Burns (1936, 18, cited in
Schwartz 1981, 43) wrote:

> The long decline was interrupted by three partial and abortive revivals.
> Of these, the first, in the early months of 1930, was brief and restricted
> mainly to automobiles, steel and heavy construction. The second, in the
> first half of 1931, had wider scope, lasted longer, and went further. It was
> especially pronounced in the textile, rubber tire, shoe, and leather indus-
> tries. The revival in the summer and autumn of 1932 was fairly general.

Gold inflows grew strongly until April 1930, then grew slowly, and practically ceased after July 1930. With no growth in active reserves supply, net reserves supply followed the same pattern (figures 9.4 and 9.5). The recession worsened (figure 7.2). In 1930, the Fed did nothing to stimulate the economy. Active reserves supply remained unchanged. Securities held by the Fed, which had averaged $709 million over the years 1926 and 1927, remained basically unchanged at an only slightly higher level of $802 million from January 1930 through June 1931 (figure 9.7). In 1930, government securities holdings remained below their peak value in December 1927.

By Fed indicators, "money policy" moved toward ease after fall 1929. By money policy, policy makers meant that they had lowered the cost and increased the availability of the funds furnished to banks. From January 1930 through June 1931, the discount rate at the New York Fed declined from 4¾ percent to 1½ percent. George Harrison, governor of the New York Fed, focused on the New York banks and money market. Meltzer (2003, 312) cited a letter sent by Harrison on July 17, 1930, to the other governors: "We believe that the important thing to be achieved in present circumstances is that the money center banks should be substantially out of debt and that there should now be some surplus funds available."

A characteristic of monetary policy in the Great Contraction is maintenance of a significantly higher marginal cost of obtaining reserves through the discount window for banks outside the New York Federal Reserve District. Borrowed reserves declined after 1929 but remained significant at banks outside of Chicago and New York (figure 9.6). That fact is significant because the Reserve Banks outside of New York lagged in reducing their discount rates. The average of the discount rates for the Reserve Banks outside New York was 4¾ percent in January 1930 and 3.4 percent in December 1930. Its lowest average value was 2¾ percent over the interval May 1931 to September 1931 (figure 6.3). There is little recorded debate over the appropriate level of the discount rate. Because interest payments were a small part of the costs of businesses, policy makers assumed that the level of interest rates was low enough not to be an impediment to borrowing.

In assessing monetary policy in the Great Contraction, it is essential to keep in mind that as long as banks either were in the window or feared reserves outflows that could force them into the window the discount rate was only the base for calculating the cost of obtaining funds through the window. The total cost was the discount rate plus both the costs imposed by Fed administrative oversight (direct pressure) and the stigma from being a financially weak bank. Because of their real bills views, the governors of the regional Reserve Banks outside New York City continued to impose costly administrative oversight. They had no intention of allowing a revival of the speculation whose collapse they presumed had caused the recession.

Clark Warburton, who worked at the FDIC in the 1930s, recalled the administrative pressure exerted on banks in the Great Depression that raised the nonpecuniary cost of borrowing at the discount window and thus raised the marginal cost of reserves to banks. Warburton (1952 [1966], 339, cited in Humphrey and Timberlake [2019, 107]) wrote:

> [Fed banks] virtually stopped rediscounting or otherwise acquiring "eligible" paper. This [cessation] was not due to any lack of eligible paper. . . . Throughout 1930, 1931, and 1932 . . . the amount of member bank borrowings was [only] about [25 to 40 percent] the magnitude of 1928 and 1929 and remained at about [5 to 10 percent] of the eligible paper held by member banks. . . . [It] was due to strenuous discouragement of continuous discounting by any member bank, "direct pressure" so strong as to amount to a virtual prohibition of rediscounting for banks which were making loans for security speculation, and a "hard-boiled" attitude toward banks in special need of rediscounts because of deposit withdrawals.

As long as the Fed kept nonborrowed reserves below the reserves demand of banks, collectively banks would have to be in the window, and monetary policy would be contractionary. Banker reluctance would keep the marginal cost of obtaining reserves elevated. Board member Adolph Miller (US Congress 1931, January 23, 156) testified, "The banks are extremely reluctant to show borrowings from Federal reserve banks. . . . Such are present conditions."

At a meeting of the New York Fed Board of Directors on November 25, 1931 (HPNY, 113–14):

> Governor Harrison . . . commented on the reluctance of banks to show borrowing in their statements under present conditions, and pointed out that banks in other districts are now rather heavily in debt at the Reserve Banks. . . . In view of the disinclination of banks to show indebtedness, he suggested that it might be desirable for the Reserve Banks to purchase Government securities in order to meet the requirements for Federal reserve credit which would develop before the year end, it being understood that securities so purchased would be resold after the turn of the year when the funds were no longer needed.

At the September 25, 1930, meeting of the Open Market Policy Conference (OMPC), which was the conference of governors organized to decide on open market operations, Governor Norris of the Philadelphia Fed summarized the real bills views of the regional Reserve Bank governors (cited in Meltzer 2003, 318):

> We have always believed that the proper function of the System was well expressed in the phrase used in the Tenth Annual Report of the Federal Reserve Board—"The Federal Reserve supplies needed additions to credit and takes up the slack in times of business recession." We have, therefore, necessarily found ourselves out of harmony with the policy recently followed of supplying unneeded additions to credit in a time of business recession, which is the exact antithesis of the rules stated above. The suggestion has been made that we should be prompt to "go into reverse" and dispose of these governments when business picks up. This is a complete and literal reversal of the policies stated in the Board's Tenth Annual Report, already quoted. We have been putting out credit in a period of depression, when it is not wanted and cannot be used, and we will have to withdraw credit when it is wanted and can be used.

Deflation had started in 1930 (figure 7.5), but policy makers thought of it as the consequence of a collapse in speculation. Earlier, Adolph Miller (US Congress 1926–27, April 30, 1926, 854) had testified:

> If there was some absolutely certain device for estopping the use of Federal reserve credit for speculative purposes, you would almost have your price stabilization so far as the Federal reserve is a factor in it. Now, there are other factors that come in that are utterly beyond the ken and control and the reach of the Federal reserve system.

Edmund Platt (US Congress 1931, January 26, 215–16), who had been a Board member from June 1920 to September 1930, testified:

> Business was speculating as well as the stock market, and the whole price level was high as well as the price of stocks. The fact that commodity price levels had not risen and were not rising, does not mean that those price levels were not too high. I think the fact they have gone down so drastically since shows they were too high. They were kept up by the speculative situation, and they had to break when the stock market situation broke.

Carl Snyder (1940, 202), a statistician at the New York Fed, characterized 1930 as a year of "hesitation and delay" because of a "fear of a renewal of speculation, and another great rise in security prices." Figure 8.1 shows a revival of brokers' loans in the first half of 1930 while the NYSE stabilized in 1929Q4 and the first half of 1930. Currie (1934b, 44) commented, "The fact that security loans increased in the first four months of 1930 probably explains why, after the initial purchases of securities during and immediately after the crash of 1929, the reserve banks abstained from any further easing measures, even though incomes and commodity prices were falling."

Hawtrey (1932 [1962], 215), wrote:

> After the Wall Street crisis, Bank rates were reduced all round. But the process was deplorably slow. The London and New York rates were not reduced to 4 per cent. till March, 1930. The vicious circle of deflation had by that time been effectively joined, and nothing but vigorous inflationary measures could have broken it. . . . Depression may become so intense that it is difficult to induce traders to borrow on any terms, and that in that event the only remedy is the purchase of securities by the central bank with a view to directly increasing the supply of money.

Hawtrey was a lone voice. Friedrich A. Hayek, the famous Austrian economist, expressed the popular view at the time that the Depression was the inevitable working out of the need to liquidate the excessive level of debt built up in the prior bubble period. Hayek (1932 [1984], 130, cited in Wheelock 1991, 101) criticized the Fed's reduction in interest rates after the October 1929 market crash as

> preventing the normal process of liquidation, and that as a result the depression has assumed more devastating forms and lasted longer than before. . . . It is quite possible that we would have been over the want long ago and that the fall in prices would never have assumed such disastrous proportions, if the process of liquidation had been allowed to take its course after the crisis of 1929.

9.4. GUARDING AGAINST A REVIVAL OF SPECULATION BY KEEPING BANKS IN THE DISCOUNT WINDOW

In 1930, policy makers waited for the demand for bank loans to revive. Hardy (1932, 56–57) expressed the prevailing sentiment:

> The primary cause of this deflation of credit was the widespread business depression. . . . In the face of this combination of a demand restricted by business depression and speculative pessimism, and credit supply enhanced by the inflow of gold, there ceased to be an effective demand

for Reserve credit. The Reserve Banks did the only thing they could do under the circumstances. They spread their wares on the bargain counter and waited for the reappearance of demand.

Why did the Reserve Banks just wait for loan demand to revive rather than supplying reserves aggressively through open market purchases of government securities until the economy recovered? A partial answer is that they feared "losing control of the market." Sufficient purchases of government securities would increase the nonborrowed reserves of banks to the point where the banks were no longer borrowing from the discount window (figure 6.1). With banks out of the window, the Fed would then not be in a position to raise market rates by raising discount rates in response to a revival in speculative activity. Senator Carter Glass asked Governor Harrison, "Why should you control the market?" Harrison replied, "For the very reason we have been discussing for two days, in the hope that we can maintain a control that will check or prevent an inordinate use of credit beyond the legitimate demands of commerce and industry" (US Congress 1931, January 22, 73).

In the 1920s, Board member Adolph Miller (US Congress 1926–27, April 30, 1926, 854) had expressed this concern given the prospect that gold inflows could increase bank reserves to the point where banks were no longer borrowing from the window: "You might have the disaster of another great inundation of gold. . . . That puts the banking situation beyond the reach, of the Federal reserve." Walter W. Stewart (US Congress 1926–27, April 22, 1926, 773–74), who had been director of research at the Board, expressed the same concern:

It is not an inconceivable situation that unless the gold standard becomes more definitely established in the various countries, and they thereby share in the new gold produced, that the Federal reserve system would have its influence very much diminished. It could adopt a policy that the member banks could not borrow except at certain high rates, but new gold would furnish member banks a basis for credit extension without use of the reserve banks.

Entirely aside from the effect of gold imports, developments in the business situation in this country might be of a character that would give rise to a credit situation almost beyond the influence of reserve-bank operations. Let us start with the present situation. If we had a decline in building activity and industry generally and a decline in prices and in pay rolls, we would have, naturally, an inflow of currency from circulation. That has the same effect as gold imports on the relation of member banks to the Federal reserve. It liquidates the system and puts the reserve banks out of touch with the market.

Behind the desire to keep control of the market by keeping banks indebted to the Reserve Banks was the perennial concern to prevent a revival of speculation. From October 1929 through March 1930, the combination of Fed open market purchases ($500 million) and currency inflows ($400 million) reduced discount window borrowing and market rates significantly (figures 9.4, 9.5, and 6.3). Why did not the Reserve Banks continue easing until the economy recovered? Harris (1933, 634, 463–64) wrote:

> The stock market boom occurred in February–March, 1930, and its effects were evident in a greater disinclination of reserve banks to follow the policy of the New York bank.... The threat of speculation in the first half of 1930 restrained them.... Rates declined in a precipitate manner, stimulating an active speculative movement and a premature development in the bond market.... In the next fifteen months (to June, 1931) no aggressive operations were undertaken and reserve credit tended to decline. Speculation had apparently frightened the authorities.

Criticism of the New York Fed did not mention contractionary monetary policy. In the real bills spirit, the presumption was that if the Fed snuffed out incipient speculation, rates would not have to rise to the level of seriously injuring business. In a letter to O. M. W. Sprague written in 1928, Strong wrote (cited in Chandler 1958, 435), "The really fundamental difficulty in a number of these matters is lack of courage to act effectively and with sufficient promptness so that the remedy is accomplished without damaging consequences." Once the speculative fever was allowed to rage, policy had waited too long, and an economic collapse was inevitable. The criticism was that the New York Fed had waited too long to raise rates, not that high rates had caused the economic contraction.

Hardy offered a window into the policy-making environment of the early Fed. The quotations are from Hardy (1932, 144–47).[2] Policy in 1928–

2. Charles O. Hardy (1844–1948) was a member of the research staff at the Brookings Institution from 1924 through 1943. His book *Credit Policies of the Federal Reserve System*, published in 1932, offers insight into contemporary thinking by economists about the Fed. The director of the Brookings Institute of Economics (Edwin G. Nourse) wrote in the preface to the book (Hardy 1932, ix) that in the 1920s the Federal Reserve System came "to be looked to by a considerable number of people as an instrumentality for accomplishing business and price stability." The book was an attempt to use the postwar experience "to test the ability of a central banking system in the United States to accom-

29 concentrated on an "attack on speculation." The objective was "to keep the stock market from absorbing more than 'its share' of the credit in the common reservoir, to the detriment of business and agriculture." When the "inevitable crash came," the liquidation of credit and business would then be less. "There were two possible ways of guarding against it" [the excess absorption of credit in the stock market]:

> One was the traditional method: make credit so expensive for all comers as to bring about a stock market liquidation even at the risk of bringing on a commercial liquidation. . . . The other alternative, which was an innovation, was to try to shut credit out of the stock market by direct action while keeping it available and not prohibitively dear for other lines of business. In 1928 the first alternative was adopted; in 1929 the second. . . . In all this controversy the one thing on which all parties were able to agree was the desirability of checking the stock market boom.

Hardy also noted that for the banking system prior to the establishment of the Fed recourse to additional reserves had to come from gold imports. Without that source of reserves, in a financial panic, banks would have to contract credit and deposits. Hardy (1932, 142) wrote:

> The creation of the Federal Reserve system had merely added another potential resource, the credit of the Reserve Banks. To the extent that this new resource was now cut off by "direct pressure," the market was thrown back on its old resources, non-banking credit and bank credit supported by newly imported gold.

What Hardy did not comprehend was that "direct pressure," which raised the marginal cost of obtaining reserves through the discount window, reduced the liquidity of the banking system. The need to restore the lost liquidity required contraction of the banking system "leading to a cancellation of deposits" just as had occurred in the pre-Fed National Banking era.

One reason that economists and policy makers came to see monetary policy as impotent in the Depression was that the economy did not revive in 1930 despite the open market operations and reductions in the discount rate following the October 1929 stock market crash. However, in 1930, member banks remained in the discount window. As long as they remained in the

---

plish the ends of economic stabilization" (Hardy 1932, ix). Contemporaries believed the experiment had failed.

window, their effort to get out of the window by reducing assets made monetary policy contractionary.

9.5. 1931: CONTRACTIONARY MONETARY POLICY BECOMES EVEN MORE CONTRACTIONARY

Contractionary monetary policy in 1930 continued into 1931 and weakened the economy until the stress on the banking system caused a nationwide crisis of confidence in banks to emerge in spring 1931. Quarterly annualized M1 growth, which had averaged 1.4 percent over the years 1928 and 1929, fell to −6.2 percent in 1930 (figure 7.4). Quarterly annualized deflation measured by the GNP deflator was −10.0 percent from 1930Q3 through 1933 Q1 (Balke and Gordon 1986). Although deflation in the Great Contraction was largely unanticipated, even a moderate degree of expected deflation produced high real rates. By Hamilton's (1992, table 7) measure based on commodity futures prices, expected inflation was −2.1 percent in 1930 and −7.1 percent in 1931. As shown in table 9.1, real rates of interest were extremely high for a recession.

Measured by annualized quarterly M2 growth (figure 8.2), the banking system contracted at a −2.2 percent rate from 1930Q2 through 1931Q1. It

Table 9.1. Nominal and Real Rate

Year	Commercial Paper Rate	Expected Inflation	Real Rate of Interest	Real GNP Growth	M1 Growth	M2 Growth
1929	5.8	−0.9	6.7	6.6	0.9	0.2
1930	3.6	−2.1	5.7	−9.6	−3.5	−2.0
1931	2.6	−7.1	9.7	−7.7	−6.6	−7.1
1932	2.7	−4.1	6.8	−13.8	−12.4	−15.4
1933T1	2.1	−6.1	8.2	−21.3	−17.8	−31.6
1933T2&T3	1.6	5.1	−3.5	14.2	6.0	4.9

Sources: Commercial paper rate is from Board of Governors (1943, table 120). Expected inflation is from Hamilton (1992, table 7). Hamilton's figures are for trimesters.
Notes: The figures are the average of expected inflation for the three trimesters of the individual years. The real rate of interest is the commercial paper rate minus expected inflation. Real GNP growth is annual growth rates from Balke and Gordon (1986). M1 and M2 growth are annual growth rates from Friedman and Schwartz (1970). The designation 1933T1 is the first trimester (four months) of 1933 and 1933T2&T3 is the last two trimesters (eight months) of 1933. For 1933T1, real GNP growth is for 1933Q1. For 1933T1&T2, it is the average of annualized quarterly growth rates for 1933Q2, 1933Q3, and 1933Q4. For 1933T1, M1 and M2 growth are the annualized growth rates from December 1932 through April 1933. For 1933T2&T3, they are the annualized growth rates from April 1933 through December 1933.

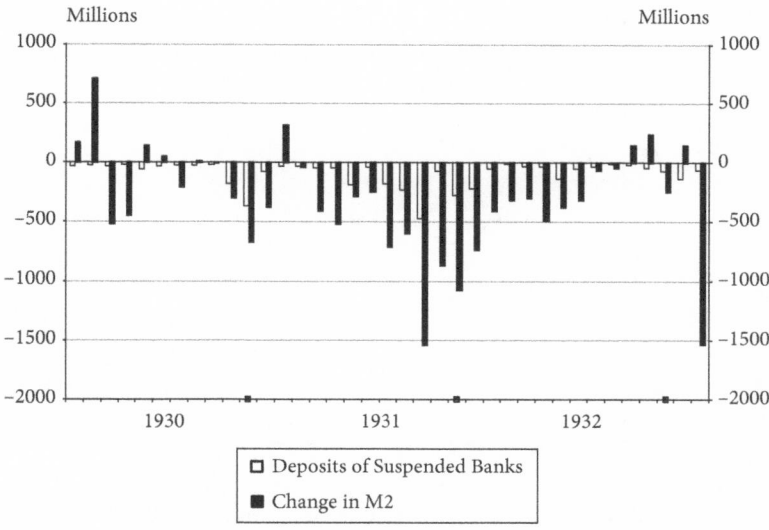

Figure 9.8. Change in M2 and Deposits of Suspended Banks
Monthly observations. Data on M2 are from Friedman and Schwartz (1970). Data on
suspended deposits are from *Federal Reserve Bulletin*, September 1936, 909, table 13.
Heavy tick marks indicate December.

then contracted at a −16.1 percent rate from 1931Q2 to 1932Q2. Figure 9.8
shows this augmented pace of the decline in M2. What produced the has-
tened pace of decline?

As a measure of public distrust of banks, Wicker (1996) used currency
in the hands of the public, which reflected currency outflows from banks.
By this measure, at the national level, public confidence in banks persisted
until March 1931 (figure 9.7). Currency outflows caused the reserves supply
schedule to shift leftward. As shown in figure 9.9, the reduction in nonborrowed reserves should have led to an increase in borrowed reserves, albeit
at a higher interest rate, IR_1. However, because of the onus on borrowing,
as shown in figures 9.5 and 9.6, borrowed reserves did not increase apart
from a short-lived increase due to the failure of the Bank of United States in
December 1930.

The stigma associated with borrowing meant that the upward sloping
segment of the reserves supply schedule possessed a steep slope. The Reserve Banks did not relax the nonpecuniary cost they imposed on use of
the discount window even during bank runs. Hardy (1932, 60) wrote: "By
encouraging the idea that a bank ought to regard the use of Reserve credit
as an emergency device or a temporary expedient, the System has made it

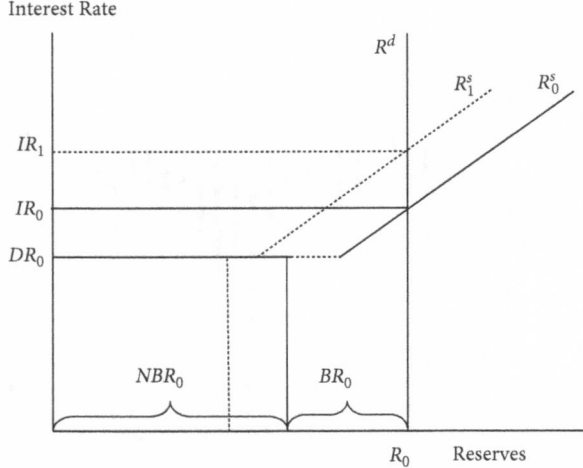

Figure 9.9. Market for Bank Reserves: Currency Outflow
R is bank reserves. R^d is the reserves demand schedule of the banking system, and R^s the reserves supply schedule of the Fed. IR is the interest rate on bank reserves. DR is the discount rate. NBR and BR are nonborrowed and borrowed reserves, respectively. The 0's and 1's subscripts denote values before and after the currency outflow.

impossible to stimulate rediscounting by low rates." Being in the window for more than a brief period remained a red flag of distress.

Bank reserves continued unchanged at their 1920s level (figure 9.10). At the same time, banks, especially those in New York, built up excess reserves (figure 9.11). As the deposits-currency ratio fell in 1931 with the bank runs, so did the deposits-reserves ratio (figure 9.3). Those declines could happen only with a contraction in bank assets and a concomitant reduction in bank deposits and required reserves.

Bagehot's dictum of lending freely at a high rate of interest in response to a bank panic was invented for the classical gold standard in which a world financial market comprising gold standard countries determined the market rate of interest provided the central bank followed the gold standard rules of the game. Central banks had to implement that interest rate by moving their discount rates to preserve international balance of payments in gold. Financial panics produced only transitory deviations from that market-determined interest rate. With the US fiat money standard, in the 1930s, the issue was not whether to lend freely at a high rate of interest but rather whether to lower the interest rate so that monetary policy was no longer contractionary. That is, the ideal policy was not to attract gold but to stop destroying bank reserves and deposits.

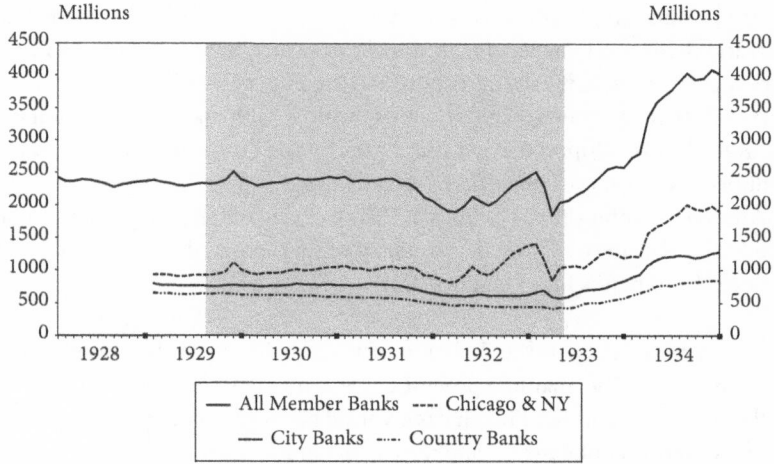

Figure 9.10. Reserves: Total and by Class of Member Bank
Monthly averages of daily figures. Heavy tick marks indicate December.
Shaded area indicates recession.
Source: Board of Governors (1943, table 105, and table 101 for 1928)

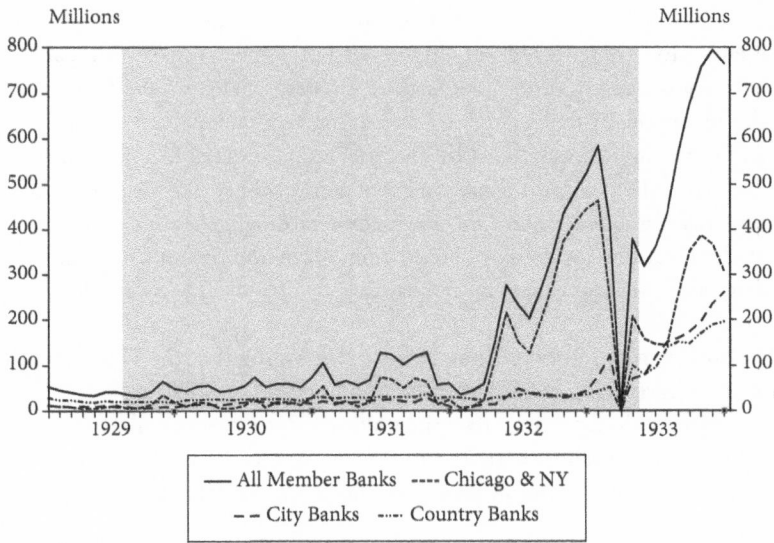

Figure 9.11. Excess Reserves: Total and by Class of Member Bank
Monthly averages of daily figures. Heavy tick marks indicate December. Shaded area
indicates recession.
Source: Board of Governors (1943, table 105)

At the same time, the criticisms of Bordo and Wheelock (2013), Friedman and Schwartz (1963a, 395), and Meltzer (2003, 730) for ignoring Bagehot's dictum possess merit. In response to the internal reserves outflow that started in 1931 and the external reserves outflow in the fall when Britain left the gold standard, open market purchases by the Fed would have kept the nonborrowed reserves of banks from declining.

Among contemporary economists, Edie (1932 [1983], 121–22) alone analyzed the pathology of the US monetary regime created by the outflow of reserves from banks into currency.

> The currency flow in the deflation of 1929–32 has been dominated by hoarding. . . . The hoarding process has accentuated the pressure for deflation for two reasons. First, it has involved heavy rediscounts in a period of weakened confidence. Member banks tend in such a period to look upon debt to the Federal as a badge of weakness, and occasionally their depositors feel uneasy about having funds in banks which are known to be rediscounting. Consequently, member banks endeavor to get out of debt to the Federal by liquidating some of their assets, a process which further depresses values. Second hoarding accentuates deflation because of the "free gold" technicality in our banking mechanism and makes the Federal Reserve reluctant to expand open market purchases of Governments. Governments are not eligible for note issue.[3] When "free gold" falls below $500,000,000, the further purchase of Governments is considered unsafe by the Federal Reserve. If the Federal buys Governments, and rediscounts are reduced by an equal amount, eligible collateral for note issue declines *pari passu*, and free gold declines likewise.[4] For the two reasons cited, therefore, currency-hoarding generates a vicious circle. Hoarding forces more liquidation, more liquidation causes more fear, and more fear causes more hoarding.

Edie, however, did not continue by recommending that the Fed offset the impact on borrowing of bank runs by open market purchases.

With Britain's departure from the gold standard in September 1931, gold flowed out of the New York banks into earmarked European accounts. Together with the earlier currency outflow, the external reserves supply

3. Note included in the original in this spot reads, "The Glass-Steagall bill has corrected this defect, but only for a period of one year."

4. Open market purchases reduced discount window borrowing and thus the real bills used as collateral for that borrowing. Note issue had to be backed by gold and real bills. Fewer real bills meant that the Reserve Banks had to back the note issue with additional amounts of gold.

plummeted (figure 9.4). From August 1931 through November 1931, the gold stock declined by almost $612 million, twice the amount of the decline from October 1919 through April 1920. Active reserves supply (open market purchases) only partially matched this decline (figure 9.4). With the decline in net reserves supply, member bank borrowing increased from its low of $154 million in April 1931 to a high of $836 million in February 1932 (figures 9.5 and 9.6). At the same time, the New York Fed raised its discount rate from 1½ percent to 3½ percent, the level of the other Reserve Banks. For the first time, the reserves of member banks declined (figure 9.10).

Fed policy makers saw their role as maintaining the confidence in the gold standard required to halt the internal and external currency drains. Harris (1933, 464) explained:

> They [the banks] met the crisis of 1931 in a courageous manner. . . . They financed withdrawals of gold, currency, and additional balances [excess reserves] inflated as a result of fear. The task of the reserve authorities was to make reserve credit available, but under conditions that would discourage excessive credit demands.

Those conditions meant a Fed willingness to supply reserves through the discount window but at an increased cost from an increase in discount rates. Market rates rose from 2 percent in September 1931 to 4 percent in November 1931 (figure 6.3).

9.6. THE GOLD STANDARD TRANSMITTED CONTRACTIONARY US MONETARY POLICY

In a boomerang effect, the contractionary monetary policy the United States forced on gold standard countries came back to ratchet up domestic contractionary monetary policy. When the Fed raised rates in 1928 and 1929, foreign central banks also had to raise rates to prevent gold from flowing to New York. Contractionary monetary policy in the United States spread to all the gold standard countries (Hamilton 1988; Eichengreen 1995). Harris (1933, 479) wrote:

> In the early part of 1929 the situation became so serious that the Bank of England raised its rate from 4½ to 5½ percent. . . . But the Bank of England, by raising its rate, conserved its gold only temporarily. . . . The German banks lost a large part of their foreign assets and gold, a loss aggravated by the impairment of confidence during a period of uncertainty concerning the future of reparations.

Despite defensive measures by foreign central banks, gold still flowed to the United States. The gold reserves of member banks increased by $860 million from January 1929 to August 1931 (Board of Governors 1943, table 101, "Member Bank Reserves. . . . ," 371).[5]

Barry Eichengreen (1986; 1995), Eichengreen and Peter Temin (2000), Douglas Irwin (2012), H. Clark Johnson (1997), and Scott Sumner (2015) pointed to monetary phenomena as major causes of the Great Depression, and all highlighted the destabilizing role played by gold. These authors highlighted how the restrictive policies of the Fed and the Banque de France absorbed gold and set off capital flows from countries on the gold bloc that forced them into monetary contraction. The reconstructed gold standard propagated monetary restriction in France and the United States to Great Britain and Germany and created a world depression.

In his book *Golden Fetters*, Eichengreen (1995, 12–13) summarized:

> In the mid-1920s, the external accounts of other countries remained tenuously balanced courtesy of long-term capital outflows from the United States. But if US lending was interrupted, the underlying weakness of other countries' external positions suddenly would be revealed. . . . As they lost gold and foreign exchange reserves, the convertibility of their currencies into gold would be threatened. Their central banks would be forced to restrict domestic credit.
>
> This is what happened when US lending was curtailed in the summer of 1928 as a result of increasingly stringent Federal Reserve monetary policy. Inauspiciously, the monetary contraction in the United States coincided with a massive flow of gold to France, where monetary policy was tight for independent reasons. Thus, gold and financial capital were drained by the United States and France from other parts of the world. Superimposed on already weak foreign balances of payments, these events provoked a greatly magnified monetary contraction abroad.

Hjalmar Schacht, governor of the Reichsbank, had just such fears. Strong summarized Schacht's concerns in a letter to Harrison on July 13, 1928 (cited in Chandler 1958, 458):

> Dr. Schacht hopes that our rate will not have to be maintained at a very high level . . . for fear of the . . . probability that it will close our investment market to German loans and lead to the crisis in reparation trans-

---

5. Eichengreen (1995) is the most comprehensive summary of the collapse of the international gold standard. See also Hetzel (2002a).

fers which he has been long anticipating. He says that much more than all that Germany has paid has been borrowed abroad. . . . He anticipates that the test of the Dawes Plan will come this winter or shortly thereafter.

The British economist D. H. Robertson (1929, 88) wrote, "A truer impression of the state of the world's monetary affairs would be given by saying that America is on an arbitrary standard [not a gold standard], while the rest of the world has climbed back painfully on to a dollar standard." In the Great Contraction, the United States would force monetary contraction, depression, and deflation on the world. Much later in the Bretton Woods era of the late 1960s and early 1970s, the United States would force inflation on the world.

In *The Midas Paradox*, Scott Sumner (2015) used an aggregate-supply/aggregate-demand framework for the determination of nominal GDP. Consistent with any standard model, declines in nominal GDP accompanied by declines in both the price level and real output signal a negative demand shock. Sumner traced the negative demand shocks of the Great Depression to the restrictive actions of central banks that increased their gold cover. He constructed an aggregate measure of the latter for the world's major central banks as the ratio of their combined monetary gold stocks to their combined stocks of currency in circulation (the gold reserve ratio).

As shown in Sumner (2015, table 2.1), central banks increased their gold reserve ratios over the entire period 1927 through 1932. From October 1929 through October 1930, approximately the first year of the Great Depression, the ratio increased by almost 10 percent. From August 1931 through December 1932, a time of intense stress due to external drains of gold particularly in Germany and Great Britain, it increased more than 4 percent. Sumner (2015, fig. 2.1) finds a strong correlation over the period October 1929 and October 1930 between the decline in industrial production and the increase in the gold reserve ratio. His measure of the gold ratio captured the worldwide character of restrictive monetary policy. Sumner (2015, 69) concluded: "The first year of the Depression, like the 1920–1921 depression, was a pure monetary policy shock."

Like Eichengreen, Sumner emphasized the stress placed on the revived international gold standard by France's absorption of gold. French policy was to move from the gold exchange standard in which central banks held reserves in the form of foreign exchange as well as gold to a pure gold standard. France's 1928 Monetary Law mandated that increases in currency had to be backed 100 percent by gold. Because of the required gold backing, increased demand for currency both in the United States and in France increased the demand for monetary gold. Sumner (2015, fig. 3.1), which shows a strong correlation between the deposits of failed banks and the gold reserve ratio, reflects on the one hand the association of the drain of bank reserves into currency with bank failures and, on the other hand, the increased demand for monetary gold.

A narrative account that gives content to the above analysis of the monetary causes of the collapse of the world economy unfolds like a Greek tragedy.[6] In *The Economic Consequences of the Peace,* Keynes (1920) predicted the havoc that would be wreaked by reparations—a havoc that played out through monetary disorder. Reeve (1943, xi) wrote:

> While the seeds of Hitlerism were many, the liquidation of the German middle class in the early post-war inflation and the wholesale unemployment during the deflation of the thirties were among the most important. Subsequently the apparent success of the unorthodox Nazi methods of monetary management helped to reconcile the German nation to the dictatorship of the Führer.[7]

Germany had to finance reparations payments in a protectionist world that discriminated against imports. The system held together because of the return flow of capital to Europe through the floating of long-term securities by Europeans in New York and through American direct investment in Europe. Everything changed starting in 1928 when monetary stringency and high interest rates in the United States reversed the capital flows. European central banks had to raise their rates to offset capital outflows. At the same time, the reconstructed gold standard was fragile in that its maintenance lacked the credibility of the late nineteenth-century standard. The credibility of the earlier standard appeared in the frankness of the comments of Horsley Palmer, who was a director of the Bank of England from 1811 until 1857 and governor from 1830 to 1833.

Palmer candidly admitted that external shocks could depress the domestic economy. In 1848, he testified to Parliament that "the raising of the rate of interest . . . stopped very largely the mercantile transactions of the country—exports as well as imports." In Parliamentary testimony, he described the consequences of raising the discount rate to counter gold outflows (citations from Hawtrey 1938 [1962], 28; see also Hetzel 2016):

6. The account follows Yeager (1966).

7. The hyperinflation of the early 1920s arose because of the unwillingness of the German public to pay taxes for reparations and the consequent use of the printing press to finance deficits. Hitler effectively abandoned the gold standard with price and exchange controls (Hetzel 2002a).

PALMER: It destroys the labour of the country; at the present moment in the neighbourhood of London and in the manufacturing districts you can hardly move in any direction without hearing universal complaints of the want of employment of the labourers of the country.

SPOONER: That you ascribe to the measures which it was necessary to adopt in order to preserve the convertibility of the note?

PALMER: I think that the present depressed state of labour is entirely owing to that circumstance.

In the early 1930s, lack of credibility for the gold standard interacted with the widespread existence of short-term debt owed foreigners held in the financial centers of countries. The new gold standard, or perhaps better a system of exchange rates pegged to the dollar, was a "gold exchange" standard in which central banks held as reserves not only gold but also foreign exchange such as sterling notes. Threat of devaluation or abandonment of the gold standard then became self-fulfilling as short-term debt flowed out of the threatened country.

Toxic international relations added to the inevitable collapse. Protectionist measures like the American Smoot-Hawley tariff, signed by President Hoover on June 17, 1930, meant that for countries like Germany even deflationary measures to lower the price level and depreciate the terms of trade drastically limited the ability of increasing export earnings to offset capital outflows. Only the United States could have altered the poisonous state of international relations by forgiving the war debts of its allies in return for their forgiving German reparations payments. That could not happen with an isolationist US Congress (Hetzel 2002a)

Belatedly, on June 20, 1931, President Hoover proposed a one-year moratorium on reparations payments and Allied war debts. However, French animosity toward Germany hindered negotiations to provide financial support to Germany and Austria. Austria and Germany had announced a customs union on March 21, 1931, but France objected regarding it as a violation of the Versailles treaty.

Contractionary US monetary policy propagated through a gold standard rendered destabilizing by capital flight created a world depression. World depression weakened the democratic German Weimar Republic and undercut the Brüning government, which was devoted to peaceful relations. The unemployment rate in Germany rose from 14.6 percent in 1930, to 22.3 percent in 1931, and to 28.1 percent in 1932 (Hetzel 2002a, table 2, "German Historical Data"). In Germany, in 1932, industrial production was 58 percent of its 1929 level (Yeager 1966, table 16.1, "Indicators of the Great Depression in Six Countries").

The initiating event in the financial panics that would force Germany into a de facto end to the gold standard through exchange controls and that would force Britain off the gold standard was a run on the Austrian bank, the Credit-Anstalt, in May 1931. "When the Austrian Parliament passed a law authorizing a government guarantee of new liabilities of the Credit-Anstalt, the shakiness of the government's own credit robbed the gesture of real significance" (Yeager 1966, 295). The concern of investors then spread to German banks. Yeager (1966, 296) wrote:

> German short-term foreign liabilities were almost double German short-term claims of foreigners. . . . On . . . July 13, the Darmstäter und National Bank closed, victim of a run touched off by failure of the largest German textile company, with which it had a close financial association. Failure of this company had converted a run mainly of Germany's foreign creditors into a flight from the mark into foreign exchange by Germans as well. . . . The Reichsbank raised its discount rate to 15 percent for August.

In August, investors began a run on the British pound. With its gold reserve having declined to its legal minimum, on September 19, Britain abandoned convertibility and the gold standard. When the pound depreciated, foreign banks, which held sterling balances, suffered significant losses, and the run spread to New York. The greatest intensification of the US monetary contraction occurred in fall 1931 when the Reserve Banks raised their discount rates in response to gold outflows.

There is an unsigned memorandum in the Harrison Papers in the archives at the New York Fed that can be taken only as critical of the lack of leadership by the New York Fed. The author recognized the fragility of the system because of the large amount of short-term balances held in different countries by foreigners. At the same time, preservation of the international gold standard was a prerequisite to world economic recovery because of the disruptive effects of a breakdown. The run on the Credit-Anstalt Bank in Austria spread to Hungary because both were Rothschild banks.

Everything would depend on dramatic leadership—leadership the New York Fed, the leader of the world's strongest central bank, abdicated. The anonymous author (HPNY, Confidential Files, June 18, 1931, 2, 15) wrote:

> Abandonment of the gold standard appeared to be inevitable unless the "run" on Austria could be checked. The best known method of stopping a run on a bank, or a banking system, or a country, is by making such a

display of strength that confidence is quickly restored and funds again flow in as well as out. The question which had to be decided in May 1931 was whether or not to try this orthodox remedy in treating the Austrian situation, a situation which had to be considered not only of itself, but in the light of the almost inevitable effects of failure there upon the weak positions in other countries. . . . Central bank credits are effective more in their creation than in their utilization.

The crisis required two kinds of leadership: one from politicians and one from central bankers. Montagu Norman, head of the Bank of England, understood the gravity of the crisis. In a separate letter, Norman told Harrison, "Unless somebody grasps the problem of reparations and debts we cannot emerge from this mess. . . . The emergency is so great that all reparations and debts should be remitted for five years. . . . There is a world crisis pending because of the situation in Germany arising out of the problem of debts and reparations" (HPNY, Confidential Files, June 18, 1931, 3).

Capital outflows then spread to Germany. Those outflows "coincided with a disturbed political situation resulting internally in Germany from agitation by the strongly supported extremist parties" [which opposed reparations]. Upon announcement on June 21, 1931, by President Hoover of a proposed moratorium on reparations and governmental war debts, "the outflow of funds from Germany was immediately arrested and confidence somewhat restored. . . . The Reichsbank actually gained slightly in its reserves" (HPNY, Confidential Files, June 18, 1931, 6).

However, French politics sabotaged the moratorium. The French right opposed all concessions, and France delayed implementation for three weeks (Eichengreen 1995, 277; Yeager 1966, 296). Given the uncertainty, the capital outflows revived. "The Reichsbank's discount rate went for a week as high as 15 percent . . . and credit restriction was practiced" (HPNY, Confidential Files, June 18, 1931, 7). On July 9, Norman told Harrison that Luther, head of the Reichsbank, had told him that "the position in Berlin is now desperate" and that without "an additional credit in 'an unlimited amount' . . . Germany will collapse" (HPNY, Confidential Files, July 9, 1931, 1).

"Towards the middle of July, at the height of the German crisis, London began acutely to experience the repercussive effects of the situation on the Continent." Those "repercussive effects" included the freezing of credits on the Continent and lenders to London who had to "recall their funds in order to fortify their cash position at home. . . . From the Scandinavian peninsula to the Balkans the free movement of funds, and consequently of goods, is hampered by public prohibition and private apprehension" (HPNY, Confidential Files, June 18, 1931, 9–10, 12). When Britain went off gold in September, the United States lost "over $700,000,000 in . . . gold during the five or six weeks ended at the close of October. The absence of obstacles in the way of the acquisition of gold here, and the calm manifested in the face of these gold sales, were rewarded by a rapid restoration of confidence in the dollar" (HPNY, Confidential Files, June 18, 1931, 12).

The author of the memo never mentioned the increase in the New York Fed discount rate from 1½ percent to 3½ percent, nor did he mention a need to maintain the Federal Reserve System gold cover. History might have unfolded differently if Harrison had led a bold rescue effort for Europe. The British crisis and the gold outflows from the United States then might not have occurred. If the United States did experience gold outflows, the Fed could have dealt with them by selling from its gold stock without raising the discount rate as "the US gold stock was at its highest level in history" (Friedman and Schwartz 1963a, 396).

Harrison worried only that his participation in a loan to Europe might result in a loss to the New York Fed. Repeatedly, he put Norman off, quibbling over details of how the loan would be secured. The Bank of England lent the Austrian government $21,000,000. Then, on May 30, 1931, central banks of eleven countries extended a loan to Austria of $14,071,000, of which the US share was only $1,083,000. The author (HPNY, Confidential Files, June 18, 1931, 14–15) of the internal New York Fed memo wrote:

> Our commitments are small in comparison with our total resources, with the domestic demands made upon our resources, and with the stakes involved. It has not been sufficiently appreciated . . . that these stakes were those of the country as a whole; the perpetuation of that degree of confidence in our present credit system which was necessary if there was not to be a complete breakdown.

When it seemed unlikely that France would participate in the Austrian loan, Harrison insisted that he could not participate without the French (HPNY, Confidential Files, June 24, 1931, 2). Leadership from Washington ended with the Hoover initiative on reparations. After the Austrian crisis, Harrison recorded that Treasury Secretary Mellon "thinks something should be done and fairly promptly, but that he is really on a vacation and other than communicating his views to Washington he did not know whether he could do anything more about it. . . . Mr. Mellon . . . knew very little about the fundamentals of the French position" (HPNY, Confidential Files, June 19, 1931, 1).

Contemporary observers associated the bank failures with the inherent instability of a capitalist system. Competitive devaluations, which favored domestic exporters but disadvantaged other countries especially those part forming the gold bloc, damaged international trade and the world economy. Speculative outflows of short-term funds destabilized currencies. The general association of currency instability in the form of devaluations and the general assumption that speculation was destabilizing created the assumption that fluctuating exchange rates would destabilize international trade and harm domestic economies.

9.7. 1932: OPEN MARKET PURCHASES AND WHAT MIGHT HAVE BEEN

With the restoration of confidence that the United States would not abandon convertibility of the dollar into gold, in early 1932, for the first time, the Fed experimented with actively supplying reserves to stimulate bank lending and the economy. From February 1932 through August 1932, the Fed's holding of government securities increased by about $1.11 billion. Offsetting this increase in *active* reserves supply and reflecting the renewed banking crisis and a renewed concern over gold convertibility, between April and August 1932, gold and currency outflows caused the *external* reserves supply to decline by $618 million (figure 9.4). However, gold inflows resumed after August 1932, and *net* reserves supply increased fairly steadily throughout 1932, and member bank borrowing declined fairly steadily (figure 9.5). Despite that fact, in January 1933 at $254 million, borrowed reserves were still well above their low point in April 1931 at $154 million (figure 9.6).

Because of the asymmetric implementation and operation of the Fed's free reserves procedures, monetary policy affected the New York banks differently than banks outside New York. Initially, monetary contraction affected the latter more severely. Because the Reserve Bank districts other than New York kept their discount rates significantly higher than New York's, member banks outside New York incurred a higher marginal cost of reserves. In June 1931, the New York bank discount rate was 1½ percent while in the other districts it averaged 2¾ percent. In January 1932, all the Reserve Bank discount rates were at 3.5 percent. By July 1932, New York had lowered its rate to 2½ percent with little change in the rates of the other Reserve Banks (figure 6.3).

In 1932, the Fed's open market purchases liberated the New York City banks from the Fed's free reserves procedures. That liberation could have been the start to ending the monetary contraction that had perpetuated the Great Contraction. For New York City banks, that liberation meant accumulating excess reserves in sufficient quantity that they did not have to worry that reserves outflows would force them into the window. With New York City banks freed from a marginal cost of reserves elevated by the fear of recourse to the discount window, the arbitrage keeping the prime commercial paper rate above the discount rate ended. With the cost of reserves determined in the New York money market by a reserves supply determined exogenously (figure 6.4), for the first time, in August 1932, the commercial paper rate fell below the New York Fed discount rate (figure 6.3). The market for bank reserves in New York then entailed a lower cost of reserves than in the other Reserve Bank districts in which banks continued to obtain the marginal dollar of reserves through periodic recourse to the discount window. (Discount window supervision prevented arbitrage whereby the New York banks would borrow from the New York Fed and relend to their respondent banks in the interior of the country.)

The New York banks were favorably placed to free themselves from recourse to the discount window. They had started to build their excess reserves in December 1930 in response to the failure of the Bank of United States. With the resolution of that failure, the process halted but resumed in June 1931 concurrently with widespread currency outflows, only to stop again after the monetary restriction in fall 1931. In April 1932, excess reserves at New York banks began to increase significantly while their use of the discount window basically dropped to zero (figures 9.11 and 9.6).

Also, the New York City banks had essentially been out of the window since the early 1930s. When in the window, it was only for a day or two.[8] Moreover, they had access to a Fed funds market (Goodfriend and Whelpley 1993). New York City banks had also succeeded better in making their portfolios more liquid. Between March 1930 and September 1931, they had decreased their loans by almost 16 percent while banks outside New York had decreased their loans by just more than 7 percent. Over this period, New York member banks had increased their holdings of government securities by about 60 percent while member banks outside New York had increased them by just less than 20 percent (figures 9.12 and 9.13). In August 1932, for central reserve city banks (New York and Chicago), only 1 percent of their total reserves came from discount window loans. In contrast, for reserve city banks and country banks, the numbers were, respectively, 22 percent and 69 percent (figures from Wheelock 1991, 109).

In 1932, as the Fed supplied reserves with open market purchases, excess reserves increased. The lessening of the pressure on the banking system

---

8. "On any given day [in the 1920s], about one-third to one-half of them [individual banks] were likely to be borrowing. Large banks were expected to repay their loans within a few days, while smaller banks could borrow for a couple of weeks at a time" (Meulendyke 1998, 24).

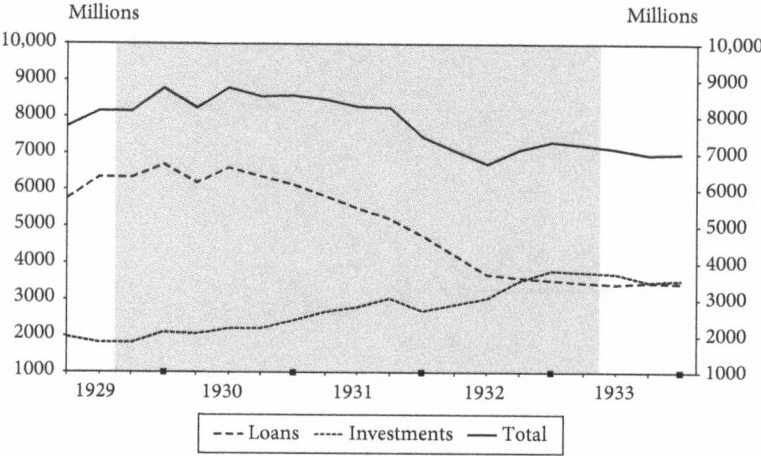

Figure 9.12. NYC Banks: Loans and Investments
Loans and investments of central reserve city banks in New York City on call dates.
Data were not collected for the March 1932 and March 1933 dates. For these dates, data
are interpolated. Heavy tick marks indicate December. Shaded area indicates recession.
Source: Board of Governors (1943, table 23)

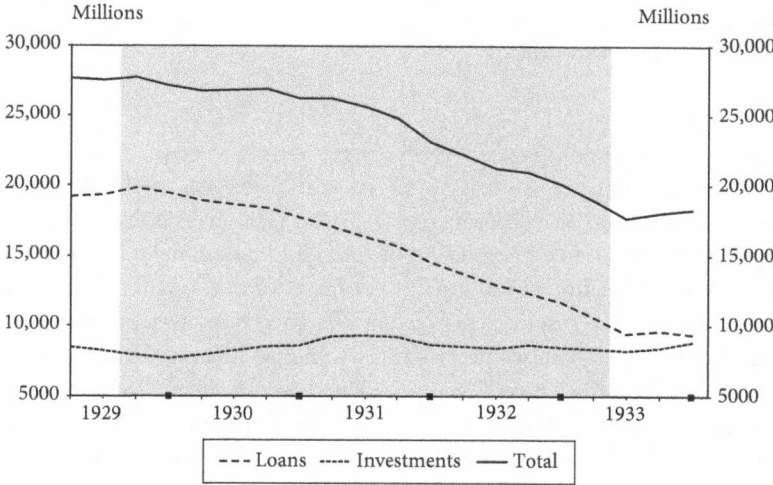

Figure 9.13. Chicago, Reserve City and Country Banks: Loans and Investments
Loans and investments of Chicago, reserve city and country banks on call dates. Data
were not collected for the March 1932 and March 1933 dates. For these dates, data are
interpolated. Heavy tick marks indicate December. Shaded area indicates recession.
Source: Board of Governors (1943, table 23)

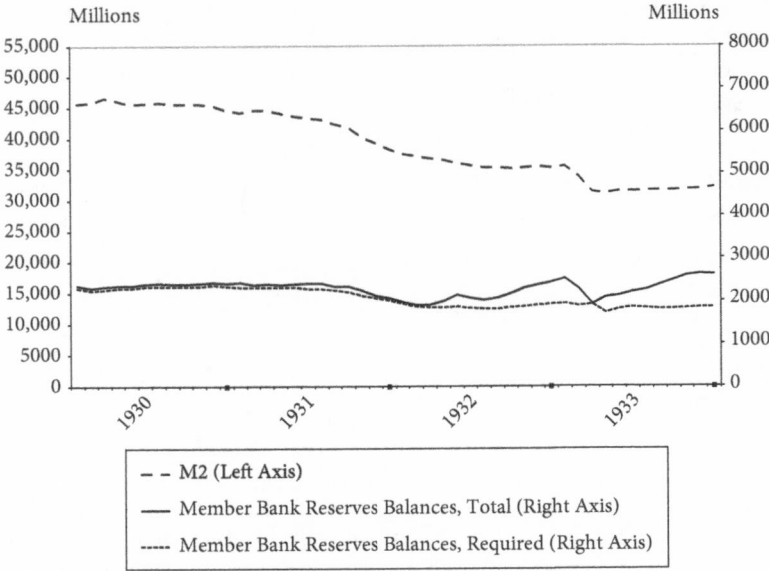

Figure 9.14. M2 and Total, Required, and Excess Reserves of Member Banks
The level of M2 and total and required reserves of member banks. The difference
between total and required reserves is excess reserves. Heavy tick marks indicate
December. Data from Friedman and Schwartz (1970, table 1) and from Board of
Governors (1943, table 101).

to contract to build up excess reserves caused M2 to cease its decline and
to stabilize. Figure 9.14 plots M2 along with series on total reserves and
required reserves. The difference in the latter two series is excess reserves.
In 1932, the move in the direction of removing monetary contraction appeared in the decline in money market rates when the commercial paper
rate fell below the discount rate, even with total borrowed reserves for all
member banks well above their 1931 lows. In mid-1932, with the increase in
excess reserves, the loans of New York City banks basically stabilized as did
investments at year-end. New York City banks no longer felt the need to
contract in order to become more liquid. At banks outside New York City,
on the other hand, loans declined until the end of the Great Contraction in
March 1933.

Annualized quarterly M1 growth, which had averaged −17.5 percent
in 1931Q4 and 1932Q1, rose to 3.8 percent in 1932Q4. Annualized quarterly nominal GNP growth, which averaged −25.1 percent from 1931Q4 to
1932Q3, rose to −10.3 percent in 1932Q4 (figure 7.4). As documented in the

Mitchell and Burns (1936) quotation above, the economy began an incipient recovery in the summer and fall of 1932.

9.8 1932: WHY DID THE FED BACK OFF IN AUGUST 1932?

Figure 9.11 offers one clue why the Fed ceased its open market purchases. Excess reserves piled up at the New York City banks but not at banks outside New York City. Much of that asymmetry came from the fact that interior banks used additional reserves to repay borrowings while the New York City banks already out of debt accumulated excess reserves (figure 9.6). Also, as a result, between December 31, 1931, and December 31, 1932, the reserves held by country and reserve city banks, which repaid borrowings, fell somewhat from $1,150 to $1,094 million. They rose at the New York and Chicago banks over this period from $825 to $1,416 million (figure 9.10).

Governors of the regional Reserve Banks outside New York City did not perceive any benefits for their banks.[9] The reserves created by the Fed's open market purchases piled up in New York City. Harris (1933, 463, 619) wrote:

> The uneven distribution of the cash distributed by reserve banks is also an obstacle: banks or sections of the country requiring additional cash may not receive it while large balances accumulate in New York. . . . Large surplus funds accumulate in the financial centers long before country banks are out of debt. In other words, the surplus cash created as a result of open market operations may find its way neither to banks heavily in debt nor to communities especially in need of the added stimulus.

Chapter 11 details the role played by Governor Harrison during the brief-lived open market purchases of spring 1932 and the reasons for their cessation. Getting the country and reserve city banks out of the discount window would have required a huge increase in the excess reserves of the New York City banks. With Harrison at the New York Fed and real bills governors at the other regional Feds, that was not going to happen, that is, not until the Roosevelt administration.

9. Harris (1933, 635–56) pointed to the reduction in the discount rate in 1932 by the New York Fed from 3.5 percent in December 1931 to 2.5 percent by July 1932 and the fact that the other Reserve Banks failed to follow as evidence that the open market purchase program was exclusively a New York Bank affair (figure 6.3). With the benefit of hindsight, 2.5 percent hardly seems to be aggressive, but New York banks were out of the window.

The remainder of this section summarizes the drama in the markets during this period. Concerned by the association between the contraction of credit and deflation with its associated negative consequences for debtors, Harrison became willing to take risks in spring 1932. After orchestrating an attempt to persuade actors in the political system to make efforts to balance the budget and cease efforts to promote the printing of money, under his leadership, the Fed began open market purchases. There ensued a contest between these purchases and gold outflows over which source would most affect bank reserves. The contest seesawed back and forth with moderate increases in bank reserves after March 1932 and sustained increases only after July 1932.

The French led in gold withdrawals over concern that open market purchases would force the United States off the gold standard. After publication in early 1932 in France of a letter calling the proposed open market purchases inflationary, the French representative of the Bank of France called on Harrison. Harrison (HPNY, Confidential Files, January 20, 1932, 2) recorded:

> Lacour-Gayet then said the real purpose of his call today was to discuss a long cable published this morning by Parker Willis in the Agence Economique et Financiere which he said had created a very considerable amount of uneasiness and nervousness in Paris financial circles. He read the article to me, which was headed by the sentence that "Inflation is now the order of the day in the United States." Lacour-Gayet said he could not over-emphasize the effects of this article in Paris and even in the Bank of France. . . . He indicated the way their minds were running by asking about the increase in our government securities holdings which had occurred since their visit in October.

Concern over whether the United States would balance its budget reinforced the gold outflows. Sumner (2015, 128–29) wrote:

> The US Congress provided another source of uncertainty for the markets . . . [as] Congress attempted to close a huge budget deficit. . . . [The] *New York Times* reflected the worsening situation: "Democratic Leaders Deplore Tax Revolt," "Leaders Are Bewildered." . . . By late March, it had become clear that with ongoing budget battles, "mischievous inferences are likely to be drawn in foreign financial centers." . . . The April 8 *New York Times* (p. 31) noted that "the foreign attack on the dollar began just before Easter [March 27], when the defeat of the sales tax in Congress led

to the widespread belief in Europe that the United States budget would not be balanced."

Populist efforts in Congress to finance expenditures through printing money disturbed markets. Sumner (2015, 129, 132) wrote:

> The financial press viewed the Bonus bill, which would have financed $2 billion in accelerated veteran's bonuses by printing fiat currency, as a reckless example of "Greenbackism" that would trigger a loss of confidence in the dollar. . . . In addition to the Bonus bill, Wall Street also faced uncertainty over the Goldsborough bill, which would have instructed the Fed to raise prices back to the average level of the mid-1920s. The May 7 *Commercial and Financial Chronicle* argued that this bill would force a devaluation of the dollar and suggested that the bill was contributing to the US gold outflow.

These concerns led to a decline in the stock market, which fell irregularly after March 8, 1932, and reached its Depression low on July 8, 1932. However, by early July, these concerns had largely dissipated. "A June 15 *New York Times* headline reported that 'France Withdraws Her Last Gold Here: Dollar Value Rises,' . . . Yet the crisis was not quite over. The markets faced one more banking panic, an additional month of congressional budget battles, and completion of the Lausanne Conference before a sustained recovery could begin in mid-July" (Sumner 2015, 135).

Bank reserves began a moderate increase after March 1932 and then a steady increase after July 1932 until peaking in January 1933 (figure 9.10). Excess reserves began a steady rise starting in April 1932 (figure 9.11). In 1932Q4, the banking system stopped contracting with growth in M2 slightly positive (figure 8.2). Industrial production ceased its precipitous decline in 1932Q2 at its Depression low and then rose slightly.

In spring 1932, markets feared that attempts to raise the price level as a way of fighting the Depression would lead to a gold crisis as had occurred in fall 1931. A year later, in contrast, when Roosevelt ended gold convertibility and the threat of a gold crisis disappeared, the markets responded in an unambiguously positive way to administration actions designed to raise the price level. Still, the open market purchases of spring 1932 contributed to the perception that expansionary monetary policy had been tried and had failed. Hardy (1932, 219–21) claimed that "the price level is not readily controlled by credit manipulation. . . . The experience of 1930–32 indicates that a price change can run very far in the face of determined efforts to reverse it by credit policy."

9.9. EARLY 1933: THE COLLAPSE OF THE BANKING SYSTEM

Monetary policy became sharply contractionary in February 1933 when currency outflows from banks (figure 9.7) and then gold drains revived and statewide banking moratoria spread panic. Figure 9.4 shows the sharp, unprecedented drop in *external* reserves supply from currency drains. *Net* reserves supply dropped, and banks were forced into the window (figures 9.5 and 9.6). As occurred after mid-1931, total reserves of banks declined (figure 9.10). The excess reserves painfully accumulated by banks disappeared (figure 9.11). The Fed fiddled while the banking system burned.

Governor Eccles (US Congress 1935a, March 18, 382) testified:

> If a bank reaches a position where the customers have called upon the bank for currency and it is unable to meet that call, that bank closes. Many of the banks in this country were unable to meet that call, not because they were not sound but because they did not have the eligible paper with which to go to the Reserve bank and get credit. . . . As the number of banks closing increased, the demand for currency increased, not because of the activity of business but because of hoarding; and the very fact that the banks were unable to go to the Reserve banks with sound assets to meet the demands of these depositors meant finally a banking collapse. Had the banks been able to pay their depositors in currency, the depositors would not have wanted the currency as was demonstrated after the bank holiday.

Eccles testimony was disingenuous. He did not mention the failure of the Fed to provide through open market operations the reserves required to prevent a decline in the nonborrowed reserves of banks. Also, it was not true that member banks lacked eligible paper as documented in the earlier Warburton (1952 [1966], 339) quotation.

The lack of comprehension within the Fed of its responsibility to ensure the stability of the banking system represented a general failure to understand the role of the Fed as a central bank. That failure appeared in the basic irrelevance of the advice urged on incoming president Roosevelt by outgoing president Hoover in early 1933. As Meltzer (2003, 383) wrote: "In mid-February, President Hoover wrote to Roosevelt to inform him about capital flight, currency drains, and the threat to the exchange rate and the gold standard. Hoover's letter blamed the problem on agitation to tinker with the financial system, publication of RFC [Reconstruction Finance Corporation] loans, and the like. The letter asked Roosevelt to commit to a policy

based on the gold standard and a balanced budget and to reassure the public
that the country would recover if the government followed sound policies."

9.10. WHAT MADE THE GREAT CONTRACTION
SO DEEP AND SO LONG?

Unlike the British gold standard, which was built on making bank reserves
respond to the international balance of payments, the US monetary standard was built on real bills principles. Unlike England then, in the United
States, member bank borrowing from the discount window provided significant amounts of the reserves of the banking system. That borrowing was
the instrument used by the Fed to enforce the allocation of bank credit to
productive rather than to speculative uses. What no one understood at the
time was that by determining the marginal cost of obtaining reserves for
banks, the Fed, not the market, determined the interest rate. The stance of
monetary policy, contractionary or expansionary, therefore, emerged out
of the way in which the interest rate interacted with the role played by the
interest rate in the operation of the price system. That role is captured by
the natural rate of interest—the interest rate that keeps output at potential.
By analogy with price fixing, an interest rate maintained above the natural
rate of interest required contraction of the banking system, measured here
by the rate of growth of M2 (figure 8.2).

According to real bills principles, banks would obtain reserves through
the discount window by discounting short-term commercial paper—real
bills. Those eligibility criteria for discounting would assure that bank lending would move goods and crops to market instead of financing speculative activity. The discounting of real bills, which are short-term commercial
paper, meant that discount window borrowing had to be short-term. The
exclusion of long-term borrowing meant that banks could not borrow to
finance speculative lending. Hardy (1932, 231) wrote:

> This tradition ["a bank ought not to borrow in order to relend at a
> profit"] is . . . in part the survival of a pre-war tradition which made *any*
> sort of borrowing by a bank a confession of weakness; and in part an
> expression of a broader traditional principle that any sort of permanent
> capital investment—industrial, commercial, or agricultural—ought to
> be financed by long-term capital instruments rather than by short-term
> borrowing. (italics in original)

Before 1929, provided banks had eligible paper to discount, borrowing
at the discount window went unchallenged as long as banks were not in the

window continuously. The New York Fed defended that principle, but in early 1929 it lost to the Board, which advocated the policy of direct pressure. The open market sales of government securities that began in 1928 required a significant increase in discount window borrowing by banks collectively and assured that all banks would be involved in the musical chairs of being in and out of the window. Direct pressure then pressured all banks by inviting scrutiny over whether their security loans were being used to finance speculation. All banks had an incentive to liquidate their assets to accumulate excess reserves. For the banking system, with the policy of direct pressure and the administrative costs that it imposed on banks, monetary policy would remain contractionary as long as banks collectively had to borrow from the discount window.

In the Great Contraction, the Fed's free reserves procedures kept the real rate of interest (the marginal cost of reserves) above the natural rate of interest.[10] Because the latter is not observable, this contention relies on events similar in spirit to semicontrolled experiments. In 1932, when open market purchases and then gold inflows allowed the New York banks to build up excess reserves and thus freed them from the fear of being forced into the discount window, M2 growth stabilized, and the economy recovered. After the cyclical trough in March 1933, the steady increase in excess reserves and reduction in discount window borrowing had the same effect of removing the determination of the market interest rate from the control of the Fed (see figures 9.6 and 9.11). Chapter 10, however, argues that cost-push shocks engineered by policies of the Roosevelt administration limited the recovery even with the end of contractionary monetary policy.

In the 1930s, no one understood the monetary regime created by the Federal Reserve Act. Policy makers were like sailors at sea whose boat had sunk and who were desperately holding on to the wooden fragments of a lost gold standard psychology.[11] As emphasized by Friedman and Schwartz,

10. Friedman and Schwartz (1963a, 311) argued that "under the pre–Federal Reserve banking system, the final months of 1930 would probably have seen a restriction, of the kind that occurred in 1907, of convertibility of deposits into currency. By cutting the vicious circle set in train by the search for liquidity, restriction would almost certainly have prevented the subsequent waves of bank failures that were destined to come in 1931, 1932, and 1933." However, if the bank runs were the consequence of the way in which a contractionary monetary policy weakened banks by weakening the economy rather than the cause of contractionary policy, albeit a factor that exacerbated monetary contraction, suspension would not have worked as it had in the pre-Fed era.

11. Temin (2007, 39, 44–45) argued that the United States was on a gold standard and policy makers did not make "policy mistakes." They knowingly accepted that the gold standard required deflation. As argued in chapter 11, in fall 1931, policy makers thought in terms of maintaining the confidence of the financial establishment assumed to be a prerequisite for economic recovery. They did not understand monetary policy as

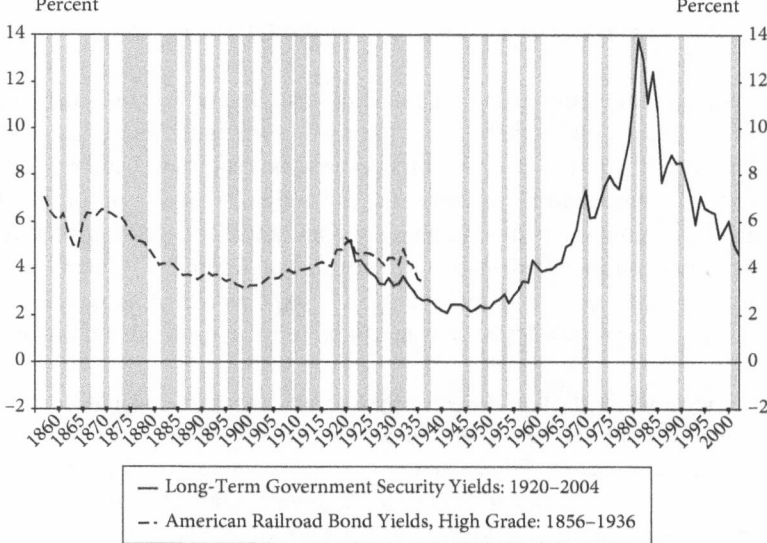

Figure 9.15. US Long-Term Interest Rates: 1856–2004
Yields on long-term government securities from 1920 until 1953 are from the Board of
Governors (1943), and those for 1941–70 from Board of Governors (1976). Thereafter,
Treasury ten-year constant maturity bonds from Board of Governors, "Selected
Interest Rates," Statistical Release G.13, are used. The railroad bond yields are from
Macaulay (1938). The shaded regions represent recessions.

at all times in the Great Contraction the Fed had the ability to end the contraction of money. In principle, the Fed could have instituted a zero-lower-
bound policy by setting discount rates at zero. It could then have undertaken purchases of long-term government securities (quantitative easing)
until all banks were out of the discount window. The market would then
determine the interest rate.

Figure 9.15 shows the behavior of long-term interest rates. They remained well above zero during the Great Contraction. Purchasing bonds
would have created money and in doing so set off the portfolio rebalancing
that would have raised asset prices and stimulated expenditure. Of course,
just to state this possibility makes evident how wildly implausible it would
have been in a world imbued with real bills principles and gold standard
psychology. The next section restates that fact.

highly contractionary. More fundamentally, Temin's assumption that policy makers understood the nature of the monetary regime implies that they understood the alternative
of stabilizing the price level. There is no support for these assumptions in the historical
record.

9.11. WHY DID LEARNING PROVE IMPOSSIBLE?

One reason that a contemporaneous understanding of the monetary origin of the Great Contraction proved impossible was that there was a ready explanation. The Great Contraction occurred as a failure to heed real bills principles. It appeared as evidence that the Fed had failed to properly implement the intended system in which the market demand for productive credit would automatically control the extension of credit. William Allan White (1938, 289–90), an iconic American newspaper editor, expressed this universally accepted real bills view in a biography of President Coolidge:

> The ideal of the Federal Reserve System was that there would never be any excess reserves and that there would never be any reserve deficiencies, that elastic Federal Reserve credit would control the volume of reserves of the member banks, letting them expand when they were needed and causing them to contract when the need was over. . . .
>
> What the [NY] Reserve Bank did [in 1927] . . . was to buy several hundred million dollars worth of government securities. The effect of this, combined with the incoming gold, was to make money rates drop. Then, as merchants had no use for additional funds, the funds began to flow into (a) collateral loans against stocks, (b) bank investments in bonds, (c) installment finance paper, (d) real estate mortgage loans in banks.
>
> The incoming gold and the excess credit created by the Federal Reserve banks created excess reserves in the hands of the member banks of the Federal Reserve System. These excess reserves became then the basis for an expansion in the superstructure of commercial bank credit on a multiple ratio.

The view expressed above dominated contemporary thinking. Garet Garrett (1931, 79, 81) wrote in the *Saturday Evening Post*:

> What the Federal Reserve System did was to force into the hands of the banking world a vast amount of surplus credit and money—much more than there was any legitimate need for. . . . The banks did not need this credit and had not asked for it. . . . Naturally, they loaned it to Wall Street brokers and speculators, and what these did with it was to foment a speculation nobody was able afterward to stop.

Benjamin Anderson (1931, 4–10, 14), an economist at Chase National Bank of New York, expressed the accepted view of recession as the required purging of prior speculative excess:

In credit matters, the equilibrium doctrine is far more interested in having a good *quality* of credit than it is in having a large *quantity* of credit. . . . The equilibrium doctrine looks upon periods of reaction and depression as periods of liquidation of credit and improvement of the quality of credit, as times for the paying of debts. . . . The great depression is due to an unbalanced economic situation. . . . In periods of crisis and depression the general rule has been that both prices and costs yield, and that, in the reduction of prices and costs, and in the restoration of a proper relation of prices to costs . . . the foundation of recovery is laid.

Just as after the 1920–21 recession, the Fed realized the cost of recession and the threat to its independence. It doubled down with the Depression. The moral drawn was the same. The Fed had to prevent the emergence of the speculation whose collapse led to recession and deflation.

Another answer to the question of why the Fed could not learn is that universally the assumption was that monetary policy was "easy" but ineffective. Hardy (1932, 55) wrote:

As soon as it was clear that the stock market boom was over and that the immediate future held threat of business depression, the Federal Reserve system adopted a policy of monetary ease. This policy was expressed both through large purchases of United States government securities and through unprecedented reductions of Reserve Bank rediscount and acceptance rates.

A misunderstanding of their primitive free reserves procedures led policy makers to believe that reductions in the discount rate were ineffective in spurring loan demand and borrowing at the window. Hardy (1932, 55) wrote, "In spite of these reductions, the volume of rediscounts fell to the lowest level in the history of the Reserve system." Policy makers did not understand the endogenous determination of borrowed reserves. Even with reductions in the discount rate, a leftward shift in the reserves demand schedule (R^d in figure 8.4) due to the recession would reduce borrowed reserves. Hardy (1932, 220–21, 239) continued:

The volume of credit outstanding is not susceptible of direct control. . . . The demand for short-term funds is inelastic and *highly* variable. In times when credit is being liquidated, the lowering of the rediscount rates has very little significance. The purchase of securities by the Reserve Banks has somewhat more effect on the volume of credit than have changes in the rediscount rate, but its primary incidence is on the rates charged in the open market. It does not produce corresponding changes in the amount of credit taken by business men. . . . The Reserve system . . . has . . . very little power to bring about an increase [in "the amount of credit extended to the public by the banks"] in time of depression. (italics in original)

In 1932, policy focused on the supply of reserves with little Federal Reserve System regard for the discount rate. Only New York lowered its discount rate, reducing it from 3.5 percent in January 1932 to 2.5 percent in July 1932. The other Reserve Banks left their discount rates at 3.5 percent. The exception was the Chicago Fed, which lowered its discount rate from 3.5 percent to 2.5 percent in June 1932. The reason, however, was because of a local banking panic (Calomiris and Mason 1997). Hardy's comment above that open market purchases affected rates in the New York money market rather than the local demand for credit undoubtedly was a factor in the lack of support by the regional Reserve Banks for the 1932 program of open market purchases.

Hardy (1932, 236) wrote, "The price data . . . show no evidence of any responsiveness to Reserve system policy. Any relationship which may exist . . . does not show itself in experiments which run only over periods of a year or two." Universally, in the United States, apart from Lauchlin Currie, everyone took the recession and the deflation as phenomena given to the Fed rather than caused by contractionary monetary policy. The only question was whether the Fed had the tools to offset them. The persistence of depression appeared to offer a negative answer.

The general belief that the transmission of monetary policy ran through the conduit of the banking system caused policy makers to conclude that "low" interest rates had failed to stimulate bank lending and expenditures of the public. With the publication of Keynes's (1936 [1964]) *General Theory of Employment, Interest and Money* in 1936, converts to Keynesianism expressed those ideas in terms of "elasticity pessimism"—the assumption that the behavior of economic agents was insensitive to relative prices in general and interest rates in particular. A Wicksellian explanation for the Great Contraction in terms of the Fed holding the real rate above the natural rate was out of the question.

In the mind of contemporaries, the 1929 stock market crash followed by the Depression cemented the idea that the Depression had resulted from an artificially high level of output supported by the speculative extension of credit. The collapse of a house of cards built on the speculative extension of credit initiated the Depression. The Fed came in for fierce criticism, but it was for allowing the speculative excess to get out of hand in 1927.

At the New York Fed, even with the benefit of hindsight, W. Randolph

Burgess, who had become deputy governor of the New York Fed in 1930, blamed the Depression on the collapse of speculative excess. Burgess (1936, 282–83) wrote:

> It now seems clear that the very economic strength and rapidity of progress of the country was its undoing, for it was this strength which supported and seemed to justify a vast speculation in securities, in which a surprisingly large number of people participated, on borrowed money. . . . This speculative orgy disturbed profoundly the country's economy.

Hawtrey (1932 [1962], 204–5) wrote of the near-universal explanation of the Depression:

> To contemporary observers of the successive trade cycles these phases were familiar and obvious. The financial crisis which was closely associated with the cycle came at the culminating point of a period of speculation or "over-trading," which was essentially an abuse of credit. Credit, having been over-expanded, had to contract, and traders who had been depending on credit were driven to liquidate. Forced sales caused a collapse of prices, and there ensued bankruptcies, general distrust and stagnation.
>
> The cycle was explained in terms not of money but of credit. The individual borrower was imprudent. He borrowed more than was in due proportion to his own capital; he bought at prices higher than he had any certain prospect of selling at; when his expectations were disappointed, he went bankrupt, and brought embarrassment to his creditors. If many people committed these imprudences at the same time, that was attributed to crowd psychology or herd instinct.
>
> The responsibility of the central bank was seen in the shape of the encouragement it gave to imprudent borrowers by its willingness to lend. The crisis was precipitated when a shortage of reserves compelled it to reverse this policy and to give a still more cogent example of unwillingness to lend.

Inside the Fed, everyone accepted this explanation for the Great Contraction. That explanation blamed the Fed for the Depression but not for the contractionary policy started in 1928. Instead, the blame originated in the Fed's not having begun a contractionary monetary policy sooner to stifle the speculative bubble before its collapse initiated the Depression. Participants in internal debates who at times advocated open market purchases had to argue that an "easy money" policy would revive the economy without sowing the seeds of another speculative bubble.

One way to understand the impossible journey required to travel from actual policy in the Depression to a stabilizing policy is to note the criticism by John Henry Williams of Keynes's *Treatise of Money*. Williams was the most distinguished economist at the New York Fed. A Harvard PhD, he joined the New York Fed in spring 1933 and, after 1934 divided his time between the New York Fed and Harvard. The criticism by Williams (1931, 578) of Keynes's use of the natural rate of interest shows how far economists were from thinking of the interest rate as part of the price system that organized the functioning of the macro economy:

> I cannot help feeling that this distinction between market rate and natural rate does not advance us at all. It sounds like a solution of the difficulty, but amounts merely to another way of stating the difficulty. If the natural rate were visible, the case might be different, but only the market rate is known. The natural rate is an abstraction; like faith, it is seen by its works.

What would have been required to give content to Williams's last statement that the natural rate "is seen by its works"? That is, what analytical framework would be required to attribute the Great Contraction to a monetary policy that kept the real rate above the natural rate? Nothing in the observation of the succession of events posed a contradiction to the speculative-excess explanations of real bills. Hawtrey (1932 [1962], vii) identified the problem: "The more intricate the subject, the more inadequate and indeed misleading is the empiricism which evolves practical precepts haphazard from the superficial uniformities of the past." What was required was an analytical framework with predictive ability and a series of experiments to test that framework. That combination came only in the post–World War II period.

What was required of such an analytical framework? First, monetary policy makers would have had to understand the difference between financial intermediation and money creation. As Representative James G. Strong (D-KS) said (US Congress 1932b, May 12, 26), "The people for and against this bill [An Act for Restoring and Maintaining the Purchasing Power of the Dollar] are composed . . . of two classes: the banker-minded who uses money as a commodity for making profit, and those who believe that money should be used as a measure of value for the purpose of exchange between the people who buy and sell their labor and their goods." Second, central bankers would have had to understand the difference between the price level and relative prices and would have had to accept their responsibility for the former. Third, they would have had to understand the interest rate as part of the price system. Furthermore, they would have had to accept that the price system worked well to provide for macroeconomic stability provided the central bank ensured an environment of nominal stability.

No doubt the human characteristic of an unwillingness to admit mistakes entailing horrific consequences reinforced the inability of policy makers to learn. Friedman (1970, 12) wrote:

> It was believed [in the Depression] . . . that monetary policy had been tried and had been found wanting. In part that view reflected the natural tendency for the monetary authorities to blame other forces for the terrible economic events that were occurring. The people who run monetary policy are human beings, even as you and I, and a common human characteristic is that if anything bad happens it is somebody else's fault.

Nevertheless, no one even outside the Fed mounted a sustained, effective attack on monetary policy as uniformly contractionary in the Depression.

The struggle to understand the Great Depression provided the stimulus for the creation of modern macroeconomics. However, only slowly following World War II did the key concepts of modern macroeconomics emerge. Only later and only slowly did economists systematize an understanding of the behavior of the economy controlled by the operation of the price system with the real (inflation-adjusted) interest rate as the intertemporal price of resources. Symptomatic of the intellectual void was the fact that the Fisher (1896) who understood the real rate of interest as the intertemporal price of resources in *Appreciation and Interest* (1896) never connected with the Fisher (1911 [1963]) of the quantity theory in *The Purchasing Power of Money*. That connection occurred only very slowly in the post–World War II period. With no understanding of the price system, early policy makers had no comprehension that markets determined well-defined values of real variables, especially a "natural" rate of interest (Friedman 1968 [1969]).

Only well into the second half of the twentieth century did economists come to think of monetary policy as a rule (reaction function) that controlled the interaction between the setting of the central bank's policy instrument (the interest rate on bank reserves or the funds rate) and the behavior of the economy. Early policy makers lacked the framework for understanding that they were setting the interest rate rather than acting as a reservoir of loanable funds. They had no way of comprehending the importance of a rule that would allow the price system to work by causing the real interest rate to track the natural rate of interest.

In the Volcker-Greenspan era, the FOMC understood the need for consistency as a prerequisite for shaping how markets responded to incoming information on the economy. That consistency made the term structure of interest rates into a stabilizing influence on economic activity. The distance separating the money policy of the early Fed and modern monetary policy appeared in the exchange between Representative Goldsborough and Governor Harrison. Harrison, always ready to pull out reserves in the event of evidence of a revival of speculation, was unwilling to commit to any sustained monetary stimulus. The exchange occurred in 1932 in the House hearings on the Goldsborough bill.

Representative Goldsborough argued that an articulated, explicit policy would render monetary policy potent through its constructive influence on expectations. In contrast, Harrison (US Congress 1932a, April 13, 462–71) took expectations as given and argued that banker pessimism about the future rendered impotent the stimulative actions (open market purchases) undertaken by the Fed:

HARRISON: That pressure [excess reserves] does not work and will not work in a period where you have bank failures, where you have panicky depositors, where you have a threat of huge foreign withdrawals, and where you have other disconcerting factors such as you have now in various sorts of legislative proposals which, however wise, the bankers feel may not be wise. You then have, in spite of the excess reserve, a resistance to its use which the reserve system can not overcome. . . .

GOLDSBOROUGH: In anything like normal times, specific directions to the Federal reserve system to use its power to maintain a given price level will tend to decrease very greatly these periods, or stop these periods of expansion and these periods of deflation which so destroy confidence and produce the very mental condition that you are talking about. . . . I do not think in the condition the country is in now we can rely upon the *action* of the Federal reserve system without the announcement of a *policy*. A banker may look at his bulletin on Saturday or on Monday morning and see that the Federal Reserve system has during the previous week purchased $25,000,000 worth of Government securities. But that does not restore his confidence under present conditions because he does not know what the board is going to do next week. . . . If this legislation . . . were passed, the Federal Reserve Board could call in the newspaper reporters and say that Congress has given us legislative directions to raise the price level to a certain point, and to use all our powers to that purpose, and we want you to announce to banks and public men at large that we propose to go into the market with the enormous reserves we now have available under the Glass-Steagall Act and buy $25,000,000 of Governments every day until the price approaches the level of that of 1926. . . . If the bankers and business men knew that was going to be the policy of the Federal reserve system, . . . it would restore confidence immediately . . . and the wheels of business would turn. . . . [italics added]

HARRISON: We have bought since the crash in the stock market approximately $800,000,000 to $850,000,000 of additional Government securities. . . . However, when after all the huge withdrawals of currency for hoarding purposes . . . we had in the system a relatively small proportion of free gold. . . . While I would have liked to proceed further and faster last year, I was adverse to doing so till we had the protection of the Glass-Steagall bill. . . . Perhaps we could have gone a little faster without clogging the banks by giving them too much excess reserve. If you give them too much excess reserve when they lack confidence it is just like flooding the carburetor of an automobile. . . .

Discounts in the system have gone down. . . . In our experience in the Federal Reserve system such a reduction in discounts or borrowings from the reserve banks operates as a real relaxation in the attitude of lending banks. . . . Let us suppose we should go. . . .

GOLDSBOROUGH: [interrupting] No; not whether you had determined to go so many millions further, but that you had announced a policy after the passage of this bill that you were going to raise the price level to a certain point and you were going to buy till that was done. That is a very different proposition.

HARRISON: Yes; I think so. I think it is a very much more difficult proposition because I do not think there is any one power or authority in the world that can say they are going to raise the price level. There are so many factors to be taken into consideration; unless you have control of all of them (even human psychology), you cannot be assured you can raise it. . . . I think to make a statement of that character [raise the price level] to the public and to the world would be one of the most unfortunate things the system could do, because primarily they would not be able to deliver all by themselves.

In later hearings, Representative Strong (US Congress 1932b, May 12, 28) testified similarly:

If the people of this country knew that through the Federal reserve system they were going to pour money out until there was a reaction, they would have a restoration of confidence. . . . I do not think they [powers given to the Fed by Congress] ought to be used to regulate the price of stocks and bonds. I think they ought to be used to stabilize the purchasing power of the dollar.

9.12. CONCLUDING COMMENT

What prevented the New York Fed from continuing to experiment with the procedures it had developed in the 1920s aimed at controlling the flow of credit as a countercyclical tool? Why did no one understand that the Fed itself was responsible for a sustained contractionary monetary policy? Even granted the hard-core real bills views of governors like McDougal at the Chicago Fed, why did the New York Fed fail to develop an effective challenge to those views?

Nothing in the experience of early policy makers provided the analytical framework required to separate financial intermediation from money creation and the association of monetary stability with procedures that allowed the price system to provide for macroeconomic stability. In the 1920s and 1930s, policy makers could always rationalize bad outcomes in terms of their existing framework. There was no framework capable of challenging their views. Only with the development of modern macroeconomics did the analytical tools exist to test hypotheses. There was a quantity theory tradition—disreputable in the eyes of policy makers because of its use by the populist/agrarian movement. Nevertheless, no one at the time put it into a form capable of challenging the Fed.

CHAPTER 10

The Roosevelt Era

Summary: A decade-long level of unemployment that imposed great human misery defined the Great Depression. Its length led to the Keynesian intellectual consensus that the price system failed to assure a level of aggregate demand consistent with full employment. Gordon and Wilcox (1981, 50) wrote, "Arguing against acceptance of an extreme monetarist interpretation [of the Great Depression] . . . [is] the apparent absence of any tendency for the mechanism of price flexibility to provide strong self-correcting forces as required by an approach that stresses monetary rules and opposes policy activism." To evaluate this viewpoint, one needs knowledge of the monetary standard during the 1930s.

There were two monetary standards during the Great Depression, although both were fiat money standards. During the first, the Great Contraction, from August 1929 through March 1933, apart from several months in 1932, monetary policy was unrelentingly contractionary. Fed procedures kept the real rate of interest above the economy's natural rate of interest. The second monetary standard lasted from April 1933 until spring 1942 when the Fed began to peg interest rates.

In the period after January 1934, the extent to which the Federal Reserve monetized gold inflows and the public demanded currency determined bank reserves. Bank demand for excess reserves then determined the amount of reserves available to support deposits. Through the standard reserves-money multiplier, the determination of money followed. Money interacted with a well-defined demand for money to determine nominal expenditure (output). The disruptive element then was twofold. First, two supply-side (markup) shocks forced up prices while monetary policy put a lid on nominal expenditure. The first shock began in May 1933 with the National Industrial Recovery Act, and the second shock began in 1935 with the Wagner Act. Output suffered, and by the start of World War II output remained well below a pre-Depression trend. The second disruptive element came from increases in reserve requirements in 1936 and 1937 that caused the banking system and money to contract.

The magnitude of the economic catastrophe represented by the Great Depression remains beyond comprehension. The decline in output per capita was unprecedented. It declined 34.1 percent from 1929 through 1933. In 1939, the figure was only slightly higher than in 1929 (figure 10.1). The unemployment rate, after peaking in May 1933 at 25.6 percent, declined only to rise again to 20 percent in June 1938 (figure 10.2). As late as April 1940,

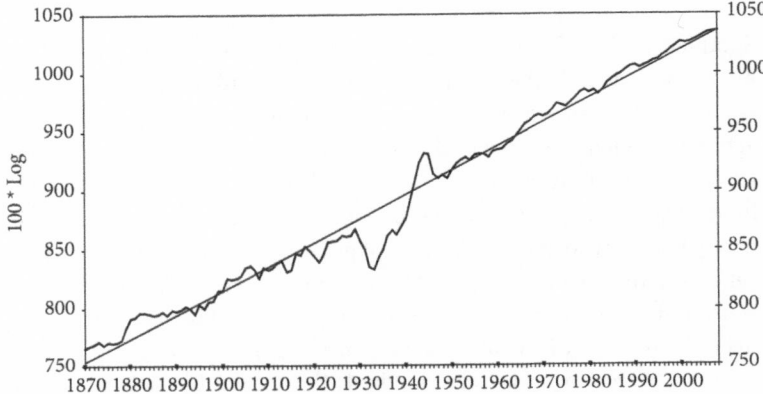

Figure 10.1. Real Output per Capita
Annual observations of one hundred times the logarithm of per capita real output and a trend line. Real output is real GNP from Balke and Gordon (1986) until 1929. Thereafter it is real GDP from the Commerce Department. "Resident population" used to calculate the per capita series is from Haver Analytics. The slope of the trend line equals 2.0.

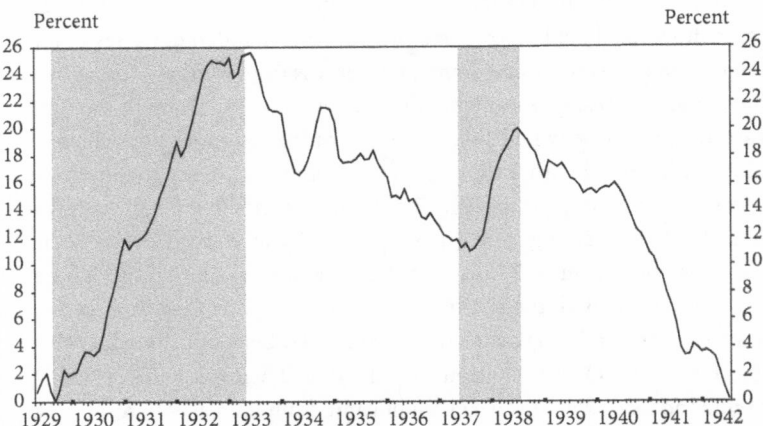

Figure 10.2. Unemployment Rate
Monthly observations of the unemployment rate. Shaded areas represent recessions. Heavy tick marks indicate December.
Sources: NBER Macrohistory Database; St. Louis FRED

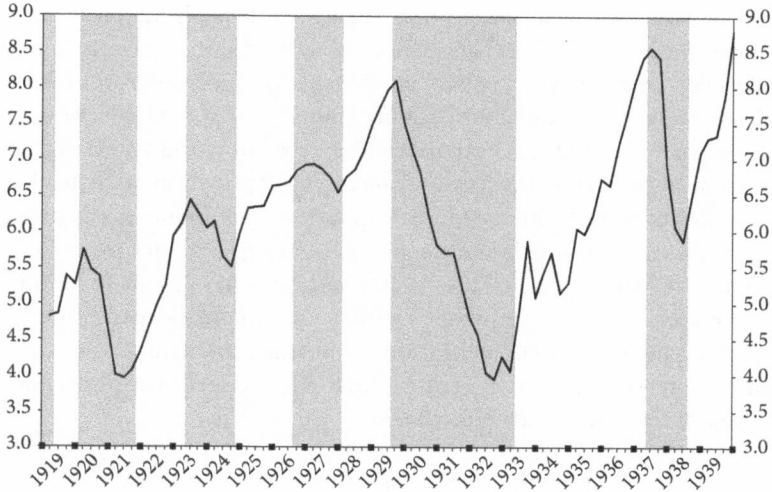

Figure 10.3. Industrial Production
Quarterly observations of industrial production. SA, 2012=100. Shaded areas represent
recessions. Heavy tick marks indicate fourth quarter.
Source: St. Louis FRED

it was 16 percent. In 1939Q4, industrial production was only slightly higher
than in 1929Q3 (figure 10.3).[1]

In the Depression, both the public and the banks wanted to become
more liquid. Given the vast amount of economic insecurity, the public's
precautionary demand for currency increased. Banks wanted excess reserves for two reasons. First, the Fed had basically shut down their two
principal sources of reserves adjustment: the call loan market and the discount window. Second, they had been burned by bank runs. From the perspective of the inelastic supply of reserves, the Fed returned the banking
system to the pre-Fed national banking system. Over the period from 1900
through 1913, national banks had held reserves averaging about 27 percent
of their deposits.[2] Banks would spend the 1930s attempting to rebuild that
reserve.

1. Based on the assumption that the secular trend in annual output growth was 1.9
percent, Ohanian (2013, 165–66) estimated that "per capita GNP was 26 percent below
trend in 1939, compared to its trough value of 38 percent below trend in 1933. In terms
of final expenditure, there was virtually no recovery in consumption of nondurables and
services, which was little changed between 1933 and 1939."

2. NBER Macrohistory Data Base, St. Louis FRED: "Ratio of Reserves to Net Deposits, National Banks, Central Reserve Cities (Reserve Cities other than Central) for
United States."

In the Great Contraction, from August 1929 through March 1933, the quantity-theoretic tension that drove down prices and output arose from the forced contraction of the banking system and bank deposits colliding with the increased demand for liquidity (money). In the remainder of the Depression from April 1933 until 1941 and the start of World War II, the tension arose in two ways. The first was the forced contraction of the banking system that occurred with the increase in reserve requirements in 1936 and 1937. The second was the limitation placed on the growth of bank reserves given by the extent to which the Fed monetized gold inflows. That limitation put a ceiling on the growth of money and nominal expenditure and output. Supply-side shocks in the form of the programs of the Roosevelt administration to force up wages and prices then produced cost-push shocks that depressed output and employment.[3]

10.1. ANOTHER MONETARY EXPERIMENT

The change in the monetary standard after March 1933 offered an extraordinary semicontrolled monetary experiment. Before then, reserves provision to banks and the marginal cost of reserves had been endogenously determined in the market for bank reserves through the interaction between a Fed reserves supply schedule and a banks' reserves demand schedule. After March 1933, reserves provision became exogenously determined. The characterization of the reserves market changed from figure 6.1 to figure 6.4. Nevertheless, despite the change in the nature of reserves provision, money growth and nominal output growth remained correlated.

According to traditional Keynesian views of money and its impotence, the positive correlation between money and nominal output should have disappeared. That is, from the Keynesian perspective, the correlation in the pre–March 1933 period with endogenous reserves supply arose because of the passive adjustment of nominal money to the public's real money demand. Temin (1976) expressed this view. As summarized by Schwartz (1981, 8), Temin argued that an exogenous decline in consumption and a fall in exports due to a worldwide depression in agriculture initiated the Great Depression. The decline in output produced a decline in real money demand, which the Fed accommodated through a decline in nominal money. If the Keynesian story is valid, the correlation between money growth and nominal output growth should have disappeared after March 1933 when reserves supply changed from passive to exogenous. It did not.

An understanding of the change in the monetary standard after March

---

3. George Selgin has an excellent series of essays entitled "The New Deal and Recovery" available in the blog post Alt-M.

1933 is also central to understanding a major puzzle of the Depression. If the Great Contraction was due to monetary disorder as evidenced by monetary contraction (figures 7.3 and 7.4) and deflation (figure 7.5), why did not the economy rebound to its potential level after March 1933? Did not the significant rates of growth of money and inflation that followed March 1933 indicate expansionary monetary policy? In terms of the Wicksellian framework, positive money growth should have indicated a real rate of interest below the natural rate.

An answer to these questions starts with the realization that after March 1933 bank reserves were exogenously given. As a consequence, so was nominal money and nominal expenditure (output). A reserves-money multiplier framework is relevant rather than a Wicksellian framework. First, it took time for banks to build up their excess reserves to achieve the liquidity they desired. That limited the money (deposit) creation associated with the given amount of reserves. The public desired to remain significantly more liquid than before the Great Contraction by holding currency. The resulting limitation on money creation limited nominal expenditure. Second, supply-side shocks created an unfavorable real-nominal breakdown in the given nominal expenditure growth.

A picture of this story can be shown graphically. Figure 10.4 shows the

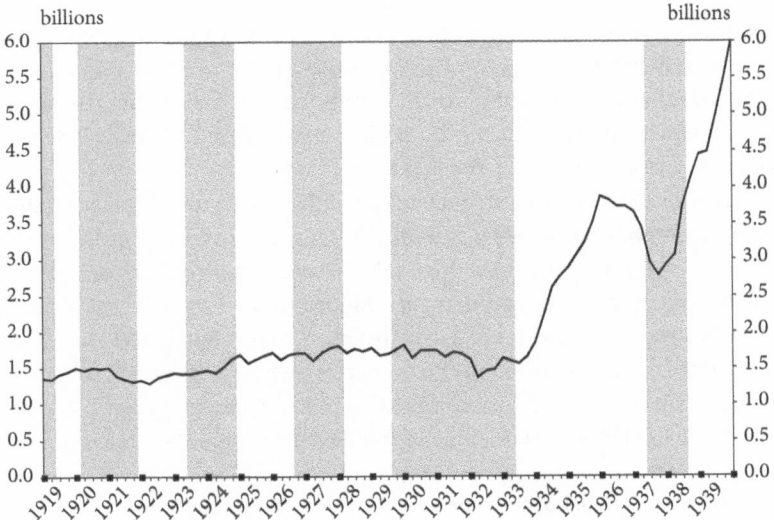

Figure 10.4. Reserves Adjusted

Quarterly observations of reserves adjusted for changes in reserve requirements, SA (see R. Anderson et al. 2003). Shaded areas represent NBER recessions. Heavy tick marks indicate fourth quarter.
Source: St. Louis FRED

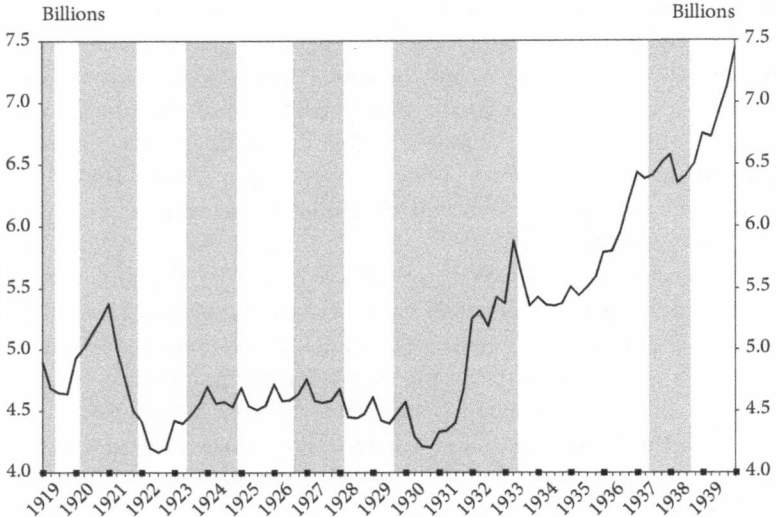

Figure 10.5. Currency
Quarterly observations of currency, NSA. Currency includes currency held in bank
vaults. Shaded areas indicate recessions. Heavy tick marks indicate
fourth quarter. *Source*: St. Louis FRED.

reserves of banks adjusted for the extent to which increases in reserve requirements removed reserves from serving as a base to expand deposits,
and conversely for decreases in reserve requirements. As shown in figure
9.7, starting in 1934, the Fed held constant its portfolio of securities. Growth
in the monetary base (currency plus bank reserves) came exclusively from
the gold inflows monetized by the Fed.[4]

The public's demand for currency reduced the extent to which increases
in the monetary base showed up as bank reserves (figure 10.5). The increase
in the excess reserves of banks reduced the extent to which increases in reserves showed up as increased deposits. Figure 10.6, "Free (Excess Minus
Borrowed) Reserves," which are excess reserves minus borrowed reserves,
tells the same story. After March 1933, the series is effectively excess reserves
because borrowed reserves are minimal. Figure 7.4 shows M1 growth, which
is exogenous. Real money demand also increased strongly (figure 10.7).

4. Monetization of gold occurs when the Treasury issues a gold certificate to the
Fed in return for adding to its Fed deposit. From January 1934 through January 1937,
gold certificates held by the Federal Reserve Banks increased at an annualized rate of 36
percent, and the monetary base increased at an annualized rate of 18.4 percent (Board of
Governors, *1935 Annual Report* and *1938 Annual Report*; Friedman and Schwartz 1963a,
appendix B, table B-3).

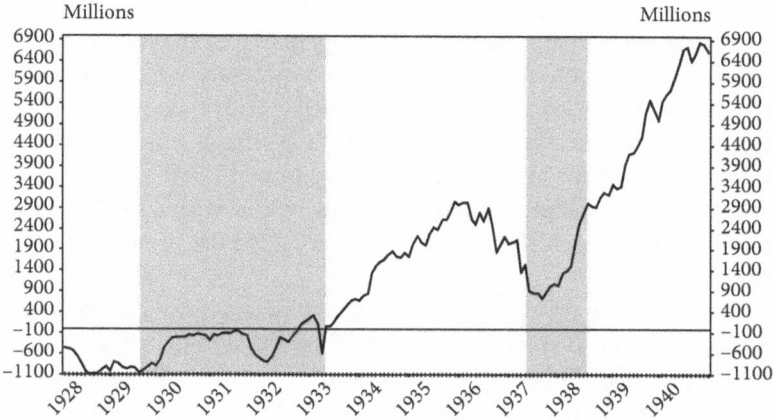

Figure 10.6. Free (Excess Minus Borrowed) Reserves

Observations are monthly. Free reserves are excess reserves minus borrowed reserves.
The series for excess reserves starts in 1929. They are small and stable until end 1930.
Shaded areas indicate recessions. Heavy tick marks indicate December. Data from
NBER Macrohistory Database and St. Louis FRED.

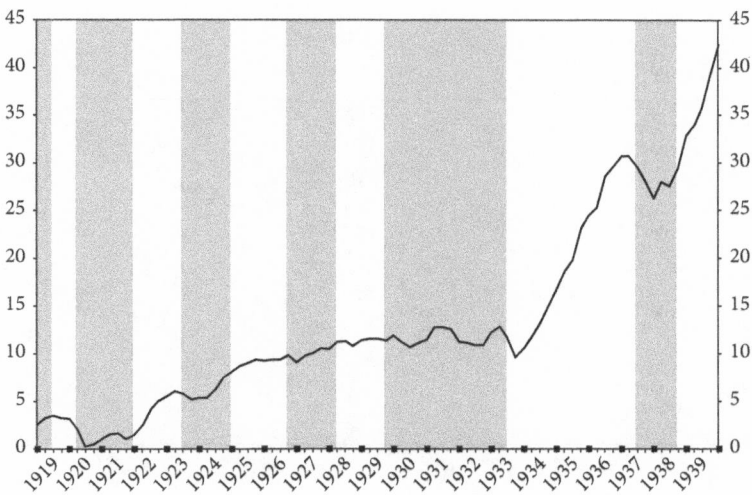

Figure 10.7. Real M1

Quarterly observations of real M1. Real M1 is nominal M1 divided by the CPI
(multiplied by 100 and subtracting 33). Shaded areas represent recessions. Heavy tick
marks indicate fourth quarter. M1 is from Friedman and Schwartz (1970), and CPI is
from NBER Macrohistory Database, St. Louis FRED.

To return to the original question, why did not output return rapidly to potential output after the cyclical trough in March 1933? As measured by industrial production, output did jump rapidly for a few months but then stalled (figure 10.3). Several authors have advanced the idea that the recovery stalled because passage of the National Industrial Recovery Act, NIRA (Cole and Ohanian 2004; Sumner 2015; and Weinstein 1981). With money determined exogenously and with velocity steady (figures 9.1 and 9.2), a cost-push shock that raised the price level would depress output.

Figure 10.8 shows real wages. They jumped sharply with the implementation of NIRA in summer 1933. Industrial production then ceased to expand (figure 10.3). Inflation jumped (figure 10.9). The real wage jumped again after passage of the Wagner Act (the National Labor Relations Act of 1935), which encouraged unionization, and the resulting wave of strikes and industrial strife. Again, inflation increased. In 1936 and 1937, the Board of Governors increased reserve requirements dramatically, and bank excess reserves declined (figure 10.4). Money growth ceased (figure 7.4). The economy went into recession in 1937Q2. The following expands on this summary.

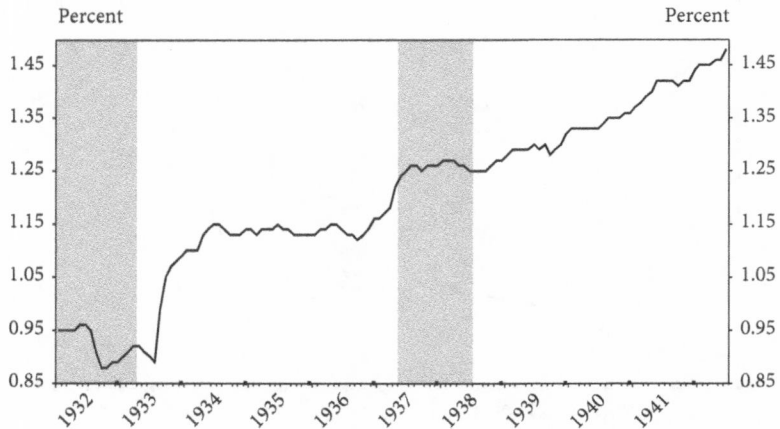

Figure 10.8. Real Wage
Monthly observations of real average hourly earnings, production workers, manufacturing for United States, 1957–59 dollars, SA. Shaded areas represent recessions. Heavy tick marks indicate December.
Sources: NBER Macrohistory Database; St. Louis FRED

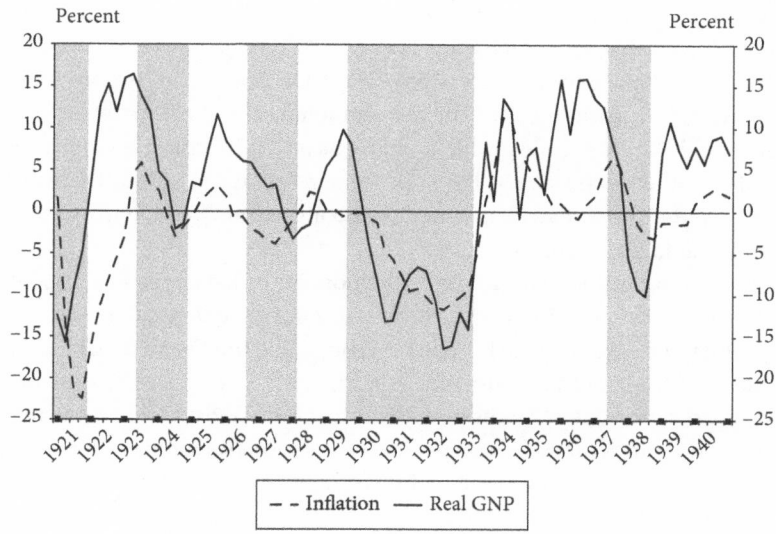

Figure 10.9. Inflation and Real GNP Growth
Quarterly observations of four-quarter percentage changes in real GNP and in the
GNP deflator. Heavy tick marks indicate fourth quarter. Shaded areas indicate NBER
recessions.
Source: Balke and Gordon (1986)

10.2. ENDING GOLD CONVERTIBILITY IN 1933:
SETTING OFF AND KILLING THE BOOM

Until spring 1933, the conservative mood of the country rendered monetary
reform and abandonment of gold convertibility politically impossible. In
early 1933, bank suspensions increased from the low level reached in fall
1932. On January 25, 1933, by publishing the names of the banks that had
received its loans, the Reconstruction Finance Corporation (RFC) created
doubts about their soundness. Until early February, deposit withdrawals from banks "represented largely transfers from weak to strong banks"
(Reeve 1943, 34). Sales of liquid assets from the weak banks, however,
caused a deterioration in the assets of the strong banks as well. On February
14, 1933, the governor of Michigan declared a statewide bank holiday to prevent withdrawals after closing a Detroit bank. His action set off bank runs
in adjoining states. The runs spread nationwide, and upon his inauguration
newly elected president Roosevelt declared a nationwide bank holiday.

The banking holiday in force for March 6–9, 1933, prohibited transactions in gold coins. Acting based on legislation passed March 9, 1933, on

March 10, 1933, Roosevelt issued an executive order prohibiting the export of gold except that licensed by the Treasury. On April 5, 1933, he issued an order that forbade private possession of gold. On April 19, at a press conference, Roosevelt announced: "The government will not allow the exportation of gold. . . . The whole problem before us is to raise commodity prices." The dollar then depreciated by 10 percent relative to sterling (Edwards 2018, 57). The nation had abandoned gold convertibility and in the popular mind the gold standard.

"It was not until January 1933 that the popular mood began to settle into an attitude of desperation which threw overboard the dogma of monetary orthodoxy" (Reeve 1943, 36). Populist groups like the Farmers' Union demanded inflation and a moratorium on farm debts. In Congress, a solid bloc of senators representing states in the South and the West and in rural areas supported their demands. At a special congressional session on March 16, 1933, the Roosevelt administration introduced a farm relief bill. Shover (1965, 20) wrote:

> Senator Frazier called for a refinancing of farm mortgages at 1½ percent through issuing fiat money; Senator Wheelock called for free and unlimited coinage of silver at 16–1. . . . An omnibus amendment sponsored by Senator Elmer Thomas, combining silver remonitization, alteration of the gold content of the dollar and the issuance of greenbacks, was soon coming to a vote. It seemed likely that inflationists could unite around it to create a Senate majority. If mandatory and uncontrolled inflation was to be avoided, the initiative lay with the White House.

Reeve (1943, 38–39) wrote similarly:

> Undoubtedly the majority sentiment in both houses of the first Roosevelt Congress favored inflation of some sort. Three minority blocs arose, one favoring paper money expansion, another wishing to "do something for silver," and the third sponsoring devaluation. This diversity in opinions enabled the President to delay action for six weeks, but no longer. On April 5, under the instigation of Senator Thomas, the Senate Committee on Agriculture and Forestry showed its dissatisfaction with the non-monetary nature of the pending administration farm bill, by voting, 15 to 0, to recommend immediate inflation of an unspecified nature. . . . Confronted with the imminent peril of either mandatory or unlimited discretionary inflation, President Roosevelt moved swiftly, taking the United States officially off the gold standard on April 19.

In a radio address on May 7, 1933, Roosevelt said, "The administration has the definite objective of raising commodity prices to such an extent that those who have borrowed money will, on the average, be able to pay in the same kind of dollar which they borrowed" (quoted in Fisher 1934, 347). The Thomas Amendment to the Farm Relief Act, enacted May 12, 1933, gave Roosevelt extensive powers to inflate. Roosevelt gained authority to (1) issue up to $3 billion in government debt and sell it directly to the Fed; (2) issue up to $3 billion in currency to retire government debt; (3) reduce the gold content of the dollar by up to 50 percent; (4) accept silver in payment of war debts and use the silver to issue silver certificates; and (5) mint silver dollars at a fixed ratio with the gold dollar. A front-page article on May 13, 1933, in the *New York Times* ran with the headline: "President signs farm bill, making inflation the law." The amendment was labeled the "inflation amendment" by the press, and Thomas replied, "My purpose is to add another plan to raise the commodity prices of the farmers and the producers of raw materials so they can live." By a vote of fifty-five to thirty-five, the Senate passed the Thomas Amendment on April 28, 1933 (Edwards 2018, 59 and 62).

In the radio address of May 7, 1933 (the Second Fireside Chat), Roosevelt noted that there were $120 billion in debt contracts outstanding with a gold clause. Devaluing the dollar by raising the dollar price of gold to raise commodity prices was not feasible as along as contracts with a gold clause were enforceable. Payment of such debts in gold would amount to an increase in the dollar amount due by the amount of the devaluation and would create widespread bankruptcies (Edwards 2018, 62–63). On May 29, 1933, Congress outlawed the gold clause in public and private contracts. As described by Shover (1965, 22), Roosevelt's conservative financial advisers opposed the inflationists.[5] The provisions of the Thomas Amendment were made optional. Nevertheless, as Fisher (1934, 360) phrased it, "the great and discretionary powers for reflation which Congress had granted" Roosevelt impacted public psychology about inflation.

Roosevelt changed the expectation of deflation to one of inflation. Abandoning the gold peg to the dollar was the cornerstone. Hardy (1932, 109)

---

5. Fed policy makers felt passionate about the dangers of inflation. Carl Snyder (1940, 331), a quantity theorist at the New York Fed, wrote:

> One symptom of this money madness is the frequently expressed view that we need a "good inflation" to end the depression which we have suffered for a decade. But inflation can never cure anything. The effect of a large increase in the quantity of money—whether greenbacks or deposits—is to give a temporary feeling of elation, much the same as that of several drinks of good whiskey.

had written, "No matter how sound a basis the budgetary and trade situation may afford for the establishment of the gold standard in any country, an essential step in stabilization is the creation in the public mind of a habit of thinking of the currency unit as the equivalent of a definite amount of gold." Going off gold changed that "habit." Hawtrey (1932 [1962], 273) wrote, "Deflation, however, is in one respect more difficult to understand [than inflation], for it arises from a change in the value of gold, whereas inflation, as soon as it goes beyond moderate limits, is clearly revealed in a change in the value of money relative to gold." Deflation with a fixed dollar price of gold was mysterious. However, the association of inflation with an increasing dollar price of gold seemed much more obvious.

The depreciation of the dollar by one-third of its previous gold value by mid-July, which raised commodity prices, and Roosevelt's charismatic confidence changed inflationary psychology from one of deflation to one of inflation. Harris (1933, 619) wrote:

> If once, the downward movement of prices is definitely checked, confidence may revive. But so long as prices decline, confidence remains at a low ebb; business men, instead of borrowing, will repay debts to their maximum capacity, and—under these circumstances—the decline of prices continues. The decline of prices is damaging to business enterprise because necessary adjustments in costs are not made.

Unfortunately, the change in psychology was not consistently supported and at times was threatened by the policies of the Fed and the administration.

Scott Sumner supported his hypothesis about the role of gold in promoting contractionary monetary policy by demonstrating how responsive financial markets were to news about abandonment of the gold peg. Especially, the behavior of the stock market offered evidence that Roosevelt's commitment to raising commodity prices changed public psychology from pessimism to optimism. For the month of January 1933, the Dow averaged 99. It declined to 91 in February but only just recovered to 101 in April, almost a month *after* Roosevelt's inauguration (figures from Sumner 2015, table 5.1). Sumner (2015, 187) wrote:

> The Dow increased by more than 65 percent between April 18 and July 3, 1933, and almost 90 percent of that increase occurred on the 10 news days shown in Table 5.2. Those "10 news days" all contained news about Roosevelt's intention to inflate. The largest four changes shown by date were as follows: 1) 4/19 "US dollar is floated" (9.0%); 2) 4/20 "Inflation

bill introduced" (5.8%); 3) 4/29 "Inflation bill passed" (6.2%); [the reference is to the Thomas Amendment, which provided various ways in which President Roosevelt could force the Fed to print money] 4) 6/19 "FDR rejects currency stabilization at WMC," World Monetary Conference (6.4%).

The World Monetary Conference (the London Economic Conference) had been convened in June 1933 to restore the international gold standard. The comments of Neville Chamberlain, chancellor of the British Exchequer, summarized the distrust of the variable exchange rates that came with the breakdown of the international gold standard (cited in Fisher 1934, 352): "The immediate objective should be to secure approximate stabilization between the currencies of the principal countries of the world in order that trade may not be hampered by violent, unpredictable fluctuations of basic currencies." On June 22, 1933, the American delegation shocked the conference with the following statement (cited in Fisher 1934, 353):

> The reason why it ["stabilization of currencies"] is considered untimely is because the American government feels that its efforts to raise prices are the most important contribution it can make and that everything that would interfere with those efforts and possibly cause a violent price recession would harm the Conference more than the lack of an immediate agreement for temporary stabilization.

On July 3, 1933, Roosevelt sent the conference a message rejecting the "old fetishes of so-called international bankers" in favor of "the kind of dollar which a generation hence will have the same purchasing power and debt-paying power as the dollar value we hope to attain in the near future." On July 5, 1933, the American delegation issued an official statement stating that "the first task is to restore prices to a level at which industry and above all agriculture can function profitably" (cited in Fisher 1934, 356 and 358). That is, the priority was reflation. However, the July 5 comment makes clear that Roosevelt focused on reflation by raising relative prices.

Powered by a change in psychology from deflation to inflation, the economy took off (Eggertsson 2008; Temin and Wigmore 1990). From April 1933 through July 1933, boosted by the depreciation of the dollar, commodity prices jumped 14.4 percent.[6] From a base in March 1933 through July 1933, industrial production jumped 57.4 percent, not annualized (figure

6. Producer price index for all commodities monthly, NSA, 1982=100, St. Louis FRED.

10.3).[7] However, by fall, the economy stalled. From July through October 1933, commodity prices rose by only 3.4 percent. From July through November 1933, industrial production fell by 18.9 percent. In July 1935, it had not quite reached the earlier July 1933 peak. What happened?

Monetary policy was only tepidly supportive of the recovery. Pressured by the Treasury, the Fed did undertake some open market purchases, and bank reserves and free reserves increased moderately (figures 10.4 and 10.6). Only in 1934Q1 did M1 just exceed its 1933Q1 value, $20.7 billion versus $20.3 billion. Only in 1935Q3 did M1 at $26.7 billion exceed its three-year average from 1926 through 1928 of $26.2 billion. With prices rising and little change in M1, real M1 fell (figure 10.7).

Harrison (HPNY, Confidential Files, September 16, 1933, 1) expressed his position to Governor Black of the Federal Reserve Board that monetary policy was easy and that the only reason for open market purchases was to head off pressure for the issue of greenbacks:

> We have now, largely through open market operations and a return flow of currency, created approximately $700,000,000 of excess reserves and a very easy money market position. . . . Our operations to date . . . have resulted in placing the banks of the country as a whole in a position to make a very substantial expansion of bank credit as soon as there is a demand for it by borrowers entitled to have it on the basis of good credit risk. . . . Making weekly purchases . . . is an . . . especially weighty factor in minimizing the risk of drastic methods of currency inflation, such as greenbacks.

Fed policy makers maintained their view that the price level was simply an average of relative prices and that increases in the price level reflected unsustainable increases in relative prices. Allan Sproul (SPNY, "Exchange Stability and Domestic Recovery," June 22, 1933, 1) at the New York Fed, later president of the New York Fed, and E. M. Despres wrote W. R. Burgess:[8]

> Growth of a speculative structure built on hopes of currency depreciation which cannot properly be realized: There are obvious limits to a movement built on speculative hopes of currency depreciation unless a complete collapse of the currency is to be contemplated. The longer such hopes are cultivated the more dangerous they are. Either they must be fed by increasingly vigorous hints of inflation to come or they will

---

7. Industrial production, SA, 2012=100, St. Louis FRED.

8. "SPNY" indicates material from the Sproul papers in the archives of the New York Fed.

give rise to a speculative reaction which again may check the recovery in business.

Perhaps, even without supportive monetary expansion the economy could still have recovered quickly to full employment. However, the policies of the Roosevelt administration created cost-push shocks that limited the extent to which the nominal expenditure of the public appeared as real expenditure. Figure 7.2 shows four-quarter percentage changes in nominal and real GNP. The excess of nominal over real growth appears especially in two periods. Over the four quarters 1933Q3 through 1934Q2, the excess of nominal over real growth was 13.7 percentage points (average of quarterly annualized growth rates). Over the four quarters 1936Q3 through 1937Q2, the comparable excess was 6.8 percentage points. These spikes in inflation appear in figure 10.9.

Figure 10.8 shows how these periods corresponded to supply shocks in the form of significant increases in real wages. In the first interval, the unemployment rate averaged 19.7 percent and in the second 12.6 percent. With this level of unemployment, there should have been no price or wage inflation. The price level and real wages should have continued to decline. The first inflation shock corresponded to implementation of the National Industrial Recovery Act (NIRA) and the second to the Wagner Act.

In a fateful decision, Roosevelt rejected the populist movements to deal with deflation and depression through fiat money creation. The Roosevelt administration's commitment to raise prices appeared through programs that entailed direct intervention in markets to raise relative prices. In agriculture, that meant reducing acreage planted. In the business sector, it meant passage of NIRA, which raised prices through price-setting agreements and cartelization of industries. In labor markets, it meant encouraging unionization as represented by NIRA and later by the Wagner Act. Such measures would interact with a nonaccommodative monetary policy to extend the Depression through the start of World War II.

The National Industrial Recovery Act, signed June 16, 1933, relaxed the Sherman Antitrust Act to allow "codes of fair competition." The act allowed cooperating industries to set "minimum rates of pay" and fix prices through trade associations. The act also guaranteed the right of labor to organize and bargain collectively. The result was "a massive wave of union organizing punctuated by employer and union violence and recognition strikes" (Wikipedia 2019). "On July 19, 1933, an impatient Roosevelt administration decided to force immediate adoption of the NIRA through the Blue Eagle program" (Sumner 2015, 212). Over the next three days, the Dow fell 19 percent.

Sumner (2015, 207) noted that nominal wages did not increase between March and July 1933 despite rising prices. They then increased by 22.3 percent over the next two months "after President Roosevelt issued an executive order creating the Blue Eagle program, which mandated that participating firms reduce hours by 20 percent with no change in total weekly wages." Ohanian (2013, 169) wrote, "The NIRA was purposefully designed to limit competition and raise prices in most of the nonfarm private economy. The NIRA accomplished this by permitting industry to cartelize provided that industry immediately raised wages and agreed to collective bargaining with workers." Cole and Ohanian (2004) calculated that about two-thirds of the shortfall from trend of output in 1939 came from NIRA's cartel policies.

Sumner (2015, 224, 285) also noted that after the Supreme Court declared NIRA unconstitutional on May 27, 1935, output rose strongly:

> During the twenty-two months from July 1933 to May 1935 the economy moved forward in a slow and erratic fashion, with industrial production actually declining slightly. Over the following twenty-two months, industrial production soared by nearly 44 percent. The December 30, 1935, *New York Times* (p. 25) noted that "trade revival started almost immediately after the 'New Deal's' vital machinery had been shattered on May 27 in the courts."

10.3. RETURN TO A GOLD PEG

In fall 1933, with the recovery stalling and continued unrest in the farm belt, Roosevelt sought to increase the prices of agricultural products. Harrison (HPNY, Confidential Files, "Telephone Conversation with Governor Norman," November 15, 1933, 1) "told Norman of the meeting at the White House. . . . The President, he said, had been in a very difficult position because of the unrest in the agricultural sections and had committed himself to a rise in farm prices. Governor Harrison added that the situation in the West was bad and that great pressure had been exerted from that quarter on the President."

Henry Morgenthau Jr., initially head of the Federal Farm Board in the Roosevelt administration and in 1934 secretary of the Treasury, introduced Roosevelt to George F. Warren, a professor of agricultural economics at Cornell. "According to him [Warren], if the government raised the price of gold, higher prices for cotton, wheat, corn, rye, barley, eggs, hogs, and other products would increase almost immediately and in the same proportion as the increase in the price of gold" (Edwards 2018, 70). In October 1933, Roosevelt began a gold purchase program with the intention of raising the price of agricultural commodities by raising the dollar price of gold. Because the Reconstruction Finance Corporation financed the purchases by issuing debt, the program had no impact on money. M1 growth did not support the surge in real GNP growth in 1933Q2 and 1933Q3 of 32.1 percent and 35.8 percent annualized growth, respectively (Balke and Gordon 1986).

Roosevelt's gold-buying program initially entailed buying newly mined domestic gold and then gold on the world market. Sumner (2015, 235–66) evaluated the program. Because the magnitude of gold purchases was so small relative to the size of the world's stock of gold, it could not realistically have been expected to raise the price of gold. However, markets could have interpreted the program as indicative of the Roosevelt administration's desire to depreciate the value of the dollar and then devalue it. The program did succeed in raising the dollar price of gold to a level of around $32.00 an ounce.

At the same time, the program caused consternation in the conservative financial community (Fisher 1934, 360). In November 1933, Treasury Secretary William Woodin, Undersecretary Dean Acheson, and Treasury adviser Oliver Sprague resigned. "Three days later, 40 orthodox economists, all 'authorities on money and banking,' organized the Economists' National Committee on Monetary policy" (Reeve 1943, 58). Alfred E. Smith (former governor of New York) attacked "baloney dollars." Uncertainty over depreciation of the dollar put pressure especially on the French franc, which was still pegged to gold. Sumner (2015, 253) suggested that the resulting private hoarding of gold depressed commodity prices abroad, potentially outweighing any positive effects from a depreciating dollar.

The New York Fed reflected the views of the financial community. Sproul (SPNY, memo to Governor Harrison, "Federal Reserve Policy," October 25, 1933, 1, 3) wrote:

> 1. The Government maintains its twin goals of raising prices and relieving the burdens of debtors. 2. The Government evidently persists in believing that, given the political facts of the case, the only feasible way to attain these goals is by monkeying with the dollar. Its most recent effort in this direction apparently is based upon the Warren idea that prices are raised, more or less automatically, by reducing the gold value of the dollar. It has been pretty well demonstrated, both in theory and in practice, that a rise in prices which is solely or largely a reflection of depreciation of the currency, and anticipation of further depreciation, causes speculation to take the place of trade and production, and ultimately collapses. . . . I am becoming more and more of the opinion that we are

traversing the usual road of inflation, while continuing to talk of sound money and unimpaired Government credit.

Lauchlin Currie (1934d) wrote a memo to Marriner Eccles: "The business and banking groups are practically unanimous in their explanation of the present hesitancy in business activity. It is 'lack of confidence.' It is said that 'If the President should declare that the budget will be balanced by July 1, 1935, and that the dollar will be stabilized immediately at its present value and definitely pegged at this figure, business confidence will immediately start the wheels of industry humming.'"

Pegging the value of the dollar at a depreciated rate in terms of gold would appease both conservative critics who disliked a variable, increasing dollar price of gold and the inflationists who wanted to raise prices. Using the authority granted by the Thomas Amendment to the New Deal's farm relief bill, on January 31, 1934, with the Gold Reserve Act of 1934, Roosevelt devalued the dollar by decreasing its gold content. The act set a fixed price at which the government would purchase gold. An undervalued dollar and political unrest in Europe caused gold to flow into the United States. The Fed monetized those inflows, and the money stock rose.

10.4. GOVERNOR MARRINER ECCLES

Roosevelt appointed Mariner S. Eccles chairman of the Federal Reserve Board on November 15, 1934. An understanding of his views, which on matters of monetary policy conformed to the views of other Fed policy makers, explains the key decision to raise required reserves in 1936 and 1937.

10.4.1. Pushing on a String

Governor Eccles (US Congress 1935a, March 13, 260) expressed the dominant view: "I think that the control of inflation is a far less difficult problem than the control of deflation." He believed that the intransigence of deflation came from the unwillingness of borrowers to borrow and spend and of the public to spend out of their money balances. Eccles (US Congress 1935a, March 13, 257, and March 15, 312) testified:

> The amount of the excess reserves held by the banks, the low discount rate, and hence the low rates that are prevailing for commercial paper, for high-grade bonds, industrial and municipal, and for Government securities, are indicative of the excess supply of money and credit in relation to the demand for it. . . . In order to expand the use of money which

is necessary for recovery, either those holding deposits in banks must be willing to spend their funds, which would increase the velocity of the total existing deposits, or borrowers who can command bank credit must be willing to go to the banks and borrow funds which they will spend, or a combination of both is necessary.

Certainly, interest rates could not be very much lower than they are now. The volume of money that is not in use is very great, and to increase it, it seems to me, would accomplish nothing toward either price raising or increasing business activity.

Or, succinctly, Eccles (US Congress 1935a, March 20, 411) testified, "When the community begins to pay its debt to the banks, it extinguishes money, deposits currency, and if that process of deflation gets under way it is more or less self-generating and it is very difficult to stop it." The boom-bust cycle was inherent to a capitalistic society. Governor Eccles (US Congress 1935a, March 18, 396) testified, "In our past history we have had periods of prosperity by the process of building up debt and then periods of depression by the process of bankruptcy and the extinguishing of debt. That has been true of all capitalistic countries."

Eccles (US Congress 1935a, March 15, 321–22) responded negatively to the suggestion that the Fed should undertake open market purchases of government securities. Congressman Farley asked Eccles, "In your judgment, we do not need any more circulating medium right now?" Eccles responded, "In my judgment, you cannot possibly force out and keep in circulation more currency than you have now. . . . The currency would go out . . . whatever amount the Government paid out in currency to retire its bonds; but the currency would immediately go into the banks and from the banks into the Federal Reserve banks and be destroyed, and you would just have additional reserves, additional excess reserves."

Eccles (1935, 50) submitted a table showing the income velocity of money in response to a request from Representative Cross (US Congress 1935a, March 13, 252), who asked, "What is the relation between actual currency . . . and check money and its velocity?" (see table 10.1). Obviously, giving content to the quantity theory would require more than a table of numbers. It would require the association of money with the behavior of the Federal Reserve not the independent liquidation of debts by banks.

10.4.2. Required Reserves, Excess Reserves, and Credit Inflation

Title II of the Banking Act of 1935 gave the Board of Governors the power to change the required reserves of banks "to prevent injurious credit

Table 10.1. Statement on National Income, Money, and Income Velocity

	National Income, Copeland[1] (Billions)	National Income, Department of Commerce (Billions)	Money[2] (Billions)	Income Velocity Based on Copeland (I÷III) (Times Per Year)	Income Velocity Based on Department of Commerce (II÷III) (Times Per Year)	Percentage Change in Income, Copeland	Percentage Change in Income, Department of Commerce	Percentage Change in Money	Percentage Change in Income Velocity, Copeland	Percentage Change in Income Velocity, Department of Commerce
	1	*2*	*3*	*4*	*5*	*6*	*7*	*8*	*9*	*10*
1921	56.8		21.7	2.62						
1922	60.3		21.5	2.81		+6.2		-1.2	+7.3	
1923	68.9		22.6	3.04		+14.3		+5.5	+8.2	
1924	70.2		23.1	3.04		+1.9		+1.8		
1925	74.5		24.6	3.03		+6.1		+6.7	-0.3	
1926	78.8		25.3	3.11		+5.8		+2.9	+2.6	
1927	80.9		26.0	3.11		+2.7		+2.8		
1928	83.3		26.4	3.16		+3.0		+1.3	+1.6	
1929	87.0	82.3	26.4	3.29	3.12	+4.4		+0.1	+4.1	
1930		75.8	25.4		2.98		-7.9	-3.8		-4.5
1931		63.3	23.8		2.66		-16.5	-6.3		-10.7
1932		49.7	20.5		2.42		-21.5	-13.9		-9.0
1933		46.8	19.9		2.35		-5.8	-2.9		-2.9
1929–33							-43.1	-24.6		-24.7

Source: US Congress (1935a, March 20, 430)

1 Less imputed nonmonetary incomes.

2 Deposits subject to check plus cash outside banks as of June 30.

expansion or contraction." Although the language mentioned "contraction," the concern was with "expansion." Eccles feared an expansion in credit that would put the United States back where it was in 1929 and produce another speculative collapse. Eccles (US Congress 1935a, March 13, 260) testified: "With the excess reserves now available, if the credit expansion should commence and continue with the use of the present existing reserves, you could get a business activity and a price level substantially higher, I think, than we had in 1926, 1927, 1928 or 1929." Although the Thomas Amendment to the Banking Act of 1933 allowed for raising required reserves, it required declaration of an emergency and consent of the president. (The provision to allow raising reserve requirements was a safeguard to deal with the possible exercise of the Thomas Amendment to the Agricultural Adjustment Act allowing the Treasury to create reserves and money by selling bonds directly to the Fed.)

As seen by the Fed, the problem was that with a high level of excess reserves it did not possess sufficient government securities to sell to extinguish all the excess reserves. Eccles (US Congress 1935a, March 13, 295–96) also highlighted the gold inflows:

> Assuming that the excess reserves of member banks greatly exceeded the amount of Government bonds which the Reserve banks held and the bills which they held . . . there would be no way of reducing or wiping out their excess reserves upon which credit inflation is built. . . . Additional gold may continue to come into the country, which would also tend to increase the reserves. So that the banking system could build up excess reserves. . . . You would have a potential agency for bank-credit inflation that would simply be terrific and no open-market operation could control it.

Eccles believed that he had invented independently the Keynesian idea of government spending to offset the failure of private spending to assure full employment. However, he also held real bills views. Eccles (US Congress 1935a, March 19, 405) testified: "One of the principal troubles or difficulties that brought about the depression was . . . the inequitable distribution of income which contributed to a speculative situation in the security markets and to an expansion of productive capacity out of relationship to the ability of the people of the country to consume under the existing distribution of income."

10.5. THE 1936–37 RECESSION

After the supply-side shock that pushed up real wages and inflation with the enactment of NIRA in June 1933, the real wage stabilized, and inflation fell to zero (figures 10.8 and 10.9). The economy then began a rapid recovery. From 1935Q3 through 1937Q1, quarterly values of four-quarter real GNP averaged 13.2 percent, up from 6.9 percent for the average of the quarterly values over the interval 1934Q1 through 1935Q2 (figure 10.9). However, the Fed and the political system would again hammer the economy with contractionary monetary policy and another supply-side shock.

With the devaluation of the dollar in January 1934 and the return to a fixed purchase price, gold flowed into the United States and bank reserves increased (figure 10.4). Given the desire of banks to rebuild liquidity, they built up their excess reserves (figure 10.6, labeled "Free [Excess Minus Borrowed] Reserves" but basically showing excess reserves when the series is positive). Friedman and Schwartz (1963a, 539) wrote, "Throughout [the period after March 1933], the high level of the discount rate relative to market rates reinforced the banks' reluctance (bred of their 1929–33 experience) to rely on borrowing from the Federal Reserve Banks for liquidity and led them instead to rely on cash reserves in excess of legal requirements and on short-term securities."

Fed policy makers viewed the buildup of excess reserves with alarm and bided their time until the Roosevelt administration was willing to reduce them. That would mean neutralizing them by increasing required reserve ratios on bank deposits. The Banking Act of 1935 reorganized the Federal Reserve System to give majority control to the Federal Open Market Committee (FOMC), which gave voting rights to all seven members of the Board of Governors and five regional Reserve Bank presidents. It transferred power away from the regional Reserve Banks to the FOMC. In the popular imagination, it transferred power away from the New York banks and the regional Reserve Banks, especially New York, thought of as having caused the Depression through encouraging speculation. Power then resided in Washington and the government.

Henry Steagall, chairman of the House Banking and Currency Committee, introduced the House version of the Banking Act.[9] Duncan Fletcher held extensive hearings on the bill. Both House and Senate versions gave the Board the power to change reserve requirements. Fletcher's comments

9. Representative T. Alan Goldsborough introduced an amendment to require the monetary authority to restore the price level to its 1921–29 average and then to maintain it at that level. By a vote of 128 to 122, the amendment was defeated (R. Phillips 1992, 38).

in the *Congressional Record* (April 22, 1935, 6104, cited in R. Phillips 1992, 36) foretold the logic of their use shortly thereafter when the Board raised reserve requirements in 1936 and 1937:

> It is common knowledge . . . that there now lies within the hands of bankers the potential makings for one of the most stupendous inflations this or any other Nation has ever experienced. And experience teaches us that banker control of monetary policy will probably give us an equally devastating financial whirlwind when the bubble is pricked.

To preempt the emergence of speculative excess, the Fed needed to raise required reserves to impound excess reserves. It would then have sufficient government securities to sell to force banks into the discount window. With banks in the discount window, an increase in the discount rate would be effective against "credit inflation." From March 1935 through March 1937, the Dow Jones rose from 100 to 187.1 (NBER Macrohistory Data Base, St. Louis FRED). Just as had been the case with the 1920–21 recession and the Depression, the New York Fed believed that tardiness to prick a speculative bubble had allowed speculative excess to proceed to the point at which its collapse caused depression. Harrison would not allow a third repetition of that presumed mistake.

As recorded by Harrison, New York Fed director Mr. Woolley (HPC, Executive Committee, February 18, 1935, 188) recounted:[10]

> He [Woolley] has a very keen memory of being terribly scalded during the vestibule period of the golden age. When we started to purchase Government securities in 1927 . . . Governor Strong expressed the view that if, when our purpose had been accomplished, we were not as insistent upon selling as we had been upon buying, we were going to drag the country into a terrible situation. We tried nobly to follow that course . . . but when it came time to act by putting up the discount rate [in early 1929], which we had been taught was the signal to reverse and to invoke remedies, we were denied the right of action.

E. A. Goldenweiser (1937, 3), director of research at the Board, wrote:

> Experience shows that monetary measures for maintaining business stability are most effective when applied in the early stages of expan-

10. "HPC" refers to the George Leslie Harrison collection at the Columbia University Rare Book Room.

sion. Timeliness of action is the essence of the matter. When speculative boom psychology prevails monetary restraints lose their effectiveness, and there is no evidence that monetary methods alone can arrest a deflation when it is under way, certainly not without support from Government activity. It is, therefore, possible that this is the one time when by proper action the Board may prevent the recurrence of a dangerous expansion with its consequent collapse.

Banks in the financial centers disliked the accumulation of excess reserves for the same reason that they disliked open market purchases by the Fed. Their concern was that excess reserves and open market purchases lowered the interest rate on the securities they held (Epstein and Ferguson 1984). Harris (1933, 621) noted that in recession "opposition to the open market policy of the reserves system arises."

In the real bills spirit, the Board acted to prevent emergence of a speculative bubble by raising required reserves. On July 14, 1936, the Board voted a 50 percent increase in required reserves ratios effective August 15. On January 30, 1937, the Board announced another increase in required reserves ratios of 33⅓ percent with half the increase effective March 1 and the other half in May 1. (At central reserve city banks, the required reserve ratio went from 13 percent to 19.5 percent on August 15, 1936, to 22.75 percent on March 1, 1937, and to 26 percent on May 1, 1937.) On December 23, 1936, the Treasury started sterilizing increases in gold from foreign inflows and domestic production. The Treasury sterilized gold purchases through financing them by borrowing from the public rather than by issuing gold certificates to the Fed.[11]

The August 1936 *Federal Reserve Bulletin* (613, 614, and 616) reported:

This action [increased reserve requirements] eliminates as a basis of possible injurious credit expansion a part of the excess reserves. . . . The present is an opportune time for the adoption of such a measure. . . . Later action when some member banks may have expanded their loans and investments and utilized their excess reserves might involve the risk of bringing about a severe liquidation and of starting a deflationary cycle. . . . The increase in reserve requirements is not a reversal of the easy-money policy pursued by the System since the beginning of the depression.

11. From January 1937 through January 1938, gold certificates held by the Fed declined slightly while the monetary base increased by only 3.7 percent (Board of Governors, *1935 Annual Report* and *1938 Annual Report*; Friedman and Schwartz 1963a, appendix B, table B-3).

The February 1937 *Federal Reserve Bulletin* (95) reported:

The Board of Governors of the Federal Reserve System today increased reserve requirements for member banks by 33⅓%. . . . By its present action the Board eliminates as a basis of possible credit expansion an estimated $1,500,000,000 of excess reserves which are superfluous for the present or prospective needs of commerce, industry, and agriculture and which, in the Board's judgment, would result in an injurious credit expansion if permitted to become the basis of a multiple expansion of bank credit.

The Board of Governors' *1938 Annual Report* (published in 1939, 22) pointed to the high level of bank excess reserves that "would make it possible for a speculative situation to get under way that would be beyond the power of the System to check or control."

The increase in reserve requirements received widespread support from economists. Irving Fisher "applauded the increases in reserve requirements" (Reeve 1943, 167). All of Viner's Treasury "brain trust," originally assembled in 1934, agreed. "As the recovery proceeded, Viner, Currie, Williams, and White agreed in considering the huge amount of excess reserves piling up in the banking system as the most relevant danger, since a sharp revival in business expectations could suddenly give rise to heavy inflationary pressures" (Alacevich et al. 2015, 402). (See also the material on Currie in chapter 12.)

Friedman and Schwartz (1963a, 526 and 510) assigned responsibility for the monetary deceleration that preceded the May 1937 cyclical peak to the Fed's action in raising reserve requirements and to the gold-sterilization program adopted by the Treasury in December 1936. Using measures of M1 and ex ante real rates of interest, Romer (1992) found that monetary policy not fiscal policy caused the 1937–38 recession. The monetary deceleration that accompanied the increases in reserve requirements and sterilization of gold inflows appeared in the quarterly annualized M1 growth rates shown in parentheses: 1936Q2 (24.1 percent), 1936Q3 (14.1 percent), 1936Q4 (7.6 percent), 1937Q1 (5 percent), 1937Q2 (−1.6 percent), 1937Q3 (−4.9 percent), and 1937Q4 (−11.9 percent).[12]

Given exogenous reserves supply deriving from the monetization of gold inflows, the deceleration in money followed directly from the money-multiplier formula as the framework for money stock determination. Gold inflows subsided in the first five months of 1935 as revealed in the plateaus

12. See table 3.5 in chapter 3.

for bank reserves and excess reserves while currency continued to grow strongly (figures 10.4, 10.5, and 10.6). Adjusted reserves declined slightly after their 1935Q4 peak but then declined sharply with the initiation of the increases in required reserves.

The fact that banks attempted to restore their excess reserves by selling securities demonstrated that they desired to hold them. Reeve (1943, 70) wrote:

> The scars which the 1933 crisis left upon the monetary and credit situation remained long after the resurrection of the great majority of the banks. Although failure of licensed banks after the summer of 1933 had virtually ceased, the pressure for liquidity continued, enhanced in some cases by the severity of bank examiners.

Figure 10.10 shows the stress placed on the banking system by the increases in reserve requirements.[13] From January 1934 through August 1936, banks had prepared for a liquidity shock by adding to their holding of securities. For the weekly reporting banks, the ratio of investments to total assets rose from 50 percent in January 1934 to 62.5 percent in August 1936.[14] When the liquidity shock came in August 1936, they sold securities to gain reserves. However, selling securities could not increase reserves for the banking system. The result was to depress the price of securities and to increase their yields to the point at which banks were collectively willing to hold the given amount of reserves.[15] Bank security holdings stabilized in late 1936 but again fell after February 1937 with the second increase in required reserves.

Interacting with a contractionary monetary policy pushing down the

13. Figure 10.10 uses monthly data for weekly reporting member banks in 101 leading cities. As of June 1934, these banks held 69 percent of all member bank loans and investments. Member banks constituted 86 percent of all insured bank loans and investments as of this date. Figures are from Board of Governors (1943, table 10, "Principal Assets and Liabilities of Banks by Population of Place in Which Located, All Insured Commercial Banks"; table 18, "All Member Banks Principal Assets and Liabilities"; and table 48, "Weekly Reporting Member Banks and 101 Leading Cities").

14. For these banks, the ratio of reserves to assets increased from 13.3 percent in January 1934 to 25.1 percent in October 1936. It then stabilized but began rising again after October 1937. It peaked at 46.2 percent in October 1939.

15. For Treasury bills, rates were as follows: for July 1936, 0.141 percent; for April 1937, 0.696 percent; and for September 1937, 0.53 percent. After that date, rates fell as the economy slowed following the May 1937 cycle peak. Figures for three-to five-year tax-exempt Treasury notes were as follows: for July 1936, 1.17 percent; for April 1937, 1.59 percent; and for September 1937, 1.5 percent. For the Depression, these increases were quite large.

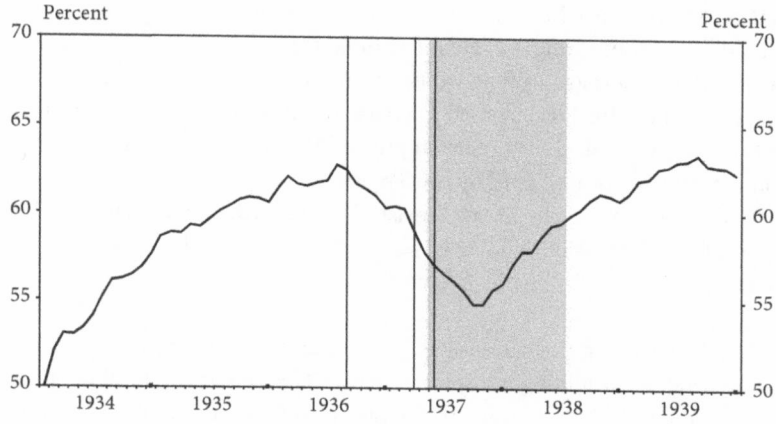

Figure 10.10. Ratio of Investments to Assets
Data from Board of Governors (1943). Investments are the sum of "US
Government Direct Obligations" and "Other Securities." Assets are "Total Loans and
Investments." Data are monthly in table 48, "Weekly Reporting Members Banks in
101 Leading Cities." Vertical lines indicate increases in reserve requirements and are
drawn at August 1936, March 1937, and May 1937. Shaded area indicates recession.
Heavy tick marks indicate December.

growth rate of aggregate nominal demand was a cost-push shock created by
the Wagner Act and the impetus it gave to union organizing and industrial
strife such as sit-down strikes. As shown in figures 10.8 and 10.9, real wages
and inflation rose autonomously (Bordo, Erceg, and Evans 2000). Meltzer
(2003, 566, 567) wrote:

> The Wagner Act (1935) strengthened trade unions and led to the orga-
> nization of labor in the steel, automobile, rubber, and other manufac-
> turing industries. Strikes and occupation of plants achieved settlements
> that recognized unions and further raised wages. In 1938 the Fair Labor
> Standards Act introduced a minimum wage and maximum hours of
> work. . . . Union membership rose from 11 percent of the labor force in
> 1933 to 27 percent in 1941. The largest jump came in 1937 ([R.] Freeman
> 1998, 292).

After the announcement on January 30, 1937, of a second increase in required reserves ratios, government bond rates began to rise when banks
sold bonds to offset the loss of excess reserves. Bond yields rose from
2.46 percent in February 1937 to 2.8 percent in April 1937 (Board of Governors, 1943, table 138). Treasury Secretary Morgenthau was upset. Harrison

(HPNY, Confidential Files, April 9, 1937) recorded that "Eccles was determined to do 'something.' . . . He mentioned three alternatives . . . (1) Repeal of the May 1 increase in reserve requirements, (2) Desterilization of imported gold by the Treasury, (3) Increase in the Reserve System's portfolio of bonds." Eccles and Morgenthau pushed for open market purchases and some desterilization of gold by the Treasury.

Led by New York, the FOMC resisted. As recorded by Harrison (HPNY, memo from J. H. Williams, April 14, 1937), at the April 3–4, 1937, FOMC meeting:

> Mr. Eccles stated that a refusal by the Committee to carry out its part of the program would be interpreted by the Treasury as a refusal to "play ball," and would result in an open break between the Reserve System and the Treasury. . . . The Committee must decide on its action by 12 o'clock, because he had agreed upon a time schedule with Mr. Morgenthau, according to which they were to see the President at 1 o'clock. . . . He [Eccles] was personally strongly in favor of open market purchases. . . . If the Committee refused to support him, he would have a choice between joining personally with the Secretary in a public statement and resigning from the Board.

In a supplementary memorandum to Harrison (HPNY, memo from John [J. H.] Williams, April 14, 1937) with the same date, Williams added that

> fears of inflationary spirals were increasing . . . [with] the prospect of a vicious circle of wage and price increases. . . . To increase excess reserves under such circumstances would be interpreted as inflationary, as inconsistent with government utterances, and as confirmatory of people's fears that our powers of monetary control, however great on paper, were rendered nil by Treasury opposition to any action which put pressure upon the government bond market.

The FOMC authorized purchases of up to $250 million of government securities.

The motivation behind eliminating excess reserves by increasing reserve requirements was to force banks to have recourse to the discount window when they expanded loans. Related to that objective was the Fed effort to persuade banks to borrow rather than to sell government bonds. The problem was the stigma surrounding borrowing that the Fed had created and that had caused banks to liquidate their asset portfolios rather than to borrow as in 1931 in response to runs. (The New York Fed also did not reduce the discount rate from the 2 percent set February 1934 until September 1937, when it set the rate at 1½ percent.) Harrison (HPNY, Confidential Files, August 27, 1937, 3) summarized a conversation with Eccles:

> I [Harrison] much preferred . . . to have the banks borrow and to show bills payable. I was confident that if the New York money market got to the point where excess reserves were pretty well wiped out and funds were short that the principal banks in New York would be willing to borrow from the Federal rather than to force liquidation of their Governments, particularly their long time Governments. . . . If we could get some of the principal New York banks to borrow . . . it would be the best thing that could happen for banks all over the country and . . . it would help to overcome the reluctance to show bills payable.

Bank reserves began to grow strongly again in 1938Q1. On April 18, 1938, at the urging of the administration, the Fed reduced reserve requirements, and "the Treasury desterilized $1.4 billion, all the remaining gold sterilized since December 1936" (Meltzer 2003, 531; Orphanides 2004b, 110). The cyclical trough occurred in June 1938. As shown in table 3.5 of chapter 3, the commercial paper rate rose from 0.75 percent to 1.0 percent in 1937Q2 but began to decline with the reduction in reserve requirements in 1938Q2, falling to 0.56 percent; in 1939Q1. The recession interrupted the ongoing decline in long-term government security yields (figure 9.15).

Carl Snyder (1940, 208–9) at the Federal Reserve Bank of New York mentioned three causes of the 1937 recession. The first sounded Keynesian. Given the absence of confidence on the part of business, there was an absence of "investment of reproductive capital." Prosperity rested on "the unstable base of government spending. The moment this was removed, the structure collapsed." The second reason "was the sharp and undesirable rise in wages. Fantastic to think that at a time of tremendous unemployment, when wage rates were already excessive, labor could ask and receive wages as high as, and in some industries higher than, in the boom year of 1929, when the volume of production and trade was much above the 1937 level."

Snyder does not consider the third reason to be the most important, but it reinforces Friedman and Schwartz (1963a). Snyder (1940, 209) wrote:

> After all the evils arising from the contraction of bank credit following the crisis of 1929, the Federal Reserve authorities again initiated a contraction of bank credit in the midst of the inadequate prosperity of 1937. By raising reserve requirements to the maximum allowed under the present law, that is, double the basic reserve requirements, the Federal

Reserve authorities compelled banks throughout the country to withdraw funds from New York. These withdrawals, together with the higher
reserves required, wiped out the excess reserves of the New York banks.
To replenish their reserves they sold government bonds. The result: a
decline in bond prices, and a rise in bond yields.

When the economy went into recession after the May 1937 cycle peak,
the Fed disavowed any responsibility. Orphanides (2004b, 111–12) found
the following in the archives of the FOMC secretariat at the Board of Governors. It was labeled "FOMC Meeting, November 29, 1937. Transcript of
notes taken on the statement by Mr. Williams."

> "We all know how it developed. There was a feeling last spring that things
> were going pretty fast. . . . We had about six months of incipient boom
> conditions with rapid rise of prices, price and wage spirals and forward
> buying and you will recall that last spring there were dangers of a run-away
> situation which would bring the recovery prematurely to a close. We all
> felt, as a result of that, that some recession was desirable. . . . We have had
> continued ease of money all through the depression. We have never had
> a recovery like that. It follows from that that we can't count upon a policy
> of monetary ease as a major corrective." . . . In response to an inquiry by
> Mr. Davis as to how the increase in reserve requirements has been in the
> picture, Mr. Williams stated that it was not the cause but rather the occa-
> sion for the change. . . . It is a coincidence in time. . . . If action is taken now
> it will be rationalized that, in the event of recovery, the action was what
> was needed and the System was the cause of the downturn. It makes a bad
> record and confused thinking. I am convinced that the thing is primarily
> non-monetary and I would like to see it through on that ground. There is
> no good reason now for a major depression and that being the case there
> is a good chance of a non-monetary program working out and I would
> rather not muddy the record with action that might be misinterpreted.

10.6. KEEPING THE REAL BILLS FAITH

Senate Resolution 125, passed on August 4, 1939, provided for questionnaires to be sent to the Federal Reserve Banks concerning "Monetary
Powers and Policies." The New York Fed response offered an excellent
summary.[16]

---

16. The references in this section are to the draft document in the Sproul papers at
the New York Fed: noted as SPNY, Questionnaire, 1939. The document is undated, but

The core of credit policy has been expressed as the promotion of the "productive" use of credit as opposed to nonproductive or speculative use, which resulted in lack of balance in production and consumption, and ultimately required drastic readjustment. . . . The Federal Reserve Board in its Annual Report for 1928 stated . . . [that] too rapid expansion of bank credit in any field may result in serious financial disorganization and it inevitably leads to increased demand for reserve bank funds. . . . Because . . . a growth of bank credit for any purpose ultimately leads to a demand for reserve bank credit, it is the duty to use its influence against undue credit expansion in any direction. (SPNY, Questionnaire, 1939, 67–68)

However, the ability to increase bank credit is limited in a recession. "While through its open market operation it [the Federal Reserve System] can increase member bank balances, it has no power to make member banks use these balances if their customers do not borrow or the banks themselves are unwilling to invest" (SPNY, Questionnaire, 1939, 74). Moreover, in response to the question "What criteria are . . . employed . . . in determining how to use its powers?" the answer was that judgment had to serve in place of explicit criteria:

The instruments . . . for influencing the availability and cost of credit are of extremely delicate nature and their application requires correct timing. . . . The best that can be done . . . is for the System to issue in advance reliable statements of prevailing business and credit conditions . . . and then to act accordingly. (SPNY, Questionnaire, 1939, 45)

The New York Fed devoted considerable effort to arguing that the price level was not an appropriate criterion for policy:

In daily transactions commodities and services are bought and sold on an individual basis, not in accordance with any average of prices, which is at best only a mathematical abstraction reflecting a mixture of fluctuations. In attempting to maintain average price levels, stability would mean deflating some prices and inflating others. The result would be artificial monetary manipulation, in many instances injurious to the producers and consumers. . . . Any such price manipulation would aggravate instability. (SPNY, Questionnaire, 1939, 70)

---

there is a table with numbers from 1940. The document is in a folder for 1939, so that is the date used here.

The New York Fed responses reproduced figures on money, prices, and interest rates for the years 1926, 1929, and 1940. It reported:

> These facts show clearly that the volume of money does not control the price level; and they show that commodity prices do not depend upon the cost of money, since interest rates of all kinds are not only sharply lower now than they were in 1926 but in the past few years have been the lowest on record. . . . Prices were fairly steady between 1921 and 1926, but during this period there developed on a large scale speculation in securities and real estate as well as inordinate lending abroad, until finally the collapse came in the fall of 1929. During this period of relatively small fluctuations in the general price level, the groundwork for one of the greatest depressions in our history was being laid. . . . The supply of currency and demand deposits, which perform the function of money, cannot be the controlling factor in the determination of prices, principally because they are more largely the effect than the cause of business activity. (SPNY, Questionnaire, 1939, 73–76)

10.7. CONCLUDING COMMENT

The coexistence of the high unemployment that persisted throughout the Great Depression and an assumed "easy" money policy on the part of the Fed underlay the Keynesian revolution. The apparent lack of the price system to work to clear markets, especially the labor market, presumably required a new theory that could explain a permanent underemployment equilibrium. Fiscal policy would provide the missing aggregate demand required to restore full employment. The contrasting explanation offered in *A Monetary History* (Friedman and Schwartz 1963a) is that the economy grew strongly as long as it was not subject to a succession of monetary shocks. In the Great Contraction, the Fed allowed the banking system and money stock to collapse. In the Roosevelt era, those shocks took the form of both supply-side shocks not accommodated by the Fed and a monetary contraction produced by the Fed with large increases in required reserve ratios.

Friedman (1997, 19) wrote:

> The contraction [August 1929 to March 1933] continued and deepened not because there were no equilibrating forces within the economy but because the economy was subjected to a series of shocks succeeding one another: a first banking crisis beginning in the fall of 1930, a second beginning in the spring of 1931, Britain's departure from gold in September 1931, and the final banking crisis beginning in January 1933—all accom-

panied by a decline in the quantity of money of 7 percent from 1930 to 1931, 17 percent from 1931 to 1932, and 12 percent from 1932 to 1933. Even after the end of the contraction and the start of revival in 1933, the shocks continued and impeded recovery: major legislative measures during Franklin Delano Roosevelt's New Deal that interfered with market adjustments and generated uncertainty within the business community. . . . Then ill-advised monetary measures in 1936 that halted the rapid rise that had been occurring in the quantity of money and produced an absolute decline from early 1937 to early 1938 that exacerbated if it did not produce the accompanying severe cyclical decline.

CHAPTER 11

The Guiding Role of Governor Harrison and the NY Fed

Summary: The confidential notes made by George Leslie Harrison, governor of the New York Fed after the death of Benjamin Strong in October 1928, offer insights into how policy makers understood their world in the Great Depression. Their internal debates provide evidence on the Friedman-Schwartz hypothesis that the knowledge required to end the Depression was available at the New York Fed but was rejected by the Federal Reserve System because of a shift of power away from New York to the governors of the other Federal Reserve Banks and to the Federal Reserve Board. Outside New York, real bills views dominated and encouraged a passivity in dealing with economic decline and deflation.

The review here of the minutes kept by Harrison suggests a more complicated picture. On the one hand, some of the staff and directors at the New York Fed wanted a more aggressive policy of open market purchases. On the other hand, Harrison resisted and did not actively promote these internal New York views to the rest of the Federal Reserve System. A review of the 1930s as seen through Harrison's eyes offers an insight into the dominant view of the world at that time. Harrison was a product of his time. He carried on the tradition of the 1920s that economic stabilization required quashing incipient speculation. According to this view, policy had failed twice in that task—once in 1919 and again in 1929.

According to Adolph Miller, under Governor Strong, not only had New York seeded the boom on the New York Stock Exchange with its cheap money policy of 1927, but also it had allowed speculation to get out of control by failing to act decisively after August 1928 when it had raised the discount rate to 5 percent. In response to the "period of optimism gone wild and cupidity gone drunk," the New York Fed had been "too slow to assume the leadership which was needed" (Miller 1935, 453). Harrison would not make the same mistakes.

11.1. WAS POLICY "INEPT" BECAUSE LEADERSHIP
SHIFTED AWAY FROM NEW YORK?

Friedman and Schwartz (1963a, 407) attributed the "ineptness" of monetary policy in the Great Contraction to a shift in power away from the New York Fed to the Federal Reserve Board and to the governors of the other Federal Reserve Banks. However, the Board lacked individuals capable of exercising that leadership. Only the New York Fed could fulfill that role. It is true that at the New York Fed Carl Snyder, W. Randolph Burgess, and some of the directors wanted a more aggressive policy to respond to the recession. George Harrison, governor of the New York Fed, did convey a New York program to the other regional Reserve Banks, but he never made a genuine effort to advance it at the meetings of the other governors. He seemed unconvinced by the views of his own staff and directors.

One factor that Friedman and Schwartz (1963a, 368) cited was the replacement after March 1930 of the Open Market Investment Committee (OMIC) with the Open Market Policy Conference (OMPC). The Open Market Investment Committee had coordinated open market operations and comprised the governors of New York, Boston, Chicago, Cleveland, and Philadelphia. At the same time, apart from New York, all the governors who had made up OMIC had hard-boiled real bills views (Fancher of Cleveland, Young of Boston, Norris of Philadelphia, and McDougal of Chicago). The Open Market Policy Conference included all the governors, and participation in open market operations was voluntary. It offered Harrison a better opportunity to build a coalition for easing if he had so desired.

Internally, at the New York Fed Carl Snyder and W. Randolph Burgess advocated open market purchases.[1] In a review of *A Monetary History*,

1. Advocacy of open market purchases did not mean disagreement with the policy of providing for economic stability by squelching speculation. Burgess (HPC, Executive Committee, June 19, 1933, 214) commented later on an increase in the index for the NYSE:

> An unstable condition, if too long continued, might build up a top-heavy speculative situation which could not be supported and would crash. In this connection he said the security markets seem to have gone wild today. Mr. Woodin [Treasury secretary] asked what is meant when you say a market has gone wild. Does it mean, he said, that something which once sold for $10,000 and which subsequently dropped in price to $500, is now selling for $1,000? . . . Mr. Burgess suggested that, nevertheless, we now have an inflation psychology and that there is danger of the movement attaining such momentum that we shall have neither the power nor, perhaps the will to stop it.

the British economist Roy Harrod (1964, 191), recounted the following anecdote:[2]

> I had luncheon with Carl Snyder and W. Randolph Burgess in the Federal Reserve Bank of New York in the late summer of 1930. . . . I pleaded with them that they should purchase $1 billion worth of government securities right away. . . . If they did not do this, the US economy would infallibly sink to lower levels, and that the great slump, which was then proceeding throughout the world, would assume unmanageable dimensions. . . . I found that they were in complete agreement with me. They spoke very frankly about the shift of power within the System. They earnestly wanted to pursue a policy of this kind, but could not do so without persuading the Banks of the "interior," and they had so far been unable to persuade them.

Friedman and Schwartz reviewed the opposition faced by New York from the Federal Reserve Board when it lowered its discount rate and from the other governors of OMIC when it engaged in open market purchases after the October 1929 stock market crash. In July 1930, Harrison wrote a letter to all the governors (quoted in Friedman and Schwartz 1963a, 370) stating that the New York Fed directors "felt so earnestly the need of continuing purchases of government securities that they have suggested that I write to you outlining some of the reasons why the Federal Reserve Bank of New York has for so many months favored having the Federal Reserve System do everything possible and within its power to facilitate a recovery of business." Harrison made the argument that New York would make often in the future that providing short-term funds to banks would encourage banks to buy bonds and thus help to revive investment. Friedman and Schwartz (1963a, 369) wrote that "faced with a clear rejection of its leadership, the New York Bank" decided "to conduct a campaign of persuasion." Harrison, however, usually seemed more in tune with the other governors than with his own New York contingent.

---

2. Roy Harrod was a Keynesian and did not accept the gravamen of *A Monetary History* that contractionary monetary policy caused the Depression. Harrod (1964, 190) highlighted the Friedman and Schwartz critique of "the feeble inertia of the Federal Reserve System in allowing the stock of money to run right down." Harrod (1964, 192), however, in his later Keynesian incarnation, questioned whether "a thing so small in relation to the world wide scene" (a $1 billion open market purchase) could have ended the recession and pointed to "more intractable forces, such as the balance between investment and saving in the world as a whole."

11.2. THE ORIGIN OF THE "NEW YORK VIEW"

Allyn Young (1927), a professor at Harvard, described a cycling of funds between banks in New York City and banks in the interior:

> Before the war, in periods of cyclical depression, bankers' deposits, and with them the country's idle cash, accumulated in New York. . . . Low interest rates generally led to a revival of long-term financing as well as (commonly a little later) to activity on the Stock Exchange. Some of the funds put at the disposal of borrowers in New York were gradually paid out in different parts of the country (as, for example, in construction expenses) and probably this was often one of the factors that helped business to get on its feet. With the recovery of industry and trade, funds were withdrawn from the New York market, and the demand for the increased amounts of money that were needed in hand-to-hand circulation also impinged upon New York. The New York banks kept on increasing their loans as long as they could, but sooner or later losses of deposits and of cash forced them to contract, and this compelled contraction in the securities market.
>
> Before the war, it was literally true that a cyclical expansion of production and trade was at the expense of speculation and long-term financing, and it was equally true that business depression created conditions which made an expansion of speculation and of long-term financing possible. This process of cyclical give-and-take between the New York money market and the interior was reflected in the timing of the expansion and contraction of general business activity. It probably accounts in part for the way in which the movement of speculation appeared to forecast the movement of business.

Snyder and some of the New York directors drew on the way in which cyclically low rates in New York led "a revival of long-term financing" and "construction expenses." Harrison drew on the way in which speculation "forecast the movement of business" by focusing on the need for a return of "confidence."

11.3. ASSESSING THE FRIEDMAN-SCHWARTZ VIEW THAT POWER SHIFTED FROM NEW YORK TO THE BOARD

Were Friedman and Schwartz correct that an explanation for the failure of the Fed to prevent a routine recession from turning into the Great Contraction was a transfer of power from a capable New York Fed to an incapable Federal Reserve Board? The contention here is that the New York Fed retained its dominant position within the Federal Reserve System. Harrison did continue to push for the New York program but not through aggressive open market purchases until spring 1932. In 1930, Harrison believed that the Fed was carrying out the New York program through maintenance of "easy" conditions in the money market. In 1931, he increasingly believed that the banks were frustrating the program through an unwillingness to utilize the reserves supplied to them. The remainder of the section selects quotes to show how under Harrison's leadership the New York Fed was not at all aggressive in pushing the regional Reserve Bank governors for open market purchases.

At the June 23, 1930, meeting of the Executive Committee of OMPC, the governors voted down the New York proposal that the Fed make open market purchases of government securities. At the next OMPC meeting in September 1930, the Conference took note of "the continued severe depression" and recommended only that it should be "the policy of the System . . . to maintain the present easy money rate position" (HPC, OMPC, September 25, 1930, 4). At the December 1930 OMPC meeting, Harrison recounted the run on the Bank of United States and noted that the New York Fed had purchased securities directly from the bank so that it would not have to show that it had borrowed from the discount window. The OMPC recommended only that "if any real need arose they would be willing to leave it to the judgment of the Federal Reserve Bank of New York whether some additional amount of government securities should be purchased" (HPC, OMPC, December 20, 1930, 2).

At the January 8, 1931, OMPC meeting, Harrison began by recounting the dire position of other gold standard countries because

> the world owes the United States on balance about $600,000,000 each year, and that payment has to be made in gold, in imports from foreign countries to us, or by borrowing from us. These countries were unable to send us much more gold, their exports to us were now limited and now financing curtailed. Their only alternative was to diminish their purchases of goods from us, which was now being done to our detriment. (HPC, OMPC, January 8, 1931, 1)

Harrison also told the governors that "the directors of the New York bank had voted at their last meeting to sell a part of the securities which had been added to the portfolio of the New York bank during the recent banking emergency. It was the general plan of the New York bank to liquidate the balance of the temporary purchases of $45,000,000 of securities" (HPC, OMPC, January 8, 1931, 2–4).

The minutes also reported:

> It should be the policy of the System to continue an easy money policy in the best interest of trade and commerce. It is the belief of the Conference, however, that the seasonal return flow of currency and credit and other factors have tended during recent weeks to make for an undue excess of funds in the principal money centers. . . . It would be desirable to dispose of some of the System holdings of government securities. . . .
>
> Governor Harrison replied that they [the surplus reserves] appeared to indicate first, little demand for funds by borrowers, and second, reluctance to employ funds. . . . Mr. Miller suggested that the banking situation might be suffering just now from excessive caution and excessive desire for liquidity. Governor Harrison replied that that was one reason why our easy money policy had not proved more effective. (HPC, OMPC, January 8, 1931, 5–6)

At the April 29, 1931, OMPC meeting, Harrison recommended granting authorization to purchase up to $100 million of government securities but with no actual purchases. At the June meeting, Harrison recounted the critical world situation:

> He [Harrison] further stated that the events of the past two weeks were in some ways the most critical which the world has passed through since the war, that there had been a threat of a general moratorium and a possible breakdown of capitalism in Europe. . . . Developments in South America had indicated the danger of a moratorium in certain countries there. In these circumstances it seemed desirable to take every possible measure available to the Federal Reserve System for improving the situation. (HPC, OMPC, Executive Committee, June 22, 1931, 2, 7)

The OMPC voted to buy the minimal amount of "up to $50,000,000 of government securities."

At the August OMPC meeting, Harrison repeated his warning about the dire condition of the world. Although he recommended that the Executive Committee of OMPC be authorized to purchase up to $300 million of government securities, he did not recommend immediate purchases. He continued to express concern that the banks would not use the additional funds:

Governor Harrison stated his belief that economic, social, and political conditions throughout the world were so very serious, the prospects for the winter indicated such severe unemployment and distress, and the threat of political and social upheavals in various parts of the world was so great that the Federal Reserve System should certainly be prepared to take any helpful steps within its power if and as soon as conditions indicated reasonable prospects of their success. Governor Harrison did not advocate immediate purchases of securities because it did not appear that the attitude of the banks and investors was such that funds thus made available would be put to work. (HPC, OMPC, August 11, 1931, 9, 3)

11.4. 1930

In 1930, the New York Fed struggled with how to respond to the recession. The fall 1929 stock market crash followed by recession unfolded as predicted by the speculative-excess explanation of recession. Within this real bills framework, the issue was whether to allow the required liquidation of business or to promote a positive psychology through "credit inflation." Because the New York banks were borrowing relatively little from the discount window, open market purchases supplying funds to the banks would push them out of the window and create excess reserves (figure 6.1). That situation would mean the end of real bills principles of supplying funds to banks through the discount window conditioned on collateral (real bills) arising out of a legitimate demand for credit.

The May 1930 meeting of the New York Executive Committee defined the issues. Although the minutes do not identify the speakers, the attribution below seems clear. Carl Snyder wanted open market purchases, and Harrison demurred. Although the directors admitted that gold inflows supported an expansion of credit not based on real bills principles, they were uncertain about a world of "managed money," that is, the creation of credit not based on market demand.

The minutes reported (HPC, Executive Committee, May 19, 1930, 11–12):

The directors admitted a recurring hesitancy to depart from the more or less commercial basis of operations in discounted papers and bankers acceptances [real bills principles] to embark upon so called credit management by means of purchases and sales of Government securities. It was generally agreed, however, that the large accumulation of gold in the United States had forced a certain amount of credit management upon the banking system. And it was further agreed that we should determine whether or not the present business depression is so serious as to warrant our assuming the risks of credit management in order to try and avoid the greater risks of prolonged depression.

At the meeting, someone who had to have been Carl Snyder challenged the real bills view that open market purchases would supply unwanted and unneeded credit:

> Nor was it unanimously agreed that purchases of Government securities at this time would represent real inflation. It was suggested that we had encouraged a deflation of credit during most of the years 1928 and 1929, that the rate of increase in total credit in use had been below normal, and that it was now proposed to help restore the amount of credit in use to more nearly normal levels.

Harrison was unwilling to represent those views before the OMPC. He made the valid point that the OMPC would reject them. However, there was not then or in the future any expression of regret or expressed opinion that the OMPC was mistaken. Harrison also expressed what would be his signature position, namely, that any attempt to supply funds to banks through open market operations would have to be done in a way that could be quickly reversed. That position reflected his concern for a revival of speculative excess:

> Finally, it was recognized that it would be most desirable to have the support of a united Federal Reserve System in any action that was taken, and that consideration must be given to the difficulty which would probably be encountered in reversing our action, which if necessary, because of the organization of the Federal Reserve System.

The directors concurred with Harrison:

> The committee discussed the desirability of taking further action—purchase of government securities—designed to foster an easier credit situation. With member bank discounts at Federal Reserve Banks practically at minimum levels, it was held that purchases of government securities would represent inflation, and that the dangers of an inflationary program were many and serious.

The New York directors did not understand how the Fed's free reserves procedures set money market interest rates. The minutes reported (HPC, BoD, June 5, 1930, 16–20):[3]

3. "BoD" refers to the full Board of Directors.

The first step in the program, as he [a director] viewed it, might well be to get the call money rate down to a dramatically low level, and, in this connection, it was suggested that there is something artificial in the present call loan rate of 3%, when time money frequently brings less than 3%. The claim was then made by another director that the call money market is a natural money market and that the present rates are in no sense artificial. . . . There is now, it was said, a balance of funds in the money market.

Adolph Miller, member of the Federal Reserve Board, in attendance, commented:

During this business recession, he [Miller] said we have not had the collapse of money rates which has characterized similar periods, partly because the Federal Reserve System has retarded liquidation. The present state of business and credit should not be considered as an independent situation, however, but as part of a long time post-war readjustment. . . . We must establish our place under a new set of conditions and there is danger, therefore, in being too optimistic concerning an early and rapid recovery of business.

At their June 1930 meeting, the New York directors supported open market purchases. The minutes (HPC, BoD, June 26, 1930, 26) reported, "[The directors] agreed unanimously that a revival of the bond and mortgage market, both logically and by precedent, is a necessary antecedent of business recovery, and they indicated their belief in the power of credit to bring about a revival in the bond market and, through it, to bring about improvement in business." However, probably as reminded by Harrison, such actions were controversial. The New York Fed continued to receive criticism for its easing actions in fall 1929. Earlier, the minutes (HPC, Executive Committee, June 9, 1930, 21) had reported the criticism "that its actions last autumn, and since, had merely delayed and prolonged necessary liquidation of an unsound business and credit situation, and that if a sharper and more natural liquidation had been permitted a more rapid recovery would have been had."

The September 1930 meeting of the New York Fed officers highlighted the differences between Harrison and both Snyder and Burgess. The minutes (HPC, Officer's Council, September 17, 1930, 46–47) reported:

Mr. Snyder called attention to the fact that . . . the figures for all member banks as of June 30 [1930] showed that there had been practically no change [in the volume of bank credit] as compared with the 1928 figures

and an actual decrease as compared with the 1929 figures. . . . In his opinion, this "deflation" should now be aggressively combatted by additional
purchases of Government securities in the hope that business would be
stimulated and the hardships of what now looks like a winter of depression diminished.

The Governor said that when banks were already borrowing minimum amounts from the Federal Reserve System, the only effect of additional purchases of Government securities was forced investments, and
the dangers of such a policy of inflation were great and the advantages
doubtful. Furthermore, he said that from a System standpoint it is a practical impossibility to embark on such a program at the present time—to
do so would mean an active division of System policy. Under the circumstances he held it wiser to maintain the present policy of keeping credit
easy and the New York City banks over in reserves, rather than to adopt
a policy of active credit creation.

[The]question was raised as to whether additional purchases of Government securities at this time could properly be called a program of
inflation—was it not more nearly correct to label it an attempt to correct
a preceding deflation. Disregarding this question of nomenclature, Mr.
Burgess said that if we were acting alone, he would be in favor of a program which involved more than merely maintaining easy money rates
and keeping the New York City banks out of debt; that by increasing the
pressure upon the banks to employ surplus funds we might give a little
impetus to business recovery.

The Governor was not convinced that present economic difficulties
could be remedied by a heavy dose of easy credit any better than the
small dose which had already been administered and he pointed out that
when all the New York City banks are more or less continuously out of
debt at the Reserve Bank over any considerable period of time it means
a very easy reserve position. He also directed attention again to the reluctance of most of the other Federal Reserve Banks to acquiesce in the
open market policy developed.

11.5. 1931

Burgess (HPC, BoD, January 15, 1931, 77) expressed the New York Fed's
policy in 1930, "namely, to keep credit so easy in the New York market that
funds would remain in or flow to the interior of the country or would, by
their redundancy in New York, stimulate investment and perhaps encourage a more liberal lending attitude on the part of the commercial banks."
Harrison (HPC, BoD, March 5, 1931, 98) remained unwilling to do more.

"The present is no time to sponsor inflation. . . . Governor Meyer of the Federal Reserve Board expressed his agreement."[4] Harrison (HPC, BoD, April 9, 1931, 113) would have been receptive "if we had such control of the throttle that we could quickly and effectively go into reverse. In the absence of ability to reverse our position, inflation would probably do more harm than good."

Harrison (HPC, BoD, May 7, 1931, 134–35) did admit that the policy was not working: "At home we have easy money in the money centers but not in the country as a whole. Credit is bottled up in New York and other cities, because of the unwillingness of bankers and investors to use it in the ordinary channels of trade and agriculture." Later in May, however, Harrison (HPC, BoD, May 28, 1931, 144–45) became willing to consider "a managed currency and credit position. . . . With conditions the world over as serious as they are now, the Governor thought that the adoption of a program of mild inflation must be considered."

However, not all the directors were willing.

Mr. Mitchell[5]. . . thought that it would be assuming a terrific responsibility, however, to charter a policy of inflation and that, if it did not work, the Federal Reserve System would suffer for what would be labeled a great mistake. He said that if it were not for the present psychology of fear, he would be more hopeful of success but that, at the moment, fear was the dominant element in business thinking and that under the circumstances money could be so soft that you could put your finger through it, and yet people would not use it except when safety was guaranteed.

At the next board meeting, Harrison (HPC, BoD, June 18, 1931, 155–56) also noted that "it [open market purchases] was the only thing left for us to do in an attempt to maintain our earning assets in the face of heavy gold imports."

New York recognized the demand for liquidity by banks given the outflow of currency from banks. The minutes (HPC, Executive Committee, August 4, 1931, 15–17) reported: "Mr. Mitchell said that the New York banks would probably not be inclined to employ the funds which they obtain as a result of System security purchases in buying second grade bonds. The

4. Eugene I. Meyer was governor of the Federal Reserve Board from September 16, 1930, to May 10, 1933.

5. Charles E. Mitchell was chairman of the City Bank of New York (now Citibank) and a director at the New York Fed from 1929 through 1931. In 1933, he was indicted for tax evasion but was found not guilty. Mitchell was the first witness in the 1933 Pecora Commission Hearings. "In November 1929, Senator Carter Glass said of him, 'Mitchell more than any 50 men is responsible for this stock crash'" (Wikipedia n.d.).

emphasis is all on liquidity at the present time, and they would in all probability, prefer to hold idle reserves rather than to employ the money in that manner." The minutes (HPC, Executive Committee, September 28, 1931, 67) recorded Governor Harrison as saying, "If each of the New York banks is going to stick to its own liquidity program and if the rest of the country looks to the New York for leadership in recovery . . . we shall not get anywhere, and banks will become no more than safe deposit boxes."

The minutes (HPC, BoD, June 18, 1931, 155–56) also reported that purchases of government securities had not expanded credit "because they were absorbed by a reduction in the earning assets of the Federal Reserve System and latterly because of a substantial increase in currency hoarding which has resulted in a similar increase in the amount of 'currency in circulation.'" Nowhere either in the minutes or in public commentary is there any recognition that a failure to provide reserves to meet a demand for excess reserves and a failure to provide reserves to offset currency outflows required a contraction of the banking system. "Mr. Mitchell said he considered that the emergency [Germany abandoning the gold standard and bank runs], which the purchase of $50,000,000 of Government securities in August was designed to meet, had long since passed, and that the excess reserves subsequently held by the New York City banks were creating an unduly sloppy money market. . . . He suggested the desirability of selling these securities" (HPC, BoD, August 20, 1931, 34–35).

One reason that banks demanded the liquidity from holding excess reserves as opposed to bonds was fear that a depreciation in the market value of bonds would prompt regulators to close them. The minutes (HPC, Executive Committee, August 4, 1931, 17) reported:

> Governor Young [Boston] said that to be effective, the purchase of Government's by the Reserve Banks would require the cooperation of commercial banks. The policy could only be effective if the commercial banks would buy bonds. They have been discouraged from the purchase of bonds by the procedure followed by the examiners with respect to charging off bond depreciation. It is questionable whether the excess reserves would be put to work. He expressed doubts about the efficacy of open market operations in general.

The minutes (HPC, BoD, August 6, 1931, 18) continued:

> Mr. Rounds, following his usual report on banks requiring special attention, said that the list of banks whose capital is impaired by reason of bond depreciation or losses in other assets is constantly being enlarged

as examination reports come in. . . . Mr. [Owen D.] Young asked, "Must
we stand by and see these banks fail?" Governor Harrison replied that
under present conditions there is no alternative if the directors or stockholders cannot be persuaded to put in additional money to restore the
capital of such institutions, or if arrangements cannot be made to have
them taken over by other banks.

Also, bankers feared that government deficits would leave government
bonds worthless. Harrison (US Congress 1932a, April 13, 504) testified:

Buying securities . . . alone accomplishes nothing because it gives excess
reserves to the member banks. . . . It is impossible to be used for expanding credit where it is used for paying off debts of a bank. That does not
change the volume of Federal reserve credit at all, but does relieve the
Bank under pressure, which tends to make it more liberal. . . . You can
not expect the bankers . . . to use that excess reserve unless they have
reasonable confidence. . . . They are not going into the bond market at all
if you have legislation pending in Congress that makes for the unbalanc-
ing of the Budget.

Owen D. Young (HPC, BoD, April 21, 1932, 201–3), one of the New York
bank directors, argued

that many people felt our program must fail if launched before the country is assured of a balanced budget. He had two criticisms of our program
both connected with this point: 1. It is hopeless to try to force credit
into use in the face of widespread fear of an unbalanced Federal budget.
2. By manufacturing an artificial market for Government securities and
facilitating their issue at low rates, obstacles are placed in the way of a
program of Government economy.

On September 19, 1931, Britain left the gold standard. Debate in the New
York Fed showed how little policy makers understood of monetary economics. Harrison (HPC, BoD, October 8, 1931, 84–85)

pointed out that during the past three months there had been a substantial increase in the demand for Federal Reserve credit [discount window
borrowing] incident to the export of gold and the hoarding of currency,
and that this increase in the demand for Federal Reserve credit had been
accompanied by a moderate rise in open market money rates. These developments made an advance in the discount rate appropriate. . . .

He . . . thought that higher rates, by improving bank earnings, might improve the psychology of bankers and increase their willingness to lend and invest funds. . . . He felt that reserve bank rates would be more nearly in touch with money market conditions.

Mr. Mitchell expressed the opinion that . . . if open market money rates could be raised to levels which would justify higher deposit rates, that might stop the withdrawals of deposits. . . . He thought that the banks would regard keeping money rates down under present conditions, as the maintenance of an artificial situation.

The only recognition that higher interest rates might negatively impact the economy was concern for a "psychological effect." Aid to banks experiencing runs would have to come from a new organization that could lend to banks: the National Credit Corporation, forerunner to the Reconstruction Finance Corporation. The minutes (HPC, BoD, October 15, 1931, 89, 91–92) reported:

Governor Harrison commented on the continued withdrawal of currency from banks and on the banking situation in various parts of the country. He pointed out that we have now come to the point where it is necessary to fight banking difficulties by every possible means, and suggested the desirability of mobilizing the liquid assets of banks in communities such as New York which are strongly situated, so that it will be possible to respond immediately to the needs of other localities. . . . Gov. Harrison . . . pointed out that the outflow of gold had continued as rapidly as in the week previous. . . . His recommendation would be for an advance of 1 per cent to a 3½ per cent [discount rate].

Governor Meyer said that the matter had been informally discussed among members of the Federal Reserve Board and that only one member of the Board had expressed fears concerning the psychological effect of bank depositors. He said that an advance in the rate was called for by every known rule, and believed that foreigners would regard it as a lack of courage if the rate were not advanced. He said he did not see how it would affect depositors in this country.

At the next directors' meeting, Harrison (HPC, BoD, November 25, 1931, 115) stated that "if there is a renewal of numerous bank failures and of currency hoarding in addition to seasonal demands during the weeks just ahead, it may become necessary to take some action to bring about cooperation between commercial banks in meeting the situation."

Harrison and the directors of the New York Fed understood the world through the eyes of bankers. Like all their contemporaries, they believed that banks, not the Fed, were responsible for the decline in bank deposits and bank credit. The minutes recorded (HPC, BoD, December 24, 1931, 124–26):

> Governor Harrison brought to the attention of the directors a record devised and maintained by the reports and statistical department of the bank showing the relation between bank credit, business volume, and the general price level. He said that on the experience of past years, these records now indicated a further decline in the general price level unless there should be an increase in volume of bank credit, and he commented on the serious aspects of any further deflation of prices.
>
> Mr. Reyburn said that he did not like to see the blame for the present situation placed upon the banking community alone, because he believes that it is the doubts and fears of industrial leaders and their absence from the forum where public opinion is formed which are primarily responsible for the declining volume of bank credit in use. . . . Mr. Mitchell stated that he did not believe that there is anything which the Federal Reserve Bank can do so long as fear is in the saddle. He said he did not like the looks of the present banking situation, that there is danger of conflagration and that in view of this condition and the difficult situation abroad he thought the Federal Reserve System should conserve its ammunition.
>
> In view of our present free gold position and the potential demands which may be made upon us at home and abroad, he [Harrison] said, the most conservative course and perhaps the wisest course to follow would be to do nothing beyond what is already being done. On the other hand, it could well be argued that if, after the turn of the year, deflation of credit and of prices continues bringing nearer the danger of complete collapse, the courageous thing to do would be to fire off our last shot in the belief that failure could be no worse than continuance of present trends. For his part, he would not want to do this unless the commercial banks would cooperate in our attempt to expand the use of credit, in which case, of course, we should have to try and measure the risks to be run by those banks. He stated his belief, at the moment, was that no further Government securities should be purchased until after the turn of the year, except to avoid a jam in the money market, but that if, after the first week in January, present trends—credit deflation, price declines, bank failures—continued, the System might well have to purchase further amounts of Government securities instead of selling those previously purchased for temporary holding over year end, as had been contemplated. Even then, we should want to guarantee the fluidity of the funds

placed in the market, he said, by securing the cooperation of the member banks in their use. This brought up the question, he thought, of whether or not we should call a meeting of principal bankers at which the situation could be placed before them and their cooperation demanded. . . . Mr. Mitchell . . . believed that the New York City bankers were almost unanimous in opposing the purchase of Government securities by the Federal Reserve System at this time.

11.6. 1932

The issues in 1932 when Harrison finally accepted the need to stimulate the extension of bank credit were twofold. First, while open market purchases in sufficient quantity could create excess reserves, there needed to be a demand for those reserves. If there was no demand, banks would not use them. Second, open market purchases reduced the gold cover. While the Federal Reserve System had ample free gold reserves, New York did not. It was not willing to undertake open market purchases on its own account without participation of the banks with ample gold cover, especially Chicago. The extent of the gold cover was a measure of the ability to supply funds. There was absolutely no question of breaching it. The gold cover gave value to the currency and was the wall separating the "gold standard" from a paper money standard of managed money.

In 1932, led by Harrison, the Fed would undertake open market purchases. However, Harrison believed that the additional reserves would be used to expand credit only if confidence returned. That belief motivated an extensive behind-the-scenes effort to shape policy in Congress. Harrison would undertake to meet the challenge defined by Governor Meyer (HPC, Executive Committee, August 4, 1931, 15–17): "Whereas in 1928 and 1929 the trouble was overconfidence and overspeculation, the trouble now is underconfidence and, in fact, too little inclination to take risks. The question now is whether we can by any action here bring about a reversal in public psychology."

The threat posed to the free gold position by open market purchases weighed on Harrison. Open market purchases of government securities would increase the deposits of banks at the New York Fed and would increase the required gold backing for those deposits. A decline in the gold cover of the New York Fed toward the legally required minimum would undermine confidence in the financial community. To be willing to take that risk, Harrison had first to be assured that banks would have the confidence to use additional reserves.

To ensure that banks would have that confidence, he organized an ambitious coordination of policy with the administration and with Congress. The Treasury wanted a reduction in the discount rate below the interest rate on government securities so that banks would have an incentive to buy debt as in WWI. In return, the Fed wanted the promise of a balanced budget. From Congress, the Fed wanted legal authority to use government securities to back currency as a way of relaxing the gold cover constraint. The Fed wanted creation of the Reconstruction Finance Corporation to lend to banks with impaired capital. It also wanted wage reductions in the railroad industry to boost the value of the railway bonds held by banks.

Harrison (HPC, BoD, February 25, 1932, 165–67) told the directors his view:

> Our chief concerns at the moment are 1. The continued hoarding of currency. . . . 2. The continued contraction of credit, which has persisted during the first two months of 1932 at much the same violent rate as in the last quarter of 1931. After two years of depression, he said, with continued declines in the value of commodities and securities, the banks of the country are pretty well tied up and yet, if present trends continued, we might have a wave of failures which would not stop with the banks but would spread to the industries and railroads of the country.
>
> Right now, he thought, we have the best opportunity we have had or may have to do what is in our power to aid in recovery. In January, he said, we mapped a program in our minds which involved organization of the Reconstruction Finance Corporation, railroad wage adjustments, support of the bond market, liberalizing the Federal Reserve Act by some such measure as the Glass-Steagall bill, a definite and sound undertaking of the Treasury to bring the Federal budget into balance.

The danger that the populist forces in Congress would force the United States onto a fiat money standard also pushed Harrison into action. The minutes (HPC, BoD, March 24, 1932, 178–79, 181) reported:

> Mr. Young said he would be very hesitant to ask the banks to embark on a program of greatly increased purchase of Government securities. The House of Representatives is on an emotional rampage, he said, and not only is there now no assurance of a balanced budget but, what is even worse, there is the possibility that it might be thrown even further out of balance than it already is. Any group, which would defeat the balancing of the budget, would also vote the soldiers bonus without providing the means of payment. That means starting the printing press. . . . So long as people are apprehensive about the budget and about a soldiers bonus to

be paid in greenbacks, there is nothing worth while which we can do. . . . Governor Harrison said that . . . it must be admitted that the best talking point for "Greenbackism" in Congress is the deflation of bank credit which we are trying to stop. Governor Harrison said that . . . we have done our part—the commercial bankers have not yet done theirs.

Later, Harrison (HPC, Executive Committee, March 29, 1932, 182) expanded on his concerns:

> There are two groups in Congress . . . 1. The soldiers bonus group, which, heretofore, has been held back because it could not see how the funds could be raised for immediate payment of the bonus. 2. The greenback group, which desires to put fiat money into circulation, and which now says to the soldiers bonus group that the money for the bonus can be supplied in this way, and that the business depression can be halted at the same time. The danger is that the two groups, together, may be able to accomplish something which either one, alone, could not have accomplished.

By April 1932, Harrison had become convinced of the need to undertake a significant program of open market purchases not only because of the deflation of prices and credit but also because of populist pressure in Congress. The problem, however, was the reticence of the other Reserve Banks. They believed that note issue unbacked by gold or real bills would be inflationary. Harrison (HPC, Executive Committee, April 4, 1932, 185–86) reported

> that the loans and investments of the banks of the country are continuing to decline, and that there is as yet no decided evidence of a change in the downward trend of business activity and commodity prices. The persistence of this movement, he said, is bringing us to the point where, not only is there heart-breaking pressure upon all debtors, but there is also a progressive deterioration in the assets of the very banks which are making the strenuous efforts to keep themselves liquid.
>
> The situation is rapidly coming to the fore in Washington, the Governor informed the directors. There are large groups in Congress which are for a soldiers' bonus payment and for inflation and, if these two groups get together, Congress is likely to take favorable action on some bill such as the Thomas bill (S.3874), which provides for the issuance of $2,400,000 of Federal reserve bank notes, collateralized by 2% Government bonds to be sold to the Federal Reserve banks. He said

that he had discussed this bill with Senator Thomas, and that the Senator, while admitting that his methods are unorthodox, had asserted a strong preference for unorthodox methods as contrasted with doing nothing. Senator Thomas had fastened on his admission that credit deflation should be checked and that prices should go up, the Governor said, and claimed that his bill provided a means of accomplishing these ends. The Senator claimed, furthermore, that if his bill is not favorably received, even more radical proposals will be forthcoming from Congress.

Governor Harrison then went on to say that it now appears as if the only way to forestall some sort of radical financial legislation by Congress, is to go further and faster with our own program.... That there are certain practical difficulties in the way of speeding up our purchases of Government securities, he admitted. First, it will be hard to get System approval. Second, even though the program is approved, many of the Federal reserve banks probably will not participate in it, leaving most of the burden upon the Federal Reserve Bank of New York. Third, if we carry the load, we shall have to take advantage of the provision of the Glass-Steagall bill which permits the use of Government securities, purchased by the Federal Reserve banks, as collateral for Federal reserve note issues. And fourth, if we are the only Federal reserve bank to do this, our critics will point to it as evidence of the determination of the New York bank to pursue a lone policy of inflation.

At the April 7, 1932, meeting, the directors were uniformly enthusiastic about increasing the rate of purchases of government securities beyond the current $25,000,000 a week. For example, Mr. Young quoted former director Mitchell as recommending that "the Federal Reserve banks make some spectacular purchases which would rivet the attention on their determination to break the back of the present credit deflation." Young continued: "He [Young] would not be at all afraid to have the New York Bank go ahead alone.... The risks of doing nothing are so great, that we must do something" (HPC, BoD, April 7, 1932, 194). Harrison (HPC, BoD, April 7, 1932, 196) noted that "Senator Thomas had indicated to him that he might be satisfied not to press for Congressional action if the System would proceed more vigorously."

As early as May 1932, Harrison (HPC, Executive Committee, May 9, 1932, 215–16) could report:

The deflation of bank credit, which was proceeding at a precipitous rate, has been checked in the country as a whole and turned in New York....

It would be fatal for the Federal Reserve System to abandon the program now....

Since the latter part of February purchases of Government securities for System account had totaled $546,000,000 and that, including a return of currency from circulation, the banks had gained funds totaling $726,000,000 during the period. These funds had been used to reduce member bank indebtedness at Reserve banks by $329,000,000, to offset the retirement of $123,000,000 of other forms of Federal reserve bank credit, to offset a net reduction of $5,000,000 in the country's gold stock and to increase member bank reserve balances by $2,690,000.

At the same time, Harrison soon began to worry about placing a limit on the purchases of government securities so that they could be undone. The balancing act was to initiate a recovery in bank lending and the economy but to stop before credit inflation could initiate another round of speculation. The goal was to provide a level of excess reserves that would encourage banks to lend but not to go beyond that level. Harrison's comments (HPC, BoD, May 18, 1932, 218) also suggest that he was nervous that if the Fed ended open market purchases Congress would pass the Goldsborough bill:[6]

> It is not possible to go forward purchasing large amounts of Government securities each week, without having some definite objective and terminal point of view. ... When the figures of member bank reserves are sufficiently high to produce adequate pressure upon the banks and to provide adequate credit for business as recovery sets in, we shall probably have done our part. If commercial banks can't or don't use the credit which we provide, that is another problem. He pointed out, however, that we must be most careful in announcing a definite objective because of the manifold possibilities of misinterpretation of such an announcement and of its use to support such legislation as the Goldsborough bill.

Given Harrison's concern for a need to undo the open market purchases, the New York Fed purchased only short-term government securities. Harrison (HPC, BoD, May 18, 1932, 220) told the directors, "With a program of the magnitude of that now being pursued, we must always have in mind the

6. The Goldsborough bill would have required "the Federal Reserve Board, the Federal reserve banks, and the Secretary of the Treasury" to "restore and maintain the average purchasing power of the dollar ... for the year 1926." In pursuit of the goal of reflation, the Fed would provide Federal Reserve notes in exchange for the deposit with it of government securities. Hearings were held in mid-May 1932.

time when a reversal of our policy will be necessary, and that a reduction of our holdings of Government securities can best be accomplished, with the least disturbance to the market, by allowing short term holdings to mature without replacement."

By the end of June 1932, New York was getting close to Harrison's objective of creating a desired level of excess reserves. Burgess (HPC, BoD, June 30, 1932, 246) reported that

> roughly, as a result of purchases of approximately $1,000,000,000 of Government securities we had offset a loss of gold of nearly $500,000,000, replaced over $400,000,000 of member bank discounts and bill holdings and increased the amount of Federal reserve credit outstanding by about $100,000,000. Mr. Young pointed out that most of our efforts had served to check a contraction of credit rather than to stimulate an expansion of credit. We have been clearing the way for action, rather than taking action, he said. Governor Harrison agreed that this had been so, and said that our program is only now getting a real test as an agency for recovery.

At the June 30, 1932, FOMC meeting, Harrison recommended continuing open market purchases but only on the condition that Boston and Chicago buy securities from the New York Fed. The directors had similar views (HPC, BoD, June 30, 1932, 257). As Harrison (HPC, BoD, April 28, 1932, 208) noted, "Most of the funds resulting from open market purchases of Government securities had gone, of course, into the New York market." The deposits of member banks at the New York Fed raised its required gold cover by 35 percent. At some point, unless Boston and Chicago with their ample gold cover bought securities from the New York Fed and transferred gold to it through the gold settlement fund, open market purchases would cause the New York Fed to breach its legal obligation to back its liabilities with gold.[7]

The Chicago and Boston Reserve Banks opposed continued open market purchases, and Philadelphia was "lukewarm," as was "a majority of the

---

7. Friedman and Schwartz (1963, 399) argued that at no time did a lack of free gold force policy makers to adopt a policy they otherwise would not have followed. That statement seems too strong. The regional Reserve Bank governors viewed an ample free gold cushion as providing them with resources to lend in a recovery and as protection against the overissue of currency, that is, managed money. The need to redistribute gold among the Reserve Banks to protect the New York gold reserves ratio gave Boston and Chicago, which were strong real bills adherents, veto power over open market purchases.

Executive Committee of the OMPC" (HPC, BoD, June 30, 1932, 254). Ironically, the bank runs in Chicago in June 1932 (Calomiris and Mason 1997) hardened the opposition of the Chicago bank to redistributing gold to New York. As shown in figure 9.9, a bank run that increased currency in circulation lowered banks' nonborrowed reserves and forced them into the discount window. Increased borrowing increased the required gold cover. Increased currency also increased the Fed's liabilities. It was true that with the passage of the Glass-Steagall Act of 1932, for one year, the Reserve Banks could collateralize currency with government securities. However, the regional Reserve Bank governors considered that a step toward a managed paper money standard.

Indicative of this attitude, Carter Glass had agreed to section 3 of the 1932 Glass-Steagall Act, but only as part of Harrison's program to restore confidence as a precondition of open market purchases. Butkiewicz (2008, 284) wrote: "In the testimony for the Banking Act of 1935, you can see Carter Glass is mad. He said he wanted on the record that he never would have reported that bill [out of the Senate Banking Committee], that is, co-sponsored the Glass-Steagall bill, had he known it was going to be used. He was told it was only for psychological purposes."

Irving Fisher (1934, 204) quoted Representative Goldsborough's comments reported in the *New York Times* of June 2, 1932:

I [Carter Glass] dissent from the view that there is any need of artificial inflation of the credit or currency of the country. . . . I distinctly disavow the belief that any of these legislative devices is necessary at this time. I simply offered the bill in question [Glass-Steagall] as a substitute for the Goldsborough Bill which I regard with the utmost aversion.

Representative Goldsborough also quoted Glass's comments on the floor of the Senate (Fisher 1934, 205): "He [Glass] would not be willing to give the power provided in this bill to any seven men that God ever made." Goldsborough then added, "Does not the Senator from Virginia know that the Federal Reserve System is now exercising these vast powers in an absolutely uncontrolled manner . . . ?" Carter Glass's attitude also appeared in a comment he made to Randolph Burgess (1964, 226) after passage of the Glass-Steagall Act. "You tell George Harrison that I am now just a corn-tassel Greenbacker."

In any event, Harrison was never willing to entertain an open-ended program of open market purchases until the economy recovered. Director Reyburn (HPC, BoD June 30, 1932, 251–52) asked Harrison "how far we could safely go on further purchases of Government securities, even if we got all of the Federal reserve banks to come in for their proportionate share of the program?" Harrison replied "that he would like to increase the excess reserves of the member banks to \$250,000,000 to \$300,000,000 and that thereafter, unless currency hoarding began again, no further purchases should be necessary until the banks begin to use their reserves." Given his inability to rally all the Reserve Banks to a united front for a program of open market purchases, Harrison settled on a goal of maintaining excess reserves at the level of \$250,000,000—an amount he believed would provide banks with an incentive to lend if loan demand revived.

Harrison realized the gravity of the banking situation. However, policy makers lacked the concept of banks forming collectively a banking system whose assets and liabilities rested on a reserves base that the Fed was responsible for maintaining. To wit (HPC, BoD, July 7, 1932, 264):

> Burgess: The excess reserves of member banks, which had built up over a period of weeks, now have been almost eliminated, largely as a result of a renewal of currency withdrawals. He said that this currency movement is offsetting whatever affirmative effects the System's open market program might had had. . . . Harrison: There is no sense . . . in our purchasing securities merely as an offset to currency hoarding. That is an impossible task and an inversion of our program, which was based on a revival of confidence in the banking and credit structure. Unless we can get the Reconstruction Finance Corporation to liberalize its operations so as to check further bank closings, he said, it is doubtful whether we should pursue our open market program further, regardless of the participation of the other Federal reserve banks.

Harrison concluded by agreeing to continue the open market purchases but only because it would look bad to stop them "in a critical situation" in which "the Federal Reserve System probably would have to bear the onus of whatever breakdown of the banking and credit machinery occurred."

The Chicago directors shared the same view of the world as Harrison. New York director Young (HPC, BoD, July 14, 1932, 273–74) related his conversation with the Chicago directors:

> They [the Chicago directors] say what is the use of going ahead if bank failures are to continue and hoarding of currency to be renewed. In these circumstances they hold it to be futile to talk of the pressure of excess upon member banks because, either there won't be any excess reserves or the banks will prefer the cost of carrying them to their use. Mr. Young said that if we must assume that hoarding is going on and bank

failures are to continue, he would agree with this stand. He said he had suggested, however, that there is now a better feeling among business men than there has been for some time and that, if the Reconstruction Finance Corporation can be prevailed upon to do its job, this might be just the time to bring excess member bank reserves and improved business sentiment together, in the hope that we may strike a spark which will bring recovery.

The directors believed that the "breakdown of the banking and credit machinery" that Harrison had referred to at their July 7, 1932, meeting came from a collapse in loan demand unrelated to Fed behavior. The success of the Fed's program of open market purchases required ruling out "the possibility of further numerous bank failures and of a renewal of currency hoarding." Ruling out that possibility would happen only if the Reconstruction Finance Corporation pursued a more liberal loan policy. "Governor Harrison said that he had pointed out to Governor Meyer . . . that there is not much use in the System going ahead with its program unless bank failures are stopped and the basis laid for a restoration of confidence" (HPC, Executive Committee, July 11, 1932, 267). However, in 1932, the Reconstruction Finance Corporation acted under legislation to prevent it from incurring losses. By overcollateralizing loans, it removed good assets from troubled banks and left them unable to borrow either in the market or from the Fed. "Mr. Rounds said that . . . the difficulty involved in working alone . . . is that in many cases the Reconstruction Finance Corporation has cornered all of the collateral of the banks and we have nothing to work on" (HPC, BoD, July 14, 1932, 272).

At the August 4, 1932, Board of Directors meeting, Harrison (HPC, BoD, August 4, 1932, 77) stated that the "open market program of security purchases is now completed." If gold inflows increased excess reserves, "we may soon have to begin to reduce our holdings of Government securities." Although the New York Fed did not begin reducing its securities portfolio, Harrison (HPC, BoD, September 8, 1932, 25) remained concerned that "in the past, we had often acted too slowly and that, if the upward momentum becomes too great, we might not be able to check the movement when we desire to do so." Harrison (HPC, BoD, December 22, 1932, 46) remained concerned that "excess reserves . . . are a cushion between the Federal reserve banks and credit control; we do not have real control . . . until member banks are forced to borrow at the reserve banks." For a variety of reasons, however, the New York Fed was reluctant to reduce its holdings of government securities. Governor Meyer (HPC, BoD, December 22, 1932, 49) noted "the tremendous sentiment for inflation now present in Congress, and which will probably be one of the most troublesome influences in the next Congress. The inflationists are hunting for a way to inflate, he [Meyer] said, and the sale of any governments at the present time would be regarded as deflation, and would be flying in the face of a predominant Congressional sentiment."

11.7. THE POLITICAL ECONOMY OF OPEN MARKET PURCHASES IN 1932

No one in the 1930s understood that the credit and deposit structure of the banking system rested on a reserves base, which the Fed controlled through its power to create and destroy reserves. (That understanding would have to await Clark Warburton.) Policy makers did not understand how their free reserves operating procedures set the marginal cost of funds to banks and how that interest rate interacted with the price system to determine deposit (money) creation. Even at the height of the Fed's open market purchases in spring 1932, Harrison was unwilling to lower the New York bank's discount rate. The minutes (HPC, BoD, April 28, 1932, 211) reported that Harrison told the directors, "It has been pretty generally agreed from the beginning that our present program is a volume program, not a rate program. . . . On the whole . . . it would be more conservative not to reduce the rate at this time." Governor Meyer (HPC, BoD, April 21, 1932, 205) said, "There is a good deal to be said by not confusing our open market policy with a cheap money program based on low discount rates. Our open market program is designed . . . to eliminate our discount and bill portfolio."

Without a restoration of confidence, the reserves provided through open market operations would presumably simply accumulate as excess reserves. The restrictive actions in fall 1931 required to maintain confidence in the gold standard, Harrison assumed, were a precondition for the addition of reserves to banks to stimulate lending and the economy. Harrison (HPC, BoD, April 21, 1932, 201) stated:

> The Federal Reserve Banks . . . cannot by themselves bring about inflation, or raise prices, or increase business activity. We may put out millions of dollars, but if they merely pile up as excess reserves they have, at that point, no influence upon business or prices. That is the reason . . . why in the past we have discussed just such a program as we are now embarked upon, without taking vigorous action. It would have been of no use to start a large open market operation if there were not a reasonable chance that the member banks would utilize the funds. And heretofore that cooperation probably would have been denied because the psychol-

ogy of the bankers, largely by reason of the breakdown in central Europe
and the suspension of the gold standard in England, was opposed to an
expansion of credit.

Most striking, Harrison argued that the periods in which there was "not
a reasonable chance that the member banks would utilize the funds" were
those periods in which reserve outflows were causing a contraction of the
banking system and money. Harrison (HPC, Executive Committee, April
4, 1932, 188) noted, "Last year [1931] . . . because of a widespread lack of
confidence with resultant bank failures and currency hoarding, the banks
would not use the excess reserves which were placed at their disposal." That
view was common. Seymour Harris (1933, 463, 624) noted about the open
market purchases of 1932, "Fear is so widespread that surplus reserves are
hoarded. . . . The excess represents hoards by banks anticipating trouble
rather than funds seeking investment as soon as a favorable opportunity appears. . . . Why supply reserves when they will not be used to expand loans?"

There was no understanding that the increased holdings of excess reserves reflected banks' desire for liquidity. Because of the way that bonds
and securities had lost value, they were not considered liquid assets. The
minutes (HPC, Executive Committee, April 11, 1932, 199–200) reported:

> Mr. Burgess asked Mr. Wiggin concerning the attitude of the banks to-
> ward the purchase of bonds other than Government bonds. Mr. Wig-
> gin said that they were dead against. . . . Mr. Reyburn said that the real
> trouble with the present situation is the general lack of confidence, and
> that he did not think the banks had any business buying anything but the
> best bonds and not too many of them. Mr. Burgess suggested that if the
> banks are going to perform the function of collecting and employing in-
> dividual savings, they must buy some bonds. One of the things which has
> hurt the bond market most, he said, was the growing feeling that banks
> should not buy bonds. . . . Mr. Wiggin said that . . . to begin buying bonds
> now would mean a complete reversal of policy on the part of most banks.

Harrison wanted only policy actions, not a committed policy of raising
the price level because he always looked ahead to when the reserves supplied purposefully by the Fed would have to be withdrawn. Fed policy makers stressed the restoration of confidence as the sine qua non of economic
recovery but were never willing to commit to a policy that made the Fed
responsible for restoration of that confidence. There was never a chance
that the observation of Governor Meyer (HPC, BoD, December 22, 1932,
50) could be considered:

Concerning the most effective pressure of excess reserves, Governor Meyer said that if the banks knew that there was going to be a constant amount of excess reserves over a long period, that amount could be relatively small and still be more effective than a much larger but uncertain amount. To be effective, he said, the pressure of excess reserves has to enter into the calculations of people who are going to use the money over a period of time. We have not obtained the full effect of recent large excess reserves because of uncertainty as to our future policy.

11.8. 1933

At no time during the Great Contraction was the failure of policy makers to understand the nature of the monetary standard so egregious as during the runs and bank closures in February 1933. Only the New York Fed could have organized a Federal Reserve System response to the panicky bank runs and closures, yet it stood by as a passive onlooker. Why did New York not rally the other regional Reserve Banks to lend freely? Summarizing the classical tradition of the Bank of England, Friedman and Schwartz (1963a, 395) referenced Bagehot (1873, 51):

> To meet an internal drain, he [Bagehot] prescribed lending freely. "A panic," he wrote, "in a word, is a species of neuralgia, and according to the rules of science you must not starve it. The holders of the cash reserve must be ready not to keep it for their own liabilities, but to advance it most freely for the liabilities of others."

Harrison did not conceive of the system of Federal Reserve Banks as a central bank with the New York bank as its head. He did not accept responsibility for the banking system, just the banks in his district. He retained the original conception of the Fed as a set of independent reservoirs of funds strictly limited by the legal obligation to protect their gold basis. Consistent with the vision of the founders of the Fed, there was effectively no central bank. Harrison (HPC, Executive Committee, February 20, 1933, 79) acknowledged the "check administered to deflation in the spring of 1932" but attributed its temporary nature to various factors that weakened confidence, "including the unsettling influence of the presidential campaign, the failure of Congress to balance the budget or to take other decisive action, the publication of Reconstruction Finance Corporation loans to banks, and the recurring talk of the inflation and devaluation."

In February 1933, Harrison continued to review "the banking situation in Detroit and the declaration of a series of bank holidays in the State of

Michigan. Currency hoarding is again in evidence and proceeding at an accelerated pace, and hoarding of gold coin has reappeared in aggravated form." He noted that withdrawals of funds by banks in the interior had caused the excess reserves of New York City banks, which had been above $300,000,000, to disappear. Rather than use the situation to rally the Reserve Banks into action, Harrison (HPC, Executive Committee, February 20, 1933, 81) only "expressed the opinion that a statement from someone high in authority in the incoming administration, to the effect that the sound money promises of the party platform and the campaign speeches are going to be strictly kept, would have an electrifying effect in restoring confidence in our currency and credit."

New York had two ways of supplying reserves to banks apart from the discount window. One was open market operations. Harrison said that the OMPC did not grant the required authority but indicated no willingness to lobby for it. The other was through the bill market. Harrison (HPC, BoD, February 23, 1933, 84) offered as the reason for not pegging a low bill rate and supplying whatever reserves banks demanded that the New York Fed would have to be "willing [to allow] our rates [to get] wholly out of line with the market."

At the February 27, 1933, meeting, Harrison (HPC, Executive Committee, February 27, 1933, 85) noted that "the New York City banks have shown a loss of over $500 million in deposits of which approximately $400 million was the result of withdrawals of balances by interior banks." Banks were selling government securities to obtain funds. Harrison (HPC, Executive Committee, February 27, 1933, 86) noted that

> the Government security market has gotten very thin. This has suggested the possibility of the Federal reserve banks going into the Government security market, purely as a market action, to prevent the development of air pockets and violent price fluctuations. A difficulty is that any such action will be interpreted by some as a part of a monetary or credit program and as being inconsistent with rising interest rates. This would be unfortunate but would have to be disregarded. Governor Harrison went on to say he had stated in Washington that, under no circumstances, would he recommend the participation of this bank in such purchases of Government securities unless the Federal Reserve Banks of Boston and Chicago agree to take more than their usual share of the total amount. They are going along with relatively large reserves while our reserve is relatively low.

By early March, Harrison noted that the internal drain had also become an external drain. Harrison (HPC, BoD, March 2, 1933, 91) "thought it best to take the orthodox step and recommended an increase in the discount rate to 3½%." By the March 3, 1933, Board meeting, the loss of gold had become unsustainable. Harrison (HPC, BoD, March 3, 1933, 95) was unwilling to suspend the gold cover and "pay out further millions of dollars of gold and currency to hoarders." Neither was he willing to suspend payment in gold, which might result in "hysteria and panic" and a general run on banks. Consultation with Treasury Secretary Mills and Governor Meyer resulted in a recommendation that "Governor Lehman be requested to declare a holiday in the State of New York."

Upon his inauguration March 5, 1933, President Roosevelt declared a national bank holiday. On March 9, Congress provided a legal basis in the Emergency Banking Act. Ironically, the Fed, which had disavowed any responsibility for keeping banks open, would have to guarantee the viability of all the banks that did open after the bank holiday. The minutes (HPC, BoD, March 10, 1933, 118) reported: "There is no escaping the fact that the Federal reserve banks will have a responsibility for keeping open banks which now are licensed to reopen. Mr. Young said . . . the Federal reserve banks become the guarantors . . . of the deposits in the banks which are reopened."

With the incoming of the Roosevelt administration, until January 31, 1934, the United States ceased pegging the price of gold and the dollar floated in the foreign exchange markets. With banks largely out of the discount window, the Fed no longer determined the marginal cost of reserves to banks and money market rates. The open market policy of the Fed determined bank reserves directly, given the demand for currency. Nothing changed, however, in how policy makers understood their world. The Fed became willing to engage in open market operations, but only grudgingly. As late as the June 8, 1933, Board meeting, Burgess (HPC, BoD, June 8, 1933, 209) reported that "looked at from a strictly monetary point of view, our recent purchases of Government securities merely have offset a runoff of other assets of the Federal reserve banks, and have not yet put any new credit into the market."

The reserves of banks declined in 1933Q2 by 1.9 percent, only slightly less than the 1933Q1 decline of 2.6 percent (figure 10.4). They increased in 1933Q3 but only by 6 percent. In January 1931, free reserves equaled $330 million and were only somewhat higher at $440 million in August 1933. Not until March 1934 did they start to grow strongly (figure 10.6). M2 grew slowly in 1933Q2 and 1933Q3 at 2.3 percent and 1.7 percent annualized, respectively. It began to pick up only in 1933Q4, growing 6.5 percent annualized (figure 8.2).

The New York minutes suggest that the new administration had not thought about monetary policy apart from requiring the Fed to support the government securities market with open market purchases. Harrison (HPC, Executive Committee, April 24, 1933, 162) told the directors that "a central bank . . . cannot go contra to the Government continuously, in perilous times, without courting destruction. The [Open Market Policy] Conference, he said, thereupon unanimously (Chicago not voting) had passed a resolution authorizing its Executive Committee to purchase up to $1,000,000,000 of Government securities if necessary to meet Treasury requirements." However, Harrison remained ignorant of what the administration would require in the way of purchases of government debt.

The May minutes (HPC, Executive Committee, May 1, 1933, 172–73) reported:

> Mr. Young asked what is the monetary policy of the United States? Governor Harrison said he did not know and had no way of finding out. . . . Governor Harrison said, further, he had told Secretary Woodin that in the absence of knowledge of the Government's monetary policy he does not know how to run the Federal Reserve Bank of New York. At present . . . the Federal Reserve Board is disorganized, and in no sense provides a means of contact with the administration.

Harrison's (HPC, Executive Committee, May 15, 1933, 188) comments indicated that the administration was not pushing for an expansionary monetary policy:

> He [Harrison] is afraid of inaction, he said, with its threat of a set-back, forced use of the various provisions of the Thomas bill, and, perhaps, uncontrolled inflation. The country expects something to be done, and he thinks it expects first a resumption of open market purchases of Government securities by the Federal Reserve System. . . . Governor Harrison said some of the other Governors are not in favor of such purchases, and that the Secretary of the Treasury has been dubious about them.

However, as commodity prices stalled, Roosevelt became desirous of open market purchases. The provisions of the Thomas Amendment allowing the president to present government securities directly to the Fed in return for Federal Reserve notes ("Greenbackism") hung over the Fed (HPC, Executive Committee, August 21, 1933, 238, 240, 244):

> Governor Harrison said that he had pointed out that the purchase of $50,000,000 of Government securities is not needed by the current

monetary position—that money is very easy and member banks now have more than $500,000,000 of excess reserves. . . . Governor Black said that farm prices had gone up rapidly when only speculators could profit, but now when the farmer has products ready for the market, prices have dropped so that the farmer gets the benefit of only a part of the rise in prices.[8] He pointed out that it is highly desirable to bring about a higher level of prices during the period when the farmer is selling his products. He repeated that he believed that the President is very desirous of enlarged open market operations by the System in the hope that prices will be strengthened. He expressed the opinion that there is great danger of radical inflationary measures otherwise.

Governor Black . . . pointed out that the Thomas bill authorized the President to direct the Secretary of the Treasury to request the Federal reserve banks to buy $3,000,000,000 of Government securities; the System has hardly made a beginning on such purchases and unless operations are conducted on a larger scale at times such as the present it is to be expected that Congressional leaders will be insistent upon the use of other measures provided by the Thomas bill.

In fall 1933, the Fed continued with open market purchases but only to head off congressional pressure to monetize debt placed directly with it by the Treasury. The minutes (HPC, Executive Committee, August 28, 1933, 252) reported, "Governor Black then said that, talking right out on the table, there was no economic justification for what we did last week [the purchase of $35,000,000 of government securities]; we did it to avoid an issue of greenbacks." The minutes (HPC, BoD, September 7, 1933, 254) of the next Board meeting reported:

> Mr. Burgess said . . . there really isn't much, if any, economic or central banking justification for the purchases. . . . Mr. Young then said that, as a normal central banking operation, our present program has no point at all; we have surrendered to a political situation and have embarked on a program of manufacturing credit as an alternative to something worse.

Harrison was part of a group appointed to formulate monetary policy (the President's Monetary Committee). It included Treasury Secretary William Woodin, Treasury undersecretary Dean Acheson, Federal Reserve

---

8. Eugene R. Black was governor of the Federal Reserve Board from May 19, 1933, to August 15, 1934.

Board governor Eugene Black, and academics Oliver Sprague of Harvard and James Rogers of Yale. New York director Young (HPC, BoD, September 21, 1933, 262) summarized Harrison's memo on the group's discussions:

> Mr. Young said that, reduced to plain English, Governor Harrison's memorandum states that there is no occasion, from a banking and credit standpoint, to buy any more Government securities and that we are going ahead because the administration in Washington thinks it is in order for use to do so, and because it thinks greenbacks are the alternative to our purchases. . . . I am concerned because the creation of excess reserves, except as a superficial gesture isn't going to accomplish the result it has to accomplish. There is no reason on earth . . . to suppose that a billion dollars of excess reserves will be any more effective than $700,000,000. . . . We can't hope to get relief by manufacturing excess reserves in banks.

A consensus developed that further open market purchases would not be helpful. That consensus left depreciation of the dollar as the alternative for combating the "inflationists." At the same time, the psychology of the gold standard still dominated conservative thought. A fixed exchange rate for the dollar gave the dollar its value and acted as a bulwark against irresponsible government deficits that would destroy its value. The compromise would be a significant devaluation of the dollar accompanied by maintenance of a fixed value.

In August 1933, Harrison (HPC, Executive Committee, August 21, 1933, 248) had expressed this proposal.

> There is some question as to whether it is not still too early to stabilize the dollar, but if the President does not make a definite devaluation and take steps to hold that level it is questionable whether he can resist the pressure from Congress in January for the use of greenbacks. . . . The System, during the past week, had done what seemed necessary, to give the President an argument against the use of greenbacks, and he believed the amount of purchases could be reduced during the coming week. . . . A rapid rise in prices might be brought about through a renewed depreciation in the dollar which would stimulate a renewed speculative rise in commodities.

In late September 1933, Harrison (HPC, Executive Committee, September 28, 1933, 4–5) noted:

There has been a decline in business and in confidence and most of the committee thought it to be largely due to doubts as to the future of the currency. Once this doubt becomes widespread . . . you will have a flight of capital [and] you won't be able to stop until the dollar goes through the floor.

[The President's Monetary Committee] . . . unanimously had reached the opinion that: The depreciation of the dollar has reached a point at which the President should let it be known that further depreciation would be disturbing and dangerous. The uncertainty of the present situation requires that immediate steps be taken with a view to stabilization of the dollar-sterling rate, with a subsequent return to gold in the background. . . . The Federal reserve banks should stop buying Government securities as such purchases are no longer necessary under existing conditions.

However, the President's Monetary Committee and the president clashed over priorities. Roosevelt wanted an immediate increase in the price of farm products and intended to continue with dollar purchases of gold to achieve that end. Harrison (HPC, BoD, October 26, 1933, 37–40) reported that

a week ago yesterday the President's monetary committee had met in Washington and had been advised through the Secretary of the Treasury that the President wished it to leave off consideration of other things and to concentrate on ways and means of raising prices. It transpired further, the Governor said, that the President was concerned mostly with raising the prices of certain agricultural products.

There was an extended discussion . . . of a paragraph which had been inserted in the report since the previous meeting of the committee, referring to the decline in prices of agricultural commodities, describing it as intolerable during the harvest season, and terming the resultant situation as a national emergency which must be met. The proposal for meeting this emergency, he said, was to authorize the Federal reserve banks to sell dollars in the market until they had been depressed to $4.86 in terms of pounds sterling. Governor Harrison said he had hit the ceiling on this new paragraph. . . . Inquiry of us had been made this morning . . . as to how the gold buying program might be extended to world markets, and we later had been informed by Mr. Morgenthau, Governor of the Farm Credit Administration, that Professor George F. Warren is coming to the bank today, at the request of the request of the President, to find out how to buy gold in the world markets.

Harrison and the New York directors worried that Roosevelt's program of buying gold to depreciate the value of the dollar would destroy confidence in the dollar and cause investors to stop buying government debt. The government would then have to print money to finance the deficit. At the November 6, 1933, meeting of the Executive Committee, Harrison (HPC, Executive Committee, November 6, 1933, 58) announced that "he had been reluctantly convinced, as had most of the President's Monetary Committee, that the easiest and best way out was to devalue the dollar and to do away with uncertainty." Similarly, Harrison (HPC, Executive Committee, December 18, 1933, 121) averred that "either we shall have to move toward some sort of monetary stability or we shall have to contemplate an issue of greenbacks." Ultimately, Roosevelt settled on a devaluation of the dollar. Harrison (HPC, BoD, December 7, 1933, 116) speculated that Roosevelt was attracted by the gold "profits" of devaluation.

11.9. THE 1936–37 INCREASES IN REQUIRED RESERVES

As the level of excess reserves mounted, Harrison became increasingly concerned about an inability to control credit in the event of a revival of speculative activity. Harrison turned to an increase in required reserves to soak up excess reserves because open market sales of securities would deplete the Federal Reserve System's portfolio and leave it without earning assets. Harrison (HPC, BoD, September 19, 1935, 72–73) told his directors:

> There is the very definite possibility that private credit expansion, once it gets underway, may be difficult to hold within wholesome bounds. Total reserves are now about double required reserves and interest rates are unprecedentedly low. . . . There is a buffer of some $2,800,000,000 of reserves between the credit structure and the required reserves that are normally supposed to govern its behavior, and the member banks are virtually entirely out of debt to the Reserve Banks. Under these conditions would not contraction of reserves through open market operations almost certainly prove to be, by itself, an inadequate means of controlling credit expansion, once such expansion got seriously under way? . . . Under these circumstances should not our first reliance be upon alteration of reserve requirements?

Harrison always said that the Fed could not act without the consent of the administration. The reasons he gave were that the administration could counter the Fed's actions through various ways of printing paper money or spending the funds in the Exchange Stabilization Fund created from the revaluation of gold. An irony was that by monetizing gold inflows the Fed was creating paper money. In effect, the Fed was running a commodity stabilization scheme financed by printing money. Policy makers, however, simply thought that because of the pegged exchange rate the Fed was on a gold standard.

When the FOMC as currently structured began in 1936, Harrison's reports to the directors became largely uninformative. He was no longer speaking for the directors, and issues of confidentiality kept him from sharing FOMC debate. However, the FOMC transcript shows that Harrison's views represented the Federal Reserve System consensus. Goldenweiser reiterated the accepted view that failure to keep on top of incipient speculation was the primary cause of recession and deflation. The minutes (Board of Governors, *FOMC Historical Minutes*, January 26, 1937, 1–7) read:[9]

> [Goldenweiser] also referred to the feeling that some action by the Federal Reserve System to absorb a substantial portion of existing excess reserves was necessary. . . . In connection with the latter point, he discussed various occasions in the past when action reversing existing policy, or in line with an agreed policy, had not been taken at the proper time or not vigorously enough, as illustrative of the utmost importance of proper timing of System action. He then expressed the opinion that the most effective time for action to prevent the development of unsound and speculative situations is in the early stages of such a movement when the situation is still susceptible of control. . . .
>
> He then expressed the opinion that an increase in reserve requirements by 33⅓% at this time would not involve a great risk on the part of the Federal Reserve System, and that this action would place the System in closer touch with the money market where it could influence the market by other means and would restore the System to the position in relation to the market which it normally should occupy.
>
> Mr. Williams . . . expressed the opinion that prior to the depression a total of $500,000,000 of excess reserves would have been regarded as an unprecedented factor in the credit situation, that this should be borne in mind in dealing with the present problem, and that some action should be taken as promptly as possible to absorb the existing substantial amount of excess reserves, which should not be held under normal con-

---

9. Goldenweiser and J. H. Williams provided the economic briefings and policy recommendations before FOMC meetings. Goldenweiser was the Board of Governors' director of research and statistics. Williams was a vice president of the New York Fed and a professor at Harvard.

ditions. Mr. Williams concluded with the statement that it appeared that
there was every argument for early action by the System.

11.10. CONCLUDING COMMENT

In summer 1931, Harrison corresponded with Norman of the Bank of England about the unfolding crisis in central Europe. Norman understood
how the fallout from the run on Credit-Anstalt was spreading to Hungary
and then Germany, and he understood the grimness of the situation. In
contrast, Harrison could think only of protecting the Fed from the risk of
default if there were to be a joint loan to Austria and Germany. Harrison ex-
emplified the American isolationist mindset. He was oblivious to the forces
in the world that were creating the strongmen who played on people's sense
of being left behind and humiliated by powerful external forces. He was
oblivious to the part played by the Fed in creating world recession. The
world was moving toward war, and there was no leadership from the Fed.

CHAPTER 12

Contemporary Critics in the Depression

Summary: In the nineteenth century in Britain, the principles of the quantity theory existed and at times found application, especially in the bullionist-antibullionist debate in the early 1800s and in debate over the Bank Charter Act of 1844 (Peel's Act). However, apart from these few instances of debate in England over the nature of the monetary standard, the quantity theory did not find empirical application. Because of the orthodoxy surrounding the gold standard, the incentive did not exist to create series on money, prices, and output and use these series to understand monetary phenomena (Hetzel 2016). With the classical gold standard, market forces determined gold production, the commodity value of gold, the price level, and the terms of trade between countries.

A few economists could use the quantity theory to understand the operation of the gold standard. However, none of them could put the quantity theory into the form required to understand the monetary regime created by the Fed. With the new monetary standard, the Fed did not follow the classical rules of the game that made money depend on the international balance of payments. Through member bank borrowing at the discount window, it set the marginal cost of reserves to banks and as a result the money market interest rate. However, the resulting interest rate did not follow a world market rate set in a world money market of countries on the gold standard. The result was a regime of fiat money creation in which money creation and destruction depended on how the market rate of interest interacted with the economy's natural rate of interest, that is, with the interest rate that functioned as part of the price system to keep output at potential.

Why was adaptation of the quantity theory so hard? With the only experience with fiat money standards those of money creation directly related to the printing press, there was no obvious model for the Fed. Because the United States maintained convertibility of gold, there was no understanding that the Fed had responsibilities formerly carried out by market forces under the classical gold standard. The Fed's operating procedures made it appear that it was supplying funds to banks and influencing financial intermediation rather than controlling money creation.

Quantity theorists not only failed to understand the monetary regime as one of fiat money creation rather than the gold standard, but also with few exceptions they did not have a monetary theory of recession. Hawtrey and Cassel, the exceptions, thought of recessions as produced by the deflation required by a rising commodity price of gold or a return to gold at an overvalued exchange rate. None of these conditions obviously applied to the United States with its ample gold cover.

Going into the Great Depression, the prevailing consensus about what caused recessions was "the collapse of speculative excess." Accordingly, the emphasis was on forestalling the emergence of "credit inflation." As the Depression ground on, intellectual attitudes changed to emphasize the lack of confidence of the business community and the impotence of monetary policy.

The review starts with opponents of the quantity theory. They viewed the price level as a simple reflection of relative prices. Recessions manifested the collapse of prior speculative excess and required a period of purging to eliminate that excess. This group includes H. Parker Willis, John H. Williams, Charles Hardy, Joseph Schumpeter, and Gottfried Haberler. The review continues with quantity theorists. They explained the price level as a monetary phenomenon but lacked a theory attributing money to the behavior of the Fed rather than to the commercial banking system. Similarly, they lacked a monetary explanation of the Depression highlighting the role of the Fed as opposed to the maladjustment of relative prices. This group includes Carl Snyder, Harold Reed, Lionel Edie, John Commons, Gustav Cassel, Ralph Hawtrey, Alan Goldsborough, and Irving Fisher. Lauchlin Currie was a solitary exception.

The great majority of economists never accepted the radical, populist idea that the Fed should control paper money creation. Reeve (1943, 191), who summarized the monetary reform movements of the 1930s, wrote:

> Advocates of most types of paper money expansion were conspicuously rare in the ranks of professional economists. A large minority, led by Fisher, however, favored issuance of additional currency to inaugurate a system of 100 per cent reserve banking. Otherwise, the only outspoken sponsors of paper money among more prominent economists were John R. Commons of the University of Wisconsin, Willford I. King of New York University and Paul H. Douglas of the University of Chicago.

What was presumed broken was the ability of the banking system to intermediate between savers and borrowers. Money creation would require bypassing financial intermediation either through 100 percent reserve banking (Fisher) or through monetization of government deficit spending (Douglas).

12.1. H. PARKER WILLIS

H. Parker Willis was an unreconstructed proponent of real bills intimately associated with the creation of the Fed. He helped Carter Glass write the Federal Reserve Act and was secretary of the Federal Reserve Board from 1918 to 1922. In the 1930s, he was a professor of banking at Columbia University. In his essay "Federal Reserve Policy in Depression," Willis (1932 [1983], 79–80) blamed the Depression on the cheap money policy the Fed followed in the two 1920s recessions. "Depression, when it comes, looks back to an anterior period of inflation. . . . There are some who would add to the functions [of a central bank] . . . that of so-called 'credit control,' meaning thereby the exerting of some influence upon prices of commodities. To this I fundamentally object."

Willis (1932 [1983], 83) favored keeping interest rates "high" in time of recession:

> The truth of the matter is that inflation is never a remedy for anything. . . . A central bank is a dangerous agency through which to undertake inflation, the more so when we remember that its operations may easily get out of hand and prove disastrous. If the efforts of reserve banks in recent years, upon occasions of expansion and overtrading, have, as most admit, proved hazardous and unsuccessful by aggravating rather than reducing such dangers, their efforts, both in recent times as well as currently, must be regarded as having very similar potentialities.

12.2. JOHN HENRY WILLIAMS

John Henry Williams was a professor at Harvard from 1921 through 1957 and an adviser to the Federal Reserve Bank of New York from 1933 through 1956. He is especially interesting because his views offer insights into the New York Fed views.

Williams (1932 [1983], 134) started by reciting real bills criticisms of the Fed:

> We are reproached again for having permitted, in depression, low rates, which retard liquidation and interfere with its necessary completion. . . . We are told by others that the founders of the Federal Reserve System

never intended its use as an agency for credit control, whether for price stabilization or any other ambitious purpose, but as an agency of elastic supply, to meet the needs of industry and trade, a view which carries the implication . . . that business under these conditions creates and extinguishes its own "legitimate" supply of credit.

At the same time, Williams (1932 [1983], 151) accepted the view that the reduction of rates in 1927 to encourage an outflow of gold started a "spiral of expansion," which required "high money rates ascribable in part to the Reserve banks' efforts to check domestic credit expansion."

Williams defended the New York view against the Board view. Although Williams did not mention Adolph Miller by name, his comments clearly side with Strong in the debate over how to limit the speculative extension of credit presumed to create an ultimately unsustainable level of economic activity. There was a need for quantitative restrictions on total credit extension to limit speculative extension of credit. Williams (1932 [1983], 138) wrote:

There is deeply embedded in the [Federal Reserve] Act the philosophy that member bank credit can be controlled by prescribing the uses to which central bank credit can be put. . . . It has now taken some eighteen years of experience, including two major booms and depressions, to reveal the fallacies inherent in this philosophy. . . . The boom of 1919–20 took primarily the form of commercial loans for commercial speculation. It should serve to explode once for all the notion that credit cannot be excessive if it is "self-liquidating" in form. . . . The boom of 1928–29 took primarily the form of secured loans for financial speculation. The Reserve System met it with an attempt to discriminate between loans for commercial and speculative purposes. Its complete failure should explode once and for all the notion that it is possible to dictate the uses to which credit is put, rather than the quantity for all purposes.

The automatic operation of the gold standard required that the price system work—a condition that did not hold. Williams (1932 [1983], 139) wrote:

In the strict theory of gold standard there is no room or need for central bank control of credit. Control is achieved automatically by the flow of gold between the banking systems. . . . It purports to give external stability conditioned upon internal flexibility. . . . The gold standard works best . . . when the demand for international products is elastic, so that a fall in prices will produce an increase in value of exports relative to

imports. . . . The collapse of the gold standard in the agricultural countries was a case of inelastic demand-supply. . . . With prices falling, the
debt payments and the imports entail a progressive increase in the quantity of exports relative to the value of exports, but increasing quantity
depresses prices farther. It becomes a case of indeterminate equilibrium,
and gold flows out persistently until collapse ensues.

Williams (1932 [1983], 153) hesitated to abandon the gold standard for
the untested perils of a paper money standard. The gold standard provided
a nominal anchor that could "exercise the only objective restraint upon that
process of evolving a costless and limitless means of payment." Williams
sounded like the Keynes, who would later argue for a managed system of
fixed exchange rates in debate over the Bretton Woods system. World trade
required the "stable exchanges" provided by the gold standard. However,
"such a system can never be automatic," especially in light of a "great increase in the international flow of short-term capital" (J. H. Williams 1932
[1983], 146, 147, and 157).

12.3. CHARLES O. HARDY

Hardy epitomized the failure of the economics profession to understand
the monetary regime and the contractionary character of monetary policy.
He rejected Fed efforts at stabilization. Hardy (1932, 215) wrote, "Little as
we know about the causes of the semi-rhythmical movement of business
activity, we can say without hesitation that the injection of new purchasing
power into the markets of the world by inflation and deflation of currency
and credit is an unstabilizing factor." Moreover, "if we cannot stabilize business activity by adjusting credit to business conditions as observed directly,
we can scarcely hope to stabilize it indirectly by action taken on the basis of
a price index which may or may not reflect the course of business" (Hardy
1932, 219).

The attempt by the Fed to control the price level had been destabilizing.
Changes in the price level have many causes. Price declines due to technological progress are desirable. Hardy (1932, 216, 219, 223) wrote that offsetting "price declines which are due to the progress of technique, invention,
and the improvement of management . . . would require the continuous
injection of new purchasing power into the market. . . . The experience of
the years from 1922 to 1929 seems to indicate that this point is . . . a fatal
objection to the use of a commodity price index as an index of the presence
of inflation or deflation. . . . Those years were years of mild credit inflation
which was offset by the downward pressure on prices exerted by technolog-

ical change." He concluded, "For these reasons I believe that the program of the stabilizers should be rejected." (Compare the comments of Haberler in section 12.5.)

12.4. JOSEPH A. SCHUMPETER

In 1934, seven of Harvard's most distinguished economists, including Joseph Schumpeter, published their views on various aspects of the Roosevelt administration's recovery program in *The Economics of the Recovery Program*. Although each essay considered a different aspect of the programs, a preface stated that "these essays had their origin in private conversations among the authors." One can infer that their views reflected a commonality of thought.

In his book on Lauchlin Currie, Roger Sandilands (1990, 40, 50) commented on Schumpeter:

> Throughout this period Schumpeter was worrying about "inflationary" monetary policies, even when the price level was falling. In fact, Currie has claimed that in the early 1930s he [Currie] was the only person on the Harvard faculty who regarded monetary policy as deflationary—though some, like Seymour Harris, later became prominent "Keynesians" when it became fashionable so to be, having earlier disdained Currie's views and sought to block his promotion. . . . Any revival which is merely due to artificial stimulus leaves part of the work of depressions undone, and adds . . . new adjustments of its own which have to be liquidated in turn, thus threatening business with another crisis ahead.

Schumpeter attributed recessions to the collapse of speculative excess that had encouraged economic excess. Recessions were required to put economic activity on a sounder footing. Schumpeter reviewed a history of financial crises, recessions, and recoveries. Schumpeter (1934, 7) started with the crisis in 1825 in England:

> The annals of the period abound with reports of all imaginable symptoms of "prosperity." . . . Then came the crash, and reaction and readjustment, both of the most typical kind. The first thing to break down was speculation. . . . Roughly three years of depression followed. Here is a case which exemplifies how much basis there is for the belief in the recuperative powers of capitalism. For Government did next to nothing. . . . Things were allowed to take their course. The inaction of government . . . contributed to recovery at least by not hampering it.

Schumpeter (1934, 8–11) then considered the US depression of 1873:

1873 and the four years of depression which followed display similarities to 1929. . . . The expenditure on railroad building was the backbone of the booms of that time. The new facilities of transportation changed the surface of the economic world. . . . They also were the center of the reckless finance and malpractice of all sorts. It was the business of railroad construction which produced that mentality, half visionary, half criminal. . . . American speculation collapsed in September. . . . There is *nothing* in what has happened in the capitalist world during the last three years which was not also present in the picture in 1873. (italics in original)

Schumpeter (1934, 13–16) concluded:

When everybody talks of new eras—blissfully unaware of the fact that soon he will be talking of the hopeless failure of capitalism—an increasing volume of business is being done on the assumption that things will continue to boom. A superstructure of such transactions rises above what is substantially sound and comes down with a crash. . . . Inflation . . . would . . . undoubtedly turn depression into . . . sham prosperity, but which . . . would, in the end, lead to a collapse worse than the one it was called in to remedy.

12.5. GOTTFRIED HABERLER

Gottfried Haberler summarized the Austrian view of the Depression. He cited Hayek, *Prices and Production*, as an elaboration of his views. Haberler (1932 [1983], 43–45) believed that booms followed by recessions were an inevitable part of a capitalist economy. "The fundamental appearance of the business cycle is a wavelike movement. . . . Periods of rapid progress are followed by periods of stagnation. . . . We have not yet got rid of this scourge of the capitalistic system." That view was common. Hayek (1925 [1999], 77) noted "the basic principle of business cycle theories, namely, that economic life can never be in a 'normal state,' but that one cycle follows the other and any given state can be understood only as a phase in this cyclical movement."

Haberler (1932 [1983], 53–56) started his explanation of the Depression by distinguishing between declines in prices "*due to an actual contraction* of the circulating medium and a fall of prices which is caused by *lowering of cost* as a consequence of inventions and technological improvements" (italics in original). Prior to the onset of the Depression, these improvements ceteris paribus would have lowered the price level. However, the low interest rates engineered by the Fed in the years 1924–27 created an amount of credit that offset the decline and resulted in price stability. "There is now an obvious presumption that it was precisely the relative inflation which brought about all the trouble. . . . The price level is a misleading guide for monetary policy."

Haberler (1932 [1983], 60–61, 73) wrote that the Fed produced an "artificial decrease of the rate of interest." That decrease produced "a credit expansion by the banks," which added to "those sums, which are deliberately saved by the public from their current income [and] come on the capital-market. . . . A reaction must inevitably set in, if this productive expansion is not financed by real, voluntary saving of individuals or corporations but by *ad hoc* created credit." The credit expansion induced

> business leaders to indulge in an excessive lengthening of the process of production. . . . A reaction is inevitably produced . . . which raises the rate of interest again to its natural level or even higher. Then these new investments are no longer profitable, and it becomes impossible to finish the new roundabout ways of production. They have to be abandoned, and productive resources are returned to the older, shorter methods of production. This process of adjustment of the vertical structure of production, which necessarily implies the loss of large amounts of fixed capital which is invested in those longer processes and cannot be shifted, takes place during, and constitutes the essence of, the period of depression.

Like real bills advocates, Haberler (1932 [1983], 70) argued that recessions represented periods of adjustment that could not be shortened through expansionary monetary policy:

> If we have, however, once realized that at the bottom of these surface phenomena lies a far-reaching dislocation of productive resources, we must lose confidence in all the economic and monetary quacks who are going around these days preaching inflationary measures which would bring almost instant relief. If we accept the proposition that the productive apparatus is out of gear, that great shifts of labor and capital are necessary to restore equilibrium, then it is emphatically not true that the business cycle is a purely monetary phenomenon . . . although monetary forces have brought about the whole trouble. Such a dislocation of real

physical capital, as distinguished from purely monetary changes, can in no case be cured in a very short time.

12.6. CARL SNYDER

Carl Snyder is especially interesting. He was a quantity theorist and did extensive empirical work on the quantity theory. Snyder constructed a price index number like that of Irving Fisher but more comprehensive. He used the series to test the Fisher version of the quantity theory. He contended that deviations of velocity (V) from a basically constant value matched deviations of transactions (T) from trend. That is, the ratio of V over T was constant. Consequently, the price level (P) varied directly with money (M): $P = (V/T) M$ or P = a constant times M in the equation of exchange.[1]

Later, Snyder (1935) reviewed price series going back to 1300. Treating the price revolution of the sixteenth and seventeenth centuries as an "experiment," he concluded that the price level is a monetary phenomenon and argued for the validity of the Fisherian equation of exchange. Relative prices had no predictive power for the price level. He also associated periods of monetary instability like the deflation from 1929 through 1933 with great social distress. Snyder answered affirmatively the question of whether a central bank could break the association between nominal and real instability through maintaining price stability.

In many ways, Snyder sounded like a precursor of monetarism. He blamed the Fed for the Depression. Snyder (1940, 188 and 190) wrote:

If in 1930 or 1931 it had been proposed deliberately to destroy one-third of the nation's currency, with which the retail business of the country is mainly carried on, there would have been an overwhelming protest. Yet we deliberately permitted the destruction of one-third of our essential bank credit, essential to the actual production of goods, without a great deal of protest, and without any adequate understanding of its inevitable effect. The proof: in the Autumn of 1931, when the depression was steadily deepening and extending all over the world, the discount rate of the Federal Reserve banks was *raised*—raised instead of lowered—in order to "protect" our gold. We had billions of gold, a huge excess, far more than we had any need for, and yet in panic we increased the pressure, forcing the banks to further contract credit. . . .

Normally the fall in the price level determines the duration of depres-

---

1. The result was a caricature of the quantity theory. I am indebted to Tom Humphrey for these points.

sions, and as this is purely a function of the monetary or credit supply, it follows that if this credit supply is properly maintained, no such fall in prices or in wages is necessary. (italics in original)

As Currie (1933a, 65) pointed out, however, Snyder did not distinguish between credit, taken as loans and investments, and money, taken as demand deposits. Snyder advocated a rule in which the Fed would maintain steady growth in bank credit. Snyder (1940, 220) advocated "maintaining its [bank credit] increase at a fixed and pre-determined rate determined by the normal rate of growth of industry and trade, which in our generation we now know has been about 4 per cent per annum." However, like the stabilization policy of the 1920s, the underlying rationale was to control speculative excess. Snyder (1940, 221) continued, "If we had used this simple rule from 1920 to 1929, we would have had no undue expansion of bank credit, no wild speculation, no crash." It was a weak foundation for a rule when confronted with the "obvious" evidence of "speculation."

Because Snyder was also head of the statistics department at the New York Fed, he had an opportunity to influence internal debate. The question then arises of why he was ineffective in influencing the New York Fed to abandon the consensus of the financial community and to adopt a program of monetary stimulus starting in 1930. What was the New York consensus that Snyder decried? Money policy operated through its influence over the cost and availability of funds supplied to banks. In 1930, the cost of funds, the discount rate, was "low." Also, in 1930, banks possessed an ample supply of funds to lend as evidence by the "low" level of borrowing at the discount window. And yet, in contrast to the three recessions of the 1920s, the economy did not recover. The problem seemed evident. The transmission of "easy" money to the business community had broken down because of the lack of confidence of businessmen who became unwilling to borrow.

The main characteristic of Snyder's view to note is that he grafted onto his monetary theory of prices a boom-bust credit cycle arising endogenously among commercial banks. Instead of making the transition to a strictly monetary-disorder understanding of recession represented later by Friedman and Schwartz, he kept with the prevalent real bills tradition. Recessions arose from the collapse of speculative excess caused by prior excessive creation of credit. Snyder then lacked a convincing retort to real bills proponents who argued that recessions were the necessary purging of prior excess. He had no framework for explaining how open market purchases would raise the money stock without at the same time creating another round of "credit inflation."

Snyder had only the conventional wisdom of the New York financial community to offer for the persistence of depression after the United States left the gold standard on April 20, 1933. Like others at the New York Fed, Snyder (1940, 189) highlighted the lack of confidence of businessmen:

> When this essential step [abandoning the gold standard] was taken, the recovery was prompt. If the government had done no more, we might readily have soon returned to the 1929 level of production and trade and continued our previous growth. But the "zeal" for mistaken "reform." The good that was accomplished by an effective monetary policy was largely offset by drastic agricultural restriction; by regulation of industrial production, of prices, wages, hours, and labor relations; by unnecessary restriction of the securities markets; by punitive taxation, that discouraged investment; by large wasteful expenditure in "priming the pump." And along with these a torrent of irresponsible denunciation of business and business men. At a time when the confidence of the country was still very low.

To convert Harrison of the New York Fed and its Board of Directors to the view that through sustained credit creation the Fed could end the Depression, Snyder would have had to persuade them to cross a vast chasm. That chasm separated the conservative eastern financial establishment from the agrarian populists in Congress. In the perspective of the time, that meant abandoning gold convertibility, which presumably gave the dollar value, for a regime of "managed money"—fiat money creation. Not even Snyder understood that the United States had been on a fiat money regime since the creation of the Fed. That regime had led to the destruction of money instead of the uncontrolled money creation and inflation feared by the eastern establishment.

Snyder's history of the Depression in his book *Capitalism the Creator* reveals how entrenched were real bills views, even in the mind of a radical quantity theorist like himself. It is also of historical interest that Snyder championed Governor Strong while not once mentioning Governor Harrison in his book. In his *Capitalism the Creator*, Snyder (1940, 198) laid out the six "noteworthy features common to all" major depressions. "Every crisis [is] preceded by a period of high prosperity. . . . Every such period [is] characterized by easy money and easy credit. . . . The rise in prices in the real estate or stock markets, or in commodity markets, is always accompanied by an outbreak of wild speculation. . . . When speculation has continued for some time . . . there is evidence of a shortage of credit. . . . There soon follows a selling movement, with a sharp fall in prices. . . . The collapse of speculation and the fall in prices leads to a sharp check to business."

Snyder (1940, 199) concluded that "the major factor, the dominant factor, leading to depression is therefore invariably the expansion of bank credit, which alone makes possible the speculative boom; and the ensuing contraction of bank credit that brings about the collapse of speculative activity." Stated more strongly, like his contemporaries, Snyder (1940, 203) attributed the Depression to the collapse of the earlier "wild speculation and perversion of our monetary system to the uses of speculators. . . . An undue expansion of bank credit brings about not only a general rise in prices, but most harmful of all, promotes speculation in securities. . . . We can no longer permit such debauchery of the share markets in this reckless fashion." That was a succinct statement of the guiding spirit of policy in the decade of the 1920s as bequeathed by Governor Strong (chap. 7).

Snyder (1940, 203–5) characterized Governor Strong as possessing a "rare combination of insight and courage" and lamented his death. Had Strong lived, Snyder believed, "we might have ended the depression in 1930." Because Snyder knew Strong, it is important to understand his argument. Irving Fisher and Friedman and Schwartz also contended that if Strong had not died in 1928 but had continued in charge of the New York Fed, the Great Depression would have been avoided. If Snyder was correct in his assumption of how Strong would have controlled policy if he had not died, then the contention of Fisher and Friedman and Schwartz, however, is less obvious.

Snyder's "if-Strong-had-lived" counterfactual began in 1927 when the New York Fed lowered its discount rate and undertook open market purchases to help the Bank of England deal with the strains of its return to the gold standard. Strong was aware of stock market speculation and credit expansion and had intended the policy of easing only to help England get through the peak seasonal demand for reserves in autumn 1927. Snyder (1940, 227–29) wrote:

> Governor Strong's plan anticipated proper repressive measures as soon as the autumnal demands upon the Bank of England had been met. However, in February 1928, Governor Strong was stricken with a fatal illness. It was not until August that, in response to his constant urgings, the New York rate had been raised to 5 per cent. Wholly inadequate. The market boom went on, gathering momentum for another year. If Governor Strong's plan of restricting reserve credit had been followed, from early 1928, the later phase of wild speculation could easily have been avoided. . . . Check the speculation in time, and we shall have no serious depressions.

The claim by Fisher and Friedman and Schwartz that if Strong had lived he would have prevented the Depression through a policy of monetary

stimulus may have merit. However, one cannot support that claim by arguing that Strong understood the world the way in which they understood it.
Snyder was on weak ground in arguing for open market purchases during
the Great Contraction. Snyder (1940, 13) wrote: "Another orgy of so-called
'prosperity,' another wild outburst of speculation, aided and only possible
through a huge expansion of bank credit, must inevitably bring us to the
brink of another cataclysm." Having accepted the consensus explanation
for the Depression that placed the blame on the Fed for having forced an
unwanted expansion of credit on banks, Snyder could not then effectively
argue that the Fed should again force an unwanted expansion of credit on
markets through open market purchases.

Finally, Snyder opposed legislation requiring the Fed to stabilize the
price level. Representative Goldsborough (US Congress 1926, April 14,
600) challenged Snyder to support a legislated mandate for the Fed to stabilize the price level:

> As I have understood the testimony on the part of Governor Strong and
> yourself, the policy of the Federal reserve system is to carry out just what
> would be this legislative direction. If that is the policy of the system and
> the system thinks it is a wise policy, but that it is doing it on its own
> initiative and exercising its own judgment in the matter of the welfare
> of the country, what is the objection to crystallizing, in legislation, that
> very policy in order to fortify the Federal reserve system in the future,
> in carrying out in the future what it thinks is a wise economic policy and
> tradition?

Snyder's response represented a classic Fed rejection of legislated rules.
Namely, monetary policy is best left to the experts. Any sort of explicit guidance would only serve to organize political pressure on the Fed. Snyder (US
Congress 1926, April 14, 99) testified: "You do not think, Mr. Congressman,
that it would inevitably build up in the public mind the idea which is so evident in hundreds of different ways, that the Federal reserve system is some
kind of an almighty power; that it can do anything?"

12.7. HAROLD REED

In 1930, Harold Reed (1930, 198, cited in Laidler 1999, 187), an economist at
Cornell, summarized the results of his book *Federal Reserve Policy 1921–1930*
as approving a policy of credit stabilization, which he associated with Carl
Snyder of the New York Fed:

In our examination of special periods we have concluded that mistakes have usually been later admitted whenever the aggregate credit supply of the country has been permitted to undergo pronounced fluctuations for any extended period of time. The stabilization of business seems to be very largely a matter of avoiding serious departures from a rate of credit enlargement corresponding roughly to the physical growth of the country's trade.

However, the persistence of the Depression gave rise to the belief that the mechanism transmitting monetary policy to bank lending had collapsed. Five years after 1930, Reed had changed his beliefs. Reed then criticized Snyder's "credit-forcing doctrine" by emphasizing both the cyclical variability in the velocity of money and the impotence of monetary policy. Reed (1935, 614) wrote:

In such a situation [a bull market] market conditions tend to pull inactive bank accounts into use. . . . Men begin to think and talk in terms of a "new era." . . . Any shock to investment confidence sets in motion contraction forces which operate with violence. . . . It is then doubtful if central banking efforts to hold up bank reserves can produce revival. Banks may have the reserves. But before they will make new loans bankers must regain confidence in borrowers' ability to repay.

12.8. LIONEL D. EDIE

Lionel D. Edie had been a professor in the business school of the University of Chicago and later was an economist at the Investment Research Corporation. As Laidler (1999, 188) noted, Edie used "credit" synonymously with "money." Edie was "concerned with the behavior of the banking system's liabilities rather than assets" but "used the time path of assets to gauge that of liabilities." Edie (1931, 102, cited in Laidler 1999, 188) wrote:

Central banks should aim at so regulating the reserves of the banking system that the outstanding credit built upon these reserves will expand at the same rate as the long-term growth of production. There is enough credit when the reserves of credit growth and production parallel each other. More than this is too much; less than this is too little.

Edie (1931, 91–92, cited in Laidler 1999, 188) expressed dismay at the dominance among central bankers of real bills views:

A symposium of central bank opinion in various countries revolves about such maxims as: "Artificial interference with the natural commercial demand for credit is dangerous and unwarranted": "It is impossible to strike a blow at speculative excesses without at the same time cutting off the credit supply to meet legitimate needs of trade"; "We can make money easy but we cannot force people to borrow it. One can lead a horse to water but one cannot make him drink."

In 1932, Edie wrote the essay "The Future of the Gold Standard" for the Harris Foundation Lectures. Like Viner and Williams, Edie understood the disastrous way in which contractionary monetary policy in the United States spread deflation and recession to the gold bloc countries. His analysis of that policy is the most perceptive of contemporaneous observers. Although the gold standard had been mismanaged, its abandonment for the alternative of "managed money" represented a radical departure from the conservative ethos of the time. Edie's essay ends with an empty plea for a solution with no proposal for reform.

Without mentioning the option of lowering the discount rate, Edie (1932 [1983], 123) noted that the reserve base "tends to be driven to excessive contraction by the automatic working of the mechanics of the banking system." Edie (1932 [1983], 126) also commented uncritically, "Furthermore, the Federal Reserve reason[s] that it would do no good to force funds on the market when the member banks are in no mood to co-operate in putting the money to constructive uses." Edie could very well have signed on to Governor Harrison's view that restoration of confidence through fiscal conservatism was a prerequisite for open market purchases to stimulate bank lending. In a footnote that updated the essay for the spring 1932 open market policy of the Fed, Edie (1932 [1983], 130) hoped that "such policy embodies a new attitude of responsibility for moderating fluctuations in the reserve base" but then concluded:

> The national budget is far out of balance. Continuation of a heavy deficit might easily impair confidence in government credit and undermine the gold standard along lines of European precedent in the post-War period. Effectiveness of Federal Reserve policy is conditioned upon a balancing of the national budget.

Like his contemporaries, Edie could not envisage a world trading system without the fixed exchange rates of the gold standard. With reference to England, Edie (1932 [1983], 111) wrote, "The injury to world-trade resulting from fluctuating exchange rates, particularly of sterling, will constitute a powerful inducement to England to lead the world back to gold parities of exchange at the earliest favorable opportunity." Breaking the golden chains of the perceived gold standard, the centerpiece of financial orthodoxy, and replacing them with a regime of paper money creation required a leap of faith that few apart from the populists were willing to take.

12.9. JOHN R. COMMONS

John R. Commons worked with Congressman Strong to draft the two Strong bills requiring the Fed to stabilize the price level. Commons, who was a professor at the University of Wisconsin, had helped to prepare an index number of the price level. He did not think of the control of prices in terms of monetary control, that is, through the control by the Fed of the deposits of banks. Commons was a quantity theorist but not in the monetarist sense. He believed that the Fed controlled prices through the way in which it controlled the velocity of money, which in turn it controlled by acting on the expectations of businessmen. Commons (US Congress 1928, March 21, 67) testified:

> I want to bring in this matter of futurity now. The reserve system, so far as its powers over credit are concerned, and over the velocity of circulation, operates through the expectations of business. . . . As soon as the public begins to get the idea that prices are going to rise, then you are going greatly to increase the velocity of business transactions . . . so that those two items which I consolidated in the two terms—velocity and futurity—are really the important instruments in the power of the reserve system.

Commons assumed that countries would remain on the gold standard but that to avoid deflation it would have to be a managed gold exchange standard. The second Strong bill explicitly authorized the Fed to work with other central banks to distribute gold among themselves to avoid deflation (US Congress 1928, March 21, 104; Fisher 1934, 171).

12.10. GUSTAV CASSEL

Gustav Cassel became a primary exponent of Wicksell's ideas. Wicksell (1898 [1962]) had exposited his idea of the cumulative inflation process in *Interest and Prices*. In a pure credit system with no currency but only bank deposits, inflation (deflation) would proceed indefinitely as long as banks held their loan rates below (above) the natural rate. Wicksell wrote without reference to a central bank. Cassel (1928, 515–17) extended the idea to a world with a central bank:

> If the supply of means of payment valid in our monetary standard were quite unlimited, any price could be paid and prices would continue to rise indefinitely. An indisputable condition of stability is, therefore, that the supply of means of payment should be limited. . . . Every monetary system is primarily characterized by the way in which it realizes the scarcity of the supply of means of payment. . . . Now, the central bank has, of course, several means whereby it is able to restrict its issue of notes. The ultimate and essential means is, however, always the price that the bank charges for its advances, that is, the bank rate.
>
> By what principles shall the central bank be guided in fixing its rate? The answer is easy enough as soon as we have perceived that there exists a definite equilibrium rate of interest. If the bank rate is lower than this equilibrium rate, people will go to the bank for covering their needs for capital, and the bank will have to issue notes in order to meet such needs. This leads to an unnecessarily large issue of notes, and fresh purchasing power is created without any more goods having been produced, and this increase of nominal purchasing power is bound to force up prices. . . . The conclusion from this is clear. Stability of prices is possible only when the bank rate is kept equal to the equilibrium rate of interest.

Cassel commented on the US experience.

Cassel (US Congress 1928, May 18, 367) testified, "We ought to begin by pointing out that the United States, first of all, has a gold standard. You have a Federal reserve system, and the most prominent function of the whole system is to keep up the gold standard." Cassel continued in arguing that the Fed had the power to control the price level because under a gold standard the central bank had to be able to vary the price level to keep the real value of a paper dollar equal to the real value of a specified amount of gold.

> There is a lot of experience confirming the fact that a central bank system has that capacity, because long before the War—in some countries almost a century—a gold standard has been kept up, and it has been kept up in no other way than that the central bank in a given country has kept the monetary unit at a purchasing power as against commodities corresponding to the purchasing power of a certain amount of gold.

Cassel thought of price stability within the framework of the gold standard. Following the above comments, he recommended that the Fed vary its gold reserve within the legal limit and vary the composition of currency between gold certificates (backed 100 percent by gold) to influence the real price of gold. Cassel (US Congress 1928, May 18, 1928, 368–69) testified:

> I know that in this country there is a certain tendency, in monetary matters, to be independent. . . . You could possibly take that view if you had decided to have a paper standard established in this country. But you are not on a paper basis. You have decided, and I venture to think once for all, that you are going to have a gold standard. . . . I have the view that we will have to face in the future an increasing scarcity in the supply of gold. . . . For that reason the cooperation between the different countries must be directed to economizing in the use of gold, and of course that can not be done in any other domain than in the monetary demand for gold.

Later, Cassel believed that the United States and France had made the gold standard into an instrument of instability. Cassel (1936 [1966], 59, 61) argued that the "world-wide deflation" that led to the "destruction" of the "new international gold-standard system" began in June 1928 when France returned to the gold standard and "the American export of capital began to run dry and the huge surplus in the American balance of payments had to be paid in gold. . . . But France and the United States did not use their newly acquired gold for a corresponding credit expansion which could have brought about the desirable rise in prices. On the contrary, the price-levels were forced down even in these countries." Cassel (1936 [1966], 63) continued:

> After the [American] crisis the directors of the Federal Reserve System gradually relaxed their restrictive policy; but they did so reluctantly and too slowly and never made it clear that they intended to stop the process of deflation. Still less did the system accept any responsibility in this respect. Under such circumstances the general fear of a further fall in prices could not be removed and conditions both in the United States and in the world at large continued to deteriorate. In 1931 the process of destruction had gone so far as to produce a tornado over the European continent

On September 19, 1931, England abandoned the gold standard. Cassel (1936 [1966], 64) cited the autobiography of Viscount Snowden, who explained that the foreign balance in London subject to withdrawal exceeded the Bank of England's gold reserve.

Like Keynes (1920) earlier, Cassel (1936 [1966], 53, 57) criticized the

reparations forced on a defeated Germany in the Versailles Treaty. Transfers of gold by Germany led to a "'maldistribution of gold' due to the huge
payments on account of reparations and War debts which, in spite of all
warnings from sensible economists, continued to be enforced by politicians
in power.... Politicians in power had so concentrated their attention upon
the question of how to enforce reparations from Germany that they had no
interest left for an investigation of the dangers threatening the stability of
the world's monetary system."

Cassel (1936 [1966], 69–70) summarized the change in the intellectual
support for capitalism but defended it as not responsible for the Depression:

> The Socialists, of course, were eager to represent the crisis as the final
> break-down of the capitalistic system. In the appalling economic disor-
> der that ensued a large amount of State Leadership and Control seemed
> to be indispensable, and the occasion was thought favorable for an agi-
> tation aiming at replacing the old social order of individual freedom by
> some form of authoritative "Planning." . . . Socialists of all shades were
> united in their condemnation of the capitalistic system that had brought
> such disaster upon the world.
>
> On closer analysis this must be found to be a singularly unfair ver-
> dict. . . . The entire War and the Peace Treaty, involving as it did calami-
> tous demands for reparations and the disintegration of the international
> trading community, were the work of the States . . . while some leading
> States and central banks were jointly responsible for the last and fatal
> process of deflation.

12.11. RALPH HAWTREY

Ralph Hawtrey stands out for his early views that the Depression was a
monetary phenomenon. Like Cassel, he had hoped that the Genoa Conference of 1922, which assembled the world's central bankers, would put into
practice the principle that central banks would manage the reconstruction
of the gold standard so that the increased demand for gold would not force
deflation. He wanted to avoid a repetition of the deflation that had occurred
after 1873 when many countries abandoned a silver standard for the gold
standard. He was disappointed, especially with the large absorption of the
world's gold supply by France when it returned to the gold standard in 1928
and by the United States when it attracted foreign capital when it raised
rates starting in 1928. Hawtrey attributed the worldwide character of the
Depression to a return to the gold standard and to a real value of gold that

had increased in the 1920s. Hawtrey (1931, 81) wrote, "The depression arises from the appreciation of gold."

Hawtrey (1932 [1962], 44) attributed the stability of the 1920s to the stabilization policies of Benjamin Strong. He attributed the start of the Great Depression to the misguided attempt by the Fed to reverse the rise in the stock market. Hawtrey attributed the rise in the NYSE to the increase in corporate profits and to the decline in long-term interest rates. Although profits did not account for the entire increase, they accounted for much of it. Like Irving Fisher (1929 [1997]), he attributed the rest to the presumed continuation of the enormous technological progress and organizational advances that had characterized the 1920s (Hawtrey 1932 [1962], 45–58).

Hawtrey (1937, 132–33, 130) wrote:

> Deflationary measures were initiated in the United States in the summer of 1928, and early in 1929 there began an intensified absorption of gold by France, and the bank rate was raised still higher in London. . . . Deflation was successfully started in the summer of 1929, and thereafter the restrictive measures were intensifying the existing tendency in that direction. . . .
>
> One is often tempted to take for granted that the volume of short-term borrowing is bound to respond to a rise or fall in the short-term rate of interest. . . . Before the War [I asked] "What if the rate of depreciation of prices is actually greater than the natural rate of interest?" . . . By the "natural" rate of interest I meant the equilibrium rate corresponding to the marginal yield of capital. The assumption was that an expected fall of prices must be set off against the natural rate to arrive at the real rate.

Initially, Hawtrey remained optimistic. Almost alone among his contemporaries, Hawtrey (1932 [1962], 172–74) advanced the idea that central banks can create money:

> It may happen that demand is so contracted and markets are so unfavourable that traders, seeing no prospect of profit, abstain from enterprise and do not borrow. . . . There appears to the money market to be a plethora of money. . . . But the low rates are merely the outward expression of the unprofitableness of business and the unwillingness of traders to borrow. . . . There is a deadlock which can best be broken by injecting money into the system.
>
> Now the central bank has the power of creating money. If it chooses to buy assets of any kind, it assumes corresponding liabilities, and its

liabilities, whether notes or deposits, are money. . . . When they [central banks] buy, they create money, and place it in the hands of the sellers. There must ultimately be a limit to the amount of money that the sellers will hold idle, and it follows that by this process the vicious cycle of deflation can always be broken, however great the stagnation of business and the reluctance of borrowers may be.

However, as the high unemployment in the 1930s dragged on, Hawtrey became pessimistic about the power of a central bank to counteract a deep depression. He accepted the prevailing view that central banks had tried to stimulate the economy, and he no longer mentioned the idea of central banks creating money. Hawtrey (1937, 133, 142) wrote:

Efforts have been made over and over again to induce that expansion of demand which is the essential condition of a revival of activity. In the United States, particularly, cheap money, open-market purchases, mounting cash reserves, public works, budget deficits on a scale reminiscent of wartime, in fact the whole apparatus of inflation has been applied, and inflation has not supervened. . . . All the inflationary measures that the wit of man has devised have together proved insufficient to overcome it [the credit deadlock].

"Mounting cash reserves" referred to the rising excess reserves of banks.

Hawtrey (1937, 142) also attached importance to the failure of the brief revival at the start of the Roosevelt presidency to last:

In the United States there was . . . a transitory interval, following the depreciation of the dollar in 1933, when revival seemed to be carrying all before it. But in July, 1933, the National Recovery Act brought an all-round increase of costs, and the expectations of profit on which the movement had been built were suddenly dissipated. Pessimism reigned once again, [and] the impetus of revival was lost.

The problem was not contractionary monetary policy. The problem was a pessimism that crushed all efforts to set off the "vicious circle of inflation," which Hawtrey (1937, 143) humorously contrasted with the common use of "vicious circle of deflation," required for economic recovery.

Despite the isolated reference above to "creating money," Hawtrey understood the central bank as operating through its influence on financial intermediation with the corollary that in depression a lack of demand for funds would limit the ability of the central bank to stimulate the economy.

The central bank would have to act early to counteract downturns while it could still affect psychology. Hawtrey (1938 [1962], 250–52) wrote:

> Bank rate can always be used to contract credit if only it be raised high enough. But there is a limit to the power of stimulating an expansion of credit by lowering Bank rate. . . . Once the rate is so low as to have practically no deterrent effect on the borrowing of money for the purchase of goods, traders will have adjusted their stocks of goods purely to suit their convenience, and cannot be induced to add to them by reducing the rate further. . . . Theoretically depression may get business into a state of deadlock, traders being so unwilling to borrow that even very cheap money would fail to start revival.
>
> It is only in recent years that the theoretical possibility of a depression too deep and persistent to be cured by cheap money has become a painful reality. The return to cheap money starting in February 1932 failed to overcome the deadlock.

Given the importance of psychology in driving cyclical instability, by acting promptly, the central bank could moderate cyclical fluctuations. However, once that psychology gained momentum, the central bank lost its leverage. Policy makers must exercise judicious discretion. Hawtrey (1938 [1962], 272, 274, 278) wrote:

> Prompt action to offset an undue expansion at the outset followed by equally prompt action to relieve the pressure when it has become effective, would do what is required. . . . Bank rate may be compared to the damper of a kitchen stove. To open the damper and increase the draft of air will stimulate combustion, provided the fuel is still alight. But if the last spark has been extinguished, no amount of air will make any difference. . . . The system has an indefinite degrees of freedom, and its inherent instability is incessantly threatening to get out of control.

With no conception of the price system as the organizing principle behind the behavior of the economy, economists invented disequilibrium theories in which the psychology of businessmen and investors (herd behavior) powered cyclical fluctuations. The concept of the central bank causing recessions by interfering with the price system lay only in the distant future. Initially, Hawtrey found encouraging the Fed's experiment in the 1920s with open market operations and economic stabilization. In reference to Hawtrey (1924, 284), Meltzer (2003, 160) noted, "The British economist Ralph Hawtrey found the new view of open market operations 'highly encouraging to those who hope for enlightened management of credit with a view to the stabilization of prices.'" By the time Hawtrey wrote in 1938, it appeared evident that the experiment had failed.

Like other contemporaries, despite the crumbling of the gold standard in the 1930s, Hawtrey wanted to hold onto fixed exchange rates. The speculation presumed inherent in a free market for foreign exchange would destabilize international commerce. Hawtrey (1938 [1962], 276–77) wrote:

> Even a country which has suspended or abandoned the gold standard cannot avoid being guided to some extent by the state of the foreign exchanges.... Now speculation in foreign exchange, if left to a free market, may materially raise or lower rates of exchange, and any variations in the foreign exchange value of a currency has immediate reactions on the prices of commodities. The whole range of foreign trade products ... is likely to be thrown out of relation to the prices of home-trade products and wages. Therefore the monetary authorities of a country which has been cut loose from any metallic or international standard find themselves compelled in some degree to regulate the foreign exchanges, either by buying and selling foreign currencies or gold, or (deplorable alternative) by applying exchange control.

Even if Hawtrey had retained his belief in the efficacy of monetary policy, he lacked a convincing theory capable of persuading others. He built up his explanation of the operation of monetary policy on the ability of the central bank to influence the inventories of traders in commodities. Hawtrey (1932 [1962], 147) wrote:

> When the banks increase or decrease their lending, they are really inducing traders, in the one case, to reinforce their balances by borrowing and to release cash, in the other, to absorb cash and reduce their indebtedness.... It is through this process of the release of cash by traders that credit regulation enlarges the consumers' income and outlay. If a trader starts releasing cash, that means he is paying away more money than he is receiving.... The release of cash by traders is an indispensable condition of an increase in the consumers' income.

Hawtrey is especially interesting because of his deep and sophisticated knowledge of central banking. The reasons for his failure to understand the Great Depression as caused by an unremittingly contractionary monetary policy are then especially interesting. In short, although he discussed both money and credit, he understood the transmission of monetary policy in terms of credit markets. Hawtrey (1931, 9) wrote:

> An acceleration or retardation of lending by the banks results *directly* in an increase or decrease in incomes; it does not have to work upon incomes through changes in the quantity of money. The changes in the quantity of money are themselves an effect of the change in the volume of lending. (italics in original)

Hawtrey (1931, 24) referred to the policies of central banks as "credit regulation." The transmission of that policy could be interrupted by the unwillingness of borrowers to borrow.

Hawtrey followed the US experiment in managed credit intensely. Just as obvious from the attention paid to it in *A Treatise*, so did Keynes. However, for both, the Great Depression demonstrated the failure of an initially promising experiment. Hawtrey (1931, 32, 65–66) wrote:

> From May 1930 till the crisis of July 1931 all the principal financial centres had cheap money. But this by itself was quite insufficient to overcome the reluctance of borrowers. . . . The present trade depression has disclosed a weak point in the power of central banks. The functioning of the superstructure of bank credit requires the cooperation of lenders and borrowers. . . . Now, however, the borrowers have become unwilling. The rediscount rate in New York is 1½ per cent. . . . [Rates] of discount and short-term interest could hardly be lower. . . . But business does not respond.

Hawtrey (1931, 24) believed that in the Depression "cheap money" failed to revive the economy. "In every trade depression without exception from 1844 to 1914 Bank rate" had rarely fallen below 2½ percent and never below 2 percent. The New York Fed discount rate fell to 2½ percent in June 1930, to 2 percent in December 1930, and to 1½ percent in May 1931.

Correction of the misperception that in the Depression a policy of easy money by the Fed had failed lay in a distant monetarist future.

12.12. T. ALAN GOLDSBOROUGH

Representative Goldsborough (D-MD) was an indefatigable promoter of the program of Irving Fisher to legislate a mandate for the Fed to stabilize the price level. Like Fisher, Goldsborough believed that instability in the price level caused social dissension. At the same time, he subscribed to real bills views of the causes of cyclical instability. As a result, like his quantity theory peers, he lacked a critique of real bills views that stabilization of the price level would interfere with the necessity of quashing speculative excess as the prerequisite to preventing the speculative collapse that leads to recession. Goldsborough (US Congress 1928, May 17, 324–29) expressed his views:

> The gradual fall in prices from 1873 to 1896 culminated in the Bryan free silver campaign, which, if successful, would have resulted and was intended to result in the paying of debts with cheap money; that is, in the partial repudiation of obligations. In the period from 1896 to 1914 we heard no more about free silver, but a wave of unrest began to spread among those with a fixed income; the clerk, the school-teacher, the salaried man of every class began to feel with ever-increasing pressure the gradual rise in the cost of living. . . .
>
> If your index number of general price levels remains constant, you are assured that your volume of money and credits are expanding only in proportion as production and turnover expands—that is, only in proportion to the legitimate needs of business—and you can be assured that when you restrain the rise of the index number you are restraining credits beyond the legitimate necessities of business, you are restraining unhealthy and abnormal production, and you are restraining business expansion within wholesome limits and stopping in its inception overproduction, waste, speculation, and collapse.
>
> The lessons of history teach of the cycle, inevitable, under our present monetary system—expansion, inflation, speculation, collapse, slow recovery. Stabilization, restraining expansion at the point of overproduction and consequent inflation, is not only an economic problem the solution of which people are ready to undertake, but is clearly a direct problem of civilization.

12.13. IRVING FISHER

Irving Fisher was a quantity theorist and one of the greatest economists the profession has known. Yet, he was ineffective as a critic of the Fed in the Depression. Why? His ineffectiveness was symptomatic of the failure of contemporary economists to understand the nature of the monetary regime that the Fed had created. Like other economists, Fisher did not understand that the Fed had replaced the gold standard with its market determination of money and prices with a fiat money standard in which the Fed determined money and prices.

Fisher comprehended many of the components required for an understanding of a modern fiat money regime. Fisher (1911 [1963]) understood the behavior of the price level as a monetary phenomenon deriving from the behavior of money. Fisher (1896 and 1907) understood the real rate of interest as the intertemporal price of resources (consumption). However, he did not have a theory of the macroeconomy that explained the role of the interest rate as equilibrating aggregate demand with the aggregate supply determined by the productive capacity of the economy. He lacked a Wicksellian version of money stock determination required to explain independent movements in money within the Fed's free reserves framework, which set the interest rate in the New York money market.

Fisher (1923) understood that monetary instability causes real instability. However, Fisher (1911 [1963], 66–77) explained the business cycle in the context of a gold standard. An inflow of gold initiates a boom because banks do not raise the interest rate they charge on their loans as much as the increase in inflation. A fall in the real rate of interest stimulates economic activity. However, with inflation, currency flows out of banks, and banks must restrict lending. They then raise their loan rates to a level that raises the real rate of interest, and recession sets in. Fisher, however, could not extend his framework to a regime of fiat money creation in which the Fed was the creator of money rather than gold flows. Fisher (1911 [1963], 70 and 71) never attributed the "belated adjustment in the interest rate" that first initiated the increased confidence in booms and then initiated the loss of confidence in recessions to the Fed.[2]

In the 1920s, the only examples of fiat money regimes were with governments printing money. Those examples ended disastrously as with the post–World War I inflations in Germany, Austria, and Hungary. No "respectable" economist could argue that the Fed was controlling "the printing press." That was tantamount to saying that the Fed encouraged speculation and ultimately runaway inflation.

Like his contemporaries, Fisher believed that the United States remained on the gold standard. On December 16, 1932, Fisher wrote Raymond Moley, an adviser to President Roosevelt, that he (Fisher) would like for the United States to leave the gold standard but that it would be difficult to change the price of gold because of the need to deal with the gold clauses in contracts (Edwards 2018, 63). Quantity theorists did not

2. See also Humphrey (2001a, 293–94).

understand how the Fed created and destroyed money as part of a fiat money standard.

The compensated-dollar plan of Fisher (1920) would have stabilized the price level by varying the gold content of a dollar proportionately to movements in a price index. The reform would have required elimination of the Fed in that Fed operating procedures would have determined an interest rate incompatible with the interest rate determined by the operation of the price system under the Fisher proposal. The Fisher proposal would also have required a floating exchange rate, something unacceptable to adherents of the gold standard.

Later, Fisher (1935, 9) advanced a proposal requiring banks to hold 100 percent reserves against their demand deposits. It would have required the elimination of commercial banking and its replacement with financial institutions holding 100 percent reserves and restricted to operating the payments system. A different set of financial institutions issuing liabilities in the capital markets would intermediate between savers and borrowers. The motivation for the proposal derived from Fisher's belief that monetary instability originated in the banking system not the Fed. Fisher lacked a theory of money-stock determination that assigned responsibility to the Fed for the control of money.

Fisher proselytized for a stable price level. At the same time, he did so without understanding the responsibility of the Fed for determining the price level. For Fisher, monetary contraction was a product of the banking system and was something to be countered by the central bank. Monetary contraction was not itself a sign of contractionary Fed monetary policy. Fisher did not blame the Fed for the deflation of the Great Contraction, and he had no program for how the Fed would control bank deposits. After noting the criticism by Mr. Shibley of the Fed in his 1934 book *Stable Money*, Fisher (1934, 158) wrote: "The present writer . . . did not share Mr. Shibley's distrust of the Federal Reserve System." Like his contemporaries, he failed to understand the monetary regime created by the Fed as one of fiat money under its control.

Fisher attributed the Depression to the stock market crash (US Congress 1932b, May 13, 127).[3] Fisher (1934, 259) characterized the contractionary actions taken by the Fed in 1928 as "corrective measures to be taken" for "the destabilizing influence of security speculation." The reason that Fisher

---

3. Lauchlin Currie was the only American economist to blame the initiation of the Great Contraction on the Fed. In the 417 pages of *Stable Money*, Fisher references Currie's accusation only in a brief footnote (page 262) and does so without comment.

failed to comprehend the contractionary nature of monetary policy is that his theory of economic instability started with instability in prices. Fisher (1925 and 1926) explained real instability by regressing a proxy for real output on a distributed lag of changes in the price level. Fisher (1926, 792, cited in Humphrey 2001b, 73) wrote, "The ups and downs of [output and] employment are the effects . . . of the rises and falls of prices, due in turn to the inflation and deflation of money and credit." For Fisher, because price stability preceded the start of the Depression, it could not be attributed to contractionary monetary policy.

Instead, Fisher understood the Depression as resulting from the collapse of an unsustainable amount of debt. The prolonged character of the Depression resulted from the way in which the liquidation of debt produced deflation, which in turn increased the real value of debt even with a diminishing nominal value (Fisher in US Congress 1932b, May 13, 126). Fisher (1933) borrowed from the real bills views of the times in explaining the Depression as a feature of a capitalistic economy prone to speculative excess leading to an excessive level of debt. There is a "vicious spiral." According to Fisher (1933, 344), when "the very effort of individuals to lessen their burden of debts increases it, because of the mass effect of the stampede to liquidate in swelling each dollar owed. Then we have the great paradox which, I submit, is the chief secret of most, if not all, great depressions: The more the debtors pay, the more they owe." The Fed's error was not one of commission but rather of omission. It did not intervene to stop the deflation. By 1932 Fisher had become agnostic about the ability of the Fed to stop deflation and raise prices. He thought that other government agencies beyond the Fed might need to add purchasing power to households (Fisher in US Congress 1932b, May 13, 127–28).

The importance Fisher attached to restraining speculation echoed the consensus view that the collapse of speculative activity had caused the Depression. Fisher (US Congress 1932b, May 13, 132) recommended the imposition of required reserves on banks that would vary based on a bank's debits to its checking accounts—a Federal Reserve proposal to restrain speculation:

> It was to base reserves on velocity, on rate of turnover, on activity of accounts. . . . That would mean that when you got a period of speculation, as in 1928 or 1929, and were exceeding the speed limit, automatically the reserve would curb the bank. The bank would find it could not extend loans or increase its deposits beyond a certain point because it was going so fast that the legal requirement would automatically check it. That would have stopped speculation in 1928 and 1929 to a large extent.

Fisher was a quantity theorist, but he did not know how to give the quantity theory substance in the new monetary standard put in place by the creation of the Fed. He struggled to understand how to control money. He had no theory making the Fed rather than the banking system responsible for the collective behavior of bank deposits. By default, Fisher advocated one of the radical plans that would separate financial intermediation from the control of money. There would be two distinct financial institutions: one with 100 percent reserves backing deposits and one issuing long-term debt to make loans. Fisher never integrated the Fed into his framework.

12.14. LAUCHLIN CURRIE

Alone among American economists, Lauchlin Currie assigned blame to the Fed for the Great Contraction. After working in Jacob Viner's brain trust at the Treasury, he became an adviser to Federal Reserve Board chairman Marriner Eccles. As an adviser, he mistakenly advocated an increase in required reserves in 1936 and 1937. Rather than admit his mistake, he converted to Keynesianism. In his earlier quantity theory incarnation, Currie's views continued to suffer from the real bills view of recession as originating in speculative excess followed by subsequent collapse.

In *The Supply and Control of Money in the United States*, Currie (1934b, 3) began by lamenting "the almost universal abandonment of the quantity theory of money" because of the presumed instability of velocity. To counter this view, Currie (1933b) constructed an annual series on the income velocity of money for the United States for the years 1921 through 1929. Currie improved on Fisher's "total transactions" version of the equation of exchange.[4] Currie (1934b, 16) pointed out that with Fisher's series, "the total number of things bought includes goods (some once, some very many times), services rendered by labor and capital, and an enormous volume of financial instruments of all kinds (bonds, stocks, and so on).... It is difficult to see how the concept of the average price of *everything* bought in a period can be in any degree significant" (italics in original).

Currie pointed out that measured by money, monetary policy leading up to 1929 was contractionary. Currie (1934b, 51, 56) wrote: "It has become almost a fashion to refer to the post-war period up to 1929 as one of inflation due not to increased velocity but to excessive expansion of the volume of credit. . . . From the viewpoint of the supply of money the period from

4. Currie (1933b) and James Angell were the first to construct series on the income velocity of money, which were published in the *Quarterly Journal of Economics* in November 1933. Currie's series was the forerunner of the current M1 and Angell's the forerunner of the current M2.

1925 on was one of increasing monetary stringency, reaching an acute stage in 1929." Currie (1933a, 69) blamed the Fed's misjudgment on the failure to distinguish between credit and money: "Growth of the means of payment under the Federal Reserve system has been largely a matter of accident."

Currie (1934b, 147–48) wrote:

> Much of the current belief in the powerlessness of the reserve banks appears to arise from a complete misreading of the monetary history of 1929–32. It is generally held that the reserve administration strove energetically to bring about expansion throughout the depression but that contraction continued despite its efforts. Actually the reserve administration's policy was one of almost complete passivity and quiescence.

In the 1930s, Currie was the only American economist to criticize the Fed for contractionary monetary policy. Currie mentioned Keynes, Hawtrey, and Cassel as European economists who criticized the Fed for restrictive policy in 1928–29. Currie (1934a, 145) wrote that "the course of events in 1930–32 is clear evidence that grave mistakes were made by the reserve administration, either by acts of commission or omission" and took "sharp issue" with the contemporaneous view that "recent experience demonstrates the inability of the central bank to influence business conditions significantly even though it pursues appropriate policies."

Currie blamed the Depression on the Fed's effort to quash perceived speculation on the NYSE. However, according to Currie, the economy did not exhibit signs of speculative excess in 1928 and 1929. Currie (1934b, 158) argued that the stock market boom reflected a healthy economy and strong corporate earnings:

> It is true that many more writers refer now to the "boom" of 1928–29. I suspect that in many cases this view may be traceable to (a) a hasty generalization from security speculation; (b) the belief that "credit" was expanding at a rate far in excess of production; and (c) the deeply rooted belief that depressions always follow booms, and since we have experienced such a catastrophic depression we must have had a boom. The rising stock prices may be explained partly by the widespread belief that a period of stability had at last been achieved and mainly by the steadily increasing earnings of corporations.

However, Currie's criticism did not entail rejection of the speculative-excess explanation of recession. The problem according to Currie was that monetary policy was restrictive in the absence of a "business boom." Currie

(1934a, 161) acknowledged that a "boom" characterized by "rising commodity prices, abnormal profits, overtime work . . . is obviously undesirable and extremely difficult to translate into a period of healthy prosperity without a depression first intervening." However, "business conditions in 1928–29 approximated . . . desirable prosperity . . . [not] an undesirable boom."

Currie lacked a theory of monetary control relevant to Fed procedures. No one understood how those procedures determined reserves and interest rates endogenously through the reserves supply and demand schedules as illustrated in figure 6.1. Instead, many quantity theorists confused the operation of the actual system with one in which a given increase in reserves would produce a multiple expansion of deposits in a fractional-reserves system. Currie (1934b, 65) referred to C. A. Phillips (1931) and "the very able and exhaustive study" of Angell and Ficek (1933). Using a reserves-money multiplier framework, they showed that an exogenous increase in bank reserves would lead to a multiple expansion of bank deposits. Using that analysis, Angell and Ficek believed that the discount rate could not exercise control over bank deposit creation. The reason was that banks could obtain reserves through the discount window. With a fractional-reserves system, the discount rate would be ineffective because the value of creating the resulting multiple of deposits would be large compared to the cost of obtaining the relatively small reserves base.

Currie (1934b, 84) restated the issue: "If every individual member bank always borrowed to meet adverse clearing house balances, every check drawn would result in a manifold expansion of deposits with no offsetting contraction and the system would quickly break down." Currie accepted the answer of Riefler (1930) to the seeming puzzle. Banks borrow from the discount window not from a profit motive but rather from a need to offset a reserves deficiency. Currie (1934b, 87–88, 89) accepted that explanation because there was no

multiple expansion of deposits when the rediscount rate is lower than the rate at which banks can safely lend. . . . It was precisely at those times when the call rates were most in excess of the rediscount rate that member bank reserves either declined or ceased to grow. . . . That *any* decline at all in deposits took place in 1928–29, however, is a powerful testimony to the strength of the non-pecuniary motives to keep down indebtedness." (italics in original)

Currie believed that the nonpecuniary costs imposed on borrowing meant that it was unprofitable for banks to borrow from the discount window even with the interest rate in the money market greater than the discount rate. Currie (1933a, 78) drew the following conclusion: "If the total [Federal Reserve credit] is composed largely of bills discounted, we may expect contraction of member bank deposits because of the repugnance of member banks to continuous indebtedness at the reserve banks; if the figure for bills discounted is small, the probabilities are that expansion of deposits will take place."

Understood within a partial equilibrium framework, that conclusion would bedevil the Fed into the 1960s. The fallacy in Currie's argument is that while a bank losing reserves with the debit of a check can borrow from the window to replace those reserves, the bank gaining the reserves can repay borrowing at the discount window with the reserves gained. What is important for the banking system is that the marginal cost to banks of using the discount window, which through arbitrage sets the interest rate in the money market, be set at a level consistent with macroeconomic equilibrium.

As shown in figure 6.1, a leftward shift in the reserves supply schedule increases borrowed reserves and produces a more restrictive monetary policy. A rightward shift in the reserves demand schedule similarly increases borrowed reserves, but without the implication that an increase in borrowed reserves means that monetary policy has tightened. In the 1950s, the Fed would use free reserves (excess reserves minus borrowed reserves) as an indicator of the stance of monetary policy—what Brunner and Meltzer (1964) termed "the Riefler-Burgess doctrine." Mistakenly, policy makers would assume that if borrowed reserves increased (free reserves turned into net borrowed reserves) monetary policy had necessarily become more restrictive.

Currie accepted the contemporaneous view that the power of monetary policy was asymmetric. It could arrest a boom but could do little to stop a recession. Currie (1934b, 144–45) wrote that the Fed's "control of money is at present such that it can normally stop an upswing of business from developing into a boom if it acts early and energetically. . . . It is undoubtedly more difficult to stop a depression than it is to stop a boom. . . . If the depression has become so severe as to entail a widespread loss of confidence in the solvency of both corporations and banks it may be impossible to bring about immediate utilization of any excess reserves given to member banks." It followed that to prevent recession it was necessary to prevent the prior boom. That belief led to the 1936–37 increase in reserve requirements.

In 1934, Currie went to the Treasury to advise Jacob Viner. Currie then left the Treasury to advise Marriner Eccles when in November 1934 Eccles became governor of the Federal Reserve Board. Currie was a key player in the drafting of the Banking Act of 1935. Currie (1934c) wrote Eccles that he (Currie) would need personal access to Eccles: "The practically unanimous view in the [Research] Division is that Federal reserve has never been too restrictive (G. [Goldenweiser] even defends or has defended the 1931 policy) but has, on the contrary, erred on the inflationary side. They are, so far as I can gather, not interested in money and have never compiled a series of money. They have done little work on velocity and nothing on income. Their main interest appears to have been in banking practice and in the character and movements of various types of bank assets."

In May 1936, Currie (1936a, 1, 7) made a case for increasing required reserves: "Excess reserves constitute a problem because they may lead to an excessive expansion of deposits. . . . It appears prudent, until we can see the way more clearly, to discourage further expansion by raising reserve requirements in the near future." Currie (1936a, 2, 3, 4, 5, 7) used "the trend of national income from 1923 to 1929 as corresponding with relatively full employment." He adjusted for "the number of workers, additions to capital equipment, efficiency, and prices" to obtain a full-employment estimate of nominal income for 1936 (between $85 to $95 billion). Currie then estimated whether the contemporaneous amount of money was sufficient to sustain full employment using "the probable turnover [velocity] of money." Currie started with the assumption that "income velocity remained steady from 1923 to 1929 at slightly under 3." However, "from 1929 to 1933 the supply of money and its income velocity both declined by about 25 percent," which reflected "an increased emphasis on liquidity." He concluded that in recovery "some increase in the income velocity can be expected." Currie drew the conclusion that "the existing supply of money . . . may very well prove adequate for conditions of relatively full employment."

By November 1936, the continued gold inflows from abroad and corresponding increase in excess reserves raised the concern that money would become excessive if banks reduced their excess reserves. Currie (1936b) believed the gold inflows would continue and recommended increasing required reserves. He hoped to return to the free reserves operating procedures of the 1920s in which the regional Fed banks exercised control over member bank lending through the pressure exercised on banks to restrict lending when their borrowing from the discount window increased. Currie (1936b, 1) wrote:

> Excess reserves are now around $2.5 billion. Experience in the past has been that in prosperous periods it is necessary to put member banks about $1 billion in debt to the reserve banks to arrest expansion of demand deposits. With the power to raise reserve requirements by $1.5 billion and the ability to sell $2 billion of securities, the System is in a posi-

tion to put member banks over $1 billion in debt if this should prove necessary. If, however, another $1 or $2 billion of gold enters the country, this will not be possible. In addition to increasing bank reserves, an inflow of gold results in a corresponding expansion of checking accounts in banks.

A month later, Currie (1936c, 3, 4) wrote:

The more orderly the upswing and the less it is characterized by price advances and speculative inventory buying, the better the chances of avoiding a boom followed by a major slump. . . . The problem will become almost insuperable if the upswing is aggravated by excessive price rises and inventory buying. . . . Expansion of private bank credit can be prevented by wiping out the bulk of the excess reserves, and if need be, by forcing banks to borrow a portion of their required reserves from the federal Reserve banks.

In early 1937, Currie remained concerned about speculative excess. Currie (1937, 1) wrote: "Commodity prices had broken out of their 1934–36 range and were moving rapidly upward. There appeared to be some danger of entering into a spiral of wage and price advances. The price advances were resulting in inventory profits and to this extent encouraged speculative inventory buying. A general inflationary psychology, fostered by the rearmament programs, was emerging."

By spring 1938, Currie had to explain the recession that had succeeded the increase in reserve requirements. Currie (1938a, 7) began by recounting how "there developed a condition in which both production and productive facilities were increasing in anticipation of price and cost advances. In other words, a speculative element of considerable dimensions entered the picture. Forward buying and inventory stocking far in excess of current needs were widely engaged upon. The speculative movement came to a close around April 1937."

Currie evaluated the increase in reserve requirements and excused them from blame for the recession. Currie (1938a, 20–21) wrote: "A body charged with the responsibility of preventing an injurious expansion of credit was in duty bound to weigh the dangerous potentialities of the situation. . . . There was . . . inflationary sentiment in the air. . . . The action may have contributed to the removal of the fear or expectation of monetary inflation and an indefinite rise in prices and hence checked a further expansion of forward buying and inventory stocking. . . . The criticism should be not that the action was taken, but rather that it was unduly delayed."

Currie dropped his earlier argument that the Fed had erred in pursuing contractionary monetary policy in 1928–29 in the absence of an inflationary boom in the economy. He completely ignored the drastic decline in money associated with the increased reserve requirements. Nothing in this exculpatory rationalization should be surprising. Policy makers are human. Given the vast human cost of mistakes, policy makers never admit to mistakes. Rather than admit his mistake, Currie abandoned the quantity theory for Keynesianism.

Warburton (1946 [1966], 83) wrote of Currie: "In his testimony before the Temporary National Economic Committee, on May 12, 1939, . . . Currie emphasized the relation of 'income-producing expenditures that offset savings to the national income,' with no mention of the relation of the quantity of money to the amount of expenditures." By 1939, Currie had converted to the secular stagnation view of Alvin Hansen. Currie (1939, 1–2, 7) wrote a memo to Eccles:

> It is now becoming clear that for the first time in our history our inability to find outlets for our potential savings on the basis of a high national income condemns us to a low national income where we can find outlets for the reduced volume of savings. The outlets for savings in the twenties arising from the rapid growth in population, the growth of the giant automobile industry, foreign loans, municipal capital expenditures, and brokers' loans are gone, and nothing comparable, apart from federal government borrowing, is in sight to take their place. . . . Consequently, any attempt by the federal government . . . to cease supplying an offset to savings will be promptly followed by stagnation or recession. . . . A program of budget balancing, given the present capacity to save in relation to the economic need for capital equipment, can have no other effect than the continuance of a low level of national income and of saving and a high level of unemployment. . . . In the absence of government action, war, or sporadic inventory bulges, the national income must remain sufficiently low so that the consequent low volume of current saving can be matched by investment.

Finally, Currie had useful advice for the qualifications required of members of the Federal Reserve Board (now the Board of Governors). Currie (1934b, 160) criticized the appointment to the Federal Reserve Board of an individual who "admitted that his previous experience had been largely in cattle paper. . . . The qualifications for the governing body would be a knowledge of advanced business cycle theory." Moreover, Currie (1934b,

161) argued that the Fed should communicate using the language of economics so that academic economists could critique its policies:

> A quarterly diagnosis of the business situation together with an account of the policy followed, the reasons the policy was followed, and the specific objects hoped to be attained would tend, I think, to make for better policy. . . . A hopeless incompetent would be exposed much more quickly than he would be under the present veil of anonymity and secrecy which cloaks the actions of the reserve administration. . . . A full discussion of policy would, moreover, enable the professional economists to make their criticisms much more informed than at present.

To that list of qualifications should be added a capacity for systematic learning from past mistakes.

CHAPTER 13

From World War II to the 1953 Recession

Summary: How deep-seated and impervious to change were the views of policy makers in the pre-1951 Accord period can be seen from their response to monetary policy after January 1934. With the monetization of gold inflows, it should have been obvious that the monetary standard was one of fiat money creation. Significant money growth allowed the economy to recover. However, no one changed their views. At the first opportunity to reassert its real bills views, the Board of Governors raised reserve requirements in 1936 and 1937. Monetary deceleration and recession followed. Through World War II, views on policy remained stagnant. The failure of the Depression to return in the postwar period had little impact. What finally put the Fed on a different course was the combination of a spike in inflation in fall 1950 and a rate peg that forced it to monetize sales by banks of their government securities.

The grand (semicontrolled) experiment in monetary economics in the twentieth century was the creation of the Federal Reserve System and the contrast between its behavior in the pre- and post-1951 Treasury-Fed Accord period. In the period after the Accord, the William McChesney Martin FOMC developed procedures labeled "lean-against-the-wind" (LAW). In the terminology of economics, the Fed invented a "reaction function." The Fed responded to new information on the economy in a routine way under the assumption of a two-way causation between its behavior and the behavior of the economy. In time, and with a long hiatus during the era of stop-go monetary policy, the FOMC accepted responsibility for how markets formed expectations of the term structure of interest rates and of inflation.

The post-Accord grand experiment was development of a reaction function by the FOMC. With a reaction function, the FOMC moves its policy variable in response to the behavior of the economy with the understanding that there is a two-way interaction. With an appropriate reaction function, the FOMC can move short-term interest rates in a way that tracks the natural rate of interest and thus allows the price system to work.

As signaled by the "Tenth Annual Report" of the Federal Reserve Board

(1924a), with the inoperability of the rules of the international gold standard, the Fed turned to stability of the domestic economy as its objective. The guiding principle became the prevention of speculative excess. As an economist for the Federal Open Market Committee (FOMC), at the January 26, 1937, meeting, in arguing for an additional increase in required reserves, Emanuel Goldenweiser expressed the guiding principle of pre-Accord economic stabilization. As cited in Friedman and Schwartz (1963a, 525), Goldenweiser stated, "The most effective time for action to prevent the development of unsound and speculative conditions is in the early stages of such a movement when the situation is still susceptible of control. . . . Action to absorb excess reserves should be taken at this time."

As events unfolded after the end of World War II, the guiding principle of quashing speculative excess in its infancy became irrelevant. With the Korean War, the issue became how to restrain aggregate demand to prevent price inflation. The experience with controls in World War II and the subsequent period made clear that controls suppressed inflation only until they came off. Inflation surged in fall 1950 with the intensification of the Korean War. Fear of World War III and the return of controls and wartime inflation caused a surge in commodity prices. Shackled by a Treasury-imposed peg on the government bond rate, the Fed watched helplessly as it created the reserves that fueled the expansion of bank credit and inflation.

With the 1951 Accord, the Fed moved to recreate its 1920s free reserves operating procedures of regulating the pressure on banks to control credit creation. In time, those procedures would develop into control of the federal funds rate. At the same time, the FOMC used its two instruments for translating the impact of free reserves into conditions in the money market (open market operations to control nonborrowed reserves and the discount rate) in a coordinated way to control conditions in the money market. That contrasted with the earlier episodic use of open market sales to force more extensive use of the discount window followed by an increase in the discount rate at times of perceived speculative excess.

After the Accord, the FOMC used its free reserves procedures to implement a policy of economic stabilization based not on quashing incipient speculative excess but rather on countering sustained deviations of growth from trend as measured in sustained changes in the economy's rate of resource utilization (leaning against the wind, or LAW). The guiding principle became the assumption that sustained growth above trend would ultimately lead to price inflation, and conversely for weakness and disinflation. The FOMC implemented LAW symmetrically in booms and recessions. The Depression belief that a pervasive hoarding psychology and bank accumulation of excess reserves in response to the absence of demand for credit faded away into irrelevance. In the changed environment of the post–World War II era, real bills beliefs gave way to a belief within the Fed that its LAW procedures should respond symmetrically to sustained strength and weakness in the economy. In sum, LAW became a reaction function.

13.1. THE POST-ACCORD GRAND EXPERIMENT

The salient fact for the grand experiment is that with a reaction function the FOMC had the rudiments of operating procedures that allowed the price system to work by allowing the real rate of interest to track the natural rate of interest. Nothing of the sort existed before the 1951 Treasury-Fed Accord. In the pre–World War II period, when the Fed had freedom of action (from November 1919 to March 1933, and from 1936 to 1937), the Fed responded episodically to the behavior of the economy. Its guiding principle was to prevent the emergence of the speculative excess whose inevitable collapse would presumably lead to recession and deflation. In essence, the Fed waged war on prosperity. As a rough visual impression portrayed through the frequency of recession, figure 9.15 reveals the reduced frequency of recession in the post-Accord period.

The early policy makers at the Fed did not understand their responsibilities under the kind of monetary regime they had created. The working of the gold standard in the pre-Fed and pre–World War I period had been largely automatic. There was no need to understand the difference between relative prices and the price level and the behavior of the price level as a monetary phenomenon. Market forces determined the behavior of interest rates in a world financial market of countries on the gold standard. Going from a gold standard operated by market forces in the absence of a central bank to a monetary regime of fiat money meant that policy makers did have responsibility for the behavior of the price level and that they did set market interest rates. The first fact implied that they should provide for a stable nominal anchor, that is, give money a well-defined and predictable value. The second fact implied that they had to have procedures for setting short-term market interest rates that respected the working of the price system.

Early policy makers comprehended nothing of the concept of a price system operating to assure macroeconomic stability. Even if early policy makers had understood their role in determination of the real rate of interest, and they did not, there existed no concept of the need to make compatible that determination with the central importance of the real rate of interest in the operation of the price system. The required analytical framework would evolve slowly only in the post–World War II period. Early policy makers simply lacked any of the conceptual framework acquired later by the economics profession regarding "monetary policy" and "macroeconomics." The idea that the price system operated to maintain output growing at potential and the idea of the real interest rate as the intertemporal price of resources varying to maintain aggregate demand at potential were yet unborn. Policy makers had no conception whatsoever of the Depression as the outcome of their interference with the stabilizing role played by the price system.

Nothing in the pre-Accord period caused the Fed to accept responsibility for the behavior of the price level. In 1939, an article in the *Federal Reserve Bulletin* (April, 258) rejected congressional efforts to require it to stabilize the price level: "Experience has shown that prices do not depend primarily on the volume or the cost of money; that the Board's control over the volume of money is not and cannot be made complete." The Board of Governors (*FOMC Historical Minutes*, May 28, 1947, 811) wrote a letter to the board of the Philadelphia Fed criticizing its plea for the Fed to take actions to restrain inflation:

> It would be most unfortunate if responsible people in the Federal Reserve System were to create the impression publicly that the System itself could at this late hour materially diminish inflationary forces. The problem is not so simple that it could be dealt with effectively by monetary policy. Outside of the monetary cranks, no one at all informed on the subject would suggest that in the great complex of economic forces there is some simple monetary device that could preserve or restore economic equilibrium.

In its 1943 *Thirtieth Annual Report*, the Board of Governors stated (10): "In the past quarter century it has been demonstrated that policies regulating the . . . cost of money cannot by themselves produce economic stability or even exert a powerful influence in that direction. The country has gone through boom conditions when . . . interest rates were extremely high, and it has continued in depression at times when . . . money was . . . cheap."

Allan Sproul (1951, 315), president of the New York Fed, argued that contractionary monetary policy would cause an unacceptable "contraction of employment and income." Sproul (1951, 298) wrote that because the increase in reserve requirements in 1936 and 1937 had preceded a renewal of recession, it was "doubtful that credit policy would thereafter be used vigorously and drastically to restrain inflationary pressures." Sproul also contended that because of the magnitude of government debt, the Fed had to support the government securities market to avoid a "bottomless market" (US Treasury 1951, 261).[1]

13.2. FROM THE END OF THE WAR TO THE ACCORD

In April 1942, after the entry of the United States into World War II in December 1941, the Fed committed to preventing a rise in the term structure of interest rates.[2] At the short end, it committed not to allow the ninety-day Treasury bill rate to exceed ⅜ percent. It also kept the one-year rate at or below ⅞ percent. The rate of long-term bonds would be kept at or below its then prevailing value of 2½ percent.[3]

Unemployment rates were low by historical standards. The unemployment rate, which was 15.5 percent in January 1940, fell to a wartime low of 1.0 percent in April 1945. Following the October 1945 cyclical trough, the unemployment rate peaked at 4.3 percent in May 1946 and then declined to 2.9 percent in October 1948 just before the cyclical peak in November 1948.[4] Inflation emerged after World War II, but the double-digit inflation of the second half of 1946 reflected the suppressed inflation released with the end of price controls.

Goodwin and Herren (1975, 9) summarized the fears that limited the ability of the Fed to raise interest rates despite low rates of unemployment: "America emerged from World War II with deep foreboding about post-war recession. An Elmo Roper poll for Fortune magazine in 1945 showed that only 41.0 percent of respondents believed that the United States would 'be able to avoid . . . a widespread depression.'" Over the interval from 1948Q4 through 1950Q1, PCE (personal consumption expenditures) inflation fell to −1.7 percent.

By the end of the war, the war effort required almost 40 percent of GNP. The fear that reconversion to a peacetime economy would bring a return to depression dominated concerns about the economy. M1 velocity fell from 2.5 in 1944 to 2.1 and to 2.0 in 1945 and 1946. Presumably, the increased demand for money reflected the expectation of postwar depression. Its failure to materialize reversed this increase in real money demand. M1 velocity rose to 2.1 in 1947 and to 2.3 in 1948 and 1949.

1. See the history of Fed-Treasury relations in US Treasury (1951, 258).
2. The material in this section summarizes Hetzel (2008), chap. 4.
3. After August 1947, the Fed with Treasury permission gradually raised the ⅜ percent bill rate. Banks sold their short-term debt and bought long-term debt, which was just as liquid given the peg. As a result, the Fed ended up with all the short-term debt. The 2½ percent ceiling on bonds remained sacrosanct.
4. Data from NBER Macrohistory Data Base, St. Louis FRED.

Fed policy makers disliked their subservience to the Treasury. However, they were powerless to challenge Treasury dominance. The Philadelphia Fed urged that the Fed act to control the "spiral of expanding credit." However, the Board (Board of Governors, *FOMC Historical Minutes*, May 28, 1947, 811) expressed its disapproval and reproached the Philadelphia Fed, arguing that to do so

> would increase enormously the charge on the budget for servicing the debt. If the Secretary of the Treasury were confronted with any such consequences . . . he would no doubt take the issue directly to the President who, in turn, would take it to the Congress. . . . There can hardly be any doubt as to what the result would be. The "System's freedom of action" would in all probability be promptly terminated.

In any event, as expressed by Goldenweiser (1945, 14), the Fed accepted the interest-rate peg on long-term debt:

> It is clear that the immediate responsibility of the monetary authorities [after the war] will be to maintain stability in the market for long-term United States Government bonds. In view of the size of the public debt and the widespread character of its ownership, we cannot permit wide fluctuations in the value of Government securities. Not only would they seriously disturb the economy but they would be a breach of faith with the individuals and institutions that have helped the war effort by lending a large part of cash resources to the Government.

Eccles held the common belief that the postwar inflation arose from the government deficits incurred in World War II. To control inflation, he urged Congress to run large surpluses to extinguish government debt (US Congress 1947). He also wanted the power to prevent banks from making loans that would add to the stock of debt. He concentrated on a futile effort to persuade Congress to impose a supplementary reserve requirement on banks.

13.3. EXPLAINING RECESSION WITH PREWAR INFLATIONARY EXPECTATIONS

Friedman and Schwartz (1963a, 577) posed the conundrum "Given the Fed's interest rate peg, what explains the post-war decline in money growth and inflation?" Average annualized quarterly M1 growth declined from 23.7 percent over the interval 1942Q1 to 1945Q1; to 10.3 percent from 1945Q2 to 1945Q4; to 4.7 percent from 1946Q1 to 1947Q4; and to −0.9 percent from

1948Q1 to 1949Q4.[5] Inflation surged with the end of postwar price controls but became negative in 1949 (figure 4.1). Understanding not only this period but also the two recessions (November 1948 to October 1949 and July 1953 to May 1954) requires understanding how the prewar experience shaped inflationary expectations. The expectation that deflation would follow inflation raised the real interest rate. The rise in the real rate precipitated the recessions that began in November 1948 and July 1953.

With monetary policy sidelined by the interest rate peg, where was the inflation in the postwar period? The answer is that the expectation of deflation kept the real interest rate relatively high even with low nominal interest rates. More generally, an understanding of the period between the end of World War II through the first recession following the 1951 Treasury-Fed Accord with cycle peak May 1953 requires an understanding of how the previous monetary standards had shaped inflationary expectations. Although inflation emerged with the end of the war, the prevailing assumption remained that "what goes up must come down." In the United States, prices rose and then declined with the War of 1812, the Civil War, and World War I. Similarly, in England, the same pattern emerged with the Napoleonic Wars and World War I. Until World War II, the secular level of prices exhibited no trend.

The stationary behavior of prices reinforced the real bills view that inflation rose with speculative activity and then fell with its collapse. Senator Robert A. Taft (R-OH) stated in hearings on the Employment Act of 1946 (quoted in Goodwin and Herren 1975, 17): "My definition of inflation has always been an activity which is artificially built up to an extent that we cannot permanently maintain." Inevitably, deflation followed inflation as asset bubbles burst. E. A. Goldenweiser (1945, 4), director of research at the Board of Governors, wrote in the first of a Board series, Postwar Economic Studies, that "the large volume of saving held by the people . . . could be used to feed the flames of inflation—which leads to ultimate collapse and disaster."

In the post–World War II period through the early 1950s, inflation created the expectation of deflation. Friedman and Schwartz (1963a, 560 and 584) wrote:

> The most widely-held expectation at the time was that prices would go
> down after the war—if this expectation seems unreasonable to us, it is

5. Friedman and Schwartz (1963a, 561) argued that during the war consumers held cash in their portfolios in place of then unavailable consumer durables. After the war as consumer durables became available, they reduced their holdings of cash by purchasing consumer durables. Given the Fed's interest-rate peg, the Fed would have accommodated the reduced demand for money.

only by hindsight. . . . The public acted from 1946 to 1948 as if it expected deflation. . . . The major source of concern about inflation at that time was . . . that what goes up must come down and that the higher the price rise now the larger the subsequent price fall.

In a speech on April 21, 1947, President Truman (Goodwin and Herren 1975, 41) said:

There is one sure formula for bringing on a recession or a depression: that is to maintain excessively high prices. Buying stops, production drops, unemployment sets in, prices collapse, profits vanish, business-men fail.

Truman began to lift price controls in February 1946 and ended them entirely in October 1946. With the end of controls, inflation surged (figure 4.1). CPI inflation rose at annualized rates of 39 percent and 23 percent in 1946Q3 and 1946Q4, respectively. In early 1946, 8 percent of households expected prices to decline, while 53 percent expected prices to rise (Board of Governors 1950).[6] In early 1947 when inflation surged with the end of controls, 46 percent of households expected prices to decline, while only 13 percent expected them to rise (*Federal Reserve Bulletin*, November 1948, 1357). Inflation produced a "deflation scare."

Using the Livingston Survey, figure 13.1 plots biannual observations of expected one-year-ahead CPI inflation and subsequently realized inflation. Economists expected deflation in the five years following the end of the war as a reaction to the postwar inflation. Using the Livingston data on expected inflation, figure 13.2 plots a real interest rate and the corresponding market interest rate. For year-end 1946 and midyear 1947, the real interest rates are, respectively, 6.5 percent and 8.0 percent. The hypothesis is that these high real rates produced a monetary deceleration and a decline in real output.

The reemergence of expected deflation in 1948 (figure 13.1) and the cor-responding rise in the real interest rate (figure 13.2) preceded the recession that began after the cyclical peak in November 1948. Measured using Liv-ingston Survey data, the real interest rate rose from 1.6 percent at year-end 1947, to 2.6 percent at midyear 1948, and to 3.9 percent at year-end 1948. Monetary deceleration accompanied the rise in the real rate (figure 13.3). The generally high real interest rates in the postwar period can explain the

6. Starting in 1946, the Board of Governors' Survey of Consumer Finances (SCF) conducted annual surveys of households including the expectation of inflation. Starting in late 1946, the Livingston Survey conducted biannual surveys of business economists including their expectations for CPI inflation for future six-month and twelve-month intervals.

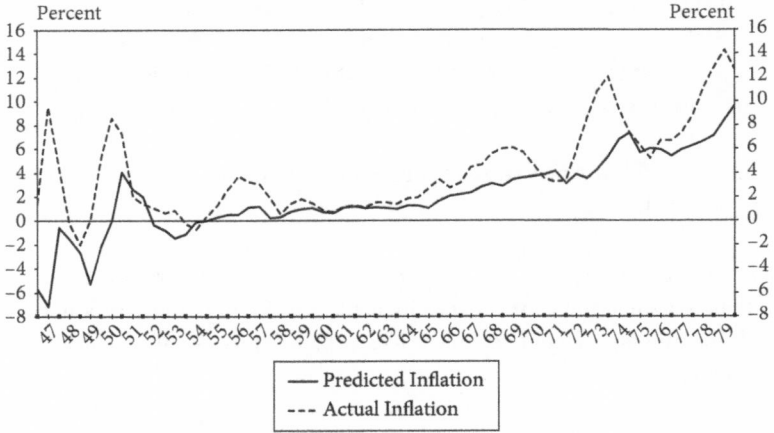

Figure 13.1. Livingston Survey: Predicted and
Subsequently Realized One Year Inflation

Predicted inflation is the mean of one-year-ahead CPI inflation predictions from
the Livingston Survey. The Philadelphia Fed maintains the survey currently (data
from www.phil.frb.org/econ1). The survey comes out in June and December. The
questionnaire is mailed early in May and November. Therefore, the one-year inflation
forecast is for the thirteen-month period from May to June of the following year for
the June release and for the thirteen-month period from November to December
of the following year for the December release. The June release inflation forecast is
matched with an average of the realized annualized monthly CPI inflation rates starting
in June of the same year and ending in June of the subsequent year. The December
release inflation forecast is matched with an average of realized annualized monthly
CPI inflation rates starting in December of the same year and ending in December of
the subsequent year; see "Real Rate of Interest (Livingston Forecasts)" in chapter 18
appendix. The light tick mark is the June release forecast, and the heavy tick mark is
the December release forecast.

disinflation that occurred starting in 1948Q3 despite the Fed's low, nominal
interest-rate peg. Over the year and a half from August 1948 through January 1950, the level of the CPI declined by 4.1 percent.

When the Chinese entered the Korean War in November 1950, inflation
surged (figure 13.3). The possibility of a Third World War generated a worldwide rise in commodity prices. The likely return of price controls and the
disappearance of consumer durables caused a surge in consumption. Inflation peaked at 14 percent in 1951Q1. Although the Fed gained the ability to
raise interest rates with the March 1951 Treasury-Fed Accord, the Korean
War period possessed a characteristic of the preceding period. Fluctuations
in the real interest rate far exceeded fluctuations in the market interest rate

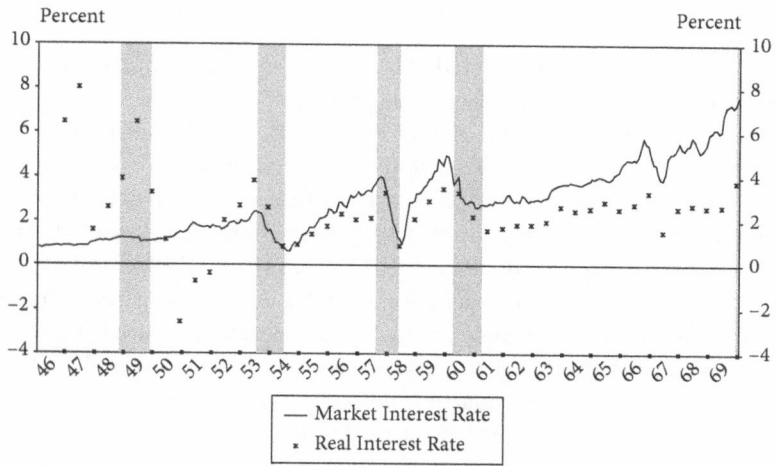

Figure 13.2. One-Year Market Interest Rate on Government Securities
and Corresponding Real Rate of Interest: 1946–69

The market rate of interest is monthly observations of the yield on US government
securities from "Short-Term Open Market Rates in New York City," in Board of
Governors (1976). Through July 1959 the series uses "9- to 12-month issues." Thereafter,
it uses "one-year Treasury bills." The series for the real rate of interest is the market rate
minus predicted CPI inflation from the Livingston Survey (figure 13.1). Observations
of predicted inflation are biannual and are for the months of May and November; see
"Real Rate of Interest (Livingston Forecasts)" in chapter 18 appendix. Shaded areas
indicate recessions. Heavy tick marks indicate the November observation.

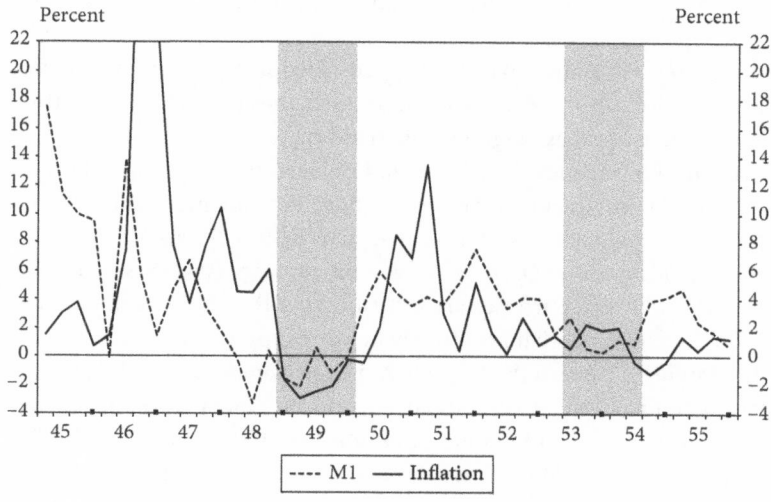

Figure 13.3. Inflation and M1 Growth

Quarterly observations of annualized percentage changes. From 1945 to 1946, the
price level is the CPI. Thereafter, it is the personal consumption expenditures deflator.
Observations for annualized inflation for 1946Q3 and 1946Q4, respectively, are 39.3
and 22.9 percent. Shaded areas indicate recessions. Heavy tick marks indicate fourth
quarter. M1 data from Friedman and Schwartz (1970).

(figure 13.2). Variation in expected inflation (deflation) rather than purposeful monetary policy actions dominated policy.

Over 1951, inflation fell and ceased by year-end. The fall appeared to confirm the view that price declines follow rises. Accordingly, in 1952, the public began to expect deflation. The Survey of Consumer Finances reported that at the beginning of 1953 only 17 percent of consumers expected price increases while 31 percent expected decreases (*Federal Reserve Bulletin*, March 1954, 249). Expected deflation raised the real interest rate (figure 13.2). Higher real rates produced monetary deceleration (figure 13.3). Average annualized quarterly M1 growth rates went from 4.25 percent in 1952 to 2.2 percent in the first two quarters of 1953 and 0.5 percent in the last two quarters. A business cycle peak occurred in July 1953.

The Fed's attempt to pursue countercyclical monetary policy began with the 1953 recession. At the time of the Accord, March 1951, the market yield on three-month Treasury bills was 1.5 percent. A year later, the Fed began to raise rates, and the bill rate peaked at 2.3 percent in early June 1953. With the onset of recession, it lowered rates to 0.6 percent by the June 1954 cyclical trough. Purposeful monetary policy actions rather than variations in expected inflation then came to dominate real interest rates and monetary policy. The era of lean-against-the-wind had begun.

13.4. FROM REAL BILLS TO LEAN-AGAINST-THE-WIND: THE CRISIS LEADING TO THE ACCORD

With the Accord, policy makers stopped viewing recessions as the inevitable reaction to prior speculative excess. Also, they began to see inflation as a consequence of excess aggregate demand rather than speculative excess. The rise in the price level with the end of wartime price controls and its subsequent failure to fall forced that change. Such inflation could not arise from asset speculation. As FOMC chairman Eccles (Board of Governors, *Minutes of the Board of Governors* November 18, 1947, 1575) reasoned, "Even loans for productive purposes are inflationary if they increase the demand for labor and material that are already in short supply."

The intensification of the Korean War in November 1950 when the Chinese crossed the Yalu River and advanced into North Korea produced a surge in expenditure and in inflation (figure 13.3). If maintained, the Fed's interest-rate peg would have sustained inflation through the monetization of government debt. That experience made clear to the Fed the importance of allowing the central bank, rather than private markets, to control reserves creation. Like World War II, that experience also moved the Fed toward thinking about inflation as resulting from excess aggregate demand rather than speculative excess. The Accord was a watershed for the Fed. The ideal of a central bank that allows an elastic currency passively to "accommodate commerce" (chap. 4) disappeared. The Fed had to control bank credit to control excessive aggregate demand and inflation.

Intensification of the Korean War in fall 1950 created the widespread fear of a World War III with the United States fighting both China and a Soviet Union moving to capture Berlin (Hetzel and Leach 2001a). Fed policy makers felt the need to raise rates to prepare for the interest-rate peg that would with certainty be imposed as in World War II. At the time of the imposition of the peg in spring 1942, considerable excess capacity still existed in the United States. In late 1950, the economy was booming, and the Fed was monetizing bank debt at the existing peg. Key Fed policy makers felt strongly that going into a World War III, the level of interest rates needed to be higher to avoid the combination of inflation and ineffective wartime controls.

In summarizing a meeting with McCabe and Snyder on January 3, 1951, Sproul (Board of Governors, *FOMC Memorandum of Discussion*, January 31, 1951, 5) stated:

> The next six months, while the Treasury will be largely out of the market, offer the best chance to get our house in order, through general credit measures. After that the requirements of credit policy and Government financing needs—refunding and new money—may be in conflict and financing needs will take precedence. . . . It is in the light of these present dangers, and in preparation for meeting the more difficult longer term of financing full scale mobilization or war, that near term policy should be determined.

Considerable ill will existed between the Treasury and the Fed in the second half of 1950 because of the Treasury practice of announcing in advance the offering rate on Treasury securities and locking the Fed into supporting the issue at the preannounced rate. The pot boiled over after a meeting with President Truman, Treasury Secretary Snyder, and Fed chair McCabe on January 18, 1951, in which McCabe voiced reservations about the bond support program. On the next day, Snyder gave a speech seemingly committing the Fed to support the bond market at the 2½ percent ceiling. Snyder (SPNY, FOMC—Meeting Comments 1951, "Snyder Talk," January 18, 1951, 2) said: "It is my view that a 2½% rate of interest on long term Treasury bonds is a fair and equitable rate. . . . We cannot afford the questionable luxury of tinkering with a market as delicately balanced as the Government security market. Now is no time for experimentation." The lack of forthrightness on the part of Truman and Snyder offended McCabe. In this instance, neither Truman nor Snyder informed McCabe of the speech despite meeting with him the day before.

Allan Sproul, president of the New York Fed, responded and criticized the Truman administration's plan to control inflation through controls (Sproul, SPNY, "Remarks, New York State Bankers Association, January 22, 1951," 1–3, 6):

> We have been told that we must have direct legal control of broad segments of our economy to promote production for defense, to insure a fair distribution of goods and services, and to prevent inflation. We have been told that these measures must include allocation of materials, and control of prices, rents and wages. . . . Direct controls couldn't do that job in the war and postwar period. . . . Direct controls may suppress inflation for a time, but they do not prevent it. . . . I am afraid that the announced debt management policy could lead us directly or indirectly into too much financing by the banks. . . . Too much of our financing would sooner or later be done with bank credit based on the ready availability of Federal reserve credit. . . . War departments are always busy fighting the last war. . . . We don't want to make that mistake on the financial front.

Governor Eccles (US Congress 1951, January 25, 158) testified:

> As long as the Federal Reserve is required to buy government securities at the will of the market for the purpose of defending a fixed pattern of interest rates established by the Treasury, it must stand ready to create new bank reserves in unlimited amount. This policy makes the entire banking system, through the action of the Federal Reserve System, an engine of inflation.

President Truman asked the FOMC to go over to the White House after its January 31, 1951, meeting. McCabe (Board of Governors, *FOMC Historical Minutes* January 31, 1951, 20) said at the FOMC meeting:

> The Secretary would like to be assured that any deficits that might grow out of the defense program during the next few years would be financed on the basis of a 2½ per cent long-term interest rate, regardless of whether the market would support such a rate, and that the Secretary felt that the Federal Reserve should commit itself to purchasing securities to whatever extent was necessary to maintain such a rate. The Chair-

man went on to say that the drop of 1/32 of a point in the price of the long-term restricted bonds on Monday of this week to which Mr. Rouse referred earlier in this meeting was, in his opinion, the thing that again had made the Secretary of the Treasury uneasy as to the procedure that would be followed by the Federal Open Market Committee and that undoubtedly this was the reason for the President's request for the meeting this afternoon.

The next day, the White House issued a statement that "the Federal Reserve Board has pledged its support to President Truman to maintain the stability of Government securities as long as the emergency lasts." Later, "a Treasury spokesman said the White House announcement means the market for Government securities will be stabilized at present levels and that these levels will be maintained during the present emergency." The FOMC had given no such assurance. Eccles released to the *New York Times* and the *Washington Post* his notes on the meeting contradicting the White House announcement (cited in Hetzel and Leach 2001a, 45).

At the February 6 to 8, 1951, meetings, Eccles was defiant. Eccles's (Board of Governors, *FOMC Historical Minutes*, February 6–August 1951, 16, 18) statement of the stakes made clear that ultimately the FOMC would, if forced to, defy the Treasury and lower the price at which it bought government bonds:

> This Committee has a public responsibility that is as important for it to discharge in trying to prevent inflation as it is that we carry out a defense program. There is going to be nothing for us to protect in this country unless we are willing to do what is necessary to protect the dollar. Our responsibility is not a minor one; it is a very great one under the conditions that exist, and if we fail, history will record that we were responsible . . . in bringing about the destruction or defeat of the very system that our defense effort is being made to protect and defend.
>
> We are almost solely responsible for this inflation. It is not deficit financing that is responsible because there has been surplus in the Treasury right along. . . . We should not think that we are going to work this out with the Treasury; we have been trying to do so for more than a year and have not worked anything out. . . . We have provided the means for the growth in the money supply, which has been directly related to the increase in cost of living and the price level.

The FOMC (Board of Governors, *FOMC Historical Minutes*, February 6–8, 1951, 26) sent a letter to the president drafted February 7, 1951:

This flood of newly created dollars in the form of credit cannot be controlled. It will overwhelm whatever price, wage, and similar controls, including selective credit measures, that may be contrived.

Sproul (SPNY, FOMC Meeting Comments, February 15, 1951, 1–2, 4, 7–8) also made clear the high stakes:

These inflationary pressures would not have gone so far nor so fast if there had been a better brake on the expansion of bank credit. . . . The tremendous and unprecedented increase in such credit—$7 billion or about 6 percent in loans and investments in 8 months (May to December inclusive)—is clear evidence to us of a speculative and inflationary demand well beyond the needs of normal current business. Our net purchases of Government securities during this period totaled approximately $3 billion. . . . Credit policy can make its contribution, *now*, in arresting further inflation—a further debasement of the dollar. Today's inflation . . . is not due to deficit financing by the Government. It is due to mounting civilian expenditures largely financed directly or indirectly by the purchase of Government securities by the Federal Reserve Banks. We must close or narrow that gap in our defenses.

If this flood of newly created dollars is not controlled it will overwhelm a "pay-as-we-go" policy, and whatever price, wage, and other controls—including selective credit controls—we may devise. If we have to go to war, and if we have to resort to deficit financing, failure to close this gap . . . will mean that the battle against wartime inflation will be largely lost before it starts. . . . With fixed buying prices for Government securities . . . the control of the Federal Reserve System over bank reserves is automatically transferred to the 14,000 odd banks of the country. . . . If there were such a thing as a bankers' romp, this would be it. . . . Unlimited Federal Reserve buying of Government securities . . . amounts to turning the public debt . . . into "printing press" money. . . . There is . . . some belief that . . . the American people, having had their pockets picked once by inflation, are ready and willing to have them picked again. . . . This is an unwarranted assumption of public stupidity.

Sproul's (SPNY, FOMC Meeting Comments, February 26, 1951, 1) notes for the FOMC dated February 26, 1951, read, "Quit providing easy reserves to the banking system to feed an inflationary expansion of credit. Quit monetizing the Federal debt."

The president and Snyder rejected any loosening of the interest-rate peg, and Snyder consistently treated McCabe and Sproul with condescension.

On February 12, 1951, Snyder entered the hospital for cataract surgery and asked the FOMC to do nothing until his release, probably in two weeks. McCabe and Sproul met with the president on February 26, 1951. Truman (Board of Governors, *FOMC Historical Minutes*, Executive Committee, February 26, 1951, 13) stalled for time:

> I [Truman] am requesting the Secretary of the Treasury, the Chairman of the Federal Reserve Board, the Director of Defense Mobilization, and the Chairman of the Council of Economic Advisers to study ways and means to provide the necessary restraint on private credit expansion and at the same time to make it possible to maintain stability in the market for Government securities. While this study is underway, I hope that no attempt will be made to change the interest rate pattern, so that stability in the government security market will be maintained.

Truman also used senators to intimidate the Fed through the threat of hearings led by Wright Patman. McCabe (Board of Governors, *FOMC Historical Minutes*, Executive Committee, February 26, 1951, 4) read from a letter sent to him by Senator O'Mahoney dated February 10: "The soviet dictators are convinced that the capitalistic world will wreck itself by economic collapse arising from the inability or unwillingness of different segments of the population to unite upon economic policy." A note from the FOMC secretary (Board of Governors, *FOMC Historical Minutes*, Executive Committee, February 26, 1951, 10) contained the Fed's defiant reply:

> As you know, inflation is perhaps the greatest force for arraying the various sectors of a capitalistic economy against each other. John Maynard Keynes stated in his "Economic Consequences of the Peace" (1919): "Lenin is said to have declared that the best way to destroy the Capitalist System was to debauch the currency. . . . Lenin was certainly right. There is no subtler, no surer means of overturning the existing basis of Society than to debauch the currency. The process engages all the hidden forces of economic law on the side of destruction, and does it in a manner which not one man in a million is able to diagnose."

McCabe (Board of Governors, *FOMC Historical Minutes*, Executive Committee, February 14, 1951, 4) also reported that "it was evident from my conversations with the Senators that they were fearful of publicity of our letter to the President and of public hearings." Truman could no longer use referral of the dispute to Congress as a threat.

The position of the Treasury was untenable. The fight between the Fed

314   CHAPTER THIRTEEN

and the Treasury was in the headlines. If markets decided that the end of the bond peg was imminent, there would be a flood of selling. Without Fed support, the price of bonds could plummet along with the future market for long-term debt. McCabe (Board of Governors, *FOMC Historical Minutes*, January 31, 1951, 9–10) had told the FOMC:

> I had received a communication from the President. This was early in December—the President telephoned me at my home about an article that had appeared in The New York Herald Tribune on December 1, 1950, which said that there was "open speculation as to whether the Federal Reserve is again undercutting the (Treasury) financing," and that it was "obviously risking another huge shake-out of long holdings such as that which followed the Christmas package of downward peg adjustments some years ago." That article seemed to have upset the President very much. He mentioned the fact that he hoped we would stick rigidly to the pegged rates on the longest bonds. I told him the dangers of that. . . . [The President said] if the Federal Reserve Board is going to pull the rug from under the Treasury on that, we certainly are faced with a most serious situation, because we are going to have an immense amount of Federal financing in the next six months. "I hope the Board will realize its responsibilities and not allow the bottom to drop from under our securities. If that happens that is exactly what Mr. Stalin wants."

At the February 14, 1951, meeting of the Executive Committee, members agreed that despite Snyder's absence due to his hospital stay, the FOMC would allow the support price of bonds to decline in the event of heavy sales to the Fed. At the same meeting, the members agreed to engage in staff-level discussions with Assistant Treasury Secretary William McChesney Martin. The result was the famous Accord, released March 4, 1951.

> The Treasury and the Federal Reserve System have reached full accord with respect to debt-management and monetary policies to be pursued in furthering their common purpose to assure the successful financing of the Government's requirements and, at the same time, to minimize monetization of the public debt.[7]

The statement simply reiterated the positions of the Fed and the Treasury. The March 1951 Treasury-Fed Accord marked the reacquisition by the

7. See Federal Reserve Bank of St. Louis, Fraser, William McChesney Martin Jr. Papers: Reports, 1949–51, box 15, folder 4.

Fed of its independence. However, that reality emerged only over time. As part of the Accord, the Truman administration had forced out Board chair Thomas McCabe and instituted its own man, William McChesney Martin. Truman and Treasury Secretary Snyder assumed that Martin would continue to support the Treasury market (Hetzel and Leach 2001a). Martin, however, asserted the Fed's independence. Later, in a chance encounter between Martin and Truman on Fifth Avenue in New York, Truman said only one word, "Traitor," and walked on (Board of Governors 1999). In one of the great turning points in the history of central banking, Martin turned out to be a servant of the public not of the Treasury.

13.5. WHAT DID THE FED BORROW FROM AND WHAT DID IT ABANDON OF ITS 1920S MONETARY POLICY?

When Thomas McCabe came from the Philadelphia Fed, where he had been chairman of the Board, to replace Marriner Eccles as chairman of the Board of Governors, he did so on the condition that Winfield Riefler accompany his as an adviser.[8] Riefler had been an economist at the Federal Reserve Board in the 1920s until he left to work in the Roosevelt administration in the early 1930s. He was author of the book *Money Rates and Money Markets in the United States*, published in 1930. Riefler remained at the Board from 1948 until his retirement in 1959. With the Treasury-Fed Accord of 1951, William McChesney Martin replaced McCabe as Board and FOMC chair. Martin and Riefler developed the procedures known as "lean-against-the-wind" (LAW).

Since March 1933, the Fed had not acted without the acquiescence of the Treasury, whose overriding concern was always the financing of government debt as cheaply as possible. Martin and Riefler had to reinvent monetary policy. To do so, they looked back to the 1920s, but in a changed intellectual environment. Real bills had vanished, and the government had a responsibility for maintaining employment. Although Martin and Riefler reinvented monetary policy along the lines of a reaction function, they also created enormous confusion about the new procedures by retaining the old language of the Fed as one influence on financial intermediation—what Brunner and Meltzer (1964) termed "the Riefler-Burgess doctrine."

The story told here of the development of the post-Accord LAW procedures begins with a review of the building blocks from the 1920s. One can then ask, "What remained, and what changed?" The recounting starts with

---

8. Truman failed to reappoint Eccles as Board chairman. Eccles, however, remained on as a governor.

an overview of policy from the New York Fed from 1934, almost certainly written by either Carl Snyder or W. Randolph Burgess.[9] The heart of what the Fed "learned" is what it "learned" from the 1920–21 recession. The guide to avoiding recession and deflation was to prevent the speculative excess whose collapse produced them. The Fed had the power to restrain the excessive extension of credit, but that power if not exercised in time was not symmetric. In depression when the demand for credit vanished, the Fed had little power to stimulate business through the extension of credit. Page 2 of the paper recounted:

In this period [1930–34] it has again been demonstrated that the supply of credit is not always the dominating factor; that demand for credit may be equally important and that there are many things, other than the availability and cost of funds, which determine what the demand for credit will be. There appears to be no instrument of control in the service of central banks which is so effective in promoting recovery from real depression, as are the weapons of credit restriction and rate increase in checking expansion. If this is so, it is obvious that the most fruitful time for the exercise of credit control in the interest of business stability is before excesses in the use of credit have developed to such an extent that a radical readjustment is necessary.

Real bills died after World War II when unlike after World War I a severe recession did not occur. A credit structure built not on real bills but rather on government debt did not yield a credit structure doomed to collapse. In the absence of the real bills philosophy with its sensitive antennae always attuned to asset-price bubbles and the need to deflate them, the FOMC could implement a LAW policy focused on unsustainable strength and weakness in the economy. The disappearance of the central real bills belief that stability required the snuffing out of incipient speculative excess gave the LAW procedures at least a chance to stabilize rather than destabilize the economy. The Fed could then pick up on the countercyclical aspects of its policy in the 1920s without the destructive elements introduced by real bills fallacies.

An earlier memo from the New York Fed offers a useful starting point for understanding Martin's views (SPNY, FRB, "Credit Policies of the Federal Reserve System 1914–1934") and material it excerpted from the question-

9. The paper is in the New York Fed archives in the Sproul papers (SPNY, FRB, "Credit Policies of the Federal Reserve System 1914–1934," December 5, 1934). A graph in the paper contains the date March 14, 1934. "FRB" pertains to papers dealing with the Federal Reserve Board.

naires submitted to Congress (US Congress 1931, "Federal Reserve Questionnaires," 762):

> The studies made by the research staff of the bank over a period of years have demonstrated that when the volume of credit grows at a rate proportionate with the long time growth of business in the country, the dangers of either inflation or deflation are least. On the other hand any expansion in credit beyond such normal growth of business and trade appears likely to result sooner or later in inflation of one form or another, not necessarily in commodity prices, but in excessive speculation. . . . This principle, we believe to be generally applicable whether a too rapid expansion of the country's credit is due to speculation in securities, to over-production or speculation in commodities, to speculation in real estate, or to an expansion in business activity or inventory beyond a normal and healthy growth. In other words whatever cause of a growth or expansion in the country's credit structure if the growth is at a rate greater than that at which experience has shown the country's business can grow on a sound and secure basis, then the Federal Reserve authorities have the responsibility, however unpopular . . . through open market operation or discount rates or both, towards restraint.

This excerpt certainly originated with Carl Snyder. It reflects the real bills views of the time. The guideline of steady growth in credit at a rate commensurate with the economy's long-run potential growth rate captures Martin's views of optimal policy.[10]

At the same time, Martin faced a political economy problem of how to maintain the Fed's independence. He needed to break from the Treasury's desire for the Fed to backstop debt issuance by buying whatever amount of debt did not sell at the Treasury's asking price. (There were no debt auctions at the time.) To propitiate the Treasury's concern for debt management, Martin had to maintain an "orderly market," including an "even keel," when the Fed would prevent interest rates from changing during the period in which the Treasury sold and in which brokers distributed Treasury debt. He could not give up control over the interest rate in the government securities market.

Martin also had to deal with the populist pressures emanating from Congress personified by Wright Patman. Populists believed that Wall Street

---

10. When the author joined the Fed in 1975, employees still viewed an old black-and-white movie that explained monetary policy by analogy to an irrigation canal. The Fed regulated the opening of a sluice gate to even out the flow of water (credit). That idea was compatible with Martin's views.

banks set interest rates at an arbitrarily high level to exploit debtors, especially farmers. They believed that the Fed had the power to set interest rates at a "low" level, as it had done in World War II. In order to control credit creation by banks, the Fed would have had to raise interest rates in a visible way (or allow them to rise by controlling total reserves). In practice, that is what the Fed did, but Martin would never admit that fact.

Given that Martin was never willing to admit that the Fed controlled short-term interest rates, he needed an alternative. Under the guidance of Winfield Riefler, the Martin FOMC developed the free reserves procedures that had emerged rough-hewn in the 1920s. They served as an operating guide for instructing the New York Desk and as way of communicating the stance of monetary policy. Over the course of the 1960s, it became clear that free reserves were an indirect way of controlling market rates of interest.

With the events surrounding the Accord, it became clear that there was a single banking system that rested on a unified reserves base. The fraught days of the rate peg during the intensification of the Korean War in which the Treasury compelled the Fed to buy the Treasury securities sold by banks made clear that the Fed controlled bank reserves creation through a bookkeeping operation. Over time, it became clear that the marginal cost of reserves was determined in the federal funds market. Through arbitrage, the federal funds rate determined the interest rate on short-term Treasury securities in a national money market centered in New York (figure 13.4).

With the changed intellectual environment produced by the Keynesian revolution, the FOMC began to implement policy through a reaction function, the LAW procedures of Martin. These conceptual changes that formed the Martin Fed laid the foundation for the idea of a modern central bank. Through its control over bank reserves and their cost, a modern central bank shapes the yield curve in the market for government securities (the risk-free interest rate and its expectation embedded in forward rates). Through arbitrage, that yield curve influences the broad spectrum of interest rates. Finally, through a reaction function that relates the funds rate to the behavior of the economy, the Fed can influence the behavior of the economy.

In the 1950s, these procedures operated in a vastly different intellectual environment than in the 1920s. Most succinctly, in the 1950s, the meaning attached to the word "inflation" changed. In the 1920s, policy makers used the word loosely to connote the expansion of credit beyond what was required for productive uses. That expansion produced a speculative excess raising asset prices and economic activity to unsustainable levels. The inevitable collapse then produced recession and deflation. In the 1950, the word "inflation" came to mean sustained increases in the price level.

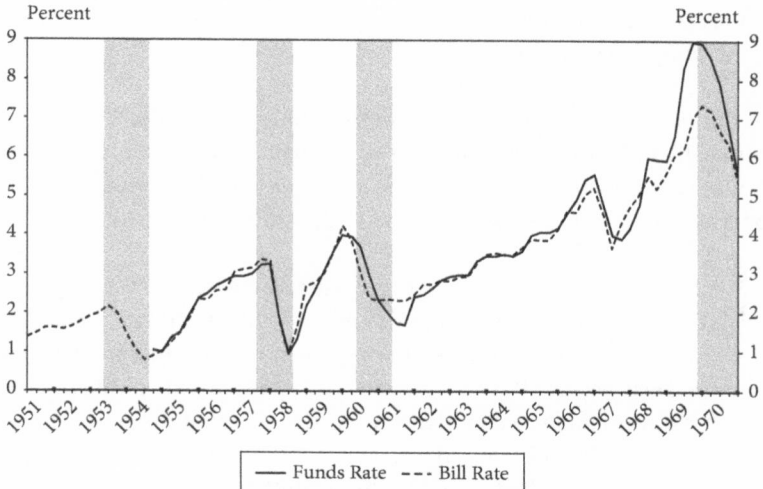

Figure 13.4. Funds Rate and Three-Month Treasury Bill Rate
Quarterly observations of three-month Treasury bill yields from 1951 to 1953 are
from Board of Governors (1943, table 101). Data from 1953 Q1 on are from Board of
Governors, "Selected Interest Rates," Statistical Release G.13. Federal funds rate from
St. Louis FRED. Shaded areas indicate recessions. Heavy tick marks indicate fourth
quarter.

Also, after the 1951 Treasury-Fed Accord, the Fed accepted the New York
market for government securities as the market transmitting the impact of
monetary policy. The role of the Open Market Desk of the New York Fed
was then to offset factors like float, Treasury deposits with the Fed, and currency outflows that affected reserves supply. While these "defensive" operations would maintain conditions in the money market, "offensive" open
market operations would "tighten" or "loosen" those conditions. Arbitrage
then influenced other interest rates in the economy.

However, the Fed's free reserves procedures created enormous confusion about the nature of the monetary regime. The Fed carried over some
of its earlier language describing monetary policy in terms of regulating
the character of financial intermediation. Ahearn (1963, 127) quoted from a
January 1955 issue of the *Federal Reserve Bulletin* summarizing Regulation
A, which governs discount window borrowing:

> In considering a request for credit accommodation, each Federal Re-
> serve Bank gives due regard to the purpose of the credit and to its prob-
> able effects upon the maintenance of sound credit conditions. . . . It con-
> siders whether . . . the bank is extending an undue amount of credit for

the speculative carrying of or trading in securities, real estate, or commodities, or otherwise.

The major source of confusion was the unwillingness of FOMC chairman William McChesney Martin to admit that the free reserves targets set by the FOMC were only an intermediate target for the variable of interest: short-term interest rates. Ahearn (1963, 37) wrote of the 1950s:

> While the Federal Reserve frequently stressed the importance of affecting bank reserves and the volume of money, it made no statement suggesting the desirability of affecting interest rates. On the contrary, the few explicit Federal Reserve statements on the subject specifically rejected direct influence on interest rates. This reflected a number of reasons. Among the most important, however, seem to be . . . the fear that any such action would degenerate into rigidly fixing yields and prices on US Government securities.

The way that the Fed characterized its operating procedures in the 1920s as one factor influencing the cost and availability of funds created similar confusion in the 1950s.

CHAPTER 14

LAW (Lean-against-the-Wind)
and Long and Variable Lags

Summary: William McChesney Martin developed the lean-against-the-wind policy of moving money market rates in a commonsense way in light of the behavior of the economy. In his March 7, 1961, testimony to the Joint Economic Committee, Martin (quoted in Maisel 1973, 63) said: "The flexible monetary policy that has been in effect now for a full decade . . . as I have capsuled it before in the shortest and simplest description I have been able to devise, is one of leaning against the winds of inflation and deflation—and with equal vigor."

Martin created the foundation of FOMC operating procedures by instituting the principle of a reaction function. Known as "lean-against-the-wind" (LAW), it entailed moving short-term interest rates (later the funds rate) in a way that countered unsustainable growth in the economy. As evidenced by sustained increases in the economy's rate of resource utilization (sustained declines in the unemployment rate), unsustainable strength requires that interest rates rise. A converse statement holds for sustained weakness. LAW works as a search procedure for causing short-term interest rates to track the natural rate of interest.

In practice, the FOMC has followed two variants, termed here LAW with credibility and LAW with trade-offs. With the first, LAW with credibility, during economic recoveries, the FOMC raises the funds rate preemptively and then aggressively in the event of evidence of overheating in labor markets to preserve price stability. Price stability creates a stable nominal anchor while allowing the real economy to determine real variables like output and unemployment. That result follows from the LAW procedures that cause short-term interest rates to track the natural rate of interest.

With the second, LAW with trade-offs, during economic recoveries, the FOMC raises the funds rate only hesitantly to avoid "aborting the recovery." It waits until the appearance of inflation to raise the funds rate aggressively. In the pre-1981 period before real money demand became unstable, LAW with trade-offs imparted procyclicality to the behavior of money. Effectively, they involved the FOMC in Phillips trade-offs between inflation and unemployment. In recoveries, monetary policy focused on reducing a negative output gap (cyclically high unemployment) by allowing inflation to emerge. When inflation emerged, monetary policy focused on maintaining a negative output gap to lower inflation.

With the Treasury-Fed Accord of March 1951, the Fed could pursue a policy of economic stabilization. Guided by Winfield Riefler, William McChesney Martin attempted to restore the New York Fed's policy of stabilization that had emerged in the 1920s but in a way that countered unsustainable growth in the economy not presumed unsustainable growth in asset prices and inventories. The Keynesian consensus dismissed monetary policy as irrelevant, a poor stepchild to fiscal policy as the instrument of aggregate-demand management. Martin and Riefler rejected that view. They reinvented monetary policy in a way influenced by the Keynesian revolution while at the same time accepting responsibility for aggregate-demand management and inflation.

14.1. LEAN-AGAINST-THE-WIND (LAW)

Martin termed the reinvention of a monetary policy aimed at economic stability "lean against the wind" (LAW). The experience leading to the Accord in which the FOMC's rate peg had forced the Fed to monetize the sales of Treasury securities by banks combined with the burst of inflation that started in late 1950 caused Martin and Riefler to accept Fed responsibility for price stability. Martin still thought of monetary policy and maintenance of price stability in terms of leaning against the wind to preempt the development of "speculative imbalances." However, the cause of those "imbalances" was unchecked growth of output above potential that increased unsustainably the economy's rate of resource utilization, and conversely for growth below potential.

In the 1920s, the Fed considered the accumulation of inventories as economic recovery progressed to be a sign of speculation. In the 1950s, the accumulation of inventories was just one factor relevant to the determination of output. There was all the difference in the 1950s view of needing a cyclically high interest rate at times of optimism and in the 1920s view of needing to suppress that optimism as a sign of speculative excess through high interest rates even at the cost of recession. The latter objective was no longer possible given the post–World War II period of heightened government responsibility for low unemployment.

LAW implemented as a reaction function gave the Fed a chance to track

the economy's natural rate of interest and to allow the price system to stabilize the economy. It did then avoid another Great Depression. However, the
United States also continued to experience recessions. What determined
whether the Fed's LAW procedures were stabilizing or destabilizing? The
answer is to distinguish two variants of LAW: LAW with trade-offs and
LAW with credibility. They differ in their application to recessions. With
LAW with trade-offs, the FOMC raises the funds rate hesitantly until inflation emerges. With LAW with credibility, the FOMC raises the funds rate
preemptively to prevent the emergence of inflation.

Economic recoveries pose a challenge to LAW procedures. Law procedures require increases in the funds rate in response to sustained growth
above potential (a sustained increase in the economy's rate of resource utilization). During a recovery, however, sustained growth above potential is
desirable to eliminate a negative output gap (excess unemployment). How
should the FOMC decide on the appropriate path for the funds rate? What
path would cause output to follow a glide path that leads to movement along
the path of potential output? LAW with trade-offs and LAW with credibility offer a stark choice. With LAW with trade-offs, in an economic recovery,
the FOMC raises the funds rate aggressively only when inflation emerges.
With LAW with credibility, the FOMC raises the funds rate preemptively
when evidence emerges that labor markets are becoming overheated. That
is, it raises the funds rate to prevent the emergence of inflation.

In the second half of the 1960s and in the 1970s, LAW with trade-offs
was the rule. LAW with trade-offs required that the FOMC manage trade-
offs between inflation and output gaps, that is, between the difference in
actual and desired inflation and the difference in actual and potential output. Monetary policy thus possessed the characteristic of an activist policy
of aggregate-demand management entailing an effort to balance the twin,
competing goals of price stability and full employment. Only with the
Volcker-Greenspan FOMCs did the policy of LAW with credibility fully
emerge.

14.2. LAW WITH TRADE-OFFS AND
LONG AND VARIABLE LAGS

Before 1981 when real M1 demand was stable, M1 serves as a measure of the
stance of monetary policy. That knowledge of monetary policy when combined with the FOMC's experimentation with monetary policy provides
a remarkable monetary laboratory lasting from 1953 to 1981. This section
summarizes the behavior of money and the economy in this period through
a series of graphs.

LAW with trade-offs, which preceded the Volcker-Greenspan era, is identifiable through lags in raising the funds rate after cyclical troughs and lags in lowering it after cyclical peaks (see the tables of the monetary contraction marker in chap. 3). The monetarist narrative identified stop-go policy with this cyclical inertia in the adjustment of the Fed's funds-rate target (see Friedman 1984, 27; and Poole 1978, 105).[1] The result was destabilizing, procyclical money growth. The "long and variable" lags associated with the impact of money growth on the economy created the stop-go pattern of monetary policy. See Friedman (1960, 88–90) for an early statement of this critique. As estimated by Friedman (1989, 31), sustained changes in money growth affect real GDP growth with a lag of two to three quarters and affect inflation with a lag of about two years.

The graphs showing money end in 1981. At that time, M1 and M2 become interest sensitive, and M1 especially ceased being a useful indicator of the stance of monetary policy.[2] The Depository Institutions Deregulation and Monetary Control Act of 1980 phased out Regulation Q ceilings on interest rates paid on bank time deposits and authorized negotiable order of withdrawal (NOW) accounts nationwide. (NOW accounts were checking accounts that pay interest.) NOW accounts possessed characteristics of both media of exchange and savings instruments. As market interest rates changed, banks changed the rates paid on NOW accounts but with a lag. As a result, in response to an increase in market rates of interest, disintermediation occurred from the deposits in M1 and M2 as investors moved out of NOW accounts and into money market instruments like Treasury bills. Analogously, reintermediation into M1 and M2 occurred when market rates declined. With these changes, money demand became sensitive to market rates of interest.

The monetary aggregates then began giving inappropriate signals about the stance of monetary policy. When the economy weakened and market

1. Fève et al. (2009, 13) repeated for Europe this monetarist critique: "The form of monetary policy, namely monetary policy inertia, has played an important role in the large and persistent increase of the real interest rate and the sizeable output losses that have followed from disinflation policies of the eighties." See also Fève et al. (2010) and chapter 23.

2. The year 1981 uses "shift-adjusted" M1, which removed from demand deposits the deposits transferred from savings instruments, which were not included in M1 (Bennett 1982). In February 2021, the Board ended the monthly limit on transfers of funds from savings deposits to other checkable deposits (retail demand deposits). With savings deposits treated as transactions deposits, the Board then combined savings deposits with other checkable deposits. Savings deposits are huge, and that caused a significant jump in M1. M2 is not affected.

interest rates declined, money growth increased, and conversely in the event of strength in the economy. By behaving countercyclically, money started giving inappropriate signals about the desirable direction of interest rates. The interest sensitivity of the monetary aggregates made the Friedman steady-money-growth rule infeasible. However, the cessation of the monetary aggregates as useful leading indicators of economic activity does not affect the validity of the classical-dichotomy monetarism defended here. Namely, the optimal rule for the central bank is to provide a stable nominal anchor and to allow the price system free rein to determine real variables. Optimal monetary policy still requires the monetary control provided by this rule.

It is useful to understand "measured" money using the existing monetary aggregates as after 1980 being a distorted measure of the liquidity of the assets represented by the public's entire portfolio of assets. However, there still exits a stable demand for a real quantity of liquidity (the natural real quantity of money demanded). To provide for price stability, the central bank must still have procedures that cause the measured monetary aggregates to grow in line with growth of this underlying natural value of real liquidity demanded.

Figures 14.1, 14.2, and 14.3 illustrate the lagged relationships identified by Friedman. Figure 14.1 shows growth rates of nominal output and money (M1) with the money series increased by 3.5 percentage points to offset the secular rise in M1 velocity. The M1 series is lagged by two quarters starting in 1956. Figure 14.2 plots real output. It shows that monetary decelerations and accelerations impact output initially and only later inflation. Figure 14.3 shows inflation and M1 growth plotted with a lag of seven quarters starting in 1956. Figures 14.4 and 14.5 show how monetary contraction preceded cycle peaks through the recession with the July 1981 cycle peak.[3]

The graphs are evidence that the Fed interfered with the working of the price system in a way that created monetary absorptions and emissions analogous to the deficiencies and excesses associated with price fixing. Maintaining the real rate of interest above the natural rate of interest requires that the Fed sell bonds to counter an excess demand for bonds and thus destroy bank reserves and money. Conversely, it creates money when it keeps the real rate below the natural rate and monetizes an excess supply of bonds.

3. An exception is the January–July 1980 recession produced by the credit controls imposed by the Carter administration on March 15, 1980 (Hetzel 2008, 155–60). Friedman and Schwartz (1963b, chart 3) created the original step function graph for money.

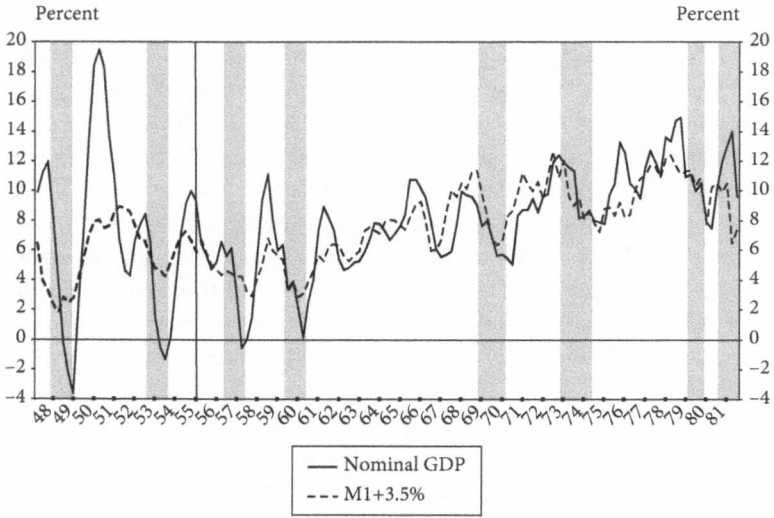

— Nominal GDP
--- M1+3.5%

Figure 14.1. Growth of Nominal Output and Lagged Money
Quarterly observations of four-quarter moving averages of nominal GDP and M1.
Beginning in 1956, M1 is lagged two quarters. The vertical line separates lagged and
unlagged M1 growth. In 1981, M1 is shift-adjusted M1 (Bennett 1982). The M1 series is
augmented by 3.5 percentage points. Shaded areas indicate NBER recessions. Heavy
tick marks indicate fourth quarter of year.
Sources: Haver Analytics; Board of Governors, Statistical Release H.6; Friedman
and Schwartz (1970)

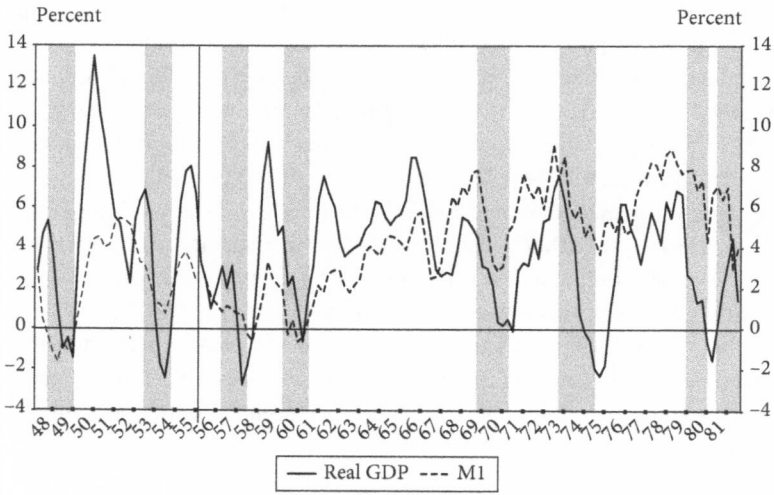

—— Real GDP --- M1

Figure 14.2. Growth of Real GDP and Lagged Money
Quarterly observations of four-quarter moving averages of quarterly annualized
percentage changes in real GDP (chain-weighted) and M1. Beginning in 1956, M1 is
lagged two quarters. The vertical line separates lagged and unlagged M1 growth. In
1981, M1 is shift-adjusted M1 (Bennett 1982). Shaded areas indicate recession. Heavy
tick marks indicate fourth quarter of year.
Source: St. Louis FRED

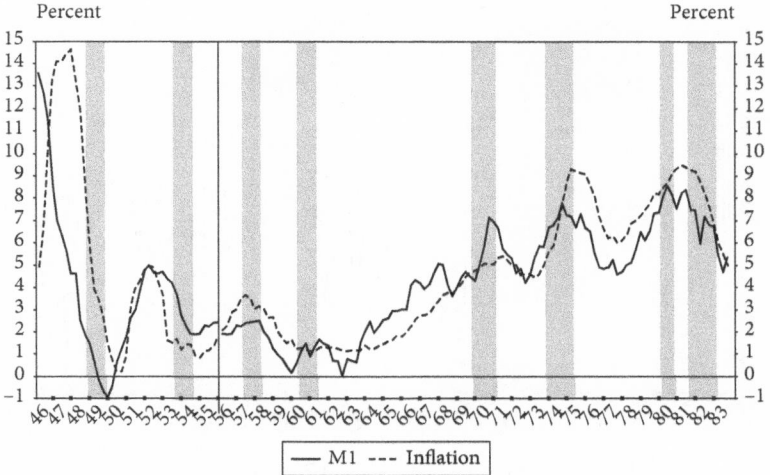

Figure 14.3. Inflation and Lagged Money Growth

Inflation is annualized percentage changes in the fixed-weight GDP deflator over an eight-quarter period. The GNP deflator from Balke and Gordon (1986) is used before 1947. Money growth is the annualized percentage change in M1 over an eight-quarter period. Beginning in 1956 M1 is lagged seven quarters. The vertical line separates lagged and unlagged M1 growth. M1 is shift-adjusted M1 for 1981 (Bennett 1982). Shaded areas indicate recession. Heavy tick marks indicate fourth quarter of year.

Sources: Friedman and Schwartz (1970); St. Louis FRED

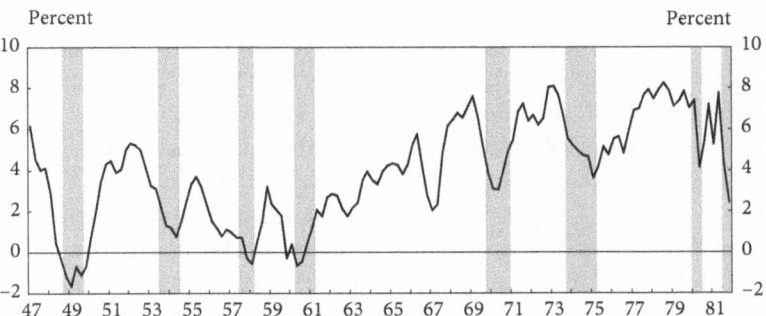

Figure 14.4. Money Growth and Recessions

Quarterly observations of four-quarter percentage changes in M1. M1 series is shift adjusted M1 for 1981 (Bennett 1982). Shaded areas indicate recessions.

Source: Friedman and Schwartz (1970)

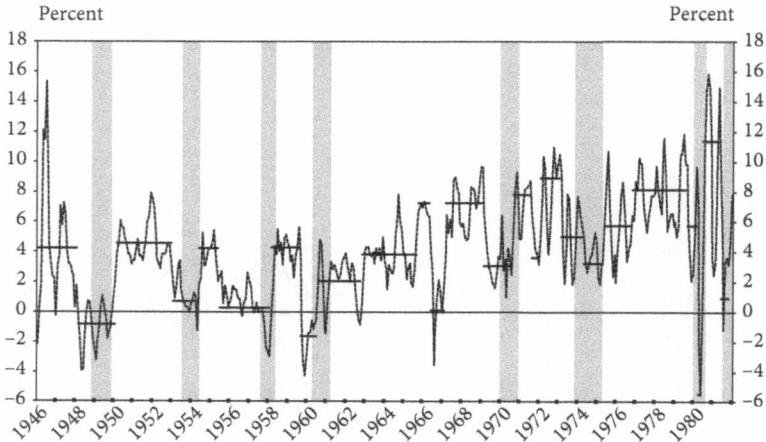

Figure 14.5. M1 Step Function and Recessions: 1946–81
Series are a three-month moving average of the annualized monthly money growth
rates and a step function fitted to monthly annualized growth rates of money. Data
on money (M1) from January 1946 to December 1958 from Friedman and Schwartz
(1970). From January 1959 to December 1980 data from Board of Governors (Statistical
Release H.6). January 1981 to December 1981 M1 is shift-adjusted M1 (Bennett 1982).
Shaded areas indicate recessions. Heavy tick marks indicate December.

14.3. LAW WITH CREDIBILITY OR LAW WITH TRADE-OFFS?

Under Martin, LAW procedures developed gradually over the 1950s. They
developed pragmatically based on the 1920s procedures but reinvented in
the new context of economic stabilization founded not on the need to quash
incipient speculation but rather on the desire to maintain growth of output
at potential. For Martin, the desideratum of policy became to have output
at potential with price stability. However, while potential output is an essential theoretical construct, it is measured with so much imprecision as to
make it useless as a target. The same comment applies to measures of full
employment or measures of the unemployment rate like NAIRU (nonaccelerating inflation rate of unemployment). Such measures are rendered am-
biguous because a strong economy can draw workers temporarily from out
of the labor force into employment. There is no close, contemporaneous
relationship between the output gap and changes in inflation. As a result,
LAW procedures emphasized changes in the economy's rate of resource
utilization rather than the magnitude of an output gap.

With LAW, the FOMC moves the funds rate in persistent, unidirectional
cycles, that is, persistently up and persistently down. Coming out of the

trough of a recession when the FOMC believes that the economy has gained enough momentum that above-trend growth is established, the FOMC begins to increase the funds rate in measured steps. The reason for initiating persistent increases is the FOMC's concern not to revive inflation. At the same time, the steps are measured in that the FOMC wants to see above-trend growth to eliminate the negative output gap incurred in the recession. The difficulty that the FOMC has felt in encouraging recovery without ultimately reviving inflation appeared in the comment of Governor Abbot Mills (Board of Governors, *FOMC Historical Minutes*, August 1, 1961, 40, cited in Meltzer 2009, 370) of the FOMC as "'groping to find a . . . policy' consistent with expansion but without 'the danger of generating subsequent inflationary pressures.'"

In an economic recovery, the issue is how to move output back to potential and then to have it grow along the path of potential output. With LAW with trade-offs, in economic recoveries, the FOMC waits to increase the funds rate aggressively until it sees inflation rise. This policy would succeed in offering the FOMC the information it needs to put output on a glide path toward and then along potential if there were a contemporaneous relationship between the output gap and inflation. However, the lags are long. LAW with trade-offs allows a negative output gap to become significantly positive before inflation rises. In figure 14.6, the path to returning to growth along potential is the overshoot path represented by ABDEF. Greenspan (US Congress 1995a, 4–5) explained the interest-rate increases in 1994 in the absence of inflation: "It is possible for the economy to exceed so called 'potential' for a time without adverse consequences by extending work hours, by deferring maintenance, and by forgoing longer-term projects. . . .

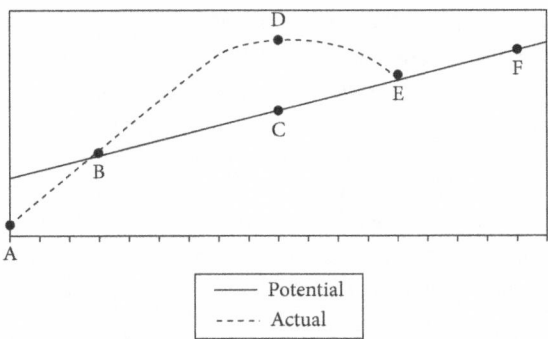

Figure 14.6. Two Alternative Paths for a Return to Growth at Potential
Two alternative strategies for returning output to potential and causing it to grow thereafter at potential in an economic recovery: overshooting and a smooth glide path.

History shows clearly that given levels of resource utilization can be associated with a wide range of inflation rates."

With LAW with trade-offs, the emergence of inflation presented a dilemma for the FOMC because of the associated rise in inflationary expectations. The FOMC then understood that to lower inflation it would have to lower expected inflation. The weakening in the economy prior to and after cyclical peaks called for a reduction in the funds rate. The FOMC, however, feared that markets would interpret the reduction as a lack of resolve to control inflation. In practice, during the stop-go era, the FOMC achieved the worst of possible outcomes. Initially, when the funds rate had risen to the point where the economy began to weaken, out of concern for inflationary expectations, it would limit reductions in the funds rate sufficiently to cause a recession. However, it would then back off, resume an expansionary monetary policy, and allow inflation to ratchet upward over the business cycle.

In 1974, Governor Mitchell expressed the dilemma to the FOMC. "The Committee had one problem with respect to its public image and credibility and another problem with respect to the effects of monetary policy on real economic activity" (cited in Mayer 1999, 49). Stephen Axilrod (1971, 27), associate economist to the FOMC, wrote earlier: "When combating inflationary psychology is taken as a primary goal of policy . . . , it becomes difficult to permit an easing in money market conditions because this might be taken as signaling an unwillingness of the System to persist in its efforts to reduce inflationary expectations."

With LAW with credibility, in contrast, during economic recoveries, when the FOMC begins to see signs of stress in measures of resource utilization, especially in the form of overheating in labor markets, it moves the funds rate up more aggressively. The intention is to move the economy along the path (figure 14.6) to avoid any increase in inflation. Policy is preemptive with respect to inflation. The FOMC is "forecasting" inflation but not based on an output gap combined with a Phillips curve but rather based on the assumption that the economy cannot grow indefinitely above trend without inflation. That assumption is evident in the comments of Governor Gramlich (Board of Governors, *FOMC Transcript*, March 22, 2005, 79) in discussing the statement language at an FOMC meeting: "The Committee perceives that if the current target for the federal funds rate were maintained for the next few quarters, it is more likely than not that output would grow at a pace faster than sustainable and that inflation pressures would pick up. That says exactly what we think."

Athanasios Orphanides (2003c) reproduced citations from Chairmen Martin and Greenspan in the spirit of LAW with credibility. Martin (1965) stated:

To me, the effective time to act against inflationary pressures is when they are in the development stage—before they have become full-blown and the damage has been done. Precautionary measures are more likely to be effective than remedial action: the old proverb that an ounce of prevention is worth a pound of cure applies to monetary policy as well as to anything else.

Greenspan (US Congress 1999b, 7) testified in the semiannual report: "For monetary policy to foster maximum sustainable economic growth, it is useful to preempt forces of imbalance before they threaten economic instability. . . . Modest preemptive actions can obviate more drastic actions at a later date that would destabilize the economy."

The implicit assumption is that allowing inflation to emerge would likely require putting the economy through a recession to lower it. Although allowing the economy to "run hot" by allowing output to overshoot potential as with the path ABDEF (figure 14.6) can temporarily lower the unemployment rate below its full employment level, the FOMC risks setting off a go-stop cycle. The tables in chapter 3 showing the "monetary contraction marker" for recessions support this view. Allowing inflation to emerge in the recovery phase of a business cycle requires limiting reductions in the funds rate at the cyclical peak. Contractionary monetary policy at cyclical peaks is signaled by a weakening of economic activity while short-term interest rates remain at cyclical highs.

Specifically, during economic recoveries, the FOMC raises short-term interest rates in a steady, measured way until the economy weakens. If at that point, its primary concern has become inflation (or the foreign exchange value of the dollar in 1960), it restrains reductions in the funds rate while the economy weakens. It maintains the (nominal and real) funds rate at a cyclical high past the cyclical peak. This behavior has characterized recessions in the lean-against-the-wind period inaugurated by William McChesney Martin (tables in chap. 3). It appears in figure 14.7 with the occurrence of cyclical peaks in real output growth (marked by +'s) that precede NBER cycle peaks. A lagged response by the FOMC in adjusting the funds rate represents interference with the operation of the price system. This behavior leads to an inversion of the yield curve (figure 14.8). The yield curve inverts because on the one hand weakness in the economy causes bond rates to decline and on the other hand the FOMC is maintaining the funds rate at its cyclical high.

In the early 1960s under Martin, FOMC procedures had evolved toward LAW with credibility. Starting with the populist pressure of President Johnson and the appointment of Keynesian governors to the Board of

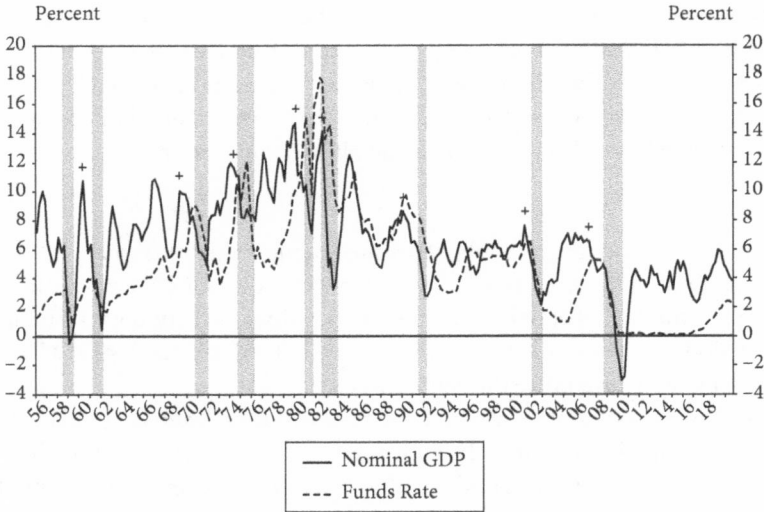

Figure 14.7. Federal Funds Rate and Growth of Nominal GDP
Quarterly observations of four-quarter growth rate of nominal GDP. Crosses mark the
weakening of growth occurring before cyclical peaks. Shaded areas indicate recessions.
Source: St. Louis FRED

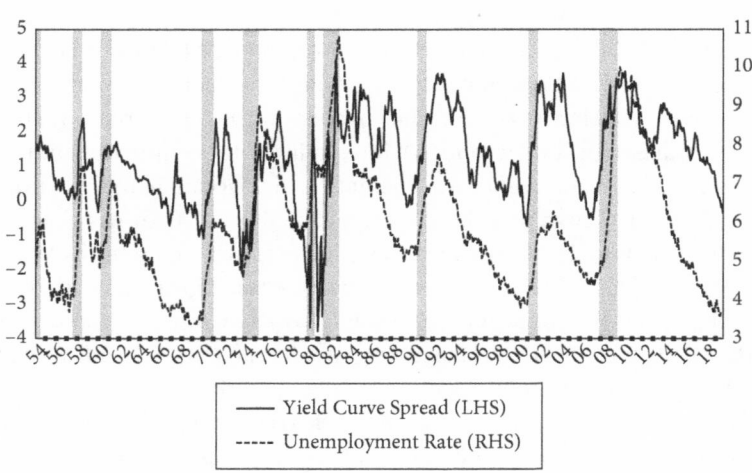

Figure 14.8. Yield Curve and Unemployment Rate
The yield curve is the ten-year Treasury yield minus the three-month Treasury Bill
Yield. Shaded areas indicate recession. Tick marks indicate December.
Source: St. Louis FRED

Governors, however, the FOMC abandoned LAW with credibility (Hetzel 2008, chap. 6). Under Martin's successors, Arthur Burns and G. William Miller, the FOMC pursued an aggregate-demand policy based on the assumption that inflation originated as nonmonetary cost-push inflation. After the Volcker disinflation, given the imperative of conditioning inflationary expectations to restore a stable nominal anchor, monetary policy became LAW with credibility.

With LAW with credibility, the indicator for funds-rate changes is persistent changes in the rate of resource utilization (growth gaps). Greenspan (US Congress 1999b, 19) testified, "We cannot tell . . . what the actual potential [growth rate] is . . . but it shouldn't be our concern. Our concern should be the imbalances that emerge." Greenspan (US Congress 2000, 14) made the same point in dismissing the criticism that raising interest rates limited growth in the economy.

> The question of how fast this economy grows is not something the central bank should be involved in. . . . What we are looking at is basically the indications that demand chronically exceeds supply. . . . The best way to measure that is to look at what is happening to the total number of people who . . . are unemployed. . . . What . . . we are concerned about is not the rate of increase in demand or the rate of increase in supply, but only the difference between the two. . . . We don't know whether the potential growth rate is 4, 5, 6, or 8 percent. What we need to focus on . . . is solely the difference between the two.

With these procedures, the FOMC does not require a structural model of the economy capable of yielding extended forecasts. The FOMC lacks the required knowledge of the structure of the economy required to make the inflation-output trade-offs inherent in the LAW with trade-offs policy. Greenspan (Board of Governors, *FOMC Transcript*, November 10, 2004, 75, 78) emphasized the limited ability of the FOMC to forecast:

> We're going to move back, I suspect, far closer to our more general position, which at one point was that we never projected the future, we merely tried to give a sense of the balance of risks. That assessment often didn't convey very much because we didn't behave as though we really viewed it as a projection; we responded largely to the data as they evolved. . . . When it comes to policy, with the increased uncertainties that we have about how the economic situation is evolving, we have to acknowledge to ourselves that our forecast is going to be wrong. It always is. We expect it to be wrong.

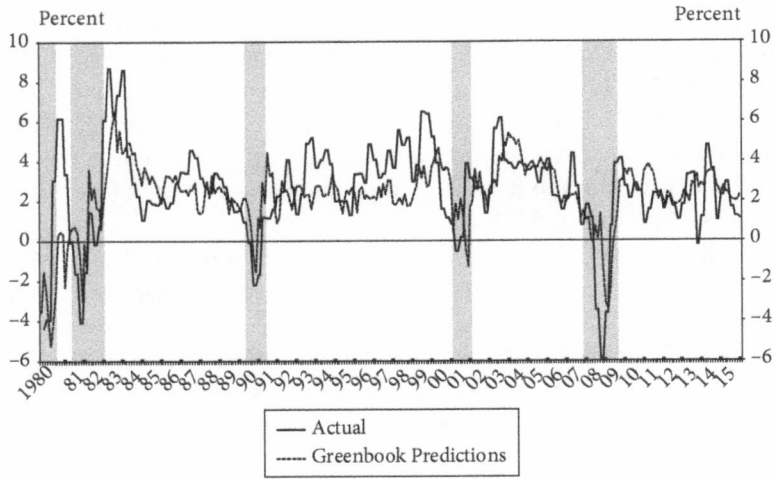

Figure 14.9. Actual and Predicted Real Output Growth
Observations correspond to FOMC meetings. Predictions are from the Greenbook and are for the annualized two-quarter rate of growth of real output (GNP before December 1991 and GDP thereafter). If an FOMC meeting is in the first two months of a quarter, the predicted growth rate is for the contemporaneous and succeeding quarter. If it is in the last month of a quarter, the predicted growth rate is for the succeeding two quarters. Actual growth is the subsequently realized growth rate, measured using the data available at the time of the publication of the "final" GDP estimate for the final quarter of the two-month growth rate. The final estimate is released in the last month of the quarter following a particular quarter. Shaded areas indicate recession. Heavy tick marks indicate a December FOMC meeting.

"Forecasting" entails putting together incoming information on various facets of the economy to understand the contemporaneous behavior of the aggregate economy. The main forecast given by the Board staff to the FOMC is the Tealbook forecast, which is judgmental rather than model based. As shown in figure 14.9 of two-quarter forecast errors in the Board staff forecasts of real output, for long periods of time, even at short time horizons, the Board staff makes significant forecast errors.[4] What is central is that the forecast generally changes in a measured, predictable way from meeting to meeting in response to new information. The spirit is "guess and correct" as new information arrives.

4. Episodes in which the FOMC has based policy on forecasts have not turned out well. In June 1968, in response to passage of the income tax surcharge, it inappropriately forecast a weakening of the economy requiring a reduction in the funds rate. After the October 1987 stock market crash and after the summer and fall 1998 Russia and Asia crisis, it similarly forecast a weakening of the economy, which did not occur.

14.4. LAW WITH CREDIBILITY AND LAW WITH TRADE-OFFS AS SEMICONTROLLED EXPERIMENTS

The monetarist-Keynesian debate reflected two competing visions of the optimal monetary standard. The Keynesian consensus advocated aggregate-demand management using the Phillips curve to trade off between competing objectives for inflation and unemployment. The difficult political economy of raising unemployment to control presumed cost-push inflation required the ongoing exercise of discretion. As formulated by Friedman (1960), the monetarist challenge advocated a rule in the form of steady money growth. At the time, the stability of real money demand and potential output growth would have ensured steady growth in nominal output. Friedman's rule would have provided for a stable nominal anchor and would have allowed market forces to determine real variables. It then was the intellectual ancestor of the rule advocated here in which the FOMC provides a stable nominal anchor in the form of the expectation of price stability and moves the funds rate to track the natural rate of interest to allow market forces an unfettered ability to determine real variables such as output and employment.

The two variants of the basic LAW procedures provide semicontrolled experiments to test these two competing visions of the optimal monetary standard. LAW with trade-offs is in the spirit of Keynesian activist aggregate-demand management. It is organized around balancing off inflation and output misses. LAW with credibility is in the monetarist spirit of Friedman. It is organized around price stability (a stable nominal anchor), which necessarily turns over the determination of real variables to the operation of the price system.

LAW with trade-offs is optimal if significant shocks to aggregate real demand and to inflation originate in the private sector. The central bank must know the structure of the economy and be able to use a feedback strategy to vary its instrument to predictably eliminate gaps between actual and targeted values of macroeconomic variables. Moreover, given the assumed nonmonetary character of an inflation driven by cost-push shocks, the central bank must be able to predictably balance off the competing objectives of price stability and full employment. There must exist a structural (hard-wired) trade-off between unemployment and inflation as captured in a structural Phillips curve.

In contrast, LAW with credibility is optimal if the structure of the economy exhibits a "classical dichotomy." That is, the central bank can follow a rule that separates the determination of the price level from the determination of relative prices and of real variables. Inflation is a monetary phenomenon not a cost-push phenomenon. Moreover, in the absence of monetary shocks that force an unpredictable evolution of the price level, the price system works well to maintain real output at potential. The central bank can guarantee aggregate nominal demand "maintenance" where aggregate nominal demand is determined as the sum of output growth at potential and of underlying trend inflation (see chap. 29). In the post-Accord period, the grand experiment was the aggregate-demand "management" of stop-go versus the aggregate-demand "maintenance" of the Great Moderation.

14.5. CONCLUDING COMMENTS

In the post-Accord period, monetary policy was of two basic kinds. With LAW with trade-offs, the FOMC actively attempted to manipulate a perceived output gap subject to presumed predicable trade-offs given by a Phillips curve. With LAW with credibility, the FOMC moved the funds rate in a persistent way in response to sustained growth gaps so as to cause the real funds rate to track the natural interest rate. A credible commitment that funds-rate changes would cumulate to whatever extent necessary to maintain trend inflation invariant to shocks provided a stable nominal anchor.

CHAPTER 15

The Early Martin Fed

Summary: William McChesney Martin was chairman of the FOMC from April 1951 until January 1970. Under his leadership, the FOMC developed its "lean-against-the-wind procedures" with which it moved short-term interest rates persistently up or down in a way designed to counter unsustainable strength or weakness in the growth of real output. Under the policy of "bills only," the Fed bought and sold only Treasury bills. With its pre–World War II real bills policies, the Fed had remained alert to incipient speculative excess evidenced by a rise in asset prices and unsustainable increases in inventories and capital expenditures. Martin changed the focus on expectations from increases in asset prices to increases in prices. The bond market, which under "bills only" fluctuated freely, then became a watchman warning of excessively expansionary monetary policy. Martin often characterized inflation as "a thief in the night" and always considered price stability to be the overriding objective.[1]

During Martin's tenure, the Keynesian intellectual consensus dominated the economics profession. That consensus held that monetary policy was an insignificant determinant of (real and nominal) aggregate demand. Belief in the impotence of monetary policy emerged out of the combination in the 1930s of sustained high unemployment and low nominal interest rates. The assumption that the government could control aggregate demand through deficit spending emerged out of the combination in World War II of low unemployment and wartime deficits.

In contrast, Martin saw the experience of the war from the perspective of price controls and suppressed inflation. As assistant secretary for international affairs at the Treasury, with the intensification of the Korean War in November 1950, Martin saw how the interest-rate peg of 2.5 percent for long-term government bonds forced the Fed to monetize the debt held by banks. Under the prewar Fed's real bills assumptions, the Fed was only one

---

1. For an overview of the life and career of Martin, the best reference is Bremner (2004).

influence on financial intermediation through the way in which it influenced the cost and availability of the reserves it supplied to banks. In the Korean War crisis, it was clear that the Fed had to control total bank credit to control inflation.

Martin chose operating procedures designed to maintain Fed independence. In part, that entailed developing the "depth, breadth, and resilience" of the government bond market so that the Fed would not have to intervene to prevent self-fulfilling declines in the prices of government bonds. Martin never admitted that the Fed controlled interest rates, not even on short-term government securities. To that end, with the help of Winfield Riefler, he reinstituted the free reserves operating procedures the Fed had pioneered in the 1920s. The idea was to prevent Treasury pressure to reinstate a rate peg. With these procedures, however, the Fed again communicated in terms of how it influenced financial intermediation through its influence on the cost and availability of the funds (reserves) it supplied to the banking system. It lacked a framework to communicate monetary policy in terms of monetary control.

As long as the conservative Eisenhower administration supported Martin's goal of price stability, the Fed maintained at least longer-run price stability. The conservative Dillon Treasury under President Kennedy, not wanting a dollar crisis, also supported Martin. However, the environment became hostile to Fed independence with the populist LBJ presidency and his Keynesian Council of Economic Advisers (CEA). Without an intellectual framework to juxtapose against these influences, the Fed drifted and did indeed become the engine of inflation it had hoped to avoid becoming with the 1951 Treasury-Fed Accord.

Under the leadership of Martin, the Fed developed into the first modern central bank. Two developments laid the groundwork. First, standing real bills precepts on their head, the Fed not only accepted but also developed a national market for reserves in New York. With the Fed's wartime and postwar peg of the interest rate on short-term government securities, the country clearly did have a national market for bank reserves. Banks adjusted their reserves positions by buying and selling Treasury bills. The New York Desk developed procedures to routinely offset factors that drained and supplied reserves to stabilize interest rates in the money market (Roosa 1956; Madden 1959, 86). Although obscured by its free reserves procedures, the FOMC eventually came to admit publicly (in 1994) that it implemented monetary policy through its control of the federal funds rate.

The second development entailed behaving predictably. That is, monetary policy came to be characterized as a reaction function relating the behavior of its policy instrument in a systematic way to the behavior of the economy. With "bills only," under which the Fed bought and sold only Treasury bills, the term structure of interest rates (the entire yield curve) would move in a way that stabilized economic activity only if the FOMC set short-term interest rates in a predictable way in response to incoming information on the economy.

15.1. THE END OF REAL BILLS

In the pre–World War II era, Fed policy makers understood monetary policy through the lens of real bills. They wanted to proportion the extension of credit to the need for productive uses. The extension of an excessive amount of credit would spill over into speculative excess whose inevitable collapse would produce recession and deflation. Credit control required keeping banks in the discount window. If evidence of speculative psychology appeared, the Fed would sell securities to create an amount of borrowing that required banks to be in the window at times for prolonged periods. The Reserve Banks would then raise their discount rates to increase the cost of credit. In addition, the policies of moral suasion and direct pressure entailed oversight of banks in the discount window to guarantee that they did not extend an excessive amount of credit and did not extend credit based on the hope of speculative gain.

The failure of depression and deflation to reemerge with the end of World War II meant the end of real bills views. Starting in 1934, bank credit expanded on a base of reserves from gold inflows. In World War II, it expanded further on a base of reserves from Fed purchases of government securities. According to real bills views, the resulting artificial expansion of bank credit should have led to an unsustainable level of economic activity followed by a collapse. After the war, there should have been an enormous depression and deflation. However, after the war, the problem was inflation, which soared with the end of price controls.

With wartime and the huge increase in military expenditures, the obvious problem became limiting total aggregate demand to the physical capacity of the economy to produce goods and services. For the Fed, that would mean limiting the expansion of total bank reserves and bank credit rather than adjusting them to the ebb and flow of legitimate (productive) uses. However, nothing could happen as long as the Fed remained subservient to the Treasury. Everything changed suddenly when in the Korean War the Chinese entered on the side of the North Koreans. In November 1950, when the Korean Army crossed the Yalu River, the world feared a World War III. Commodity prices soared, and markets feared shortages due to the reimposition of price controls. The Fed watched from the sidelines while inflation jumped.

With its rate peg, the Fed had to create the reserves that stoked the fires of inflation. Restricting reserves creation to the discounting of real bills was impossible given the Fed's obligation to monetize Treasury debt. The Fed defied the Treasury and the White House when in early 1951 it refused to support the price of long-term government debt to keep rates from rising above 2½ percent. At the time, Congress was at odds with President Truman over the firing of General MacArthur. Congress refused to support the administration. The Fed and the Treasury negotiated the March 1951 Treasury-Fed Accord, which gave the Fed its independence conditioned on a phased end to support for the Treasury market (Hetzel and Leach 2001a).

After the March 1951 Treasury-Fed Accord, the Fed's new leader, William McChesney Martin, created the modern central bank. The concern for economic stability remained unchanged from prewar real bills days. However, the Fed's intermediate target changed from the prevention of speculative excess to leaning against unsustainable growth in aggregate demand that persistently either reduced the rate of resource utilization in the economy or increased it. Martin retained the real bills concern for speculative psychology, but with two momentous changes. First, he focused on the stability of goods prices not asset prices. Second, he looked to the bond market not the stock market for evidence on expectations.

With the end of the ceiling on bond rates in March 1951, the Martin FOMC worked to make the government bond market into the world's largest market for liquidity. The bills only policy of not conducting open market operations in the bond market made the bond market into a useful measure of investor sentiment. The real bills preoccupation with a central money market that could divert funds into stock market speculation disappeared. The Fed could then understand the transmission of monetary policy as occurring through the money market. Martin worked to develop the "depth, breadth, and resilience" of the New York market for Treasury securities to obviate any need for the Fed to intervene to support the issue of Treasury debt. In support of that program, the New York Desk developed procedures by which it routinely offset factors that drained and supplied reserves to the banking system (Meulendyke 1998).

What survived from real bills was the (mis)understanding of monetary policy as the regulation of financial intermediation. The concept of monetary control was still a bridge too far into the populist domain of banks as creators of paper money. Travel from the idea of credit control through the control of borrowing from the discount window to monetary control through the control of reserves creation was too radical a leap. The instrument of control that emerged after the Accord remained the free reserves concept of the 1920s. Policy makers understood the amount of free reserves as a measure of the pressure on the reserve position of banks that regulated the incentive of banks to extend credit—what (Brunner and Meltzer 1964) termed "the Riefler-Burgess doctrine."

15.2. FREE RESERVES AS THE INTERMEDIATE TARGET AND BILLS ONLY

After the Accord, the Fed had to establish and then to maintain its independence against a Treasury wanting support for the market for government debt. The Treasury was unwilling to sell long-term debt at auction, which would have allowed the market to set the interest rate on the debt. At the time, the fear was that a drop in the price of Treasury bonds could set off an "explosive overnight run from debts to real assets" (E. Wood 1954, 3).

The Fed was not going to peg the price of a government security. The use of free reserves (excess reserves minus borrowed reserves) as an instrument and as an indicator of the stance of policy solved this problem. The Fed could continue to use its prewar real bills language of monetary policy operating through the presumed influence on the cost and availability of funds to banks. Sproul (SPNY, memo from Allan Sproul to Dr. Williams and Mr. Roosa, May 17, 1954, 1) explained:

> I have blamed it ["the inflation which occurred after the war"] on the swollen money supply created during the war. . . . Our support operations during the postwar 40's . . . not only gave the commercial banks automatic or semi-automatic access to reserve funds, but also gave others such as insurance companies and saving banks the same sort of access. . . .
>
> There are guides to policy other than interest rates. . . . At times of credit ease, this would mean . . . infrequent and minor borrowing in response to temporary needs of individual banks. At times of credit restraint, it would mean . . . member banks having to borrow fairly frequently and in relatively large amounts so that, in the aggregate, they would be in debt more or less continuously.

Free reserves procedures would do the work of controlling reserves through the tradition of banker reluctance to be in the discount window. In the debate leading up to the Accord, Sproul (SPNY, February 15, 1951, 5) advocated abandoning the rate peg in favor of free reserves procedures:

> Under this policy, banks would be expected to obtain needed reserves more largely, and eventually primarily, by borrowing from the Federal Reserve Banks. If demands for expansion of bank credit and bank

reserves continue, . . . short term rates of interest would adjust to a level around the discount rate. . . . This would bring to the support of our policy the powerful tradition of the member banks against large and continuous borrowing.

Although in the 1950s the FOMC developed a reaction function in the form of lean-against-the-wind (LAW), its use of free reserves operating procedures created problems with the way in which policy makers and the Fed understood monetary policy. The FOMC continued to understand policy in terms of its influence on financial intermediation rather than in terms of monetary control. Also, free reserves were defective as an indicator variable.[2] The underlying problem was that policy makers did not understand the endogeneity of free reserves. A leftward shift in the reserves demand schedule (R^d in figure 6.1) due to weakening loan demand arising in turn out of a weakening economy would lower borrowed reserves. The FOMC interpreted the reduction in borrowed reserves and the associated reduction in interest rates as an easing of monetary policy. That reduction did not necessarily imply that interest rates were declining sufficiently to track a decline in the natural rate of interest. These procedures introduced a destabilizing procyclicality into movements in the money stock.

Although agreed on the use of free reserves, until Sproul's retirement in 1956, the Board and the New York Fed engaged in a heated argument over the Martin policy of "bills only" (Hetzel and Leach 2001b). Martin wanted open market operations confined to Treasury bills with the influence on long-term rates occurring through arbitrage. The Fed would deal with Treasury concerns through developing a market in government securities exhibiting "depth, breadth, and resilience." Sproul wanted the freedom to undertake open market operations at all maturities. The difference was over the effectiveness of arbitrage between short-term rates and future-forward rates. Sproul assumed a "preferred habitat" world in which the Fed could influence the cost and availability of credit and thus could move long rates independently of short rates.

2. Wheelock (1991, 477) explained:

The notion that banks are reluctant to borrow reserves, and do so only when forced to, is fundamental to the Fed's use of borrowed reserves as a policy guide. If this theory is correct, then the level of borrowing will indicate accurately the degree of monetary ease or restraint. Relatively heavy borrowing will reflect pressure on bank reserve positions and tight money, while little borrowing will reflect monetary ease.

At the June 11, 1953, FOMC meeting, Sproul (Board of Governors, *FOMC Historical Minutes*, June 11, 1953, 14–15) challenged Martin:

> I don't think we can do it [develop a market with depth, breadth, and resilience] if we continue . . . to confine ourselves at all times to operations in Treasury bills. We have been told that operations in bills would have prompt and pervasive effects throughout the market. That was the theory of perfect fluidity—perfect arbitrage. I think historical records and current observation indicate that a prompt and invariable response between short and long markets can not always be expected. . . . It seems to me that we must either still be reacting violently against market pegging or embracing a somewhat doctrinaire attitude on free markets.

The debate over bills only also concerned where control of monetary policy would lie. If the New York Desk were to possess the authority to intervene judgmentally at all maturities, New York and the Desk would possess significant control over monetary policy. An instruction to the Desk framed exclusively in terms of free reserves with open market operations confined to Treasury bills would keep control with the FOMC, which Martin dominated. The heated character of the dispute appeared in a memo Tilford Gaines wrote for Allan Sproul in response to a memo from Martin criticizing the New York Fed's position on bills only. Gaines (1956, 1, 16) wrote:

> The position he [Martin] has taken . . . would in a court of law or logic, give you [Sproul] the case. He has twisted your central theme, the "nudge," to make it mean arbitrarily imposed and artificially sustained "rigging" of rates. . . . But in the course of his argument against the twisted version of your views, he concedes the whole point you really want to make. That is, he concedes that System operations in the long market could at least have a temporary influence in moving interest rates (and altering credit availabilities) more rapidly in one direction or another than could be achieved through operations at the short end alone. . . .
>
> You stated categorically that one reason for the need for flexibility in System operations is the fact that we do not have the kind of arbitrage in the Government securities market that formed the basis of a good deal of the hopeful speculation in the Ad Hoc Subcommittee report. You added that so long as the System recognizes the existence of a need, at times, for being interested in what happens in the long-term markets, and to long-term rates, there will be times when action confined to the short end

of the market must take an extreme form it if is to exert even a remote influence at the longer end. Chairman Martin's only reference to this line of discussion was . . . a statement that the Federal Reserve System really effectuates its policy . . . primarily by the effects it has on the banking system's ability to lend.

Elmer Wood (1954) at the University of Missouri expressed Sproul's position:

> The only sensible position for the monetary authorities is to admit that they can and do control the level of market interest rates. . . . It is important that such buying and selling prices be established for Governments in all maturity ranges. In this respect, the final outcome of the recent Sproul-Martin controversy—that the System should execute open market operations only in bills—is to be deplored. Long-term bond yields are too important a factor in the economy to be left to the unpredictable influences of market arbitrage and attitudes. In part, long-term yields reflect anticipations of the future level of all rates. . . . During depressions the only expansionary opportunity available to the central bank in the rate structure may be in the long-term area. Short-term rates may be depressed to nearly zero because of investor demand for near-money assets. Long-term rates, however, would be higher, and hence susceptible to further reductions through System purchases of longer maturities.

Later, policy makers came to understand that having a reaction function that moved the funds rate predictably in response to incoming information on the economy would move the entire yield curve in a stabilizing manner.

Although the Fed denied having an interest-rate target, it is clear that policy makers (and the Treasury) cared about interest rates. For example, at the June 23, 1953 meeting of the FOMC Executive Committee, Sproul (SPNY, Board Executive Committee June 23, 1953, 6) said:

> The critical point in all this analysis is whether the market is going to expect further significant increases in interest rates and further declines in security prices during the remainder of the year. If System actions do not quickly dispel such expectations, our present credit policy is going to fail and the Treasury's debt management problems are going to be almost insuperable. To confine open market operations to Treasury bills in such circumstances may defeat the legitimate aims of credit policy and debt management.

Sproul also used the occasion to make his criticism of bills only as opposed to intervention in long-term bonds to ensure that long-term rates moved in the desired direction. If the Fed's only concern was with free reserves, there would never have been any need for a pitched battle between the Board and New York over at what maturities to allow the Desk to buy and sell.

In choosing the format for discussion in FOMC meetings, Martin restricted the policy recommendations to the value of free reserves. That format enhanced Martin's control over monetary policy in that the unsatisfactoriness of free reserves as an instrument for controlling the interest rate on short-term Treasury debt made mandatory the New York Desk routine of looking through free reserves to market rates. The actual provision of reserves then depended on a "morning call" between the manager of the New York Desk and Martin or his assistant. (Sproul and Martin fought over whether the manager should be responsible to the FOMC or to the president of the New York Fed for this reason.)

Malcolm Bryan (Board of Governors, *FOMC Historical Minutes*, August 21, 1956, 26) described the deficiencies of free reserves as a target:

> The past has demonstrated that a given level of free reserves means one thing at one time and another thing at another time, so that policy decisions aimed at a given level of free reserves often produce unpredictable money rate effects; and that fundamental difficulty is compounded because the factors affecting free reserves often exhibit erratic and unpredictable behavior from day to day, so that, regardless of our difficulty in appraising the monetary effect of an aimed-at level of free reserves, we are even unable in the short-run to effect the intended level of free reserves with any substantial degree of precision. Mr. Bryan hoped that the management of the account in trying to estimate its actions would not have in mind any level of free reserves but would have in mind the behavior of the market which should be related to the interest rate.

Also, free reserves possessed significance only given the level of the discount rate, and market rates fluctuated around the discount rate (figure 6.1). At the same meeting, Governor Abbot Mills (Board of Governors, *FOMC Historical Minutes*, August 21, 1956, 21) said that

> it was his belief that a retreat should be made, to the end of bringing the level of negative free reserves down toward a $200 million level, but on a gradual basis that would test the response of the market to such actions by the System and in that way guide the System to the point at which the

market for US Government securities would stabilize. It was Mr. Mills' opinion that such a point of stability would fall realistically in line with a 3 per cent discount rate.

Throughout the decade of the 1960s, members of the FOMC would argue without success for an ability to formulate a well-defined directive to the Desk that would not require intermeeting judgmental interpretation by the Desk and, behind the Desk, Martin. An advantage of lack of a meaningful directive for Martin was that he could then speak for an FOMC consensus even if such a consensus did not exist. Meltzer (2009, 332) reproduced comments made in response to a proposal by Eliot Swan, president of the San Francisco Fed, that the FOMC should tell the public "what the System is trying to do, how it tried to do it, and what seems to have been accomplished." George Clay, president of the Kansas City Fed, responded arguing that "efforts to be completely specific may make it more difficult to arrive at a consensus. But lack of specific directions shifts the responsibility of interpretation to the Trading Desk." Meltzer (2009, 333) also quoted a letter from Frederick Deming, president of the Federal Reserve Bank of Minneapolis, to Board economist Ralph Young: "An attempt to write directives in specifics would push uncomfortably close to mechanistic policy-making."

At the January 26, 1960, FOMC meeting, A. James Meigs (1976, 449–50, 453) recounted one attempt by Malcolm Bryan, president of the Federal Reserve Bank of Atlanta, to give substance to the directive the FOMC issued to the New York Desk. (Bryan's specific proposal reflected the desire of the FOMC at that time to pursue a restrictive policy.)

> Based on his concept of total effective reserves . . . he suggested a 2 percent rate of growth for the time being, as compared with the 3.6 percent average rate of growth in the postwar period. . . . President Hayes, of New York, said . . . "the problem got into terms of the feel, color, and tone of the market." . . . President Hayes returned to his criticism of the proposed reserves and money supply targets at the March 1 meeting. . . . "Our usual instructions couched in terms of 'the same degree of restraint' of 'more' or 'less' are sufficiently precise and make it possible for the Manager to react to changing developments flexibly." . . . At the October 4 meeting, Robert Rouse, Manager of the Open Market Account, reported, "As the Committee has instructed, we have been operating primarily on the feel of the market rather than on the basis of reserve statistics."

In the absence of a meaningful directive, after the Accord, practical control rested with the Executive Committee, which was dominated by Martin and Sproul. The FOMC only characterized the state of the economy and by implication the direction of change in conditions in the money market. For example, at the March 4–5, 1953, FOMC meeting, the FOMC directed the Executive Committee "to arrange for such [open market] transactions . . . with a view to exercising restraint upon inflationary developments" (see the Board of Governors' *Fortieth Annual Report*, Record of Policy Actions, March 4–5, 1953, published 1954, 86).[3] At the June 11, 1953, meeting, the language changed "to avoiding deflationary tendencies without encouraging a renewal of inflationary developments" (Board of Governors' *Fortieth Annual Report*, published 1954, 92). At the September 24, 1953, FOMC meeting, the latter sentence omitted the last part about "encouraging a renewal of inflationary developments." The Executive Committee, which met every several weeks, then issued guidelines to the New York Desk putting limits on the amount of securities it could buy or sell. With the abolition of the Executive Committee after the June 6, 1955, meeting, Martin's control was complete.

15.3. CONCLUDING COMMENT

In the second half of the 1960s, the Martin FOMC got pushed off track by the pressures of a populist president, Lyndon Johnson, and his Keynesian Council of Economic Advisers. Martin was not an intellectual. One reason that the Fed could be pushed off into the dead end of a policy of stop-go monetary policy with secularly rising inflation was that Martin could not articulate a rationale for the procedures he had developed. He could not express them as a rule directed toward price stability. The resulting intellectual vacuum would then be filled by a Keynesian view of the world that promised low unemployment with only a small amount of inflation.

Meltzer (2009, 254) wrote, "The FOMC minutes and other Federal Reserve documents show no evidence that the Federal Reserve developed or systematically applied any theory or framework in the 1950s." Martin developed the practice whereby FOMC chairs retain control over monetary policy by limiting the format of FOMC meetings to a decision about whether to move the policy variable away from its existing value based on a judgment of whether the economy's more serious problem is inflation or recession. The need to impose consistency over time on individual policy actions then is the sole responsibility of the chair. The chair's communication with the public consists of forecasts of the economy over a long enough time ho-

3. The Executive Committee comprised the FOMC chairman (Martin) and vice chairman (Sproul) and three governors.

rizon so that the Fed achieves all desirable objectives. Martin's views did not change in the 1960s from favoring price stability to favoring inflation. As the single individual responsible for maintaining a continuity of policy and lacking an ability to articulate and defend such continuity, he was overwhelmed by political pressures.

CHAPTER 16

From Price Stability to Inflation

Summary: The 1957 recession provided the pattern for post-Accord recessions. Coming out of a cyclical trough, the FOMC raised interest rates in steps, moderately but persistently, until the economy weakened. At that point, if concerned about inflation or the foreign exchange value of the dollar, it then imparted inertia to downward movements in rates past the cyclical peak. Effectively, the FOMC attempted to create a negative output gap to lower inflation (see chap. 3, tables of the monetary contraction marker).

Little changed for the Fed with the election in 1960 of John F. Kennedy because the Douglas Dillon Treasury was concerned with gold outflows and Kennedy did not want a dollar crisis added to the Cuban missile crisis. Everything changed after the assassination of Kennedy in the fall of 1963 and the accession of Lyndon Johnson to the presidency. Now, influence within the administration shifted from the Treasury to the Heller CEA, which campaigned for a national goal of 4 percent unemployment. The 1964 election of Johnson as president also produced a Democratic majority in both houses of Congress. The passage in early 1964 of the Kennedy tax cuts created pressure on the Fed not to "thwart" the united will of the political system by offsetting with higher interest rates the fiscal stimulus needed to restore full employment. In the second half of the 1960s, society fractured over a combination of anti–Vietnam War protests, urban riots, and growing militancy in the civil rights movement. "Low" unemployment would ease social tensions. Keynesian economics, which had waited in the wings since World War II, promised to provide that low unemployment at a socially acceptable cost in terms of inflation.

Inflation revived toward the end of 1965. Initially, the Fed responded as it had in the mid-1950s by raising interest rates. However, in 1967, confronted this time by a hostile political system, it retreated. Martin, who believed that he could ultimately prevail through tactical compromise, made two fateful pacts: one with Keynesian economics and one with the administration. First, Martin listened to an increasingly Keynesian Board of Governors and staff who found convincing the "optimal instrument" implications of Keynesian models. A mix of easy monetary policy and tight fiscal policy would deliver an amount of aggregate demand sufficient for full employment but with the moderate interest rates desirable to promote investment and appease the housing lobby.

Second, Martin, who thought of inflation as arising from the speculative excess allowed by the excessive creation of credit, bargained with the administration and the Congress for a tax hike by holding out the promise of lower interest rates. President Johnson finally agreed, but the required congressional cooperation snagged over the difficulty of finding agreement between President Johnson and Wilbur Mills, chairman of the House Appropriations Committee. Mills wanted cuts in Johnson's Great Society programs in return for a tax increase. Only in June 1968 did Congress enact a tax surcharge, and the Fed did lower the discount rate.

By then, money growth had risen over most of a decade, and inflation rose to 6 percent in 1970. In 1969, Martin turned to contractionary monetary policy to restore price stability. However, his time ran out. In February 1970, Arthur Burns replaced Martin as FOMC chairman.

Martin had views on monetary policy that foreshadowed those of Volcker and Greenspan. He stressed raising short-term rates in a way that preempts inflation, that is, early on during periods of economic expansion.[1] The desirability of a preemptive monetary policy came from a belief that "easy money" permits an inflationary psychology to develop in credit markets and inflationary psychology produces inflation. Greenspan's (US Congress 1999c, 10) statement sounded like Martin: "For monetary policy to foster maximum sustainable growth, it is useful to preempt forces of imbalance before they threaten economic stability." Martin (US Congress 1958, 384) assumed responsibility for the inflation of 1956 and 1957 by having allowed "inflationary excesses."

Given Martin's unquestionable commitment to price stability, how could he have ushered in the era of rising inflation that lasted through the decade of the 1970s? Any answer to this question should also address the issue of whether there is a rule that can prevent such a major mistake.

16.1. BACK-TO-BACK RECESSIONS: 1957Q3 TO 1958Q2 AND 1960Q2 TO 1961Q1

With the 1953 recession, Martin began implementation of the LAW procedures with which the FOMC lowered money market rates in measured

1. Romer and Romer (2002 and 2004) express a similar view.

steps in response to sustained declines in rates of resource utilization, and conversely raised rates when economic recovery began. As the economy slowed with the July 1953 cycle peak, the Fed lowered market rates (figure 16.1). Figure 16.2 shows the corresponding behavior of free reserves, which increased. Chapter 13 presented the argument that the 1953 recession originated in the expectation of deflation conditioned by pre–World War II expectations that deflation would follow inflation. The expectation of deflation corresponded to an increase in the real rate of interest (figure 13.2). Figure 14.1 shows the sharp swing in nominal GDP. In the recovery, inflation rose from slightly negative values to 3 percent (figure 16.3).

What caused the inflation? When the recession turned out to be short-lived and mild rather than becoming another depression with significant deflation, predicted inflation ceased being negative and turned positive (figure 13.1). High real interest rates then declined to below 1 percent (figure 13.2). Although M1 growth declined before and during the recession, it rose again at the start of the recovery (figures 14.4 and 14.5). Probably, the best way to explain the rise in inflation in the recovery (figure 16.3) is as a manifestation of the relatively high M1 growth in the three-year period

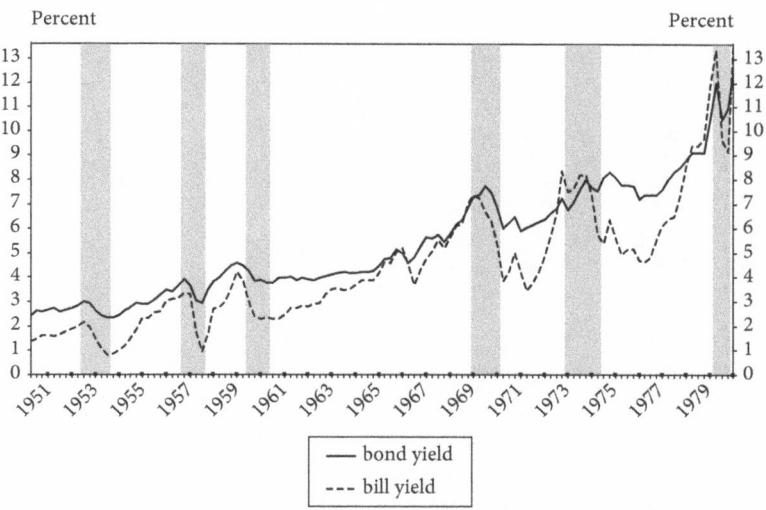

Figure 16.1. Government Bond and Three-Month Treasury Bill Yield
Quarterly observations of US (long-term) government bonds from 1951 to 1953 from Board of Governors (1976). Data from 1953Q1 on are US Treasury ten-year constant maturity bond yields from Board of Governors, "Selected Interest Rates," Statistical Release G.13. Shaded areas indicate recessions. Heavy tick marks indicate fourth quarter.

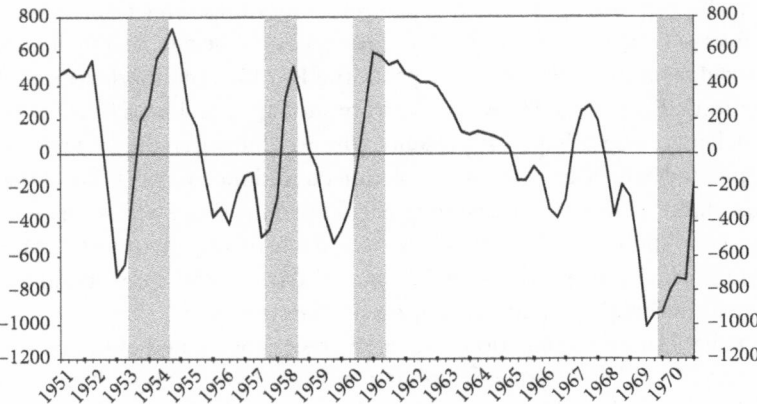

Figure 16.2. Free Reserves

Excess reserves minus borrowed reserves of commercial banks. Data for 1951–59
obtained from Board of Governors (1976). Data for 1959–70 from Board of Governors,
Statistical Release H.3. Shaded areas indicate recession. Heavy tick marks indicate
fourth quarter.

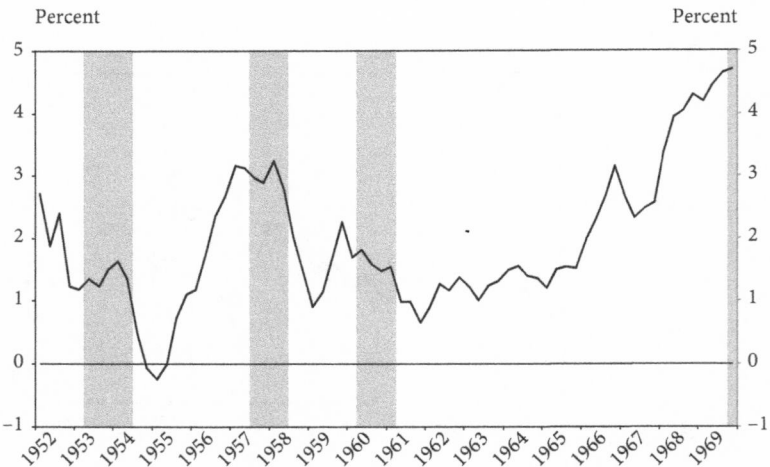

Figure 16.3. Inflation

Quarterly observations of four-quarter percentage changes in the personal
consumption expenditures chain-type price index. Shaded areas indicate recession.
Tick marks indicate fourth quarter.
Source: St. Louis FRED

1950–52 and then again immediately following the cycle trough in May 1954 (figure 14.4). The relatively high M1 steps surrounding the 1953–54 recession were 4.6 percent and 4.2 percent (figure 14.5).

The FOMC moved aggressively to restore price stability. Market rates rose steadily following the May 1954 cycle trough, and free reserves declined (figures 16.1 and 16.2). As market rates rose, money (M1) growth declined (figures 14.4 and 14.5). The Reserve Banks raised their discount rates in August 1957, the date of the cyclical peak. M1 decelerated sharply and declined in the subsequent recession with cycle peak in August 1957. For Al Hayes (Board of Governors, *FOMC Historical Minutes*, July 30, 1957, 11–12), president of the New York Fed, that fact represented maintenance of an appropriate degree of restraint given persistent inflation:

> The money supply will not show any appreciable net growth for the year as a whole.... It is exceedingly frustrating to see prices edging up month after month in spite of our best efforts, and I can see the natural appeal of the argument that what we should do is to tighten credit further and see if that will prove any more effective.... We must give serious thought to the consequences to the System if we are later blamed for recession and substantial unemployment.... It seems to me clear that the prudent course is to continue ... preventing any national expansion in bank credit and the money supply and allowing reduced liquidity to take effect on the economy.

Despite the monetary deceleration, the FOMC raised short-term interest rates steadily continuing past the cyclical peak in August 1957 (figure 16.1 and table 3.9).

With respect to cyclical inertia in interest rates (but not with respect to a ratcheting upward in inflation), the 1957 recession presaged the stop-go era. Board economist Ralph Young (Board of Governors, *FOMC Historical Minutes*, March 26, 1957, 15–16, cited in Meltzer 2009, 153) stated the view that going into recession, the FOMC had to choose between price stability and economic stability: "The Committee needs to consider carefully at this time whether it should not regard the objective of a stable value of the dollar as overriding the objective of adjusting flexibly and promptly to short-run cyclical changes in activity. It needs to weigh the risk that monetary policy may lose strategic opportunity to make its discipline effective."

Among policy makers, the belief was that the inflation that arose in 1956 came from tardiness in raising rates after the May 1954 cycle trough.[2] More-

2. See Hargrove and Morley 1984, Saulnier interview, 150–51; H. Stein 1990, 344. The best overview of this period is Burns and Samuelson (1967).

over, sustained outflows of gold led to the belief within the Fed and the administration that markets were losing confidence in both the internal and the external value of the dollar. With the cyclical trough in April 1958, the Fed began raising market interest rates (figure 16.1).

Burns and Samuelson (1967, 7–9) described the overriding concern with inflation in 1959:

A cash deficit of $13 billion, which still stands as the largest annual deficit since 1946, piled up in the fiscal year ending in June, 1959—a year of continuous business expansion. This emergence of a huge deficit at a time of rather rapid economic advance was merely the most dramatic of a series of developments that cast doubt on the financial policy of the government. . . . In the recession of 1957–58 wholesale prices . . . actually rose, and thus gave fresh support to the widely held theory that we are living in an age of inflation. This somber view about the future was reinforced by the deterioration in the balance of payments. During 1958 . . . our stocks of gold were cut by two billion dollars. More ominous still, foreign financiers, who hitherto appeared to have unbounded faith in American finances, began to whisper serious doubts whether the integrity of the dollar could be counted on in the future.

Financial developments during 1958 and the fears which they engendered thus strengthened the determination of governmental authorities to try to prevent, now that the economy was again advancing, the sort of excesses that had led to the inflationary boom during 1956–57. . . . Having moved too slowly to restrain the preceding expansion, they were ready to move with all necessary speed this time.

Pressure on [bank] reserves was sharply intensified during 1959. . . . The budget moved from an enormous deficit in early 1959 to a sizable surplus 12 months later. Taken together, these fiscal and monetary measures accomplished one of the most violent shifts on record from a policy of stimulation to a policy of restraint. . . . Largely as a result of their actions, the economic expansion that started in April, 1958, came to a premature end. . . . The very abruptness and magnitude of the policy shift routed an inflationary psychology, demonstrated that ours need not be an age of inflation . . . and thus reestablished stability in costs and prices.

Martin believed that the speculative psychology of markets provided a key early warning signal for inflation. Raising interest rates in the beginning of the recovery phase of the business cycle would prevent that speculative psychology and inflation. Martin (US Congress 1959, 462 and 467) testified to Congress:

About this time [summer 1959] inflationary expectations began to spread. The abrupt upward shift of interest levels in central money markets . . . reflected investor demand for an interest premium to cover the risk of a depreciating purchasing power of invested funds. . . . With inflationary and speculative psychology spreading, the Federal Reserve, during the summer, began to moderate the policy of credit ease with a view to tempering the rate of bank credit and monetary expansion. . . . The experience in the government bond market . . . is a vivid example of the influence of inflationary expectations in financial markets. To the extent that such attitudes come to be reflected in decisions on wages, prices, consumption, and investment, they help to bring about their own realization.

Concern for confidence in the value of the dollar (internal and external) appeared in a speech Martin (1958, 1, 4, and 9–10) gave in December 1958.

During the past year, we have had both recession and recovery and now, once again, fear of inflation. . . . A recent trip to several countries of the Far East gave me a welcomed opportunity to see ourselves as others see us. One distressing experience was to find among intelligent and perceptive men in those countries a growing distrust over the future of the American dollar. . . . It is important to recognize that this feeling exists. To the foreigner, much more than to Americans, the dollar is a symbol of this country's strength. A decline in the value of the dollar would suggest to him a decline in the faith and credit of the United States, signaling in his mind a decline not only in American economic strength but also in moral force.

Now I want to go one step further and talk about the most difficult aspect of all of our problems. This is the subject of confidence. . . . Confidence is perhaps the fundamental factor in money and currency. Those of us who are charged with responsibility for our monetary affairs recognize this clearly. . . . The fear of inflation is earnest, and it is having a damaging impact already. . . . We do have it within our power to maintain the integrity of the American dollar if we have the will to do it. . . . I can pledge to all of you that the Federal Reserve System will do everything in its power to safeguard our currency.

In the 1960 recession with cycle peak April 1960, the FOMC lowered interest rates hesitantly out of concern for gold outflows. Under the Bretton Woods system, the United States committed to maintaining convertibility between the dollar and gold at the price of $35 per ounce. Other countries set the value of their currencies in terms of gold thereby pegging their exchange rates. The system of pegged exchange rates then rested on the US commitment to maintain convertibility of the dollar into gold at $35 per ounce. If there were to be a run on the dollar and foreign holders of dollar assets collectively asked for an amount of gold in excess of the US gold stock, the dollar price of gold would depreciate. The belief was that the system of pegged exchange rates would collapse as the run spread.

The Bretton Woods system became operational only in 1959 as at the end of 1958 the major European countries allowed their currencies to be freely convertible into foreign currencies for current account transactions. With convertibility, countries needed reserves to maintain their IMF currency parities. However, with world gold production falling far short of growth in the need for international reserves to finance international trade, countries accumulated dollar balances. In what became known as the Triffin dilemma, foreign holdings of dollar balances grew relative to US gold holdings (Bordo 1993). Edwin (Ted) Truman (2017, 9), who headed the Division of International Finance at the Federal Reserve Board from 1997 to 1998, wrote:

> Ominously, the foreign official and private holdings of short-term dollar assets (bank deposits and US treasury obligations) had reached $17.4 billion by the end of 1960, an increase of $5.5 billion over two years, and those holdings were approximately equal to US gold holdings of $17.8 billion. . . . By the end of 1961, US gold reserves had dropped $5.9 billion from the end of 1957. . . . The international monetary system faced a confidence problem in terms of the ability and willingness of the United States to meet all the claims on its gold stock—to maintain the convertibility of the US dollar into gold for official foreign holders.

In 1959, 1960, and 1961, the need to maintain confidence in the dollar weighed on the Treasury and the Martin FOMC. Figure 16.4 shows that the current account deteriorated sharply after 1957 and became negative in 1959.

Concern over the balance of payments appeared in the briefings on the international situation that Arthur W. Marget (Board of Governors, *FOMC Historical Minutes*, October 13, 1959, 11–12, and February 9, 1960, 11)) gave the FOMC:

> [Treasury] Secretary Anderson's speech at the Annual Meeting of the International Monetary Fund two weeks ago [showed that his] sense of concern, if not alarm, is obviously genuine. . . . Our figures for gold and

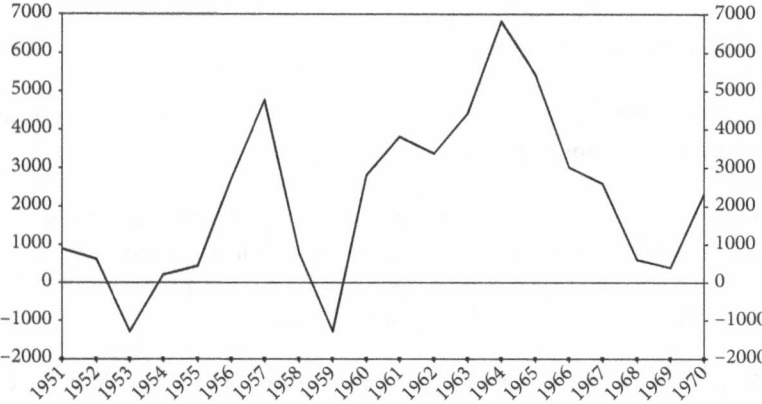

Figure 16.4. Current Account
Annual observations of the current account. US international transactions: balance on
goods and services, income, and net unilateral transfers. Millions of dollars.
Source: St. Louis FRED

dollar movements in July to September of this year . . . would suggest
that the over-all balance-of-payments deficit for that period was still in
the neighborhood of $4 billion seasonally adjusted annual rate. That is
still a long way from the average deficit of $1.5 billion that we ran from
1950 to 1957. . . .

The basis of this confidence is the belief that balance of payments developments depend, to a very large extent, upon the policies pursued
by the monetary and fiscal authorities of the country experiencing the
balance of payments difficulties. In the present instance, that means a belief that the fiscal and monetary authorities, in determining their actions,
are not likely to confuse evidence that a salutary process of adjustment
is under way with a conclusion that the adjustment has been virtually
completed.

In the same address, Marget commented on Chairman Martin's response
to a letter from Senator Javits, who asked for comment on a "much discussed" *New York Times* article stating

that because of our balance-of-payments position "a US recession in the
near future would be allowed to drift into severe unemployment because
the Government would be afraid to act vigorously against it." This . . .
"would come about because anti-recession action-chiefly an aggressive
easy-money policy—could bring on the feared run on gold. This coun-

try's freedom of action domestically will be limited by the fact that the dollar is a reserve world currency."

Martin (Board of Governors, *FOMC Historical Minutes*, March 1, 1960, 30) gave a classic Fed nonresponse:

What is needed today is not so much to discuss ways to meet a hypothetical dilemma as to see to it that we continue to follow policies designed to ensure the domestic and international financial equilibrium of the United States, so that the dilemma will not arise.

The *Times* was right. Figure 16.1 shows the aggressive increase in interest rates coming out of the April 1958 cycle trough. The funds rate went from about 1 percent in 1958Q2 to 4 percent in 1959Q4 (figure 13.4). M1 growth did rise after the cyclical trough (figures 14.4 and 14.5) but became negative with the sharp increase in the funds rate. (Four-quarter) inflation rose from 0.9 percent in 1959Q1 to 2.3 percent in 1959Q4, but then declined steadily reaching a trough in 1961Q4 of 0.6 percent (figure 16.3). Concern for the deterioration of the current account deficit (figure 16.4) outweighed concern for the unemployment rate, which started rising from a cycle low of 5.1 percent in 1960Q1 (figure 16.5).

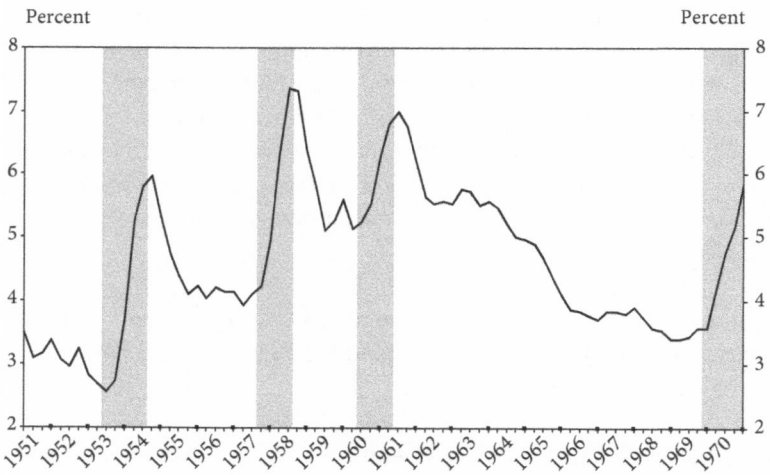

Figure 16.5. Unemployment Rate
Civilian unemployment rate. Shaded areas indicate recession. Heavy tick marks indicate fourth quarter.
Source: St. Louis FRED

The level of M1 declined 2 percent over the one and a half years from July 1959 through January 1961, and the economy entered recession in April 1960. Back-to-back recessions "routed an inflationary psychology" (Burns in Burns and Samuelson 1967, 9). Bond yields remained at 4 percent from 1960 through 1964 (figure 16.1). The expansionary monetary policy that began in earnest in 1964 then took place in an environment of expected price stability.

16.2. HOW DID THE EARLY MARTIN FED LOSE ITS WAY IN THE SECOND HALF OF THE 1960S?

Unquestionably, Martin was committed to a policy of price stability. How then did he end his term in early 1970 with 5 percent inflation? An answer must combine an understanding of the weaknesses in how Martin understood the world, the political pressures he endured, and the faulty compromise he made with the Johnson administration. Martin was not an economist. He thought in terms of metaphors rather than abstractions. Sherman Maisel (1973, 118), who was a member of the Board of Governors from 1965 until 1972, quoted Martin as saying, "One might picture the Federal Reserve as operating like a giant rubber band: As the markets become too ebullient or expansionary, they would have to push harder and harder against the restraining action of Federal Reserve policy."

Martin thought of monetary policy as affecting the cost and availability of credit. Robert V. Roosa (1960, 262), vice president of the Federal Reserve Bank of New York, captured how the Martin FOMC thought about the transmission of monetary policy through the credit markets:

> The Federal Reserve has had to rely primarily on experimental probing, to gauge the balance between the current forces of credit demand and the current availability of new credit supply. Utilizing its own qualitative concept of pressure, it has withheld or released new bank reserves in response to a composite reading of market rates, member bank borrowing, the "feel" arising from participation in the securities markets, and broader judgments of current economic and credit trends.

Maisel (1973, 68) described Martin's view in which inflation could arise from excess credit demands by government and business:

> Government was not the only source of inflationary danger. . . . Speculative activity in the financial and business sectors also led to large and unfortunate booms. Since overspending in the private sector depends upon

the creation of excess money and credit, the Federal Reserve must guard against excessive private as well as government credit. . . . The necessary and proper amount [of credit] could be estimated by careful observation of events in the financial and credit markets. . . . People trying to borrow extra money to profit from a boom or inflation had to be stopped.

Inflation, Martin believed, developed from speculative credit extension that in turn derived from an inflationary psychology. Unlike Keynesians, he did not see monetary policy as balancing the conflicting goals of inflation and unemployment. He believed that inflation led to recession. Easy money meant a too easy availability of credit and tolerance of an inflationary psychology conducive to speculation. Speculation led to inflation and then, as a reaction, recession.

Martin had no use for the money supply. At the December 15, 1959, FOMC meeting, Board economist Woodlief Thomas noted that M1 was "only about one percent higher than a year ago" (Board of Governors, *FOMC Historical Minutes*, December 15, 1959, 14). Alfred Hayes (Board of Governors, *FOMC Historical Minutes*, December 15, 1959, 16), president of the New York Fed, noted "that the economy is still operating well below capacity without any strong upward price pressures." In his summary of FOMC discussion, Martin (Board of Governors, *FOMC Historical Minutes*, December 15, 1959, 44) said:

Where he came out was that the System was going well, that it should keep steady in the boat, and that the problem was one of rolling with the punches at this juncture. This was not in any sense to say that the Committee should disregard Mr. Mills' basic point regarding the quantity of the money supply. For the year as a whole the increase in the money supply appeared to have been less than one per cent. . . . Personally, he did not know just how to measure the money supply. . . . Like many others, he was unable to make heads or tails of the money supply on either a quantitative or a qualitative basis. . . . One should not go overboard on the money supply question unless he was certain that the velocity factor was not playing a part. Personally, he felt that money supply factors in terms of velocity were the crucial points that the System must take into consideration at this time.[3]

3. The New York Fed had an especially strong aversion to the use of money in formulating monetary policy or to the idea of rules. In a letter dated April 27, 1959, former New York Fed president Allan Sproul wrote to Roosa in regard to Atlanta Fed president Malcolm Bryan, who had expressed concern over the lack of money growth, that Bryan's views were "a legacy of a fundamentalist religious slant as bent and twisted by

As the decade of the 1960s progressed, the political establishment became increasingly hostile to Martin's overriding objective of price stability. John Kennedy became president in the 1960 election with a promise to "get the country moving again." Walter Heller persuaded Kennedy to set 4 percent as a goal for unemployment. Initially, Martin had an ally in the conservative Treasury headed by Douglas Dillon with former New York Fed vice president Robert Roosa as Treasury undersecretary for monetary affairs. Kennedy, preoccupied by the Cuban missile crisis, feared an attack on the dollar, which was still pegged to gold. The main concession of the Fed to the administration was Operation Twist, in which the Fed abandoned bills only by selling Treasury bills and buying Treasury bonds. The goal was to keep bond rates steady at 4 percent while maintaining short-term rates at a level that would encourage capital inflows to support the foreign exchange value of the dollar.

16.3. MARTIN'S ILL-FATED BARGAIN

Martin wanted to work with a consensus that included the administration. He was never aggressive about moving interest rates without it. He pushed for a restrictive monetary policy in 1959 and 1969, but with the support of the administration. Walter Heller (Hargrove and Morley 1984, 190–91) later recalled Martin's participation in the Quadriad, which included Martin; Walter Heller, who was the head of the Council of Economic Advisers (CEA); the head of the Bureau of the Budget; and the president:

> The Quadriad worked out well because it was a true dialogue. Bill would come in and tell us what he thought about fiscal policy, we'd tell him what we thought about monetary policy. . . . Basically, there was give and take; it was not just a one-way street with Martin. Martin . . . was on the President's team.

Ultimately, Martin would stumble in his willingness to work with the administration to obtain a tax hike from Congress in return for delaying interest-rate increases.

With the assassination of Kennedy in fall 1963 and the accession of a president, Lyndon Baines Johnson, with populist attitudes, Martin found himself isolated. In early 1964, Congress passed a tax cut originally proposed by Kennedy. A political consensus then developed that the Fed should allow the resulting stimulative fiscal policy to lower the unemployment rate.

---

the University of Chicago, but it is also a consequence of his having had no experience in a money market" (cited in Meltzer 2009, 81).

Populist congressmen like Henry Reuss and Wright Patman charged that increasing interest rates would thwart the will of Congress. The administration turned to capital controls to deal with the dollar and balance of payments. A statement by Martin that the Fed would not finance a tax cut created a congressional backlash. The LBJ White House and Democratic Congress united in opposition to rate increases.

Martin believed that to prevent the emergence of inflationary psychology and inflation the FOMC needed to begin raising short-term interest rates at the onset of economic recovery. In opposition, the Johnson CEA believed that the Fed should wait to raise rates until the unemployment rate neared 4 percent. Even then, the CEA preferred restraining excess aggregate demand through fiscal policy. As the decade progressed, the political consensus for sustained high growth and low interest rates hardened. Johnson wanted to fight a war in Vietnam and to fund Great Society programs. He wanted guns and butter. Urban riots and an increasingly strident civil rights movement plus Vietnam War protests produced a fractured America. A strong economy and low unemployment seemed a necessary condition for social accord.

Keynesian economics promised just what the political system wanted. It promised sustained high growth and low unemployment with a moderate amount of inflation. Moreover, Keynesian economics highlighted the "optimal instrument policy." If fiscal policy were tight, monetary policy could be easy, and easy monetary policy could help keep the politically potent housing lobby at bay.

Martin also had to deal with divisions in his own house. Appointments to the Board of Governors by Kennedy and Johnson tilted the Board toward Keynesian views. The prior "banker view" had emphasized internal and external stability of the dollar. Martin could not challenge the political consensus in favor of sustained high growth and low unemployment with a divided Board. At the October 1965 FOMC meeting (Board of Governors, *FOMC Historical Minutes*, October 12, 1965, 69, cited in Calomiris and Wheelock 1998, 50–51), "with a divided committee and in the face of strong Administration opposition [Martin said] he did not believe it would be appropriate for him to lend his support to those who favored a change in policy now."

Over the course of 1965, it became evident that the economy was growing unsustainably fast as the unemployment rate declined from 5 percent early in the year to 4 percent by year-end. In December 1965, Martin achieved agreement among Board members and agreed to Reserve Bank hikes in the discount rate. Johnson reacted angrily and called Martin down to his Texas ranch. At the November FOMC meeting, Martin (Board of

Governors, *FOMC Historical Minutes*, November 23, 1965, 85, cited in Calomiris and Wheelock 1998, 50–51) had told the FOMC that "the country was in a period of creeping inflation. . . . The economy was growing too fast." Yet, at the May 1966 meeting, in an uncharacteristic statement, Martin (Board of Governors, *FOMC Historical Minutes*, May 10, 1966, 94–95, cited in Calomiris and Wheelock 1998, 51) told the FOMC, "The Committee should not press too hard in the belief that monetary policy alone could achieve price stability."

Although Martin did not say so, he was negotiating with the administration over sending legislation to Congress for a tax hike. Initially, nothing happened. In summer 1966, the FOMC raised interest rates, and in early 1967 the economy slowed. Martin then entered a fateful pact with the Johnson economic advisers and the Treasury. Working closely with Treasury Secretary Henry Fowler, Martin agreed to hold off on raising interest rates if the Johnson administration would submit to Congress a proposal for a tax increase. Martin presumed that changing a budget deficit to a surplus would reduce credit demands and lessen the pressure on interest rates. Even if that presumption had been correct, politics stood in the way. Achieving agreement between Wilbur Mills, chairman of the House Ways and Means Committee, and Johnson became a protracted process. As a condition for a tax hike, Mills wanted cuts in Johnson's Great Society programs, and Johnson refused (Hetzel 2008).

With the tax hike stalled, the FOMC began again to raise rates. Prompted by a run on gold that threatened the Bretton Woods system, Congress finally passed an income tax surcharge in June 1968 that turned a government deficit into a surplus. Fearful of recession, prompted by a Keynesian Board staff, and mindful of its promise to Congress that a tax surcharge would lessen the need to raise interest rates, the Board of Governors approved a reduction in discount rates. Sustained high money growth, however, trumped contractionary fiscal policy. The economy continued to grow strongly, and inflation rose steadily. Inflation (PCE, personal consumption expenditures deflator), which had averaged 1.3 percent in the first half of the decade, rose to about 5 percent by the end of decade.

Martin tried to restore price stability in 1969 with a highly restrictive monetary policy. Sounding like the future Paul Volcker, Martin (US Congress 1969, February 26, 668, 669, and 685) testified to Congress:

Expectations of inflation are deeply embedded. . . . A slowing in expansion that is widely expected to be temporary is not likely to be enough to eradicate such expectations. The experience of early 1967 is a lesson in point. Moderation in economic activity . . . did indeed produce a significant slowing in the rate at which prices advanced. But the moderation was short-lived. As economic activity accelerated after midyear, so did prices. . . . The critical test for stabilization policies in 1969 will be their ability to keep such a rebound in activity and prices from developing. If we were to dissipate again the benefits derived from a reduction in excessive demands, the credibility . . . of Government economic policies would be severely strained. . . . A credibility gap has developed over our capacity and willingness to maintain restraint. . . . We have been unwilling to take any real risks. . . . We have raised . . . the ghost of overkill. . . . We have got to take some risk.

Martin's testimony was a cry in the wilderness. The Fed would spend a decade wandering in the wilderness. His term as chairman ended in January 1970. He ran out of time. At the end of his term, in the Board library, he told the other governors that he had failed (Board of Governors 1999).

CHAPTER 17

The Burns Fed

Summary: Arthur Burns succeeded William McChesney Martin as FOMC chairman in February 1970. Although Burns was not a Keynesian, he conducted an activist policy of aggregate-demand management. Like Keynesians, he understood inflation as a nonmonetary phenomenon. Faced with cost-push shocks from labor unions and large corporations that produced exogenous increases in prices, monetary policy presumably had to manage aggregate demand in order to find a balance between limiting it to control inflation and expanding it to prevent a socially unacceptable amount of unemployment.

Burns came out of the NBER tradition of "measurement without theory." From his perspective, the psychology of the businessman powered the business cycle. Burns thought of himself as the one person who could reconcile the low unemployment required for social harmony with the low inflation needed to give the businessman the confidence to invest. Burns concentrated on the control of inflationary expectations but not through the pursuit of a consistent, credible monetary policy. Rather, his concern was managing inflationary expectations through addressing the conventional concerns of the businessman: wage pressures and a balanced budget.

Burns and the Keynesians joined forces on the desirability of wage and price controls. Controls would relax the discipline of the Phillips curve trade-off between inflation and unemployment by mitigating cost-push shocks and especially the wage-push shocks Burns believed came from the unions (Nelson 2005; Nelson and Nikolov 2004). To achieve his ends, Burns traded monetary policy for influence over incomes and fiscal policy. The exception came during the Ford presidency because of the opposition to controls of CEA chairman Alan Greenspan.

According to Burns, not only union power but also a permissive welfare state imparted an inflationary bias to expectations and inflation. Burns became the preeminent advocate of "incomes policies," which entailed government intervention in the price setting of the private sector. In August 1971, Burns entered a Faustian bargain with President Richard Nixon. Burns got wage and price controls, and Nixon got an expansionary monetary policy.

Before becoming FOMC chairman, Arthur Burns had had extensive experience in government. President Eisenhower made him head of the Council of Economic Advisers (CEA) after the 1952 election. Because of the partisanship and advocacy of central planning by Truman's chairman, Leon Keyserling, the CEA had fallen into disrepute. Burns saved the CEA from an end to congressional funding and restored its standing through his professionalism. Burns took naturally to the role of counselor to the president. "Burns says he could feel himself coming down with 'Potomac fever,' becoming attached to the bustle of government crisis, being infected with a sense of his own importance" (Viorst 1969, 32). Burns became an adviser to Nixon during Nixon's 1968 presidential campaign. When Nixon assumed the presidency, he put Burns in charge of development of the agenda for domestic legislation.

From January 31, 1970, through March 8, 1978, Arthur F. Burns dominated the FOMC. Prior to joining the Fed, he had had an extraordinarily distinguished career. He had been head of the National Bureau of Economic Research, president of the American Economic Association, and head of the Council of Economic Advisers under President Eisenhower. Burns saw himself as the foremost opponent of inflation; nevertheless, over his tenure as FOMC chair, inflation reigned. How could he have let that happen?[1]

17.1. THE POLITICAL AND INTELLECTUAL ENVIRONMENT

When Arthur Burns became FOMC chairman, US society was fractured over the issues of race and the Vietnam War. A nearly universal consensus existed that a 4 percent unemployment rate corresponded to full employment and that the government had a responsibility to maintain unemployment at that level or lower. A political consensus prevailed that the United States required unemployment at least that low to deal with its social malaise. When Burns became FOMC chair, the unemployment rate was not far from its cyclical high of 6.1 percent reached in December 1970. At the same time, the inflation rate had risen from 1.5 percent at the end of 1965 to 5 percent at the start of 1970 (figure 17.1).

In the language of the recent moon landing, it was supposed to be the time of the "soft landing." The Keynesian consensus promised that the Fed could keep the unemployment rate moderately over its full employment level of 4 percent and work inflation down over time. However, the sharp rise in the unemployment rate over the course of the 1970 recession to 6 percent did not lead to disinflation (figure 17.1). Burns drew the con-

1. The following draws on Hetzel (1998).

Figure 17.1. Unemployment Rate and Inflation
Quarterly observations of the civilian unemployment rate and four-quarter percentage changes in the personal consumption expenditures implicit price deflator. Shaded areas indicate recessions. Heavy tick marks indicate fourth quarter.
Source: St. Louis FRED

clusion that the contemporaneous inflation arose primarily from a rise in wages due to the exercise of monopoly power by labor unions. In a speech before the American Economic Association in December 1972, Burns (1972 [1978], "The Problem of Inflation," 143–54) stated:

> The hard fact is that market forces no longer can be counted on to check the upward course of wages and prices even when the aggregate demand for goods and services declines in the course of a business recession. During the recession of 1970 and the weak recovery of early 1971, the pace of wage increases did not at all abate as unemployment rose. . . . The rate of inflation was almost as high in the first half of 1971, when unemployment averaged 6 percent of the labor force, as it was in 1969, when the unemployment rate averaged 3½ percent. . . . Cost-push inflation, while a comparatively new phenomenon on the American scene, has been altering the economic environment in fundamental ways. . . . If some form of effective control over wages and prices were not retained in 1973, major collective bargaining settlements and business efforts to increase profits could reinforce the pressures on costs and prices that

normally come into play when the economy is advancing briskly, and thus generate a new wave of inflation. If monetary and fiscal policy became sufficiently restrictive to deal with the situation by choking off growth in aggregate demand, the cost in terms of rising unemployment, lost output, and shattered confidence would be enormous.

Burns would be the public face of the argument for controls to deal with what appeared to be a cost-push inflation rather than an aggregate-demand inflation. Burns (Board of Governors, *Minutes of the Board of Governors*, November 6, 1970, 3115–17) told the Board of Governors in November 1970 that

> prospects were dim for any easing of the cost-push inflation generated by union demands. However, the Federal Reserve could not do anything about those influences except to impose monetary restraint, and he [Burns] did not believe the country was willing to accept for any long period an unemployment rate in the area of 6 percent. Therefore, he believed that the Federal Reserve should not take on the responsibility for attempting to accomplish by itself, under its existing powers, a reduction in the rate of inflation to, say, 2 percent. . . . He did not believe that the Federal Reserve should be expected to cope with inflation single-handedly. The only effective answer, in his opinion, lay in some form of incomes policy.[2]

Burns was not a Keynesian; nevertheless, monetary policy ended up being an experiment in activist aggregate-demand management to balance off the presumed competing goals of unemployment and inflation. Why? Burns and Keynesians believed that the lack of competitive markets meant that the market power of corporations and unions raised prices and inflation in the absence of restrictive monetary policy. There was therefore a trade-off between unemployment and inflation. Incomes policy could relax the harsh inflation-unemployment trade-offs and allow a more expansive monetary policy. Burns (US Congress 1973a, February 7, 485 and 504) testified:

> There is a need for legislation permitting some direct controls over wages and prices. . . . The structure of our economy—in particular, the power of many corporations and trade unions to exact rewards that exceed what

2. "Incomes policy" is a general expression for various forms of direct intervention by the government in the price setting of firms to control prices from public pressure to actual controls.

could be achieved under conditions of active competition—does expose us to upward pressure on costs and prices that may be cumulative and self-reinforcing.

17.2. BURNS'S VIEW OF THE BUSINESS CYCLE AND ECONOMIC STABILIZATION

Like the majority of economists who came of age in the Depression, Burns (1973, 792–93) held standard views about the need to manage the economy:[3]

> Our economy is inherently unstable. . . . Experience has demonstrated repeatedly that blind reliance on the self-correcting properties of our economic system can lead to serious trouble. . . . Flexible fiscal and monetary policies, therefore, are often needed to cope with undesirable economic developments.
>
> The principal practical problem of our generation is the maintenance of employment, and it has now become—as it long should have been—the principal problem of economic theory.

What distinguished Burns was his belief that an understanding of the psychology of the businessman gave him an ability to understand the evolution of the business cycle. For Burns, managing the business cycle meant managing the confidence of the businessman.

Burns's understanding of the business cycle came from the empirical regularities he derived from examining the cyclical behavior of a large number of statistical series. He imparted an inner logic to the evolution of these series through his knowledge of human psychology. At the same time, he believed that each cycle possessed unique features. Burns (Viorst 1969, 123) told a reporter:

> I suspect that some of my colleagues are unduly fascinated by economic instruments and have given insufficient attention to the workings of the business mind of America. I weigh that heavily in questions of policy. . . . Before I judge whether some proposal is good or bad, I ask how the businessman is going to react. I've studied the businessman of America. He has his strengths and he has his weaknesses, but it is within the framework of his psychology that the economist in America must operate. . . . The well-being of the country . . . depends upon the favorable expecta-

3. See also Burns (1946 [1954], 4).

tions of the investing class. . . . As I see it, the role of Government must
be to shape policy to improve these expectations.

Burns organized an explanation of the business cycle around the timing
of relationships between the specific cycles of individual sectors and the
general reference cycle. Burns (Burns 1950 [1954], 111) explained that the
cycle is a "consensus of specific cycles." Among the individual sectors, as
the cycle develops, an accumulation of imbalances occurs that affects the
psychology of the businessman. Recoveries turn into recessions as imbalances develop from the way that costs overtake prices, depress profits, and
sour the mood of the businessman. Burns (1950 [1954], 127–28) wrote:

> As prosperity cumulates, unit costs tend to mount for business firms
> generally; and since in many instances selling prices cannot be raised,
> profit margins here and there will narrow. . . . Errors pile up as mounting
> optimism warps the judgment of an increasing number of businessmen
> concerning the sales that can be made at profitable prices.

According to Burns (1969, 27–28, 33, and 41), alternating mood swings of
the consumer and businessman drive the process of moving from recovery
to recession:

> [During expansion phases] firms will find their profit margins rising
> handsomely [and] people [have] a feeling of confidence about the eco-
> nomic future—a mood that may gradually change from optimism to exu-
> berance. . . . The new spirit of enterprise fosters more new projects. . . .
> Over stocking and overbuilding . . . are likely to be bunched when enthu-
> siasm has infected a large and widening circle of businessmen. . . . The
> stubborn human trait of optimism begins to give way. . . . Once many
> men begin to lose faith in themselves or in the institutions of their so-
> ciety, full recovery may need to wait on substantial innovations or an
> actual reduction in the stock of fixed capital.

Most often, in recessions, imbalances correct and prompt recovery. In
the Depression, however, the economy fell into a downward spiral. Burns
(1969, 36) explained the spiral:

> As a decline in one sector reacts on another, the economy may begin
> spiraling downward. . . . The likelihood that a depression will develop
> depends on numerous factors—among them, the scale of speculation
> during the preceding phase of prosperity, the extent to which credit was

permitted to grow, whether or not the quality of credit suffered significant deterioration, whether any markets became temporarily saturated,
how much excess capacity had been created before the recession started.

Burns's views disposed him to an interventionist approach to managing
the business cycle. Especially important was acting early at the onset of recession to maintain the optimism of the businessman. Burns (1950 [1954],
132–33) wrote:

> To glimpse economic catastrophe when it is imminent may prevent its
> occurrence: this is the challenge facing business cycle theory and pol-
> icy. . . . The crucial problem of our times is the prevention of severe de-
> pressions. . . . Developments during "prosperity"—which may cumulate
> over one or more expansions—shape the character of a depression.

Burns (1957, 30–31 and 69) believed that under his leadership the Eisenhower administration had prevented the 1953 recession from developing
into depression:

> When economic clouds began to gather in the late spring of 1953, the gov-
> ernment was alert to the possible danger of depression. . . . In its new role
> of responsibility for the maintenance of the nation's prosperity, the fed-
> eral government deliberately took speedy and massive actions to build
> confidence and pave the way for renewed economic growth. . . . This
> unequivocal declaration of tax policy, like the earlier moves in the credit
> sphere, was made when the unemployment rate was 2½ percent. . . . The
> President recommended a broad program of legislation. . . . Whenever
> the economy shows signs of faltering, the government must honor by its
> actions the broad principles of combatting recession which served us so
> well during the decline of 1953–54.

The way in which Burns understood the business cycle caused him to
emphasize microeconomic tools to control unemployment and inflation.
For example, Burns (US Congress 1973b, June 27, 179) recommended forced
savings to deal with inflation:

> I would look with some favor on a fiscal measure that does not quite fall
> in the tax category. This would be a plan for compulsory savings, but
> again of a flexible type. Let us say corporations would be required to
> put aside 10 percent of the amount of their corporate taxes. That sum
> would be locked up in the Federal Reserve in such a way that it could be

released in the event of a downturn in the economy. In other words, my concept is that we ought to try to siphon off some purchasing power but we ought to do it in such fashion that we could reverse gears and do so rather quickly if the economic need arose.

Burns (1973 [1978], 157–58, "Some Problems of Central Banking") also regularly advocated a variable investment tax credit.

The other side of Burns's emphasis on microeconomic tools as the appropriate instruments of countercyclical stabilization was his deemphasis of the traditional tools of aggregate-demand management, namely, monetary and fiscal policy. Burns believed that monetary policy worked through the cost and availability of credit, which has only a minimal effect on the decisions of businessmen. Burns (1957, 46) wrote, "Many business firms are able to finance their requirements without any borrowing. . . . Interest charges are rarely a large element in business costs, and their practical importance has tended to become smaller as a result of high taxes." Burns (US Congress 1973a, February 20, 400) testified:

> The proper role of monetary policy in the achievement of our national economic objectives is a comparatively modest one. Monetary policy can help to establish a financial climate in which prosperity and stable prices are attainable. But it cannot guarantee the desired outcome: the task is much too large.

Although Burns minimized the direct effects of monetary and fiscal policy, he stressed their psychological effects on the confidence of the businessman. Burns especially highlighted the psychological effect of the government deficit on the confidence of the businessman and his willingness to invest. Money did not exercise a major independent influence on economic activity or inflation. What was important was the velocity of money, which varied with the confidence of businessmen. Burns (Board of Governors, *FOMC Memorandum of Discussion,*
December 17, 1974, 79, 104) told the FOMC:

> The willingness to use money—that is, the rate at which money turned over, or its velocity—underwent tremendous fluctuations; velocity was a much more dynamic variable than the stock of money, and when no account was taken of it, any judgment about the growth rate of M1 was likely to be highly incomplete. . . . Fundamentally, velocity depended on confidence in economic prospects. When confidence was weak, a large addition to the money stock might lie idle, but when confidence

strengthened, the existing stock of money could finance an enormous expansion in economic activity.

17.3. BURNS AS FOMC CHAIRMAN

Burns's failure as FOMC chairman came about above all because of his belief that inflation reflected cost-push shocks. Other beliefs and characteristics also contributed, however. They included a self-confidence in his ability to forecast the economy; a belief that economic recoveries were fragile; and the related belief that sharp increases in interest rates would impair the confidence of the business community. Based on the assumed importance of the president's ability to influence the psychological mood of the businessman especially through control over wages and the assumed importance of the deficit in influencing the willingness of business to invest, Burns wanted to remain influential not only within the executive branch but also within Congress.

Because of the work on leading indicators done with Wesley Clair Mitchell, Burns was confident of his ability to predict the behavior of the economy. Burns believed that he could read the course of the economy by following the mix of weak and strong economic series. Burns (1950 [1954], 113) explained how the mix of strong and weak series turns a recession into an economic recovery:

> The substitution of one of these majorities for the other takes place gradually, and indeed follows a definite cyclical course. . . . Rising series are only a thin majority at the beginning of a business cycle expansion. Their number swells as aggregate activity increases, though expansion reaches its widest scope not when aggregate activity is at a peak, but perhaps six months or a year earlier. In the neighborhood of a peak, crosscurrents are the outstanding feature of the business situation.

Unwilling to risk injuring the confidence of the businessman, Burns was willing to raise interest rates only gradually during economic recoveries. Burns (US Congress 1971, July 20, 256) testified:

> This March and April, the Federal Reserve System faced a dilemma. Information available at that time suggested that high rates of monetary growth might well persist under existing conditions in the money market. Interest rates, however, were already displaying a tendency to rise, and vigorous action to restrain monetary growth might have raised them sharply further. In view of the delicate state of the economic recovery,

which was just getting under way, it seemed desirable to prevent the possible adverse effects of sharply higher interest rates on expenditure plans and public psychology.

Burns (1947 [1954]) wrote that "economics is a very serious subject when the economist assumes the role of counselor to nations." As that counselor, Burns believed that he could achieve low unemployment while maintaining moderate inflation. The problem, as Burns understood it, was that monetary policy constituted only one of the instruments he needed. Burns wanted to influence fiscal policy to achieve a balanced budget, and he especially wanted an incomes policy to lessen the unemployment cost of restoring price stability. In that spirit, Burns saw himself as the one who could prod the Nixon administration into the bold leadership that he believed the country needed. For example, Burns (Board of Governors, *FOMC Memorandum of Discussion*, July 18, 1972, 734–35) had a dramatic effect on stabilizing foreign exchange markets with a speech delivered at an IMF conference:

> His [Burns's] remarks had received world-wide acclaim, not because of their intrinsic merit, but because of the widespread hunger for leadership; they represented the first outgoing, constructive statement by a senior US official indicating a willingness on this country's part to help in reestablishing monetary order. . . . There were times for blowing a trumpet within the halls of Government, and this was one of them.

17.4. INFLATION AS A COST-PUSH PHENOMENON

In *Prosperity without Inflation*, Burns (1957, 71) stated that there that "there is . . . not one cause of the post-war inflation but many." Nevertheless, Burns (1957, 71) most often explained inflation by reference to a wage-price spiral initiated by the expectation of inflation. "One of the main factors in the inflation that we have had since the end of World War II is that many consumers, businessmen, and trade union leaders expected prices to rise and therefore acted in ways that helped to bring about this result." The fundamental source of inflationary expectations arose from a belief that government would protect individual groups from competition. Labor unions especially could then force increases in wage rates with impunity. Burns (1970b [1978], 93–94) told the American Bankers Association:

> The root of the difficulty [inflationary bias] seems to be the broadening of the social aspirations that have been shaping our national economic policies, and especially the commitment to maintain high levels of em-

ployment and rapid economic growth. . . . Another source of inflationary pressure in recent years has been the rise of governmental expenditures for social welfare. . . . The present world-wide inflationary trend may thus be ascribed to the humanitarian impulses that have reached such full expression in our times.

If inflation is driven by powerful cost-push forces, then suppressing it requires raising unemployment. High unemployment, however, was socially unacceptable. Monetary policy then became an ongoing decision about how to trade off between "high" unemployment and "low" inflation. In 1979, after having left the Fed, Burns gave a speech called "The Anguish of Central Banking." Burns (1979 [1987], 690–92) said:

> Once it was established that the key function of government was to solve problems and relieve hardships—not only for society at large but also for troubled industries, regions, occupations, or social groups—a great and growing body of problems and hardships became candidates for governmental solution. . . . Their [government programs] cumulative effect . . . was to impart a strong inflationary bias to the American economy. . . . The pursuit of costly social reforms often went hand in hand with the pursuit of full employment. . . . This weighting of the scales of government policy inevitably gave an inflationary twist to the economy, and so did the expanding role of government regulation. . . .
>
> If the Federal Reserve then sought to create a monetary environment that fell seriously short of accommodating the upward pressures that were being released or reinforced by governmental action, severe difficulties could be quickly produced in the economy. . . . Monetary policy came to be governed by the principle of undernourishing the inflationary process while still accommodating a good part of the pressures of the marketplace.
>
> My conclusion that it is illusory to expect central banks to put an end to the inflation that now afflicts the industrial economies does not mean that central banks are incapable of stabilizing actions; it simply means that their practical capacity for curbing an inflation that is driven by political forces is very limited.

In 1973 and 1974, with the sharp rise in inflation, Burns became sensitive to monetarist criticism of the Fed for allowing high rates of growth of M1. In 1973 and the first half of 1974, the FOMC moderated the rate of growth rate of M1. However, while acknowledging that inflation could not continue without rapid money growth, Burns challenged the monetarists by arguing that rapid money growth had followed inflation, rather than preceding it. Burns (US Congress 1974b, July 30, 257) testified:

> The current inflationary problem emerged in the middle 1960's when our government was pursuing a dangerously expansive fiscal policy. Massive tax reductions occurred in 1964 and the first half of 1965, and they were immediately followed by an explosion of Federal spending. . . . Our underlying inflationary problem, I believe, stems in very large part from loose fiscal policies, but it has been greatly aggravated during the past year or two by . . . special factors. . . . From a purely theoretical point of view, it would have been possible for monetary policy to offset the influence that lax fiscal policies and the special factors have exerted on the general level of prices. One may, therefore, argue that relatively high rates of monetary expansion may have been a permissive factor in the accelerated pace of inflation. I have no quarrel with this view. But an effort to use harsh policies of monetary restraint to offset the exceptionally powerful inflationary forces of recent years would have caused serious financial disorder and dislocation.

Over his tenure as FOMC chairman, Burns would alter his explanation for inflation, but he always attributed it to nonmonetary sources. An initial problem for Burns was that the wage and price controls that he so coveted did work to restrain wage growth but failed to restrain inflation. The controls program that began with a wage and price freeze on August 15, 1971, did restrain the growth of unit labor costs of corporations with wage guidelines of 5.5 percent, along with strong productivity growth. Moreover, the program limited the price increases of corporations. Although it permitted corporations to raise prices in line with increases in costs, they could do so only subject to a profits test. A Cost of Living Council had to approve price increases by large corporations (Kosters 1975). Despite working as intended, the controls did not prevent a rise in inflation.

In early 1973, world commodity prices rose rapidly. Burns (US Congress 1974a, February 1, 669–70) attributed the resulting inflation to a variety of special factors:

> In retrospect, it might be argued that monetary and fiscal policies should have been somewhat less expansive during 1972, but it is my considered judgment that possible excesses of this sort were swamped by powerful special factors that added a new dimension to our inflationary problem. . . . A major source of the inflationary problem last year was the coincidence of booming economic activity in the United States and in

other countries. . . . Another complicating factor was the devaluation of the dollar. . . . Disappointing harvests in 1972—both here and abroad—caused a sharp run-up in prices. . . . In short, the character of inflation in 1973 was very different from the inflation that troubled us in different years. A worldwide boom was in process; the dollar was again devalued; agricultural products, basic industrial materials, and oil were all in short supply.

If inflation were due to special factors, it should have receded in 1974. However, inflation remained in the low double digits throughout 1974. With controls on wages but not commodity prices, Congress turned against the program. On April 30, 1974, Congress allowed the president's authority to impose controls to lapse. Moreover, Gerald Ford became president in August 1974. The new CEA chairman, Alan Greenspan, and Treasury Secretary William Simon opposed incomes policies. Although Burns lobbied for a new incomes policy, such policies had been discredited politically.

Initially, Burns (US Congress 1974b, July 30, 258) lobbied for reestablishment of an incomes policy. However, the price controls program had become discredited in Congress. In the Ford administration, with incomes policies no longer an option and with continued inflation, Burns turned to government deficits as the underlying cause of inflation. Burns (US Congress 1974d, August 21, 213; and US Congress 1974e, September 25, 119) testified:

The current inflation began in the middle 1960s when our government embarked on a highly expansive fiscal policy. . . .

Special factors have played a prominent role of late, but they do not account for all of our inflation. For many years, our economy and that of most other nations has been subject to an underlying inflationary bias. . . . The roots of that bias lie in the rising expectations of people everywhere. . . . Individuals and business firms have in recent times come to depend more and more on government, and less and less on their own initiative, to achieve their economic objectives. In responding to the insistent demands for economic and social improvement, governments have often lost control of their budgets, and deficit spending has become a habitual practice. Deficit spending . . . becomes a source of economic instability . . . during a period of exuberant activity.[4]

4. In reality, deficits had not been especially large. As a percentage of GNP, the government (federal, state, and local) surplus or deficit (−) was 1.1 in 1969, −1.0 in 1970, −1.7 in 1971, −0.3 in 1972, 0.5 in 1973, and 0.2 in 1974. The 1970 and 1971 deficits resulted from

For Burns, the deficit represented government indiscipline, which vitiated the discipline required of businessmen to hold down wages and, as a consequence, prices. Burns (US Congress 1974c, August 6, 225–26 and 229) testified:

> If the Congress . . . proceeded to cut the budget . . . then confidence of business people, and of heads of our households, that the inflation problem will be brought under control would be greatly enhanced. In this new psychological environment, our trade unions may not push quite so hard for a large increase in wage rates, since they would no longer be anticipating a higher inflation rate. And in this new psychological environment, our business people would not agree to large wage increases quite so quickly.

Burns carried over the beliefs in the Depression of the conservative business community about the importance of conservative government policies to restore the confidence of the business community (chap. 11). He only modified them to deal with a world of inflation rather than deflation.

17.5. "MACROECONOMETRIC FAILURE ON A GRAND SCALE"

Burns had opposed the profession's embrace of Keynesianism and was a fervent believer in price stability. Nevertheless, the Burnsian FOMC gave the world an extraordinary experiment in the validity of a key Keynesian principle: the existence of a structural Phillips curve presenting policy makers with an "exploitable" (predictable) relationship between inflation and unemployment.[5] The FOMC never communicates in terms of trade-offs. In the "long run," the FOMC always fulfills the dual mandate. However, under Burns, the FOMC believed that by accommodating perceived cost-push inflation it was avoiding higher unemployment rates. In the event, as evidenced by the term "stagflation," there was no trade-off.

The failure to achieve moderate, stable unemployment purchased at the cost of a moderate amount of inflation produced the rational-expectations challenge to the Keynesian consensus. As subsumed in the rules versus discretion debate, the issue was the nature of inflationary expectations. Are those expectations given to the policy maker, and do they then drive a

---

recession. Burns made the deficits appear larger by including the lending of government-sponsored agencies like the Federal National Mortgage Association.

5. The expression that serves as the heading for this section is from Lucas and Sargent (1978 [1981], 303).

wage-price spiral? Alternatively, can the policy maker shape those expectations with a credible rule?

How did this seminal experiment unfold, and what was Burns's role? In the 1960s, Burns (1966, 61) had opposed wage and price controls as "a grim expedient that would indeed suppress inflation for a time, but at the cost of impairing efficiency as well as crushing economic freedom." Absent controls, the control of inflation must reside with the Fed. Why did Burns change his views when he became FOMC chairman?

Burns (1957, 17) believed that the behavior of the business cycle entailed a rise of prices during expansions and a decline in contractions: "Experience both before and after 1933 suggests . . . that when expansions are long or vigorous, the price level tends to rise substantially, and that when contractions are brief and mild, the decline in the price level tends to be small." In the 1970 recession, however, inflation failed to decline. Burns believed that the continued inflation derived from the market power of labor unions.

Burns believed that an incomes policy would engender a reduction in inflationary psychology, which would produce both a decline in inflation and an economic recovery. Burns (1970a [1978], 103–5 and 113–15) stated:

[Inflation first arose because of] the imprudent policies and practices pursued by the business and financial community during the latter half of the 1960s [and because of the] mood of speculative exuberance. [More recently] the inflation that we are still experiencing is no longer due to excess demand. It rests rather on the upward push of costs—mainly, sharply rising wage rates. Wage increases have not moderated.

In a society such as ours, which rightly values full employment, monetary and fiscal tools are inadequate for dealing with sources of price inflation such as are plaguing us now—that is, pressures on costs arising from excessive wage increases. . . . We should consider the scope of an incomes policy quite broadly. . . . We are dealing . . . with a new problem— namely, persistent inflation in the face of substantial unemployment— and . . . the classical remedies may not work well enough or fast enough in this case. Monetary and fiscal policies can readily cope with inflation alone or with recession alone; but, within the limits of our national patience, they cannot by themselves now be counted on to restore full employment, without at the same time releasing a new wave of inflation.

Burns (US Congress 1971, July 20, 259) testified before Congress:

The present inflation in the midst of substantial unemployment poses a problem that traditional monetary and fiscal policy remedies cannot solve as quickly as the national interest demands. That is what has led me . . . to urge additional governmental actions involving wages and prices. . . . The problem of cost-push inflation, in which escalating wages lead to escalating prices in a never-ending circle, is the most difficult economic issue of our time.

17.6. CONCLUDING COMMENT

Burns did not consider monetary policy to be the driving force behind inflation. He believed that inflation emanated primarily from an inflationary psychology produced by a lack of discipline in government fiscal policy and from private monopoly power, especially of labor unions. It followed that if government would intervene directly in private markets to restrain price increases the Federal Reserve could pursue a stimulative monetary policy without exacerbating inflation. When Burns got the controls he had lobbied for, he was effectively committed to continue the expansionary monetary policy that had begun early in 1971. In August 1971 in a Faustian bargain with President Richard Nixon, Burns accepted expansionary monetary policy in return for wage and price controls.

The decade of the 1970s offered an experiment in monetary policy based on the assumption that inflation is a nonmonetary phenomenon. Wage and price controls worked as intended by restraining wage growth and the price increases of large corporations (Kosters 1975). Nevertheless, by the end of 1973, inflation had risen to double digits. Burns then resorted to special factors such as increases in food prices due to poor harvests and in oil prices due to the restriction of oil production as the explanation for inflation. However, as the effect of these one-time events dissipated, inflation should have fallen. Yet, it remained at double-digit levels. Finally, Burns blamed inflation on government deficits. However, those deficits were small in 1973 and 1974. Finally, when Paul Volcker became FOMC chairman, the Fed would turn to monetary control to control inflation.

CHAPTER 18

Stop-Go and Collapse of a Stable Nominal Anchor

Summary: The Kennedy Council of Economic Advisers (CEA) gave the country a numerical target for full unemployment: 4 percent. At the end of the 1960s, the empirically estimated Phillips curve promised to deliver only modest inflation for 4 percent unemployment. However, in the recession year of 1970, the country got 6 percent inflation and 6 percent unemployment. The combination produced turmoil within the economics profession and the political system. Keynesians rallied around cost-push inflation as the explanation for inflation with excess unemployment (Nelson 2005). The Phillips curve had shifted upward because of the monopoly power of unions and corporations. Restricting aggregate demand to lower inflation would come at the cost of a level of unemployment that was socially wasteful and politically unacceptable. Incomes policy was the essential additional instrument. Controls would allow the Fed to achieve a socially acceptable balance between inflation and unemployment.

When G. William Miller succeeded Arthur Burns as FOMC chairman in early 1978, inflation was again increasing. In December 1978, an oil price shock augmented inflation. Out of concern for a recession, the Miller FOMC kept the funds rate unchanged. As inflation rose, inflationary expectations became untethered. Instead of expecting increases in inflation to be transitory, expected inflation ratcheted up with actual inflation. The stable nominal anchor inherited from a commodity standard and the Bretton Woods system disappeared.

Paul Volcker, who became FOMC chairman in August 1979, accepted responsibility for inflation and inflationary expectations. Discussion about whether inflation was cost-push inflation or aggregate-demand inflation and discussion of a wage-price spiral became irrelevant. If the Fed did not get inflationary expectations under control, they would pass into negotiated wage settlements and lock in high inflation. In the 1980s, the bond market vigilantes made certain that the FOMC removed inertia from its lean-against-the-wind procedures. The Volcker-Greenspan

FOMCs created a monetary standard in which the nominal anchor took the form of a rule that stabilized the expectation of the price level.

The Keynesian consensus presumed that the price system failed to maintain full employment. A negative output gap could persist indefinitely. During the go phases of stop-go monetary policy, the FOMC attempted to eliminate a negative output gap based on an assumption that potential output was consistent with 4 percent unemployment. In the go phases, the FOMC waited to begin raising the funds rate until well after cyclical troughs and then only cautiously out of concern for aborting the recovery. Monetary policy was stimulative and in time inflation rose. In response to the inflation, the FOMC raised the funds rate persistently until the economy weakened. In the resulting stop phases, the FOMC lowered the funds rate but only well after the cyclical peak. In the conduct of its lean-against-the-wind (LAW) procedures, the FOMC introduced significant lags into short-term interest rates relative to cyclical turning points (see monetary contraction markers in chap. 3).

18.1. THE COMPLICATED POLITICS OF AN INCOMES POLICY AND STOP-GO MONETARY POLICY

The political dynamic that created the demand for "low" unemployment began with the fracturing of the social polity in the 1960s over the Vietnam War and a militant civil rights movement and urban riots. Keynesians had been waiting in the wings and promised to deliver such a policy with a policy of aggregate-demand management based on Phillips curve trade-offs relaxed by incomes policies.

The inflation of the second half of the 1960s itself added to the fracturing of society and created additional political pressures on monetary policy. The transition from a world of assumed price stability to one of inflation created by stimulative monetary policy produced destabilizing income transfers between workers and the owners of capital. Recovery from the 1960–61 recession and later a stimulative monetary policy in an environment of expected price stability raised the markup of businesses (lowered their unit labor costs by raising output per worker with little change in wages). However, the resulting redistribution from workers to firms could not last and reversed starting in early 1966 and especially in 1968 when the markup fell (figure 18.1). The counterpart to these markup changes appears in labor's share of income, which declined through early 1966 and then rose sharply (figure 18.2). It was then natural for the business community to blame inflation on the wage-push pressures they were confronting caused

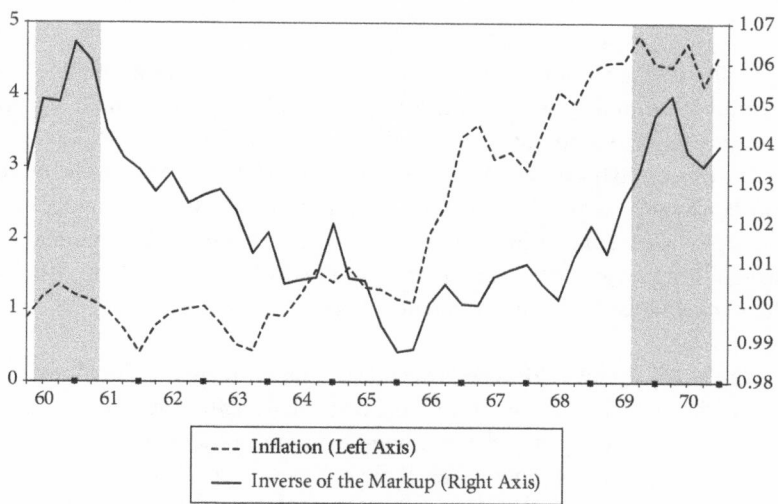

Figure 18.1. Inflation and Inverse of the Markup

Inflation is four-quarter percentage changes in the implicit price deflator for the nonfarm business sector. The inverse of the markup is the ratio of unit labor costs and the price level. Unit labor costs are total compensation divided by total hours worked for the nonfarm business sector. The price level is the deflator for the nonfarm business sector. The shaded areas indicate recessions. Heavy tick marks indicate the fourth quarter.
Source: St. Louis FRED

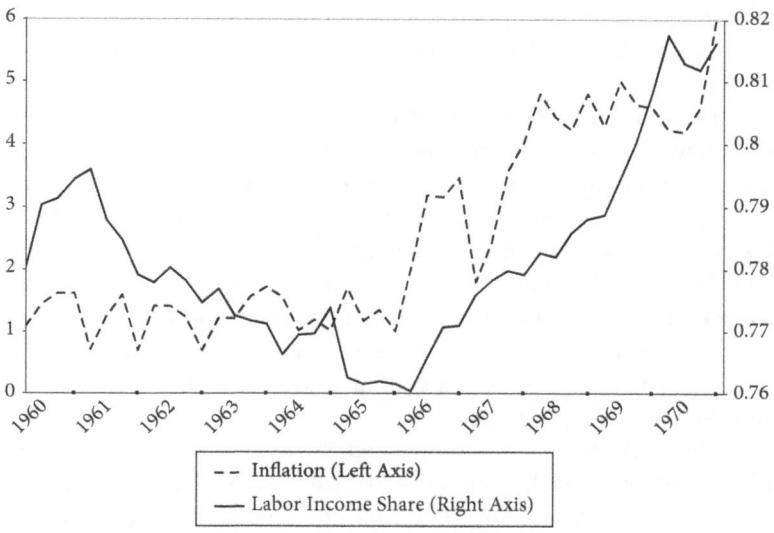

Figure 18.2. Inflation and Labor's Share of Income

The labor income share is calculated as the ratio of compensation to employees over national income minus proprietors income. Inflation is annualized growth rates of the PCE price index before 1959 and the core PCE price index from 1959 onward.
Source: St. Louis FRED

by militant labor unions. Burns, who was the unofficial spokesman for the business community, became the foremost public advocate of incomes policies designed to moderate presumed wage-push inflation.

Burns started his tenure as FOMC chairman with policy premised on the soft-landing strategy. The Fed could engineer a moderate amount of excess unemployment (unemployment above 4 percent) and produce a measured disinflation. In 1970, the Council of Economic Advisers stated the policy in the *Economic Report of the President* (57–58):

> The policy problem for 1970 is to take actions in the first half of the year which will place the economy on the sustainable path of moderately rising output and significantly declining inflation in the second half. . . . By mid-1970 the economy, after three quarters of very little increase of real output, would be producing significantly below its potential. Such a GNP gap places a downward pressure on the rate of inflation.

Policy makers believed that policy could manage real aggregate demand to produce a desirable outcome between inflation and unemployment. The desirable outcome did not happen. The FOMC lowered the funds rate from 9 percent in February 1970, Burns's first month as FOMC chairman, to 3.7 percent in February 1971 (figure 18.3). However, the unemployment rate rose steadily, reaching 5.9 percent in 1971Q2 and then remained stubbornly high near that plateau through 1972Q1 (figure 17.1). At 4.4 percent (PCE deflator) inflation remained near a plateau through 1971Q3 (figure 18.3).

The economics profession and the Nixon administration, which was looking forward to the 1972 presidential election, were thrown into a state of consternation. In the 1960s, when a declining unemployment rate had neared 4 percent, inflation began a steady rise (figure 17.1). Samuelson and Solow (1960 [1966], 1344) had asked whether the Phillips curve was a "reversible behavior equation?" They and the profession believed that it was. Why then did not inflation decline as the unemployment rate rose? In a universal acclamation, the answer arose from the business community, the economics profession, the Nixon administration, and most importantly, Arthur Burns: "wage-push inflation."

Burns believed that the country needed him as a "councilor to the President" (Hetzel 1998, 26). He could heal the rift between labor and business by lowering inflation without significant unemployment. To do that, he needed an incomes policy. Also, Democrats attacked the administration for dealing with inflation by raising unemployment rather than through an incomes policy. Under the influence of George Shultz, who had started as

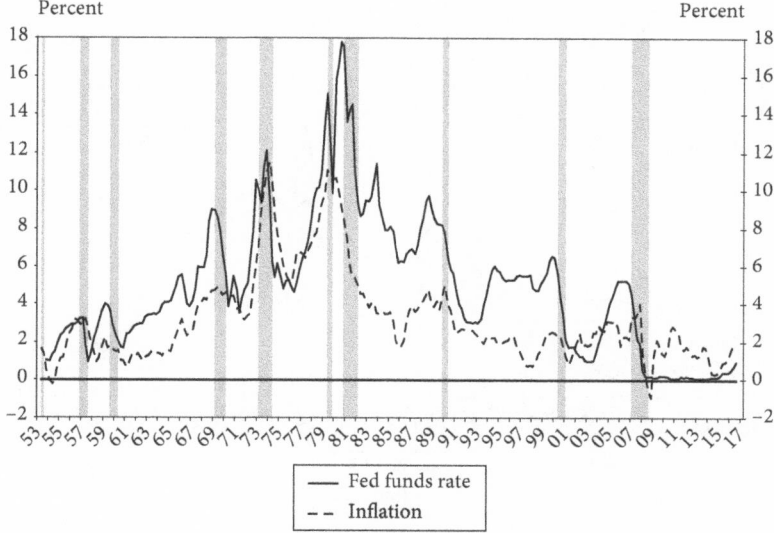

Figure 18.3. Federal Funds Rate and Inflation
Quarterly observations of the effective federal funds rate. Inflation is four-quarter percentage changes in the personal consumption expenditures (PCE) deflator. Shaded areas indicate NBER recessions. Tick marks indicate fourth quarter.
Source: St. Louis FRED

labor secretary and had become head of the OMB (Office of Management and Budget), the Nixon administration had resisted calls for an incomes policy. However, as the 1972 election approached, Nixon needed an expansionary monetary policy to lower an unemployment rate above 4 percent. The dance then began between Nixon and Burns.

Although by early 1971 the Fed was delivering the monetary acceleration desired by the Nixon administration, in May 1971 bond rates ceased declining and rose signaling an increase in inflationary expectations (figure 18.4). The administration feared that such an increase would frustrate an expansionary monetary policy. In congressional testimony, Burns (US Congress 1971, July 23, 252–54 and 259) challenged the administration to institute the controls he so much wanted:

> A year or two ago it was generally expected that extensive slack of resource use . . . would lead to significant moderation in the inflationary spiral. This has not happened. . . . The rules of economics are not working in quite the way they used to. . . . The increased militancy of workers . . . has probably led to wider and faster diffusion of excessive wage rate increases.

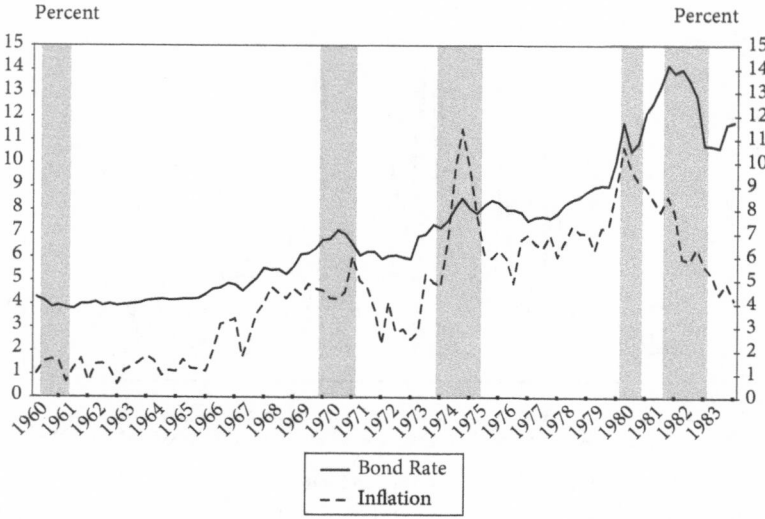

Percent   Percent

Figure 18.4. Bond Rate and Inflation
Quarterly observations of annualized quarterly growth rates of the personal
consumption expenditures deflator. From 1960 through 1977Q1, the bond rate is the
twenty-year constant maturity Treasury bond yield and thereafter the thirty-year
constant maturity yield. Shaded areas indicate recessions. Heavy tick marks indicate
fourth quarter.
Source: Board of Governors, Statistical Release H.15

Nixon then brought Burns on board. Burns believed that controls would
allow for the expansionary monetary policy required to lower the unemployment rate to 4 percent while also restraining inflation. Nixon would
deliver wage and price controls in return for expansionary monetary policy.
On August 15, 1971, at Camp David, Burns got the price controls for which
he had lobbied. The 1972 *US Economic Report of the President* (56) could
state, "After August 15 the success of the New Economic Policy became one
more goal of monetary policy."

18.2. LEAN-AGAINST-THE-WIND WITH TRADE-OFFS OR STOP-GO MONETARY POLICY: A TAXONOMY

Stop-go monetary policy took shape with the 1970 recession. The 1970 recession illustrated the characteristic restrictive monetary policy that preceded recessions. In response to rising inflation, the FOMC raised the funds
rate persistently to a level sufficient to produce a monetary deceleration
and create a recession (figures 16.1, 14.4 and 14.5). The FOMC maintained

relatively high real rates of interest past the cyclical peak (figure 18.5, and table 3.11 in chap. 3).

A desire to lower inflation and the resulting contractionary monetary policy produced the following recessions: August 1957–April 1958, December 1969–November 1970, November 1973–March 1975, July 1981–November 1982, July 1990–March 1991, and December 2007–June 2009. As shown by the tables in chapter 3 of the monetary contraction marker, the level of short-term rates lags cyclical peaks. Although the FOMC never communicates in terms of trade-offs, in reality, this fact represented attempts to create a negative output gap to lower inflation. Contributing to the lag was a concern that a reduction in the funds rate consequent upon economic weakness would signal a lack of resolve to lower inflation and impede a reduction in expected inflation.

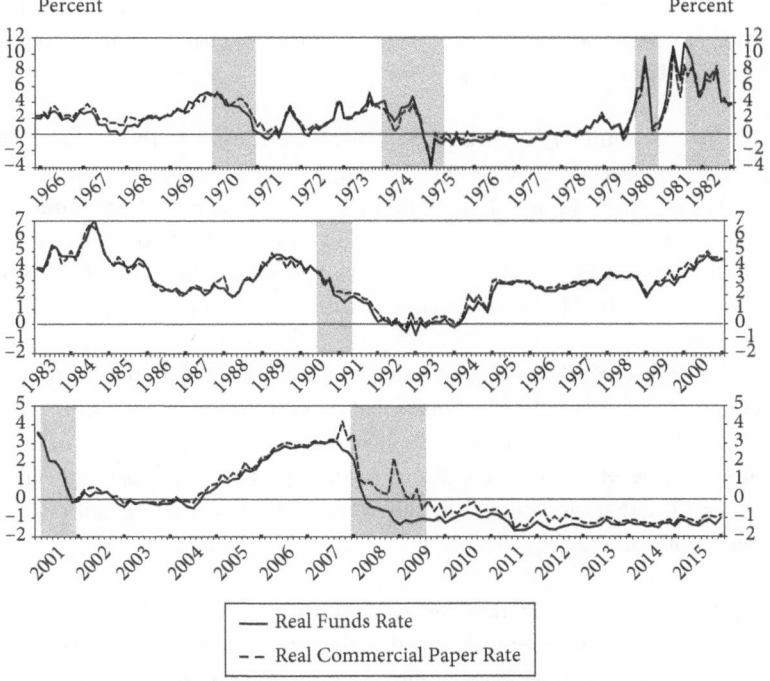

Figure 18.5. Real Funds Rate and Commercial Paper Rate
The real interest rate series is either the federal funds rate or the commercial paper rate minus the inflation forecast made by the staff of the Board of Governors in the Greenbook (later Tealbook). For a description of the series, see "Real Rate of Interest (Greenbook Forecasts)" in chapter 18 appendix. Forecasted inflation is for an overall index through 1979 and thereafter for a core index excluding food and energy. Shaded areas indicate recessions. Heavy tick marks indicate December FOMC meetings.

The association of a reduction in the funds rate with a presumed willingness to accept inflation arose from the discretionary character of monetary policy. Absent an explicit, credible rule, the FOMC had to demonstrate its commitment through policy actions. Stephen Axilrod (1971, 23), later staff director at the Board of Governors, observed:

> Concentration on money market conditions in the operating paragraph of the directive has led both the Committee and the market at times to interpret these conditions as policy itself. . . . When this occurs, the System often tends to get locked in, because it feels that any change in money market conditions will be interpreted as a change in policy and, therefore, lead to overreactions by market participants and others. This is particularly true in periods, such as 1969, when abatement of inflationary psychology appeared to be the ultimate aim of monetary policy. With that aim, there seemed to be fear that any change in money market conditions would be interpreted itself as signaling a change in policy and thus would fuel inflationary psychology.

In the November 1973–March 1975 recession, even with the intensification of the recession, the FOMC found it hard to lower the funds rate with high inflation (figure 18.3). After the July 14, 1974, FOMC meeting, the funds rate reached 13 percent, and real interest rates climbed back to cyclical highs (figure 18.5). Al Hayes, New York Fed president, stated (Board of Governors, *FOMC Memorandum of Discussion*, October 15, 1974, 64–66):

> Policy had to remain basically restrictive. . . . The Committee continued to be up against the old danger that modest slackening of monetary restraint might be overinterpreted by the market and might lead to an unwanted acceleration of inflationary expectations. . . . It was of crucial importance that the System not undermine the belief that it meant business about combating inflation.

Attempts to create a moderate negative output gap to put inflation on a declining path never succeeded. Viewed as attempts to exploit a Phillips curve relationship, stop-go monetary policy demonstrated that monetary policy cannot exercise predictable control over real output.

Figures 18.6 and 18.7 summarize the stop-go character of monetary policy in the decade and a half after 1965. Figure 18.6 measures the fall-off in consumption relative to trend that starts before a cyclical peak in the business cycle. In figure 18.7, deviations in consumption from trend appear as the dashed line. In the December 1969–November 1970 recession, the real

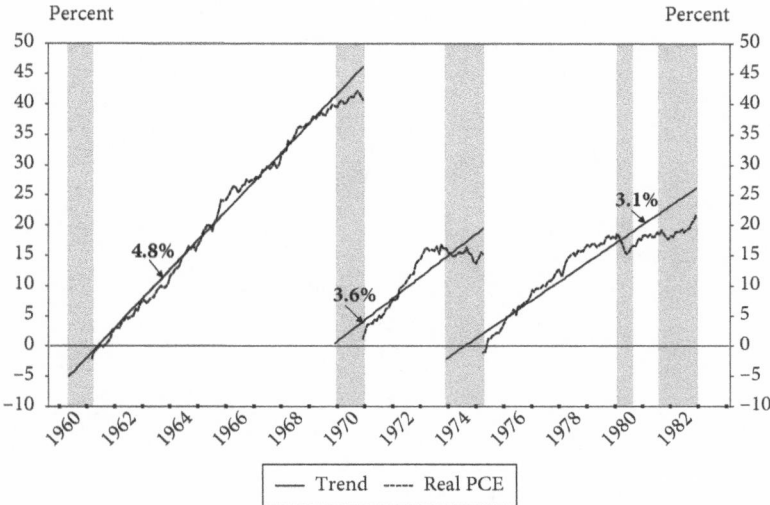

Figure 18.6. Real Personal Consumption Expenditures and Trend
Observations are the natural logarithm of monthly observations of real personal
consumption expenditures (PCE) normalized using the value at the prior business
cycle trough. Trend lines are fitted to these observations from the prior cycle peak
to the subsequent cycle peak and extended through the subsequent recession.
The business cycles with peaks at January 1980 and July 1981 are treated as a single
recession. Shaded areas indicate recessions. Heavy tick marks indicate December. Data
from the Commerce Department via Haver Analytics.

rate of interest (the diamonds) rose prior to the cyclical peak of the business
cycle and then remained at a cyclical high for most of the recession. With
inflation remaining at its cyclical high, the FOMC was reluctant to lower
the funds rate with the slowing of output (consumption) prior to the cycle
peak (chap. 3, table 3.11). That interference with the operation of the price
system created the monetary decelerations associated with stop-go policy.

18.3. BURNS'S JUGGLING ACT

At Camp David on August 15, 1971, starting with a wage and price freeze,
Burns got the controls he wanted.[1] Ironically, the initial effect of the price
controls program was to make monetary policy contractionary. Concerned

1. The history in the remainder of the chapter summarizes Hetzel (2008, chaps. 8
and 10). Nelson (2005) emphasized the prevalent Keynesian view of inflation as a nonmonetary phenomenon. Orphanides (2002 and 2003b) emphasized how a policy of
aggregate-demand management requires information on the structure of the economy
such as the level of employment corresponding to full employment not possessed by the

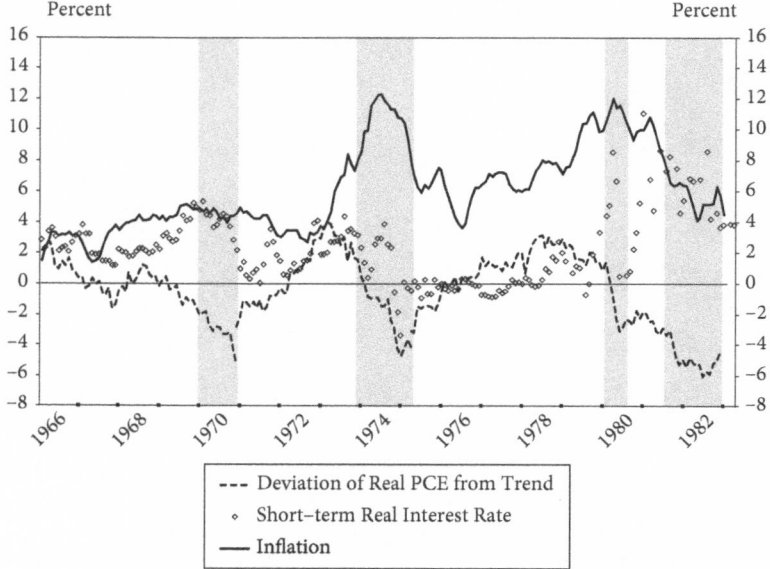

Figure 18.7. Deviation of Real PCE from Trend, Short-
Term Real Interest Rate, and Inflation: 1966–82
"Deviation of real PCE from trend" is the difference between the actual values and
trend lines shown in figure 18.6. Inflation is twelve-month percentage changes in the
personal consumption expenditures deflator. The "Short-Term Real Interest Rate" is
the commercial paper rate minus the corresponding inflation forecast made by the staff
of the Board of Governors (figure 18.5). Shaded areas indicate recessions. Heavy tick
marks indicate December. Data from Haver Analytics.

about appearances, the FOMC left its funds-rate target unchanged while the
announcement of controls lowered expected inflation and raised the real interest rate (figures 18.5 and 18.7). M1 growth declined (the low step in figure
14.5). Nixon wrote Burns reminding him of how he (Nixon) had lost the
November 1960 election because of an increase in unemployment. "Many
elections in this country have been determined because of an increase in
unemployment which resulted in the voters turning out the party in power.
I cannot think of one election where inflation had any effect whatever in
determining the result" (Hetzel 2008, chap. 8, note 12). Despite especially
intense opposition by the New York Fed, which was concerned about maintaining the new exchange-rate parities in the Bretton Woods system set in
the fall, Burns forced through steady decreases in the funds rate. It fell from

policy maker. More generally, the era of stop-go monetary policy reflected the Keynesian temper of that time not just the mistakes of Arthur Burns.

5⅝ percent after the August 24, 1971, FOMC meeting to 3¼ percent after the February 15, 1972, meeting (figure 18.3).

Although money growth surged starting in early 1972 (figure 14.5), Burns opposed increases in the funds rate. He told the FOMC that an increase in the funds rate would lead to an increase in mortgage rates and prevent the Pay Board from keeping wage increases within its pay guidelines. Although Burns allowed the Fed to become enmeshed in the politics of controls, at the time, his actions could be rationalized as necessary to make the controls program a success. Apart from Milton Friedman and a few monetarists, that program enjoyed almost universal support. For example, Governor Brimmer (Board of Governors, *FOMC Memorandum of Discussion*, April 18, 1972, 448) told the FOMC:

> The significant point was that the Administration had decided at that time [August 15, 1971]—with the support of the Congress and the Federal Reserve—that the way to solve the problem of inflation was to apply direct controls rather than to slow the rate of economic growth and increase excess capacity. If more effective means of fighting inflation were needed, they should be sought in tighter controls . . . not through monetary policy.

In 1972, expansionary monetary policy combined with controls generated high real growth and low inflation. M1 growth (fourth quarter to fourth quarter) was 8.4 percent and M2 growth 12.8 percent. Real GDP increased 5.1 percent while CPI inflation increased 3.2 percent, and the unemployment rate declined to 5.2 percent in December 1972. The 1973 *US Economic Report of the President* (63) boasted that "American anti-inflation policy had become the marvel of the rest of the world." Encouraged, the administration moved to a relaxation of the controls in a Phase 3. However, in 1973 inflation soared with quarterly rates of CPI inflation of 6.4 percent, 8.6 percent, 8.2 percent, and 10.5 percent. The surge came primarily from the price of food and energy, which because their markets were international were not subject to controls.

Although much of the commentary on this period has focused on whether the Fed lost its independence because of Burns's relationship with Nixon (Ferrell 2013), an understanding of the monetary policy from this time should remain focused on the guiding spirit of inflation as a nonmonetary phenomenon. Accordingly, policy needed to target an amount of real aggregate demand that achieved the right balance between unemployment and inflation as informed by the Phillips curve and inferred from social preferences. The Board staff used the then standard version of the Samuelson and Solow (1960 [1966]) Phillips curve. At the April 17, 1973, FOMC meeting (Board of Governors, *FOMC Memorandum of Discussion*, April 17, 1973, 9–10), the Board staff commented:

> Mr. Black [vice president of the Richmond Fed] asked whether the trade-off between unemployment and the rate of advance in prices had become less favorable recently, so that a higher rate of price advance would now be associated with a reduction in unemployment to an acceptable level.
> [Charles Partee, senior economist, replied that according to "the Board's econometric model"] calculations indicated that in the foreseeable future—over, say, the next 2 or 3 years—an unemployment rate in a 4½ to 5 per cent range was likely to be associated with a rate of price advance of 4 to 4½ per cent.

The November 1973–March 1975 recession arose from the interaction of tight monetary control and an inflation shock produced by the combined effect of an oil price shock and a surge in inflation from the end of price controls. Although the FOMC had two-quarter benchmarks for M1 growth, it had ignored them. Beginning with the April 17, 1973, FOMC meeting, it began to restrain money growth by making the benchmarks bind. Dissatisfaction with a perceived unwillingness and inability to enforce the controls by the administration led Burns to see the responsibility for controlling inflation as resting with the Fed. He was unhappy with what he saw as lax enforcement of Phase 3 of the controls. More important, in spring 1973, Watergate had begun to erode Nixon's moral authority as president and in Burns's opinion Nixon's ability to rally public support for the enforcement of controls. Burns (Board of Governors, *FOMC Memorandum of Discussion*, April 17, 1973, 91) told the FOMC, "Trust in government had declined dangerously. Those developments had increased the weight of the System's obligations." The Watergate drama would continue until Nixon's resignation in August 1973. A year later, Burns (Board of Governors, *FOMC Memorandum of Discussion*, March 19, 1974, 139) told the FOMC:

> Governments were weak in all of the democratic countries. . . . Because weak governments could not cope with the problem of inflation, the task had become the inevitable responsibility of central banks. Although their ability to deal with inflation was limited, central banks were discharging that responsibility at present.

In a letter to the president written June 1, 1973, Burns urged Nixon to reassert his leadership by decreeing a new price freeze (Burns Papers, Nixon File, Ford Library). Nixon followed his advice and on June 13, 1973, decreed a sixty-day price freeze with controls on agricultural exports. This time, however, with an overheated economy, the controls created shortages and eroded public support. Businessmen, who had initially supported controls, tired of the bureaucracy. With the end of the freeze, with Phase 4 of the controls, the administration began phasing out controls in a way intended to prevent a bulge in prices The controls lapsed on April 30, 1974.

In October 1973, war broke out in the Middle East. Motivated by a desire for the United States to end the oil embargo through diplomatic means, Burns did not want the administration to believe that the Fed would offset the economic disruption. He therefore left the funds rate unchanged. Burns (Board of Governors, *FOMC Memorandum of Discussion*, November 19–20, 1973, 84, and January 22, 1974, 109) told the FOMC that

> any easing of policy at this time could prove mischievous, because it might well be interpreted as suggesting that monetary policy could make a significant contribution toward resolving current economic problems and thus lead to confusion and misdirected effort in the private economy and perhaps in the Government as well. . . .
>
> The economy was suffering from a shortage of oil . . . rather than a shortage of money.

Until summer 1974, the FOMC concentrated on moving the funds rate to maintain moderate money growth. From 1973Q1 through 1974Q2, M1 growth almost equaled the FOMC's target of 5.5 percent. In summer and fall 1994, below-target M1 growth called for a reduction in the funds rate. Burns, however, was trying to persuade Congress to accompany tax reductions with expenditure reductions and wanted to use funds-rate reductions as a bargaining chip (Board of Governors, *FOMC Memorandum of Discussion*, July 16, 1974, 60–61):

> Chairman Burns said his purpose could be simply stated. If the funds rate . . . were to decline . . . the drop would be likely to be interpreted by the market as an easing of Federal Reserve policy. Such an interpretation would be unfortunate. . . . In private conversations with both Administration officials and Congressmen, he had been urging that some steps be taken in the direction of fiscal restraint. . . . That possibility would be reduced if at this juncture the System were to take actions that were publicly interpreted as easing.

At the September 1974, FOMC meeting Al Hayes (Board of Governors, *FOMC Memorandum of Discussion*, September 10, 1974, 58), New York Fed president, said that "fiscal restraint was not yet by any means assured, and a relaxation of monetary policy in advance of its realization could be taken as an implied reduction in the need for fiscal restraint."

Money growth declined significantly prior to and during the November 1973–March 1975 recession (figures 14.4 and 14.5). Despite shortfalls from the FOMC's money targets, Burns was unwilling to lower the funds rate in the absence of congressional action to restrain spending. The funds rate peaked after the July 16, 1974, FOMC meeting at 13 percent (figure 18.3). The real rate of interest rose prior to the cycle peak, initially declined with the peak, and then recovered in late summer and fall 1974. Starting well before the cycle peak, real personal consumption expenditures declined steadily below trend. Inflation remained in double digits throughout 1974 (figure 18.7).

Gerald Ford became president August 9, 1974, and Alan Greenspan became head of the CEA and Ford's key economics policy maker. Burns and Greenspan, the latter having been a student of Burns's at Columbia in the late 1940s, had much in common. Both believed the expectations of the businessman were essential. Increased business confidence would promote capital expenditures and hasten economic recovery. Both believed fiscal discipline was critical. The difference was that Greenspan and thus Ford would have nothing to do with incomes policies. With nothing to bargain for from the administration, monetary policy in the Ford presidency was disinflationary (see figure 20.1 on p. 426). That would change under Carter, when Burns would again have something to trade for with monetary policy.

Jimmy Carter became president in January 1977. During the Carter presidency and for the remainder of his tenure as FOMC chairman, Burns concentrated on sustaining economic recovery. For Burns, that task required maintaining the confidence of the businessman. As Burns (Board of Governors, *FOMC Transcript*, January 17, 1978, 18) told the FOMC, "What happens in the sphere of profits—and what expectations are with regard to profits—is still the main driving force of the economy." For Burns, those expectations made economic recovery fragile. At the trough of the recession, Burns (Board of Governors, *FOMC Memorandum of Discussion*, March 18, 1975, 69) had told the FOMC, "The recovery might appear to be so delicate, fragile and uncertain that it would be hard to face up to a course that would bring about rising interest rates." Also, maintaining a lid on interest rates again became a bargaining chip even though money growth consistently exceeded the FOMC's targets. Burns seemed to be making progress on inflation when, in April 1977, Carter announced a program "to convince labor and business to cooperate voluntarily in moderating price and cost increases" (Biven 2002, 130).

18.4. G. WILLIAM MILLER

G. William Miller became FOMC chairman in March 1978. He joined a thoroughly Keynesian Board of Governors with a thoroughly Keynesian staff. The statement of Board member J. Charles Partee (Board of Governors, *FOMC Memorandum of Discussion*, July 18, 1978, 26) in explaining why the FOMC had to accept above-target money growth to prevent interest rates from rising is representative. "The honest, rational, intelligent thing to do is to recognize that M1 growth has exceeded the target over a protracted period and that is because there has been a great deal of inflation in the system, which is induced by wage increases and government actions and things like that." At the March 1978 FOMC meeting, President Willis of the Minneapolis Fed asked Chairman Miller, "What are the chances for an effective anti-inflation policy from the administration?" Miller answered, "If the administration doesn't act, inflation will be left to the Federal Reserve and that is bad news." As long as the unemployment rate was 6 percent or higher (figure 17.1), the Miller FOMC was unwilling to tighten monetary policy (Hetzel 2008, 124).

That reticence changed briefly in fall 1978. In 1977, the US current account turned negative, and the dollar began to depreciate in late 1977. Under pressure from US domestic allies and public opinion, President Carter called for wage and price guidelines. Disappointed markets reacted adversely, and the dollar depreciated sharply. In coordination with the administration, the Fed and the Treasury intervened to buy dollars in the foreign exchange market, and the FOMC raised the funds rate. The real funds rate, which had been slightly negative or zero from 1975 through mid-1978, moved up to just above 2 percent in December 1978 (figure 18.5).

However, in December 1978, OPEC announced an increase in oil prices of 14.5 percent. The dominant concern of the FOMC then changed to fear of recession. From its December 1978 value of 10 percent, the FOMC at its May 1979 meeting raised the funds rate only to 10.25 percent, where it remained until the August 1979 meeting, when Paul Volcker took over as chairman. CPI inflation rose from 9.5 percent at the end of 1978 and averaged 13.5 percent over the last three quarters of 1979. The inflation rate expected by the markets rose steadily and reached 10 percent in 1979Q1 (figure 13.1). Four-quarter M1 growth reached almost 8 percent in 1979Q3 (figure 14.4). The real funds rate, which had risen to 2.2 percent in November 1978, fell steadily, and by the July 1979 FOMC meeting, which was Miller's last, it was slightly negative (figure 18.5).

18.5. THE COST OF ALLOWING INFLATION
TO EMERGE IN ECONOMIC RECOVERY

The stop phase of stop-go monetary policy arose from allowing inflation to emerge in the go phase. Reducing inflation was costly because of the need to reverse an increase in inflationary expectations. The Board's econometric models quantified the cost in terms of a sacrifice ratio. In reference to the FRB/US model of the staff of the Board of Governors, Kiley et al. (2006) noted:

> Inflation is only modestly responsive in the short run to changes in resource utilization. Together these effects cause the long-run sacrifice ratio in FRB/US to be relatively large: Permanently reducing the inflation rate in FRB/US by 1 percentage point requires keeping the unemployment rate above the NAIRU by roughly a full percentage point for six years.

Governor Yellen (Board of Governors, *FOMC Transcript*, July 2, 1996, 42) told the FOMC, "The sacrifice ratio in our new FRB-US model without credibility effects is 2.5, resulting in an output cost of about 5 percent of GDP per point of inflation [reduction]."

The contractionary monetary policy required to reduce inflation necessitated increasing the unemployment rate. In the past, the FOMC has never been able to increase the unemployment rate in a measured, moderate way to achieve a soft landing, that is, spread a moderate amount of excess unemployment over an extended period of time. Instead, it has created a recession. Figure 18.8 plots the unemployment rate. The black squares demarcate increases in the unemployment rate that cumulated to 40 basis points or more and that did not immediately precede a business cycle peak or follow a business cycle trough. What is striking is the paucity of increases in the unemployment rate not associated with recession.[2] The Volcker-Greenspan

2. The four squares shown in the figure may indicate incipient recessions forestalled by other events. The November 1951 increase demarcated the date when the Korean War intensified with the entry of the Chinese in crossing the Yalu River. It set off fears of World War III with the return of price controls and created an intense demand for any goods that could be stockpiled. The August 1952 increase occurred during the Korean War. The February 1963 increase marked an economic slowdown, which convinced President Kennedy of the need for a tax cut. January 1967 does not meet the criterion for a nontrivial increase in the unemployment rate although the downward movement in the unemployment rate stalled. However, in summer 1966, the Fed tightened to snuff out a rise in inflation. When President Johnson agreed to a tax hike, the Martin FOMC

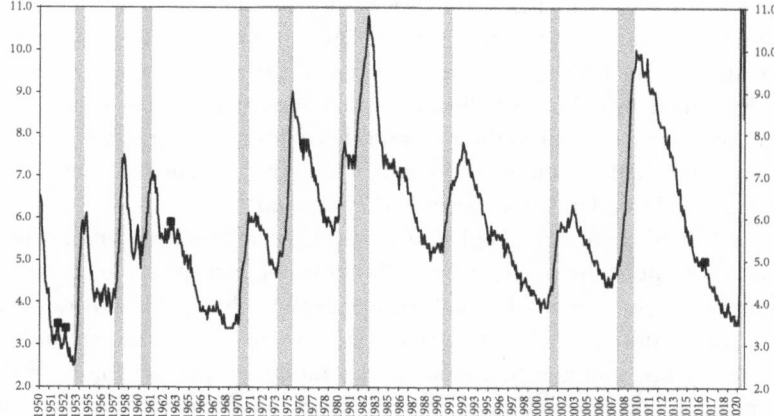

Figure 18.8. Unemployment Rate and Rises Not Associated with Recession
Monthly observations of the unemployment rate. The black squares demarcate
intervals of increases in the unemployment rate that cumulate to 40 basis points or
more and that do not immediately precede a recession peak or follow a recession
trough. They fall on the following dates: November 1951, August 1952, February 1963,
and July 1976. Shaded areas indicate recessions. Heavy tick marks indicate December.
Source: St. Louis FRED

policy of preemptive increases in the funds rate during economic recovery
to prevent the emergence of inflation recognized this reality.

18.6. CONCLUDING COMMENT

James Tobin's views on inflation represented the prevailing belief that inflation was not caused by the Fed and rapid money growth. In a *New York
Times* essay entitled "There Are Three Types of Inflation: We Have Two,"
Tobin (1974) wrote: "Three decades of experience tell us that inflation is
endemic to modern democratic industrial societies." Tobin continued to
"distinguish three types of inflation: a) 'excess demand inflation,' b) 'the
wage-price-wage spiral,' and c) 'shortages and price increases in important
commodities.'" Tobin concluded that the 1970s inflation was a combination
of the last two. The overwhelming Keynesian consensus held that nonmonetary forces drove inflation.

Moreover, "excess demand inflation" need not arise from "too much
money chasing too few goods." In the Keynesian world, excess aggregate

---

backed off tightening. The July 1976 increase remains a puzzle. The economy seemed to
stall but then picked up again in the fall after the election.

nominal demand can arise from government deficit spending, an investment boom, an export boom, and so on. Only later would economic models explain how the Fed can restrain real aggregate demand to equal potential with a monetary policy that allows the price system to work by keeping the real interest rate equal to the natural rate of interest. Aggregate nominal demand would then emerge as the sum of growth in potential real aggregate demand and trend inflation controlled by the Fed.

As FOMC chairman, Paul Volcker brought inflation down and held it down without the need for periodic socially unacceptable increases in unemployment. The intellectual consensus then changed in favor of Milton Friedman's belief that the price system works well in the absence of monetary disorder and that inflation is a monetary phenomenon. In the terminology employed here, the Fed abandoned the idea of "activist aggregate-demand management" and replaced it with "aggregate-demand maintenance." With the latter, the Fed's reaction function causes the real interest rate to track the natural rate of interest and thereby turns over to market forces the unfettered determination of real variables like employment and output. Credibility for price stability shapes the way that firms in the sticky-price sector set prices for multiple periods (Aoki 2001). Absent the noise from inflation determined in the flexible-price sector, aggregate nominal demand then emerges as the sum of market-determined potential real aggregate demand and monetary-determined inflation from the sticky-price sector.

In his article "Poor Hand or Poor Play?" François Velde (2004) expressed the debate over the causes of the inflation and real instability in the 1970s in terms of either supply shocks ("Poor Hand") or faulty monetary policy ("Poor Play"). The consensus in favor of the latter came only afterward with the policy of Paul Volcker, which abandoned inflation-unemployment trade-offs in favor of price stability (low, stable inflation).

APPENDIX: REAL RATE OF INTEREST
Real Rate of Interest (Livingston Forecasts)

The Livingston Survey commenced in 1947 and is currently conducted by the Federal Reserve Bank of Philadelphia.[3] Twice annually in June and December the survey publishes forecasts from about fifty business economists of the level of the CPI at six- and twelve-month horizons. The forecasts of inflation in the paper follow Carlson (1977). Carlson noted that the December survey is mailed early in November, when respondents have available

---

3. This appendix is adapted from Hetzel 2008, chap. 4 appendix.

the October CPI. The respondents forecast the level of the CPI for the following June. The forecast of inflation, therefore, is assumed to be the annualized rate of growth of the CPI over the eight-month period from October to June. Similarly, the inflation forecast based on the forecasted December level of the CPI for the following year is assumed to be the annualized rate of growth of the CPI over the fourteen-month period ending in December of the following year.

Real Rate of Interest (Hoey Forecasts)

Richard B. Hoey in "Decision Makers Poll" conducted irregularly timed surveys of inflation expectations when he worked, respectively, for Bache, Halsey, Stuart and Shields; Warburg, Paribus, and Becker; Drexel, Burnham, Lambert; and Barclays de Zoete Wedd Research. The first ten-year inflation forecast is from September 1978. The survey begins collecting shorter-term (approximately one-year) forecasts beginning in October 1980. The number of respondents varied between 175 and 500 and included chief investment officers, corporate financial officers, bond and stock portfolio managers, industry analysts, and economists. The survey dates are dates when the polls were mailed to Hoey. The survey was discontinued in March 1991, begun again in March 1993, and ended again definitively after five months.

Real Rate of Interest (Philadelphia Fed Forecasts)

The Survey of Professional Forecasters is currently conducted quarterly by the Federal Reserve Bank of Philadelphia. It was conducted formerly by the American Statistical Association and the National Bureau of Economic Research and began in 1968Q4. In 1981Q3, the survey began collecting forecasts of four-quarter rates of CPI inflation. In 1991Q4, it began to collect forecasts of CPI inflation over the next ten years.

Real Rate of Interest (Greenbook Forecasts)

The real interest rate is the difference between the commercial paper rate and Greenbook inflation forecasts. The Greenbook contains forecasts of the National Income and Product Accounts prepared by the staff of the Board of Governors before FOMC meetings. The maturity of the real rate varies from somewhat more than one quarter to somewhat less than two quarters. The commercial paper rate is for prime nonfinancial paper placed through dealers (A1/P1). The dates for the interest rates match the publication dates of the Greenbooks. From 1965 through 1969, interest-rate data are from the New York Fed release "Commercial Paper." Subsequently, they are from the Board's FAME database or from Bloomberg. From 1965 through April 1971, the paper rate is for four- to six-month paper. Thereafter, if there are fewer than 135 days from the Greenbook date to the end of the subsequent quarter, the three-month paper rate is used; otherwise, the six-month paper rate is used.

Predicted inflation is for changes in the implicit GNP (GDP from 1992 on) deflator until August 1992. Thereafter, the fixed-weight deflator is used until March 1996. Thereafter, the GDP chain-weighted price index is used. A weighted-average inflation rate for the period from the Greenbook date to the end of the succeeding quarter is calculated from the Greenbook's inflation forecasts for the current and succeeding quarter. The weight given to the current quarter's inflation rate is the ratio of the number of days left in the current quarter to the number of days from the Greenbook date until the end of the succeeding quarter. The weight given to the succeeding quarter's inflation rate is the ratio of the number of days in that quarter to the number of days from the Greenbook date until the end of the succeeding quarter. This weighted-average expected inflation rate is subtracted from the market rate of interest.

In the 1960s, the FOMC usually met more than twelve times per year. For example, it met fifteen times in 1965. In order to make the real-rate series monthly through 1978, if there was more than one meeting per month, an observation was recorded only for the first meeting of the month. The FOMC met only nine times in 1979. (Because the October 6, 1979, meeting was unscheduled, there was no Greenbook, and no real rate is calculated for this date.) It met eleven times in 1980. Starting in 1981, it has met eight times a year. For this reason, starting in 1979, the observations of the Greenbook real-rate series are less frequent than monthly.

The real-rate series begins in November 1965 because the Greenbook first began to report predictions of inflation for the November 1965 meeting. Until November 1968, for FOMC meetings in the first two months of a quarter, the Greenbook often reported a forecast of inflation only for the contemporaneous quarter. For this reason, for the following FOMC meeting dates, the real rate calculated is only for the period to the end of the contemporaneous quarter, not to the end of the succeeding quarter: November 23, 1965; January 11, 1966; February 8, 1966; April 12, 1966; May 10, 1966; June 7, 1966; July 26, 1966; November 1, 1966; December 13, 1966; January 10, 1967; July 18, 1967; October 24, 1967; November 14, 1967; January 9, 1968; February 6, 1968; April 30, 1968; May 28, 1968; July 16, 1968; October 8, 1968; October 17, 1972; and November 20–21, 1972. For these dates, the maturity of the interest rate used to calculate the real rate varies between one and three months. For other dates, the maturity varies between three and six months. For this reason, some of the variation in real rates reflects term structure considerations. This variation is a consequence of the fact that the FOMC meets at different times within a quarter and the Greenbook inflation forecasts are for quarters.

CHAPTER 19

The Volcker Fed and the Birth of a New Monetary Standard

Summary: In 1952, Paul Volcker became an economist at the New York Fed. His mentor there, Robert Roosa, later joined the Treasury in the Kennedy administration. Roosa brought Volcker to the Treasury, where in the 1960s as Treasury undersecretary for international affairs he helped manage the Bretton Woods system. Volcker believed that a strong dollar was the financial counterpart to American strength in the Cold War. His experiences at the Desk of the New York Fed and at the Treasury defending the external value of the dollar imbued him with the importance of expectations. In August 1979, Volcker succeeded G. William Miller as FOMC chairman.

As FOMC chairman, Volcker rejected the 1970s policy of activist aggregate-demand management with its goal of "low," stable unemployment achieved by allowing a "moderate" amount of inflation. By 1979, unhinged inflationary expectations made such a trade-off impossible. Inflation had ratcheted up over the course of successive business cycles, and inflationary expectations followed. By summer 1979, markets had come to anticipate that higher inflation would follow expansionary monetary policy. Volcker determined to recreate a stable nominal anchor for the dollar by recreating nominal expectational stability invariant to cyclical fluctuations and to transitory fluctuations in inflation.

Initially, he tried to do so through substantive money targets, which did not drift upward as actual money growth exceeded targeted money growth. With the deregulation of interest rates in 1981, however, the monetary aggregate M1 lost its value as an indicator of monetary policy. Real M1 demand became interest sensitive so that when the economy weakened and market interest rates fell, real M1 demand increased. The corresponding increased growth in M1 then gave the wrong signal about the appropriate direction of short-term rates. Volcker created a stable nominal anchor in the form of consistency in policy directed toward low, stable inflation. That consistency created a stable nominal anchor in the form of nominal expectational stability: low, stable expected inflation.

The 1970s monetary policy of activist aggregate-demand management assumed the feasibility of achieving "low" unemployment at a "moderate" cost in terms of inflation based on estimated Phillips curve trade-offs. The presumed counterfactual, which assumed cost-push inflation, was that a monetary policy focused on price stability would require regular recourse to socially unacceptable high rates of unemployment. Arthur Burns and his successor, G. William Miller, delivered the Keynesian experiment in activist aggregate-demand management. In his attempt to recreate the stable nominal anchor lost in the 1970s, Volcker delivered the monetarist/rational-expectations experiment. After the Volcker disinflation, the result was the Great Moderation.

Paul Volcker understood the crucial role of expectations. In a way epitomized by Charlie Coombs (1976), head of the Foreign Exchange Desk at the New York Fed, central banks had traditionally viewed market speculation as destabilizing. Speculators attacked the exchange rates set by Bretton Woods and had to be fought. Volcker realized that unmoored expectations of inflation made expectations destabilizing. Breaking with the Keynesian consensus, he rejected the idea of a wage-price spiral driven by inflationary expectations given exogenously to the Fed. Volcker accepted central bank responsibility for disciplining inflationary expectations.

In the Volcker-Greenspan era, the primary objective became low, stable inflation. The belief by both Volcker and Greenspan that this objective required nominal expectational stability imposed consistency on policy. Monetary policy became "rule-like."

19.1. RESTORING A STABLE NOMINAL ANCHOR

In August 1979, when Volcker moved from president of the New York Fed to FOMC chairman, he had accepted that inflationary expectations had become destabilizing. The reason was that financial markets had come to expect that in recession an expansionary monetary policy would raise inflation. As a result, in recession, bond rates rose and defeated expansionary monetary policy. Countercyclical monetary policy that worked off Phillips curve trade-offs based on excess capacity in recession (an unemployment rate above the NAIRU) now destabilized expectations.

In the past, the Fed had put the economy through recessions to lower inflation. Volcker knew that reducing double-digit inflation would require a recession. However, disinflation was not sufficient. To restore nominal expectational stability, the stop-go cycle had to end. For that to happen, the country had to endure a recession *and* a recovery without the stimulative monetary policy that in past cycles had revived inflation. Abandonment of Keynesian activist aggregate-demand management followed from Volcker's acceptance of Fed responsibility for inflationary expectations and for stabilizing them over the business cycle.

Acceptance of responsibility for inflationary expectations also rendered pointless whether inflation was cost-push or demand-pull. The source of a presumed wage-price spiral was irrelevant. The Fed had to get control of inflationary expectations, or they would pass into negotiated wage settlements and perpetuate inflation. Initially, Volcker instituted money targets to demonstrate the credibility of policy. A commitment to low money growth would assure sustained low inflation.

After the Volcker disinflation, the Fed created a new monetary standard in which the nominal anchor constituted a rule that stabilized the expectation of the future price level. In doing so, the FOMC followed its traditional lean-against-the-wind procedures but implemented them in a way that removed the cyclical inertia in interest rates that had characterized the stop-go era. In the terminology used here, the FOMC went from LAW with trade-offs to LAW with credibility (chap. 14).

With the 1970s policy of LAW with trade-offs, in the go phase, cyclical inertia in interest rates arose after the trough of recessions from a reluctance to raise rates because of the desire to stimulate economic activity. Stimulative monetary policy appeared as rapid money growth. In response to a subsequent rise in inflation, the FOMC raised interest rates steadily until the economy weakened. In stop phases, despite the weakening in economic activity, inertia arose from a reluctance to lower interest rates until inflation abated. Although the Fed never used the language of Phillips curve trade-offs, it followed a policy of stimulus in economic recoveries to eliminate a negative output gap followed by a policy of contraction as inflation rose to create a negative output gap. Milton Friedman associated the accompanying interest-rate inertia with procyclical money growth and argued that it created the business cycle rather than mitigated it. His argument was known under the rubric of "long and variable lags" (Friedman 1960, 87).

Volcker looked to the behavior of bond rates as a test of whether policy was restoring nominal expectational stability. Sharp jumps ("inflation scares") indicated that markets believed that the FOMC was implementing stimulative and ultimately inflationary monetary policy (Goodfriend 1993). The bond market vigilantes then pushed the FOMC into raising the funds rate early during the cyclical recovery from the 1982–83 recession. A clear demonstration of the new policy came with the May 1983 inflation scare. Despite an unemployment rate of 11 percent and falling inflation, the FOMC raised the funds rate when bond rates jumped. Over time, the Fed created a new nominal anchor in the form of a widespread expectation of low, stable trend inflation.

The success of the Volcker-Greenspan standard (LAW with credibility) in contrast with the stop-go standard in which the FOMC had allowed high and rising inflation in an attempt to maintain "low" unemployment (LAW with trade-offs) changed the professional consensus. The foundation of the stop-go monetary policy of the 1970s rested on the Keynesian view of cost-push inflation setting off a wage-price spiral perpetuated by inflationary expectations untethered by monetary policy. Countering inflation driven by the exercise of market power by large corporations and labor unions to maintain price stability would require socially unacceptable high levels of unemployment. In contrast, a monetary policy resting on the foundation of nominal expectational stability assumed that inflationary expectations would conform to rule-like monetary policy. The exercise of monopoly power could cause a one-time change in relative prices but not persistent inflation.

At the time, the outcome of the Volcker policy of disinflation followed by low, stable inflation was uncertain. It was not foregone that Congress and President Ronald Reagan would support Fed independence through disinflation and recession. There was little belief within the economics profession that disinflation followed by sustained low and stable inflation would be compatible with low unemployment. If the experiment had failed, the United States would have endured perpetual inflation beset by on-and-off price controls. A free market economy would have been the casualty.

19.2. CREATING A NEW MONETARY STANDARD: LAW WITH CREDIBILITY

The Volcker disinflation constituted one of the most significant monetary experiments in history, comparable to the gold standard reforms that ended hyperinflations in the 1920s (Sargent 1982). The dramatic disinflation shows in figures 18.3 and 18.4. Over time, the FOMC had to reduce the dollar expenditure of the public. Figure 19.1 shows four-quarter rates of growth of nominal and real GDP, and figure 19.2 shows the difference in these series, which is inflation measured by the GDP deflator. Over time, the difference shows the progress made in restoring near price stability.

Figures 19.1 and 19.2 show the dramatic experiment conducted by the Fed. Through the 1960s and 1970s, the Fed allowed the nominal (dollar) expenditure of the public to rise based on the belief that it was accommodating relatively high real growth and low unemployment. Starting with the Volcker disinflation, the Fed lowered nominal expenditure and maintained

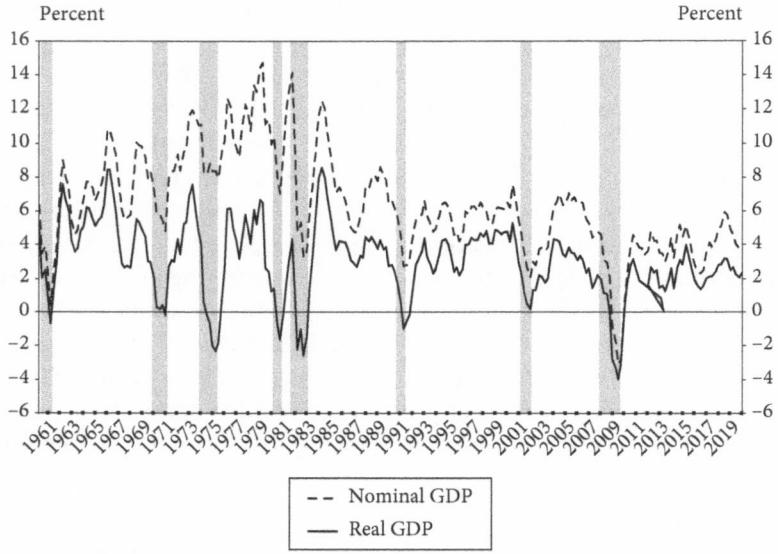

Figure 19.1. Growth Rates of Nominal and Real GDP
Quarterly observations of four-quarter percentage changes of real and nominal GDP.
Shaded areas represent recessions. Heavy tick marks indicate fourth quarters.
Source: St. Louis FRED

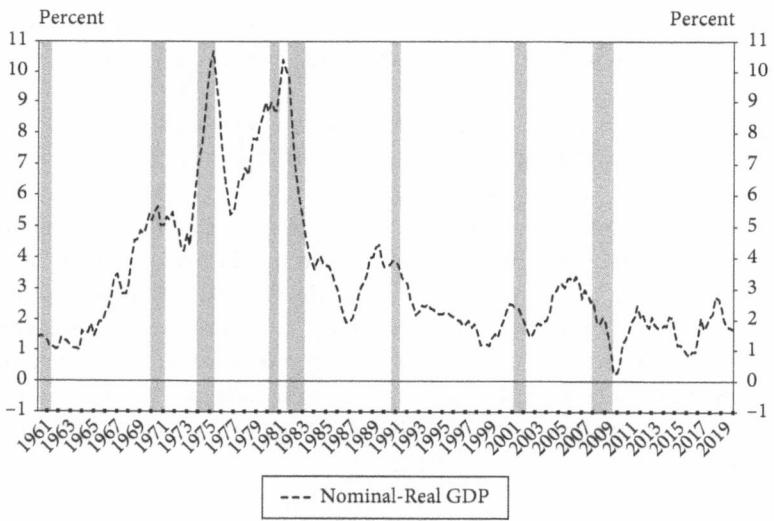

Figure 19.2. Nominal GDP Growth Minus Real GDP Growth
Quarterly observations of four-quarter percentage changes in nominal GDP minus
four-quarter percentage changes in real GDP. Shaded areas represent recessions. Heavy
tick marks indicate fourth quarters. Data from St. Louis FRED.

it at a relatively low level. Figure 19.2, which shows the difference between nominal and real expenditure, highlights the rise in inflation, the disinflation, and then the relative stability of low inflation.

The 1970s spirit of policy appeared in *The 1979 Joint Economic Report* (US Congress 1979, 45):

> Inflation . . . cannot be dealt with . . . through demand restriction alone without exacting intolerable costs in terms of lost output and high unemployment. . . . Clearly, demand restriction does not address supply-related inflation triggered by rising energy and food costs, increases in government regulation, substandard productivity gains, and a declining international value of the dollar—which is propelled onward by subsequent spirals of wages and prices attempting to keep up with each other.

If this nonmonetary understanding of inflation were correct, monetary policy entailed an agonizing period-by-period choice of the extent to which to accommodate inflation by creating unemployment.

Volcker challenged this perception through policy based on a commitment to sustain low, stable inflation. That commitment would discipline inflationary expectations. Supply shocks could pass into the price level but would not propagate as inflation. Untethered inflationary expectations would not power a wage-price spiral. Volcker (1980a, 3, 10, 11) explained how through credible commitment monetary policy would restore the stable nominal anchor lost in the 1970s:

> Our policy . . . rests on a simple premise—one documented by centuries of experience—that the inflationary process is ultimately related to excessive growth in money and credit. . . . The question I receive most frequently is . . . "Will the Fed stick with it?" . . . My own short and simple answer . . . is yes. "It" is restraint of the money supply. . . . One expectation that has come to be almost universally shared is that prices would move higher—and so long as that expectation is held it tends to become a self-fulfilling prophecy. . . . To break that cycle, we need to change expectations. One indispensable element in the process is singularly in the domain of the Federal Reserve—we must have a credible and disciplined monetary policy that is characterized by sustained moderation of growth in money.

The visible commitment to achieving money targets committed the FOMC to raising interest rates by whatever extent necessary to lower inflation (Volcker 1994, 160). The new policy also had to be preemptive. Policy makers had to be willing to raise the funds rate significantly before the appearance of inflation.[1]

At his first FOMC meeting as chairman in August 1979, Volcker made clear his commitment to creating credibility. It was essential that markets not associate a reduction in the funds rate with an eventual increase in inflation. Volcker (Board of Governors, *FOMC Transcript*, August 14, 1979, 21, 27) said:

> I am impressed myself by an intangible: the degree to which inflationary psychology has really changed. . . . That's important to us because it does produce . . . paradoxical reactions to policy. . . . The ordinary response one expects to easing actions . . . won't work if they're interpreted as inflationary; and much of the stimulus will come out in prices rather than activity. . . . If a tightening action is interpreted as a responsible action . . . long-term rates tend to move favorably. . . . Economic policy in general has a kind of crisis of credibility. . . . Can we restore the feeling that inflation will decline over a period of time? . . . [Recession is] manageable . . . if long-term expectations are not upset . . . by any decline in interest rates.

The FOMC raised the funds rate from 10.25 percent to 11 percent at its August 1979 meeting and then to 11.5 percent at its September 1979 meeting. In addition, the Board accepted an increase in the discount rate from 7.25 percent to 8 percent, but with three dissents on the seven-member Board. Later, Volcker (2001, 447) said that the deciding factor in the decision to move to new operating procedures was a divided Board. Credibility required a united Fed. That was not possible as long as debate took place over the level of the funds rate. On October 6, 1979, in a special, highly secret meeting, the FOMC adopted nonborrowed reserves operating procedures, which did not entail setting a target for the funds rate.

The new operating procedures revived the free reserves procedures of the 1950s and 1920s (figure 6.1). Because Volcker had been at the New York Fed in the 1950s, he understood how they would work. He understood the endogenous determination of money market rates as the outcome of bank reserves supply and demand. Given lagged-reserves accounting with which required reserves depended on deposits with a two-week lag, reserves demand was given in the reserves accounting period. With the new procedures, the FOMC specified a target for nonborrowed reserves. It followed that borrowed reserves were then determined. Given reserves demand, the

1. The narrative draws on Hetzel (2008, chap. 13). See also Goodfriend and King (2005).

funds rate was determined as the sum of the discount rate and a surcharge reflecting the administrative cost imposed on banks for using the discount window. Strength in the rate of growth of M1 would increase bank deposits, increase reserves demand, and raise the funds rate by raising borrowed reserves (Hetzel 1982).

Although Volcker billed the new procedures as operating automatically to control money with the funds rate determined by market forces, in practice, he exercised considerable discretionary control over the determination of the funds rate through changes in the discount rate (Cook 1989). Increases in the discount rate increased the funds rate one for one. Still, the medium was the message. Volcker wrote (Volcker and Gyohten 1992, 167–68):

> Among the most important [benefits] would be to discipline ourselves. Once the Federal Reserve put more emphasis on the money supply, not just by publicly announcing the target but by actually changing its operating techniques to increase the chances of actually hitting it, we would find it difficult to back off even if our decisions led to painfully high interest rates. More focus on the money supply also would be a way of telling the public that we meant business. People don't need an advanced course in economics to understand that inflation has something to do with too much money.

Only in retrospect did it become clear that the Fed would persist in a policy of disinflation and indeed that the Fed could control inflation without an unacceptably high rate of unemployment. There was no assurance that the political system would allow the Fed to maintain its independence through a severe recession. Credibility would require recovering from a recession without a revival of inflation. As it turned out, the Fed did not make headway in creating credibility until summer 1982. Initially, everything went wrong. Although Volcker's achievement in initiating a new monetary standard was epochal, his tenure as FOMC chairman would start and end badly.

The thirty-year bond rate, which was 9 percent in August 1979 when Volcker became FOMC chairman, rose to 9.9 percent in October 1979 and 12.3 percent in March 1980. In December 1979, the Soviet Union invaded Afghanistan. Bond rates rose over skepticism that President Carter would achieve a balanced budget despite increased defense spending (figure 18.4). For 1979, CPI inflation came in at 13 percent. At the time, Volcker was working with the administration on a budget that promised additional fiscal constraint. Being part of the team tripped Volcker up twice. First, he did not guide the FOMC into raising the funds rate in response to the December inflation scare evidenced by the increase in bond rates. Only in mid-February 1980 did the funds rate increase significantly. Second, and more serious, Volcker signed on to the Carter administration's credit control program.

With its promise of fiscal constraint, President Carter's economic program had a conservative cast. His advisers, who wanted to balance it with a populist component, seized on credit controls. In 1969, Democrats wanting to embarrass Nixon for not acting on inflation and believing that he would not invoke the controls, passed the Credit Control Act. Volcker was negatively disposed to the program but felt that he had to go along after Carter had accepted his recommendation for a conservative budget (Hetzel 2008, 156). On March 14, 1980, the Board of Governors announced the Special Credit Restraint Program (SCRP).

Prior to the SCRP, the economy had already begun to slow. The average of quarterly annualized rates of growth of real GDP declined from 6.2 percent from 1978Q2 through 1979Q1 to 1.9 percent from 1979Q2 through 1980Q1 (figure 19.1). Although the NBER cycle peak occurred in January 1980, the controls program sent the economy into a precipitous decline. The SCRP had complicated provisions for limiting the extension of credit by banks and money market funds (Schreft 1990). What counted, however, was the televised appeal by Carter asking the public to refrain from using credit. Volcker (2001, 448) later recounted:

> We put them [controls] on one day, with a big White House announcement by the President, and the economy collapses the next day. . . . To the very day, to the very week, there was a sharp reaction. Suddenly the stuff that was covered, like I guess automobile trailers or mobile homes, sales went to zero the next week. People were tearing up their credit cards and sending them in to the White House. "Mr. President we want to be patriotic." Consumption just collapsed.

Measured by the funds rate, monetary policy tightened prior to the SCRP. The funds rate rose from 10.2 percent after the July 11, 1979, FOMC meeting to 13.6 percent after the February 5, 1980, FOMC meeting (prior to introduction of the SCRP). After the March 18, 1980, FOMC meeting, which followed the introduction of the SCRP, the funds rate jumped to 17.8 percent. Although part of the increase reflected a 1 percentage point increase in the discount rate, most of the increase reflected credit stringency introduced by the controls. Banks feared the consequences of exceeding their credit limits. Because the FOMC was not directly controlling the funds rate, that fear increased credit stringency as reflected in the funds rate (Hetzel 1982). Like other recessions, the short-term real interest rate (funds rate) was at a cyclical high in the recession, going from −0.1 percent after the July 1979 FOMC meeting to 9.6 percent at the March 1980 meeting (figure 18.5). Unlike other recessions, however, the decline in money growth occurred with the peak in the business cycle rather than preceding it (figures 14.4 and 14.5).

When it became clear that the economy was in recession, on July 3, 1980, the Board ended the SCRP program. The subsequent rapid recovery in the economy became evident to the FOMC only in fall 1980. The Board staff forecast basically unchanged real GDP while actual real GDP came in at 7.7 percent and 8.1 percent in 1980Q4 and 1981Q1, respectively (figure 14.9). M1 growth also surged with the four-quarter growth rates averaging 6.4 percent over the quarters 1980Q3 to 1981Q2 (figure 14.4).

Despite genuine determination to break the cycle of go-stop monetary policy, the SCRP had initiated just such a cycle. As measured by bond rates, the Fed had lost credibility. In 1979, the thirty-year bond rate had reached a high of 10.5 percent. In 1981, it reached a high of 15.2 percent (figure 19.3). Volcker (2001, 449) explained what had happened in an interview:

VOLCKER: The economy just took off as fast as it had gone down. Then we really got behind the eight ball. . . . It was a sad experience, because we basically lost . . . 8 months.

MEHRLING: So it took 3 years instead of 2 years before you could really change expectations.

VOLCKER: Exactly.

Volcker (1994, 148) repeated the assessment later, "It was . . . a mostly wasted year [for] restoring credibility in the attack on inflation." The next time he would be in control. The funds rate went from 9 percent after the July 9, 1980, FOMC meeting to 20 percent after the May 18, 1981, meeting (figure 19.4, which shows quarterly averages).

When combined, the back-to-back recessions with cycle peaks in January 1980 and July 1981 exhibit the characteristics identified as the monetary contraction marker. The decline in real and nominal GDP started before the January 1980 cyclical peak (figure 19.1). Using the fall-off from trend in real personal consumption as a measure of the negative output gap, the economy entered a recession in January 1980 (figure 18.7). Figures 18.5 and 18.7 show the cyclically high level of short-term real interest rates in the back-to-back recessions. The short-term real interest rate (the real commercial paper rate) started rising strongly with the September 1979 FOMC meeting and peaked at 6.9 percent in March 1980 with the introduction of

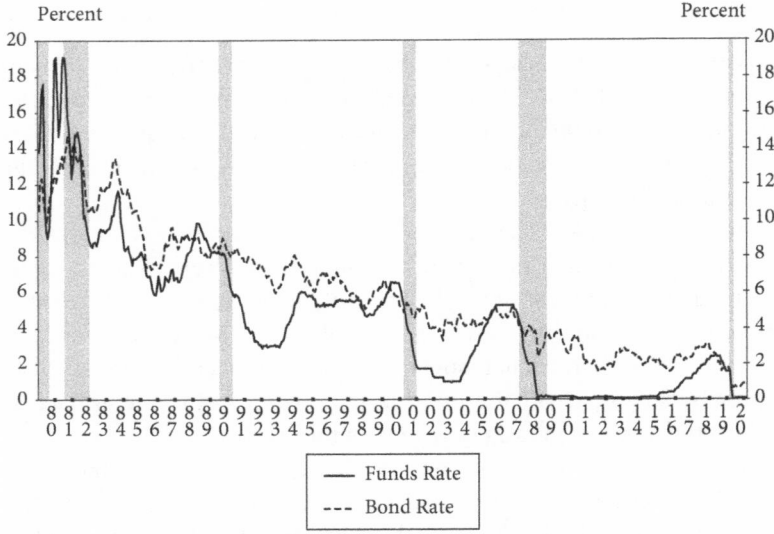

Figure 19.3. Funds Rate and Bond Rate

Monthly observations of the funds rate and the bond rate. Prior to 2000, the bond rate is the thirty-year Treasury constant maturity rate; thereafter, it is the ten-year Treasury constant maturity rate. Shaded areas indicate recessions. Heavy tick marks indicate December.

Source: St. Louis FRED

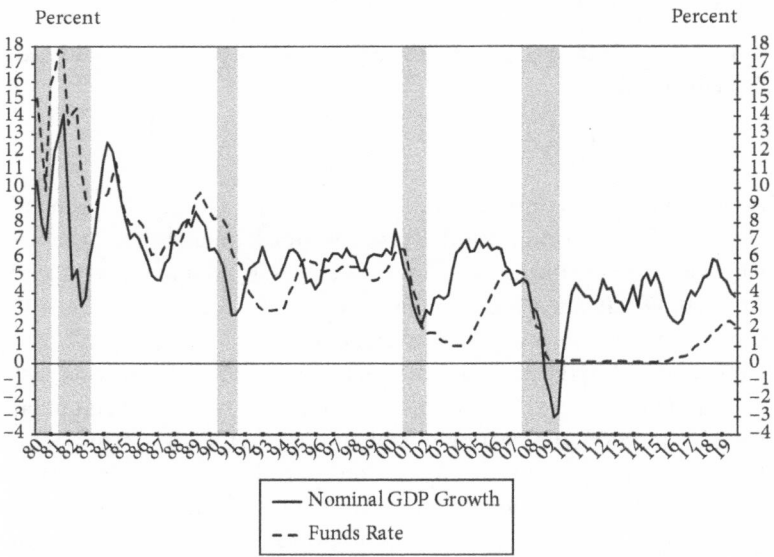

Figure 19.4. Funds Rate and Nominal GDP Growth

Quarterly observations of funds rate and four-quarter percentage changes in nominal GDP. Heavy tick marks indicate fourth quarter. Shaded areas indicate recession.

Source: St. Louis FRED

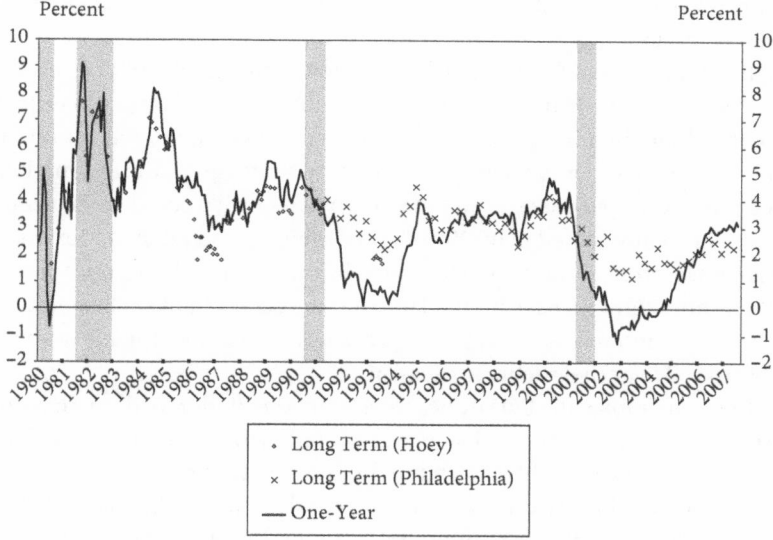

Figure 19.5. Long-Term and Short-Term Real Treasury Security Rates
The long-term real rate (Hoey) is the ten-year constant-maturity US Treasury bond
yield minus the predicted ten-year inflation rate from the "Decision Makers Poll"
conducted in the 1980s by Richard B. Hoey. Starting in October 1991, the long-term
real rate (Philadelphia) is the ten-year constant-maturity US Treasury bond yield
minus the predicted ten-year inflation rate from the Survey of Professional Forecasters.
This survey is conducted quarterly by the Federal Reserve Bank of Philadelphia
(formerly conducted by the American Statistical Association and the National Bureau
of Economic Research) and measures expected CPI inflation for a ten-year horizon.
The one-year real rate is monthly observations of the one-year constant maturity US
Treasury yield minus predicted one-year-ahead inflation from Global Insight. For a
description of the series, see chapter 18 appendix, "Real Rate of Interest." Heavy tick
marks indicate last observation of the year. Shaded areas indicate recession.

the SCRP. Figure 19.5 shows the cyclically elevated level of the one-year and
long-term real rates of interest for the latter recession.

The interaction between the FOMC's nonborrowed (free) reserves
procedures for targeting M1 and the decline in M1 with the introduction
of the SCRP caused a sharp decline in interest rates that lasted from May
1980 through September 1980 with the one-year real interest rate slightly
negative over this period (figures 14.4 and 19.5). Short-term real interest
rates then resumed a sharp rise peaking in May 1981 with a real funds rate
over 11 percent (figure 18.5). M1 growth, which had rebounded during the
period of low real interest rates (May 1980 through September 1980), declined sharply in 1981. Growth in four-quarter (shift-adjusted) M1 went

from 7.7 percent in 1981Q2, to 4.2 percent in 1981Q3, and 2.4 percent in 1981Q3 (figure 14.4).

In fall 1982, the FOMC formally abandoned the nonborrowed reserves procedures adopted in October 1979. Although the primary concern was the instability in money demand that had emerged with deregulation, the immediate catalyst was a need to lower interest rates given the international debt crisis that had emerged in June 1982 when Mexico could no longer pay its dollar-denominated debt. Brazil and Argentina soon joined Mexico. To finance a current account deficit created by oil imports, these countries had taken short-term loans from the large money center banks. The combination of high interest rates and an appreciation of the dollar made it impossible to roll over their debts to the banks.

In summer 1982, the FOMC began to lower the funds rate through reductions in the discount rate and increases in nonborrowed reserves. The bond market responded positively, and bond rates fell (figure 19.3). The FOMC had gained credibility through a significant decline in inflation underway since 1981Q2 (figure 19.6). The FOMC ceased lowering the funds rate in December 1982 when a reduction in the discount rate did not produce a reduction in bond rates.

The FOMC formally abandoned its money targets in fall 1983. The Monetary Control Act of 1980 rendered money targets infeasible. By phasing out Regulation Q, the act phased out interest-rate ceilings on savings deposits and allowed payment of interest on checkable deposits (NOW accounts). Checkable deposits (the NOW accounts) gained the characteristics of money market instruments. Because banks change the interest rates they pay on their deposits sluggishly relative to interest paid on money market instruments, when money market rates of interest rise, investors withdraw funds from bank deposits. Similarly, when market rates decline, investors reintermediate those funds into bank deposits. Consequently, money growth declines in booms when market rates rise relative to bank deposit rates, and conversely. This countercyclical behavior of money growth sends misleading signals for the Fed's interest-rate target. The Fed does not want to lower interest rates in a boom when money growth declines or raise rates in a recession when money growth rises.[2]

It is possible to date the start of the new monetary standard to a particular FOMC meeting, May 1983. At that meeting, the data indicated that the economy had begun to recover from the recession. The March 23, 1983,

2. For 1981, the Board staff constructed a "shift-adjusted" M1 series that removed such transfers. In 1981, the FOMC targeted this shift-adjusted series (Bennett 1982). Using shift-adjusted M1 for 1981 makes it possible to extend by one year the time over which M1 growth could serve as a measure of the stance of monetary policy.

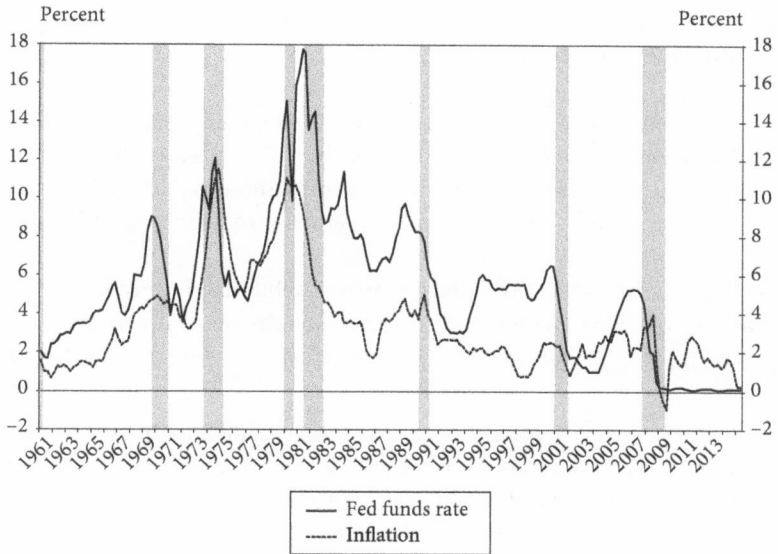

Figure 19.6. Fed Funds Rate and Inflation
Quarterly observations of four-quarter percentage changes in the personal
consumption expenditures deflator. Shaded areas indicate recessions. Heavy tick
marks indicate fourth quarter.
Source: St. Louis FRED

Greenbook (Board of Governors, Tealbook [formerly Greenbook], I-1) had
begun: "Incoming data confirm that the economy has begun to recover
from the prolonged contraction. . . . Production and employment showed
moderate gains on balance between December and February." The May 18,
1983, Greenbook (I-1) began: "The recovery in economic activity recently
has shown signs of greater vitality, with strong gains in production and employment in April."

Signs of incipient economic recovery, however, produced an inflation
scare. On March 3, 1983, the ten-year Treasury rate had been 10.23 percent.
On May 23, 1983, the day before the FOMC meeting, the rate had risen to
10.57 percent. The thirty-year bond rate went from 10.5 percent in April
1983 to 11.8 percent in August 1983 (figure 19.3). By all historical precedent, the FOMC should have left the funds rate unchanged. Signs of economic recovery were too recent to assure that the recovery would be self-
sustaining. Core PCE (personal consumption expenditures) inflation had
fallen steadily from a peak in February 1980 of 12.6 percent to 5.3 percent
over the first four months of 1983 (figure 18.4). Although the unemployment

rate had declined, it was still above 10 percent (figure 14.8). The May 1983 Greenbook reported:

> Labor demand is projected to continue to expand only gradually, in line with the moderate economic recovery projected. . . . As a result, the civilian jobless rate is projected to hover near 10½% through the middle of this year and then to decline slowly, remaining above 9% at the end of 1984.

Finally, the LDC (less developed countries) debt crisis festered.

Minnesota Fed president Gerald Corrigan (Board of Governors, *FOMC Transcript*, May 24, 1983, 27, 35–38) stated the issue while the FOMC split:

> CORRIGAN: Internationally, the case is overwhelming that we would be better off with lower interest rates and a lower exchange rate. . . . What will happen to bond rates if we do snug up a little, recognizing that they have already increased 50 basis points in the last two weeks? On the other hand, what would happen to bond rates if we didn't do anything? . . . That is the $64 question.

> SOLOMON (N.Y. PRESIDENT): It will look as though we're trying to spoil the recovery. . . . People are just not going to understand.

> ROBERTS (ST. LOUIS PRESIDENT): . . . Snugging would be positively interpreted. . . . We would more likely to get a decline in [long] rates than an increase.

> GOV. TEETERS: I have never seen the short-term rates go up without the long-term rates going up. . . . If we want the long rate down . . . we need to lower the federal funds rate, not increase it.

The FOMC did raise the funds rate in steps from 8.5 percent at the March 1983 meeting, to 8.75 percent at the May 1983 meeting, to 9.375 percent at the July 1983 meeting, and to 9.5 percent at the August 1983 meeting. In doing so, the Volcker FOMC changed policy to being preemptive with respect to inflation. In the terminology here, LAW with trade-offs became LAW with credibility. Volcker (1983, 4–5, 7, 9, 11–12) told economists:

> The years of inflation . . . have understandably left deep scars. . . . As the economy grows . . . there will be stronger temptations to anticipate inflation. . . . Progress against inflation is . . . typically reversed in the second year of expansion, with further acceleration expected before the next recession. . . . The need remains to convey a sense of conviction. . . .

Growth in nominal GNP and money and credit will need to be reduced over time. . . . Both our policy decisions . . . and your expectations . . . should be strongly conditioned by that broad objective and strategy—I am tempted to say by that "general rule."

In 1984, financial markets handed the FOMC another inflation scare. The thirty-year bond rate rose from 11.75 percent in January 1984 to 13.44 percent in June and remained high at 13.21 percent in July (figure 19.3). The recovery gained momentum with the four-quarter growth rate of real GDP for the quarters 1983Q4 to 1984Q3 averaging 7.3 percent (figure 19.1). Inflation also stopped declining with four-quarter PCE inflation averaging 4.3 percent over the quarters 1982Q4 to 1984Q2 (figure 19.6). The FOMC raised the funds rate from 9.375 percent after the January 1984 FOMC meeting to 11.625 percent after the August 1984 meeting. Given the perilous state of the financial system, those increases displayed the determination of the Volcker FOMC to master inflationary expectations. In May 1984, a run began on Continental Illinois, which had made loans to Penn Square in Oklahoma. Penn Square defaulted when oil prices declined. By August 1984, Continental had borrowed $7.5 billion from the Fed (Hetzel 2012a, chap. 9).

Despite the noise created by the short stop-go cycle associated with the Carter credit controls initiated on March 15, 1980, and abandoned shortly afterward in July, the Volcker disinflation is the poster child for a recession caused by the FOMC engineering cyclically high real rates of interest and then maintaining them past the cycle peak. This pattern, labeled here the monetary contraction marker, appears in table 3.14 in chapter 3 for the recession with the cyclical peak in 1981Q3. Figure 18.5 shows the real rate of interest, and figures 14.4 and 14.5 show the monetary deceleration.

19.3. THE LOUVRE ACCORD

The Volcker era ended with expansionary monetary policy out of concern for the foreign exchange value of the dollar (Hetzel 2008, chaps. 14 and 17). With the Louvre Accord in early 1987, the FOMC became reluctant to raise the funds rate out of a desire to encourage stimulative policy in Germany and Japan. Inflation trended down in the first part of the 1980s but rose starting in 1987 (figure 19.6). A full return to near price stability and credibility fell to the Greenspan FOMC.

In an effort parallel to that of producing disinflation, Volcker worked to protect the solvency of the large money center banks in New York as well as the Bank of America. For a while, he seemed successful, but then everything started to unravel in 1985 and 1986. The seeds of the problem sprouted in

the 1970s with OPEC-engineered rises in the price of oil. The OPEC countries, which ran current account surpluses, placed their oil revenues in large
money center banks, which lent the funds to the LDCs (less developed countries) importing oil and running current account deficits. That LDC debt became unmanageable with the rise in interest rates and the appreciation of the
dollar in the early 1980s. Volcker promoted IMF loans to the LDCs, which
the LDCs used to make the interest payments on their debt. The longer-run
solution was supposed to be internal reform in the LDCs to reduce structural internal deficits and to increase their exports to generate the foreign
exchange required to repay the IMF lending. Protectionism in developed
countries impeded the ability of the LDCs to increase their exports.

The United States economy recovered more rapidly than the economies
of the other OECD countries, which remained focused on disinflation. As
a result, the United States incurred large current account deficits. The appreciation of the dollar associated with capital inflows due to the Reagan
tax cuts, which reduced taxes on capital, reduced US exports. Protectionist sentiment grew in Congress. Unchecked, US protectionism would limit
the ability of the LDCs to export and repay their debts to the money center
banks and to the IMF. Volcker wanted the developed countries, especially
Germany and Japan, to pursue stimulative policies, which would expand
their economies and increase their imports.

In return, these countries wanted a lower US government deficit. The
prevailing belief was in the "twin deficits." A large government deficit produced capital inflows that created a current account deficit and a strong
dollar. The LDC debt crisis festered, and in early 1987 Brazil threatened to
default on its debt. Domestic and international pressures in favor of a depreciated dollar and lower interest rates in the United States increased. The
initial response was the Plaza Accord, signed in September 1985, designed
to depreciate the dollar through foreign exchange intervention. The dollar did depreciate, but the depreciation did not eliminate the US current
account deficit. The result was the Louvre Accord. Ultimately, it set off a
developed-country go-stop cycle.[3]

19.4. A GRAPHICAL OVERVIEW OF MONETARY POLICY IN THE GREAT MODERATION

Formula 19.1 summarizes the consistent part of the Volcker-Greenspan
monetary policy:

3. For the way in which the Louvre Accord initiated inflationary monetary policies
in Japan and Germany, see Hetzel (1999, 2002b, 2003, and 2004).

$$(19.1) \ i_t = i_{t-1} + a(\pi_t^e - \pi^*) + \beta \Delta RU_t, a, \beta > 0,$$

where i_t is the funds rate, π_t^e is expected inflation, π^* an implicit inflation target, and ΔRU_t an estimate of the persistent change in resource utilization. It captures a growth gap—the extent to which output is growing faster (slower) than potential output. Formula 19.1 should be understood in the context of the Volcker-Greenspan era before the Fed earned credibility. That is, expected inflation, π_t^e, did not come from the FOMC's rule but was a positive function of actual inflation and the growth gap, ΔRU_t.

In a later formulation (equation 29.1, in chap. 29) for a regime of complete credibility, the latter two right-hand-side variables are expressed as the FOMC's forecasts. Also, the later formulation includes an output gap missing in formula 19.1. Not until after 1994, when the Fed finally established credibility for price stability, could the FOMC respond to emergence of a negative output gap with sharp reductions in the funds rate. It did so in in the 2001 recession when it lowered the funds rate from 6.5 percent in December 2000 to 1.75 percent in December 2001 with no adverse reaction from bond markets.

With formula 19.1, the FOMC moves the funds rate away from its current value in response to a growth gap (the difference between "actual" and "sustainable" real growth) and a credibility gap (the difference between expected inflation and the FOMC's implicit inflation target). Figure 19.7 plots proxies for actual and sustainable real growth (GDP). The proxy for actual real growth comes from forecasts contained in the Greenbook. For FOMC meetings in the first or second month of the quarter, it is the forecast of growth for the contemporaneous quarter. For FOMC meetings in the last month of the quarter, it is the forecast for the succeeding quarter. The proxy for "sustainable" real growth uses longer-run Greenbook forecasts for real output growth. For FOMC meetings in the first five months of the year, it is the forecasted value in the January Greenbook for growth between the fourth quarters of the prior year and current year. For the remainder of the meetings, it is the annualized two-quarter growth rate in the June Greenbook for growth between the second and fourth quarters of the current year. Although these figures are forecasts, they are contingent on a funds rate path consistent with maintaining the staff's best guess of the inflation rate the FOMC considers acceptable. They are taken as proxies for sustainable growth.

Figure 19.8 plots changes in the funds rate and the growth gap (the difference between the actual and sustainable growth proxies from figure 19.7). Diamonds mark instances of funds-rate increases not associated with positive growth gaps—inflation scares. As shown in table 19.1, a regression of

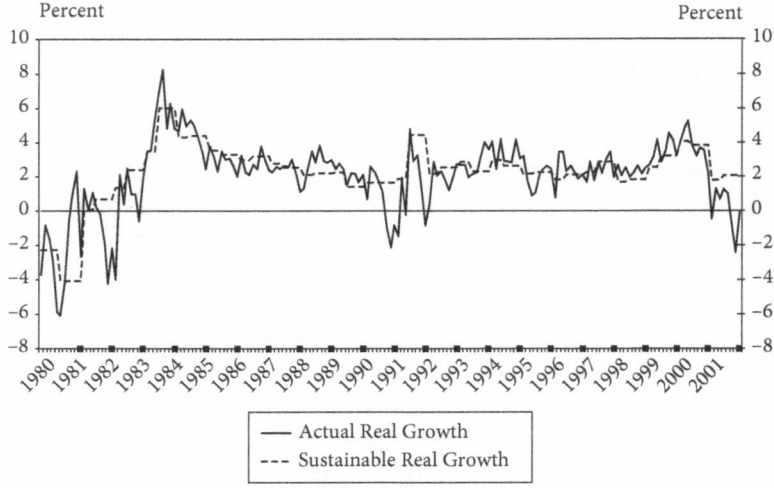

Percent ... Percent

- Actual Real Growth
- - - Sustainable Real Growth

Figure 19.7. Actual and Sustainable Real Output Growth

Actual real output growth is an estimate of the annualized quarterly rate of growth of real output (GNP before 1992, GDP thereafter) available at FOMC meetings. If an FOMC meeting is in one of the first two months of a quarter, it is for the contemporaneous quarter. If the meeting is in the last month of a quarter, it is for the succeeding quarter. Sustainable growth is a longer-run forecast of real output growth from the Greenbook. For the first three FOMC meetings in a year, it is the real output growth predicted to occur over the four-quarter period ending in the fourth quarter found in the January Greenbook. For the remainder of the meetings, it is the two-quarter annualized growth rate ending in the fourth quarter found in the June Greenbook. Observations correspond to FOMC meetings. Heavy tick marks indicate December FOMC meeting.

Table 19.1. A Funds-Rate Reaction Function

Δ FR = 0.15 GG + 0.016 MISSI + 0.32 Δ BR + 0.15 Δ BRL1 + û				
(8.0)	(0.42)	(5.2)	(2.5)	
CRSQ = 0.45	SEE = 0.26	DW = 1.6	DF = 148	Dates: 2/1983 to 12/2001

Notes: Δ FR is the change in the funds rate following FOMC meetings. GG is the growth gap: the difference between actual and sustainable real output growth shown in figure 19.8. MISSI is the difference between "actual" and "targeted" inflation. It is calculated analogously to the calculation of the growth gap. Δ BR is the change in the thirty-year bond rate from the day after the prior FOMC meeting to the day prior to the FOMC meeting and is set equal to zero after 1995. Δ BRL1 is the lagged value of the change in the bond rate. Inflation predictions are for the implicit GNP deflator prior to 1988, CPI less food and energy from 1989 through May 2000, and PCE less food and energy chain-weighted price index thereafter. Parentheses enclose *t*-statistics. CRSQ is the corrected R-squared; SEE, the standard error of estimate; DW, the Durbin-Watson statistic; and DF, degrees of freedom. Absolute values of *t*-statistics are in parentheses.

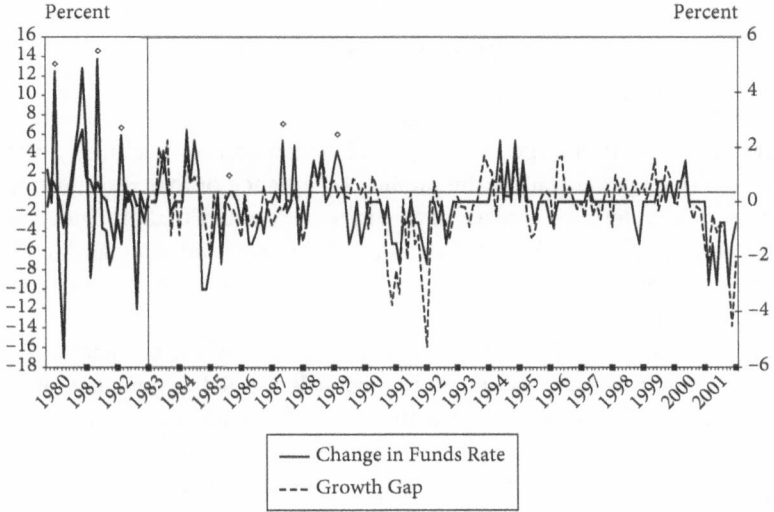

Figure 19.8. Growth Gap and Funds Rate Changes
The growth gap is the difference between the actual and sustainable values shown in
figure 19.7. Left scale is for the 1980–82 period. Right scale is for the subsequent period.
The funds rate is the target set at FOMC meetings. Changes in the funds rate are
multiplied by three. Diamonds mark the following dates: (1) March 1980; (2) May 1981;
(3) February 1982; (4) August 1985; (5) May 1987; (6) February 1989. Heavy tick marks
indicate December FOMC meetings.

changes in the funds rate on the growth gap shows a statistically significant
relationship (regression from Hetzel 2008, table 21.1, 265). As a proxy for
the credibility gap, the regression uses changes in bond rates, which are
also statistically significant. The bond-rate variable is set to zero after 1995.
Establishment of credibility after the 1994 inflation scare caused the bond
rate to lose its explanatory power. The regression runs from February 1983
through December 2001. A positive correlation exists between changes in
the funds-rate target and the two independent variables: the growth gap
and bond-rate changes.[4]

4. Taylor rules embed the assumption that the FOMC controlled inflation in the
Volcker-Greenspan era through responding to realized inflation combined with a willingness to increase the funds rate more than increases in realized inflation. However,
the Taylor rule fails to capture the preemptive character of policy according to which
the FOMC raised the funds rate in response to increases in expected inflation signaled
by inflation scares even when actual inflation remained quiescent. To test this feature
of the Taylor rule, the regression equation included a proxy for the gap between actual
inflation and a proxy for an implicit FOMC inflation target. The implicit target keeps
inflation on a path consistent with a longer-run target of price stability. The proxy for
the miss between actual and targeted (implicit) inflation was constructed analogously

19.5. A NEW MONETARY STANDARD

The FOMC chairmanships of Volcker and Greenspan created a new monetary standard. It emerged because each accepted responsibility for the inflationary expectations of the public. Acceptance of that responsibility imposed an underlying consistency on monetary policy that precluded any attempt to exploit Phillips curve trade-offs between inflation and unemployment. Compare the statements of each. Volcker (1980b, 4) observed:

> The idea of a sustainable "trade off" between inflation and prosperity . . . broke down as businessmen and individuals learned to anticipate inflation, and to act in this anticipation. . . . The result is that orthodox monetary or fiscal measures designed to stimulate could potentially be thwarted by the self-protective instincts of financial and other markets. Quite specifically, when financial markets jump to anticipate inflationary consequences, and workers and businesses act on the same assumption, there is room for grave doubt that the traditional measures of purely demand stimulus can succeed in their avowed purpose of enhancing real growth.

Greenspan (US Congress 1993a, 55–56) observed:

> The effects of policy on the economy depend critically on how market participants react to actions taken by the Federal Reserve, as well as on expectations of our future actions. . . . The huge losses suffered by bondholders during the 1970s and early 1980s sensitized them to the slightest sign . . . of rising inflation. . . . An overly expansionary monetary policy, or even its anticipation, is embedded fairly soon in higher inflationary expectations and nominal bond yields. Producers incorporate expected cost increases quickly into their own prices, and eventually any increase in output disappears as inflation rises.

In the 1970s, the policy-making and professional consensus prevailed that inflation arose from cost-push inflation propagated through a wage-price spiral. The inflationary expectations that drove the spiral emerged out of a competition among large corporations and unions with market power

---

to the proxy for actual and sustainable real output growth. The statistically insignificant coefficient on the inflation gap contradicts the Taylor rule assumption that the FOMC responded directly to observed inflation.

that competed to increase their share of a given economic pie. This expectational environment presumably forced the Fed into making painful choices between unemployment and inflation. The monetary control required for price stability would require socially harmful "high" interest rates that would punish housing and implement price stability "on the backs of the workers." The result was "stagflation"—the combination of high inflation with no payoff in the form of lowered unemployment.

Monetarists challenged this nonmonetary theory of inflation. According to Milton Friedman, the monetary control required for price stability would allow the price system an unfettered ability to work to provide for economic stability. Starting with Robert Lucas, under the banner of rational expectations, a small group of economists attributed stagflation to a lack of central bank credibility for the control of inflation. Although monetarists and rational-expectations adherents constituted a small minority in the 1970s, the success of the Volcker disinflation altered profoundly the intellectual environment. The argument conducted by Keynesians about whether inflation arose from aggregate-demand (demand-pull) or cost-push pressures with the implication that incomes policies should be used to deal with the latter lost relevance when the Volcker FOMC simply accepted responsibility for inflation. Nonmonetary theories of inflation lost relevance when Volcker demonstrated that the central bank could control inflation without periodic recourse to "high" unemployment. The demonstrated success of central bank control of inflation through consistent application of policy (a rule) gave credence to the ideas of Lucas (1972 [1981]; 1976 [1981]; and 1980 [1981]) and of Kydland and Prescott (1977).

A preemptive monetary policy focused on preventing the emergence of inflation implied a reaction function for the funds rate that caused the real funds rate to track the economy's natural rate of interest. Such a monetary policy contrasted with the activist aggregate-demand management of the stop-go era in which the FOMC effectively moved the short-term real interest rate relative to its natural value in an attempt to control a trade-off between inflation and output. Monetary policy went from superseding the working of the price system to allowing it to work unimpeded.

CHAPTER 20

The Greenspan FOMC

Summary: Under Paul Volcker and Alan Greenspan, the monetary standard evolved toward LAW with credibility. With these procedures, the
FOMC moves the funds rate in a measured but persistent way to counter unsustainable strength or weakness in the economy subject to the
discipline that bond markets believe that those changes will cumulate
to whatever extent required to maintain price stability. Like Volcker,
Greenspan believed in the fundamental necessity of monetary policy to
shape inflationary expectations. Coming out of the 1990 recession, he
lowered the funds rate only cautiously because the inflation premiums
built into bond rates were inconsistent with his goal of returning to price
stability. The strong funds-rate increases in 1994 were the FOMC's decisive response to an inflation scare and the need to establish credibility.
Credibility allowed Greenspan to depart from these procedures at the
time of the Asia crisis, but in the context of his entire tenure the departure was brief.

Like Volcker, Greenspan wanted to create a monetary standard characterized by expectational stability for prices. To this end, Greenspan
treated the inflation premium in long-term bond rates as an intermediate target. A stable nominal anchor in the form of expectational stability
for prices required elimination of a positive correlation between cyclical
strength in the economy and expected trend inflation. Similarly, it required elimination of a positive correlation between inflation shocks and
expected trend inflation. Restoration of nominal expectational stability
required the implementation of monetary policy through a consistent
strategy. The result was reduced variability in both inflation and real output relative to the stop-go period.

Because central bankers operate in the money market, they naturally
seek expectational stability. However, is the central bank responsible for
the expectational stability of asset prices or of goods prices? By choosing the latter, William McChesney Martin moved the Fed away from real
bills views. Burns also placed great weight on inflationary expectations,
but he wanted fiscal policy and incomes policies to control them. Volcker brought the Fed back to Martin's choice of using inflationary expec-

tations in financial markets as the canary in the coal mine. The desire
to restore nominal expectational stability imposed a discipline on monetary policy in the Volcker and Greenspan eras.

Alan Greenspan was a student of Arthur Burns in the late 1940s at Columbia
University. Greenspan understood the world through the NBER framework
of Burns and Mitchell with cyclical fluctuations driven by the psychology of
the businessman. Greenspan's defining difference from Burns was his liber-
tarian view making unacceptable the control of inflation through interference with the price setting of firms. Although Greenspan at the time of the
Asia crisis departed from the policy labeled here "LAW with credibility,"
which takes price stability as the goal of a central bank, the departure was
brief. His desire to achieve the nominal expectational stability he associated with the gold standard imposed a rule-like consistency to policy that
restored credibility for price stability.

Greenspan (US Congress 1999a, 61) testified to Congress: "Our current
discretionary monetary policy has difficulty anchoring the price level over
time in the same way that the gold standard did in the last century." Greenspan (US Congress 1993b, 47–49) testified: "The process of easing monetary policy . . . had to be closely controlled and generally gradual because
of the constraint imposed by the marketplace's acute sensitivity to inflation. . . . . The role of expectations in the inflation process is crucial."

Greenspan was FOMC chairman from August 1987 to January 2006.
His great achievement was to finish the work of Paul Volcker by creating a
monetary standard with a stable nominal anchor. To achieve that goal, he
initiated the recession with a July 1990 cycle peak. In 1994, with dramatic
increases in the funds rate in response to an inflation scare, he restored Fed
credibility for near price stability. In response to the Asia crisis, Greenspan
initiated a mini-go-stop cycle, with the 2001 recession the stop phase of
monetary policy. The departure from a policy focused on price stability was
a brief one, however. Figure 20.1 shows how Paul Volcker and Alan Greenspan restored the price stability lost in the prior stop-go era of monetary
policy.

20.1. RESTORING A STABLE NOMINAL ANCHOR

The desire to restore the nominal expectational stability lost in the stop-go
era imposed an overall consistency on monetary policy in the Greenspan
era. That consistency is summarized here as LAW with credibility. Greenspan (2005, 2) said, "The Federal Reserve and most other central banks
generally pursue price stability and, consistent with that goal, ease when

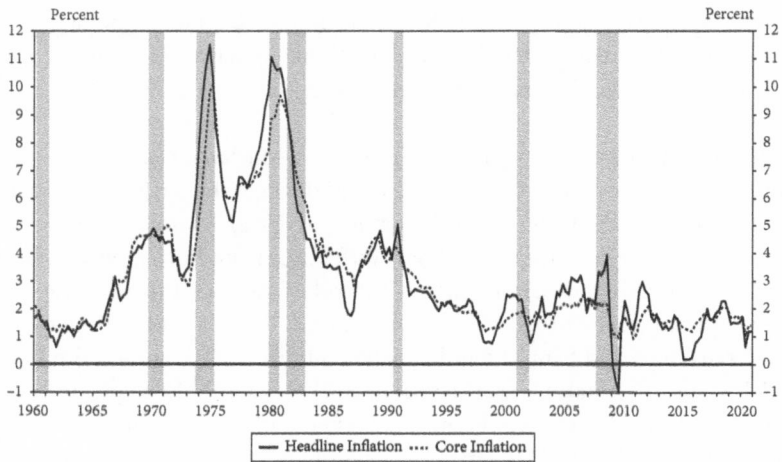

Figure 20.1. Headline and Core PCE Inflation: 1960–2020
Quarterly observations of four-quarter percentage changes in headline and core
personal consumption expenditures (PCE) deflator. Shaded areas indicate recessions.
Tick marks indicate fourth quarter.
Source: St. Louis FRED

economic conditions soften and tighten when they firm." Until the early
1990s, Greenspan and the FOMC set target ranges for M2 to establish credibility for restraining growth in aggregate nominal demand over time to
return to price stability. When M2 demand became unstable, Greenspan
watched aggregate nominal demand. Greenspan (Board of Governors,
FOMC Transcript, November 17, 1992, 45–46):

> There is no debate within this Committee . . . that a non-inflationary
> environment is best. . . . We have seen that to drive nominal GDP, let's
> assume at 4½ percent, in our old philosophy we would have said that
> [requires] 4½ percent growth in M2. . . . I'm basically arguing that we are
> really . . . using a nominal GDP goal of which the money supply relation-
> ships are technical mechanisms to achieve that.

Concern for the behavior of bond rates also provided consistency.
Greenspan (US Congress 1993a, 55–56) testified:

> The [Humphrey-Hawkins] Act . . . requires the Federal Reserve "to pro-
> mote effectively the goals of maximum employment, stable prices, and
> moderate long-term interest rates." The goal of moderate long-term in-
> terest rates is particularly relevant. . . . Lower intermediate- and long-

term interest rates and inflation are essential to the structural adjustments in our economy and monetary policy thus has given considerable
weight to helping such rates move lower.

LAW with trade-offs became LAW with credibility in the Volcker-
Greenspan era because of the rejection of attempts to trade off between
output gaps and inflation. Such attempts would have revived the association created in the prior stop-go era between activist aggregate-demand
management and inflation. Price stability required a preemptive monetary
policy. Indicative of the change was the transformation of the unemployment rate from a target to an indicator. Greenspan (US Congress 1999c,
16) testified: "Focusing on a specific unemployment rate as an economic
goal . . . is very shortsighted. I think what you try to do is to get maximum
sustainable growth. . . . What unemployment rate falls out as a consequence
of that policy . . . would be the appropriate unemployment rate."
Similarly, Greenspan (US Congress 1999c, 44) testified:

> Surges in economic growth are not necessarily unsustainable—provided
> they do not exceed the sum of the rate of growth in the labor force and
> productivity for a protracted period. However, when productivity is ac-
> celerating, it is very difficult to gauge when an economy is in the process
> of overheating. In such circumstances, assessing conditions in labor mar-
> kets can be helpful in forming those judgments. Employment growth has
> exceeded the growth in working-age population this past year by almost
> ½ percentage point. . . . It implies that real GDP is growing faster than
> its potential. . . . There can be little doubt that, if the pool of job seek-
> ers shrinks sufficiently, upward pressures on wage costs are inevitable,
> short . . . of a repeal of the law of supply and demand.

The focus on growth gaps constrained the FOMC's reaction function to
move the funds rate in a way that tracked the natural rate of interest.

20.2. A ROCKY START WITH LOUVRE AND
THE 1987 STOCK MARKET CRASH

The Louvre Accord turned into a landmine for Greenspan (Hetzel 2008,
chap. 14). Under the agreement, as desired by the United States, the countries with large current account surpluses, Germany and Japan, would
stimulate their economies to increase imports. In return, the United States
would reduce its fiscal deficit. All the signatories, including Germany, Japan,
Canada, France, and Britain, agreed to intervene in the foreign exchange

markets to prevent additional depreciation of the dollar. However, the foundation was structurally flawed.

The US commitment in the form of Gramm-Rudman to reduce the deficit appeared to support the agreement. However, domestic politics upended Gramm-Rudman. A Supreme Court decision invalidated the requirement for automatic spending cuts. The Republican administration feared that congressional Democrats would use it to force a tax hike and cuts in the defense budget. Congress drew from a deep bag of tricks to prevent spending cuts. Also, Louvre effectively required that the behavior of the US economy not require the Fed to raise interest rates. Higher rates in the United States would cause the dollar to appreciate. The other side of that was a depreciation in the German mark, which the Bundesbank disliked because of the belief that it would cause inflation in Germany. To complicate the situation, the Japanese wanted a weaker yen to stimulate exports. However, the US Treasury did not want the Japanese to believe that would occur through a hike in US rates rather than a reduction in Japanese rates.

The complicated fabric of the Louvre Accord began to unravel in spring 1987. The dollar had ceased depreciating with the announcement of the Accord on February 22, 1987. Depreciation resumed, however, when the United States threatened Japan with 100 percent tariffs on its electronic products. Dollar depreciation revived fears of inflation in the bond market. Depreciation also threatened the capital inflows from Japan that supported the bond and equity markets. The inflation scare began in April 1987 when the thirty-year bond rate rose from 7.4 percent at the beginning of the year to 8.5 percent. Unlike previous inflation scares, the FOMC responded with only a limited increase in the funds rate (figure 19.3).

Volcker later expressed regret at not having raised the discount rate (Volcker and Gyohten 1992, 284). However, the politics of Louvre stood in the way. The Treasury and the Fed wanted to pressure Germany and Japan to lower their interest rates and did not want to send a contradictory message with higher domestic rates. During the inflation scare, President Reagan surprised markets by failing to reappoint Volcker. Instead, he appointed Alan Greenspan as Board of Governors chairman. Although he had been Gerald Ford's head of the CEA, at this time Greenspan lacked Volcker's stature, and markets feared he would not be independent of the administration. Such transition issues always arise when there is no rule to guarantee continuity across different leadership.

The rise in bond rates that preceded the stock market crash on October 19 warned of an inflation scare that the Fed failed to address. The *New York Times* (Wyatt 1997, sec. 3, 1) later quoted then governor Wayne Angell:

By the time Federal Reserve policy makers agreed that inflation was pick-
ing up again, "we were behind the curve," Mr. Angell said. . . . Mr. Greenspan took office in mid-August and the Fed finally raised rates on Sept. 4,
but by then world markets had lost confidence in its resolve. "I think
there was a question about the Federal Reserve's credibility," Mr. Angell
said. "The 30-year bond rate would not have been able to rise will above
10 percent without some people making pretty heavy bets that monetary
policy would not be able to bring inflation down."

Greenspan responded to the rise in bond rates by raising the funds rate
by ¾ of a percentage point to 7⅜ percent at the September 1987 FOMC
meeting. The thirty-year bond rate, however, continued to rise peaking at
10.25 percent on October 19. Louvre crashed on October 15 when Treasury
Secretary Baker threatened to depreciate the dollar in retaliation for the
unwillingness of Germany to lower interest rates. The dollar depreciated.
The willingness of the US Treasury to threaten a depreciation of the dollar
backfired. The threat disrupted capital inflows from Japan and produced
higher bond rates. Governor Angell (*Wall Street Journal* 1994) said later,
"The precipitating factor in the 1987 stock market crash was the notion that
the administration would accept a depreciating currency." The high level of
bond rates left the stock market overvalued. Figure 20.2 shows the ten-year
bond yield and the ratio of forecasted earnings for the S&P 500 companies
to the S&P 500 price index. The market crash appears in the sharp rise in
the S&P 500 E/P ratio in late 1987.

Because of Louvre, the FOMC was slow to respond to a pickup in nominal GDP growth. From 1986Q4 to 1987Q4, nominal GDP growth rose from
3.7 percent to 5.9 percent while the funds rate rose only from 6 percent to
6.8 percent (figure 19.4). The FOMC feared a slowdown in the economy
because of the stock market crash. Greenbook forecasts of growth fell to
just under 1.5 percent (figure 14.9). The FOMC lowered the funds rate from
7⅜ percent after the September 1987 FOMC meeting to 6½ percent after
the February 1988 meeting. The real funds rate fell to 1.9 percent with the
March 1988 FOMC meeting (figure 18.5). However, strength in output
growth flat footed the FOMC with four-quarter rates of growth of real GDP
averaging 4.3 percent over the quarters 1987Q4 through 1988Q3. Inflation
(four-quarter core PCE) went from 2.8 percent in 1987Q1 to 4.7 percent
in 1989Q1 (figure 20.1). That rise significantly increased the difficulty the
Greenspan FOMC would confront in returning to price stability.

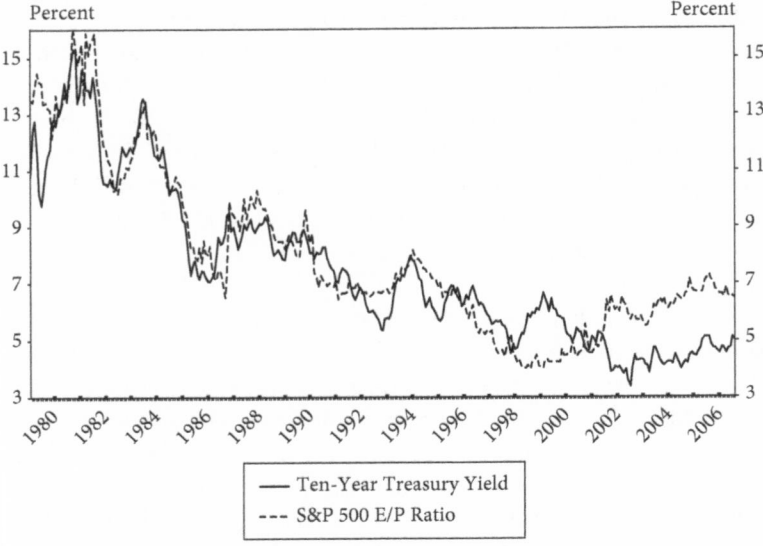

Figure 20.2. S&P 500 Earnings/Price Ratio (Forward)
and Ten-Year Treasury Bond Yield

The bond yield is the ten-year Treasury constant maturity yield. The earnings-price
ratio is the I/B/E/S International Inc. consensus estimate of earnings over the coming
twelve months divided by the S&P 500 price index. Observations are monthly and
reflect midmonth prices.

20.3. THE 1990 RECESSION, THE JOBLESS RECOVERY, AN INFLATION SCARE, AND FINALLY CREDIBILITY

By the March 1988 FOMC meeting, it had become obvious that the feared
slowdown subsequent to the stock market crash had not occurred, and
that the economy was growing strongly (figures 14.9 and 20.3). Moreover,
markets handed Greenspan an inflation scare with the thirty-year bond rate
going from 8.4 percent in February 1988 to 9.2 percent in April 1988. Greenspan had to pursue his goal of restoring price stability with these handi-
caps. Early in 1989, Greenspan (US Congress 1989, February 22, 167–68)
told Congress, "Let me stress that the current rate of inflation, let alone an
increase, is not acceptable, and our policies are designed to reduce inflation in coming years. This restraint will involve containing pressures on our
productive resources."

The 1990 recession displays the hallmarks of contractionary monetary
policy labeled as the monetary contraction marker (table 3.15 and figure 20.3). With the March 1988 FOMC meeting, Greenspan began to raise

the funds rate. It went from 6½ percent at the February 1988 meeting to 9⅞ percent at the May 1989 meeting. Against a backdrop of undesirably high inflation, the FOMC raised the short-term real rate of interest while the economy weakened and a negative output gap arose (figure 20.3). Figures 18.5 and 19.5, respectively, show relatively high short-term and long-term rates of interest persisting past the cyclical peak of July 1990.

The Greenspan FOMC brought down (four-quarter core PCE) infla-tion from 4.6 percent in 1989Q1 to 1.3 percent over the interval 1998Q2 to 1999Q3. After the contractionary monetary policy of the recession (cycle peak in July 1990 and cycle trough in March 1991), Greenspan lowered the funds rate only cautiously out of concern that the slow reduction in

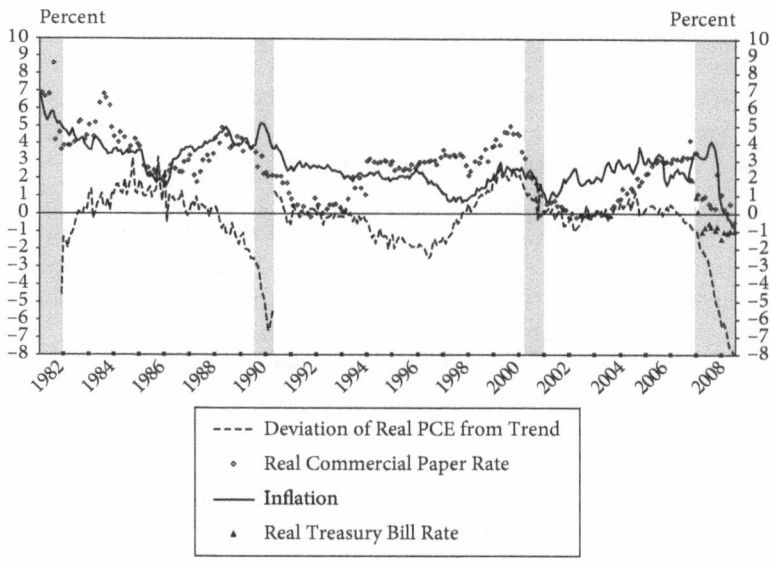

Figure 20.3. Deviation of Real PCE from Trend, Short-
Term Real Interest Rate, and Inflation: 1982–2008

For the series "deviation of real PCE from trend," observations are calculated using the natural logarithm of monthly observations of real personal consumption expenditures (PCE) normalized using the value at the prior business cycle trough. Trend lines are fitted to these observations from the prior cycle peak to the subsequent cycle peak and extended through the subsequent recession. Deviation of real PCE from trend is the difference between the actual values and trend lines. Inflation is twelve-month percentage changes in the personal consumption expenditures deflator. The real interest rate is the commercial paper rate (and the Treasury bill rate in the 2008–9 recession) minus the corresponding inflation forecast made by the staff of the Board of Governors (figure 18.5). Data on PCE and the PCE deflator from Haver Analytics. Shaded areas indicate recessions. Heavy tick marks indicate December.

bond rates indicated inflationary expectations inconsistent with the move to price stability. The result earned the term "jobless recovery." The unemployment rate had reached a cyclical low in March 1989 of 5 percent, climbed to 7.8 percent in June 1992, and in May 1993, almost three years after the cyclical peak, was still relatively high at 7.1 percent.

Greenspan observed bond rates throughout the recovery not just during inflation scares. At the November 1992 FOMC meeting, when Richmond president Robert Black (Board of Governors, *FOMC Transcript*, November 17, 1992, 45–46) said that he doubted that the public expected a return to price stability, Greenspan replied, "We will know they are convinced when we see the 30-year Treasury at 5½ percent." Greenspan (1993) told the Economic Club:

> The goal of low-to-moderate long-term interest rates is particularly relevant. . . . We have eased in measured steps . . . to reassure investors that inflation is likely to remain subdued, thereby fostering the decline in longer-term interest rates. . . . Monetary policy . . . has given considerable weight to encouraging the downtrend of such rates.

Persistent reductions in the funds rate lowered the real interest rate, which neared zero at the end of 1991 (figure 18.5). The economy grew steadily in 1992 and 1993 (figure 19.1). In November 1993, bond rates started to rise again, going from 5.9 percent to 8.1 percent in November 1994 (figure 19.3). Earlier, in late 1987, when the unemployment rate fell below 6 percent, inflation had begun to rise. Based on that experience and given the steady decline in the unemployment rate, which reached 6.6 percent in January 1994, policy makers believed that inflation would start rising in 1994. The May 1994 Greenbook reported a staff estimate for the NAIRU of 6.5 percent. In the event, in a contradiction of a stable Phillips curve relationship, (four-quarter core PCE) inflation fell to 1.2 percent in 1998Q2 while the unemployment fell to 4.4 percent in that quarter (figure 18.3 and figure 14.8).

Initially in 1994, the FOMC failed to quell the inflation scare. After quarter-point increases in the funds rate at the February and March FOMC meetings, the FOMC became significantly more aggressive. It hiked the funds rate ½ of a percentage point at the May 1994 meeting, ½ of a percentage point at the August meeting, ¾ of a percentage point at the November meeting, and ½ of a percentage point at the February 1995 meeting. By the February 1995 meeting, the funds rate had risen from 3 percent to 6 percent. In 1994, monetary policy was "preemptive" in that the FOMC raised the funds rate without having first observed an increase in inflation. In doing so, the Fed finally vanquished the bond market vigilantes and achieved credibility.

20.4. THE ASIA CRISIS AND THE 2000 RECESSION

The baseline monetary policy that emerged under Greenspan was LAW (lean-against-the-wind) with credibility. Given a stable nominal anchor in the form of the expectation of price stability, the FOMC moved the funds rate in a way designed to maintain output growing at potential. The latter is implied in Greenspan's dictum (Greenspan 1997, 965):

> The law of supply and demand has not been repealed. . . . Short of a marked slowing in the demand for goods and services . . . the imbalance between the growth in labor demand and expansion of potential labor supply . . . must eventually erode the current state of inflation quiescence.

Starting in 1997, the real GDP grew strongly (figure 19.1). Measured by deviations of consumption from trend, the output gap diminished and became increasingly positive in fall 1998 (figure 20.3). The unemployment rate declined steadily (figure 14.8). With the economy growing above potential, LAW with credibility called for an increase in the funds rate. However, the Asia crisis intervened (Hetzel 2008, chaps. 16–19). The FOMC refrained from increases in the funds rate for fear that an appreciation of the dollar in the foreign exchange markets would disrupt the IMF programs undertaken in order to stabilize the Asian economies by making it harder for them to repay their dollar-denominated debt. Greenspan (US Congress 1998a, 32) told Congress, "We need to be aware that monetary policy tightening actions in the United States could have outsized effects on very sensitive financial markets in Asia." Stanley Fischer, first managing IMF director, cautioned the United States not to raise interest rates as they were "the prime determinant of capital flows to the developing countries" (*Financial Times* 1998). The Russian debt default in August 1998 worsened the problem of capital flight from emerging markets.

With an unchanged funds rate of 5.5 percent from the March 1997 FOMC meeting to the August 1998 meeting, a reduction in expected inflation raised the real funds rate to 3.3 percent from fall 1997 to fall 1998 (figure 18.5). However, the economy continued to grow above potential. The FOMC relied on a repeated argument in the Greenbook's staff forecast that weakness in Asia would spread to the United States. Net exports would fall because of a widening of the current account surpluses of Asian countries. Declining corporate profits would reduce corporate investment and produce a fall in the stock market. Consumption would then fall. The December 16, 1997, Greenbook sounded the refrain: "Virtually all signs point to a continuation this quarter of the economic pattern we have been witnessing for some time: strong growth of real GDP, huge gains in jobs. . . . We are predicting a marked deceleration [in real GDP growth] in the near term." From the September 1996 FOMC meeting to the December 1998 meeting, actual real GDP growth exceeded the Greenbook forecasts on average by more than 2 percentage points (figure 14.9).

The FOMC lowered the funds rate in September 1998 in an attempt to offset capital outflows from emerging markets into the United States. Only by the end of 1999 did the real rate exceed its summer 1998 value (figure 18.5). The *New York Times* (1998a) noted the departure from the FOMC's standard procedures: "Had the Fed been looking strictly at recent economic data, it would almost certainly not have cut rates. . . . 'Where is the slowdown?' asked Peter Canelo, United States investment strategist at Morgan Stanley Dean Witter." Another *New York Times* (1998b) article talked about a "game plan in a world economic defense":

> The Federal Reserve's decision to cut interest rates again marks the completion of a three-part strategy, put together over the last seven weeks by the Clinton Administration and Alan Greenspan. . . . "We had to deal first with rebuilding confidence, so that capital would stop flowing out of countries," Treasury Secretary Robert E. Rubin told a group of business executives. . . . Washington's strategy, which appeared to have been carefully coordinated, was laid out in pieces, first in speeches by President Clinton and Mr. Greenspan and then fleshed out by Mr. Rubin and his aides. Part 1 was to cut interest rates. . . . Part 2 was to stabilize Brazil, with a $41.5 billion bailout package.

The combination of an expansionary monetary policy in an environment of low inflation stimulated the stock market. The earnings/price ratio for the S&P went from 8.2 in December 1994 to 4 in January 2000 (figure 20.2). The wealth effect of equity prices contributed to the rise in consumption above trend (figure 20.3). Core inflation also stopped declining (figure 20.1). However, the reduction in world commodity prices, which lowered headline inflation in the Asia crisis, to some extent passed through to core inflation. With the end of the Asia crisis, headline inflation rose, and core inflation recovered.

At its June 1999 meeting, the FOMC began moving the funds rate up from 4.75 percent to 6.5 percent at the May 2000 meeting. The real funds rate moved up from a low of somewhat less than 2 percent in December

1998 to a peak in August 2000 of 4¾ percent. Short-term real interest rates remained relatively high until the cycle peak (figures 18.5 and 20.3, and table 3.16). The FOMC was hesitant to lower the funds rate when the cyclical expansion began to slow. Greenspan (2001, 4) commented:

> By summer of last year [2000], it was finally becoming apparent that the growth of demand was slowing and its evident excess over the growth of potential supply, as proxied by a diminishing pool of available labor, was being contained. . . . Had we moved the funds rate lower at the first sign of economic slowing, we would have created distortions threatening an even greater economic adjustment at a later date. . . . We took our first easing action on January 3 [2001].

When it became clear that the economy was going into recession, the FOMC lowered the funds rate sharply. Although the recession with cycle peak in March 2001 does not display the same degree of persistence of cyclically high real rates of interest past the cycle peak as typified by other recessions, as shown in table 3.16 by the figures on real GDP and industrial production, real short-term interest rates were at cyclical highs when significant weakening in the economy began.

20.5. BALANCING PRICE STABILITY
WITH COST-PUSH PRESSURES

How should one characterize the FOMC's reaction function and its implicit inflation target during Greenspan's tenure as chairman? Because Greenspan like other chairmen never placed funds-rate changes in the context of a strategy for achieving explicit objectives, this task falls to the historian. Although Greenspan moved decisively toward price stability when he became FOMC chairman, he was never willing for the FOMC to adopt an inflation target. Examination of documentary evidence and the actual realization of inflation yield several conclusions about his implicit inflation target. Greenspan wanted price stability subject to the proviso that at low rates of inflation productivity growth would be high enough to restrain growth in unit labor costs to be consistent with moderate wage growth. He feared that with price stability wage compression coming from an inability to cut nominal wages would increase unemployment. The reason was the presumed unwillingness of workers to accept cuts in real wages through cuts in nominal wages although they would be willing to accept cuts arising from unchanged nominal wages with inflation. For Greenspan, a prerequisite for price stability was that productivity would rise with price stability.

Although Greenspan resisted FOMC discussion of an inflation target, formal or informal, he had to make an exception at the January 1996 meeting because he needed to speak for the FOMC in responding to legislation by Senator Mack requiring the Fed to achieve price stability. The staff presented the standard Keynesian view of the sacrifice ratio in lowering inflation. As summarized by Kathy Minehan (Board of Governors, *FOMC Transcript*, January 30–31, 1996, 39), president of the Boston Fed, "Moving from 3 percent to 1 percent inflation by the year 2002 results in a full 8 percentage point loss of economic growth in this period." Al Broaddus (Board of Governors, *FOMC Transcript*, January 30–31, 1996, 39), president of the Richmond Fed, suggested that Greenspan, in the Humphrey-Hawkins report, state "that the Committee wants and expects the CPI inflation rate to remain below 3 percent on average over the two-year 1996–1997 period and that beyond that we intend to take steps to bring the inflation rate down further over time." At the July 1996 FOMC, Broaddus again raised the suggestion. At this meeting, as a result of the debate between Governor Yellen and President Broaddus, the FOMC reached a consensus over an interim target for CPI inflation of 2 percent.

Greenspan (Board of Governors, *FOMC Transcript*, July 2, 1996, 72) warned the FOMC, "If the 2 percent inflation figure gets out of this room, it is going to create more problems for us than I think any of you might anticipate." Why did Greenspan express such concern, and more generally what did the debate reveal about his own views? When Yellen (Board of Governors, *FOMC Transcript*, July 2, 1996, 50) asked Greenspan to assign a number to the objective of price stability, he replied, "I would say the number is zero, if inflation is properly measured." One can infer that Greenspan associated price stability with measured inflation of about ¾ percent.[1] As noted above, Greenspan believed that price stability (a 1 percent inflation rate) would require an increase in productivity growth high enough to allow nominal wage growth high enough to permit real wage cuts to occur with no change in nominal wages.

Greenspan was optimistic about this outcome. Greenspan (US Congress 1994, 17) told Congress, "The rate of inflation is associated inversely with the rate of growth of productivity." Nevertheless, he was not confident enough to try the experiment of moving completely to price stability without imperiling the FOMC's independence. Greenspan (Board of Governors, *FOMC Transcript*, July 2–3, 1996, 67) told the FOMC:

1. Greenspan (US Congress 2004, 29) testified, "We know there are significant biases remaining in the price indexes we use so that true price stability would be reflected in price indexes which are positive, probably somewhere between .5 percent and a little under a full percentage point."

My own view, as I have stated many times, is that our goal should be price stability. But I do not think we should have a naïve view as to what is required to get there or what it means when we get there and what we do when it is no longer rhetoric but action that we need to maintain it. . . . It is not that low or stable prices are an environment that is conducive to capital investment to reduce costs, but rather that it is an environment that forces productivity enhancements. . . . The question is basically whether we are willing to move on to price stability. The question really is whether we as an institution can make the unilateral decision to do that. . . . I think the type of choice is so fundamental to a society that in a democratic society we as unelected officials do not have the right to make that decision. Indeed, if we tried to, we would find that our mandate would get remarkably altered.

The result was a 2 percent minus informal inflation target. However, for Greenspan, at low rates of inflation, the amount of inflation that the FOMC would tolerate would vary inversely over time with the rate of productivity growth.

Risk management was also a determinant of policy. The FOMC raised the funds rate to 5.5 percent in March 1997. Despite the steady fall in the unemployment rate from 5.2 percent in March 1997 to 4.0 percent by end 1999, it did not raise the funds rate above 5.5 percent until February 2000. Greenspan did not consider inflation a threat because he believed that productivity growth was restraining inflation. The FOMC could then concentrate on the financial volatility engendered by the Asia crisis. The Asia crisis also limited concern for inflation because of the way in which the worldwide decline in commodity prices lowered measured inflation. Inflation (four-quarter core PCE) went from 4.5 percent in 1989 to almost 1 percent at the end of 1998 (figure 20.1). Taking account of the bias in price indices for their failure to account for improvements in quality, the FOMC had achieved price stability.

Greenspan (US Congress 1999a, 61–62) testified:

Recent restrained inflation may be emanating more from employers than from employees. . . . Businesses . . . have lost pricing power. . . . Price relief evidently has not been available in recent years. But relief from cost pressures has. The newer technologies have made capital investment distinctly more profitable. . . . Since neither firms nor their competitors can count any longer on a general inflationary tendency to validate decisions to raise their own prices, each company feels compelled to concentrate on efforts to hold down costs. The availability of new technology to each company and its rivals affords both the opportunity and the competitive necessity of taking steps to boost productivity.

Like Arthur Burns (Hetzel 1998, 28; see also chap. 17), Greenspan believed that alternating waves of optimism and pessimism created the business cycle. The policy maker had to use judgment to decide when to counter cyclical instability produced by excessive investor pessimism.[2] Greenspan (US Congress 1996, 22; US Congress 1997, 10; and US Congress 2001, 55–56) testified:

> [Because] people get excessively exuberant on occasion and inordinately depressed on occasion, you get a cycle.
>
> Excessive optimism sows the seeds of its own reversal in the form of imbalances. . . . When unwarranted expectations ultimately are not realized, the unwinding of these financial excesses can . . . amplify a downturn.
>
> Can fiscal and monetary policy . . . eliminate the business cycle? . . . The answer . . . is no because there is no tool to change human nature. Too often people are prone to recurring bouts of optimism and pessimism that manifest themselves . . . in the build up or cessation of speculative excesses. . . . Our only realistic response to a speculative bubble is to lean against the economic pressures that may accompany a rise in asset prices . . . and address forcefully the consequences of a sharp deflation of asset prices.

Or more simply, "The business cycle is essentially a function of human nature" (Greenspan in US Congress 1995b, 23).

20.6. FEAR OF DEFLATION

In 2003, the FOMC concentrated on the fear of deflation and a zero lower bound (ZLB) on the funds rate. As a business forecaster, Greenspan understood inflation as a product of the growth in unit labor costs and the "pricing power" of corporations, that is, their power to pass on their increase in costs as higher product prices. From 2001Q1 to 2002Q1, quarterly changes in unit labor costs averaged −3.6 percent. From 2002Q2 to 2003Q3, the number still was only 0.4 percent. Because the economy recovered slowly from the cyclical trough, the output gap remained negative. As late as Feb-

2. More specifically, the issue is whether policy makers should respond directly to asset prices or only indirectly as they influence real output.

ruary 2004, nonfarm payroll employment remained 2.35 million below the March 2001 peak. Low growth in unit labor costs combined with a negative output gap created fear of deflation.

Governor Ben Bernanke (2003, 3–4) wrote of the situation

> in which aggregate demand is insufficient to sustain strong growth, even when the short-term real interest rate is zero or negative. . . . [As] a consequence of the well-known zero-lower-bound constraint on nominal interest rates . . . deflation might grow worse as economic slack led to more aggressive wage- and price-cutting. Because the short-term nominal interest rate cannot be reduced further, worsening deflation would raise the real short-term interest rate. . . . The higher real interest rate might further reduce aggregate demand, exacerbating the deflation and continuing the downward spiral.

Greenspan (US Congress 2003, 49) testified to "an especially pernicious . . . scenario in which inflation turns negative . . . engendering a corrosive deflationary spiral."[3] Greenspan (US Congress 2004, 28) reiterated, "Were it [deflation] to happen, the consequences would be extraordinarily negative."

At its June 2003 meeting, the FOMC discussed ways of conducting policy with a funds rate at zero but reached no consensus. What emerged was an attempt to lower the yield curve without reducing the funds rate. To this end, the FOMC made public statements that the funds rate was likely to remain low for an extended period. At its August 12, 2003, meeting, the FOMC issued a statement containing the phrase "policy accommodation can be maintained for a considerable period" (Board of Governors, *FOMC Transcript*). The longer-lasting consequence of this episode was a desire to maintain some inflation in excess of price stability. Greenspan (Meyer 2004, 193) talked about a "firebreak," and Bernanke (2002b, 4) said, "the Fed should try to preserve a buffer zone for the inflation rate." As it turned out, the FOMC incurred an inflation scare not a deflation scare.

Following standard LAW procedures, which entail raising the funds rate from its cyclical low when it becomes evident that an economic recovery is self-sustaining, the FOMC began raising the funds rate at its June 2004 meeting. Although the unemployment rate had fallen from its cyclical high of 6.3 percent, reached in June 2003, at the June meeting it seemed stuck at around 5.7 percent. However, using three-month annualized growth in

---

3. These concerns implicitly assume that at the ZLB a policy of money creation through open market purchases of illiquid assets will be ineffective in stimulating aggregate nominal demand.

payroll employment available to the FOMC at the time of its meetings, in spring 2004, employment had finally begun to grow faster than the labor force. The FOMC then persisted in quarter-point increases in the funds rate even when the recovery seemed to falter. For example, the Greenbook ("Summary and Outlook," part 1, August 5, 2004, I-1) for the August 2004 FOMC meeting began:

> The bulk of the data that we have received since the June Greenbook have been decidedly softer than we had expected. Notably, employment growth slowed substantially in June, manufacturing output contracted slightly, and consumer spending fell sharply. All told, real GDP increased only 3 percent at an annual rate in the second quarter—1½ percentage points less than our projection in the June Greenbook.

The importance assigned to stable expectations of inflation appeared in the following. Greenspan (Board of Governors, *FOMC Transcript*, June 29–30, 2004, 148) commented, "Measures of long-term inflation expectations are remarkably contained. Indeed, the measure that I find most useful in that regard is the forward rate on one-year maturities nine years out. In other words, it's the yield associated with the last one-year tranche of a ten-year note. That yield has barely moved." Bernanke (Board of Governors, *FOMC Transcript*, August 10, 2004, 54) commented:

> The finding that long-horizon inflation expectations appear to respond to short-term economic developments, whether real or nominal, raises the possibility that long-term inflation expectations in the United States are not as firmly anchored as we would like. This brings me back to the current situation. If inflation expectations are, indeed, imperfectly anchored, it is very important that we continue to demonstrate in word and deed our commitment to price stability.

20.7. DID EXPANSIONARY MONETARY POLICY CAUSE A HOUSING BUBBLE?

Proper interpretation of monetary policy during Greenspan's last years as FOMC chairman ending in January 2006 is essential for evaluating the revival of the speculative-excess theories of cyclical fluctuations that prevailed in the 1920s and 1930s. For example, Brunnermeier and Schnabel (2016, abstract, 493) wrote:

> The historical evidence suggests that the emergence of bubbles is often preceded or accompanied by an expansionary monetary policy, lend-

ing booms, capital inflows, and financial innovation or deregulation. We find that the severity of the economic crisis following the bursting of a bubble is less linked to the type of asset than to the financing of the bubble—crises are most severe when they are accompanied by a lending boom, high leverage of market players, and when financial institutions themselves are participating in the buying frenzy. Past experience also suggests that a purely passive "cleaning up the mess" stance towards inflating bubbles in many cases is costly.

Although often advanced as self-evident, just as after the 1929 stock market crash, the contention that monetary policy was "easy" prior to the Great Recession with cyclical peak December 2007 is not obvious. The purported evidence is that house prices increased. However, the obvious cause of that increase was the increased demand for houses spurred by government policy to increase the rate of home ownership that began in the Clinton administration and continued in the Bush administration. The home ownership rate, which had been steady at 64 percent from 1986 through 1995, then began to rise and peaked at 69 percent in 2005. With the supply of houses inelastic, the real price of houses began to rise in 1997 and peaked in 2006. At the same time, a financial safety net that encouraged banks to take risk by concentrating their assets in housing provided ample funding for subprime mortgages (Hetzel 2012a, chaps. 9 and 10; Wallison 2016).

A review of the macroeconomic data does not indicate expansionary monetary policy. The cyclically high value of the real funds rate of 4¾ percent reached in August 2000 and the slowness with which it declined are consistent with contractionary monetary policy (figure 18.5). Not until November 2002 did short-term real interest rates become consistently negative. Over the interval 2003Q2 to 2003Q4, four-quarter percentage changes in the core PCE deflator averaged 1.35 percent.

The recovery from the 2001Q4 trough was weak by postwar standards. In the two years following the trough, real GDP increased by 7.1 percent, the same amount as in the 1991 jobless recovery. For the recoveries in the in the 1949–82 period, the comparable figure was 14.5 percent (not including the 1980 recovery, which was shorter than two years). For the same two-year period, payroll employment declined by 0.9 percent. The FOMC pushed the funds rate down to 1 percent in June 2003 and left it there until June 2004. Given the initial weak recovery, that rate does not in retrospect appear inappropriately low.

Short-term real rates of interest were near zero from fall 2002 through summer 2004 (figure 18.5). However, a characteristic of monetary policy in the twenty-first century is that zero and negative interest rates have not signaled expansionary monetary policy. Economists have offered various reasons for the prevalence of low real rates of interest. The conjecture here is that worldwide wealthy investors concentrated on wealth preservation. A sustained flight to safety has lowered returns on safe assets, especially the debt of politically stable countries like the United States and Germany.

In the twenty-first century, the world seemed to risk disintegrating. On September 11, 2001, the attack on the World Trade Center in New York killed almost three thousand people and initiated the American invasion of Afghanistan. The Iraq War started in March 2003. Moderate US Treasury bond rates of around 4 percent in the years 2003 to 2005 (figure 20.2), not seen since the first half of the 1960s and attributed to a "global savings glut," reflected their safe haven status. With the Great Recession, it became obvious that moderate recessions had not replaced severe recessions. The shock of the prolonged unemployment of the Great Recession combined with the dislocation of low-skilled workers set off by the integration of China into the world economy created alienation among workers on the losing side of globalization.

If monetary policy was not expansionary in Greenspan's last years as FOMC chairman, how can one account for the increase in inflation that began in 2004Q1? Similarly, what accounts for the rapid increase in the four-quarter growth rate of nominal GDP starting in 2003Q3 with funds-rate increases occurring only starting in 2004Q3 (figure 19.4)? The answer lies in the giant inflation shock that shook the world following the integration of the BRIC (Brazil, Russia, India, and China) countries into the world economy and that continued into 2008. The result was high headline inflation produced by commodity price inflation, which in turn passed through into core inflation (figure 20.4). The Board staff recognized the pass-through in the Greenbook ("Summary and Outlook," part 1, June 23, 2004, I-1): "We still think that recent increases in core prices have been exacerbated by transitory factors, such as the pass-through of large increases in energy prices and non-energy import prices."

Governor Bernanke (Board of Governors, *FOMC Transcript*, June 29–30, 2004, 137) elaborated:

> With nonmarket prices excluded, more than 100 percent of the acceleration in core PCE inflation between 2003:H2 and 2004:H1 can be accounted for by higher inflation or less deflation in goods prices, particularly durable goods prices. In contrast, the inflation in services excluding energy, whether inclusive of housing services or not, has actually decelerated in the past six months. As it seems likely that goods prices would be relatively more affected by changes in the value of the dollar and in the prices of energy and raw materials, this pattern seems consistent with

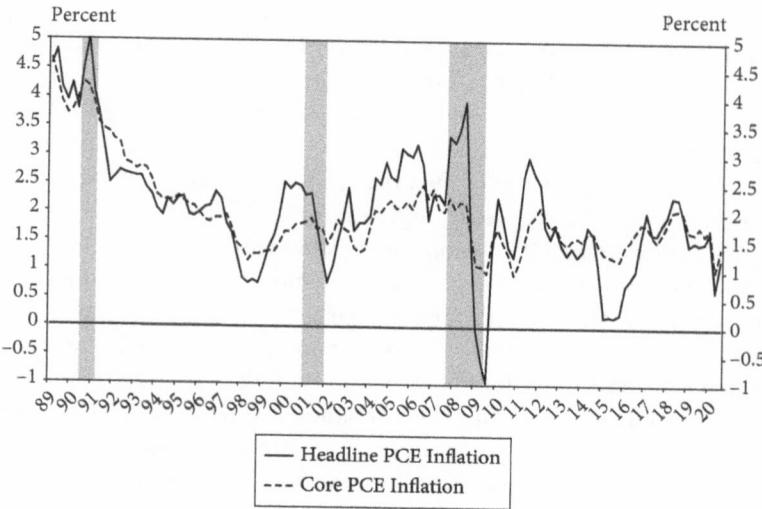

Figure 20.4. Headline and Core PCE Inflation: 1989–2020
Quarterly observations of four-quarter percentage changes in headline and core
personal consumption expenditures (PCE) deflator. Shaded areas indicate NBER
recessions. Tick marks indicate fourth quarter.
Source: St. Louis FRED

the inference that the recent increase in inflation is due more to these
factors than to a generalized increase in aggregate demand or higher labor costs.

Although the short-term real rate of interest fluctuated around zero before June 2004 (figure 18.5), what was important was that markets assumed
that the FOMC would move to "normalize" rates. At the August 2004 meeting, Greenspan (Board of Governors, *FOMC Transcript*, August 10, 2004,
73–74) said:

This leads me to what I think policy ought to be, which—if you'll excuse
the expression—I've termed "opportunistic disaccommodation." . . . We
should be choosing to raise rates, and we should endeavor to get back to
a neutral policy stance as quickly as we can. . . . The sooner we can get
back to neutral, the better positioned we will be. We were required to
ease very aggressively to offset the events of 2000 and 2001, and we took
the funds rate down to extraordinarily low levels with the thought in the
back of our minds, and often said around this table, that we could always
reverse our actions.

The fact that through 2007 bond rates remained fairly steady at a level not seen since the early 1960s provided evidence that the markets did not believe monetary policy was inflationary (figure 19.3). While short-term real rates declined to cyclical lows, long-term rates remained relatively high (figure 19.5). Real personal consumption expenditures grew steadily at trend through 2006 rather than rising above trend during the recovery contrary to previous recoveries (figure 20.3).

The FOMC's implicit inflation target likely moved from price stability to around 2 percent minus after the 2003 deflation scare. At a time when the Greenbook ("Summary and Outlook," part 1, March 16, 2005) was forecasting for 2005Q1 core PCE inflation of 2.1 percent and core CPI inflation of 2.2 percent, Bernanke (Board of Governors, *FOMC Transcript*, March 22, 2005, 58) told the FOMC that "core inflation is approaching the top of my comfort zone, and I would not like to see it go much higher."

With the benefit of hindsight, one can conjecture that it would have been better for the FOMC to have stayed with an objective of price stability rather than one of low inflation. The inflation shock raised headline inflation. With a lower level of core inflation, the headline inflation number might not have seemed so threatening to the FOMC of its credibility. If so, it might not have pursued the contractionary monetary policy that caused the Great Recession.

CHAPTER 21

The Great Recession

Summary: As captured by the term "financial crisis," popular commentary has attributed the Great Recession to a disruption of financial intermediation. A common criticism of the Fed is that "inflation targeting" was at fault by preventing a concern for financial stability (Curdia and Woodford 2009). Such criticism often starts with the assumption that low interest rates in the early 2000s initiated a boom-bust cycle in housing whose collapse caused the Great Recession (Taylor 2009). The explanation here is that contractionary monetary policy caused the Great Recession. The FOMC, concerned about high headline inflation, limited reductions in the funds rate while the economy developed a negative output gap. As in past recessions, the attempted soft landing failed as the FOMC misjudged its ability to manage an inflation-output gap.

The Great Recession, with cyclical peak in December 2007 and cyclical trough in June 2009, shattered the common belief that severe recessions were events of the past. Although newspaper accounts, which referred to the financial crisis, blamed the recession on a disruption to financial intermediation, contractionary monetary policy offers an explanation more consistent with events. The Great Recession followed in the pattern of the 1957, 1960, 1970, 1973, 1981, and 1990 recessions. During the economic recoveries, to normalize the level of short-term interest rates lowered in response to the preceding recession, the FOMC raised the funds rate until the economy weakened. At that point, out of concern for rising inflation (the foreign exchange value of the dollar in 1960), the FOMC limited downward movements in the funds rate despite weakness in the economy (see chap. 3). Although eschewing the language of trade-offs, the FOMC attempted to create a negative output gap to lower inflation.

The Great Recession departed from the pattern of earlier recessions in that the inflation of concern to the FOMC arose from a gigantic inflation shock. It came in the form of commodity price inflation produced by the integration into the world economy of China in particular. In summer 2008, headline inflation reached 4 percent although core inflation remained just over 2 percent. The FOMC, concerned about loss of credibility for price stability, limited reductions in the funds rate after May 2008. As explained in Aoki (2001), the FOMC should have allowed the inflation shock to pass through to headline inflation to facilitate the setting of relative prices. That is, it should have concentrated on stabilizing inflation in the "sticky-price" sector, that is, among firms that set prices for multiple periods. To deal with the issue of credibility, it could have made explicit an inflation target for core inflation and a strategy for achieving it.

The combination of a decline in output and disinflation was evidence of contractionary monetary policy. The persistent decline in inflation after 2008 had to reflect contractionary monetary policy. Core PCE (four-quarter) inflation fell from 2.2 percent in 2008Q3 to 1 percent over the interval 2009Q1 to 2009Q3 and to about 1.5 percent over the interval 2009Q4 to 2016Q1 (figure 20.4).

21.1. AN OVERVIEW: THIS TIME WAS NOT DIFFERENT FROM PAST RECESSIONS

Over the interval from 1994 to 2018, core PCE inflation fluctuated narrowly between a range of 1 percent and a little over 2 percent (figure 20.4). However, core PCE inflation (four-quarter percentage changes) rose from 1.3 percent in 2003Q3 to an average of 2.2 percent over the interval from 2006Q2 to 2008Q3. The reason for the increase was a prolonged, enormous inflation shock that took hold in early 2004. The integration of the BRIC (Brazil, Russia, India, and China) countries into the world economy produced a strong demand for commodities and an increase in their prices. The price of oil (WTI) rose from $20 a barrel in January 2002 to $134 a barrel in June 2008 (figure 21.1 shows the real price of oil). Headline PCE (four-quarter) inflation went from 0.8 percent in 2002Q1 to almost 4 percent in 2008Q3 (figure 20.4).

From mid-2004 to mid-2006, the FOMC steadily raised the funds rate, and the short-term real rate of interest rose from zero to 3 percent (figures 19.5 and 18.5). The economy began to weaken prior to the funds-rate peak. Nominal GDP growth began to fall after 2006Q2 (figure 14.7). The difference between nominal and real GDP growth began its decline at the same time, a decline that lasted three years (figure 19.2). That is, that FOMC was forcing down inflation (the difference between nominal and real GDP growth) despite an inflation shock. Real disposable personal income stopped growing in March 2007 and remained stagnant until the Bush rebates in May 2008. Real personal consumption expenditures began to fall below trend at the same time (figure 20.3).

By summer 2008, before the disruption in financial markets due to the Lehman bankruptcy on September 15, the United States and the world

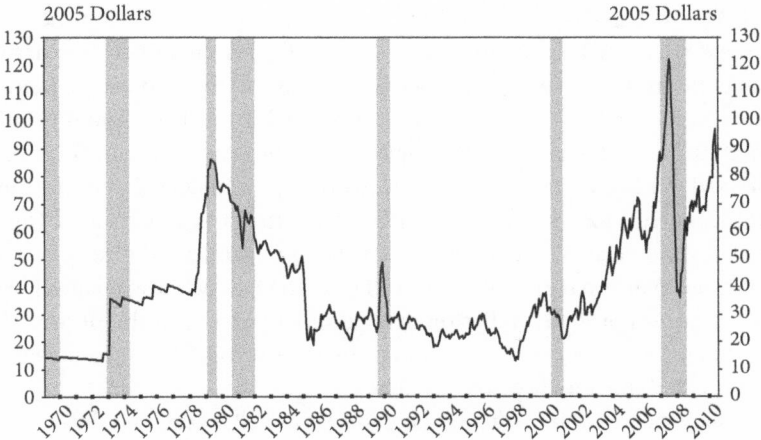

Figure 21.1. Real Price of Oil
Monthly observations of West Texas intermediate crude oil spot price per barrel deflated by the personal consumption expenditures price index. Shaded areas indicate NBER recessions. Heavy tick marks indicate December. Data from the *Wall Street Journal* and the Commerce Department via Haver Analytics.

economy had entered a serious recession. From June 2007 through December 2007, annualized monthly changes in nonfarm payrolls averaged only 0.5 percent. They deteriorated steadily after January 2008. In September 2008, they declined 3.9 percent (annual rate). (The September survey was conducted before the Lehman bankruptcy.) The decline occurred even with the Bush tax cut, which increased real disposable personal income by $562.1 billion in May 2008.

In October 2008, the Fed began to pay interest on the excess reserves of banks (IOER). Significantly, under the belief that monetary policy was stimulative, it did so to prevent the reserves created as part of its credit programs from lowering the funds rate. Even once recession had begun in December 2007, the FOMC was slow to realize that, despite a near-zero short-term real rate of interest, monetary policy was contractionary (Selgin 2018). A neutral monetary policy would require a significantly negative short-term real interest rate combined with quantitative easing (QE) and forward guidance to markets signaling the persistence of low negative real rates (chap. 24).

Just prior to the onset of the recession in December 2007, the real funds rate declined (figure 18.5). However, it did not become significantly negative until October 2008 when it reached −1.1 percent. Only at its December 2008 meeting did the FOMC lower the funds rate to the zero lower bound

(ZLB) by setting a range from 0 to ¼ percent.[1] Only much later did it become evident that the combination of a decline in the underlying natural rate of interest along with the shocks of a decline in the value of the housing stock and a decline in real disposable income due to the commodity-price inflation shock required both a significantly negative real funds rate and forward guidance to tilt down the slope of the yield curve. The real funds rate averaged −1.2 percent from January 2009 through January 2014 (figure 18.5). Evidence available after the fact that a negative real rate of interest was not expansionary came from two facts. The first was low inflation, with four-quarter core PCE inflation averaging 1.3 percent in the period after the end of the recession from 2009Q3 through 2011Q1. The second was the weakness of the initial recovery (chap. 24).

Policy makers and markets expected a V-shaped recession. Always in the past, a sharp upturn had followed a sharp contraction. That presumption caused the Treasury bond rate to remain relatively high. Not until after July 2011 did the ten-year Treasury yield fall below 3 percent in a sustained way. For monetary policy to have been stimulative, the FOMC would have had to have telegraphed to markets that a significantly negative real funds rate would persist. The Fed's experiment with forward guidance, however, did not begin in a determined way until quite late. At its March 2009 meeting, the FOMC adopted statement language that read "economic conditions are likely to warrant exceptionally low levels of the federal funds rate for an extended period" (Board of Governors, *FOMC Transcript*). The FOMC basically kept that qualitative language until the August 2011 meeting, when it changed the sentence to date-based guidance by adding "for at least through mid-2013" (chap. 24) (Board of Governors, *FOMC Transcript*).[2]

21.2. A CHRONOLOGY OF THE GREAT RECESSION

From a low of 1 percent in June 2004, the FOMC raised the funds rate steadily to its cyclical peak of 5.25 percent in June 2006.[3] The FOMC kept the

---

1. The unwillingness to consider a negative funds rate reflected the Fed's credit view. Former Fed governor Alan Blinder (2012) remarked that a negative IOER (interest on excess reserves) is "viewed at the Fed as a frightening prospect . . . but for the life of me I can't understand why." The article that quoted Blinder also quoted a Fed official: "'You're going to put the money funds out of business' if the Fed stops paying a positive IOER. . . . Cutting the IOER to zero or making it negative 'takes away the margin they need to keep going.'"

2. At the initiative of Chairman Bernanke, the Open Market Desk began buying MBS and agency debt in late November 2008. However, the purchases were intended solely to help the mortgage market because financial institutions "were actively dumping MBS on the market" (Bernanke 2015, 32).

3. For the chronology of the Great Recession, see Hetzel 2012a and 2020; and Hetzel and Richardson 2018. Sumner (2021) offers a critique similar in spirit.

funds rate unchanged when consumption began to weaken in March 2007 (figure 20.3). In fall 2007, the flight to liquidity of cash investors away from funding the off-balance sheet entities created by banks to hold mortgage-backed securities raised commercial paper rates and lowered Treasury bill rates. Neither series then is representative of the stance of monetary policy. However, in retrospect, the unprecedented decline in the natural rate of interest misled policy makers about the degree of ease represented by zero or negative interest rates.

Because of concern that a disruption to the flow of credit to mortgage markets would weaken growth, at its September 2007 meeting, the FOMC began reducing the funds rate from its cyclical peak. As of the April 2008 meeting, the FOMC had lowered the funds rate to 2 percent. Fatefully, at that meeting, the FOMC communicated to markets that easing had ended. One factor misleading the FOMC about the stance of monetary policy was an apparent stabilization of the economy in 2008Q2. Two factors provided temporary stimulus to the economy. First, a reduction in the magnitude of net exports boosted GDP. Second, the Bush tax cut provided an enormous fillip to disposable income and temporarily halted the decline in real personal consumption expenditures that had begun in December 2007.

Table 21.1 shows figures for annualized growth rates of monthly real PCE: In March, April, and May 2008, the negative growth rates turned positive boosted by the increase in disposable income from the tax cut. Although President Bush signed the tax cut into law on February 12, 2008, and the rebates arrived in May, households anticipated their arrival. From January 2007 through September 2007, real personal disposable income had increased at an average monthly rate of $12.1 billion. From October 2007 through April 2008, the rate declined to $6.6 billion. However, it then jumped by $562.1 billion in May 2008. Transitory tax cuts impose a cost by obscuring the underlying state of the economy.

With its April 2008 meeting, the FOMC delivered the message to markets that the easing cycle had ended and that the next change in the funds rate would likely by an increase. Behind the message was the concern that high headline inflation would raise inflationary expectations. The message changed dramatically compared to that of the March FOMC

Table 21.1. Annualized Growth Rate of
Real Personal Consumption Expenditures

12/2007–2/2008	−1.9%
3/2008–5/2008	1.7%
6/2008–9/2008	−3.8%
10/2008–12/2008	−4.5%

meeting. For the March meeting, the Greenbook ("Summary and Outlook," part 1, March 13, 2008, I-7) forecast that growth in real final sales to private domestic purchasers for the entire year 2008 would be negative (−1.6 percent).

> We are anticipating a further retrenchment in consumer spending in the next few months: Consumer confidence has plummeted; soaring energy prices are biting into household purchasing power; the labor market is weakening; and real estate values are dropping. As a result, we expect that real PCE [personal consumption expenditures] will be little changed in the first quarter.

The March 2008 FOMC minutes (Board of Governors, *FOMC Minutes*, April 8, 2008, 7) expressed a primary concern for recession:[4]

> Most members judged that a substantial easing in the stance of monetary policy was warranted at this meeting. The outlook for economic activity had weakened considerably since the January meeting, and members viewed the downside risks to economic growth as having increased. Indeed, some believed that a prolonged and severe economic downturn could not be ruled out.

The statement issued at the end of the March FOMC meeting had expressed the belief that inflation would soon moderate. That did not happen. Headline PCE inflation (four-quarter) increased from 2.4 percent in July 2007 to 4.4 percent in July 2008 (figure 20.4). The Greenbook ("Summary and Outlook," part 1, April 23, 2008, I-6 and I-9) for the April FOMC meeting continued to project a pessimistic future and forecast that the stimulative effects of the Bush tax cut would be short-lived:

> With mounting job losses and outsized increases in energy prices holding down real income, falling home values cutting into household net worth, and consumer sentiment deteriorating further, we would, all else equal, expect a noticeable decline in PCE [personal consumption expenditures] in the second quarter. However, the tax rebates are anticipated to boost the change in spending by 1½ percentage points in the second quarter, leading us to project PCE to increase at an annual rate of ¼ per-

4. FOMC "minutes" refers to the summary of an FOMC meeting released shortly after an FOMC meeting. An FOMC "transcript" is released only with a lag of five calendar years.

cent. . . . Abstracting from the effects of the tax rebates, real PCE is expected to remain weak throughout the year.

Despite the pessimistic outlook for the economy, the minutes (Board of Governors, *FOMC Minutes*, April 29–30, 2008, 9) for the April 29–30 FOMC meeting sent the message to markets that the easing cycle was ending:

> Although downside risks to growth remained, members were also concerned about the upside risks to the inflation outlook, given the continued increases in oil and commodity prices and the fact that some indicators suggested that inflation expectations had risen in recent months. . . . Risks to growth were now thought to be more closely balanced by the risks to inflation. Accordingly, the Committee felt that it was no longer appropriate for the statement to emphasize the downside risks to growth. . . . In that regard, several members noted that it was unlikely to be appropriate to ease policy in response to information suggesting that the economy was slowing further or even contracting slightly in the near term, unless economic and financial developments indicated a significant weakening of the economic outlook.

The end-of-meeting statement repeated the language from the prior statement about the expectation for "inflation to moderate" but added the qualification: "Uncertainty about the inflation outlook remains high. It will be necessary to continue to monitor inflation developments carefully" (Board of Governors, *FOMC Transcript*).

The yield curve jumped after the April 2008 FOMC meeting based on this message. For both the three-month and the six-month Treasury bill rate, figure 21.2 plots the difference with the funds-rate target using observations the day following an FOMC meeting. When markets expect that the FOMC wants to stimulate growth, the difference is negative because markets anticipate future declines in the funds rate. Conversely, when markets expect that the FOMC wants to restrain growth, the difference is positive because markets anticipate future increases in the funds rate. As shown by the sharp jump in the series, the latter was the case after the April 2008 meeting.

The minutes for the June FOMC meeting were revealing of an anti-inflation sentiment that would last into the fall of 2008. All participants believed that a zero real funds rate (a 2 percent funds rate minus contemporaneous 2 percent core inflation) meant that monetary policy was accommodative. Doves believed that such a funds rate just balanced off financial

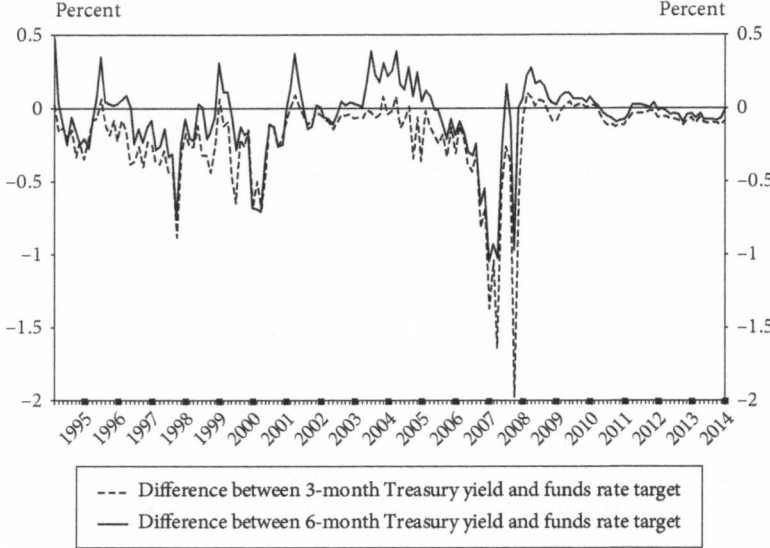

Figure 21.2. Term Structure of Interest Rates: Three-Month and Six-Month
The series are the difference between the three-month and six-month Treasury
yields and the funds-rate target. Treasury yields are from Board of Governors,
Statistical Releases H.15, starting January 7, 2002, and G.13 before. Starting October 2,
2001, yields are constant maturity. Before, they are the three-month and six-month
yields. Observations are for the day after an FOMC meeting. Heavy tick marks indicate
December.

frictions and relatively high credit spreads. Hawks believed that monetary
policy was expansionary and ultimately inflationary. Despite the division,
the consensus held that the next move in the funds rate would be upward.
The minutes (Board of Governors, *FOMC Minutes*, June 24–25, 2008, 6–8)
recorded:

> Participants continued to see significant downside risks to growth. At
> the same time, however, the outlook for inflation had deteriorated. Re-
> cent increases in energy and some other commodity prices would boost
> inflation sharply in coming months. . . . Participants had become more
> concerned about upside risks to the inflation outlook—including the
> possibility that persistent advances in energy and food prices could spur
> increases in long-run inflation expectations. . . . Participants agreed that
> the possibilities of greater pass through of cost increases into prices,
> higher long-run inflation expectations feeding into labor costs and other
> prices, and further increases in energy prices all posed upside risks to
> inflation that had intensified since the time of the April FOMC meeting.

Some participants noted that certain measures of the real federal funds rate, especially those using actual or forecasted headline inflation, were now negative, and very low by historical standards. In the view of these participants, the current stance of monetary policy was providing considerable support to aggregate demand and, if the negative real federal funds rate was maintained, it could well lead to higher trend inflation. . . . However, other participants observed that the high level of risk spreads and the restricted availability of credit suggested that overall financial conditions were not especially accommodative; indeed, borrowing costs for many households and businesses were higher than they had been last summer. . . . With increased upside risks to inflation and inflation expectations, members believed that the next change in the stance of policy could well be an increase in the funds rate.

Chairman Bernanke (2008b) stated:

Another significant upside risk to inflation is that high headline inflation, if sustained, might lead the public to expect higher long-term inflation rates, an expectation that could ultimately become self-confirming. . . . We are attentive to the implications of changes in the value of the dollar for inflation and inflation expectations and will continue to formulate policy to guard against risks to both parts of our dual mandate, including the risk of an erosion in longer-term inflation expectations.

For the August 5, 2008, FOMC meeting, despite a weakening economy, the market's expectation of the future funds-rate path rose because of Fed hawkish language about inflation and concern for a depreciation of the dollar. On April 3, 2008, the six-month contract for Fed funds futures implied a funds rate in September 2008 of somewhat below 2 percent. On July 3, 2008, the six-month futures contract implied a funds rate above 2.25 percent in December 2008.[5] The ten-year constant-maturity Treasury nominal bond yield was 3.3 percent on March 24, 2008, and 3.8 percent on August 29, 2008, while real (inflation-indexed) bond yields increased from 1.0 percent to 2.2 percent over the same interval.[6]

For the August 5, 2008, meeting, despite the deterioration in the economy, the Board staff assumed that the next change in the funds rate would be an increase. The staff wrote in the Greenbook ("Summary and Outlook,"

5. See Federal Reserve Bank of St. Louis *US Financial Data*, various weekly issues.
6. Figures are from Board of Governors, Statistical Release H.15, "Selected Interest Rates."

part 1, July 30, 2008, I-1, I-2, and I-15), "Considering the totality of the evidence, we continue to think that a significant weakening of activity is in train. . . . As before, we assume that the federal funds rate will remain at 2 percent over the rest of 2008 and be raised to 2¾% over the first half of 2009." As part of the long-term outlook, the staff forecast that "the federal funds rate continues to climb to just above 4 percent by the end of 2012."

The Great Recession followed the pattern of other recessions in that the FOMC allowed a negative output to develop with the intention of lowering inflation. The August 2008 FOMC meeting illustrates. For both quarters 2008Q3 and 2008Q4, the Greenbook forecast 2.6 percent inflation for the core (not including food and energy) PCE ("Outlook and Summary," "Changes in Prices and Costs," July 30, 2008, I-29). At the same time, the Greenbook forecast an output gap growing in magnitude from −0.3 percent in 2008Q2, to −1.3 percent in 2008Q4, and reaching −1.6 percent in 2009Q3 ("Outlook and Summary," "Other Macroeconomic Indicators," July 30, 2008, I-30). Because of increased slack, the Greenbook forecast a decline in core PCE inflation to 2.1 percent by 2009Q1.

At the August 2008 FOMC meeting, Tim Geithner (Board of Governors, *FOMC Minutes*, August 5, 2008, 75), president of the Federal Reserve Bank of New York, stated:

> On balance, the rate of growth in underlying inflation suggests that growth in demand in the United States will have to be below potential for a longer period of time if inflation expectations are to come down sufficiently. This means that we will have to tighten monetary policy relatively soon compared with our previous behavior in recoveries—perhaps before we see the actual bottom in house prices and the actual peak in unemployment.

In a break with precedence, the Bluebook ("Monetary Policy: Strategy and Alternatives," July 31, 2008) prepared for the August FOMC meeting did not contain an Alternative A, which would customarily have allowed for a reduction in the funds rate. The only monetary policy actions considered then were maintenance of the existing 2 percent funds-rate target and an increase.[7] Governor Kohn (Board of Governors, *FOMC Minutes*, August 5, 2008, 76) stated, "About the output gap, the incoming information strongly suggests that we are on a trajectory that at least for some time will have the

7. The omission is indicative of the range of FOMC participants' attitudes. Input from the regional Reserve Bank presidents as part of the creation of the Bluebook assures that the Bluebook alternatives span their views.

THE GREAT RECESSION   >   455

economy growing appreciably below the growth rate of its potential. The most obvious evidence is the persistence of a soft labor market." Because of the FOMC's concern for inflation, discussion focused on when to raise the funds rate. Hawks wanted an immediate increase while doves wanted a later increase. Chairman Bernanke (Board of Governors, *FOMC Minutes*, August 5, 2008, 98, 100–101) stated:

> The unemployment rate . . . has risen as quickly as in previous episodes, and any look at the unemployment rate would suggest that this is something close to a normal recession dynamic. . . . So overall I think there is still significant downside risk to growth. . . . The speed at which we remove the accommodation—and I think it is clear we do have to do that relatively soon—should depend to some extent on how inflation evolves. . . . I welcome the ongoing discussion we should have about the pace of withdrawal of accommodation.

The minutes (Board of Governors, *FOMC Minutes*, August 5, 2008, 5–6, and September 16, 2008, 6) for the August and September meetings, respectively, captured the FOMC's willingness to allow a negative output gap to develop to counter inflation:

> Retail sales had weakened during late spring and auto sales had dropped sharply in both June and July. The unemployment rate jumped during the intermeeting period. Participants expressed significant concerns about the upside risks to inflation, especially the risk that persistently high headline inflation could result in an unmooring of long-run inflation expectations. . . .
>
> With elevated inflation still a concern and growth expected to pick up next year if financial strains diminished, the Committee should also remain prepared to reverse the policy easing put in place over the past year in a timely fashion.

Newspaper stories conflated the Great Recession and the financial turmoil that developed in the fall. However, the timing of events is consistent with the severity of the recession coming from contractionary monetary policy not a disruption to financial intermediation. The reason is that in the United States the recession became a major recession in summer 2008 when financial intermediation was still working well (chap. 22). Sharp declines in annualized real GDP growth for 2008Q4 and 2009Q1, which came to −5.4 percent and −6.4 percent, respectively, were already guaranteed in summer 2008 by the dynamics of the inventory cycle. In summer 2008, the

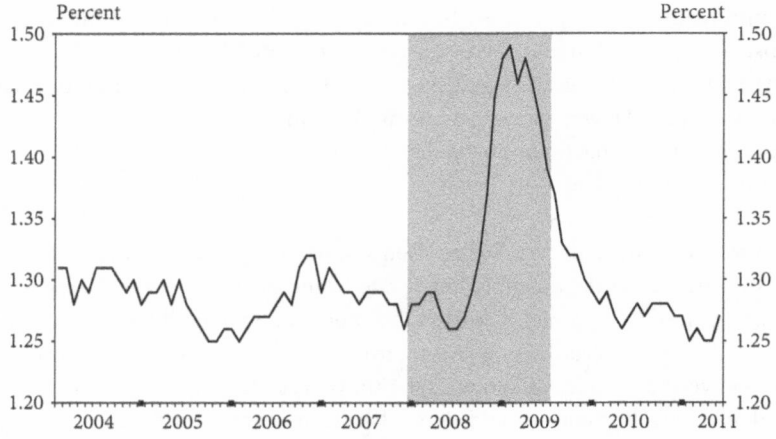

Figure 21.3. Business Inventory/Sales Ratio
Monthly observations of inventories divided by sales for all businesses. Shaded area indicates recession. Heavy tick marks indicate December. Data from the Census Bureau via Haver Analytics.

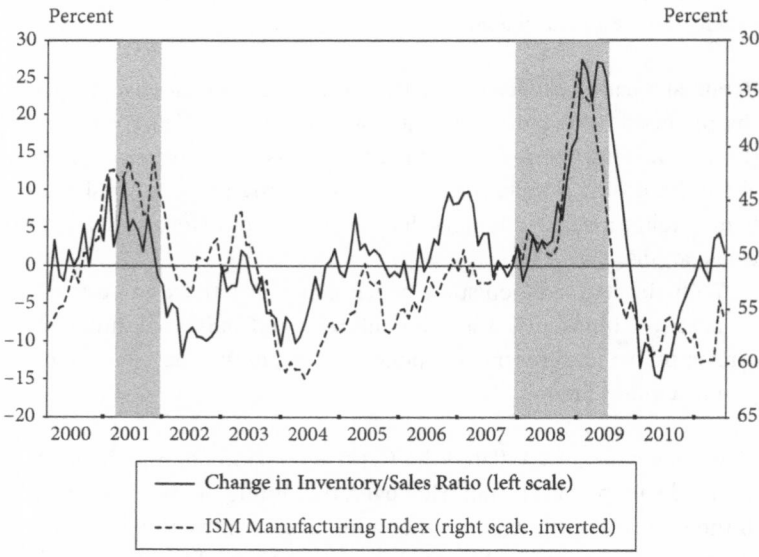

Change in Inventory/Sales Ratio (left scale)

- - - - ISM Manufacturing Index (right scale, inverted)

Figure 21.4. Change in Inventory/Sales Ratio and ISM Manufacturing Index
Monthly observations of annualized percentage changes in the inventory/sales ratio for the durable goods sector and monthly observations of the Institute for Supply Management (ISM) index for the manufacturing sector (shown on an inverted scale). Shaded areas indicate recessions. Heavy tick marks indicate December. Data from the Census Bureau and Institute of Supply Management via Haver Analytics.

increase in inventories required a reduction in output to align production with demand.

By summer 2008, a shortfall in aggregate demand led to businesses accumulating unwanted inventories. Starting in July 2008, from 1.27, inventory/sales ratios (total business) climbed to 1.46 by year-end (figure 21.3). Figure 21.4 plots percentage changes in the inventory/sales ratio for the durable goods sector along with percentage changes in the ISM (Institute of Supply Management) index for activity in the manufacturing sector (inverted scale). The latter shows the deterioration in the economy that began in summer 2008.

21.3. FALL 2008, THE LEHMAN BANKRUPTCY, AND THE FLIGHT OF THE CASH INVESTORS

The failure of Lehman Brothers rocked the markets' perception of what had seemed an immutable policy of not allowing financial institutions to fail. A clear retraction of the financial safety net had occurred, but no one knew to what new boundaries. Even Bernanke (Board of Governors, *FOMC Transcript*, September 16, 2008, 74–75) privately expressed the confusion to the FOMC:

> We don't have a set of criteria, we don't have fiscal backstops, and we don't have clear congressional intent. So in each event, in each instance, even though there is this sort of unavoidable ad hoc character to it, we are trying to make a judgment about the costs—from a fiscal perspective, from a moral hazard perspective, and so on—of taking action versus the real possibility in some cases that you might have very severe consequences for the financial system and, therefore, for the economy of not taking action. Frankly, I am decidedly confused and very muddled about this.

Financial market participants were placed in the impossible position of suddenly having to evaluate the solvency of their counterparties. Governor Betsy Duke (Board of Governors, *FOMC Transcript*, October 28–29, 2008, 108) captured the resulting disruption:

> They had a sense of being unable to predict who was going to be saved, who was going to get whacked, and who would be the winners and the losers. So subsequently both the banks and their customers froze, and there has been very little activity since then. All the banks I talked to

reported having stopped doing business with one or more counterparties and that one or more counterparties had stopped doing business
with them, and they were shocked by both of those things.

The insurance company / hedge fund AIG dramatized the issue. After September 16, 2008, markets had to sort out why the Fed had allowed
Lehman to fail but had rescued AIG. It was not the case that the Fed considered Lehman insolvent but AIG solvent. Rather, it seemed to be that
the Fed had backed off from bailing out financial institutions based on the
criterion of "too interconnected to fail" but had stayed with the "too big to
fail" criterion. That perception reinforced the flight of the cash investors
from financial institutions with asset portfolios consisting of hard-to-value,
long-term assets to the obviously too-big-to-fail banks.

William Dudley (Board of Governors, *FOMC Transcript*, September 16,
2008, 5), manager of the Federal Reserve Bank of New York System Open
Market Account, told the FOMC: "A lot of times when people look closer at
the books they find out that the liquidity crisis may also be a solvency issue.
I think it is still a little unclear whether AIG's problems are confined just to
liquidity. It also may be an issue of how much this company is really worth."
Governor Kevin Warsh (Board of Governors, *FOMC Transcript*, September
16, 2008, 62–63) highlighted the fact that AIG's AAA credit rating had had
been worthless: "If an AAA company like AIG were really fundamentally
insolvent, the direct losses to a range of institutions, particularly those that
are not just wholesale institutions but are retail institutions, could be very
significant. I don't think we know the answer yet to the question of whether
AIG speaks to a broader loss of confidence that could affect the foundations
of the US financial system."

The apparent retraction of the financial safety net caused short-term
cash investors either to flee to the undisputedly safe side of the financial
safety net or to lend overnight. They abandoned the prime money funds for
government money funds and abandoned the investment banks with illiquid, long-term investments, especially subprime mortgages for the conservatively managed too-big-to-fail institutions such as JPMorgan Chase (Hetzel 2012a, chap. 13). They also abandoned foreign banks that funded dollar
loans not with dollar deposits but by borrowing in the wholesale market
from US banks, money funds, and hedge funds. The Fed undid this flight
to the safe side of the financial safety net with lending through a variety of
credit programs such as the Term Auction Facility (TAF), the Commercial
Paper Funding Facility (CPFF), and swap lines to foreign central banks,
which re-lent the funds to their banks.

Evidence of a generalized demand for liquidity appeared in the way in which corporations drew on their lines of credit with banks. McCracken and Enrich (2008, 1–2) wrote:

> Fearful of tightening credit and bank failures, a growing number of companies are hoarding cash by taking the unusual step of tapping credit lines they don't actually need. . . . This corporate-cash stockpiling stems directly from the collapse of Lehman Brothers Holdings Inc. last week, which continues to reverberate in unforeseen ways. . . . The bigger impact [than on a bank's capital] is on a bank's liquidity. Bank treasurers are generally charged with gauging the likelihood that specific loans will be drawn down, and the expected demands that will place on the balance sheet. That in turn influences the bank's decisions about whether to make new loans to other borrowers.

Banks tightened lending standards out of fear that corporations would draw on their credit lines to make payments and the banks would then lose reserves. Fed policy attempted to offset the tightening of lending standards induced by the demand for liquidity through programs that substituted use of its balance sheet to provide credit to financial institutions and to firms that had formerly relied on short-term funding from the cash investors. What the FOMC did not do was to flood the market with liquidity through open market purchases and to implement an expansionary monetary policy. The failure to pursue an aggressive monetary easing came from continued FOMC concern for inflation.

To illustrate, contrast the more aggressive actions of the Fed with the onset of the pandemic in March 2020 with those of fall 2008. Securities held outright by the Fed increased by $9.8 billion over the two months from September 11, 2008, to November 10, 2008. In contrast, over the two months from March 11, 2020, to May 13, 2020, they increased by $1.783 trillion. M2 increased by $220 billion over the two months from September 15, 2008, to November 17, 2008. Over the two months from March 9, 2020, to May 4, 2020, M2 increased by $2.031 trillion. From September 15, 2008, to October 7, 2008 (when the Fed began paying interest on excess reserves), the effective federal funds rate averaged 1.6 percent. After the March 2020 reduction, the funds rate averaged less than 0.1 percent (Board of Governors, Statistical Release H.4.1; remaining series are from St. Louis FRED).

21.4. MONETARY POLICY TAKES A BACK SEAT

In fall 2008, the FOMC wanted to ensure that the reserves creation from its credit programs would not cause it to lose control over bank reserves and prevent it from raising the funds rate. At the September 16, 2008, FOMC meeting, the day after Lehman's bankruptcy, St. Louis Fed president Jim Bullard (Board of Governors, *FOMC Transcript*, September 16, 2008, 36) said:

> An inflation problem is brewing. The headline CPI inflation rate, the one consumers actually face, is about 6¼ percent year-to-date. . . . This is against the federal funds target of 2 percent. While it makes sense to focus on financial markets for the time being, it is essential that we keep in position to put downward pressure on inflation going forward.

In his summary of FOMC opinion, Bernanke (Board of Governors, *FOMC Transcript*, September 16, 2008, 72, 76–77) said, "Inflation risks are still in play and remain a concern for the Committee. Some participants reiterated their concern that maintaining rates too low for too long risks compromising our credibility and stimulating inflation over the medium run." Bernanke then added, "I also agree with those who say that, when the time comes, we do need to be prompt at removing accommodation. It is just as much a mistake to move too late and allow inflation, and perhaps even financial imbalances, to grow as it is to move too early and be premature in terms of assuming a recovery. . . . Overall I believe that our current funds rate setting is appropriate, and I don't really see any reason to change."

Bernanke (Board of Governors, *FOMC Transcript*, October 7, 2008, 14) expressed surprise when on a conference call on October 7, 2008, a weakening economy caused him to recommend a reduction in the funds rate:

> I think the macro outlook has shifted decisively toward output risks and away from inflation risks, and on that basis, I think that a policy move is justified. I should say that this comes as a surprise to me. I very much expected that we could stay at 2 percent for a long time, and then when the economy began to recover, we could begin to normalize interest rates. But clearly things have gone off in a direction that is quite worrisome.

Bernanke (Board of Governors, *FOMC Transcript*, October 7, 2008, 15) told the FOMC that the reduction in the funds rate from 2 percent to 1½ percent had a "tactical" objective. The European Central Bank (ECB) could not get a consensus to lower their policy rate. However, having a "coordinated" reduction in interest rates would give "them an opportunity to get out of the corner into which they are somewhat painted." Also, a reduction in the funds rate would hopefully provide some "reassurance" until the fiscal support became available "to solve this problem."

The challenge for the New York Desk was how to prevent the reserves created by the Fed's special credit programs from pushing the funds rate below the FOMC's target. Until the Lehman bankruptcy, the Desk had sold Treasury securities to sterilize the reserves creation from these programs. However, partly because of the Treasury Securities Lending Facility (TSLF) in which the Desk exchanged Treasuries for other less attractive collateral used by securities dealers in doing RPs, the Desk was running out of securities to sell. After Lehman, with the Supplementary Financing Program (SFP), the Treasury sold securities and placed the reserves gained on deposit with the New York Fed, thereby draining reserves. By the end of October 2008, the SFP had sterilized $559 billion in reserves. However, the Treasury was limited in the amount of securities it could sell by the debt ceiling.

The solution to preventing reserves creation from pushing down the funds rate was payment of interest on bank reserves.[8] According to Dudley (Board of Governors, *FOMC Transcript*, September 29, 2008, 15, 11), paying interest on reserves "should put a floor . . . under the funds rate and thereby allow the Federal Reserve to conduct monetary policy appropriately while providing liquidity consistent with financial stability. . . . We have a very important tool that will allow us to expand the balance sheet but maintain control of the federal funds rate. So we're not going to be compromising monetary policy."

Under Bernanke's guidance, the FOMC remained convinced that the cause of the recession was a disruption to financial intermediation, which the Fed could meet through its various credit facilities, but only in part. The solution was not an expansionary monetary policy but rather a government financed recapitalization of the banking system. At the October 2008 FOMC meeting, Tim Geithner (Board of Governors, *FOMC Transcript*, October 7, 2008, 12), president of the New York Fed, stated:

> You could think about the use of our balance sheet as a necessary but not sufficient condition to . . . stabilize the financial system and make sure that intermediation begins again and that people are willing to start lending again on a scale necessary to support some reasonable outcome for the economy going forward. Our basic judgment—and I think everybody's judgment—is that it is going to require capital from the government in some mix of forms for that to happen.

8. The Financial Services Regulatory Act of 2006 had granted the Fed authority to pay interest on reserves starting in October 2011. The Emergency Economic Stabilization Act of 2008, which created TARP (Troubled Asset Relief Program), moved the date up to October 1, 2008.

At the September 16, 2008, FOMC meeting, Bernanke began to consider a policy of adding to the capital of the banking system to promote economic recovery. At some point, the Fed could no longer use its balance sheet to aid financial institutions but needed to ask Congress for fiscal support. The question was when. Bernanke (Board of Governors, *FOMC Transcript*, September 16, 2008, 49) told the FOMC:

> Historically, if we look at situations like Japan and Scandinavia, ultimately there comes a point at which the banking system is decapitalized and dysfunctional and the government intervenes on a large scale. Those interventions have been very expensive, but in those cases I mentioned, they have generally restored the banking system to health and have helped the economy recover.

Although the Fed provided reserves, before March 2009, it did not do so freely through open market purchases but rather indirectly through loans that would have to be repaid (figure 21.5). Loans required the surrender of good collateral and were costly. Loans obtained by selling commercial paper to the Commercial Paper Funding Facility (CPFF) had a cost of OIS (basically the funds rate) plus 200 basis points for nonfinancial and financial issuers and OIS plus 300 basis points for asset-backed commercial paper (ABCP). Loans from the Term Auction Facility (TAF) had a maturity of eighty-four days. Discount window borrowing, which required pledging good collateral, carries significant stigma. It is evidence of weakness. Borrowing from the window peaked in the week ending October 29, 2008, at $112 billion. Only after the week ending January 7, 2009, when discount window borrowing was at $88 billion, did borrowing begin a steady decline. The Fed announced the purchase of agency (Fannie and Freddie) debt on November 25, 2008. However, by December 31, 2008, such debt amounted to only $20.3 billion, just a sliver of the reserves provided by the special credit programs (figure 21.6).

21.5. BERNANKE AND THE CREDIT CHANNEL

During the Great Recession, drawing on his work on the Depression, Bernanke emphasized the restriction of output through a credit channel. Bernanke (2015, 200, 206, and 208) believed that the Great Recession, which began after December 2007, originated in financial instability, not contractionary monetary policy:

> Animal spirits, sentiment, psychology . . . [were] central to the economic and financial story in February and March [2008]. . . . The

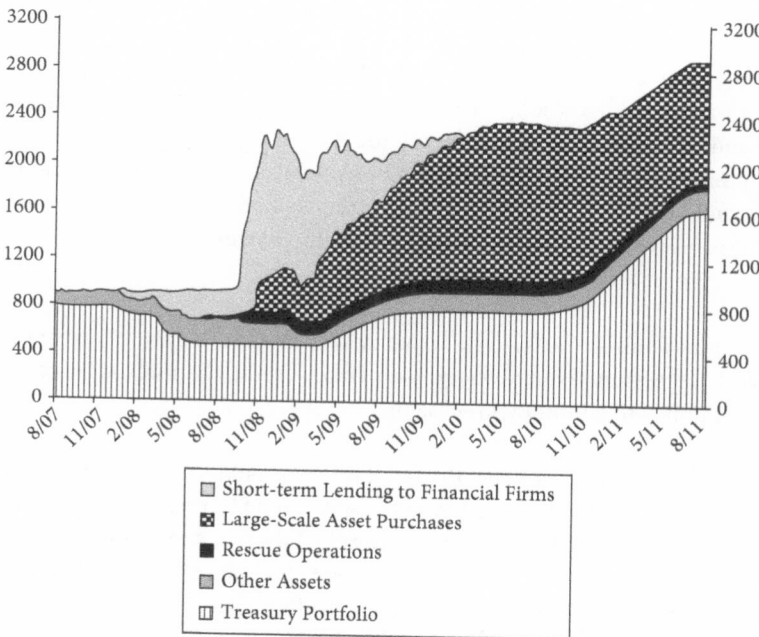

Figure 21.5. Federal Reserve System Assets
Data from Board of Governors, "Factors Affecting Reserve Balances," Statistical Release H.4.1. Short-term lending includes the Term Auction Facility, Discount window, Commercial Paper Funding Facility, Term Asset-Backed Securities Loan Facility, and the Primary Dealer Credit Facility. Large-scale asset purchases are open market purchases of agency debt and agency mortgage-backed securities (MBS). Rescue operations include Maiden Lanes I, II, and III and other AIG-related credit.

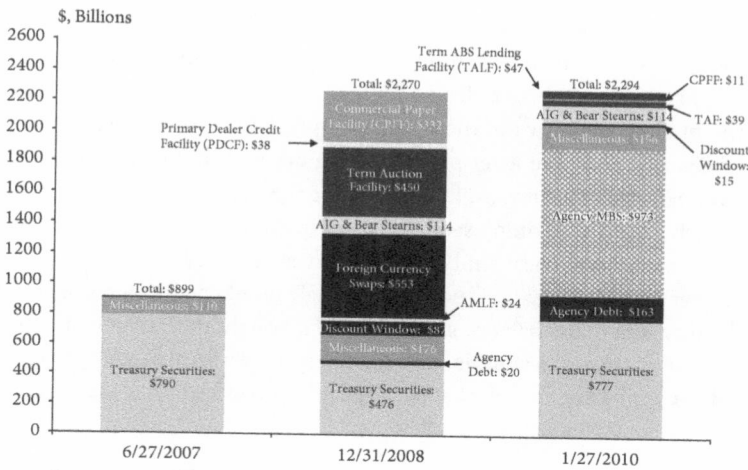

Figure 21.6. Changing Composition of Federal Reserve System Assets
Data from Board of Governors, Statistical Release H.4.1, "Factors Affecting Reserve Balances." AMLF is the ABCP Money Market Liquidity Facility.

economy and credit markets were increasingly mired in their own destructive feedback loop—bad economic news fueled financial turmoil,
and the turmoil in turn disrupted the flow of credit that powered economic activity. . . . Financial instability, contracting credit, and falling
confidence were seriously damaging the economy. . . . Market turmoil
was . . . what I called "self-feeding liquidity dynamics." In other words,
fear begat fear.

Henry Paulson (2013, 337), Treasury secretary during the first year of the
Great Recession, expressed the Bernanke "credit channel" view of using
credit policy to counteract recession:

The [Troubled Asset Relief Program] money would stretch much further
if it were injected as capital that the banks could leverage. . . . [9] [Assum-
ing] banks had a ten-to-one leverage ratio, injecting $70 billion in equity
would give us as much impact as buying $700 billion in assets. This was
the fastest way . . . to get them [banks] lending again.

Bernanke argued that the Fed should turn to credit policy rather than to
monetary policy. Bernanke (Board of Governors, *FOMC Transcript*, December 15–16, 2008, 25, 27) told the FOMC:

What we're doing is fundamentally different from the Japanese approach. . . . The Japanese approach, the quantitative easing approach,
was focused on the liability side of the balance sheet—specifically the
quantity of bank reserves. . . . The theory behind quantitative easing was
that providing enormous amounts of very cheap liquidity to banks . . .
would encourage them to lend and that lending, in turn, would increase
the broader measures of the money supply, which in turn would raise
prices and stimulate asset prices, and so on, and that would suffice to
stimulate the economy. . . . I think that the verdict on quantitative easing
is fairly negative. It didn't seem to have a great deal of effect, mostly because banks would not lend out the reserves that they were holding. . . .
Rather than looking at . . . [policy] as a single number, as a measure of the
liability side of the balance sheet, I think we ought to think about it as a
portfolio of assets, a combination of things that we are doing on the asset
side of our balance sheet, that have specific purposes.

9. The Troubled Asset Relief Program consisted of the $700 billion Congress ap-
propriated initially to buy mortgage-backed securities (MBS) from banks. In the event,
the Treasury used the money to put equity into banks.

The fundamental conceptual error during the Depression was to understand the role of the Fed as influencing the financial intermediation of banks rather than as controlling money creation. Nevertheless, to a significant extent, Bernanke accepted many of the themes common in the Great Depression. In the spirit of real bills, he accepted the idea that recessions reflected the collapse of speculative excess. The economist Henry Kaufman asked Bernanke, "How will the Federal Reserve respond to further financial speculative activities." Bernanke (2009b) replied, "You just introduced perhaps the most difficult problem in monetary policy of the decade, which is how to deal with asset bubbles. We've had two big asset bubbles in this decade, and both have resulted in severe downturns, particularly the credit bubble."

In the Depression, the belief prevailed that because of the uncertainty of their sales and possible interruption of their cash flow, businesses became unwilling to borrow from banks. Banks were not lending the reserves supplied to them by the Fed not only because of lack of demand for loans but also because they worried about their own capital adequacy. The low level of interest rates presumably indicated the ample supply of reserves to banks by the Fed (Hetzel 2012a, chaps. 3–4).

Because monetary policy was understood through the lens of financial intermediation, the presumed breakdown of financial intermediation during the Great Depression encouraged a general presumption that monetary policy was impotent. Based on this (mis)understanding, policy turned toward encouraging financial intermediation. Congress created the Reconstruction Finance Corporation in 1932 to supply capital to banks. (It was the forerunner of the Troubled Asset Relief Program created in September 2008.) Also, in 1932, the Federal Home Loan Bank Act created the Federal Home Loan Bank Board, the Federal Savings and Loan Insurance Corporation, and the Federal National Mortgage Association (Fannie Mae). The Farm Credit Administration, created in 1933, provided credit to farmers. It also put the 13(3) language into the Federal Reserve Act.[10]

21.6. REVIVING REAL BILLS THEORIES OF THE COLLAPSE OF SPECULATIVE EXCESS

Until December 2008, the Fed did not implement an expansionary monetary policy. Especially in fall 2008, it could have undertaken massive open

10. Fettig (2002) wrote, "Tucked inside a highway construction bill in 1932 was an amendment to the Federal Reserve Act [section 13(3)] allowing the Fed to allocate credit to individuals, partnerships and corporations in emergency situations. . . . This 1932 emergency authority . . . was used sparingly, and just 123 loans were made over four years by all 12 banks, totaling about $1.5 million." See also Selgin (2020b).

market purchases to provide banks with reserves. It could have reduced the discount rate to zero as a way of removing the stigma from using it and made clear to banks that the window was freely available as it had done in the May 1970 Penn Central crisis. It could have dealt with its concern that it would fail to control inflation by announcing an inflation target as a way of assuring the public that an expansionary monetary policy was a short-term expedient to deal with the recession and financial disorder.

In the Great Recession, however, through fall 2008, the FOMC believed that monetary policy was "accommodative" because with a funds rate of 2 percent and with underlying inflation (core PCE) just above 2 percent, the realized real rate of interest was zero. The FOMC therefore believed that the recession came from an interruption to financial intermediation. As a result, the Fed concentrated its efforts on programs to promote financial intermediation, especially after the disruption caused by the failure of Lehman Brothers on September 15, 2008.

The Great Recession revived real bills ideas, which highlight the collapse of speculative excess as the cause of recession. According to real bills, the herd behavior of investors drives an alternation of market psychology between excessive euphoria and excessive pessimism. In the initial periods of irrational exuberance, debt levels rise to unsustainable heights. The resulting imbalances cumulate until an inevitable correction occurs. A period of purging of these excesses must follow taking the form of deleveraging, recession, and deflation. It follows that central banks have a responsibility to prevent speculative excess.

According to this story, the reduction of the funds rate to 1 percent in June 2003 set in train the events that caused the Great Recession. Low interest rates encouraged financial institutions to fund portfolios of long-term illiquid assets concentrated in MBS (mortgage-backed securities) with short-term borrowing in the form of commercial paper and repurchase agreements (RPs). The resulting demand for mortgage debt created a bubble in house prices whose collapse set off the recession. Gary Gorton (2010) emphasized disruption to financial intermediation caused by a collapse of the "shadow banking system." Atif Mian and Amir Sufi (2010a; 2010b; 2011) emphasized a decline in the expenditures of liquidity-constrained households impacted by falling house prices that rendered their mortgages "underwater."[11]

11. Measured by the Federal Finance Housing Agency (FHFA) index, which excludes wealthy households that are not credit constrained, from 1997Q1 to 2007Q1, house prices rose 92 percent. House prices then fell 1.4 percent from their 2007Q1 peak prices to the 2007Q4 cycle peak. The minimal size of the decline seems hardly likely to have

21.7. CONTRACTIONARY MONETARY POLICY

Contractionary monetary policy caused the Great Recession. The classical-dichotomy (divine-coincidence) version of the New Keynesian model applies directly to the Great Recession (Goodfriend and King 1997; see also chap. 29). This model classifies firms into those in the sticky-price sector and those in the flexible-price sector. Firms in the sticky-price sector change prices only infrequently while firms in the flexible-price sector operate in auction markets in which prices are determined continuously. By targeting inflation in the sticky-price sector while allowing inflation originating in the flexible-price sector to pass through to headline inflation, the central bank gives free rein to the price system to determine relative prices.

Presciently, Aoki (2001, 75) had written earlier:

> Suppose there is an increase in the price of food and energy . . . putting an upward pressure on aggregate inflation. . . . The central bank could respond with a sharp contractionary policy and reduce aggregate demand by a large amount so as to decrease prices in the sticky-price sector. . . . However, our model shows that such a policy is not optimal. The optimal policy is to stabilize core inflation.

The FOMC should have been concerned only with the slight overshoot of core inflation from its implicit inflation target not with the higher headline inflation.

In summer 2008, four-quarter core PCE inflation peaked at 2.2 percent while headline inflation peaked at 4.2 percent (figure 20.4). Some of the core inflation likely represented transitory pass-through from the commodity price inflation shock. The FOMC, however, was concerned that high headline inflation would raise inflationary expectations and cause it to lose credibility. In retrospect, it would have been better to have announced an explicit inflation target to address the concern with credibility. The FOMC could have waited for the inflation shock to dissipate. If the FOMC did nevertheless lose credibility, it could then have initiated a contractionary policy.

Popular narrative attributes the Great Recession to a Great Financial Crisis. Much of the appeal of this assignment of causality to an interruption in financial intermediation derives from the timing of events. The recession

---

initiated the recession although the Mian-Sufi evidence indicates that declines in house prices depressed output during the recession.

worsened in 2008Q4 after the Lehman bankruptcy and AIG bailouts in September. However, until early October, the presumption had prevailed that because the subprime housing debacle had occurred in the United States, the recession would be primarily a US phenomenon. In the first part of October, as data came in from abroad, it became evident that the recession was worldwide. The Wilshire 5000 (Total Market Full Cap Index from St. Louis FRED) declined by 22.7 percent from October 1 through October 10.

The severity of the 2008–9 recession derived from the combined contractionary monetary policies of all the world's central banks. The world economy entered recession in 2008Q2 as shown in figure 21.7, which displays real GDP growth for G7 countries minus the United States. Because of a common concern for high headline inflation, foreign central banks maintained their policy rates at cyclically high levels while their economies weakened (figure 21.8). Foreign central banks kept their policy rates basically unchanged until October 2008. The ECB (European Central Bank) raised rates in July 2008 (Hetzel 2012a, 215).[12] At a world level, this behavior illustrated the empirical phenomenon documented by the monetary contraction marker for the United States in chapter 3. Recessions occur after central banks have raised their policy rates to cyclically high levels and then maintain them at a relatively high level while the economy weakens.

Three factors eliminated a contractionary monetary policy and allowed the economy to recover. First, at its December 16, 2008, meeting, the FOMC reduced the funds rate to the ZLB. Second, at that meeting, the FOMC used the statement to start forward guidance. The statement language read, "The Committee anticipates that weak economic conditions are likely to warrant exceptionally low levels of the federal funds rate for some time" (Board of Governors, *FOMC Transcript*, December 16, 2008). Third, especially with its March 2009, meeting, through open market purchases, the FOMC began to provide the liquidity desired by banks in a way that did not require collateralized short-term borrowing.

In 2008, the FOMC failed to understand the powerful forces that were affecting the world economy. The natural rate of interest declined dramatically. No one understood that a negative real rate of interest could be consistent with contractionary monetary policy. In the past, such as the second half of the 1970s, negative real rates had been expansionary (figure 18.5). At the same time, the assumption through fall 2008 that monetary policy

12. The Fed, the Bank of England, and the ECB cut their rates on October 8, 2008, by ½ a percentage point. The Bank of Japan did not follow. "The BOJ decided it was better to stand pat and guard against the potential risks of any rate cut, such as an asset bubble" (*Nikkei Weekly* 2008).

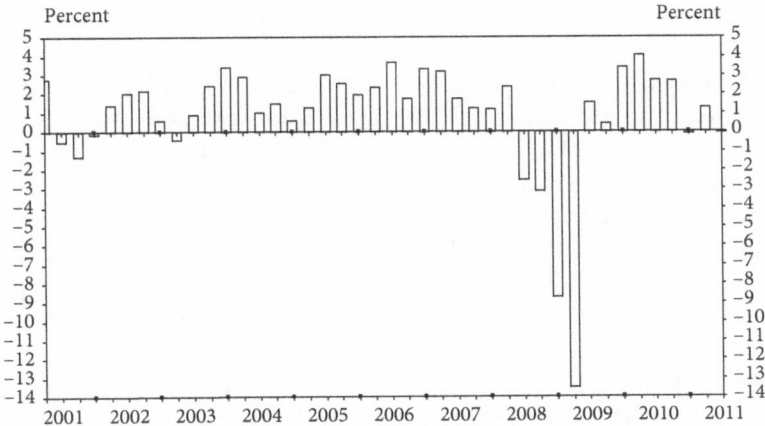

Figure 21.7. International Growth

Annualized quarterly growth in real gross domestic product for G7 countries excluding
the United States (Canada, France, Germany, Italy, Japan, and the United Kingdom).
Data are from the OECD via OECD Stat (http://stats.oecd.org/index.aspx), item
"B1_GE:VPVOBARSA." Heavy tick marks indicate fourth quarter.

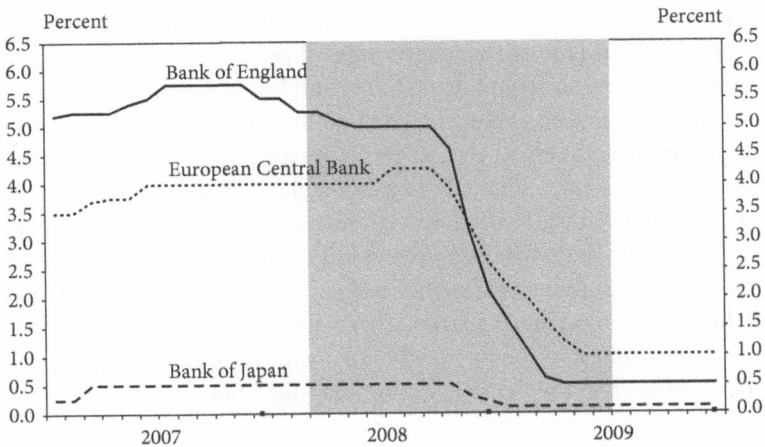

Figure 21.8. Central Bank Policy Rates

Foreign central bank interest-rate targets. Shaded area indicates recession. It
demarcates the Eurozone recession from a peak in March 2008 to a trough in June
2009. Heavy tick marks indicate December. Data from Bloomberg.

was expansionary coincided with high headline inflation caused by a giant inflation shock.

With the inflation shock, the FOMC could have let the higher inflation pass through to higher nominal GDP growth. However, the FOMC feared losing credibility for low inflation. For much of 2008, it signaled to markets that the easing cycle had ended and that an increase in the funds rate was imminent. As events unfolded, contractionary monetary policy caused a decline in nominal GDP growth (figure 19.1). In fact, inflationary expectations were well anchored. As a result, monetary contraction appeared primarily as a reduction in real output and only to a much lesser extent as a reduction in trend inflation (figure 20.4).

Bernanke (2007, 66) summarized the conclusions he drew from Friedman and Schwartz's *A Monetary History*. The first lesson was

> that a central bank's primary responsibility is the maintenance of price stability . . . and particularly to avoid the instability of expectations associated with an unanchored price level. The second lesson is that the financial industry is a special industry in terms of its role in macroeconomic stability. Major upheavals in the financial system can be extremely disruptive to the economy.

Unfortunately, Bernanke stumbled in implementing the first lesson. He ignored Friedman's advice not to interpret a "low" interest rate as indicative of expansionary monetary policy. The second lesson is pure Bernanke not Friedman. Friedman and Schwartz attributed the length and severity of the Great Contraction solely to restrictive monetary policy.[13] Bernanke, drawing on Bernanke (1983), highlighted a credit channel and extrapolated it to 2008. As a result, in 2008, after the March 2008 FOMC meeting, Bernanke ignored contractionary monetary policy as a cause of the recession (see also Selgin 2018 and Sumner 2021). After the Lehman failure, he concentrated stimulus measures on credit market interventions. That was easy to do because of the turmoil in the financial markets, but it sidelined quantitative easing at the ZLB as the FOMC's major weapon to fight recession.

---

13. They contrasted the experience of the United States with that of Canada, which experienced no bank runs or bank closures. Because of its fixed exchange rate with the dollar, Canada endured the same contractionary monetary policy as the United States. Friedman and Schwartz (1963a, 352) wrote: "If the bank failures deserve special attention, it is clearly because they were the mechanism through which the drastic decline in the stock of money was produced." That is, Friedman and Schwartz dismissed a credit channel.

CHAPTER 22

The 2008 Financial Crisis

Summary: The period from summer 2007 through summer 2008 was one of deleveraging. Banks took the mortgage-backed securities (MBS) in their off-balance-sheet structured investment vehicles (SIVs) onto their own balance sheets and wrote down their market value. Because of the uncertainty of the extent of the write-downs and the resulting credit-worthiness of the banks, banks limited lending to each other apart from short maturities. Banks wanted to be liquid. After summer 2007, the major uncertainty lay with European banks. With the failure of Lehman Brothers on September 15, 2008, the giant carry trade entailed by financing portfolios of long-term, hard-to-value, illiquid assets with short-term liabilities like repurchase agreements and commercial paper unraveled. The cash investors that had provided the financing fled to the safe side of the financial safety net, that is, to the too-big-to-fail banks and government money funds. Regulators spent the rest of 2008 trying to undo the flight by extending the financial safety net and by devising special lending facilities.

In fall 2008, monetary policy makers acted on the belief that they could separate the implementation of monetary policy and credit policy. The FOMC led by Ben Bernanke believed that monetary policy was expansionary and potentially inflationary as evidenced by a real funds rate near zero (a funds rate of 2 percent and core inflation near 2 percent). The recession, which had begun in December 2007, then had to come from disruption to financial intermediation. With the failure of Lehman in September 2008, the Fed instituted numerous programs designed to undo the flight of the cash investors and to maintain the flow of credit. However, the ad hoc nature of these programs created uncertainty and diverted the attention of policy makers from the responsibility of monetary policy for the recession.

Although the industrialized world had already entered a deep recession in summer 2008, because of the lags in reporting on GDP, that information became known only in early October. As a result, newspapers reported simultaneously on the world recession and on the disruption to financial markets caused by the flight of the cash investors to the safe havens. That coincidence along with the announcement by the Fed, Treasury, and FDIC of programs to undo that flight created the impression that the recession originated in a disruption to financial intermediation. However, if effective, the credit programs should have preempted the disruption to financial intermediation. They did not keep monetary policy from being contractionary.

The Great Recession imposed enormous costs in terms of the human suffering caused by high unemployment. In addition, it imposed costs by discrediting a free market economy. Ironically, with its heavy government regulation and the moral hazard created by the financial safety net, the financial sector was not a free market.

Financial markets are not inherently fragile but become fragile through the way in which the financial safety net encourages risk taking: the phenomenon of moral hazard. In the absence of a financial safety net, debt holders monitor the risk taking of the owners (equity holders) of a firm. The riskier the investments, the higher the risk premium debt that debt holders charge (Jensen and Meckling 1976). The financial safety net short circuits that monitoring and leaves it to regulators. As became evident in the Great Financial Crisis of 2008, regulators were not up to the task.

When house prices began to fall in 2006, the solvency of the entities created to hold illiquid MBS became problematic, and their debt holders (the cash investors) stopped rolling over the debt. In 2007 and 2008, the whole superstructure of illiquid assets financed by short-term, runnable debt unraveled.[1] Commentators use the term "shadow banking system" to summarize financial intermediation occurring outside of the banking system financed by cash investors, that is, funded by short-term liabilities. However, in 2007–8, especially foreign banks as well as nonbanks like the prime money funds and the investment banks were subject to runs by the cash investors that had supplied short-term dollar funding. The shadow banking system was only one manifestation of a worldwide "dollar carry trade."

1. The 1998 Asian crisis illustrated the pattern (Hetzel 2008, chap. 16). The banks in Asian countries like Thailand and Korea with fixed exchange rates had borrowed short term from American banks to finance illiquid loan portfolios. Foreign debt holders ceased rolling over debt when it became clear that the exchange rates of these countries were overvalued. This "carry trade" was made possible by the assumption, which turned out to be correct, by the debt holders that the IMF would bail them out in the event of a crisis. In 2008, the Fed played the role of the IMF. During the Asian crisis, Tim Geithner worked with Treasury Secretary Rubin. In 2008, Geithner was president of the New York Fed and worked to bail out the financial institutions abandoned by the short-term debt holders.

22.1. THE FINANCIAL SAFETY NET AND MORAL HAZARD

The housing crash that weakened the balance sheets of financial institutions arose as two blades of a scissors. One blade was the second grand failure of the government's attempt to allocate credit to housing. (The first was the S&L debacle of the 1980s.) Using the GSEs (government-sponsored enterprises) and the FHLBs (Federal Home Loan Banks), the government attempted to increase home ownership. The chief tool for making housing affordable was to reduce the requirement for down payments on home mortgages. An increased demand for housing with a limited supply created a sustained rise in house prices. That price rise made subprime mortgages seem like viable investments.

The second blade of the scissors was a financial safety net that encouraged risk taking. The financial safety net limits the discipline on risk taking by removing the monitoring of financial institutions by its debt holders. It subsidizes risk taking by socializing losses while privatizing gains. The result was nondiversified bank portfolios and a giant dollar carry trade in which banks or their off-balance-sheet progeny, the SIVs, financed illiquid, long-term, hard-to-value private MBS with short-term liquid debt.

The excessive risk taking encouraged by moral hazard assumed a variety of forms. Banks held disproportionate amounts of housing mortgages rather than diversifying their asset portfolios. European banks funded their dollar lending in the wholesale market by selling CDs, commercial paper, and engaging in foreign exchange swaps with US banks, hedge funds, and prime money market funds. Banks set up off-balance-sheet structured investment vehicles (SIVs) to hold mortgages as a way of lowering their required capital (Hetzel 2008, chap. 10). The investment companies (Bear Stearns, Merrill Lynch, and Lehman Brothers especially) levered up by taking on lots of short-term debt like commercial paper and repurchase agreements (RPs). The main avenue for risk taking took the form of financing illiquid, opaque portfolios of long-term mortgages with short-term debt.[2]

The moral hazard created by the financial safety net created a fragile financial system in which significant amounts of financial intermediation occurred outside of the regular banking system. First, starting with the failure of Franklin National in 1974, too-big-to-fail (TBTF) became a bedrock principle (even if unarticulated) among regulators of the financial system. The term TBTF, however, is better expressed as too-indebted-to-fail (TITF).

---

2. Books on the financial crisis include Ball (2018), Bernanke et al. (2019), Blinder (2013), Paulson (2013), Sorkin (2018), Tooze (2019), and Wessel (2009).

In the case of Franklin National, the Fed and the FDIC bailed out the debt holders of the bank holding company as well as the depositors of the bank. Although the term TBTF was invented after the bailout of Continental in 1984, it had already taken on mammoth proportions with the bailout of the large New York City banks and Bank of America at the time of the less-developed-country (LDC) debt crisis, which emerged in 1982 (Hetzel 1991; Nurisso and Prescott 2020).

Second, starting in the late 1980s, regulators became concerned that American banks operated at a disadvantage relative to foreign banks. The latter could be universal banks while American banks operated subject to the disadvantage of the separation of commercial banking and deposit banking (Hetzel 1991). US regulators looked on benignly when American banks created off-balance-sheet entities to hold mortgages to reduce required capital. Third, starting with the Clinton administration and continuing with the Bush administration, government used the GSEs (government-sponsored enterprises—Fannie Mae and Freddie Mac) to expand home ownership.

A result of these policies was an increased investment in real estate. From 1986 through 1995, the home ownership rate was steady at about 64 percent. It then began to rise and peaked at 69 percent in 2005. In real terms, house prices had remained steady from 1950 through 1997. They then rose more than 50 percent through the end of 2006 (Hetzel 2012a, figs. 10.1 and 10.2). Over the decade of the 1990s, real estate loans (residential and commercial) of commercial bank assets remained stable at 30 percent but then rose until reaching over 40 percent in 2007 not counting holdings of MBS. The real estate loans of FDIC-insured institutions (banks and thrifts) as a ratio of loans and leases were 47.6 percent in 2002Q2 and rose to 55 percent in 2008Q2 with the increase accounted for by banks with assets of more than $1 billion (Hetzel 2012a, 179).

22.2. THE CASH INVESTORS RUN THE SIVS IN SUMMER 2007

Indirectly through their SIVs, commercial banks held significant amounts of the AAA-rated tranches of subprime mortgages (MBS). The large investment banks and prime money funds held them directly. They financed these opaque, illiquid portfolios through issuing short-term debt. In August 2007, the holders of this debt, the cash investors, stopped believing in the AAA rating of the MBSs. The triggering event occurred on August 9 when the French bank BNP Paribus ceased redemptions from funds holding subprime mortgages.

Given the stable net asset values (NAVs or redemption at a par dollar value) of the prime money funds, the cash investors had an incentive to be the first out in a self-fulfilling anticipation of a run. If there were a run, the illiquid MBS could only be sold at a steep discount, and the funds would "break the buck," that is, be unable to redeem shares at par. Cash investors supplying funds through RPs feared that they would be left holding the illiquid MBS because the funds could not readily sell them. In the event of a run, they would be left with frozen debt.

The SIVs had lines of credit with their sponsoring banks. Those banks brought the mortgages onto their own balance sheets when the cash investors fled. European banks were affected because their dollar lending was financed by commercial paper issued in dollars. Great uncertainty existed over which European banks were holding MBS in their portfolios and what losses they would incur. Correspondingly, the cost of dollar funding of European banks rose. Issuance of asset-backed commercial paper became mainly overnight while interbank funding became primarily short-term.

As long as uncertainty existed over how many of the MBS would be coming onto bank portfolios from their SIVs, short-term funding contracted to short maturities, especially overnight. Because banks wanted to remain liquid, the interest rate on term lending in the federal funds market rose relative to the overnight rate. The Fed wanted to encourage banks to borrow from the discount window to reduce any funding difficulties associated with bringing MBS onto their balance sheets while winding down their SIVs. Because the discount rate was 100 basis points over the funds rate, apart from an overnight surprise outflow of funds, borrowing from the discount window sent a message to markets that the bank was having funding troubles. Through a reduction of the discount rate by 50 basis points on August 17, 2007, the Fed hoped to reduce the stigma associated with borrowing.

The Fed encouraged some large banks to borrow at the discount window with the hope of making such borrowing appear routine. However, because the spread over the discount rate remained at 50 basis points, the stigma remained. The Board of Governors could have lowered the discount rate to equal the funds rate. On March 15, 2020, in dealing with a surge in the demand for liquidity, it lowered the discount rate to the top of the funds-rate range, 0.25 percent. However, in August 2007, a discount rate equal to the funds rate would have encouraged borrowing and reserves creation. That reserves creation would have been difficult to sterilize and thus would have depressed the funds rate. The Fed did not want to send a signal that could be interpreted as an easing of monetary policy.

At its September 18, 2007, meeting, the FOMC began discussing an alternative to the discount window, which would allow term borrowing and which would not carry stigma. The Desk would auction off a set amount of funds. Because the interest rate on the loan would be determined competitively, such borrowing would not carry stigma. The resulting loan facility, the Term Auction Facility (TAF) began operation on December 12, 2007. In the meantime, the Federal Home Loan Bank System lent to banks experiencing funding difficulties (Ashcraft et al. 2010). However, that option was not available to European banks. To a significant extent, TAF was introduced to deal with funding issues in the US-dollar-denominated interbank market used by European banks. As measured by the widening of the interbank-deposit/OIS spread, the main problem was with funding the short-term debt of European banks.[3]

When the Fed announced TAF, it also announced swap lines with the European Central Bank (ECB) and the Swiss National Bank (SNB), which then announced auctions of dollars to their banks. The Fed sterilized the reserves creation from TAF and swap line borrowings. The fact that the Desk did not have to create additional reserves to keep the funds rate from rising meant that there was no system-wide panicky demand for liquidity. TAF and the swap lines were instruments for allocating credit to banks, especially European banks, that had funding difficulties because the markets did not know their MBS exposure. It was significant that TAF borrowing could be collateralized in euros with euro-denominated government debt, German Jumbo Pfandbriefe, and foreign government guaranteed securities. Agency-backed mortgage securities and nonagency residential-backed securities were also accepted as collateral (LHM 2020a).

The United States was pulling the chestnuts out of the fire for European regulators who did not require transparency for the books of their banks. Bernanke (2015, 184) wrote:

> ECB president Jean-Claude Trichet wanted the TAF and swaps announcements out at the same time to foster the impression that the swap lines were part of a solution to a US problem, rather than an instance of the Fed helping out Europe. His goal was to avoid highlighting the dollar funding difficulties faced by European banks. . . . [Not] only did the $24 billion initially distributed through the swaps go to Europe, all but about $3 billion of the $40 billion distributed in the first two TAF auc-

---

3. For example, for a maturity of one month, the interbank-deposit rate is the rate paid by a bank to borrow funds for one month from another bank. The OIS rate is the rate paid in return for the average funds rate realized for the month.

tions went to European and other foreign institutions operating in the United States, with German banks leading the way.

The Term Auction Facility and the dollar swaps were emblematic of the Fed's credit market interventions. It highlighted the difference between allocating reserves to distressed banks as part of a bailout and the traditional lender-of-last-resort function of a central bank to meet a generalized need by the banking system for additional reserves in a financial panic. TAF firmly extended the financial safety net to the dollar carry trade engaged in by European banks. In December 2008, dollar swaps came to $580 billion, "35 percent of the Fed's balance sheet. . . . Not the least remarkable thing about the Fed's crisis response was its politics, or rather the lack of political legitimation. The emergency liquidity provision to the international economy by the Fed between 2007 and 2009 was shrouded in as much obscurity as possible" (Sorkin 2018, 212, 215).

The FOMC was aware that TAF would attract the troubled banks. Eric Rosengren (Board of Governors, *FOMC Transcript*, August 18, 2007, 135), president of the Boston Fed, said, "If we had this auction, who would be the most likely to want to take the money out? I could imagine a situation in which you would have five borrowers taking out the full $20 billion. If those five were Countrywide, Washington Mutual, and three European banks, it would certainly give the perception that we were focused on financial institutions that had significant risks." Governor Kohn (Board of Governors, *FOMC Transcript*, September 18, 2007, 161) followed up:

> It's an issue for two reasons. One is that it could facilitate the runoff of uninsured liability holders, and the Congress has told us not to do that [likely a reference to FDICIA passed in 1991 in reaction to the S&L bailout], and we shouldn't do it. That's a moral hazard problem. The second is that it might allow the banks that aren't being run well to make that last bet—to do some other things that would put them at greater risk.

The Term Auction Facility was the first of the credit facilities that allowed the Fed to allocate credit. It supported the market presumption that regulators would not allow troubled financial institutions to fail but would merge them with stronger, better-capitalized firms. Bank of America's purchase of Countrywide in January 2008 reinforced that presumption. In fall 2007 and early 2008, the write-downs that banks incurred from taking the MBS of their SIVs onto their own balance sheets created no concerns among regulators about either the level of bank capital or the ability of large banks to raise capital (Bernanke 2008a). The acquisition of Bear Stearns by JPMorgan Chase in March 2008 added to the certainty.

22.3. FROM BEAR STEARNS TO LEHMAN BROTHERS

In early March 2008, the prices of subprime MBS continued to decline with the higher tranches of the securitized MBS also affected. Portfolios of MBS financed with MBS as collateral required higher haircuts. The investment bank Bear Stearns was especially affected. The run on Bear, which began in earnest on Thursday, March 13, 2008, started with a downgrade by Moody's Investors Service of the MBS that Bear held. The New York Fed ended the run by lending to Bear. It did so indirectly through JPMorgan Chase. JPMorgan lent to Bear with Bear's MBS as collateral. The New York Fed lent to JP Morgan with that same MBS as collateral. The Fed loan was a "nonrecourse" loan so that if Bear went into bankruptcy the Fed would be left with the collateral and would be fully repaid only if the sale of the MBS covered the amount of the loan.

The Fed initiated three programs intended to maintain market confidence in the weaker nonbank primary dealers (Bear and also Morgan Stanley, Lehman, and Merrill Lynch). Announced March 7, the Single-Tranche Term Repurchase program offered twenty-eight-day RPs with primary dealers. The key was that the dealers could deliver as collateral MBS to the Fed, their least attractive collateral for RPs with markets. The Term Securities Lending Facility (TSLF), announced March 11, lent the primary dealers Treasury securities in return for their MBS. The loans were for twenty-eight days rather than overnight as had been the case previously. The dealers could then use the Treasury securities in their RP financing rather than the securities requiring large haircuts. The Primary Dealer Credit Facility (PDCF), announced March 16, offered loans up to ninety days to primary dealers collateralized by mortgage-backed and asset-backed securities. The PDCF was unprecedented in that the investment banks were not regulated by the Fed but by the SEC. It required use of the 13(3) "unusual and exigent" authority.

The Fed loan to Bear via JPMorgan and the new lending programs did not stop the run. The Friday loan would just get Bear through the weekend. Bear needed a buyer with deep pockets that could credibly guarantee its borrowing. On such short notice, there was only one potential buyer with knowledge of Bear's books, JPMorgan, which was Bear's clearing bank. Wessel (2009, 167) wrote: "As for Jamie Dimon [CEO of JPMorgan], he held the best cards, and he knew it. The government wanted to sell Bear

Stearns before the markets in Asia opened, and Morgan was the only potential buyer left. Ergo, the government was going to have to subsidize the
deal."

Subsidizing the deal meant that the Fed would buy "a $30 billion pile of
dodgy mortgage-related assets of uncertain value, and putting the taxpayers
at risk for any losses" (Blinder 2013, 107). Wessel (2009, 167) wrote: "The
fact was, the Fed was about to purchase assets that it would likely hold for
up to ten years, assets that had more than a little stink on them. But the
spirit of the law was clear: the Fed should not make a deal if it anticipated a
loss." The uncertain value of the MBS appeared in the fact that "three more
months would pass before JPMorgan Chase and the Fed—working with the
money manager it had hired, BlackRock, and the auditing firm of Ernst &
Young—agreed on what was in and what wasn't. . . . By the end of 2008, the
Fed said the portfolio had lost another $3.2 billion in value" (Wessel 2009,
172–73) (beyond the $1 billion less than it had been valued at in mid-March).

New York Fed president Geithner could not get a current balance sheet
for Bear from Bear's regulator, the SEC (Wessel 2009, 171). Paradoxically,
the New York Fed had itself earlier ended a program that would have offered
it that information. Morgenson and Rosner (2011, 43) wrote:

> In January 1992, the Fed ended a program called dealer surveillance that
> it had long used to audit and inspect these Wall Street firms. . . . From
> this moment on, the Fed would no longer be able to conduct its own due
> diligence on dealer firms. . . . It was, to some Fed officials, a dangerous
> delegation [to the SEC] of an important duty that had given the cen-
> tral banks access to crucial information about the soundness of the Wall
> Street firms it was dealing with.

The Federal Reserve Act prohibited the Fed from buying Bear's MBS
assets. So, as Wessel (2009, 167–69) wrote:

> The lawyers would devise language to get around the requirements that
> the Fed could make loans, not buy assets. But that would be legal seman-
> tics. . . . To satisfy Fed lawyers, the Fed subsidy was cast in the rhetoric
> of a loan. But the Fed was effectively spending $30 billion of its money to
> buy mortgage linked securities that JPMorgan didn't want. . . . Because
> the Fed was not supposed to buy the securities outright, it borrowed a
> tool from the financial engineers whose handiwork had led to the Great
> Panic. It created a "special purpose vehicle" to hold the assets. Then it
> made a loan to that entity [Maiden Lane].

The loan to Bear Stearns was unprecedented in that it was the first time that the Fed had lent directly to prevent the failure of a financial institution that was not a bank. Shortly after the Fed bailed out Bear Stearns, Paul Volcker (2008) commented that the Fed had approached "the very edge of its lawful and implied powers."

Because of its relatively small size, Bear was not the problem. Sheila Bair (2012, 5), head of the FDIC, called it "a perimeter player at best." The real fear was that if Bear went into bankruptcy, the cash investors financing the repo market would draw back from Lehman Brothers and Merrill Lynch, which were especially highly leveraged and held significant amounts of MBS. At the same time, after the Bear bailout, Lehman and Merrill knew that if they got into trouble the Fed would rescue them by bringing money to the table to arrange a merger. They then did not need to sacrifice on their share prices in looking for a merger partner.

If the Fed had not bailed out Bear, then Merrill Lynch and Lehman, which also held significant amounts of MBS, would have had an incentive to find a buyer with deep pockets. The *Wall Street Journal* (2008a) headlined: "Lehman Is Seeking Overseas Capital, as Its Stock Declines, Wall Street Firm Expands Search for Cash, May Tap Korea." However, Lehman spurned offers from the Korea Development Bank to buy the firm and rejected the offer from China's Citic to buy half of it (J. Freeman 2009). Given the Fed's bailout of Bear, Dick Fuld, Lehman's chairman, could hold out for a good price. Vincent Reinhart, former FOMC secretary and economist, "called it [the Bear bailout] 'the worst policy mistake in a generation.' It meant that the Fed would always be expected to bring money to the table when trying to arrange the rescue of a big financial firm" (Wessel 2009, 174).

The *Washington Post* (2008a) reported, "We're not predicting that Lehman will fail—it won't, because of the Federal Reserve, which has let it be known that it will lend Lehman . . . enough money to avoid collapsing, the way Bear Stearns did." Similarly, the *Wall Street Journal* (2008b) reported: "In the summer of 2008, Mr. Fuld remained confident, particularly given the security of the Fed's discount window. 'We have access to Fed funds,' Mr. Fuld told executives at the time. 'We can't fail now.'" Treasury Secretary Paulson (2013, 158) wrote, "Dick [Fuld] was looking for an unreasonable price."

In June 2008, Jeffrey Lacker (2008), Richmond Fed president, wrote presciently: "In the short-term, governments and central banks may be able to alleviate financial market strains, but such intervention may affect financial intermediaries' choices in a way that makes financial stress more likely." The climax of Lacker's warning would come with the Lehman bankruptcy. The Fed created the worst of all possible outcomes. It did so by building the moral-hazard foundation for the dollar carry trade (shadow banking system) over many years and suddenly exploding the foundation with the Lehman bankruptcy. The cash investors then ran for the cover of the government money funds and the too-big-to-fail banks.

Although this was unknowable at the time, the Bear bailout would make a later bailout of Lehman politically inadvisable for the Fed. With Bear, what the public saw was a Fed without any congressional appropriation risking almost $30 billion of taxpayer money to facilitate the sale of Bear to JPMorgan. Because JPMorgan was the only bidder and because it knew that the Fed was unwilling for Bear to fail, it could get a highly advantageous deal. At the same time, there would be no help for the home owners losing their homes to foreclosure. The path from Bear to Lehman runs through the GSE (Fannie and Freddie) bailout.

In early July, financial markets became concerned about the solvency of the GSEs because of losses on their holdings of MBSs. On July 13, 2008, Paulson proposed that the Treasury be granted authority to purchase unlimited amounts of equity in the GSEs. In making the proposal, Paulson (2013, 147) feared that "by asking for these powers we would confirm just how fragile the GSEs were and spook investors." Paulson asked Bernanke to open the discount window to the GSEs. "Ben Bernanke made clear that this was properly a fiscal matter," but he agreed if Paulson (2013, 147) could assure him that Congress would approve the authority Paulson requested.

Paulson believed that asking for an unlimited capacity to inject capital would reassure investors. On July 15 before the Senate Banking Committee, Paulson (2013, 148–51) said, "If you've got a squirt gun in your pocket, you may have to take it out. If you've got a bazooka, and people know you've got it, you may not have to take it out." Paulson (2013, 151) later said that those words "would come back to haunt me." Congressmen disliked the fact that the authority would require the federal debt limit to be waived. Republican congressmen like Senator Richard Shelby disliked ceding fiscal authority to the executive branch. Paulson (2013, 153) wrote, "Shelby was right. Even though we said we never intended to use it, we were asking for an unprecedented blank check—and Congress was understandably wary of signing one over to us." On July 23, 2008, Congress passed the requested legislation.

With the announcement of losses in early August, the legislation did not restore confidence in the GSEs. Sorkin (2008) argued that reference to the bazooka produced the contrary result that fearful of government intervention private investors would no longer put additional capital into the GSEs. Sorkin quoted Doug A. Dachille, CEO of First Principles Capital Management: "He never laid out a roadmap. . . . Because of the uncertainty nobody was willing to put in money."

As government-sponsored enterprises, investors believed that the government would guarantee the debt of Fannie and Freddie. That assurance allowed them to operate with a vast amount of leverage, but the decline in the value of MBS brought to the fore that the guarantee was only implicit. Tooze (2019, 172) wrote:

> The vast bulk of the Fannie Mae and Freddie Mac balance sheet consisted of top-quality conforming mortgages. If they had had conventional balance sheets, they ought to have been able to ride out the storm. The problem was that they did not. In 2008 Fannie Mae and Freddie Mac held MBS valued at $1.8 trillion and guaranteed another $3.7 trillion on the basis of shareholder equity, which in the case of Fannie Mae came to only $41.2 billion, and in the case of Freddie Mac, to $12.9 billion.

Allowing debt holders to incur losses on GSE debt was unacceptable to the Treasury. It would have created an international crisis. Paulson (2013, 159, 161) explained that foreign investors, especially Japan, China, and Russia, held more than $1 trillion in GSE debt. They considered a debt default to be "expropriation," and Russia approached China about selling "big chunks" of the debt to force US intervention. One commentator quipped "too Chinese to fail" (Tooze 2019, 172). On September 7, 2008, the Treasury and the newly created Federal Housing Finance Agency (FHFA) placed Fannie and Freddie into conservatorship. Equity holders were wiped out, but debt holders were protected.

Nationalizing the GSEs did not calm the market. Instead, it exacerbated fears about the value of all MBS and consequently about the solvency of the financial institutions holding them. When Paulson actually exercised the authority given him by Congress, congressmen believed they had been misled. Congressional reaction was negative. With the GSE bailout, Paulson lost Republican support in Congress for another bank bailout. Paulson (2013, 181) wrote: "All of us were well aware that after Fannie and Freddie, the country, Congress, and both parties were fed up with bailouts. Obama and McCain, neck and neck in the national polls, each spoke out against them on the campaign trail. . . . I'd spoken with [Senator] Chris Dodd, who told me . . . don't bail Lehman out."

In response to the criticism from Republicans in Congress, Paulson made known that there would be no more public money for bank bailouts. Paulson "had been following a public strategy that specifically ruled out government support for a Lehman rescue" (Wallison 2016, 326) and presumably for other financial institutions. When Lehman ran into trouble in mid-September, he gambled that by announcing that the government would not aid in a rescue, the Treasury and the Fed could put together an LTCM style rescue in which the large banks would provide the guarantees required to restore confidence in Lehman. Time ran out, and the gamble failed.

Paulson had hoped that Bank of America would buy Lehman. When it decided instead to buy Merrill Lynch, that hope vanished. Only the British bank Barclays remained as a potential buyer. Barclays wanted a clean deal, that is, a Lehman without the mortgages and real estate. "Paulson and Geithner had repeatedly told Diamond [Barclay's CEO] in no uncertain terms that the US government was not going to help" (Sorkin 2018, 326). Paulson (2013, 186–87) had his aides leak to the press that there would be no "government checkbook" to bail out Lehman. He also used CNBC's Steve Liesman to reiterate that "there will be no government money in the resolution of this situation." Wall Street banks would have to finance a bad bank.

To get that clean deal, the hope was to persuade the large banks to finance a "bad" bank to take mortgage debt off Lehman's books as had happened in 1998 when the Fed arranged a bailout of LTCM. The Fed did assemble the bankers to set up such a bad bank. On Saturday, September 13, 2008, "at the Fed, Barclays, against all odds appeared to be making progress. . . . As unbelievable as it seemed to all the bleary-eyed bankers in the room, they were inching toward a possible deal" (Sorkin 2018, 338–39).

However, at the last moment, the talks collapsed. The sticking point was that Barclay's shareholders would have to sign off on a deal and a vote could take a month. Without a deal, there would be no deep-pocketed firm to guarantee Lehman's debt, and its trading partners, the hedge funds, would leave, and the firm would have no value. The British regulator, the Financial Services Administration, refused to become involved.

The Fed did lend Lehman's broker-deal subsidiary $60 billion to unwind its repo positions. However, according to Lehman executives, the Fed was unwilling to allow Lehman to transfer assets from the rest of the firm to serve as additional collateral sufficient to stop the run. The SEC regulated Lehman. Paulson persuaded its head, Chris Cox, to call Fuld Sunday night to tell him that Lehman had no alternative but to file for bankruptcy, which it did at 1:45 a.m. Monday.

Paulson's public stance against bailouts would have left the Fed isolated if it had lent sufficient funds to Lehman to prevent its bailout. Wessel (2009, 14) wrote:

In a conference call with Bernanke and Geithner, Paulson had stated unequivocally that he would not publicly support spending taxpayers' money—the Fed's included—to save Lehman. "I'm being called

Mr. Bailout," he said. "I can't do it again." Though Paulson had no legal authority to stop the Fed, Bernanke and other officials were extremely reluctant to put money into any Lehman deal over the Treasury secretary's objections.

On September 23, 2008, Bernanke made his first public comments on the Lehman failure in testimony before the Senate Banking Committee. Ball (2018, 123) commented: "In saying the Fed 'declined' to assist Lehman, Bernanke suggests that it could have done so if it had wanted to. He does not cite legal barriers, saying instead that the expected effects of Lehman's failure were not sufficiently dire to warrant a rescue because 'the troubles at Lehman had been well known for some time.'" The day after the Lehman failure, the *New York Times* (Andrews et al. 2008) wrote, "Asked why Lehman was allowed to fail, but A.I.G. was not, a Fed staffer said the markets were more prepared for the failure of an investment bank."

In a summary of his exhaustive study of the Lehman bankruptcy, Ball (2018, xii) wrote about the "claim of Fed officials that they did not rescue Lehman because the firm lacked the collateral needed to make the loan legal": "This claim is wrong: the evidence shows clearly that issues of collateral and legality were *not* important factors in the decisions of Fed officials. In addition, Lehman actually *did* have ample collateral for a loan that would have averted its sudden bankruptcy" (italics in original).

Ball (2018) and Wallison (2016) make the case that because the Fed did not have an inventory of Lehman's securities acceptable as collateral, Bernanke's claim is unsupported. Through its earlier actions, in voluntarily relinquishing oversight of the dealer community, the Fed was responsible for its own ignorance. Christopher Whalen (2013, 1) wrote: "neither the Fed nor the other regulators understood the scale of the disarray and absence of internal controls inside Lehman. The firm's assets were undocumented and could not be sold, a fact that surprised federal officials who tried to bail out the crippled institution. Why was this a new revelation? Because in the early 1990s, then New York Fed president Gerald Corrigan had ended surveillance of primary dealers."

Wallison (2016, 326) explained how the Bear bailout had weakened the financial system. Because Bear was the smallest of the investment banks, it would be inconsistent not to save a larger firm like Lehman. The prime money fund, Primary Reserve, then had no reason to sell the Lehman paper it held. With their share prices depressed, none of the large financial institutions would find it opportune to raise capital. Regulators seemed to have had no conception that the moral hazard created by the financial safety net required financial institutions to hold significant amounts of capital. Calomiris (2017, 60, fig. 1) showed the significant declines in the ratio of market equity to assets of the large financial institutions that occurred starting in summer 2007 when the declining value of mortgage debt began lowering the value of their capital. These institutions included AIG, Bank of America, Bear Stearns, Citigroup, Lehman Brothers, Merrill Lynch, WAMU, Morgan Stanley, Wachovia, and Wells Fargo.

Bernanke and Paulson judged correctly that Lehman was not too interconnected to fail. Alan Blinder (2013, 125), vice chair of the Board of Governors from June 1994 to January 1996, wrote: "They [regulators] first enunciated the belief that because six months had elapsed since Bear Stearns, the *markets had ample time to prepare*—both financially and psychologically— for the possible demise of Lehman Brothers" (italics in original). Blinder then quoted Bernanke's testimony before the House Financial Services Committee: "The troubles at Lehman had been well known for some time. . . . Thus, we judged that investors and counterparties had had time to take precautionary measures." What Bernanke and Paulson failed to understand was that the action would undermine the vast dollar carry trade of borrowing short to fund risky asset portfolios. Instead of the hitherto reasonably controlled unwinding of this shadow banking system that had started in August 2007, the flight of the cash investors that provided the short-term funding occurred in a sudden, discrete way.

Blinder (2013, 128) concluded:

> The market had acquired the view that the government was not going to let any financial giant fail messily. . . . The Lehman decision abruptly and surprisingly tore the perceived rulebook into pieces and tossed it out the window. Market participants thus were cut adrift, no longer knowing what game they were playing. That's a formula for panic.

A safety net that had previously insured all the debt incurred by financial institutions not just FDIC-insured deposits had created a fragile financial system. With the money market and the capital market, financial intermediation had always occurred outside of the banking system. What made the system fragile was the moral-hazard incentives that encouraged the funding of long-term, illiquid, opaque asset portfolios with short-term, runnable debt. In addition to the maturity mismatch, financial institutions operated with high levels of leverage, the ratio of debt to assets.

The failure of Lehman Brothers marked the first time in the post–World War II period that regulators had allowed a financial institution to fail with losses to its debt holders. That bankruptcy undercut the foundation of the dollar carry trade based on leveraging illiquid assets with short-term debt.

Cash investors fled to money funds holding government securities and to the too-big-to-fail (TBTF) banks.

22.4. AFTER LEHMAN

Bernanke thought of the Fed as possessing two tools. (Note the discussion in section 21.5, "Bernanke and the Credit Channel.") One tool, the funds rate, served its traditional role of macroeconomic stabilization and had to balance off the FOMC's dual goals of maximum employment and price stability. In fall 2008, concern by the FOMC over inflation limited how aggressive it would be in using that tool to counter economic weakness. The other tool was credit policy. The FOMC could counter weakness in the economy by maintaining and encouraging the flow of credit through the financial system. On the Tuesday after the Monday bankruptcy of Lehman, the Fed got two pieces of bad news: AIG was on the edge of bankruptcy, and a prime money fund "broke the buck" and had imposed limits on withdrawals by its shareholders. The potential disruption to the money markets and financial intermediation caused Bernanke and Paulson to reverse course on bailouts. They would pursue an aggressive credit policy by ensuring that no more financial institutions failed.

The first negative repercussion from the Lehman default was news from London that the British administrator of Lehman's bankruptcy had seized the collateral held for the hedge funds that used Lehman as their prime broker. Unlike in the United States where customer accounts are kept out of bankruptcy, all accounts were frozen. Hedge funds were then sure to flee Goldman Sachs and Morgan Stanley.

Also on Tuesday, September 16, the Primary Reserve Fund, which held Lehman debt, "broke the buck" and temporarily suspended payment. Because investors had always considered money funds to offer risk-free investments, the drop in net asset value (NAV) from \$1.00 to \$.97 was a shock. Primary Reserve was a prime institutional fund that held short-term paper rather than a government money fund that held only government securities. Because the other prime money funds offered stable NAV, there was a rush to be first out before they too broke the buck. With no cost to transferring funds from a prime to a government money fund, investors withdrew from the prime funds and moved to the government funds. The prime funds not only lost funds but also became uncertain about future withdrawals. Consequently, they ceased buying commercial paper except at the shortest maturities.

A disruption to the commercial paper market should not have been a problem. Corporations that issue commercial paper have backup lines of credit with banks. The problem was uncertainty over whether banks were well capitalized enough to take over the additional lending. As described above, to lower their required capital, banks had created off-balance-sheet entities, the SIVs. The SIVs held debt created by the bundling of debt such as mortgages, credit card and auto loans. They funded the debt with asset-backed-commercial paper (ABCP). Since August 2007, banks had been putting this debt on their own balance sheets and increasing their capital needs. As a result, between August 2007 and September 2008, commercial paper outstanding had declined by about $435 billion (Wallison 2016, 318).

On Tuesday, September 16, AIG, the global insurance giant, was fast running out of cash because of a failure to roll over its commercial paper. The problems originated with AIG's Financial Products Division (AIGFP). Prescott (2013, 148) wrote: "AIG's securities lending program took the investment-grade securities that its various insurance subsidiaries owned and then lent them out for cash collateral. They then took this cash and, rather than lend it against safe securities like short-term Treasury securities, they lent it against risky securities such as subprime mortgage-backed securities." Also, AIGFP sold insurance (credit default swaps) to protect against defaults on MBS, junk bonds, and collateralized debt obligations (CDOs). (CDOs are packages of loans—auto, credit card, corporate, and mortgage.) To do so, AIG had to post collateral. Declines in the value of the collateral resulting from credit downgrades by the rating agencies required increased collateral.

Because AIG had acquired some small savings banks, it was regulated by the Office of Thrift Supervision (OTS), but only in a pro forma way. The OTS did not require AIGFP to hold any capital against potential losses on the CDS that it sold (Blinder 2013, 132). Paulson (2013, 236) recounted how in explaining to a skeptical President Bush why an insurance company should be systemically important Bernanke described the Financial Products division as "a hedge fund sitting on top of an insurance company." In a review of two books dealing with AIG and Merrill Lynch, Prescott (2013, summary) wrote: "Both firms were vulnerable to managerial failures because they were inefficiently large, complex, and leveraged, that is, 'too big to manage.' The review also argues that these firms were able to get to that point because 40 years of governmental interventions in financial markets created the expectation that large financial firms are too big to fail."

Late on Tuesday, September 16, with an $85 billion loan, the Fed bailed out AIG.[4] Eventually, aided by the TARP money appropriated by Congress

4. Only in 1991 did the Fed obtain authority to lend to investment banks and insurance companies. Ironically, the authority came in a provision of FDICIA—legislation

to buy the subprime mortgages of banks, the loan commitment reached $183 billion. Just as the Primary Reserve Fund held Lehman paper, many prime funds held AIG paper. The Fed was concerned that an AIG failure would exacerbate a run on the prime money funds (Dudley in Board of Governors *FOMC Transcript* September 16, 2008, 4–5). The Fed feared that a run on the funds would force debt onto bank balance sheets and strain their ability to lend because of capital constraints. Given AIG's size and sudden loss of AAA status, the Fed also feared that an AIG bankruptcy could cause a general loss of confidence in large financial institutions. AIG's conventional insurance business would have survived in bankruptcy because the states regulated and required adequate reserves for its insurance subsidiaries. The bailout saved the Financial Products division and its creditors.

William Dudley (Board of Governors, *FOMC Transcript*, September 16, 2008, 5), then manager of the System Open Market Account, told the FOMC: "The liquidity crisis may also be a solvency issue. I think it is still a little unclear whether AIG's problems are confined just to liquidity. It also may be an issue of how much this company is really worth." Governor Kevin Warsh (Board of Governors, *FOMC Transcript*, September 16, 2008, 63) seconded Dudley: "If an AAA company like AIG were really fundamentally insolvent, the direct losses to a range of institutions, particularly those that are not just wholesale institutions but are retail institutions, could be very significant . . . [and produce] a broader loss of confidence that could affect the foundations of the US financial system."

The Fed bailed out AIG and all its creditors but not Lehman and its creditors. Investors had to sort out the distinction. Allowing Lehman to fail had to imply that regulators had retracted the safety net from the too-interconnected-to-fail criterion in place at least since the 1984 bailout of Continental Bank and its holding company. AIGs solvency was also in question. Rescuing AIG reinforced the belief that the safety net still covered too-big-to-fail financial institutions. The result was a flight of the cash investors from the remaining investment banks (Morgan Stanley and Goldman Sachs) to large, conservatively managed banks like JP Morgan Chase.

Paulson (2013, 242) wrote, "Our intervention with AIG didn't calm

intended by Congress to eliminate future bailouts such as the S&L bailout it had just legislated. Wessel (2009, 161) wrote that it was inserted "at the urging of Goldman Sachs lobbyists." Morgenson and Rosner (2011, 41) attributed the language to H. Rodgin Cohen, whose law firm represented all the large financial companies including AIG, Goldman Sachs, Bear Stearns, and Lehman Brothers. See Todd (1993). Morgenson and Rosner (2011, 43) wrote, "Even as Congress was writing legislation to allow investment banks and insurance companies to tap the Federal Reserve in times of crisis, the Federal Reserve Bank of New York . . . was reducing its oversight of the Wall Street firms it did business with."

markets—if anything it aggravated the situation." By bailing out all of AIG's debt holders, it also raised the moral hazard of the financial safety net to a whole new level. "Most generous of all was the resolution of the CDS portfolio, which was accomplished by buying out the dangerous CDO on which AIG had written insurance. . . . The counterparties received payment at 100 percent of par on $62.2 billion in toxic mortgage-backed securities." Sorkin (2018, 178). "When creditors who lent to, and the counterparties who dealt with, AIG without bothering to worry about its creditworthiness are bailed out 100 percent, the government is inviting creditors and counterparties of other companies to assume the same" (Blinder 2013, 138). The Fed then used its credit facilities to bail out the remaining two investment banks: Morgan Stanley and Goldman Sachs, which became bank holding companies on Sunday night, September 21, 2008.

Blinder (2013, 137) termed the AIG bailout "the most reviled of all the emergency actions taken by the Federal Reserve and the Treasury." One reason was "that a significant share of the original loan passed through directly to Goldman Sachs," formerly headed by Paulson. Blinder (2013, 137) quoted the Financial Crisis Inquiry Commission or FCIC (US Department of the Treasury 2009, 350) report: "With AIG, the Federal Reserve and the Treasury broke new ground. They put the US taxpayer on the line for the full cost and full risk of rescuing a failing company." The ability of the Fed overnight to make an $85 billion loan made clear that it was engaging in fiscal policy, the province of Congress."

The Fed had fully entered the realm of fiscal policy—an activity nowhere authorized in the Federal Reserve Act. Bernanke admitted as much when he told Paulson, "We can't keep doing this. Both because we at the Fed don't have the necessary resources and for reasons of democratic legitimacy, it's important that Congress come in and take control of the situation" (Sorkin 2018, 431). Bernanke and Paulson then decided to go to Congress to ask for an appropriation of money in a program that would come to be known as TARP.

22.5. PUTTING OUT THE FIRES IN FALL 2008

Bernanke and Paulson believed that the recession had to derive from the way in which the problematic subprime mortgages on bank balance sheets limited the willingness of banks to lend. Monetary policy could not be the problem. The FOMC statement issued after the September 16, 2008, meeting referred to "the substantial easing of monetary policy," that is, the reduction of the funds rate to 2 percent at the April 2008 meeting (Board of Governors, *FOMC Transcript*, September 16, 2008). Paulson (2013, 256–57,

260) later wrote, "We all knew that the root cause lay in the housing market collapse that had clogged bank balance sheets with toxic mortgages that made them unwilling to lend. . . . The situation called for fiscal policy. . . . We wanted . . . [banks to] clean up their balance sheets, and break the logjam of credit."

Fearful of Republican criticism that using government money to put equity into banks amounted to nationalizing them, Paulson opted to ask Congress for money to buy the toxic (subprime) mortgages from banks. On September 18, Paulson and Bernanke went to congressional leaders requesting funding for what became known as TARP (the Troubled Asset Relief Program). In one of the great ironies of the financial crisis, TARP only worsened the crisis through the fear it engendered by suggesting that regulators feared a collapse of the banking system. TARP became a vehicle for funding the bailout of Citi and AIG. It did not strengthen the banking system but instead eroded confidence in it.

Paulson knew that Congress would be hostile to a request for money perceived as bailing out the large banks. Moreover, concerned about preserving its constitutional prerogative to control spending, Congress would resist giving the Treasury a blank check to spend money at its discretion. The original three-page request was a carte blanche request for $700 billion to purchase mortgage-backed securities from banks at the discretion of the Treasury. After the unlimited authorization to bail out the GSEs, Congress was hostile. To persuade Congress to act, Bernanke and Paulson had to claim that the financial system was close to a collapse that would cause the economy to collapse. Later, that claim would become a Fed narrative of how the Fed had saved the economy from another Great Depression. Paulson (2013, 282) wrote, "We faced a real dilemma. To get Congress to act we needed to make dire predictions about what would happen to the economy if they didn't give us the authorities we wanted. But doing so could backfire. . . . Investors could lose the final shred of confidence."

With the top leadership of Congress at the September 18 meeting, Bernanke and Paulson did indeed scare those present. Bernanke began (Sorkin 2018, 446), "I spent my career as an academic studying great depressions. I can tell you from history that if we don't act in a big way, you can expect another great depression, and this time it is going to be far, far worse." Paulson continued, "I don't want to think about what will happen if we don't do this. If it doesn't pass, then heaven help us all" (Sorkin 2018, 446). Bernanke continued in emphasizing "how the financial crisis could spill into the real economy. As stocks dropped perhaps a further 20 percent, General Motors would go bankrupt, an unemployment would rise. . . . It is a matter of days before there is a meltdown in the global financial system" (Paulson 2013,

259). According to Paulson, members of Congress were left "ashen-faced" (Paulson 2013, 259). Buying toxic assets with TARP money would "break the logjam of credit" (Paulson 2013, 260).

On September 29, after Senate passage, the House rejected the TARP bill. That rejection, spurred by popular resentment at Wall Street bailouts, increased fears in financial markets that regulators would no longer protect the debt holders of financial institutions from loss. The *Wall Street Journal* (Power and Fields 2008) reported, "The defeat in Congress of a proposed $700 billion economic-rescue package followed an intense outpouring of voter anger, fanned by politicians, interest groups and media on the left and right, that overwhelmed calls from the president and top lawmakers to pass the deal. . . . 'The vast majority of my voters looked at this as a bailout for Wall Street,' said Representative Darrell Issa of California, one of the most outspoken Republican critics of the proposal."

Wessel (2009, 227) wrote: "The vote was a stunning rebuke of Bernanke and Paulson, who had told everyone that the economy as we knew it would end if Congress rejected the proposal. The markets believed the prediction." Stock markets fell with the S&P falling almost 9 percent. On October 3, the House reconsidered and passed the TARP legislation. After passage, nevertheless, "the Dow dropped 157 points, for a total of 818 points lost over the week" (Paulson 2013, 329).

Paulson had wanted TARP money to buy toxic assets from banks. On September 19, Paulson (Sorkin 2018, 449) said, "These illiquid assets are choking off the flow of credit that is so vitally important to our economy. . . . As illiquid mortgage assets block the system, the clogging of our financial markets has the potential to have significant effects on our financial system and our economy." However, the auctions envisaged for purchasing the private MBS from banks were a political minefield. If the Treasury purchased them at their diminished market value, banks still holding them would be under pressure to write down their value and take a hit to their capital. If the Treasury purchased them at a price above the market price, it would be subsidizing the banks at the expense of the taxpayer. Moreover, designing an auction was time consuming.

On October 12, after the passage of TARP, Paulson announced that the TARP money would be used to inject capital into banks rather than to buy toxic assets. The challenge was to avoid having the acceptance of TARP money carry a stigma of being a weak bank. Paulson therefore ordered nine of the most systemically important financial institutions to appear at the Treasury on October 13. Collectively, they held over 50 percent of US deposits (Paulson 2013, 359). The well-capitalized institutions would have to take the TARP money to cover for the weak institutions (Citigroup and

Morgan Stanley). Together, the nine banks could also make taking TARP money respectable for smaller, weaker banks. Unfortunately, the market knew which were the weak banks.

At the Treasury, the heads of the nine banks confronted their regulators: Bernanke, Geithner, Paulson, Bair (FDIC), and John Dugan (from the Office of the Comptroller of the Currency, OCC). Each bank was instructed on how much capital it would receive. Paulson made clear that if any bank refused, regulators would declare their bank deficient in capital. If the bank had trouble raising capital, their regulators would force it on them on harsh terms. Paulson explained, "But let me be clear: If you don't take it and you aren't able to raise the capital that they [the regulators] say you need in the market, then I'm going to give you a second helping and you're not going to like the terms on that" (Sorkin 2018, 527). Bair explained the additional program (Temporary Liquidity Guarantee Program) to be announced the next day that would guarantee the debt of banks and their holding companies. "Tim [Geithner] emphasized that the capital and debt programs were linked: you couldn't have one without the other" (Paulson 2013, 364). If a bank did not take TARP money, its competitors but not itself would have its debt guaranteed by the FDIC.

The Troubled Asset Relief Program may have provided banks with cheap capital, but it aroused public enmity toward them. The message was that they caused the recession by refusing to lend. TARP contained nothing to force banks to lend and did nothing to mitigate the wave of home foreclosures. "The errors continued with the wasteful decision to force-feed capital into banks that neither wanted nor needed it—on the foolish theory that doing so would avoid stigmatizing other TARP recipients. . . . Forcing capital on banks that didn't want or need it wasted a precious resource" (Blinder 2013, 208, 203). TARP never had more than $360 billion outstanding at any one time (Blinder 2013, 205). It did help get the Fed out of AIG, provide asset guarantees for Citi and Bank of America, and provide financing to General Motors and Chrysler until Congress could bail them out.

Sorkin (2018, 533) wrote, "Instead of restoring confidence, the [TARP] bailout had, perversely, the opposite effect. . . . Investors emotions and imaginations—the forces that John Maynard Keynes famously described as 'animal spirits'—ran wild. Even after President Bush signed TARP into law, the Dow Jones Industrial average went on to lose as much as 37 percent of its value."

On September 19, 2008, the Treasury announced the Temporary Guarantee Loan Program. It used funds in the Exchange Stabilization Fund to guarantee shareholders in money market mutual funds against loss. Wallison (2016, 319–20) wrote: "The Federal Reserve had permitted them [banks] to evade normal capital requirements by placing mortgages in these off-balance sheet vehicles and issuing commercial paper backed by these as- sets to short-term lenders like primary money market funds. If the primary funds lost too many investors to government money funds, the banks . . . would have to take immediate losses by . . . bringing the loans back on their own balance sheets." Given the Fed's belief that encouraging bank lend- ing was key to stimulating the economy, the resulting hit to bank capital would have had the undesirable effect of limiting bank lending. Ironically, "The money market fund industry itself was split on the question of govern- ment aid. The biggest funds thought they could protect themselves and the $1-a-share value and didn't want to pay for government insurance" (Wessel 2009, 208).

A consequence unanticipated by the Treasury was to encourage the transfer of funds from banks, which offered deposit insurance just up to $100,000, to the money funds. To counter that incentive, the Treasury changed the guarantee to apply only to money fund shares already held. However, "the episode didn't instill confidence in the United States Trea- sury" (Blinder 2013, 147). In addition, to prevent an outflow of funds from community banks to the too-big-to-fail banks, on October 3, 2008, the FDIC raised the limit on insured deposits for banks and credit unions to $250,000 (Bair 2012, 112). Because small businesses often held deposits in excess of $250,000, on October 14, 2008, the FDIC began to insure indi- vidual deposit accounts without any size limit.

The same day, September 19, the Fed announced the Asset Backed Com- mercial Paper Money Market Mutual Fund Liquidity Facility (AMLF). With it, the Fed made nonrecourse loans to banks using as collateral asset-backed commercial paper (ABCP) purchased from the prime money market funds. "Nonrecourse" meant that if ABCP suffered losses, the Fed not the banks would incur the losses. That is, the AMLF involved the Fed in fiscal policy. Unlike the Fed's response to the May 1970 Penn Central disruption to the commercial paper market, the AMLF allowed banks to fund the purchase of ABCP without recourse to the discount window.

On October 7, 2008, the Board of Governors announced the Commercial Paper Funding Facility (CPFF) to purchase commercial paper from banks and corporations. From 1934 through 1958, when Congress rescinded the authority, section 13(b) of the Federal Reserve Act authorized Fed banks to make loans to corporations. With the CPFF, the Fed again started lending to corporations using section 13(3). The CPFF also added to TAF and swap lines in helping foreign banks. "The three biggest foreign borrowers turned out to be the troubled institutions UBS (Switzerland), Dexia (Belgium), and BNP Paribus (France)" (Blinder 2013, 149). On October 21, 2008, the

Fed announced the Money Market Investor Funding Facility (MMIFF) to purchase commercial paper from money market mutual funds. Both worked through SIVs. Table 22.1 (from Hetzel 2012a, 258) lists the various credit programs as of November 26, 2008.

On October 14, 2008, the FDIC announced the Temporary Liquidity Guarantee Program (TLGP), which guaranteed newly issued senior debt of all financial institutions ("banks, thrifts, and holding companies"). With the TLGP, the FDIC ventured far beyond its original mandate to insure bank deposits up to a limit. The FDIC found the authority for the TLGP in the 1991 Federal Deposit Insurance Corporation Improvement Act (FDICIA). Congress had intended FDICIA to prevent the kind of bailouts forced on it by the 1980s S&L crisis. It did so by requiring the FDIC to use least-cost resolution when it closed a bank. However, it could depart from that requirement if a bank posed a "systemic risk."

To authorize the TLGP, the FDIC would have to apply the systemic risk designation, which FDICIA had intended to apply to a single bank. The FDIC would have to stretch hard to argue that the banking system rather than an individual bank was threatened. However inaccurate, the designation could only create distrust of the banking system. By guaranteeing the debt issued by all financial institutions, the FDIC could guarantee the debt issued by Morgan Stanley, Goldman Sachs, and Citigroup without attaching any bailout stigma.

Paulson, Bernanke, and Geithner pressured Bair to set up the program. Paulson (2013, 340, 357) said that Bair characterized their meeting with her as an "ambush." Paulson said he would meet separately with Bair "when the tension between Tim and her got too high." Paulson had to reassure her "that Treasury would use TARP to prevent bank holding companies from failing." Despite the "systemic risk" rationale, the banking system was never threatened with a Depression-style bank run. The TLGP provided cover to aid a few large, troubled financial institutions. Bair (2012, 114) wrote:

> The truth is, there were only three major institutions at that time that were clearly insolvent with no options for accessing capital from non-government sources: Merrill Lynch, Citi, and AIG. Morgan Stanley and Goldman Sachs were having problems, but they had been able to access additional capital from "deep pockets" (Warren Buffett for Goldman Sachs and the giant Japanese bank Mitsubishi for Morgan Stanley).

Bernanke wanted the debt guarantees as a tool to use financial intermediation to provide economic stimulus. Bair (2012, 14) wrote, "If there was a reason to provide the debt guarantee (indeed, the only reason to provide

Table 22.1. Programs to Stimulate Financial Intermediation as of November 26, 2008

Federal Reserve Programs		
Use	Maximum Dollar Commitment	Funds Used as of 11/26/2008
Commercial paper funding facility	$1.8 trillion	271 billion
Term auction facility	$900 billion	$415 billion
Term securities lending	$250 billion	$190 billion
Credit extension to American International Group (AIG)	$123 billion	$87 billion
Money market investor funding facility	$540 billion	$0 billion
Citigroup bailout	$291 billion	$291 billion
Discount window lending to commercial banks, primary credit		$92 billion
Asset-backed commercial paper money market mutual fund liquidity facility	$62 billion	$62 billion
Primary dealer credit facility	$50 billion	$50 billion
Bear Stearns' assets (covered when bought by JPMorgan Chase)	$29 billion	$27 billion

FDIC Programs		
Use	Maximum Dollar Commitment	Funds Used as of 11/26/2008
Loan guarantees	$1.4 trillion	
Guarantee to GE Capital	$139 billion	$139 billion
Citigroup bailout	$10 billion	$10 billion

Treasury Department Programs		
Use	Maximum Dollar Commitment	Funds Used as of 11/26/2008
Troubled Asset Relief Program (TARP)	$700 billion	$375 billion
Stimulus package	$168 billion	$168 billion
Exchange Stabilization Fund—money market fund share guarantees	$50 billion	$50 billion
Tax breaks for banks	$29 billion	$29 billion

Source: *Washington Post* (2008b)

the debt guarantee), it was to keep the banks in a position of continuing to lend. Geithner especially wanted to aid Citigroup, which he regulated." Bair (2012, 117) wrote, "Tim [Geithner] wanted us [the FDIC] to guarantee the debt not only of banks and their regulated holding companies but also of any affiliate organizations within the holding company structure. . . . All that was being driven by Citi's special needs."

On November 25, the Fed announced a new program to revive the shadow banking system: the Term Asset-Backed Securities Loan Facility (TALF). Under TALF, the New York Fed set up a SIV that would buy asset-backed securities (ABS) collateralized by loans to small businesses and consumers. The New York Fed would lend on a nonrecourse basis to the SIV. Originally, the Fed would lend up to $200 billion. The maximum amount lent at any one time was not more than $49 billion, and lending stopped in July 2010. In a similar program, with the Public-Private Investment Program (PPIP), announced on March 23, 2009, the Fed planned to buy up to $1 trillion of toxic assets from banks' balance sheets (Wikipedia 2020). Although these programs never financed a significant amount of ABS, they are indicative of how the Fed thought of economic stimulus in terms of subsidizing financial intermediation by taking risk onto its own balance sheet.

22.6. BANK BAILOUTS

Washington Mutual (WaMu) was the largest US thrift. It held significant amounts of option-adjustable-rate mortgages (ARMs), which gave the borrower the ability to postpone payments by adding to the principal of the loan. Bair (2012, 93) wrote, "WaMu had been terribly mismanaged and was a major player in the kind of abusive, unaffordable, and at times potentially fraudulent lending that had driven the subprime crisis." WaMu was closed on September 25, 2008, by the FDIC and was sold to JPMorgan Chase. The Fed could bail out Bear and AIG but not WaMu because it was an FDIC-insured institution. That meant that the head of the FDIC, Shelia Bair, had the authority to close it. In arranging a merger with JPMorgan Chase, she imposed losses on the unsecured creditors of WaMu's holding company. "WaMu debt holders got about 55 cents on the dollar, roughly what the securities had been trading for" (Paulson 2013, 293).

In 2006, Wachovia, a commercial bank, had purchased Golden West, which held significant amounts of option ARMs and concentrated its mortgages in California. Wachovia's wholesale funding dried up after September 25, 2008. The FDIC arranged a sale of Wachovia first to Citigroup on September 29 but then switched the buyer to Wells Fargo when the latter made an offer that did not require government assistance.

On November 23, the Fed, the Treasury, and the FDIC bailed out Citi again, that is, beyond the TARP money. Failure to buy Wachovia with its stable deposit base hurt Citi. With $500 billion in uninsured foreign deposits (Paulson 2013, 412), it possessed characteristics of a hedge funds engaged in the dollar carry trade. Bair (2012, 121–22, 124–25) wrote:

> Its [Citi's] losses were not attributable to uncontrollable "market conditions"; they were attributable to weak management, high levels of leverage, and excessive risk taking. It had major losses driven by their exposures to a virtual hit list of high-risk lending: subprime mortgages, "Alt-A" mortgages, "designer" credit cards, leveraged loans, and poorly underwritten commercial real estate. It had loaded up on exotic CDO's and auction rate securities. It was taking losses on credit default swaps entered into with weak counterparties, and it had relied on unstable, volatile funding—a lot of short-term loans and foreign deposits. . . . What's more, virtually no meaningful supervisory measures had been taken against the bank by either the OCC or the NY Fed. . . . It had been hijacked by an investment banking culture that made profits through high-stakes betting. . . . Its failure would be not just a domestic but an international embarrassment for those two regulators [the OCC and the New York Fed]. . . . So many decisions were being made through the prism of that one institution's needs.

With the bailout, Citi set aside $306 billion in a pool of mortgage assets. Beyond $29 billion in initial losses for Citi, the Treasury and the FDIC would absorb the next $15 billion. The Fed made a nonrecourse loan to Citi, which meant that if losses exceeded the covered amount, Citi would turn the mortgages over to the Fed. The Fed got the downside and Citi got the upside.

At the time of the Lehman bankruptcy, Bank of America had agreed to buy Merrill Lynch, one of the remaining threatened investment banks. Bank of America had not done its due diligence. In the fourth quarter, Merrill announced large losses on its mortgage portfolio, and Bank of America threatened not to complete the deal. To keep Bank of America engaged, the Fed, Treasury, and the FDIC announced a "ring-fencing" arrangement of its MBS like that of Citi.

On February 10, 2009, Geithner, who had become Treasury secretary, announced the Supervisory Capital Assessment Program (SCAP). Under SCAP, bank regulators would examine the balance sheets of banks to determine their capital adequacy under a worst-case scenario that the recession would worsen significantly. Banks undercapitalized based on this draconian assumption would have to raise new capital. Failure to raise the required capital would lead to a government recapitalization with unknown conditions. Ironically, the stress tests only added to the stress of the banking system. Markets reacted badly to the lack of details about the program, and the Dow Jones fell almost 5 percent.

In a case of unintended consequences, SCAP made it practically impossible for banks to raise new capital. Investors feared that if they put new equity into a bank that subsequently received government capital their shares would be diluted. Just as concerning was the fear that government capital would amount to a nationalization of the bank. That is, the government would run the bank. The *New York Times* (Andrews 2009, B1) wrote, "If policy makers were even remotely honest, analysts said, they would force banks to take huge write-downs and insist on a high price in return for taking bailout money. For practical purposes, that could mean nationalization."

The Fed revealed the results of the stress tests on May 7, 2009. Even assuming a worsening of the recession, the banking system was well capitalized. The total additional capital required for the nineteen banks examined came to only $75 billion with $59.1 billion accounted for by just three institutions: Bank of America ($33.9 billion), GMAC ($11.5 billion), and Wells Fargo ($13.7 billion) (Board of Governors 2009b).

Banks did supply the credit needs of their business customers. Figure 22.1 (from Hetzel 2012a, fig. 12.23) shows survey data from small busi-

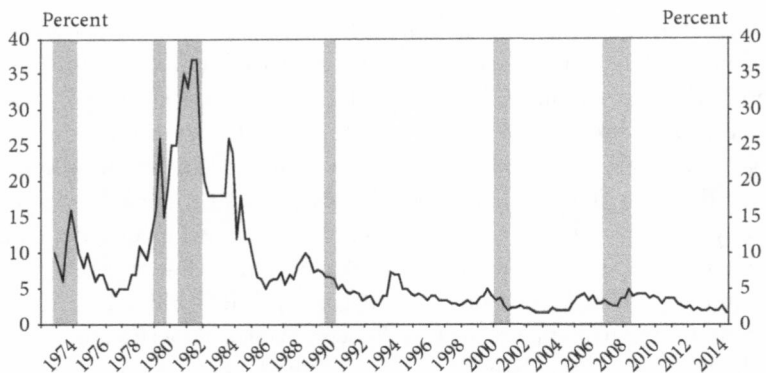

Figure 22.1. NFIB Single Most Important Problem:
Percentage Reporting Financial and Interest Rates
Percentage of small businesses reporting "financial and interest rates" in response to the question, "What is the single most important problem facing your business today?" Survey conducted by the National Federation of Independent Businesses, Small Business Economic Trends. Shaded areas indicate recessions. Heavy tick marks indicate December. Data from Haver Analytics as gathered by the National Federation of Independent Businesses.

nesses gathered by the National Federation of Independent Businesses. It shows the percentage of firms that reported obtaining credit as their primary problem. In the recession, this series remained well below the levels reached in the 1980s and peaked at only 6 percent at the end of the recession.

22.7. THE POLITICAL ECONOMY OF CREDIT POLICY

Why should there be any limits placed by law on the power of the Fed to intervene in credit markets? Should not the Fed have unlimited power to act in a financial crisis? An answer to these questions touches on the foundations of a constitutional democracy with its separation of powers (Hetzel 1997).

Any discussion of the role of the Fed within the democratic institutions of the United States must distinguish between monetary policy and credit policy (Goodfriend 1994). Monetary policy concerns how the Fed conditions markets to form expectations of the future risk-free rate of interest embodied in the forward rates of the term structure. The resulting term structure of interest rates interacts with the (natural) term structure to determine the impact of monetary policy. (The natural term structure is the real yield curve that that distributes aggregate demand intertemporally to maintain aggregate real demand equal to potential output.) The ability of the Fed to implement monetary policy derives from its ability to create bank reserves through its bookkeeping operations.

Credit policy is different. It concerns the ability of the Fed to act as a financial intermediary. It can allocate its asset portfolio in a way that influences the allocation of credit among competing uses. By holding only Treasury securities, the Fed leaves the allocation of credit to the marketplace. In contrast, through holding assets like MBS, it allocates credit to a particular sector, housing. The lending created by bailouts overrides the market allocation of credit. The Fed is using its seigniorage power, which derives from its ability to create reserves, to transfer resources. There are winners and losers. In the case of bailouts, the winners are the stockholders and unsecured creditors of the bailed-out financial institutions, and the losers are the taxpayers. Credit policy is fiscal policy, not monetary policy. The US Constitution reserves fiscal policy to Congress.

Bailing out financial institutions undercuts the principles of free markets. Free markets require free entry *and* free exit if a firm fails to meet the competition of a free market. Moral hazard—excessive risk taking—arises when regulators stand ready to bail out the stockholders and debt holders of financial firms. Those debt holders then have no incentive to exercise control over the risk taking of the firms. The managers of the firms, however, have an incentive to take on excessive risk knowing that they reap the gains of their bets while the taxpayers incur the losses. The Fed subsidizes private sector risk taking.

The bailouts contributed to the widespread public sentiment that capitalism is a system rigged in favor of the rich and powerful. For example, in the case of Bear, the public saw that Bernanke and Geithner were willing to risk $30 billion of taxpayer money to create a favorable buying opportunity for JP Morgan Chase. At the same time, helping home owners underwater on their home mortgages was infeasible. No policy maker pointed out that a vast financial safety and the moral hazard it creates are not an inherent part of capitalism. More than any bailout, AIG caused the public to think that capitalism was rigged.

Bair (2012, 188) stated, "Everybody should have the freedom to fail in a market economy. Without that freedom, capitalism doesn't work." In contrast, the culture in the Fed in the post–World War II period is that leaving the decision about the viability of a bank to the discipline of the marketplace is unacceptable. A failure of a bank precipitated by bank debt holders is messy and unnecessary. Regulators can always work with a troubled bank to fix its problems. Moreover, financial markets are presumed inherently unstable. "In a panic, runs on a few institutions soon become contagious. . . . Consequently, like a row of dominoes toppling, one institution's failure may cause others" (Bernanke 2015, 399). Perhaps the real concern is that in the event of a large shock investors move funds from weak to strong banks.

The "no fail" culture created a vast dollar carry trade around the ambiguity of the line drawn by the financial safety net. Money market funds advertised themselves as banks from the point of view of safety. They could offer higher returns than banks but still in a crisis be treated as banks because of the moral hazard created by the de facto policy of bailing out all troubled financial institutions. In summer 2007, the intermediation that had been conducted through this system began to unravel as intermediation returned to banks (Hetzel 1991; 2012, chaps. 9 and 13). In fall 2008, contractionary monetary policy by all the world's major central banks and the surprise of regulators allowing Lehman to fail set off a precipitate unraveling.

22.8. CREDIT POLICY CROWDED OUT MONETARY POLICY

In the Great Recession, policy makers focused on maintaining the flow of credit as an instrument of macroeconomic stabilization. Instead, if they had been willing to implement an expansionary monetary policy, they would not have made the mistake of implementing a contractionary monetary policy. Regulators could have dealt with any disruption to financial intermediation by preventing the failure of financial institutions in ways that nevertheless imposed losses on stockholders and debt holders.

Central banks have two sides to their balance sheet and two ways of conducting policy. Bernanke changed the focus to the left side, the asset side. Credit policy deals with the way in which the composition of central bank assets directs credit to particular sectors under the presumption that financial markets fail to supply funds to credit worthy borrowers. Credit policy was supposed to prevent a second Depression. However, prevention of a second Depression set a low bar for measuring the performance of the Fed and regulators.

Monetary policy concerns the right side of the central bank's balance sheet: its liabilities. Those liabilities, which include the reserves held with it by banks, along with currency, constitute the monetary base, the foundation of the money stock. Control over the money stock gives the central bank control over the nominal (dollar) expenditure of the public. In the Great Recession, the common decline in nominal and real expenditure signaled a failure of monetary policy.

In May 1970, with the failure of Penn Central and the resulting disruption to the commercial paper market, the Fed opened the discount window and encouraged banks to borrow to fund the lines of credit drawn on by corporations replacing the funds lost from not issuing commercial paper. The Fed could have responded similarly after the Lehman bankruptcy. All corporations that issue commercial paper have lines of credit with banks. Opening the discount window for banks to borrow freely would have allowed banks to replace funding in the commercial paper market as well as allowing them to support the off-balance-sheet SIVs they had created.

The immediate hindrance was that discount window borrowing had come to be associated with stigma as a sign of weakness. In the 1980s, Continental Bank and the Bank of New England had borrowed heavily from the discount window when wholesale funding disappeared in response to their insolvency. Nevertheless, the Board of Governors could have removed the stigma from borrowing at the window through a dramatic lowering of the discount rate. However, in fall 2008, the FOMC remained concerned about a revival of inflation and lowered the funds rate only reluctantly (chap. 21). Even at the September 16, 2008, FOMC meeting, the day after the Lehman failure, the FOMC statement read: "The inflation outlook remains highly uncertain. The downside risks to growth and the upside risks to inflation are both of significant concern to the Committee" (Board of Governors, *FOMC Transcript*, September 16, 2008).

Bernanke's two-tool toolbox view of policy was decisive. The primary tool for dealing with the recession would be maintenance of financial intermediation by using bailouts and special credit programs. On October 8, 2008, along with other central banks, the FOMC lowered the funds rate by ½ a percentage point from 2 percent to 1½ percent. In response, the Dow

Jones lost 2 percent. Wessel (2009, 231) reported Bernanke as saying, "It obviously didn't calm the markets. . . . What it told me was that monetary policy wasn't the only tool. . . . And monetary policy works with a lag."

Bank loans, however, are a poor indicator of economic activity. Loans at banks declined steadily after the cyclical trough in June 2009 and did not start to grow again until two years later in June 2011.[5] Loans are demand determined. The concept of a central bank as a creator of money never appeared. The economy did recover after the FOMC pushed the funds rate down to the ZLB and engaged in open market purchases, but these actions, implemented timidly, always focused on financial conditions. The severity of the recession points to the decision to concentrate on financial intermediation to stimulate the economy as the major mistake of the Great Recession.

22.9. CROSSING THE RUBICON TO ALLOCATING CREDIT

In the financial crisis of fall 2008, the Fed made credit allocation an integral part of managing aggregate demand. Why was this expansion of Fed intervention into financial markets a dramatic departure from past practice? It is true that the Fed had been involved in allocating credit through bank bailouts such as Franklin National and Continental. Through discount window borrowing to troubled banks, the Fed let the short-term debt holders of these banks escape without losses. The FDIC then then took the Fed out and incurred the losses itself. Such bailouts were the foundation for the moral hazard that created the dollar carry trade known as the shadow banking system.

As unfortunate as these bailouts were, they did not cross a line in which the Fed took credit risk onto its own portfolio to allocate credit to particular sectors of the economy. The spirit of the Federal Reserve Act is to prohibit lending that is not risk-free. The reason is to prevent the extension of credit promoting speculation. The constraint that the Fed not make risky loans possesses a political economy implication. Lending to an insolvent bank like the Bank of New England in 1989 was risky only for the FDIC. The FDIC makes up losses through the premiums charged on banks. Taking over the MBS held by Bear was crossing the Rubicon for the Fed in that losses would be passed on to taxpayers in the reduction of the seigniorage revenues that the Fed turned over to the Treasury. Once the Fed is willing to incur credit risk, it is free to allocate credit among competing uses. The sea

5. The data are "loans and leases in bank credit, all commercial banks" from St. Louis FRED taken from the Board of Governors release H.8. Because of reclassification, there is a significant discontinuity on March 31, 2010, with an increase of $442 billion. The cited decline abstracts from this increase.

change in Fed policy appears in the willingness to allocate credit to housing. At the start of 2009, the Fed held no MBS in its portfolio. By mid-June 2010, it held $1.2 trillion in its portfolio.

The change in the conception of the appropriate role for a central bank appears in the change in Bernanke's characterization of monetary policy. Before 2008, Bernanke's views reflected the consensus organized around Woodford (2003). (See also comments by Stanley Fischer in chap. 28.) Monetary policy operates through the way in which the FOMC communicates to markets the path of the risk-free interest rate. Confined to such communication, monetary policy leaves the allocation of credit to the marketplace. The spirit of this division of labor between the Fed and markets is in the spirit of William McChesney Martin's policy of bills only (chap. 15).

Before the financial crisis, Bernanke (2005, 8) wrote:

Because financial conditions depend on the expected future path of the policy rate as well as (or even more than) its current value, central bankers must be continuously aware of how their actions shape the public's policy expectations. The crucial role of expectations in the making of monetary policy, in normal times as well as when the policy rate is near the ZLB, has recently been stressed in two important papers by Gauti Eggertsson and Michael Woodford (EW) [Eggertsson and Woodford 2003a and 2003b]. Indeed, in the context of their theoretical model, EW obtain the strong result that shaping the interest rate expectations of the public is essentially the only tool that central bankers have—not only when the ZLB binds, but under normal conditions as well.

Bernanke (2005, 6) elaborated:

The Fed controls very short-term interest rates quite effectively, but the long-term rates that really matter for the economy depend not on the current short-term rate but on the whole trajectory of future short-term rates expected by market participants. Thus, to affect long-term rates, the FOMC must somehow signal to the financial markets its plans for setting future short-term rates. . . . The FOMC has two general ways to help financial market participants divine the long-run course of policy. First, to the extent practical, the FOMC strives to be consistent in how it responds to particular configurations of economic conditions and transparent in explaining the reasons for its response. . . . Second . . . comments by FOMC officials about the Committee's general policy framework . . . help the public deduce how policy is likely to respond to future economic circumstances.

At the ZLB, the Fed could resort to direct money creation. Bernanke (2002b) wrote:

> Like gold, US dollars have value only to the extent that they are strictly limited in supply. But the US government has a technology, called a printing press (or, today, its electronic equivalent), that allows it to produce as many US dollars as it wishes at essentially no cost. By increasing the number of US dollars in circulation, or even by credibly threatening to do so, the US government can also reduce the value of a dollar in terms of goods and services, which is equivalent to raising the prices in dollars of those goods and services. We conclude that, under a paper-money system, a determined government can always generate higher spending and hence positive inflation. . . . A central bank whose accustomed policy rate has been forced down to zero has most definitely *not* run out of ammunition. (italics in original)

However, by early 2009, Bernanke had reoriented policy toward allocating credit instead of focusing on the operation of the price system summarized in a reaction function communicating a path to markets for the risk-free interest rate. Bernanke (2009a) wrote:

> The provision of ample liquidity to banks and primary dealers is no panacea. Today, concerns about capital, asset quality, and credit risk continue to limit the willingness of many intermediaries to extend credit, even when liquidity is ample. Moreover, providing liquidity to financial institutions does not address directly instability or declining credit availability in critical nonbank markets, such as the commercial paper market or the market for asset-backed securities, both of which normally play major roles in the extension of credit in the United States. To address these issues, the Federal Reserve has developed a second set of policy tools, which involve the provision of liquidity directly to borrowers and investors in key credit markets.

What happened? An answer must be conjectural. Bernanke had to explain why a severe recession had occurred while he was in charge. Why did not the FOMC push the funds rate to the ZLB earlier and then resort to money creation to stimulate demand? One answer would be that policy makers assumed, just as they had in the Depression, that banks would not employ additional reserves to make loans. Just as in the Depression when Congress created the GSEs, the Fed created programs to allocate credit to markets that the banks were presumably no longer serving. The association of the financial turmoil following the Lehman bankruptcy with a worsening recession naturally pointed to a breakdown in financial intermediation as a cause of the recession. Bernanke could argue that policy had successfully prevented another Great Depression. Such an argument would also deflect populist criticism for bailing out AIG·and Citibank.

22.10. THE GREAT FINANCIAL CRISIS AND EROSION OF SUPPORT FOR FREE MARKETS

In the Great Depression, policy makers failed to understand how the creation of a fiat money standard made the Fed responsible for determination of the reserves and the deposits of the banking system. They failed to understand how the destruction of reserves and money created recession and deflation. The public associated the failure of the banks with speculative excess and a failure of a free market economy.

In the Great Recession, policy makers failed to understand how the moral hazard of the financial safety net had created a fragile system of financial intermediation through the encouragement of risk taking. They failed to understand how monetary policy could be contractionary with a low level of short-term interest rates. As with the Depression, the public associated bank bailouts with a failure of a free market economy. Tooze (2019, 166–67, 170) wrote:

> The financial crisis in 2008 . . . was a devastating blow to the complacent belief in the great moderation, a shocking overturning of prevailing laissez-faire ideology. To mobilize trillions of dollars on the credit of the taxpayer to save banks from the consequences of their own folly and greed violated maxims of fairness and good government. . . . Having done so, however, how could they [countries] ever go back to the idea that markets were efficient, self-regulating and best left to their own devices? . . . No longer did wisdom lie in devising predictable rules to curtail the arbitrary discretion of policy makers.
>
> The crisis snapped the fragile bond between the GOP's managerial, big-business elite and its right-wing mass base. . . . The fracture of the American Right would in due course have profound consequences both for America and for the wider world.

In an address on the ninetieth birthday of Milton Friedman, Bernanke (2002a) ended by saying, "I would like to say to Milton and Anna: Regarding the Great Depression. You're right, we did it. We're very sorry. But thanks to you, we won't do it again." Parting ways with Friedman, however, Bernanke fell into the Fed tradition of thinking of low interest rates as stimulative and of understanding monetary policy in terms of the Fed's influence on financial intermediation.

On September 16, 2008, Paulson (2013, 235, 237) talked to President Bush, who asked him: "How did we get to this point? . . . Someday you guys are going to have to tell me how we ended up with a system like this and what we need to do to fix it." Unfortunately, the Fed cannot answer that question. The language of discretion allows it to portray each individual policy action as optimal. The presumption then is that the concatenation of those individual actions leads to an optimal regulatory and monetary policy. Adverse outcomes come from external shocks, which the Fed mitigates. Because the Fed cannot admit mistakes, it has no systematic way of learning from the past.

CHAPTER 23

The Eurozone Crisis

Summary: Because episodes of economic instability do not arise from controlled experiments that hold constant a variety of forces, they inevitably can be explained by a multiplicity of theories.[1] Although this book is devoted to US monetary policy, the experience of the Eurozone counterpart to the Great Recession offers one test of the validity of the explanation here of the recession as caused by contractionary monetary policy. This chapter makes the point that the European Central Bank (ECB) and the Fed followed the same monetary policy focused on preventing the high headline inflation caused by the world commodity price inflation from raising inflationary expectations and thus passing permanently into a higher inflation rate. If both the United States and the Eurozone had experienced recession with different monetary policies, a disruption to financial intermediation would emerge as the more likely cause of recession.

The Eurozone experienced two recessions, which together constituted the "Great Recession." The combination of a decline in output and disinflation as well as a persistent decline in inflation implies that contractionary monetary policy was the dominant factor. This chapter reinforces two methodological points. First, in analyzing the causes of the Great Recession, it is important to distinguish between credit and monetary policy. Second, a multiplicity of estimated models can "explain" the Great Recession. In practice, economists choose between models through an associated narrative that adds additional information about causation.

The experience in the Eurozone is consistent with the characterization of the optimal monetary standard in this book. The central bank should implement a credible rule that conditions price setting in the sticky-price sector of the economy to conform to the expectation of price stability. It then moves its interest-rate instrument in a lean-against-the-wind way to offset sustained strength or weakness in the economy. Monetary instability arises when the central bank responds directly to

---

1. This chapter reproduces material from Hetzel (2019).

inflation and introduces inertia into its interest-rate instrument by failing to lower it in response to weakness in the economy. In doing so, it attempts to balance the creation of a negative output gap with a reduction in inflation.

The Eurozone Great Recession is especially interesting because the monetary policy of the ECB entailed moving its interest-rate target in direct response to the behavior of inflation. Much earlier, Friedman (1960, 87) had argued that such a policy would founder given the phenomenon of "long and variable lags." Chapter 29 ("What Is the Optimal Monetary Standard?") explores the issue of how central banks can target inflation without running afoul of the Friedman critique.

In the Eurozone, the Great Recession encompassed back-to-back recessions. Given the prominence of disruptions to financial markets, it has generated controversy about the desirability of central bank "inflation targeting." Especially, should central banks add a measure of financial stability to their traditional objectives for output and inflation (Curdia and Woodford 2009; Woodford 2012).[2] Answers are complicated if the origin of the Great Recession lay in a combination of contractionary monetary policy and disruption to financial intermediation.

Just as with the discussion of the Great recession in the United States, it is essential to distinguish monetary policy from credit policy. "Monetary policy," considered as the central bank reaction function for setting its policy rate, exercises its influence on the nominal expenditure of the public through its influence on the term structure of the risk-free interest rate. The "stance" of monetary policy, the central bank's impact on stabilizing or changing growth in nominal expenditure, derives from the interaction of this risk-free term structure with the "natural" term structure. The latter is derived under the assumption of perfectly flexible prices and reflects the way in which the real rate of interest reconciles the desire of households to smooth consumption with unevenness in the expected availability of the consumption good. "Credit policy" concerns how the central bank influences financial intermediation. In terms

---

2. Rivas and Perez-Quiros (2015, 557) are critical of incorporating macroprudential policy:

> The comparison of the forecast performance of models that include credit with other global models shows that there is no significant gain from introducing credit. . . . Our results indicate that the role of credit in the identification of the economic cycle . . . is very limited. . . . Credit can describe the past but not infer the future.

of New Keynesian models, credit policies affect the external finance premium that firms face.[3]

Also, narrative complements model. While identification of the shocks that produce a recession requires a model, all models are abstractions and incorrect in significant ways. Moreover, a multiplicity of models exists capable of fitting the macroeconomic time series. It is important to use a model in conjunction with a narrative. The narrative brings in information from outside the model that renders plausible the association of a model's shocks, which are unobservable, with observable time series. The narrative here suggests that the monetary policy of the ECB was contractionary at times even though its credit policies were stimulative.

The narrative in section 23.1 highlights how in 2008 and 2011 the ECB effectively attempted to lower headline inflation by creating a negative output gap. Section 23.2 discusses the credit policies of the ECB. Section 23.3 puts the decline in output associated with the decline in inflation in the Great Recession into the perspective of estimates of the "sacrifice ratio."

23.1. A NARRATIVE ACCOUNT OF THE GREAT RECESSION IN THE EUROZONE

Like its counterpart the Fed, the ECB failed to understand the Great Recession as a reflection of contractionary monetary policy because of confusion arising out of the belief that monetary policy and credit policy were both valid tools for maintaining aggregate nominal demand. The ECB directed monetary policy, embodied in its reaction function used to set its interest-rate target, toward control of headline inflation. In doing so, it failed to recognize the long lags of almost two years, highlighted by Friedman (1989, 31), relating the stance of monetary policy to changes in inflation. In contrast, credit policy stems from the ability of the central bank to allocate savings

---

3. The analytical distinction made here is not common among policy makers. The more common practice is to characterize monetary policy in terms of the level of the interest rate and to characterize credit policies as "liquidity" enhancing programs that facilitate the "transmission" of monetary policy. In the United States, it is natural to think about how the Federal Reserve's reaction function shapes the behavior of the risk-free term structure of interest rates because there is a term structure for government securities. In the Eurozone, in contrast, with the absence of a supranational risk-free Euro bond, the focus of attention is more naturally on the disparate banking systems of each member of the Eurozone. Credit market interventions appear attractive as a way of facilitating the "transmission" of monetary policy and appear less abstract than monetary policy. The arguments here, however, point to the importance of a clear distinction between monetary and credit policy and to the importance of getting monetary policy right as the foundation.

through its function as a financial intermediary. The belief that credit policy could serve to maintain aggregate demand misled the ECB into believing that its policies were stimulative rather than contractionary.

In the Great Recession, following its "separation principle," the ECB focused monetary policy on headline inflation and focused credit (liquidity) policy on maintaining financial intermediation.[4] Cahn et al. (2014, 3) noted:[5]

> In response to the 2008–2009 crisis, central banks in most advanced countries embarked in large-scale asset purchase programs. In the euro area . . . instead, the bulk of non-standard interventions took the form of long-term refinancing operations (LTROs). . . . Through these operations, the ECB aimed at increasing the average maturity of outstanding liquidity, from approximately 20 days before the crisis to more than 200 days in the second half of 2009.

Figure 23.1 shows real GDP growth for the Eurozone with cyclical peaks in 2008Q1 and 2011Q1. Figure 23.2 shows real GDP growth for the core countries of the Eurozone such as Germany and the main peripherals such as Greece. For the first recession, the basic coincidence of the series between the core and peripheral countries indicates a common shock among Eurozone countries. Similarly, in the second recession, the near coincidence of peaks also suggests a common shock, but the severity of the downturn for the peripheral countries indicates the intensity of the capital flight they experienced (Hetzel 2014b).[6]

Figure 23.3 shows the real (inflation-adjusted) one-year Euribor rate constructed by subtracting forecasted inflation using the ECB's Survey of Professional Forecasters from the Euribor rate. Use of the one-year Euribor rate accounts for the forecast by financial markets of the near-term path

4. For an overview of the latter, see European Central Bank (2010b) and Gonzalez-Páremo (2013).

5. The authors use a dynamic, stochastic, general equilibrium model (DSGE) in which credit policies are stimulative by reducing the interest-rate wedge imposed by banks on financial intermediation. Cahn et al. (2014, 2) find that the LTROs (long-term refinancing operations) "can have large macroeconomic effects . . . when the separation principle is breached . . . that is to say when we force monetary policy not to react to the stimulative effects of LTROs."

6. One common explanation for the Great Recession points to a collapse of speculative excess in the peripherals characterized as a "boom-bust cycle . . . not unlike the subprime bubble" (Honkapohja 2014, 261–62). This explanation suggests counterfactually that for the first recession the initial decline in output should have started in the peripheral countries and spread subsequently to the core countries and that the decline in output should have been significantly more pronounced in the peripheral countries.

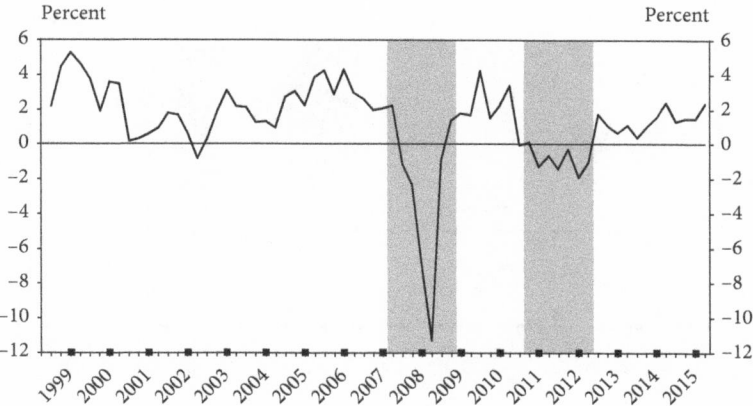

Figure 23.1. Growth in Eurozone Real GDP
Quarterly observations of quarterly annualized percentage changes in real GDP.
Shaded areas mark recessions with cycle peaks 2008Q1 and 2011Q3. Heavy tick marks
indicate fourth quarter.
Source: Haver Analytics

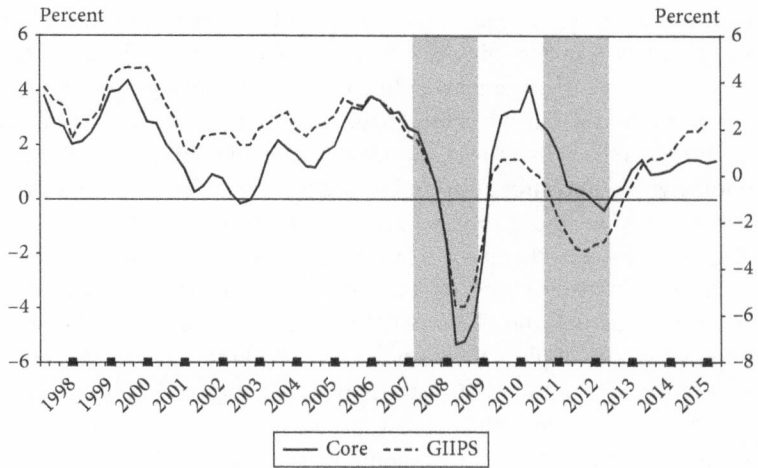

Figure 23.2. Growth in Real GDP for Core and GIIPS Countries
Four-quarter percentage change in real GDP for core countries (Austria, Belgium,
Finland, France, Germany, and Netherlands) and the GIIPS (Greece, Ireland, Italy,
Portugal, and Spain). Shaded areas indicate recessions. Heavy tick marks indicate
fourth quarter.
Source: Haver Analytics

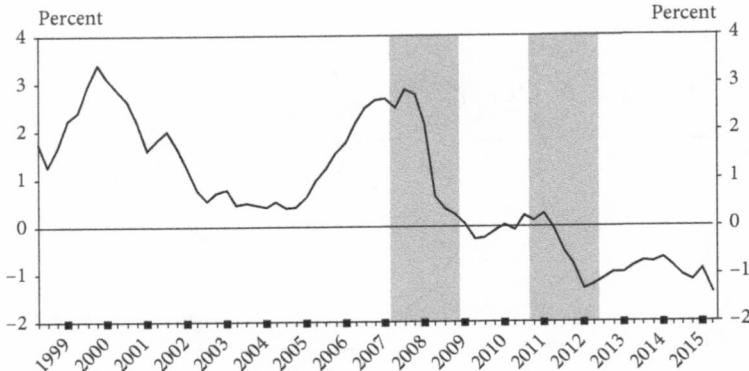

Figure 23.3. Real Euribor Interest Rate
Quarterly observations of real one-year Euribor interest rates constructed using one-year-ahead inflation forecasts from ECB Survey of Professional Forecasters mean point estimates. Heavy tick marks indicate fourth quarter.
Sources: ECB; Haver Analytics

of the ECB's MRO (main refinancing operations) rate. With each recession, the real interest rate declined significantly only well after the cyclical peak. That fact is in accord with US recession experience documented in the monetary contraction marker in chapter 3. Monetary contraction appears in the inertia that the central bank imparts to the reduction in short-term interest rates when the economy weakens. In contrast, the Eurozone economy weakened after 2001Q1, but the real rate of interest had already begun a steady decline after 2000Q3. No recession occurred.

Figure 23.4 shows that prior to 2008 the ECB had moved its policy rate in a "lean-against-the-wind" way without imparting significant inertia to it. It plots changes in the ECB's MRO rate as a bar chart. As a measure of economic activity, it plots the growth rate in real retail sales.[7] The two periods of increases in the MRO rate (February 2000 to October 2000 and December 2005 to June 2007) correspond to growth measured by retail sales strong enough to lower the unemployment rate (figure 23.5). The two periods of decreases in the MRO rate (May 2001 to November 2001 and December 2002 and June 2003) correspond to growth weak enough to raise the unemployment rate.

Econometric evidence is consistent with the hypothesis that the ECB's control of inflation occurred mainly through the way in which a credible

---

7. The Markit purchasing manager's index, PMI, and industrial production yield similar graphs.

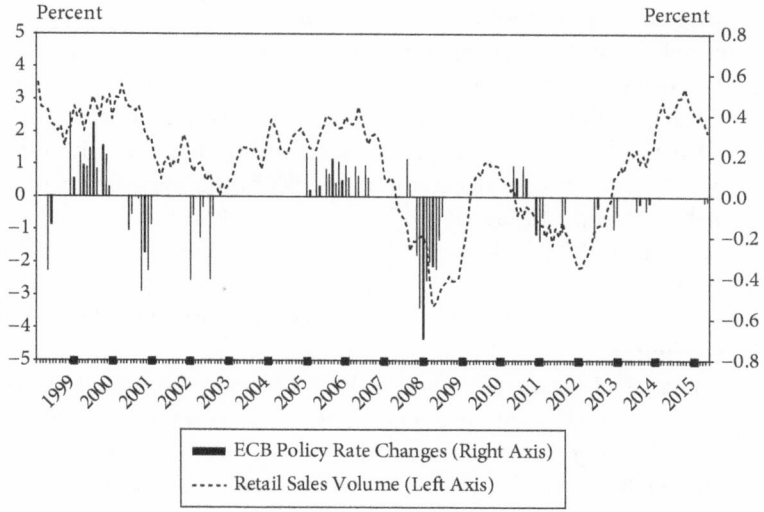

Figure 23.4. Retail Sales and ECB Policy Rate

Retail sales volume is the three-month moving average of the year-over-year percentage change in the EA 17: Retail Sales Volume Index (SA/WDA, 2010=100). ECB policy rate is the main refinancing operations (MRO) rate. Because changes in the MRO rate occur within the month and data are monthly, the changes are distributed over two months. Heavy tick marks indicate fourth quarter.

Sources: Eurostat; Haver Analytics

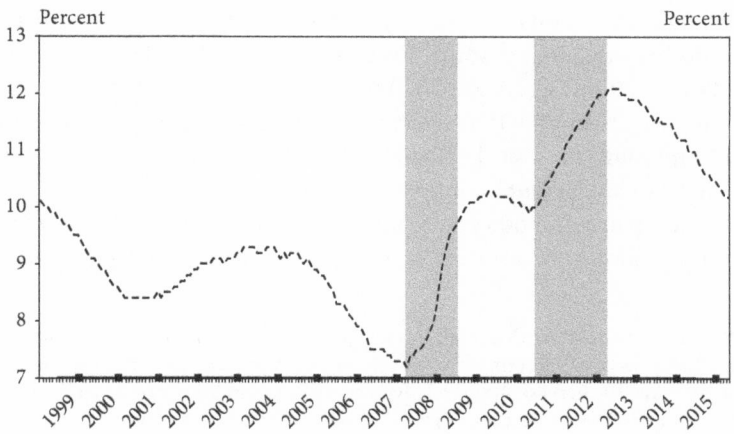

Figure 23.5. Eurozone Unemployment Rate

Heavy tick marks indicate fourth quarter. Shaded areas indicate recessions.

Source: Haver Analytics

rule conditioned price setting in the sticky-price sector (firms setting prices for multiple periods) rather than through manipulation of an output gap. Based on estimation of a Taylor rule, as an average over the first decade of the ECB's operation, Aastrup and Jensen (2010, abstract) concluded: "We show that the ECB's interest-rate changes during 1999–2010 have been mainly driven by changes in economic activity in the Euro area. Changes in actual or expected future HICP [harmonized index of consumer prices] inflation play a minor, if any, role." That is, with credibility, the central bank does not have to react to actual inflation. Changes in the interest-rate target respond to the evolution of economic activity in a way that tracks the natural rate of interest.

Goldman Sachs (2016a, "Exhibit 1: ECB's Response to Inflation Varies across Time") highlighted the departure in the 2008 period by estimating a Taylor rule using real-time data with a rolling coefficient on core inflation. The coefficients on the inflation term fluctuate around zero until 2008, when they jump to two, and decline to zero only at the end of 2012. That is, in 2008 when the ECB became concerned about headline inflation well above its target, it began to respond directly to inflation and as a result to create a negative output gap.

In 2008, both core inflation and expected inflation remained close to the objective of 2 percent or somewhat less with the latter declining only after mid-2013 (figures 23.6 and 23.7). As shown in figure 23.8, which graphs the euro price of oil and the CRB (Commodity Research Bureau) index of prices of nineteen commodities summarized in the Commodity Spot Price Index, the price of oil began to rise in 2004 followed by commodity prices in 2006.[8] Starting in late 2007, this commodity price inflation passed into headline inflation (figure 23.6).[9] This inflation shock produced by a rise in commodity prices with the integration of the BRICs (Brazil, Russia, India, and China) into the world economy caused all the major central banks of the world to implement a contractionary monetary policy.

The jump in commodity price inflation reduced household real income. Figure 23.9 shows the cessation in 2007Q3 of the prior steady increase in real

8. In early 2004, the price of oil was €25 per barrel. It rose to €85 per barrel in June 2008. The growth of emerging market economies, especially China, India, and Brazil, accounted for the increase in the relative price of commodities. For example, in 2000, China accounted for 12 percent of global consumption of copper. In 2012, the number had grown to 42 percent (*Financial Times* 2013a).

9. Initially, the commodity-price shock did not pass through to headline inflation presumably because of an offsetting appreciation of the euro. From 2002 until mid-2008, the euro appreciated from less than 0.9 dollars/euro to almost 1.6 dollars/euro.

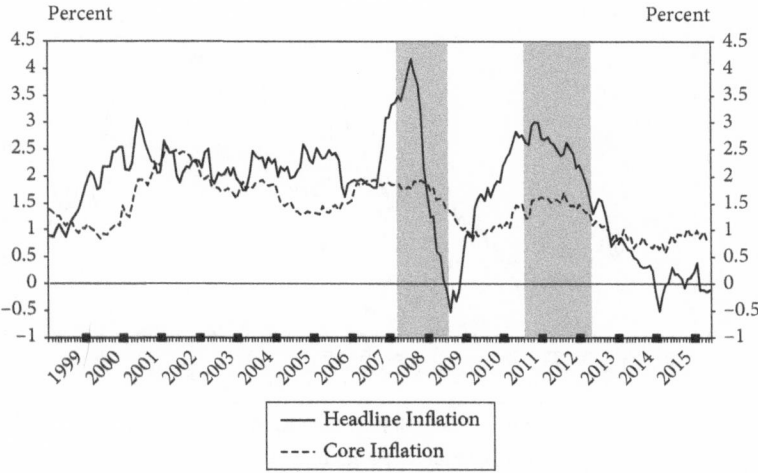

Figure 23.6. Eurozone Headline and Core Inflation

Monthly observations of twelve-month percentage changes. Headline inflation is the harmonized CPI. Core inflation excludes energy, food, alcohol, and tobacco. Shaded areas indicate recessions. Heavy tick marks indicate December.
Sources: ECB; Haver Analytics

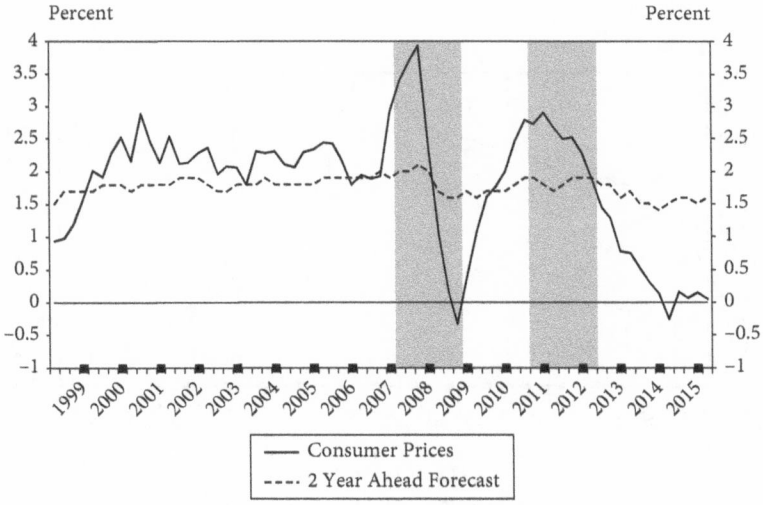

Figure 23.7. Expected and Realized Inflation

Quarterly observations of four-quarter percentage changes in Harmonized Index of Consumer Prices. Inflation forecast is from ECB Survey of Professional Forecasters mean point estimates: two years ahead. Shaded areas indicate recession. Heavy tick marks indicate fourth quarter.
Sources: ECB; Haver Analytics

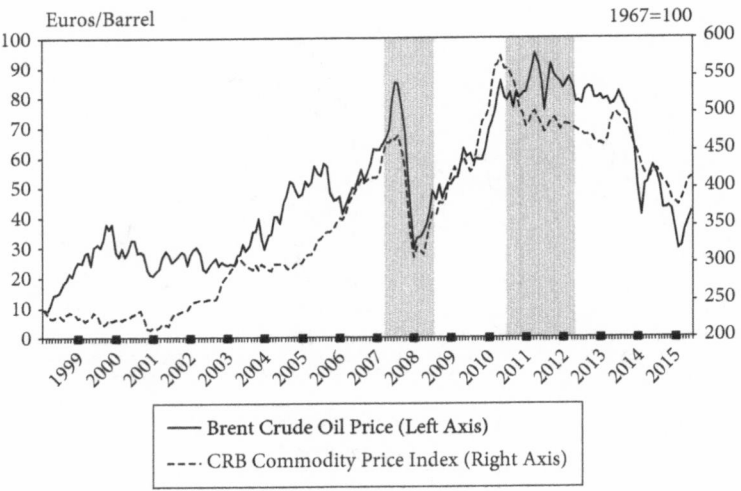

Figure 23.8. Brent Crude Oil Price in Euros and CRB Commodity Spot Price Index
Brent crude oil price multiplied by the EUR/US$ spot exchange rate. CRB Spot
Commodity Price Index: All Commodities (1967=100). Heavy tick marks indicate
December. Shaded areas indicate recession.
Sources: Reuters-CRB Commodity Index Report; Haver Analytics

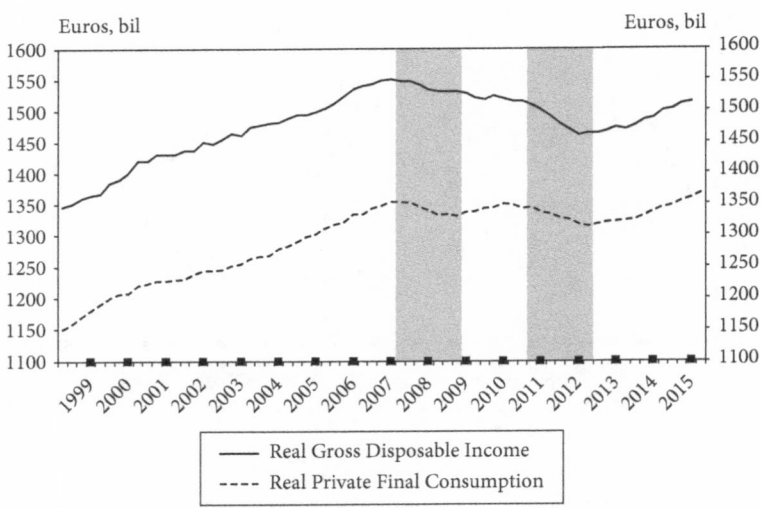

Figure 23.9. Real Gross Disposable Income and Private Consumption
Real gross disposable income is gross disposable income divided by the harmonized
consumer price index times 100. Heavy tick marks indicate fourth quarter. Shaded
areas indicate recession.
Sources: Eurostat; Haver Analytics

disposable income. Growth in real consumption declined after 2007Q3.[10] The smoothed, year-over-year percentage change in real retail sales was 2.8 percent in April 2007 (figure 23.4). It then declined steadily, became negative in April 2008, and was −1.6 percent in August 2008. Consumer confidence (Economic Sentiment Indicator) peaked in May 2007 and then fell rapidly.[11] The resulting pessimism of households about their future income prospects required a lower real interest rate.[12]

Despite a weakening economy after mid-2007, the ECB failed to lower its policy rate. Instead, in July 2008, it raised the MRO rate from 4.0 percent to 4.25 percent (figure 23.11). Moreover, the ECB's communications caused markets to anticipate further increases in rates. Figure 23.10, which plots the difference between twelve-month and one-month Euribor rates, suggests that from the beginning of 2008 until fall 2008 markets expected a significant increase in rates. The ECB lowered rates only when headline inflation fell (figure 23.11). The decline in 2009 both in real output and in core inflation is consistent with contractionary monetary policy (figures 23.1 and 23.6).

The ECB explained its actions in 2008 by a concern that high headline inflation would exacerbate wage demands of French and German unions.[13] Wage inflation (year-over-year in the business sector) had increased from

10. Over the interval 2004Q4 through 2007Q3, real personal consumption expenditures (PCE) grew at an annualized rate of 2 percent. Annualized real PCE growth then declined as follows: 1.6 percent (2007Q4), 0.2 percent (2008Q1), −0.6 percent (2008Q2), and −1.9 percent (2008Q3).

11. Data from Economic and Financial Affairs page of the European Commission website, https://ec.europa.eu/info/departments/economic-and-financial-affairs_en.

12. As shown in figure 23.9, the persistent decline in real income after 2007Q3 is consistent with households forecasting a persistent decline in their income and consequently a reduction in the natural rate of interest. Blanchard and Gali (2007, 36) noted, "The effects of changes in factors such as the price of oil . . . appear through their effects on natural output." The persistence of the commodity price shock first from 2004 through summer 2008 and then from 2009 through 2011 suggests a reduction in the natural rate of interest through pessimism about growth in natural output. It is also plausible that the risk of a disastrous outcome due to the possible breakup of the Eurozone in 2011 and 2012 exacerbated pessimism about future growth. For a discussion of how left-tail risk can lower the natural rate of interest, see Rietz (1988) and Guvenen et al. (2014).

13. See *Financial Times* (2013b). Lucas Papademos (2013, 510), vice president of the ECB, explained, "For more than a year after the outbreak of the global financial crisis, the ECB did not ease monetary policy, as determined by its key interest rates, mainly because it was concerned about the materialization of second-round effects of supply shocks on wage- and price-setting and the potential unanchoring of inflation expectations." The ECB (European Central Bank July 2008a, 6) noted: "This worrying level of inflation rates results largely from sharp increases in energy and food prices at the global level. . . . There is a . . . very strong concern that price and wage-setting behaviour could add to inflationary pressures via broadly based second-round effects."

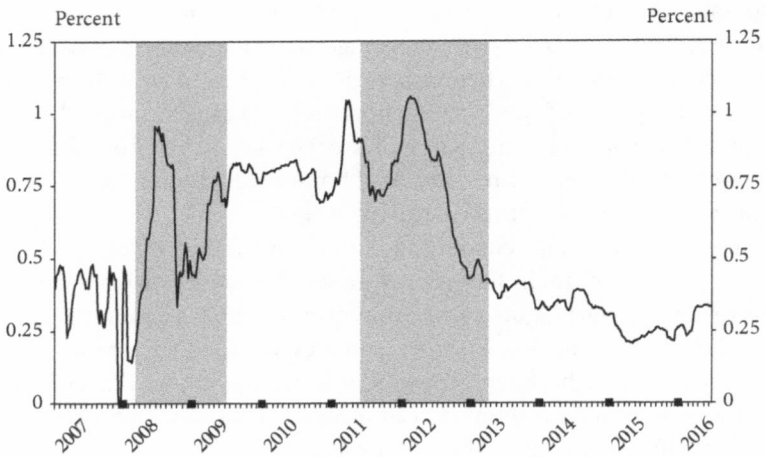

Figure 23.10. Euribor Term Structure
Difference between twelve-month and one-month Euribor interest rates. Heavy tick
marks indicate December. Shaded areas indicate recessions.
Sources: ECB; Haver Analytics

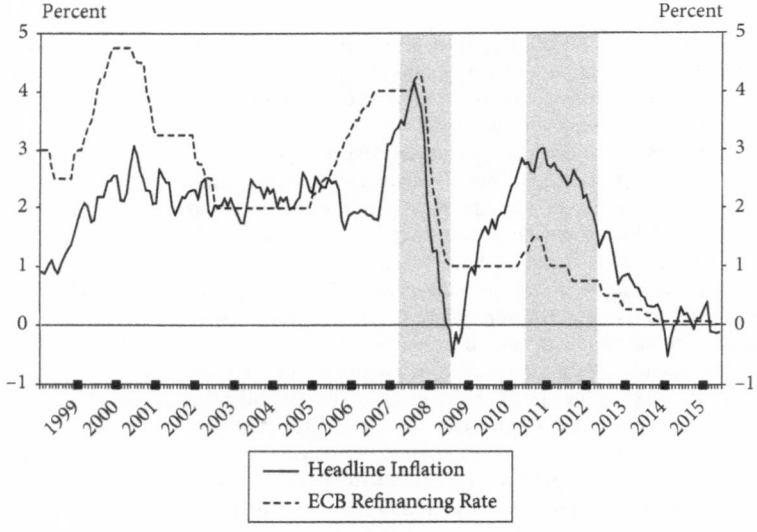

Figure 23.11. Inflation and ECB Policy Rate
Monthly observations of twelve-month percentage changes in Harmonized Index of
Consumer Prices. ECB refinancing rate is the main refinancing operations rate. Shaded
areas indicate recessions. Heavy tick marks indicate December.
Sources: ECB; Haver Analytics

3.2 percent over the interval 2003Q1 through 2007Q4 to 4.1 percent in the first three quarters of 2008. ECB actions reflected the belief that a cost-push shock would increase inflation. The ECB created a negative output gap to keep headline inflation at 2 percent. It did so by raising rather than lowering its policy rate when the economy went into recession.

When the world economy began to recover in 2009, commodity-price inflation rose once more (figure 23.8). Starting in early 2011, turmoil in the Middle East also caused oil prices to rise. Headline inflation, which had fallen to −0.5 percent in 2009, rose to 3 percent by the end of 2011 although core inflation remained well below target (figure 23.6). The second commodity-price shock intensified the ongoing decline in real disposable income after 2010Q4. Consumption, which had been recovering slowly, again began to decline after 2010Q4 (figure 23.9). Real retail sales peaked in September 2010 (figure 23.4). Growth in real GDP peaked in 2011Q1 (figure 23.1). Given its focus on headline inflation, the ECB raised its policy rate twice in 2011, from 1 percent to 1.25 percent in April and to 1.5 percent in July.

Monetary contraction as an explanation of the dual recessions has the advantage of simplicity in that it offers a common explanation of each recession. First, monetary contraction is consistent with the observed decline in core inflation and in output in both recessions. Second, the ECB responded to the commodity-price shock in the same way in each recession. Moreover, repeated monetary contraction can explain why in contrast to past experience a strong recovery did not follow a deep recession.

If the central bank follows a rule that keeps the real rate of interest equal to the natural rate, given the accommodation of money supply to money demand implied by an interest rate target, nominal money grows at a rate consistent with the central bank's inflation target. Money then offers no information about the evolution of the economy. However, if the central bank creates a difference between the natural and real rates of interest, the behavior of money becomes informative.

The monetary aggregate M1 offers a better measure of transactions demand than M3, which includes a significant amount of debt.[14] Banks issue debt to finance loan growth when loan demand is high. As shown in figure 23.12, apart from 2002–3 and 2012–13 when banks made up for weak loan demand by holding more government securities, M3 growth and loan growth

---

14. M1 includes currency in circulation and overnight deposits. M3 includes M1 plus time deposits with maturity up to two years, deposits redeemable given notification up to three months, repurchase agreements, money market fund shares, and debt instruments with maturity up to two years.

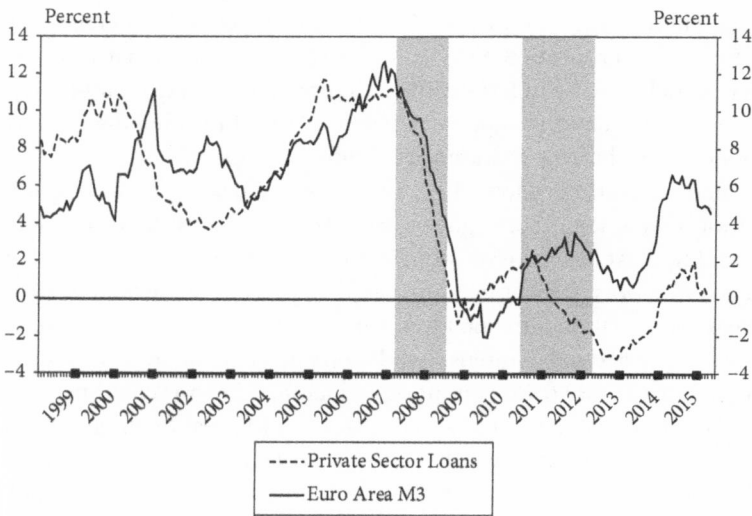

Figure 23.12. M3 and Private Loan Growth
Monthly observations of twelve-month percentage changes in M3 and loans to private sector by monetary financial institutions. Shaded areas indicate recessions. Heavy tick marks indicate December.
Sources: Eurostat; Haver Analytics

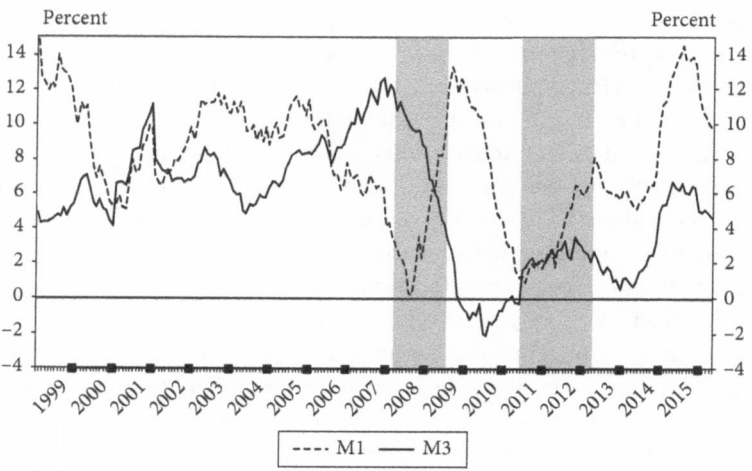

Figure 23.13. Money Supply
Monthly observations of twelve-month percentage changes in M1 and M3. Shaded areas indicate recessions. Heavy tick marks indicate December.
Sources: Eurostat; Haver Analytics

move together. For this reason, it is hard to disentangle money and credit. M3 is mainly a contemporaneous indicator of the state of the economy.

M1 growth slowed starting in mid-2006 and slowed sharply at the end of 2007 (figure 23.13).[15] Real GDP growth then declined from an annualized rate of 2.2 percent in 2008Q1 to −1.2 percent in 2008Q2. After falling to near zero in 2008Q3, M1 growth revived. Real GDP growth then reached a trough in 2009Q1 with annualized growth of −11.3 percent. M1 growth fell sharply starting in 2010Q3. Real GDP growth then declined from an annualized growth rate of 3.4 percent in 2011Q1 to −1.3 percent in 2011Q4.

Despite possessing some predictive value, the signal to noise ratio is low for M1. In a time of financial turmoil when market participants desire liquidity, they transfer out of the illiquid debt instruments in the non-M1 part of M3 into the liquid demand deposits of M1 thus inflating M1 growth. One is on firmer ground using M1 growth as a measure of the stance of monetary policy in the first half of 2008, when growth in M1 and M3 both declined, and after May 2010 through early 2012, when M1 growth declined while M3 growth remained low (figure 23.13).

23.2. THE INTERACTION OF FINANCIAL CRISIS AND CONTRACTIONARY MONETARY POLICY

While financial market disruption must have impacted economic activity adversely in the Great Recession, the first cycle peak in March 2008 preceded any significant disruption. Real GDP fell at annualized rates of −1.3 percent and −2.2 percent in 2008Q2 and 2008Q3, respectively. Industrial production including construction peaked in February 2008. Monetary contraction preceded any significant disruption to financial intermediation.

In the United States, in August 2007, when cash investors ceased buying the commercial paper that financed the holding of subprime mortgages in US banks' off-balance-sheet entities, banks moved them onto their own balance sheets. European banks also held many of these illiquid mortgages (Hetzel 2012a, 179, 242). Uncertainty over the extent to which banks held them lessened the willingness of European banks to lend to each other in

---

15. In May 2003, the ECB demoted the behavior of money (M3) to a "cross-check" from one of its two "pillars," the other pillar being the behavior of the economy (Deutsche Bank 2013). For example, despite the absence of M3 growth, the editorial in the July 2010 ECB *Monthly Bulletin* (European Central Bank 2010a, 6) noted, "The annual growth rate of M3 was unchanged at −0.2 percent in May 2010. . . . These data continue to support the assessment that the underlying pace of monetary expansion is moderate and that inflationary pressures over the medium term are contained." The ECB Governing Council left its policy rate unchanged.

the interbank market. Instead of relying on interbank loans to meet liquidity needs, they began to hold additional excess reserves (Heider et al. 2009). The ECB accommodated that increased demand. In August 2007, it introduced fixed-rate/full-allotment tenders and in October 2008 made them standard. The EONIA rate (the euro equivalent of the funds rate) remained fixed at the ECB's MRO rate.

The Federal Reserve and the ECB cooperated to relieve funding pressures on European banks with dollar liabilities. With the Term Auction Facility (TAF), the Fed auctioned dollars to the US branches of European banks. Through swap lines, the Fed provided dollars to the ECB, which it re-lent to European banks to replace the dollar funding no longer supplied by money market mutual funds (Hetzel 2012a, 244, 267). Only with the Lehman bankruptcy in September 2008, well after the cycle peak, did the amounts outstanding in this facility jump significantly.[16] That is, funding pressures arose after the commencement of the recession.

Loan growth remained healthy until after the economy entered recession in 2008Q1. Bank loans to the private sector (MFIs) averaged 10.7 percent year over year from May 2006 through May 2008 (figure 23.12). Only in June 2008 did growth fall below 10 percent.[17] By these measures, funding pressures were manageable through the cycle peak. After the recovery took hold in 2009Q3, loan growth recovered steadily until peaking in 2011Q3. Economic recovery, however, aborted earlier. Growth in real GDP fell from 3.4 percent in 2011Q1 to zero in 2011Q2 and Q3 and to −1.3 percent in 2011Q4.

From midsummer 2011 to midsummer 2012, investors fled the sovereign debt markets of the peripheral countries, most noticeably Italy and Spain, out of fear that they would exit the Eurozone. Sovereign credit default swap spreads for Italy and Spain started their climb to alarming levels in mid-2011. In early July 2011, the spread of two-year yields on Italian over German debt climbed above 2 percent, and it reached 7 percent in late November 2011. However, the Eurozone economy had already begun to weaken after 2011Q1 (figure 23.1). The timing suggests causation going from the economic weakness to a debt crisis rather than the reverse.

The spread in the interest rates on loans made to corporations in Italy

16. Before Lehman, swap amounts outstanding averaged about $50 billion (Goldberg et al. 2010).

17. In recession, it is hard to separate disruption to financial intermediation as a causal factor from reduced demand due to a weakening economic outlook. The July 2008 Euro Area Bank Lending Survey (European Central Bank 2008b) reported:

> The most important factor in the net tightening continued to be a deterioration in expectations about the economic outlook. . . . Banks reported that net demand for loans to enterprises and households continued to be negative in the second quarter of 2008.

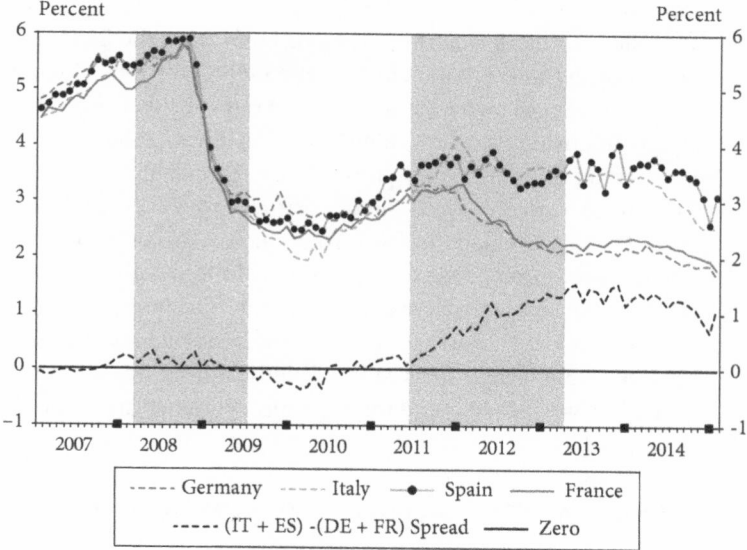

Figure 23.14. Average Interest on New Loans to Nonfinancial Corporations.
Spread is between the average of Italy plus Spain minus Germany plus France. Shaded
areas indicate recessions. Heavy tick marks indicate fourth quarter of year.
Sources: ECB; Haver Analytics

and Spain compared to Germany and France began to widen only in July
2011, along with, not prior to, the end of recovery from the first recession
(figure 23.14). In 2011, the unemployment rate rose sharply in Italy and was
already above 20 percent in Spain. Plausibly, this interest-rate spread reflected a normal risk premium and was therefore not indicative of a failure
of financial intermediation.

The year 2011 illustrates the difference between monetary and credit
policy. In the second half of 2011, ECB lending to banks in the peripheral
countries jumped. Consider ECB lending to Spanish banks, which replaced
loans previously made by German banks. German banks placed the reserves
gained from calling in their loans in the ECB's deposit facility. The ECB then
became the indirect conduit for lending by German banks to Spanish banks.
The increase in the size of the ECB's balance sheet indicated a stimulative
credit policy, that is, a supportive influence on financial intermediation. The
ECB's credit policies were largely successful in limiting increases in money
market spreads like Euribor-OIS (Goldman Sachs 2016b).[18]

18. De Andoain et al. (2014) sought instances of "fragmentation": episodes in which
banks in some Eurozone countries paid a premium to borrow in the interbank market. The most significant occurred at year-end 2011 before the introduction of LTROs
(long-term refinancing operations) on December 8, 2011, providing three-year financing

Also in 2011, in April and July, the ECB tightened monetary policy by raising its policy rate. As late as the April 2012 editorial in the ECB *Monthly Bulletin* (European Central Bank 2012, 5), the ECB Governing Council retained hawkish language on inflation: "Inflation rates are likely to stay above 2% in 2012, with upside risks prevailing." Only in July 2012 did the Governing Council guide the EONIA rate toward zero by cutting the MRO rate from 1 percent to ¾ percent and the deposit rate to zero. As late as May 2012, the ECB had still ruled out forward guidance, the essence of which is precommitment. In response to a question, Mario Draghi (2012, 4) responded, "As we always say, we never pre-commit."[19] As implied by indexed swap markets, in mid-2011 the expected time for inflation to return to 2 percent was almost nine years. After falling briefly, in mid-2012, it returned to that value but then rose to twenty years after summer 2014 (Goldman Sachs 2015).

23.3. THE QUANTITATIVE IMPACT OF A MONETARY SHOCK

With expected inflation the dominant determinant of trend inflation, contractionary monetary policy in an environment of central bank credibility implies a high sacrifice ratio, which measures the cost in terms of lost output produced by a reduction in inflation. The first thing to note is that estimated Phillips curves have become flat, a fact that implies a high sacrifice ratio. Atkeson and Ohanian (2001) noted that lagged inflation does a better job of predicting inflation than do Phillips curves, which include resource slack as an explanatory variable.

For the first recession, from 2008Q1 through 2010Q2, the unemployment rate rose 3 percentage points from 7.3 percent to 10.3 percent while the inflation rate in the services sector (a proxy for the sticky-price sector in which firms change prices only infrequently) fell 1.3 percentage points

---

to banks by the ECB. They concluded, that "overall, the evidence suggests that nonstandard measures such as long-term liquidity operations were broadly effective in dampening market tensions" (De Andoain et al. 2014, 11).

19. Kang et al. (2015) documented that equity markets responded positively to the Fed's interest-rate cuts but negatively on average to the ECB's rate cuts. They attributed the difference to the belief by markets that the cuts by the Fed manifested its commitment to restore full employment while the cuts by the ECB simply conveyed pessimism about the economy. Kang et al. (2015, 45) used ECB communication to argue that "when commodity prices were pushing inflation up, the ECB sought to nip it in the bud; but when commodity prices pushed inflation down, the ECB preferred to wait in anticipation of a return to more normal inflation rates." In contrast, after the 2009 cycle trough, the FOMC sought to anchor expected inflation while using forward guidance to stimulate the economy.

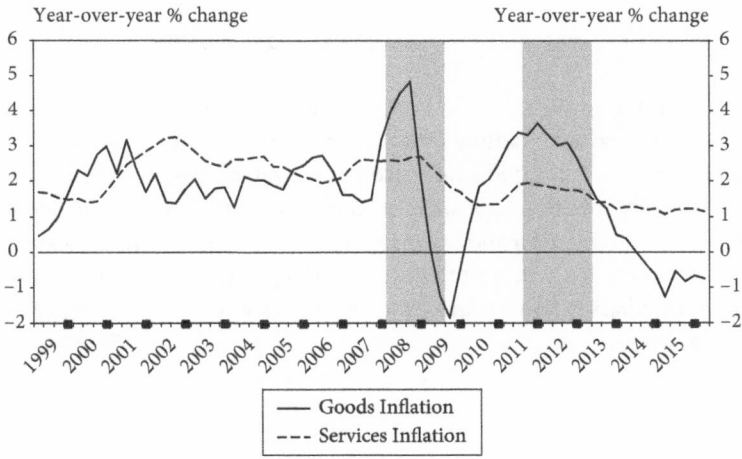

Figure 23.15. Eurozone Goods and Services Inflation
Quarterly observations of harmonized CPI. Shaded areas indicate recessions. Heavy
tick marks indicate fourth quarter.
Sources: Eurostat; Haver Analytics

from 2.6 percent to 1.3 percent (figures 23.6 and 23.15). With 7.3 percent
as the NAIRU and average unemployment over this period of 8.8 percent, unemployment averaged 1.5 percentage points above NAIRU for
2.25 years. Roughly, the sacrifice ratio would be 2.6 (the man-years of excess unemployment required to lower inflation by 1 percentage point). For
the second recession, from 2011Q1 through 2013Q2, the unemployment
rate rose 2.1 percentage points from 10.0 percent to 12.1 percent while
the inflation rate in the services sector fell 0.2 percentage points from
1.6 percent to 1.4 percent. With 10.0 percent as the NAIRU and average
unemployment over this period of 11.1 percent, unemployment averaged
1.05 percentage points over NAIRU for 2.25 years. Roughly, the sacrifice
ratio would be about 12.

The estimated sacrifice ratio for the first recession appears consistent
with historical experience while the estimated sacrifice ratio for the second recession appears implausibly high (see also Ball and Mazumder 2015).
For the second recession, it thus seems likely that the increase in the unemployment rate originated to a significant extent in the disruption to financial intermediation associated with the capital flight crisis in 2011–12
(Hetzel 2014b). At the same time, the decline in services sector inflation to
1.3 percent in 2016Q1 is inconsistent with the expansionary monetary policy
appropriate if the central bank's reaction function includes mitigation of
financial frictions (Carlstrom et al. 2010).

23.4. CONCLUDING COMMENT

In 2008 and again in 2011, the Eurozone experienced a commodity-price shock, which raised headline inflation. Rather than concentrating on core inflation, the ECB created a negative output gap to keep headline inflation at its 2 percent inflation target. Optimal policy would have entailed concentrating on core inflation and lowering the policy rate instead of raising it in order to maintain a zero output gap. In both episodes, disruptions to financial intermediation would have called for expansionary not contractionary monetary policy.

CHAPTER 24

Recovery from the Great Recession

Summary: In August 2020, monetary policy makers articulated a new framework for conducting monetary policy.[1] That framework reflected the conclusion drawn from the recovery from the Great Recession that monetary policy had erred in pursuing preemptive increases in the funds rate. Starting in December 2015, the FOMC had raised the funds rate off the zero lower bound (ZLB). As it turned out, inflation continued to run below the FOMC's 2 percent target. Because such preemptive increases had been a hallmark of the Volcker-Greenspan era and had guided the policy of returning to price stability, the new framework represented a significant departure from policy in the Great Moderation.

Going forward, the FOMC committed to forgoing preemptive funds-rate increases to ensure an overshoot of its inflation target for some persistent but unspecified period. That overshoot would indicate that the FOMC had achieved the goal of "maximum employment." Given that the unemployment rate prior to the start of the pandemic had reached a low of 3.5 percent with inflation remaining less than 2 percent, this policy was presumed to allow the FOMC to achieve its expanded goal of an unemployment rate low enough to ensure full employment in minority communities.

What should policy makers have learned from the recovery from the Great Recession? The first thing to note is that it was a period of considerable nominal and real stability. In part, that stability was an artifact of an initially moderately contractionary monetary policy that limited the strength of the recovery from the Great Recession. However, the preemptive increases in the funds rate intended to prevent an overshoot of inflation from the 2 percent target contributed to the desirable stability exhibited in the recovery. It was desirable to maintain a noninflationary recovery. That price stability provided the foundation for the significant decline in the unemployment rate during the recovery. Moreover, dur-

---

1. A version of this chapter first appeared as Robert L. Hetzel, "Recovery from the Great Recession" (Mercatus Working Paper, Mercatus Center at George Mason University, Arlington, VA, February 2021).

ing the recovery, the ZLB on the funds rate did not undermine the efficacy of monetary policy. The inflationary expectations of the public did not become unanchored to the downside.

Based on the experience of the recovery from the Great Recession, the FOMC revised its policy framework. Chair Powell (2020d) summarized the conclusions drawn from the recovery in the policy of flexible-average-inflation targeting (FAIT). A characteristic of the recovery period was a funds rate at the ZLB for seven years with inflation running mainly below the FOMC's 2 percent inflation target. Moreover, a steady decline in the unemployment rate failed to raise inflation to the 2 percent target. The FOMC drew two conclusions. First, at the ZLB, there is a danger that the public's expectation of inflation will become unanchored to the downside of 2 percent.

Second, the level of unemployment consistent with the mandate of maximum employment could be achieved only through the experiment of running down the unemployment rate through an expansionary monetary policy. The emergence of inflation persistently more than the 2 percent inflation target would reveal this mandate-consistent level of unemployment. These two features of FAIT are complementary in that the inflation overshoot signaling achievement of maximum employment would prevent an undesirable reduction in the inflationary expectations of the public through a period of above-target inflation compensating for the prior period of below-target inflation.

An implication of FAIT is the undesirability of preemptive increases in the funds rate intended to prevent the emergence of inflation. Such preemptive increases had been a hallmark of the Volcker-Greenspan era and had guided the policy of returning to price stability (chaps. 19–20). A motivation for the revised policy was the belief that the preemptive increases in the funds rate that started with an increase in December 2015 and then resumed in December 2016 limited job creation. The narrative here provides an alternative version of what policy makers should have learned from the recovery from the Great Recession.

The first characteristic of the recovery to note is that it was a period of considerable nominal and real stability. In part, that stability was an artifact of an initial, moderately contractionary monetary policy that limited a vigorous economic rebound. Also, the preemptive increases in the funds rate that were intended to prevent an overshoot of inflation from the 2 percent target contributed to the stability exhibited in the recovery. It was desirable to maintain a noninflationary recovery. Price stability provided the foundation for the significant decline in the unemployment rate during the recovery. Moreover, during the recovery, a funds rate at the ZLB did not undermine the efficacy of monetary policy. Inflationary expectations never became unanchored. They remained anchored at the level of near price stability produced by the earlier policy aimed at restoring price stability.

When a V-shaped recovery failed to emerge, a common fear was that, with the funds rate pressed against the ZLB, the FOMC was "out of ammunition." That is, at the ZLB, the FOMC could not pursue an expansionary monetary policy to offset contractionary "headwinds" impeding a strong recovery. In fact, the FOMC's "unconventional" monetary policies of forward guidance and quantitative easing (QE) maintained the efficacy of monetary policy even at the ZLB. It follows that there is no need to abandon genuine price stability by raising inflation and thereby raising nominal interest rates to avoid running into the ZLB.

24.1. MONETARY POLICY WAS INITIALLY MODERATELY CONTRACTIONARY IN THE RECOVERY

Monetary policy was contractionary in the Great Recession as evidenced by the decline in both real output and inflation (figures 24.1, 24.2, and 20.4). In 2009Q2, real GDP growth (four-quarter percentage change) declined to −3.2 percent while in 2009Q4 core PCE inflation (four-quarter percentage change) fell to 0.95 percent (four-quarter percentage change).

In fall 2008, Chairman Bernanke would maintain the FOMC consensus by lowering the funds rate only reluctantly given the shared concern for inflation. After the Lehman bankruptcy in September, the emphasis was on programs to channel credit to ensure the availability of credit. A key point is that in 2008 no FOMC participant considered that monetary policy could be contractionary with a zero real interest rate. As shown in figure 24.2, from December 2008 through 2016, however, the realized real interest rate averaged around −2 percent. Although the FOMC judged monetary policy to be "accommodative," the duration of such a negative rate without inflation could have occurred only from a decline in the natural rate of interest.

Nothing in their historical experience prepared policy makers for a sharp, sudden decline in the natural rate of interest to a negative value. In the 1970s, a negative realized real rate of interest was inflationary (figure 18.5). Starting with the Volcker disinflation and prior to the Great Recession, the realized real rate of interest was consistently, significantly positive. The exception occurred in the years 2003 to 2004. However, that period was considered to be one in which a low funds rate had encouraged excessive risk taking and a housing bubble. It seemed obvious that a negative realized real interest rate was expansionary. That belief carried over into the

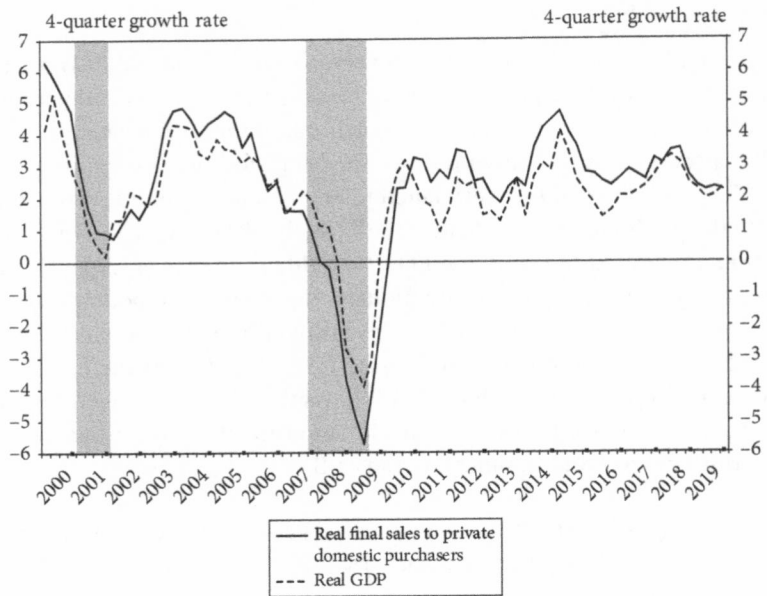

Figure 24.1. Growth Rates of Real GDP and Real Final
Sales to Private Domestic Purchasers

Quarterly observations of four-quarter percentage changes. Shaded areas indicate
recession. Heavy tick marks indicate the fourth quarter.
Source: St. Louis FRED

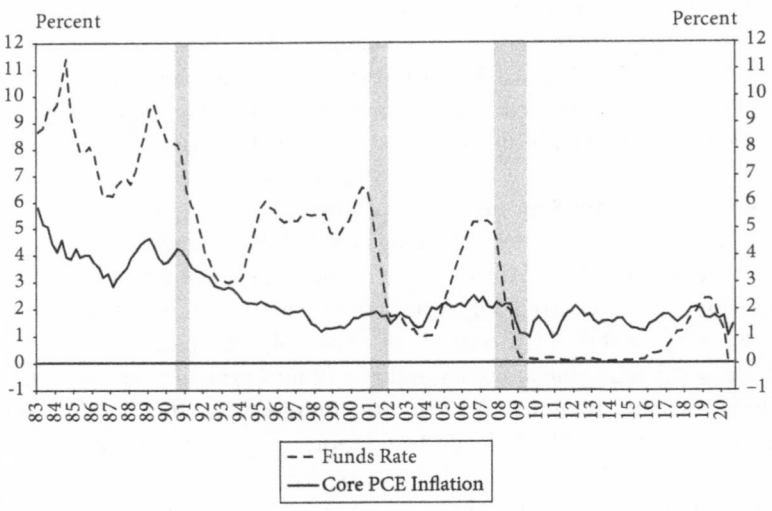

Figure 24.2. Funds Rate and Core PCE Inflation

Quarterly observations of four-quarter percentage changes in core personal
consumption expenditures (PCE) deflator. Tick marks indicate fourth quarter. Shaded
areas indicate recessions.
Source: St. Louis FRED

recovery and allowed policy makers to believe that a moderately contractionary monetary policy was stimulative.

The contention that monetary policy was moderately contractionary early in the recovery is supported by the failure of output to rebound in a V-shaped recovery as had always occurred in the past when a vigorous recovery followed a sharp decline in output. After an initial rebound, over the interval 2010Q1 through 2014Q1, real GDP growth (four-quarter percentage changes) averaged only 2 percent, well below the nearly 5 percent in the prior recovery for the years 2003 through 2005. A tepid recovery combined with a reduction in inflation. For 2008Q3 through 2017Q3, core PCE inflation (four-quarter percentage changes) averaged 1.5 percent. Over the preceding period, 2004Q2 through 2008Q3, the corresponding number was 2.2 percent. The most straightforward explanation of the tepid recovery combined with a decline in inflation is a moderately contractionary monetary policy.

The initial failure of the FOMC to realize that the natural rate of interest had fallen to historic lows appears in the Summary of Economic Projections (SEP). The median value of the longer-run funds rate contained in the SEP, a proxy for the assumed natural rate, was 4.3 percent at the January 2012 FOMC meeting and still at a relatively high 3.8 percent for March 2014 meeting. Similarly, forecasts of FOMC participants for real GDP growth started relatively high in line with a normalization of the funds rate requiring a significant increase. In January 2010, FOMC participants' "central tendency" (the midpoint of the "central tendency range") for growth in real GDP was 4 percent for both 2011 and 2012. The actual growth rates (averages of quarterly annualized rates of growth) for these years came in significantly lower at 1.6 percent for 2011 and 1.5 percent for 2012.

As shown in figure 24.3 (from Sløk 2020), in the early years of the recovery until December 2016, markets also consistently forecasted an imminent rise in the funds rate. That misforecast in turn derived from the past observation that recoveries from sharp recessions had all been strong, or V-shaped. The resulting upward tilt to the yield curve acted to make monetary policy restrictive.

Figure 24.4 (from Sløk 2017a) shows that this ex post upward bias in forecasts of the funds rate carried over to the forecasts by market professionals of bond rates. FOMC participants learned only slowly that the natural rate of interest had fallen. The resulting upward sloping term structure of interest rates initially made policy moderately contractionary. Consequently, the economic recovery was relatively slow and prolonged.

One piece of evidence for the lack of a stimulative monetary policy was the lack of vigorous growth in M2. Initially, as cash investors fled nonbank

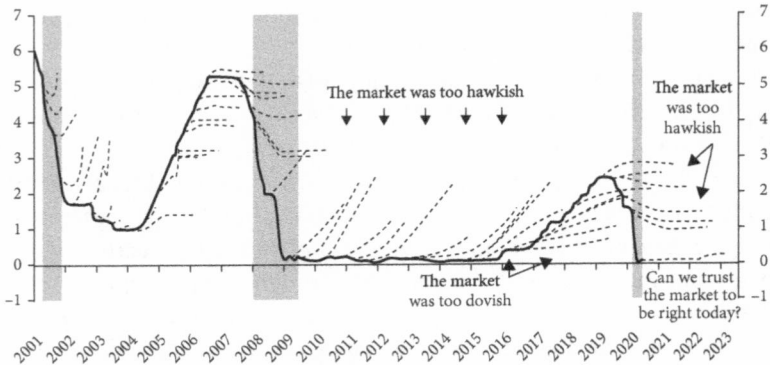

Figure 24.3. Fed Funds Rate: Actual and Forecasted from Fed Funds Futures Market
Figure from Sløk (2020). Tick marks indicate December. Shaded areas indicate
recession.

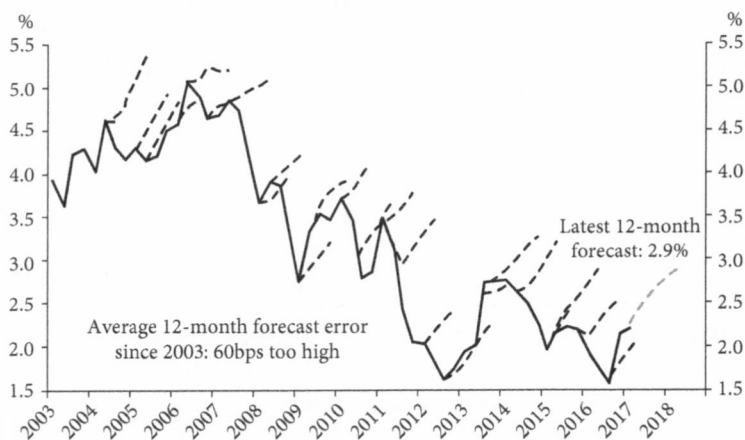

Figure 24.4. Actual Ten-Year Treasury Rate and Forecasts from
Survey of Professional Forecasters
Figure from Sløk (2017a).

financial intermediaries in favor of the too-big-to-fail banks, M2 growth
surged. However, from June 2009 to July 2010, annualized monthly growth
rates for M2 averaged only 1.9 percent. From August 2010 to January 2020,
the number was 6.4 percent. The decline in market rates of interest, the
desire among households and corporations for liquidity, and the ongoing
secular decline in M2 velocity should have resulted in vigorous M2 growth
in the year after the recession trough of June 2009.

The FOMC never considered the possibility that monetary policy might be restrictive. From the FOMC's perspective, "headwinds" had lowered the natural (neutral) rate of interest, and it had followed the decline with a lower funds rate to offset those headwinds. Chair Yellen (2015, 13) stated:

> This expectation [of rate increases] is consistent with an implicit assessment that the neutral nominal federal funds rate . . . is currently low by historical standards and is likely to rise only gradually over time. The marked decline in the neutral federal funds rate [r^*] after the crisis may be partially attributable to a range of persistent headwinds . . . [including] tighter underwriting standards and limited access to credit for some borrowers, deleveraging by many households to reduce debt burdens, contractionary fiscal policy at all levels of government, weak growth abroad coupled with a significant appreciation of the dollar, slower productivity and labor force growth, and elevated uncertainty about the economic outlook. As the restraint from these headwinds further abates, I anticipate that the neutral federal funds rate will gradually move higher.

Although the economy recovered after the cycle trough in June 2009, a V-shaped recovery did not occur. In June 2013, four years after the cyclical trough, the unemployment rate was 7.5 percent. One reason for the restrained recovery was another inflation shock, which the FOMC did not accommodate with expansionary monetary policy. Headline PCE inflation (four-quarter) rose sharply in two peaks (figure 20.4). It first went from −1 percent in 2009Q3 to 2.3 percent in 2010Q1. It then declined to 1.2 percent in 2010Q4 before rising to 3 percent in 2011Q3. Economic stimulus measures in China produced strong Chinese growth, which raised world commodity prices. The resulting high headline inflation in the United States passed into core inflation.[2] Plausibly, the post–Great Recession inflation shock was one factor in limiting the recovery in real personal consumption expenditures after summer 2011 (figure 24.5). The 2015 surge then reflected catch-up.

---

2. The annual growth rate of real GDP in China rose from 7.6 percent in 2008 to 13 percent in 2010. Yearly M2 growth for China, which had averaged 16.6 percent for the years 2004 through 2008, rose to 26.5 percent and 20.6 percent, respectively, in 2009 and 2010. Annual changes in the world price of commodities averaged 19.6 percent for the years 2003 through 2008, fell to −28.4 percent in 2009, and then rose back to 25 percent in 2010 and 2011. The world commodity inflation rate then subsided to −10.6 over the years 2012 through 2016. The figures are from St. Louis FRED: (1) 2010, University of Groningen and University of California, Davis, real GDP at constant prices for China; (2) IMF, M2 for China; (3) IMF Global Price Index of All Commodities.

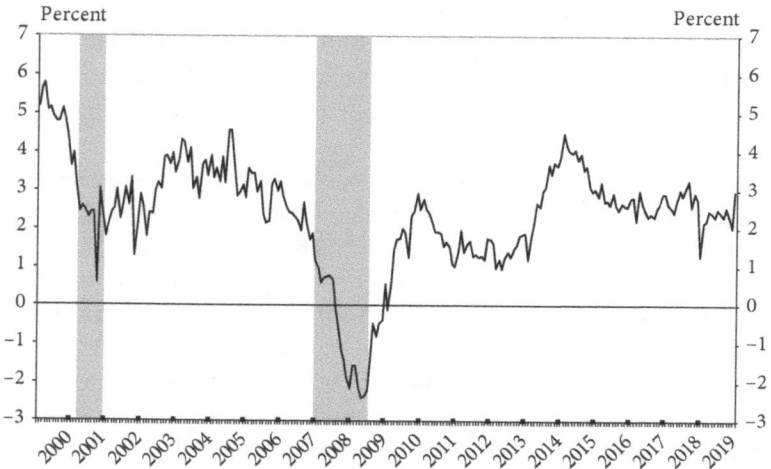

Figure 24.5. Growth of Real Personal Consumption Expenditures
Twelve-month percentage changes in real personal consumption expenditures (PCE).
Shaded areas indicate recessions. Heavy tick marks indicate December.
Source: St. Louis FRED

24.2. A SLOW START TO THE RECOVERY AND
PREEMPTIVE INCREASES IN THE FUNDS RATE

Starting in December 2008 with the statement language that "weak economic conditions are likely to warrant exceptionally low levels of the federal funds rate for an extended period," the FOMC experimented with forward guidance (Board of Governors, *FOMC Transcript*, December 15–16,
2008). Initially, this communication focused on guiding the market's forecast of the liftoff date for the funds rate from the ZLB. The market's expectation of the number of months to liftoff influenced the ten-year bond rate
until August 2013 (figure 24.6). Postponing the expectation of liftoff was
the equivalent of reducing the funds rate. Starting in August 2013, however,
the number of months to liftoff declined while the ten-year Treasury yield
(plotted on an inverted scale) also declined. Both core and headline PCE
inflation declined after this date (figure 20.4). Plausibly, without a concern
for a revival of inflation, the approach of liftoff did not cause markets to
raise their expectation of the required level of long-term interest rates. A
Deutsche Bank newsletter wrote, "The present narrative in markets that
'long rates in the US will stay low, even when the Fed hikes rates' is normally
based on the view that the US is experiencing secular stagnation and the
terminal fed funds rate is low" (Sløk 2015).

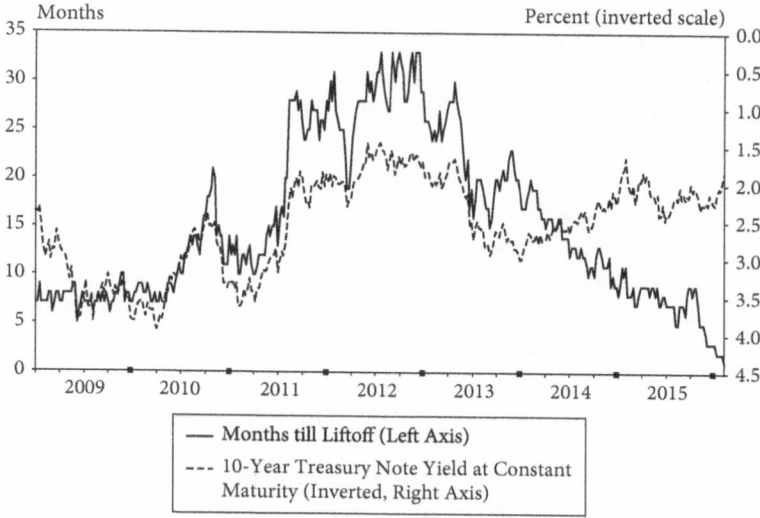

Figure 24.6. Months until Expected Fed Tightening
versus Ten-Year Treasury Note Yield
Torsten Sløk of Deutsche Bank Securities provided the idea. Months until liftoff refers
to the number of months at or below 38 basis points on federal funds futures contracts.
Heavy tick marks indicate the end of fourth quarter.
Sources: Fed Funds Futures via Bloomberg; Ten-Year Treasury Yield via Haver
Analytics

At the August 2011 meeting, the FOMC adopted date-based forward
guidance with the statement that economic conditions were "likely to
warrant exceptionally low levels for the federal funds rate at least through
mid-2013" (Board of Governors, *FOMC Transcript*, August 9, 2011). At the
November 2011 FOMC meeting, Charles Evans, president of the Chicago
Fed, revived an idea advanced earlier by then Governor Yellen for outcome-
based forward guidance using as a threshold the unemployment rate. At
the December 2012 FOMC meeting, the FOMC adopted such forward
guidance with statement language reading, "The Committee decided to
keep the target range for the federal funds rate at 0 to ¼% and currently
anticipates that this exceptionally low range for the federal funds rate will
be appropriate at least as long as the unemployment rate remains above
6½%, inflation between one and two years ahead is projected to be no more
than half a percentage point above the Committee's 2 percent longer-run
goal, and longer-term inflation expectations continue to be well anchored"
(Board of Governors, *FOMC Transcript*, December 11–12, 2012).

In January 2012, the FOMC decided on an explicit inflation target of

2 percent. In the first three months of 2012, twelve-month core PCE inflation reached 2.1 percent when the inflation shock referred to above passed
through into core inflation. The 2 percent target then seemed to ratify the
status quo. However, the strength in inflation was transitory.

As described by Jeffrey Lacker (2019), former president of the Richmond
Fed, inflation hawks on the FOMC felt uncomfortable with the FOMC's efforts at stimulus in the form of QE and forward guidance without an explicit
inflation target. After the initiation of QE2 in November 2010, inflation
hawk Charles Plosser, president of the Philadelphia Fed, with Chairman
Bernanke's blessing, had negotiated a draft of what became the document
"Longer-Run Goals and Policy Strategy" released in January 2012. Lacker
(2019, 10) wrote, "Adopting an inflation objective seemed to be a prerequisite to formulating forward guidance in terms of an unemployment threshold without confusing the public."

In 2014, the funds-rate path projected by the FOMC in the SEP and in
the public statements of FOMC chair Yellen rose, but funds-rate futures
failed to follow. Part of the political economy of monetary policy is to communicate the need to raise the funds rate solely in terms of the need to restrain inflation rather than in terms of the need to slow economic growth
and employment. However, markets did not believe that inflation was a
problem. As evidenced by the behavior of the ten-year yield on Treasury
securities and the increase in global debt with negative interest rates starting in 2015 and especially in 2016, deflation scares replaced the earlier inflation scares. Sløk (2014) summarized: "She [Yellen] is basically saying the
following: 'I know that when capacity utilization is at 2005–2006 levels,
ISM is around 60, the unemployment rate close to NAIRU, [growth in]
nonfarm payrolls is above 300k and GDP is around 4 percent then I feel
very confident that it won't be long before we see a move up in inflation.'
To this the markets say: 'Ok, but we have not seen inflation for the past six
years, and you have been too optimistic for the past six years, so why should
inflation be a problem in 2015?'"

Starting in 2014, it became clear that the economy was growing above
potential, which argued for a normalization of the funds rate by moving up
from the ZLB. The numbers were strong. From March 2014 through December 2018, the monthly average of total nonfarm payroll employment was
210,000, twice the sustainable rate, and the unemployment rate continued
to decline. Hatzius (2017) wrote: "Measures [of unemployment] such as U3,
U6, job openings, quits, reported skill shortages, and household job market
perceptions all send a similar message—the labor market is about as tight as
in the full-employment years 2006 and 1989. . . . All this suggests that further
labor market tightening is likely to result in a significant overshoot of full

employment." Real median household income increased, rising 18.5 percent from 2014 through 2019. An optimistic outlook for the future increases the natural rate of interest. At the same time, markets forecast only a minimal rise in the funds rate, and the ten-year Treasury constant maturity yield declined from 3.0 percent on January 3, 2014, to 1.4 percent on July 11, 2016. (It then rose and reached a peak of 3.2 percent on November 9, 2018.)

The *Financial Times* (R. Harding 2014) reported in an interview with St. Louis Fed president James Bullard:

> The median forecast on the FOMC expects an interest rate of 1 per cent to 1.25 per cent by the end of 2015, and Mr. Bullard said he was "worried" to see markets expecting a slower path for rate rises. "I do think that's a mistake on the part of the market," he said. "I think the committee means what it says. To have markets trading more dovishly than what the com-mittee is intending I think suggests there will be a day of reckoning at some point in the future—either for us or for them."

Yellen's roots were Keynesian. She naturally used the framework out-lined by Modigliani and Papademos (1975; 1976), which makes changes in inflation depend on the difference between the unemployment rate and a benchmark for full employment known as the nonaccelerating inflation rate of unemployment (NAIRU). With the NAIRU taken as the median value of FOMC participants' SEP projections for the longer-run unemploy-ment rate, as of the December 2015 FOMC meeting, the Fed's proxy for the NAIRU was 4.9 percent. In December 2015 also, the unemployment rate was 5.0 percent. At the December FOMC meeting, the FOMC raised the funds rate off the ZLB.

Even given her Keynesian roots, Yellen had absorbed the lessons of the Great Inflation incorporated by Volcker and Greenspan in their policy of preemptive increases in the funds rate to forestall a rise in inflation (Hetzel 2008). Yellen (2017b, 16) said:

> We should also be wary of moving too gradually. Job gains continue to run well ahead of the longer-run pace we estimate would be sufficient, on average, to provide jobs for new entrants to the labor force. Thus, without further modest increases in the federal funds rate over time, there is a risk that the labor market could eventually become overheated, potentially creating an inflationary problem down the road that might be difficult to overcome without triggering a recession. Persistently easy monetary policy might also eventually lead to increased leverage and other developments, with adverse implications for financial stability. For

these reasons, and given that monetary policy affects economic activity and inflation with a substantial lag, it would be imprudent to keep monetary policy on hold until inflation is back to 2 percent.

Yellen (2017a) summarized, "If the economy ends up over heating and inflation threatens to rise well above our target, we don't want to be in a position where we have to raise rates rapidly, which could conceivably cause another recession. So we want to be ahead of the curve and not behind it."

Yellen was replaying the earlier policy of the 1990s when the Greenspan FOMC raised the funds rate preemptively. From 7.8 percent in June 1992 to 3.8 percent in April 2000, the unemployment rate fell while inflation changed only minimally. Inflation, measured by the core PCE, went from 2.2 percent in 1992Q2 to 1.3 percent in 2000Q2. Measured by the headline PCE deflator, it remained unchanged over this period at 1.8 percent. Greenspan, however, did not give up on a policy of preemption. Without evidence of inflation, the FOMC raised the funds-rate target from 3 percent at its December 1993 meeting to 6 percent at its February 1995 meeting (figure 24.2). Again, without evidence of inflation, the FOMC raised the funds rate at its June 1999 FOMC meeting (Hetzel 2008, chaps. 15 and 17).

Greenspan was not running the economy "hot" to lower the unemployment rate to a minimal level indicated by an increase in inflation. Along with his predecessor Paul Volcker, he had renounced any attempt to balance off inflation and unemployment based on a Phillips curve. To recreate the stable nominal anchor lost in the stop-go era, Greenspan had to let the price system work without interference to determine real variables such as unemployment (Hetzel 2008, chap. 21).

24.3. SECULAR STAGNATION, FEAR OF GLOBAL RECESSION, AND CENTRAL BANKS OUT OF AMMUNITION

Starting in fall 2015, concern grew in financial markets that an adverse shock to the world economy perhaps from a recession in China or from a geopolitical crisis would push the world back into recession. The fear was that monetary policy lacked the capacity to respond. Central banks had to rely on unconventional and untested policies such as quantitative easing and negative interest rates. Low interest rates created the fear that central banks would lack the ability to stimulate aggregate demand in the event of a recession,

Larry Summers argued that the US economy had entered what Alvin Hansen in the late 1930s called secular stagnation (see Hansen 1939). The future norm would be low real growth, low inflation, and near-zero rates of interest. This view rationalized the observation that across countries, real GDP growth was anemic, inflation was below central bank targets, and yet interest rates were low or even negative. Central banks were supposedly "out of ammunition."[3] A common theme was that expansionary monetary policy works through weakening the foreign exchange value of the currency. However, that channel is a zero-sum game for countries collectively. The *Financial Times* (2016) reported:

> The yen touched new highs yesterday, defying Tokyo's effort to weaken the Japanese currency in the latest sign policy makers in leading economies are running out of tools to kick-start growth and battle the threat of deflation. . . . Like the BoJ, the European Central Bank has intervened in capital markets at unprecedented levels to little effect on the EU's common currency or inflation. . . . Aggressive monetary policies in general, and negative interest rates in particular, have long been seen as a means to depreciate currencies and raise inflation. . . . But despite the aggressive BoJ and ECB moves, global inflation remains lackluster.

With a surprise devaluation of the renminbi (yuan) in August 2015, financial markets became preoccupied with the state of the Chinese economy. China's foreign exchange reserves reached a peak in 2014 at $4.0 trillion and then ran steadily down to just over $3.0 trillion in 2016 (Hooper et al. 2017). In September 2015, Citibank (Spence 2015) warned: "A 'hard landing' for the Chinese economy will likely lead the world into a recession in the next year. . . . They [Citi's economists] anticipate the global economy to slide into recessionary territory during the next year, and remain there for most of 2017." Markets feared that a recession in China with low real growth in the world economy could push the world back into recession. (A China shock could have come from maintaining an overvalued yuan or from the collapse of its housing market.) The concern for China recognized its importance to

3. In five major countries, central banks instituted a negative-rate policy in which commercial banks pay to maintain their reserves at the central bank. In the Eurozone, year-over-year growth in real GDP in 2015Q4 was 1.6 percent, barely enough to lower an unemployment rate of 10.3 percent in early 2016. The Eurozone year-over-year growth in the CPI through March 2016 was −0.1 percent. The other countries with negative policy rates (and their corresponding year-over-year figures) were Japan (0.7 percent GDP growth through 2015Q4 and 0.3 percent CPI inflation through February 2016); Denmark (0.5 percent GDP growth through 2015Q4 and 0 percent CPI inflation through March 2016); and Switzerland (0.4 percent GDP growth through 2015Q4 and −0.9 percent CPI inflation through March 2016). (Sweden is an outlier. Despite strong real GDP growth for 2015 near 4 percent and inflation near 1 percent, the Riksbank implemented negative interest rates to prevent an appreciation of the Krona.

the world economy. Deutsche Bank estimated that in 2016 of the estimated growth in world real GDP of 3.2 percent, China would contribute 1 percentage point and the United States 0.6 percentage points (Sløk 2016).

In January 2016, RBS (the Royal Bank of Scotland) issued the warning. "RBS has advised clients to brace for a 'cataclysmic year' and a global deflationary crisis, warning that major stock markets could fall by a fifth and oil may plummet to $16 a barrel. The bank's credit team said markets are flashing stress alerts akin to the turbulent months before the Lehman crisis. 'Sell everything except high quality bonds. This is about return of capital, not return on capital. In a crowded hall, exit doors are small,' it said in a client note" (Evans-Pritchard 2016). The price of oil measured the state of the world economy. Its price went from $102 a barrel in August 2014 (averaging $110 over the years 2011 to August 2014) to $31 in January 2016 (global price of Brent crude from St. Louis FRED).

With the Great Recession, markets associated recession with deflation. Investors bought insurance with nominally denominated Treasuries, which do well in recession. Bonds trading at negative interest rates first appeared in nontrivial amounts in 2015. Over 2016, worldwide, the percentage of bonds trading at negative interest rates went from less than 5 percent to about 28 percent (Sløk 2019a). For most of the recovery, world financial markets were in a "risk-off" or wealth-preservation mood. Low and negative bond rates reflected fear of adverse tail risk.

In 2018 and 2019, market fears concentrated on a trade war. Starting in 2018 with tariffs on solar panels and washing machines, the United States began imposing tariffs on numerous countries. Countries retaliated with their own tariffs. Eisenbeis (2020) wrote: "The scope and scale of the tariffs have been large, with a total of over 20,000 products (12,043 imports and 8,073 exports) amounting to over $400 million in goods being impacted." Donnan and Leonard (2019) wrote:

What began as method [the calibrated imposition of tariffs on Chinese exports] looks more and more like madness. A tit-for-tat tariff war has ensnared more that 70% of bilateral trade in goods and raised the specter of a decoupling of two economies that once seemed destined to become progressively more intertwined. . . . That tariff round [additional tariffs threatened for December 15, 2019] could jeopardize America's record-long expansion.

In the recovery, the general spirit of market commentary was fear of a self-reinforcing negative feedback loop between pessimism and recession. The International Monetary Fund (2016, Executive Summary, ix) captured the prevailing mood about the fragility of the world economy: "In such circumstances [a recurrence of market turmoil], rising risk premiums may tighten financial conditions further, creating a pernicious feedback loop of fragile confidence, weaker growth, lower inflation, and rising debt burdens. Disruptions to global asset markets could increase the risks of tipping into a more serious and prolonged slowdown marked by financial and economic stagnation."

Chairman Bernanke (sec. 21.5) expressed these views in his explanation of the Great Recession. Numerous external shocks threatened confidence in the recovery from the Great Recession. They included the euro crisis in 2011 and 2012, the Brexit vote in June 2016, the devaluation of the renminbi by China in August 2015, and the trade war in 2018 and 2019. However, if the economy was inherently unstable because of the Keynesian animal spirits of financial markets, such shocks should have set off recessions. The lesson is that the price system is resilient to shocks in the presence of stabilizing (the absence of contractionary) monetary policy.

24.4. QUANTITATIVE EASING

The great benefit of the Greenspan FOMC in finally achieving credibility for price stability was to eliminate market fears that aggressive reductions in the funds rate would revive inflation. As long as the funds rate was well above the ZLB, the FOMC could then make clear that it would pursue funds-rate reductions in the event of weakness in the economy until the economy recovered. However, with the funds rate at the ZLB in the recovery from the Great Recession, the FOMC turned to QE not only as a tool for creating monetary stimulus but also as a way of conveying to markets the "whatever it takes" message that despite the constraint imposed by the ZLB, monetary policy would ensure a recovery. The challenge was to convey the message to markets that a more pessimistic reading of the economy and a consequent lengthening of the estimated liftoff date of the funds rate from the ZLB was embedded in a policy of "whatever it takes" to maintain the recovery. The FOMC had to avoid a message of pessimism that would dampen economic activity.[4] This chapter's appendix ("The FOMC's QE Programs") summarizes the FOMC's QE programs in which it bought long-term securities (see Chen 2015; Engen et al. 2015; and Rosengren 2019, fig. 4.1).

Numerous papers evaluate the announcement effects of QE, for example, Gagnon et al. (2011) and Vissing-Jorgensen and Krishnamurthy (2011). They found significant announcement effects on long-term interest rates.

---

4. Swanson (2017) found that both forward guidance and QE raised stock prices. That is, markets did not interpret them as information that the economy was worse than had been expected.

Others, like Daniel Thornton (2017) have pointed out that the reduction in long-term rates was short-lived. However, if QE is stimulative, one would expect that it would strengthen the economy and, in the process, raise long-term rates. QE works through a portfolio balance effect in which replacing an illiquid asset like a mortgage-backed security (MBS) with a liquid bank deposit causes investors to rebalance their portfolios by purchasing illiquid assets like stocks, houses, consumer durables, and so on. The effects then would be hard to disentangle from other forces.

Some FOMC participants have doubted the power of quantitative easing (QE, or the purchase of long-term assets) given that IOR that prevents the resulting reserves creation from lowering the funds rate. The assumption is that QE lowers the yield on long-term Treasury securities. It does so by lowering their term premium, which is the excess yield beyond the risk-free interest rate. The excess yield compensates for the risk that interest rates will increase over their lifetime. However, term premiums were already negative in 2020.[5] The FOMC minutes for the June 2020 meeting (Board of Governors, *FOMC Minutes*, June 9–10, 2020, 4) stated:

> Participants agreed that asset purchase programs can promote accommodative financial conditions by putting downward pressure on term premiums and longer-term yields. Several participants remarked that declines in the neutral rate of interest and in term premiums over the past decade and prevailing low levels of longer-term yields would likely act as constraints on the effectiveness of asset purchases.

The argument for the efficacy of QE is indirect. Assume that the natural rate of interest was extremely low and negative at least through 2015 as suggested by figure 24.2. As noted, there were significant, negative shocks in the recovery period. Other things equal, they likely would have required a significantly negative real interest rate. Because the Fed was unwilling to consider a negative funds rate, something had to substitute for a reduction in the real rate of interest. The stability exhibited in the post–Great Recession period despite the constraint imposed by the ZLB then likely derives to a significant extent from the Fed's three QE programs.

The fact that at first the FOMC used forward guidance and QE only tentatively is consistent with the claim that initially in the recovery monetary policy was moderately contractionary. The open market purchases announced November 25, 2008, and expanded March 18, 2009, only replaced

---

5. The model of D. Kim and Wright (2005) yields a value of −0.91 for July 24, 2020. See Board of Governors, "Term Premium on a 10 Year Zero Coupon Bond [THREEFYTP10]," available on FRED (Federal Reserve Bank of St. Louis), https://fred.stlouisfed.org/series/THREEFYTP10.

the reserves supplied by the Fed's various liquidity facilities. That is, the size of the Fed's asset portfolio did not expand after November 25, 2008, but expanded only with the commencement of QE2 announced November 3, 2010.[6] As J. C. Williams (2013, 1) noted "from 2009 to mid-2011, expectations from financial markets showed the federal funds rate lifting off from zero within just a few quarters." However, not until August 2011 did the FOMC use forward guidance "to push back against these excessively tight policy expectations" (J. C. Williams 2013, 1). It did so with the August 2011 statement containing the language that economic conditions were "likely to warrant exceptionally low levels for the federal funds rate at least through mid-2013" (see chap. 28) (Board of Governors, *FOMC Transcript*, August 9, 2011).

The fact that initially the FOMC did not "push back against these excessively tight policy expectations" means that the FOMC, like the markets, expected a strong V-shaped recovery. Forward guidance conveying the FOMC's consensus forecast is an important determinant of market expectations. Note the sharp rise in the ten-year Treasury yield in May 2013 associated with the "taper tantrum" (figure 24.7). Comments by Chairman Bernanke that the FOMC would begin reducing the size of its QE purchases caused the markets to advance the timing of the expected liftoff date of the funds rate from the ZLB. The rise in the ten-year Treasury yield demonstrates the importance of this kind of forward guidance.

The stability of the post–Great Recession period despite the ZLB suggests that QE compensated for the FOMC's inability to implement a negative funds rate. The work of Wu and Xia (2016) shows that the largest-magnitude negative shadow rate of −3 percent occurred in 2014. The total announced QE purchases came to about $4 trillion (see this chapter's appendix), which in the event amounted to $3.35 trillion since January 2008 (Sløk 2017b). They apparently sufficed to offset the FOMC's inability to lower the funds rate to −3 percent. Deutsche Bank (Luzzetti et al. 2020, 4) summarized: "One well-known estimate of the shadow fed funds rate—the Wu-Xia shadow rate—indicates that during the period of the Fed's unconventional tools, a roughly $3.5tn expansion of the Fed's balance sheet post the global financial crisis coincided with a shadow fed funds rate trough of −3%." K. Kim et al. (2020, abstract) found "that absent the LSAP3 [large-scale asset purchase] program implemented between late 2012 and 2014, CPI inflation would have been about 1 percentage point lower, while the

6. On November 26, 2008, the reserve bank credit in the Fed's portfolio was $2.1 trillion, and securities held outright was just less than 0.5 trillion. On November 3, 2010, reserve bank credit was only slightly larger at $2.3 trillion, and securities held outright came to about $2 trillion. The increase in securities mainly replaced the bank reserves that had been supplied by the FOMC's credit programs.

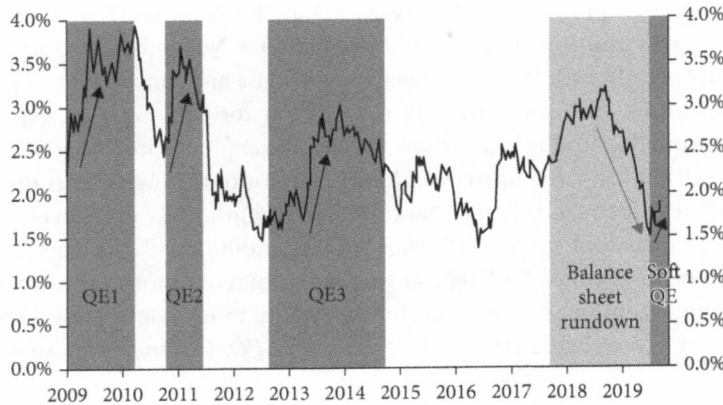

Figure 24.7. Ten-Year Treasury Yield and QE Periods
Figure from Sløk (2019c). Tick marks indicate first observation of the year.

unemployment rate would have been about 4 percentage points higher, by the end of 2015."

A criticism of QE is that with low long-term interest rates it has a limited impact. However, QE undertaken in sufficient magnitude will still exercise a stimulative portfolio balance effect (chap. 26). Hudepohl et al. (2019) found a positive effect on stock prices in the Euro area from QE after controlling for macroeconomic fundamentals. For the period from October 9, 2019, to December 25, 2019, when the Fed engaged in open market purchases in response to a spike in repurchase agreement (RP) rates, Sløk (2019b) found "a 1% increase in the Fed balance sheet has been associated with a 0.9% increase in the S&P 500."

24.5. WHAT ACCOUNTS FOR THE NEAR PRICE STABILITY IN THE RECOVERY FROM THE GREAT RECESSION?

In his August 2020 speech, Chair Powell (2020d) expressed concern that without the makeup of inflation shortfalls provided for in FAIT, the public's expectations of inflation would become unanchored to the downside. Despite the duration of the funds rate at the ZLB, there is no evidence in the recovery from the Great Recession of such unanchoring. The public's expectation of near price stability reflected the longer-run effort of the FOMC to restore the price stability lost in the Great Inflation.[7] Although the FOMC

---

7. Measurement of price stability must take account of upward bias in the price indices due to inadequate controls for quality changes in goods and services. The Boskin Commission (1996) estimated the bias at 1.1 percent.

adopted a 2 percent inflation target in January 2012, monetary policy continued to be consistent with a somewhat lower rate of inflation, that is, with near price stability of about 1.5 percent.

Headline inflation is a combination of inflation in the sticky-price sector, in which firms set prices for multiple periods based on their expectation of inflation, and in the flexible-price sector (Aoki 2001; Mankiw and Reis 2003). The Atlanta Fed constructs a proxy for these inflation series based on frequency of price changes of the individual components (figure 24.8). Figure 24.9 offers an alternative measure assuming that prices in the services sector are changed less frequently than those in the goods sector. As shown in figure 24.8, starting with the Volcker disinflation and lasting through the Asia crisis at the end of the 1990s, apart from the period after the Louvre Accord in February 1987, monetary policy lowered sticky-price inflation. Inflation in the sticky-price sector declined after the Great Recession. Going into the Great Recession, from 2007Q1 through 2008Q3, PCE services inflation averaged 3.2 percent. In the subsequent period, 2008Q4 through 2019Q4, it declined to 2.1 percent (figure 24.9).

Until the adoption of an explicit inflation target in January 2012, the FOMC's implicit inflation objective was somewhat less than 2 percent. The

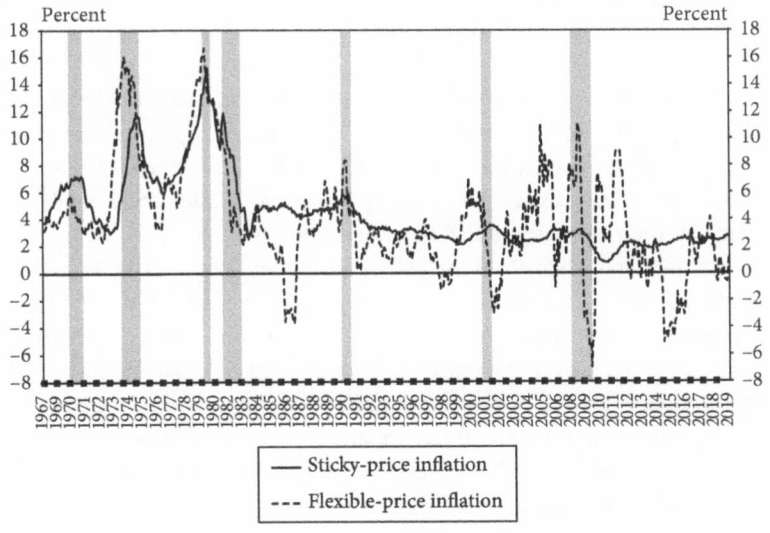

Figure 24.8. Sticky-Price and Flexible-Price Inflation
Observations are twelve-month percentage changes in sticky-price and flexible-price inflation. Shaded areas indicate recession. Heavy tick marks indicate December. For construction of the series, see Bryan and Meyer (2010).
Source: Federal Reserve Bank of Atlanta

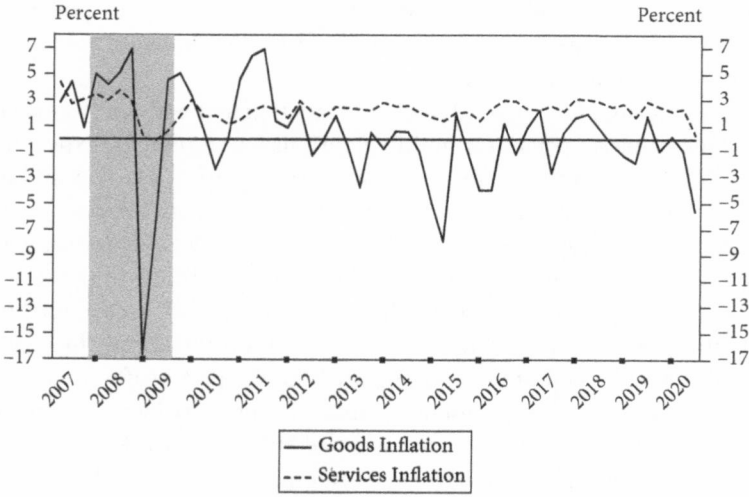

Figure 24.9. PCE Goods and Services Inflation
Quarterly observations of annualized percentage changes in the goods and services
personal consumption expenditures (PCE) implicit price deflator. Shaded area
indicates recession. Heavy tick marks indicate fourth quarter.
Source: St. Louis FRED

near price stability that prevailed in the recovery period then should be
expected. Shapiro and Wilson (2019a) wrote:

> In this *Economic Letter*, we summarize FOMC meeting deliberations
> leading up to the 2012 explicit target announcement, as examined in
> our recent study, Shapiro and Wilson (2019b). In numerous instances
> during deliberations, FOMC participants made explicit statements re-
> garding their preferred inflation target. For example, in the March 21,
> 2007, meeting, then-President of the San Francisco Fed Janet Yellen
> stated, "I remain comfortable with the goal that I enunciated some time
> ago—a long-run inflation objective of 1½% for the core PCE inflation
> rate." Searching over the entire archive of publicly available historical
> transcripts of FOMC meetings, we track the explicit statements made by
> participants about their preferred inflation target. . . . The analysis shows
> that participants generally expressed a preference for an inflation target
> around 1½% from 2000 to at least 2007.

San Francisco Fed president Janet Yellen (2005) wrote: "I would characterize a long-run inflation objective centered on 1.5% for core PCE inflation
as a 'modal' [FOMC] view." From 2000Q1 through 2004Q1, core PCE infla-

tion (four-quarter averages) averaged 1.7 percent. In a discussion of a deflation trap, Chairman Bernanke (Board of Governors, *FOMC Transcript*,
October 28–29, 2008, 153) said, "The best two ways to avoid it are, first,
as President Lacker suggested, reaffirm our commitment to price stability defined as 1½ to 2%." (The second was to move aggressively if deflation
threatened.) In discussing inflation targeting, Bernanke pointed out that
the long-run projections for inflation contained in the FOMC's Summary
of Economic Projections (SEP) made quarterly by FOMC participants substituted for an explicit inflation target. Bernanke (2015, 174) wrote, "The
first set of projections under the new system [at the October 2007 meeting]
would show most FOMC members forecasting inflation in three years (in
2010) to be between 1.6% and 1.9%."

Following the recovery from the 2001 recession, flexible-price inflation
significantly exceeded sticky-price inflation. Similarly, headline PCE inflation generally exceeded core PCE inflation. The integration of the BRICs
(Brazil, Russia, India, and China) into the world economy raised flexible-
price inflation by increasing the demand for commodities. From 2004Q2
through 2008Q3, core PCE inflation rose to 2.2 percent while headline PCE
inflation rose to 2.8 percent (figure 20.4). By concentrating on headline inflation, central banks through restrictive monetary policy lowered core inflation (see chap. 21; and Hetzel 2012a). Trend inflation in the sticky-price
sector fell from around 3 percent going into the 2008 recession to around 2
percent afterward (figure 24.8).

In updating the statistical decomposition of inflation into a time-varying
trend and into transitory changes in Stock and Watson (2007), Cecchetti
et al. (2017) found that the trend for core PCE inflation declined after the
Great Recession to about 1½ percent. A weak world economy starting in
2012 kept inflation in the flexible-price sector low through weak commodity prices, especially oil. The combination of stable but low inflation in the
sticky-price sector and low inflation and even deflation in the flexible-price
sector generally kept headline inflation below 2 percent. The disinflation of
the Great Recession firmly embedded the public's expectation of near price
stability.

The recovery from the Great Recession provides no support for the fear
that this expectation of near price stability could become unanchored to
the downside. Measures of expected inflation declined slightly as evidence
accumulated that historically low interest rates did not produce inflation.
In the University of Michigan Surveys of Consumers, the median expected
price change for the next twelve months averaged 3.2 percent for the period
January 2012 to December 2014. It then declined to 2.6 percent over the
interval January 2015 to February 2020 (2.7 percent for the period March

2020 to October 2020). The five-year, five-year forward expectation of inflation calculated from ten-year and five-year nominal and Treasury inflation protected securities (TIPS) averaged 2.6 percent over the period November 2009 through September 2014. It then declined to 2.0 percent over the period October 2014 to February 2020.[8]

24.6. CONCLUDING COMMENT

In August 2020 in a speech at the Jackson Hole Conference, Chair Powell used a revision of the FOMC's Statement on Longer-Run Goals and Monetary Policy Strategy to announce a new strategy for monetary policy. According to Powell, the FOMC can run an expansionary monetary policy to achieve an unemployment rate low enough to achieve socially desirable goals. The reason is that the world has changed so that even with low levels of unemployment inflation does not emerge. (The Phillips curve is flat down to historically low levels of unemployment.) To discover this minimal level of unemployment, monetary policy should be expansionary until inflation rises persistently above the FOMC's 2 percent inflation target. The new policy required rejection of the Volcker-Greenspan FOMC's policy of preemption—that is, raising the funds rate during economic recoveries to forestall the emergence of inflation.

Much of the inspiration for this changed policy rested on the quiescence of inflation in the prior period of economic recovery. Inflationary expectations remained centered on near price stability. For the period from December 2008 through December 2016, the funds rate remained at and then close to the ZLB, and yet inflation generally remained somewhat less than the FOMC's inflation target of 2 percent. Moreover, the unemployment rate fell from a peak in October 2009 of 10.0 percent to 3.5 percent in February 2020. The narrative here is consistent with a monetary policy either moderately contractionary or neutral. Nothing in this experience suggests that the FOMC can run an expansionary monetary policy until the unemployment rate has declined sufficiently to cause a controlled, moderate overshoot of the 2 percent target.

The recovery from the Great Recession was a period of considerable economic stability. The FOMC should ask what it did right, not what it did

8. Data are from St. Louis FRED. From August 2020 through November 2020, the five-year, five-year forward expectation of inflation averaged 1.8 percent. The reason for omitting the observations at the start of the pandemic is that in times of financial stress, TIPS become relatively illiquid so that their yield rises. At the same time, the on-the-run ten-year Treasury yields decline because of the demand for safety and liquidity. It then appears as though expected inflation has declined.

wrong. Preemptive increases in the funds rate did not prevent a decline in the unemployment rate to a historically low level. Inflationary expectations did not become unanchored to the downside. Nothing in this period or in the more distant past demonstrates that the FOMC can successfully pursue an expansionary monetary policy to lower the unemployment rate to a minimal level without destabilizing inflation and the economy.

APPENDIX: THE FOMC'S QE PROGRAMS

QE1: The Fed announced QE1 on November 25, 2008. It targeted total purchases of up to $100 billion in agency debt and $500 billion in agency MBS. On March 18, 2009, the FOMC increased substantially the size of the program. It committed to buying an additional $100 billion in agency debt and $750 billion in agency MBS through December 2009, and $300 billion in longer-term Treasury securities through September 2009.[9] From November 2008 through year-end 2009, the Fed purchased $1.75 trillion of securities (10.8 percent of GDP).

QE2: On November 3, 2010, the Fed announced the purchase of $600 billion of long-term treasuries terminating December 31, 2012 (3.9 percent of GDP).

MEP (Maturity Extension Program): The Fed exchanged $667 billion of short-term Treasuries for long-term treasuries with no change in the size of its balance sheet. The FOMC announced the program in September 2011 and continued it through the year-end 2012.

QE 3: From September 2012 to October 2014, the Fed purchased about $1.6 trillion of assets consisting of approximately equal amounts of agency MBS and long-term Treasury securities. On September 13, 2012, the Fed announced monthly purchases of $40 billion of MBS and $85 billion of long-term Treasuries in aggregate as part of the Maturity Extension Program (twist). In December 2012, it continued the monthly purchases of $40 billion per month for agency MBS plus $45 billion per month for Treasuries. QE3 purchases amounted to 9.3 percent of GDP.

9. The heavy preponderance of purchases of MBS as opposed to Treasury securities reflected the belief that the problem was not contractionary monetary policy but rather a failure of financial intermediation centered on the housing market. QE1 still caused many in financial markets to worry about "runaway inflation" (Torres and Boesler 2016). Purchasing Treasury securities was presumed inflationary because it financed the government's deficit.

CHAPTER 25

Covid-19 and the Fed's Credit Policy

Summary: In March 2020, with the realization of the enormity of the threat posed by the Covid-19 virus, financial markets exhibited unusual volatility.[1] According to the Federal Reserve's narrative, financial markets became dysfunctional. That narrative implies that markets could no longer assess risk appropriately. However, nothing in market volatility implies that private markets can no longer assess risk or allocate credit; nevertheless, the Fed responded with numerous programs to intervene in private credit markets. This chapter examines the causes of the financial market volatility, discusses the moral hazard entailed by intervening in private credit markets, and explores whether credit market interventions could undermine the Fed's political independence. The Fed promoted its 13(3) programs as providing resources to sectors of the economy where markets failed to do so, but the Fed's credit programs can only allocate credit, not increase real resources. It was monetary policy actions that calmed financial markets, not the announcement of future credit market interventions. Involvement in credit policy drags the Fed into the political arena; therefore, to maintain its independence, the Fed should return to the sole job of monetary policy.

A signal feature of the Federal Reserve's response to the Covid-19 recession was the creation of programs to intervene in credit markets with the intent of sustaining financial intermediation. With credit policy, the Fed attempts to influence financial intermediation, that is, the transfer of resources from households (savers) to firms or government (borrowers). The essential characteristic of credit policy is the way in which the Fed influences how the resources made available by households get allocated among competing uses.[2] That response raises difficult questions. One must address the underlying premise of the interventions. Did the ability of private credit

1. A version of this chapter first appeared as Robert L. Hetzel, "COVID-19 and the Fed's Credit Policy" (Mercatus Working Paper, Mercatus Center at George Mason University, Arlington, VA, July 2020).
2. Through its influence on the term structure of interest rates, in contrast, monetary policy influences the intertemporal distribution of the aggregate demand for resources

markets to assess risk fail so that the Fed had to maintain the flow of credit by transferring risk from private balance sheets to the public's (taxpayers') balance sheet (the combined balance sheet of the Fed and the Treasury)? If, upon reflection, one decides that the assessment of risk would better have been left to the marketplace, how should the Fed have responded to maintain the stability of financial markets?

Just as troublesome are the issues of the role of an independent central bank in a constitutional democracy. Credit policy supplants the market allocation of private savings. Through its redistribution of the resources allocated to investors, it is fiscal policy not monetary policy. The opaqueness of the resulting transfers limits the transparency and thus the accountability desirable for a central bank. Asking for its credit programs to be funded through congressionally authorized debt, as was done with the 1932 Reconstruction Finance Corporation (Todd 1996) or with the 2008 Troubled Asset Relief Program (TARP) would have increased transparency. Moreover, in the longer run, the moral hazard that credit policies create encourages excessive risk taking, especially in the shadow banking system (financial institutions with the characteristics of banks but not regulated as banks).

Applied to the credit market interventions of a central bank, the fundamental idea expressed here is that the real quantity of household savings is determined independently of the central bank. The central bank can supersede the working of financial markets by allocating household savings among competing uses, but it cannot increase the aggregate amount of available savings.

Section 25.1 summarizes the Fed's narrative of the events in financial markets in March 2020. That is, financial markets became dysfunctional because of a presumed inability of market participants to assess risk. Section 25.2 shows how instability created by the shadow banking system created much of the volatility in financial markets in March 2020. It explains the existence of the prime money market funds as a manifestation of moral hazard. Nothing in market volatility implied that private markets could no longer assess risk and allocate credit.

Section 25.3 makes the argument that the Fed's monetary policy actions—namely, its massive open market operations, not the announcement of future interventions into credit markets—calmed financial markets. It also asks whether the Fed's credit programs worsened market function by exacerbating a two-tier credit market favoring relatively riskless assets over relatively risky ones. Section 25.4 illustrates how the Fed's credit programs

in a way that aids in maintaining that demand equal to potential output and that maintains price stability.

allocate credit without increasing the aggregate supply of credit. It also explains how paying interest on reserves (IOR) expands the ability of the Fed to become a financial intermediary like the housing government-sponsored enterprises (GSEs).

Section 25.5 illustrates the standard response of a central bank to a financial panic of freely creating reserves by comparing that aspect of the Fed's response in March 2020 with its response to the default of Penn Central Transportation Company in May 1970. When the commercial paper market ceased functioning in May 1970, the Fed made certain that the banks could lend freely. This alternative would still assure markets of the uninterrupted continuation of financial intermediation while avoiding Fed involvement in the allocation of credit and attendant risks to its independence. Section 25.6 questions whether the Fed can retain its independence given a heavy involvement in credit markets. An appendix documents the past reluctance of the Fed to be drawn into credit policy (preceded by an appendix of program definitions).

25.1. CHAIR POWELL DEFINES THE NARRATIVE

The Fed's narrative for its unprecedented intervention into private credit markets is that financial intermediation to households and businesses ceased in mid-March, and the Fed's programs restored the flow of credit. Chair Powell (2020e) stated:

> Some essential financial markets had begun to sink into dysfunction, and many channels that households, businesses, and state and local governments rely on for credit had simply stopped working. We acted forcefully to get our markets working again.... When ... private markets and institutions are once again able to perform their vital functions of channeling credit and supporting economic growth, we will put these emergency tools away.

Powell (2020c) defended the need for the credit programs with similar assertions. He noted that when markets realized that the virus would not be contained in China, they became "volatile." He further claimed that "investors fled from any kind of risk and really markets stopped functioning" and that "companies and households couldn't borrow, couldn't roll over debt. Markets kind of closed. They stopped working." When financial markets actually did continue to function, Powell claimed that it was because of an announcement to the effect that the programs would become operational in the future. Powell (2020c) stated, "Even before we began lending, [markets] started to work again. There's a confidence factor."

The FOMC meeting minutes are interesting because they summarize FOMC views just at the start of announcements of the various credit programs (Board of Governors, *FOMC Minutes*, March 15, 2020, 5):

> Corporate bond issuance came to a near standstill around late February in the midst of elevated volatility following the escalation of concerns about the coronavirus outbreak. Later in the intermeeting period [January 29 to March 15, 2020], investment-grade bond issuance resumed intermittently, but speculative-grade issuance and leveraged loan issuance virtually stopped. . . . Credit quality indicators . . . deteriorated following the escalation of the coronavirus outbreak, particularly for the speculative-grade and energy segments of the market.

Lorie Logan (2020), executive vice president at the New York Fed, stated her view: "In early to mid-March, amid extreme volatility across the financial system, the functioning of Treasury and agency MBS markets became severely impaired. Given the importance of these markets, continued dysfunction would have led to an even deeper and broader seizing up of credit markets and ultimately worsened the financial hardships that many Americans have been experiencing as a result of the pandemic." Logan expressed the traditional New York Fed view that equates market volatility (formerly denoted as "disorderly markets") with market failure requiring Fed intervention. It is right that the New York Desk has a responsibility to maintain the short-term funding of brokers and dealers, which supports the government securities market. However, massive open market purchases by the Desk rectified that "dysfunction." While it may be correct that "continued dysfunction would have led to an even deeper and broader seizing up of credit markets," nothing in her account of markets indicated the necessity of the Board's broad array of 13(3) programs. Chair Powell (2021b) wrote Senator Rick Scott (R-FL): "By staving off severe financial-market stress, our actions, taken together, helped unlock more than $2 trillion in funding from private sources to support businesses large and small, nonprofits, and state and local governments between April and December."

The Powell-FOMC narrative raises many questions. What evidence is there of a breakdown in the ability of markets to perform the function of financial intermediation? Was Governor Clarida (2020, 4) right that the Fed's credit market programs were required to "support the flow of credit to households and businesses" by "supporting lending throughout the economy?" It is natural that the issuance of long-term securities would cease while investors evaluated the risk that the Covid-19 virus would shut down the world economy. The question is whether investors looked beyond the Covid-19 crisis to the return of a normal world and therefore continued to be able to price risk and allocate resources. Alternatively, did markets cease to function because investors feared an end-of-the-world, apocalyptic outcome?

In fact, market trading did continue, and markets did continue to price risk. Measured by junk bonds, yields were not high relative to the past periods of market stress.[3] The yield on junk bonds peaked at 11.4 percent on March 23, 2020. During the fall 2008 financial turmoil, they peaked at 22.9 percent, on December 12, 2008; they peaked at 10.1 percent on October 4, 2011, during the Eurozone crisis; and at 10.1 percent on February 11, 2016, with fear of a world recession. Yields on high-grade commercial paper show that the period of unusual market volatility was short-lived. The yield on high-grade paper rose above 1.5 percent on March 11, 2020, and then declined below 1.5 percent after April 6.[4] The Board of Governors created the 13(3) programs well before it could possibly have had any evidence that financial intermediation had broken down. Policy makers based that conclusion on market "volatility." One must then ask whether volatility in response to increased risk provides evidence of a breakdown in financial intermediation.

25.2. WHAT DESTABILIZED FINANCIAL MARKETS IN MARCH 2020?

The increase in risk measures in mid-March 2020 reflected the sudden apparition of the Covid-19 virus and its devastating impact on the real economy. Measured using credit card data, starting abruptly on March 13, "total spending by all consumers" declined by more than 30 percent before steadying in early April.[5] At the same time, the tumult in credit markets also reflected regulatory features that reduced the resilience of the system to respond to shocks. The rise of the shadow banking system as embodied in the prime money market funds, municipal bond market funds, and REITs (real estate investment trusts) made credit markets unstable. In addition, the

3. ICE BofA US High Yield Index Effective Yield [BAMLH0A0HYM2EY], St. Louis FRED.

4. Board of Governors of the Federal Reserve System, "Overnight A2/P2 Nonfinancial Commercial Paper Interest Rate," St. Louis FRED.

5. Data from www.tracktherecovery.org, which tracks real time data. The website is Opportunity Insights Economic Tracker, put together by Raj Chetty, John N. Friedman, Nathaniel Hendren, and Michael Stepner of Harvard University.

Table 25.1. Fed Balance Sheet (Billions of $)

	Mar 18	Mar 25	Apr 1	Apr 8	Apr 22	May 20
Securities	3,929	4,187	4,605	4,973	5,452	5,873
Repo outstanding	389	388	302	228	172	162
Discount window	7	40	50	44	35	21
Swap lines	45	169	328	385	406	446
PDCF		14	34	33	31	9
MMLF		7	47	54	50	38
CPFF					3	4
PPPLF					3	43

Basel III Accords ironically made financial markets less resilient through the LCR (liquidity coverage ratio) and especially the SLR (supplementary leverage ratio).[6]

The Fed's balance sheet offers evidence on the causes of market instability in March 2020. Table 25.1 shows the balance sheet on selected dates. The most important entry increasing the size of the balance sheet was the Fed's security holdings, which increased by almost two trillion dollars from the March 18 to the May 20 statement week. The Fed's special credit programs, few of which had yet begun operation, contributed little.[7] Striking is the increase in the swap lines, which grew by $401 billion. That increase signaled a run on short-term dollar funding for foreign banks and a corresponding fragility in the financial system. What is the source of that fragility?

25.2.1. Why Were the Swap Lines Needed?

The first clue to answering this question is to note that the swap lines have ballooned three times, starting with the fall 2008 financial crisis. They pro-

6. The LCR for large systemically important financial institutions (SIFIs) emerged as a reform after the fall 2008 financial crisis. Some individual banks and investment houses lacked sufficient liquid assets to survive a funding shortfall. Under Basel III, banks with more than $250 billion in assets had to hold enough high-quality liquid assets (HQLA) to substitute for a lack of short-term funding for thirty days. Level 1 HQLA, whose value is not discounted, include deposits with the Fed (reserves). The SLR, which requires a minimum ratio of capital to total assets, was intended to provide an additional safeguard to prevent banks from manipulating capital ratios based on risk weightings for assets.

7. As of May 6, 2020, the total of lending by the CPFF, the PDCF, the PPPLF, and the MMLF amounted to only $91 billion (Board of Governors, Statistical Release H.4.1). The MLF, MSLF, PMCCF, SMCCF, and TALF were not yet operational.

vided dollars to replace the suddenly unavailable dollars formerly obtained from the prime money funds, which buy the CDs and commercial paper of foreign banks. In the first episode, drawings on swap lines reached a peak of $586 billion on December 4, 2008 (US GAO 2011, "Figure 25: Overview of Dollar Swap Lines," 201). In addition, TAF (Term Auction Facility) offered dollars to foreign banks directly through auctions. TAF borrowing peaked at $493 billion on March 4, 2009 (US GAO 2011, "What GAO Found"). According to the report (US GAO 2011, fig. 30, "Top 25 Largest TAF Borrowers," 231), 41.7 percent of the borrowing originated in foreign banks. Using that percentage, of the $493 billion of peak TAF borrowing, TAF supplied $206 billion dollars to foreign banks.

In the second episode, drawings on the swap lines went from zero at the end of September 2011 to $108 billion in the statement week of February 22, 2012.[8] In the third episode, March 2020, fearing outflows, the prime money funds reduced buying of foreign bank debt except at short maturities. The foreign banks then replaced the funds obtained from the prime money funds by dollars made available by their own central banks, which drew on their swap lines. In all three episodes, the sudden withdrawal of dollar funding by the prime money market funds forced foreign banks to look to their central banks to provide them with the lost dollar funding (Eren et al. 2020a and 2020b).

25.2.2. Moral Hazard and the Shadow Banking System

The financial system is fragile because in a financial crisis while there is a flight to safety into the deposits of large banks there is a corresponding flight from the suddenly illiquid prime money funds. The money funds are a creature of moral hazard. Moral hazard results from the Fed's unwillingness to allow any financial institution including the money funds to fail when that failure would

8. Jeremy Stein (2012, 3, 6) wrote:

In the second half of 2011, when the credit quality of a number of large euro-area banks became a concern . . . US prime money market funds sharply reduced their lending to those banks. In a span of four months, the exposure of money funds to euro-area banks fell by half, from about $400 billion in May to about $200 billion in September.

The central role played by money market funds in the 2011 episode is a reminder of the fragility of these funds themselves—and of the risk created by their combination of risky asset holdings, stable-value demandable liabilities, and zero-capital buffers. The events following the Lehman Brothers bankruptcy in 2008 provide even starker evidence of the risks that money market funds pose for the broader financial system.

impose losses on debt holders.[9] The common feature of prime money funds is the financing with short-term debt of a portfolio of assets that become illiquid in periods of financial stress. Often, the assets are hard to value and have long-term maturities. Money funds remove financial intermediation from banks by selling themselves as banks. They offer transactions services and shares redeemable upon demand. Although not regulated as banks, investors know that the Fed will bail them out in periods of stress. While the common term is TBTF (too big to fail), a better term is TITF (too indebted to fail).

In reaction to the use of the financial safety net to protect sophisticated investors in the turmoil of fall 2008, Congress imposed restrictions on the Treasury's Exchange Stabilization Fund (ESF) to prevent its use to backstop money funds, restrictions removed in the 2020 CARES Act. The *Wall Street Journal* (2020a) quoted Aaron Klein, a former Obama administration Treasury official: "There was widespread agreement following the [2008] financial crisis that money market funds would bear losses in the future, and postcrisis regulatory changes were meant to impress upon investors the risks they were taking. . . . The Exchange Stabilization Fund was created to stabilize the value of the dollar, not to be used for domestic purposes."

With the Covid-19 crisis, the institutional prime money funds again found themselves in a situation like September 2008. The commercial paper market was normal on March 12 with thirty-day A2/P2 nonfinancial paper selling at 1.9 percent (with seven-day and one-day at basically the same rate). The rate then rose each day through March 18 when it reached 3.47 percent (seven-day and one-day at 3.59 percent and 3.07 percent, respectively). After March 12, the institutional money market funds experienced outflows. The shareholders in those funds are institutional investors, for example, companies and pension funds. Fearing cash-flow shortfalls themselves, it was natural to withdraw funds and place them in banks or government money funds. The prime funds then ceased to buy commercial paper. Foreign banks, which had obtained their dollar funding from the money funds, obtained that funding from their own central banks, which drew on the dollars made available by swap lines. US corporations that would have issued commercial paper instead drew on their bank lines of credit.

9. "Mr. Clarida (vice chair of the Board of Governors) also dismissed a question about whether the central bank had created a 'moral hazard' that encouraged risky investor behavior when the Fed moved quickly to backstop swaths of credit markets. 'This is entirely an exogenous event,' said Mr. Clarida, noting how the virus—not private-sector behavior—had forced widespread business closures and revenue losses" (*Wall Street Journal* 2020c). This argument is like claiming that, if one builds a house in a flood plain because of government insurance, there is no moral hazard because floods are exogenous events.

The money funds could have imposed a "gate" to limit withdrawals to the amount of their maturing paper. In 2014, the SEC had required the prime money market funds to adopt a floating share price and gave them the ability to impose fees on redemptions and even freeze redemptions. As reported by the *Wall Street Journal* (2020b), the intention was to make "it more apparent to investors that they could suffer losses." However, that would have made the funds unattractive in the future to their investors, who want the liquidity offered by bank deposits but with higher returns than are available on bank deposits.

To again bail out the prime money market funds, the Fed announced the CPFF (Commercial Paper Funding Facility) and the MMLF (Money Market Mutual Fund Liquidity Facility). In a *Wall Street Journal* (2020b) article, Jonah Crane, a Treasury Department official in the Obama administration, said, "It is déjà vu. At this point, investors in money funds can just assume that the Fed is going to backstop them." In the same article, Sheila Bair, former head of the FDIC, said, "It's just frustrating that we never really fixed this stuff. . . . The industry lobbyists came in and persuaded regulators to do half measures. And we're back in the soup again."[10]

Real estate investment trusts (REITs) illustrate the same moral hazard. Thomas Barrack (2020, 4–5), executive chairman of Colony Capital, explained that after 2008 increased capital requirements for mortgages held by banks caused the banks, which originate the mortgages, to place them in REITs, which turn around and fund them with RPs (repos or overnight repurchase agreements) with the banks: "Since 2013, bank financing through repurchase agreements has surged—the top six publicly-traded mortgage REITs alone reported over $42.5 billion in total loan originations and $20 billion in repurchase borrowings in 2019." These mortgage REITs were in trouble in March 2020 because of the requirement that they mark-to-market the MBS used in their RPs and post additional collateral as the value of the MBS declined. Just like their SIV (structured investment vehicle) predecessors, the basic problem was funding long-term, illiquid assets with short-term debt. In March 2020, the Fed bailed out the mortgage REITS by purchasing enormous quantities of MBS.[11] From the statement week end-

10. The obvious reform is to regulate the money funds as banks as suggested in the Group of 30, Working Group on Financial Reform (2009). By offering transaction services, withdrawal on demand, and a stable net asset value, they offer the services of banks. However, they do so as the modern equivalent of "wildcat" banks.

11. Under pressure from Congress, the Fed bought some FNMA and Freddie Mac debt in the 1970s. The Fed ceased the purchases in the 1980s but then revived them in November 2008 at the instigation of FOMC chairman Bernanke.

ing February 26 to the statement week ending May 27, the Fed increased its holdings of MBS by $476 billion.

The question arises of why banks could not recycle the funds they gained from the flight from the money funds and the REITs to buy debt sold by these entities. The answer lies in the perverse operation of the LCR and SLR regulations, which were designed for a funding shortfall by an individual bank. Broker-dealers, the trading arms of the large bank holding companies, lacked the balance sheet capacity to add the debt instruments sold by the money funds and the REITs.

In addition, banks had entered interest-rate swap contracts that offered insurance to companies against an increase in interest rates on their sales of future debt. When market rates fell in March, those companies had to post additional collateral, which added to bank assets and made the SLR more of a problem. Banks had also lent to REITs to increase the leverage of the latter. The decline in the value of MBS forced the REITs to post additional collateral, which again added to bank assets.

Finally, hedge funds increased market volatility by suddenly adding to the supply of Treasury securities. Using as a model LTCM, which became insolvent in September 1998, hedge funds arbitrage the small yield difference between on-the-run-treasuries (newly issued) and off-the-run-treasuries (secondary market). Using repo financing, they buy the latter and enter a futures contract to deliver the former. Although the yield differences are small, leverage by a factor of 100 normally allows a profitable carry trade. However, in March, the futures market became illiquid. The hedge funds became subject to margin calls and had to sell their treasuries. Foreign central banks also sold treasuries to acquire dollars to support their currencies. As a result, at a time of a flight to safety, the yields on coupon treasuries rose instead of falling (Schrimpf et al. 2020).

With the SLR binding, broker-dealers lacked the balance sheet capacity to absorb the supply of Treasuries coming on the market (Duffie 2020).[12] Because of the stress caused by balance sheet constraints, bid-ask spreads increased by a factor of 10. The Fed relieved market stress with its enormous purchases of Treasury securities. Although stressed, short-term fund-

---

12. The *Wall Street Journal* (Baer 2020) reported:

Senior executives . . . wouldn't trade. . . . There was no room to buy bonds and other assets and still remain in compliance with tougher guidelines imposed by regulators after the previous financial crisis. In other words, capital rules intended to make the financial system safer were . . . draining liquidity from the markets. One senior bank executive leveled . . . "We can't bid on anything that adds to the balance sheet right now."

ing markets continued to function.[13] The trading volumes of broker-dealers *increased* (Duffie 2020). However, a shadow banking system created by the moral hazard of TITF and perverse regulatory constraints increased the stresses in the money market in mid-March. The resulting volatility did not indicate that markets had lost the ability to assess risk and allocate resources.

In the long run, the Fed's credit programs also contribute to moral hazard. For example, with interest rates low after 2008, corporations had an incentive to take on debt and engage in share buybacks. Especially for highly leveraged firms, an increase in risk premiums increases their debt service costs. The Fed's CCP (Corporate Credit Programs) put a floor under bond prices and thus encourage firms to "lever up" in times of low interest rates—a "Powell put." More generally, the moral hazard of bailing out banks or the various forms of funds in the shadow banking system destroys the institutional capital required of a market economy. A market economy requires free entry and its twin, free exit. Free exit requires that creditors that have their own capital at stake make the "pull the plug" decision.

William Dudley (2020), former president of the New York Fed, highlighted how the Fed has exacerbated moral hazard:

> The Fed's enormous purchases of Treasuries . . . [were] a backdoor bailout of highly leveraged hedge funds. . . . Real-estate investment trusts . . . were forced sellers as they struggled to meet margin calls. Again, the Fed purchases [of MBS] helped limit their losses. . . . Heavily indebted corporations also got a helping hand.

25.3. WHAT CALMED FINANCIAL MARKETS IN MARCH 2020?

The fundamental issue in appraising the Fed's response to financial market volatility in March 2020 is whether that volatility arose from a scramble for liquidity or from a breakdown in the ability of markets to evaluate risk and thus to sustain the flow of credit from households to firms and state and local governments. Assuming the former, the only required response was the traditional one of supplying liquidity through open market purchases

13. One measure of stress in the short-term funding markets is the amount of overnight RPs made by the New York Desk with broker-dealers. Over the period March 3 to March 17, overnight RPs averaged $68 billion. Fall 2019 was also a period of stress due to a maldistribution of reserves. From October 16 to December 5, overnight RPs averaged $57 billion. Although somewhat less than in March 2020, the RPs persisted over a longer period (data from St. Louis FRED).

of Treasuries. Assuming the latter, the Board of Governors appropriately introduced an array of programs to intervene in individual credit markets.

John Mousseau (2020a), CEO of Cumberland Advisors and manager of their bond portfolio, argued for the former: "That was not a . . . selloff [of] people thinking 'Oh my God, credit is going to hell, [an] erosion of [creditworthiness of] state and local governments or corporations.' What this was was a selloff of people wanting cash as the stock market was imploding." Later, Mousseau (2020b) wrote: "This was a liquidity event, not a credit event." Investors wanted to be liquid. For example, investors wanting certain access to cash moved out of muni funds into government money funds. As funds flowed out of the muni funds, yields on munis rose relative to yields on Treasuries. However, "the cheapness didn't last long. Private money moved into the space abandoned by the bond funds, and it happened in a fairly short period of time. The rebound at the end of March was one of the most vigorous muni rallies ever witnessed" (Mousseau 2020b). The Fed's open market purchases provided the reserves that accommodated the demand for liquidity. The Fed's 13(3) programs did not replace an inability of markets to evaluate risk and to conduct financial intermediation. Opportunistically, the Fed claimed credit for restoring a breakdown in financial intermediation. However, the 13(3) programs were really meant as credit policy to provide for macroeconomic stimulus (chap. 26).[14]

The Fed had not planned for how monetary policy would respond to a pandemic.[15] Although 13(3) programs are undertaken by authority of the Board with Treasury consent, they have implications for the Fed's portfolio and thus monetary policy. The 13(3) programs that entailed outright credit provision such as the MSLF, the PMCCF, and the SMCCF as opposed to programs like the CPFF, the MMLF, and the PDCF that entailed liquidity provision in short-term funding markets were novel. There is no indication in FOMC minutes or the available transcripts that the FOMC ever discussed the criteria for evaluating when a breakdown in financial intermediation had occurred that would necessitate such intervention. When the FOMC did respond to the pandemic, markets interpreted the response as

14. Of course, the Fed's bond-buying programs for corporate bonds boosted the prices of bonds because the Fed took the tail risk. That fact does not imply any kind of breakdown in bond markets.

15. Lack of planning for the response of monetary policy to a pandemic is consistent with Fed practice of treating monetary policy as made discretionarily period by period. With the language of discretion, the Fed can control the historical narrative. That is, each period, it responds optimally to shocks arising externally. In contrast, thinking about policy as a rule requires examination of how the rule produces a mutual interaction between the behavior of the Fed and the behavior of the economy. One can then learn from the past about which rules stabilized or destabilized the economy.

a message that the situation was much worse than perceived. A key role of the central bank is to assure investors of the stability of the financial system. However, by startling markets, the Fed precipitated a panic.[16]

25.3.1. Increased Risk Spreads Do Not Indicate That Financial Intermediation Has Broken Down

Table 25.2 presents daily measures of risk in financial markets from February 20, 2020, through April 8, 2020. The February 20 BAA-10Y yield spread of 2.05 serves as a benchmark for a normal level of risk. In March 2020, risk spreads increased when default risk increased. For example, on March 11, when the World Health Organization (WHO) declared Covid-19 a pandemic and countries imposed international travel restrictions, the BAA-10Y spread increased, and the S&P 500 declined from the day before to the day after (table 25.2). The Fed associated the increase in risk spreads with market dysfunction. LHM (2020b) reported, "The Fed is here to close spreads." Widening credit spreads, however, did not mean that market specialists could no longer evaluate risk and allocate credit.

When it became obvious that financial markets were in fact continuing to function, Chair Powell attributed their functioning to the announcement of the Fed's credit programs.[17] However, market risk spreads *increased* after the Board started to announce its credit programs. On March 17, the Board announced the establishment of the PDCF (Primary Dealer Credit Facility), which lends to primary dealers collateralized by a wide variety of collateral. It also announced the CPFF (Commercial Paper Funding Facility), which purchases commercial paper. From the day before the announcement to the day after, the A2/P2 paper rate increased from 3.05 to

16. The *Wall Street Journal* (Baer 2020) reported:

The Federal Reserve set the stage for the downturn on Sunday, March 15. Most investors were expecting the central bank to announce its latest response to the crisis the following Wednesday [the date of the FOMC meeting]. Instead, it announced at 5 p.m. that evening that it was slashing interest rates and planning to buy $700 billion in bonds to help unclog the markets. Rather than take comfort in the Fed's actions, many companies, governments, bankers and investors viewed the decision as reason to prepare for the worst possible outcome from the coronavirus pandemic. A downdraft in bonds was now a rout. The Dow Jones Industrial Average plunged nearly 13% that day [Monday, March 16], the second-biggest one-day fall in history. . . . "On that first day, the Fed got completely run over by the market," said Dan Ivascyn, who manages one of the world's biggest bond funds.

17. LHM (2020h) reported, "Powell noted the powerful easing effect of the mere announcement of such facilities. He pointed to the easing in market conditions that has occurred even though the facilities are not even operational yet."

Table 25.2. Measures of Market Stress

2020 Date	BAA-10Y	S&P 500	Oil Brent
2/20	2.05	3,373	59.57
2/21	2.09	3,338	58.60
2/24	2.13	3,226	56.71
2/25	2.19	3,128	55.29
2/26	2.20	3,116	54.96
2/27	2.27	2,979	52.19
2/28	2.38	2,954	51.31
3/2	2.44	3,090	52.52
3/3	2.48	3,003	52.24
3/4	2.47	3,130	51.86
3/5	2.52	3,024	51.29
3/6	2.55	2,972	45.60
3/9	2.93	2,747	35.33
3/10	2.93	2,882	35.57
3/11	2.99	2,741	34.45
3/12	3.20	2,481	31.02
3/13	3.30	2,711	32.25
3/16	3.38	2,386	27.98
3/17	3.49	2,529	27.97
3/18	3.81	2,398	22.79
3/19	4.01	2,409	23.98
3/20	4.23	2,305	25.55
P 3/23	4.31	2,237	23.75
3/24	4.19	2,447	24.50
3/25	4.13	2,476	25.62
3/26	4.04	2,630	23.55
3/27	3.98	2,541	22.39
3/30	3.89	2,627	19.19
3/31	3.93	2,585	14.85
4/1	3.97	2,471	14.97
4/2	3.92	2,527	20.24
4/3	3.92	2,489	24.33
4/6	3.91	2,664	22.58
4/7	3.79	2,659	22.1
4/8	3.75	2,750	25.22

Note: The first column is the difference between the BAA corporate bond rate and the ten-year treasury constant maturity yield; the second is the S&P 500 index; and the third is the Brent-Europe price of crude oil used as a measure of the state of the world economy. The "P" marks the peak value of the BAA-10Y spread.

Source: Federal Reserve Economic Data, St. Louis Fed, "Moody's Seasoned Baa Corporate Bond Yield Relative to Yield on 10-Year Treasury Constant Maturity [BAA10Y]"; "S&P Dow Jones Indices LLC, S&P 500 [SP500]"; "U.S. Energy Information Administration, Crude Oil Prices: Brent-Europe [DCOILBRENTEU]"

3.47. On March 18, it announced the MMLF (Money Market Mutual Fund Liquidity Facility), which makes loans to banks secured by commercial paper. On March 19, it announced the swap lines. On March 20, the Board announced that the MMLF would make loans to banks secured by collateral from states and municipalities (again, see this chapter's appendix "Program Definitions" for a list of programs). Only after March 23, however, did risk spreads begin to decline.

When it became obvious not only that markets were functioning but also that they were pricing risk, the Fed argued that it could better assess risk than the market. LHM (2020i) reported about the Fed's program to purchase corporate bonds: "The Fed will buy [corporate] bonds/loans directly from the issuer only if the issuer certified it is 'unable' to secure 'adequate credit accommodations' from banks and the capital markets. 'Lack of adequate credit' does not mean that no credit is available. The standard is not as high as a total credit freeze, but merely pricing or terms 'inconsistent with a normal, well-functioning market.'"

25.3.2. Separating Credit Market Interventions from Open Market Operations

The problem for evaluating the Fed's credit market interventions is that news arrived as a mixture of congressional fiscal policy and of Fed monetary policy, not just Fed credit policy. On Monday, March 23, the Board announced additional facilities for credit market interventions: the PMCCF (Primary Market Corporate Credit Facility), the SMCCF (Secondary Market Corporate Credit Facility), and the TALF (Term Asset-Backed Securities Loan Facility). At the same time, it announced expansionary monetary policy measures. "The Fed removed the guidance for asset purchases to make it open ended (from 'at least' $500bn UST and 'at least' $200bn MBS [mortgage-backed securities])" (LHM 2020e). "If this rate is sustained 'over coming months,' the expansion of the balance sheet from these assets alone would sum to $4.5tn" (LHM 2020d). (In late March, the Fed was purchasing $75 billion in Treasuries daily.)

Speculation about the CARES Act, which was passed on Friday, March 27, filled the airwaves. AP News (2020) reported that after talks lasting until midnight Monday, March 23, Treasury Secretary Mnuchin announced the likelihood of a deal the next day (Tuesday). A draft of the CARES Act circulated Thursday, March 25. It contained significant provisions for fiscal policy and the Fed's credit policy. By including $454 billion for the ESF, it would allow the Fed's 13(3) special purpose vehicles (SPVs) to extend loans to beneficiaries up to ten times their allocated ESF amount. The CARES legislation buoyed confidence by showing that despite a bitter partisan divide, Congress could come together to enact legislation dealing with the crisis.

There is then no way to isolate the announcement effect of the Fed's credit programs from the Fed's monetary policy actions and from the fiscal policies in the CARES Act. Moreover, a Fed program to buy, say, corporate or municipal securities should buoy their prices. Investors benefit from a "Powell put" on the price of the asset. However, that fact does not imply that the enhanced price better measures the riskiness of the asset.

It is striking how little market risk (the BAA-10Y spread) declined in response to the Fed's credit programs. The spread was 2.05 on February 20 and remained at an elevated 3.91 on April 6. The modest decline in perceived market risk despite all the combined firepower of Fed credit and monetary policy and congressional fiscal policy suggests that the increase in market risk spreads reflected not market dysfunction but rather real risk created by the unknown impact of the Covid-19 virus.

The decline immediately following April 6 followed good news about the spread of the Covid-19 virus. Stanley (2020) wrote, "Finally, there is unambiguously good news to report. Yesterday might turn out to be a turning point globally. . . . The US got some surprisingly good news yesterday. The number of new cases and deaths yesterday both fell, and by a sizable amount." In the end, what likely calmed markets the most was news that the Covid-19 virus while devastating could be contained. Buoyed by optimism that the Covid-19 crisis could be contained, financial intermediation remained robust. For example, despite the minimal use of the programs to support asset-backed commercial paper (table 25.1) for the MMLF (Money Market Fund Liquidity Facility) and the CPFF (Commercial Paper Funding Facility) programs, the structured finance market was healthy in April.[18]

Similarly, despite the non-operational status of the two programs designed to support corporate borrowing (the Primary and Secondary Market Corporate Credit Facilities, PMCCF and SMCCP), the corporate bond market remained healthy. "Companies last month sold more than $227 billion of investment-grade corporate bonds in the US market, breaking the previous record of $194 billion set a month earlier, according to Dealogic"

---

18. S&P Global (2020) reported:

The credit quality of US ABCP issuance remains stable. From the total outstanding 48 ABCP programs, 85% are fully supported by liquidity, while the remaining 15% are well-diversified partially supported assets. . . . Banks and non-bank institutions providing liquidity to US ABCP programs are diversified and highly-rated entities. . . . The credit quality of the [structured finance] issuances remains stable.

(*Wall Street Journal* 2020g). Newspaper accounts indicated that markets continued to evaluate credit worthiness from a long-term perspective.[19]

Financial markets retained their long-run perspective in the evaluation of risk because of a return of confidence that the Covid-19 crisis would pass. As shown in table 25.2, from March 23 through April 8, the S&P 500 rose from 2,237 to 2,750. That rise likely reflected the general return of confidence rather than the promise of the Fed's 13(3) programs becoming operational in the future.

Financial intermediation did not break down in March 2020. Although the Fed's actions were critical, it seems likely that it was the monetary policy actions that made the difference. For the three statement weeks ending March 4, 2020, the New York Desk's purchases of securities added an average of $27.5 billion a week. For the three statement weeks ending April 8, security purchases added on average $347.9 billion a week. As explained in the previous section, purchases of treasuries by the Fed helped to relieve market stress by absorbing much of the supply coming on the market from the hedge funds. Also, the addition of reserves added to banks' HQLAs (high-quality liquid assets) and thereby relaxed the balance sheet constraint on their broker-dealers. And, most important, the reserves provision allowed the banking system to expand its deposits to meet the increased liquidity demanded by businesses.

In mid-March, the immediate concern was continued short-term funding in the money markets. The Fed dealt with that concern through its traditional tools. As shown in table 25.1, these tools (securities holdings, repos, discount window borrowing, and swap lines) added almost one trillion dollars ($978 billion) to bank reserves between the statement weeks ending March 18 and April 1. Nothing in this response required involvement in financial intermediation, heretofore conducted by banks and capital markets. The fact that the maximum increase in discount window lending was only $43 billion shows that the Fed's reserves provision met the liquidity demands of financial markets (table 25.1). In his public pronouncements, Chair Powell could have maintained public confidence in the functioning of financial markets by stressing these dramatic actions.

19. The *Wall Street Journal* (2020h) reported:

The aviation industry is selling debt at a record pace, reflecting investors' continuing willingness to buy debt from companies hard-hit by the pandemic—at the right price. "The investor base is not fixated on the status quo, it's focused on where these companies will be when the virus is managed," said Mr. Foley, whose team helped lead the debt sales on behalf of Boeing and Delta. . . . The market is saying this is inherently a good business and willing to price that risk," said Mr. Foley.

Powell could have said that he was monitoring whether private markets had broken down and could no longer evaluate credit risk and allocate credit to productive uses. He could have created the 13(3) programs. With a determination allowed by the passage of, say, two weeks that financial intermediation had broken down, Powell could have implemented them. Instead, he simply assumed that increased credit spreads indicated a breakdown in financial intermediation.

25.3.3. *The Fed Reinvents Itself as a Financial Intermediary*

In a three-week period, between March 4 and March 23, the threat of the Covid-19 virus went from being perceived as a nuisance that might disrupt global supply chains to being understood as a possible killer of millions and a destroyer of the world economy. That three-week period is dated here from March 4, when the S&P was at 3,130 to March 23, when the S&P sank to 2,237. On March 17, the Board established the CPFF (Commercial Paper Funding Facility) and the PDCF (Primary Dealer Credit Facility) and on March 20 the MMLF (Money Market Mutual Lending Facility). Those programs reflected a concern for maintaining short-term funding in the money market. It was on March 23 that the Board of Governors advanced toward making the Fed into a full-fledged financial intermediary.

On that date, March 23, in a press release, the Board announced the "establishment of two facilities to support credit to large employers—the Primary Market Corporate Credit Facility (PMCCF) for new bond and loan issuance and the Secondary Market Corporate Credit Facility (SMCCF)." It also announced "the Term Asset-Backed Securities Loan Facility (TALF), to support the flow of credit to consumers and businesses." Finally, it stated that "the Federal Reserve expects to announce soon the establishment of a Main Street Business Lending Program to support lending to eligible small-and-medium sized businesses, complementing efforts by the SBA." On April 9, in a press release, the Board announced, "that it is creating the Municipal Liquidity Facility (MLF), a tool to help states and localities deal with budgetary stresses."[20]

The pre–March 23 programs, the first tier, reflected the Fed's traditional concern with the functioning of the money market. The March 23 and subsequent programs, the second tier, were completely different. Chairman Powell (2020c) must have had the latter in mind when he said, "We crossed a lot of red lines that had not been crossed before. . . . You do that and you

---

20. See Board of Governors of the Federal Reserve System, News and Events, Press Releases for the selected dates on the website, https://www.federalreserve.gov/.

figure it out afterward." Menand (2020) illustrates how extreme is the departure from the Fed's "baseline statutory framework." As characterized by Daleep Singh (2020, 12), executive vice president and head of the Markets Group at the New York Fed, "Our first obligation is to make sure the financial system is functioning. And then afterwards our work isn't done. We have to make sure we try to provide credit to particular parts of the economy that aren't really getting a near-term benefit from Treasury market stabilizing and that's where the targeted support comes in."

This change in the conception of the role of the Fed was striking. The focus of monetary policy had been on influencing the expenditure of the public through the FOMC's influence on the term structure of interest rates. As a separate tool, the Fed added credit policy. Like a giant, multifaceted GSE, the Fed would control the flow of credit from households to particular sectors of the economy. The change happened in a remarkably short period of time. The puzzle is why the Board of Governors did not wait until it had evidence that financial intermediation had broken down. It could have announced the second tier of programs as available but to be made operational only in the event of such a breakdown.

The optimism that sustained financial markets likely derived from the belief that, despite the severity of the shock, the economy would recover, rather than from the Fed's entry into the business of credit allocation. Giglio et al. (2020) offered evidence to support this assertion. They surveyed investor sentiment on March 11–12. That date was near the height of the financial turmoil but before the announcement of the Fed's credit programs and thus before one can ascribe a renewal of optimism to the Board's 13(3) programs.

> We surveyed retail investors who are clients of Vanguard . . . on March 11–12, after the stock market had collapsed by over 20%. . . . Following the crash, the average investor turned more pessimistic about the short-run performance of both the stock market and the real economy. . . . In contrast, investor expectations about long-run (10-year) economic and stock market outcomes remained largely unchanged, and, if anything, improved.

25.3.4. Did Lender of Last Resort Require Becoming Financial Intermediary of Last Resort?

The Fed's credit programs may have made a bad situation worse. With the Covid-19 crisis, apart from Treasury securities and FDIC-insured bank deposits, all debt became riskier. At the same time, Fed programs favored the less risky assets.[21] Its programs thus helped to reinforce a two-tier market for debt: relatively less risky and relatively more risky.[22] If market "dysfunction" was a problem, then the Fed's credit programs exacerbated it by drawing funds into the relatively safe (more functional) part.[23] Similarly, for its open market portfolio, as of April 9, 2020, the Fed had $1,459,202 million in GSE residential MBS and none of the riskier CMBS, that is, commercial mortgage-backed securities (Board of Governors, Statistical Release H.4.1, April 9, 2020). Acharya and Steffen (2020) documented the two-tier character of credit markets by showing that at the height of the crisis highly rated firms were issuing bonds to deal with anticipated cash shortfalls while lower-rated firms had to draw on lines of credit.

25.4. CREDIT POLICY DOES NOT DRAW FORTH REAL RESOURCES

The Fed's credit programs convey to the public a power to create resources—a power that it does not possess. The Fed can only allocate credit between competing uses. On March 26, 2020, on NBC's *Today Show*, Powell explained that the Fed could lend unlimited amounts to the private sector because of an unlimited ability to expand the size of its asset portfolio. The only limit was the amount of ESF funds to backstop its lending.[24] Similar to

21. For example, the PMCCF (Primary Market Corporate Credit Facility) accepted corporate bonds rated at least BBB/Baa3, that is, investment grade (Board Press Release March 23, 2020). The MMLF (Money Market Mutual Fund Liquidity Facility), which opened March 23, accepted ABCP (asset-backed commercial paper) "in the top rating category (not lower than A1, F1, or P1)" (Board Press Release March 18, 2020). The CPFF (Commercial Paper Funding Facility) accepted commercial paper rated at least A1/P1/F1) (Board Press Release March 17, 2020). For the SMCCF (Secondary Market Corporate Credit Facility), "The preponderance of ETF [exchange traded funds] holdings will be of . . . investment-grade corporate bonds" (Board Press Release March 23, 2020).

22. Davies et al. (2020, 3) wrote, "One of the Fed's programs buys new commercial paper from companies and banks that had top credit rating when the program was announced. . . . That excludes lower-rate companies such as Marriott International Inc. that need cash the most. . . . It's the tier-two guys: They're the ones that will need the cash."

23. The Board announced its SIV to buy corporate bonds on Monday, March 23. On Friday, March 20, the AAA corporate bond yield was 3.36 percent, and on Tuesday, March 24, it was 2.776 percent, a decline of 0.6 percentage points. Over this same interval, the junk bond yield *rose* from 10.75 percent to 11.13 percent.

24. LHM (2020f) printed an informal transcript of the exchange between Powell and the moderator:

> Savannah: . . . "You do have the ability to conjure money out of thin air. . . . Is there any limit to the amount of money the Fed is willing to put into this economy . . . ?
> Powell: Essentially, the answer to your question is . . . "No." . . . Effectively, $1 of

the comment of Savannah Guthrie on the NBC *Today Show*, in commenting on the CARES Act nearing passage in Congress, Senator Patrick Toomey (R-PA) expressed the objective of levering up "the unlimited balance sheet of the Fed" (Torres 2020).

Newspapers repeated the misconception that because the Fed can create reserves and bank deposits through a bookkeeping operation it can expand the aggregate of real resources made available to borrowers through financial intermediation. The *Wall Street Journal* (2020f) reported, "The Fed has a unique power, the ability to create money by crediting banks with funds they can lend. That helps it guide the cost of money, which is the interest rate." The misconception appeared in an article in the *Wall Street Journal* (2020c) reporting comments by Governor Richard Clarida: "The Fed last week announced an expansion of nine different programs it has unveiled to support lending to US states and businesses. It has said those programs will enable $2.3 trillion in new lending" (see Board of Governors 2020c; see also Selgin 2020a).

Financial intermediation transfers resources from savers to borrowers. The Fed's programs did not draw forth any additional savings. Confusion within Congress and also within the Fed may lead to expectations in future crises that the Fed cannot fulfill. Paul Tucker (2020, 4) wrote, "The more central banks acquiesce (even revel) in the 'only game in town' label, the easier it becomes for politicians to give them more to do, and so undo them." The Fed should not mislead Congress that it has an ability to create credit (create household savings) as opposed to directing it.

The Fed has packaged its 13(3) lending programs not as the allocation of resources among competing uses but rather as adding to the total of resources available to borrowers and making those additional resources available to borrowers in sectors shunned by financial markets. Sorting out the fallacies underlying the presumption of the central bank as a creator of real resources requires clarification of basic analytical concepts. The most basic concept is the nominal/real distinction and its application to the difference between financial intermediation and money creation.[25]

A nominal variable is a dollar amount. A real variable is a physical quantity or a relative price (the rate of exchange between two goods). The de-

---

loss absorption of backstop from the Treasury is enough to support $10 worth of loans. . . . When it comes to this lending, we're not going to run out of ammunition. . . . We've cut them [short-term interest rates] to 0 now. We still have policy room in other dimensions to support the economy but the main thing we're doing now is really with our lending programs.

25. For the author, the analysis here came from the money and banking course offered by Milton Friedman at the University of Chicago in 1967.

posits that households hold with banks constitute not only savings but also media of exchange. What the public cares about is the real purchasing power of its deposits not the number of nominal units. If the nominal (dollar) amount of deposits corresponds to a real amount that differs from what households desire to hold, the price level adjusts to eliminate the difference. Increasing the nominal quantity of bank deposits then does not make available additional resources to the banks' borrowers.

Like a commercial bank, the Fed possesses a balance sheet with assets on the left-hand side and deposits on the right-hand side. Since the era of FOMC chairman William McChesney Martin and until recently, the Fed has eschewed credit allocation. It has done so by holding primarily Treasury securities as assets. Its deposits are those of the commercial banks. Those deposits, bank reserves, constitute the media of exchange that banks use to effect finality of payment. Moreover, with a fixed exchange rate between bank reserves and currency, the total of bank reserves and of currency held by the public constitutes the monetary base. The monetary base, as the name suggests, constitutes the support for bank deposits and thus the money stock—the media of exchange used by the public to effect finality in transactions.

Although both commercial banks and the central bank have similar-looking balance sheets with assets on the left and deposits on the right, there is a critical difference. A commercial bank competes for the savings of households by offering interest and transactions services on its deposits. The central bank creates the deposits held with it by commercial banks. If a commercial bank buys a Treasury security, it likely loses deposits. If the central bank buys a Treasury security, it adds to its deposits, bank reserves, through a bookkeeping operation. Competitive market forces limit the deposits of a commercial bank. Only an externally imposed rule, not the marketplace, can limit the deposit creation of the central bank. With this quantity-theoretic framework, one can understand the origin of the fallacy that a central bank can increase the flow of savings from households to investors rather than simply affect its allocation. Although the central bank can increase the nominal quantity of bank deposits, apart from transitory nonneutralities, it cannot increase the real quantity.[26]

With an open market purchase of a Treasury security, instead of send-

26. Seigniorage does not change the situation. As the economy grows, the public desires to hold additional currency. The Fed adds that currency by purchasing Treasury securities from the public. With less debt now held by the public, the Treasury can issue debt to restore the original total. At this point, the Treasury has additional funds in its Fed account and the public, which has bought the Treasury security, no additional currency. When the Treasury spends those funds, it obtains real resources in exchange for

ing the interest payments on the newly acquired Treasury debt back to the Treasury, the Fed could instead allocate them to selected borrowers by lending at subsidized interest rates. It would then transfer less to the Treasury and more to selected borrowers. However, maintaining seigniorage revenue is sacrosanct for the Fed. A sharp reduction in Fed transfers to the Treasury could draw congressional attention and generate efforts to put the Fed on budget as a way of reducing its expenditures and restoring seigniorage. This concern appears in the Fed dictum that it can lend only if it does so with enough collateral that it cannot incur a loss. The CARES Act met this concern by providing ESF money for the first 10 percent of losses on 13(3) loans. However, for evaluating fiscal policy, one should combine the balance sheets of the Fed and the Treasury. Regardless of whether a loss is booked to the Fed or to the ESF, it is a loss to government revenue. Even though Fed transfers to the Treasury do not decline if the ESF incurs the loss, lending at a loss still does not make additional resources available to borrowers. Losses increase the deficit and the issuance of Treasury debt, which competes for private saving.

The reality that the Fed can allocate savings but not create them is evident with its traditional operating procedures. With those procedures, the size of its asset portfolio was constrained by the necessity of creating just the amount of reserves required to achieve the funds-rate target. To illustrate, consider first the purchase by the Fed of an MBS from a bank. The bank then replaces the MBS with deposits at the Fed (reserves) on the left side of its balance sheet. The additional reserves created by the Fed with the MBS purchase lower the funds rate, causing the Fed to sell a Treasury security to the bank to defend its funds-rate target. The bank now has a Treasury security in place of an MBS, and the Fed has an MBS in place of a Treasury security. Intermediation by the Fed that provides funds to the housing market replaces the intermediation formerly done by the bank.

Assume alternatively that the Fed purchases the MBS from the public. The sellers deposit the check received from the Fed with their bank, which creates a deposit. The bank sends the check to the Fed and gains additional reserves. Again, the Fed must sell a Treasury security to prevent a decline in the funds rate. Intermediation by the Fed that provides funds to the housing market replaces the intermediation formerly done by the individuals. The Fed has replaced a Treasury security with an MBS in its portfolio while the public has replaced an MBS with a Treasury security in their portfolio.

---

adding the additional currency demanded by the public. (Up to a point, higher inflation increases seigniorage revenues; however, an inflation target eliminates that option.)

With IOR (interest on reserves paid to banks by the Fed), the Fed can create additional reserves and bank deposits without lowering the funds rate below its interest-rate target. Those additional bank deposits also do not increase money in a way that creates inflation if the FOMC keeps the funds rate at its natural value. Do not these last two facts overturn the above conclusion that "increasing bank deposits will not increase the real resources available to bank borrowers"? Is IOR a kind of magic that draws forth additional saving by households? In fact, nothing changes with IOR and an expansive Fed balance sheet. Intermediation by the Fed that provides funds to, say, the housing market through the purchase of MBS only replaces intermediation formerly conducted through the private sector.

Assume that the Fed buys an MBS in the secondary market. Using the check received from the Fed, the sellers buy a CD from their bank. Because of the interest paid on reserves through IOR, the bank impounds as additional desired reserves the reserves created by the Fed's MBS purchase. The IOR interest paid to the bank is in turn passed on as interest paid on the CD held by the sellers of the MBS. The sterilized reserves are the equivalent in the above examples of the Fed extinguishing additional reserves creation from an MBS purchase by selling a Treasury security. Again, there is simply a change in what party is doing the intermediation. Nothing changes in this argument when IOR sets the funds rate at the ZLB.

When long-term interest rates are above short-term rates (the interest rate on MBS exceeds the IOR rate), the Fed is engaged in a carry trade and can send additional profits to the Treasury. These are not profits due to seigniorage, however. There is no corresponding purchase of goods and services by the government monetized by the Fed with the money creation to meet a demand for currency. Profits will turn to losses if short-term rates rise and exceed long-term rates. The way to think of the Fed as a financial intermediary is as a GSE involved in a carry trade.

25.5. SUPPORTING FINANCIAL MARKETS WHILE AVOIDING CREDIT ALLOCATION

The Fed/Powell narrative is that financial markets ceased to function in mid-March 2020 but were revived by the announcement of 13(3) programs. The narrative here is that markets continued to function. The Fed played a key role in that continued functioning. However, its role was the traditional one of supplying ample reserves, not allocating credit.

In March 2020, banks accommodated the public's increased precautionary demand for deposits. Businesses wanted an increase in their cash reserves (deposits) in the event of an interruption to cash flow. Through a bookkeeping operation, the banks increased their deposits.[27] When confidence returns with the end of the pandemic, this money (deposit) creation needs to reverse. Failure to unwind indicates that the Fed is keeping interest rates below their natural (sustainable) value.

An alternative to the Fed's response in March 2020 that would not have entailed taking over financial intermediation from private markets would have been something akin to the Fed's response to the failure of Penn Central Railroad in May 1970 (Maisel 1973). The default by Penn Central on its commercial paper surprised markets and interrupted the demand for commercial paper. In response, the Fed encouraged banks to lend freely and made clear its support by emphasizing that the discount window was wide open for borrowing. All nonfinancial firms of any economic significance have a relationship with a bank and a line of credit. In an emergency, they draw on those lines. With the Penn Central model, the Fed would make clear that that discount window borrowing would amount to "whatever it takes."[28] With that funding, there is no limit to the ability of the banking system to expand its balance sheet. Regulators would relax capital requirements for banks and the LCR and SLR.

The role of the Fed in a period of stress should be to make certain that intermediation formerly conducted through the money market can occur through the banking system rather than becoming itself a financial intermediary. Banks undergo regular stress tests to make certain that they can handle a major period of stress. Press releases from the Board (Board of Governors 2020a and 2020b, respectively) did not indicate that the Fed needed to become a parallel system of intermediation:

27. There is a reverse process. As confidence returns, corporations will attempt to reduce their cash balances. The corresponding reduction in the demand for bank reserves will lower the funds rate below the IOR of 0.1 percent. The New York Desk will then undertake ON RRPs (overnight reverse repurchase agreements) with the money funds to drain reserves. Deposits will be extinguished. Note that if the real interest rate dictated by the price system, the natural interest rate, rises and the FOMC does not follow that rise by raising the funds rate, the decline in money demand can still produce a decline in the money stock. At the same time, the nominal quantity of money will exceed the nominal quantity of money demanded and nominal expenditure and ultimately inflation will rise. The fact that money declines while inflation rises does not mean that inflation is not a monetary phenomenon.

28. The discount window can be used to keep insolvent banks afloat as was the case with banks in New England in the late 1980s with the real estate slump (Schwartz 1992). To prevent moral hazard, it is appropriate that there is a stigma attached to borrowing at the window. However, in a financial panic, lowering the discount rate to the funds rate appropriately removes that stigma.

The Federal Reserve Board on Thursday released the hypothetical scenarios for the 2020 stress test exercises, which ensure that large banks have adequate capital and processes so that they can continue lending to households and businesses, even during a severe recession. The harshest scenario includes a severe global recession with heightened stresses in corporate debt markets and commercial real estate, and for banks with large trading operations, additional pressure on leveraged loans. . . . Additionally, banks with large trading operations will be required to factor in a global market shock component as part of their scenarios. This year's shock features, among other things, heightened stress to trading book exposures to leveraged loans. Additionally, firms with substantial trading or processing operations will be required to incorporate a counterparty default scenario component.

US bank holding companies have built up substantial levels of capital and liquidity in excess of regulatory minimums and buffers. The largest firms have $1.3 trillion in common equity and hold $2.9 trillion in high quality liquid assets.

It is also important to remember that for distressed corporations there are sources of funding other than banks. In addition to highlighting the record amount of debt issuance by investment-grade firms, Chappatta (2020, 4) pointed out the extent to which private equity firms were still willing to lend to firms in industries like hospitality particularly hard hit by the Covid-19 virus. Of course, such funding can require restructuring that imposes costs on bond holders. However, a capitalist system works only if those who gain the rewards in good times bear the losses in bad times.[29]

---

29. The *Wall Street Journal* (2020d) reported:

Working to the industry's advantage is a record-high mountain of unspent cash—around $2 trillion across global private markets, with most of that dedicated to private equity, according to investment-advisory firm Hamilton Lance Inc. Blackstone could be among the best positioned to capitalize on market disruption: It has yet to spend a dollar of the record $26 billion private-equity fund it raised last year. . . . Buyout firms have submitted proposals to invest in cruise lines, casinos, airlines and other hard-hit sectors of the economy, but corporate chefs have so far been hesitant to accept financing under their onerous terms.

It continued four days later (*Wall Street Journal* 2020e):

As of December, private investment firms of all types, including venture capital and private equity, were sitting on around $2.5 trillion in unspent capital, according to a Bain & Co. report released in February. It said buyout firms held $830 billion.

25.6. CAN THE FED MAINTAIN ITS INDEPENDENCE?

What will happen to Fed independence when Congress realizes that it can remake the Fed into a hybrid central bank and GSE serving its constituencies?[30] In 2020, the amounts were large. If all the Fed's 13(3) programs had been fully levered up with ESF money, of the $2 trillion in loans, more than $1 trillion would have been divided between the politically sensitive sectors of the SMEs (small and medium-sized enterprises) and state and local governments (LHM 2020g).[31] Congress has an incentive to transfer risk to the Fed's books where it is invisible to taxpayers.

If the Fed is going to forswear intervention in credit markets in the future, it will have to abandon its historic aversion to commitment and rules. Without such commitment, moral hazard reigns. If the Fed committed to not bailing out the prime money funds in the future, then regulators would have to regulate them like banks and eliminate the inherent instability they impart to the financial system. The commonly repeated statement of Bernanke (2015, 168) makes this point: "There are no atheists in foxholes or ideologues in a financial crisis." That comment makes the obvious point that without institutional constraints regulators will always follow a bailout policy.

Bernanke (2015, 219 and 342) articulated the time-consistency issue creating moral hazard:

> We wanted creditors that funded financial institutions, large as well as small, to be careful about where they put their money. That they might not, because they expected any failing firm to be bailed out, was the moral hazard problem. In the short run, though, we couldn't risk a general panic in the repo market and other funding markets.
>
> The Fed had traditionally opposed expanding deposit insurance, on the grounds that it would increase moral hazard. But during the crisis, insuring the checking accounts used by businesses, municipalities, and nonprofit organizations . . . made a lot of sense. Without it, these entities might rapidly shift their deposits from smaller banks perceived to be at risk to banks perceived as too big to fail.

30. For additional commentary on the political economy of credit policy, see Broaddus and Goodfriend (2004); Goodfriend and King (1988); Schwartz (1992); Goodfriend (1994); Cecchetti and Schoenholtz (2020); Todd (2019); and Selgin (2020a).

31. Fully levered up, the MSLF (Main Street Lending Facility) could loan up to $600 billion and the MLF (Municipal Liquidity Facility) up to $500 billion.

In reference to the Fed's role in facilitating a privately financed rescue of LTCM, which made highly leveraged bets on differences in yield spreads, Barney Frank (D-MA) (US Congress 1998b, 81, 83) commented:

> Mr. Greenspan has said that this may happen again. So then the question is, if it was so important as to justify this intervention now, how do you persuade us to do absolutely nothing except wait again and trust entirely in your discretion to deal with it if it happens again? . . . You intervened in a way that left the mistake-makers better off. . . . A consequence . . . was to leave some of the richest people in this country better off than they would have been if the Federal Government hadn't intervened; and that rankles a lot of us . . . when we are told we can't do anything similar for people much needier. . . . I am disappointed that you tell us we can do nothing except allow for repetitions of this.

There are changes that would assure that Congress not the Fed conducted fiscal policy in a future crisis. First, Congress should eliminate the authorization for the Board of Governors to pay interest of reserves (IOR). In doing so, the Fed would have to restrict the size of its balance sheet to the amount required to conduct monetary policy (Selgin 2020a and 2020b). Second, Congress should eliminate the 13(3) authorization for the Fed to lend to nonbanks. Third, the prime money market funds and REITs, which amplify instability of the financial system in a period of stress, should be regulated like banks.

Congress could also end the Fed's authority to arrange swap lines with other central banks. All the large foreign banks have US branches and thus can borrow from the Fed's discount window. It would be desirable to phase out the swap lines with the understanding that in a financial panic large foreign banks would use their US branches to borrow at the discount window subject to supervision by the New York Fed. There would be an advantage to the United States in that the financing of foreign trade invoiced in dollars would come to be centered in New York in the way that it was centered in London before World War I. The advantage of having the dollar as a reserve currency comes from the seigniorage of foreign individuals holding dollars in the form of currency as an emergency store of value. That would not be affected by ending the swap lines.

25.7. CONCLUDING COMMENT

The Fed's bookkeeping powers allow it to create bank reserves through the purchase of debt instruments. Nothing in a bookkeeping operation allows it to conjure up real resources. It follows that the Fed's credit programs can only allocate credit among competing uses, not increase the real resources made available through financial intermediation. Such actions are subject to only limited public debate. They therefore limit Fed accountability.

The payment of interest on reserves (IOR) enhances the ability of the Fed to engage in financial intermediation by buying private debt. However, to an offsetting extent, its financial intermediation reduces intermediation in the private sector. Nevertheless, the Fed has not communicated its 13(3) programs as allocating credit. Instead, it promotes them as making resources available to sectors of the economy where markets have failed to provide resources through market dysfunction. The absence of any talk of trade-offs implies that the Fed's involvement in financial intermediation augments the total transfer of resources from households to businesses and state and local governments. Such a message can only encourage Congress to require the Fed to allocate credit to politically important constituencies.

In March 2020, the Fed's monetary policy actions consisting of massive purchases of treasuries and of RPs were critically important. Chair Powell, however, should have waited to see whether these actions kept financial market working. Instead, he assumed that markets would no longer be able to evaluate risk and direct credit flows to productive uses. The Fed's credit programs may have worsened market function by reinforcing a two-tier market favoring the allocation of credit to the investment-grade (safer) part of the market. William Dudley (2020) dramatized the need to address the issue of moral hazard: "The moral hazard issue needs to be debated and addressed. Big crises seem to be occurring more often and Fed interventions are growing ever bigger in size and broader in scope. Whatever you thought was the size of the moral-hazard problem before, now it's gotten even larger."

Inevitably, because of the way in which the allocation of credit apportions losses and windfalls, involvement in credit policy drags the Fed into the political arena. To maintain its independence, it is important that the Fed return to the sole job of monetary policy. The Covid-19 crisis has greatly increased the role of government in the economy. The Fed policy of commandeering the allocative role of private credit markets is a major contributor to this expansion of state power. If the political system comes to expect the Fed to allocate credit to favored constituencies, the Covid-19 crisis will mark a permanent movement away from a free market system.

APPENDIX: PROGRAM DEFINITIONS
13(3) Programs

CPFF (Commercial Paper Funding Facility). The CPFF was an SPV (special purpose vehicle) that purchased unsecured and asset-backed commercial paper rated A1/P1, through funds supplied by the Federal Reserve Bank of New York. It was established March 17, 2020. The ESF provided $10 billion in funds.

MLF (Municipal Liquidity Facility). The MLF established an SPV to buy state and local government debt. It could purchase up to $500 billion of short-term notes directly from states and from counties (as originally announced) with a population of at least two million residents, and from US cities with a population of at least one million residents. On April 27, the Fed reduced the minimum city size from one million to 250,000 and reduced the minimum county size from two million to 500,000.

MMLF (Money Market Mutual Fund Liquidity Facility). Through the Federal Reserve Bank of Boston, the MMLF made loans to banks collateralized by commercial paper, especially ABCP (asset-backed commercial paper), purchased from money market funds. It was established March 18, 2020, and became operational March 23. The ESF provided $10 billion in funds. Under the program, a bank (depository institution, bank holding company, US branch and agency of a foreign bank) purchased the assets used as collateral for the Fed loan from an eligible MMMF (money market mutual fund), which includes prime, single-state, or tax-exempt money market funds. Loans are nonrecourse. Eligible assets include ABCP rated not lower than A1, F1, or P1.

MSLF (Main Street Lending Facility). The MSLF established an SPV to buy loans from banks. Eligible loans consisted of loans to firms employing ten thousand or fewer workers or firms with revenues less than $2.5 billion. Loans were for four-year terms with deferral of principal and interest payments for one year. Banks retained 5 percent of the loans on their books. The SPV could purchase up to $600 billion of loans.

PDCF (Primary Dealer Credit Facility). On March 17, 2020, the Fed resurrected the PDCF. It supplied funds to primary dealers through repurchase agreements. (A primary dealer engages in open market transactions with the New York Fed.) Loans are made with recourse. Eligible collateral includes commercial paper (investment grade, that is, rated A2/P2/F2); investment-grade corporate debt securities, international agency securities, municipal securities, mortgage-backed securities, and asset-backed securities; and equity securities. Commercial mortgage-backed securities

(CMBS), collateralized loan obligations (CLOs), and collateralized debt obligations (CDOs) must be rated AAA.

PMCCF (Primary Market Corporate Credit Facility). The PMCCF was an SPV that purchased bonds and syndicated loans directly from investment-grade corporations. The bonds had to be rated at least BBB/Baa3 as of March 22, 2008. Thus, firms having been downgraded were included. The Treasury ESF would make a $75 billion investment. It was established March 23, 2020.

PPPLF (Paycheck Protection Program Liquidity Facility) The PPPLF established an SPV to lend to the SBA (Small Business Administration) by providing term financing for PPP loans. There were no haircuts on the loans serving as collateral. It became operational April 16, 2020.

SMCCF (Secondary Market Corporate Facility). The SMCCF was an SPV that bought investment-grade corporate bonds on the secondary market. It also bought shares in corporate bond ETF's (exchange traded funds), which included high-yield bonds. The individual corporate bonds had to be rated at least BBB/Baa3, and the ETFs had to buy investment-grade corporate bonds. The Treasury's ESF initially invested $10 billion. It was established March 23, 2020.

TALF (Term Asset-Backed Securities Loan Facility). The TALF was an SPV. It held investment-grade (AAA-rated) asset-backed securities (ABS): private student loans, auto loans and leases, consumer and corporate credit card receivables, and specified loans guaranteed by the SBA (Small Business Administration). It was established March 22, 2020. Effective April 9, 2020, TALF began to accept as eligible collateral-leveraged loans and commercial mortgages. The $10 billion in funds supplied by the Treasury's ESF incurred the first loss. Although loans to the SIV were recourse, the TALF loans to the issuers of the ABS were nonrecourse. If the ABS declined sufficiently in value below the value of the loan, after deducting the ESF contribution, the Fed would suffer a partial default, and the loan would be effectively nonrecourse. On April 9, 2020, the Board broadened eligible collateral to include AAA CMBS (commercial mortgage-backed securities) and newly issued CLOs (collateralized loan obligations).

Fed Non-13(3) Programs

Swap Lines. A swap line is an agreement between central banks to exchange their currencies and later reverse the transactions. When a foreign central bank draws on its swap line with the New York Fed, it receives dollars. At the same time, it agrees to buy back at a later date its currency with dollars at an unchanged exchange rate.

Government

PPP (Paycheck Protection Program). PPP was a $349 billion relief program designed to help small business owners keep their workers employed. It lent to businesses with fewer than five employees. Loans covered up to two months of payroll and were capped at $10 million. The Small Business Administration administered the program through approved lenders. Loans were forgiven if the business maintained its payroll for eight weeks after receipt of the loan at the level that existed before the pandemic.

TARP (Troubled Asset Relief Program). TARP was a program to buy MBS from banks. President Bush signed it into law on October 3, 2008. It was funded with $700 billion.

Miscellaneous Terms

LCR (Liquidity Coverage Ratio). The idea of the LCR is that a bank will have sufficient liquid assets to offset thirty days of a run on its deposits. It is the ratio of the bank's liquid assets to net cash flows over a two-day period.

REITs (Real Estate Investment Trusts). A REIT is a mutual fund that owns properties that generate income, for example, apartment buildings and hotels. Most are publicly traded.

SLR (Supplementary Leverage Ratio). The Basel III Accords require that large banks hold a minimum of capital relative to all assets. For large bank holding companies, the ratio is 5 percent.

APPENDIX: THE POLITICAL ECONOMY OF CREDIT POLICY

Arthur Burns (1975, 65–66), who was FOMC chairman from February 1970 until March 1978, made some of the strongest statements on the dangers to the Fed of involvement in the allocation of credit. The following came in response to a bill, H.R. 212, that would have required the Fed to allocate credit toward "national priority uses." It should serve as a warning for any Fed involvement in a policy that requires it to supplant the market allocation of credit with its own judgment.

> Our financial markets are highly competitive and they have served our Nation well over the years. As we read H.R. 212, it envisages a comprehensive intrusion of the Federal Government into private credit markets. . . . The bill delegates enormous and virtually dictatorial power to the Federal Reserve. Implementation of the bill could undermine the market system and wreck all chances for economic recovery. And it is

even highly doubtful whether H.R. 212 could achieve the objectives being sought—that is, larger credit flows to certain uses, such as essential
capital investment, small businesses, and agriculture, at low interest
rates.

Decisions as to social priorities in the use of credit are inherently political in character. If such decisions are to be made at all, they should be
made by the Congress—not by an administrative and nonpolitical body
such as the Federal Reserve. After all, tilting credit in favor of some borrowers implies denying credit to someone else. Our economy has developed by relying mainly on the market to make such decisions. The market reflects the interaction of many thousands of borrowers and lenders.
If the day ever arrives when governmental decisions are to be substituted
for individual preferences expressed in the marketplace, then the priorities should be set explicitly by the Congress.

The specifications of H.R. 212 are so vague and general that they
would inevitably involve the Board in political judgments—an area in
which it obviously has no special competence.

More succinctly, Burns (US Congress 1974b, July 30, 263) commented:

The concept of credit allocation implies a degree of knowledge of social
priorities that I for one am quite certain that we at the Federal Reserve
Board do not have. I think the Congress would not be well advised to
give us a power that we simply do not know how to exercise properly.
If we are to have credit allocation in this country, then I think credit allocation should proceed according to the rules devised by the Congress.
But there again, I must say, in all humility, that I am not at all sure that
Congress has the wisdom to substitute its rules for the workings of the
marketplace.

In early 2009, the Board of Governors (2009a) issued a statement jointly
with the Treasury. The section headed "The Federal Reserve to avoid credit
risk and credit allocation" included the language: "The Federal Reserve's
lender-of-last-resort responsibilities . . . should improve financial or credit
conditions broadly, not . . . allocate credit to narrowly-defined sectors or
classes of borrowers. Government decisions to influence the allocation of
credit are the province of fiscal authorities." FOMC chairman Ben Bernanke (2015, 156) stated in his August 2007 Jackson Hole speech, "It is not
the responsibility of the Federal Reserve—nor would it be appropriate—to
protect lenders and investors from the consequences of their financial
decisions."

In May 1975, New York City petitioned the federal government for financial aid to prevent bankruptcy and a default on its debt. At the time, New York politicians made dire predictions that a default by New York City would disrupt the entire municipal bond market. Other mayors of large cities warned that their cities could fall in a domino effect if New York City defaulted. New York politicians pressed the Fed to open its discount window to New York, but the Fed refused. Peter Sternlight (Board of Governors, *FOMC Memorandum of Discussion*, April 15, 1975, 70), deputy manager for domestic operations, told the FOMC, "It has been made clear . . . that there is no likelihood of direct Federal Reserve assistance to New York City."

FOMC chairman Jerome Powell (2020a) engaged in the following exchange with congresswoman Rashida Tlaib (D-MI):

TLAIB: Can you explain to me why we shouldn't, the Federal Reserve, ensure that state and local governments have access to funding during time of stress.

POWELL: As you know, we have limited authority. . . . A series of FOMC chairs in all kinds of different political environments have thought of that as something that's not appropriate really for us in the sense that it's government. . . . It's to be dealt with by fiscal authorities rather than the monetary authority. We focus on the job you've given us . . . as opposed to the solvency of state and local governments. . . .

TLAIB: Yes or no, does the Federal Reserve retain the ability to give emergency lending facilities? Is that accurate in stabilizing the economy?

POWELL: Yes, to financial institutions, we do.

TLAIB: So, when the Fed steps in to rescue banks in a crisis is that because you believe their role in the economy is vital? . . . Do you not believe that the governments of Detroit and Puerto Rico also play a vital role that should be preserved even if a financial crisis makes it hard for them to borrow money?

POWELL: What I believe is that's not a job for the Fed. It has a particular role and particular authorities. Lending to state and local governments and supporting them when they are in bankruptcy. . . .

TLAIB: Yeah. . . . I'm afraid that's simply not good enough. . . . Look, the federal government is supposed to be about people.

CHAPTER 26

Covid-19 and the Fed's Monetary Policy

Flexible-Average-Inflation Targeting

Summary: In August 2020, FOMC chair Jerome Powell announced a strategy for achieving an inclusive value of the FOMC's goal of maximum employment. The strategy rested on discovering the minimal value of sustainable unemployment by running the economy above potential until the unemployment rate declined to a level that initiates an inflation overshoot from the FOMC's longer-run 2 percent target. There was no contradiction with an FOMC target for inflation of 2 percent. The new strategy of average inflation targeting (AIT) required that an inflation overshoot would compensate for prior undershoots of the 2 percent target.

The framework is reminiscent of the 1970s. With a country fractured over the Vietnam War and a militant civil rights movement, a socially desirable low unemployment rate became a political imperative. FOMC chairman Arthur Burns accepted the challenge (Hetzel 1998; 2008, chap. 8). The Keynesian consensus of the time promised to deliver a socially desirable rate of unemployment at least as low as 4 percent at the cost of only moderate inflation. This desirable Phillips curve trade-off between unemployment and inflation became the centerpiece of monetary policy. Modigliani and Papademos (1975; 1976) provided the organizing principle for monetary policy. Namely, there is a predictable and "exploitable" trade-off in which changes in inflation depend on the difference between the unemployment rate and a full-employment rate termed "the nonaccelerating inflation rate of unemployment" (NAIRU).

The intellectual and political environment were also reminiscent of the earlier Keynesian environment. The Powell Fed reverted to its 1950s "cost and availability" view of monetary transmission. There was also a widespread belief that inflation is a nonmonetary phenomenon. In Keynesian terms, because the Phillips curve, which relates inflation and unemployment, was presumed to be flat, the Fed could push the unemployment rate down to at least its prepandemic low without raising inflation. FOMC chair Jerome Powell asserted that the course of the recovery would be dictated by the behavior of the virus. That made sense in that the recession arose as a shock to potential output. Powell and the FOMC, however, treated the recession as if it originated in a large negative aggregate-demand shock requiring stimulative monetary policy.

On August 27, 2020, FOMC chair Jerome Powell (Board of Governors 2020f) announced a revision to the FOMC's Statement on Longer-Run Goals and Monetary Policy Strategy termed "flexible-average-inflation targeting" (FAIT). The revision entailed an aggressive monetary policy to restore the prepandemic low level of unemployment reinforced by a willingness to raise inflation above the FOMC's 2 percent target for some persistent period. This change in monetary policy came from mistakes presumed to have been made in the prior economic recovery that left inflation below the 2 percent target. Namely, the FOMC should not have engaged in preemptive increases in the funds rate. That is, it should not have raised the funds rate off the zero lower bound (ZLB) based on sustained growth in output above potential but instead should have waited for inflation to increase.

The chapter starts by summarizing the Powell view of the world. It reflects a nonmonetary theory of inflation summarized in the assumption that the empirical correlations of the Phillips curve relating unemployment to inflation are structural.

26.1. FOMC COMMENTARY

Chair Powell (2021a) explained how the new strategy is based on a structural Phillips curve that is flat down to a low level of unemployment and that lacks inflation persistence. Similarly, Powell (LHM 2021a, 3) testified to Congress:

> We have had inflation dynamics in our economy for . . . three decades, which consists of a very flat Phillips curve, meaning a weak relationship between high resource utilization, low unemployment, and inflation. But also low persistence of inflation critically. You go back to, when you and I were in college, you had a steep Phillips curve. But you also had the situation where, if inflation went up, it would stay up, because expectations were not anchored. And so people would expect inflation and that would make it go up.

An implication of a flat Phillips curve is that an expansionary monetary policy can push the unemployment rate to low levels without danger of an undesirably large increases in inflation. Richard Clarida (2021), Board of Governors vice chair, explained how this assumption meant that the FOMC would not raise the funds rate off the ZLB in response to declines in the unemployment rate. He highlighted the change in the wording of the FOMC's Statement on Longer-Run Goals and Monetary Policy Strategy of "'*shortfalls*' of employment from its maximum level'—not 'deviations.' This language means that going forward, a low unemployment rate, in and of itself, will not be sufficient to trigger a tightening of monetary policy" (Clarida, 2021, 4, italics in original).

Specifically, the FOMC rejected the Volcker-Greenspan policy of pre-emptive increases in the funds rate to prevent the emergence of inflation. As summarized by Larry Meyer (LHM 2020l): "The switch to a maximum employment threshold reflects that, while a *rise* in the unemployment rate is always 'bad' in the normal [new] regime, a *decline* in the unemployment rate is always 'good.' Given that a lower unemployment rate is recognized as *always good*, there is no preemptive rise in the funds rate when the unemployment rate falls" (italics in original).

Governor Lael Brainard (2021) made clear that the FOMC treats inclusive employment as an independent goal:

> Two years ago, the Federal Reserve began an in-depth review of its monetary policy framework. . . . Our review was prompted by changes in key long-run features of the economy: The recognition that price inflation is much less sensitive to labor market tightness than historically—that is, a flat Phillips curve. . . . In response, we have made changes to monetary policy that can be expected to support fuller and broader-based employment than in earlier recoveries, improving opportunities for workers who have faced structural challenges in the labor market. . . . The new policy approach, by avoiding the need to tighten preemptively, could support labor market conditions that help to reduce persistent disparities.

Even before Powell's Jackson Hole speech, Brainard (2020) had rejected a policy of preemptively raising the funds rate before the emergence of inflation:

> And with inflation exhibiting low sensitivity to labor market tightness, policy should not preemptively withdraw support based on a historically steeper Phillips curve that is not currently in evidence. Instead, policy should seek to achieve employment outcomes with the kind of breadth and depth that were only achieved late in the previous recovery.

Mary Daly (2021), president of the San Francisco Fed, reiterated the abandonment of preemption:

> We are not going to . . . take the punch bowl away from the economy when we have inflation running consistently below 2 percent . . . just because we get to the levels of unemployment that have traditionally, historically meant that wage inflation would push up and that price inflation would be right behind it. . . . In an era when we have a pretty flat Phillips curve, and I want to add for full disclosure I still believe in the Phillips curve, . . . what we have learned [is that] the labor market is far more elastic than we thought.

The new strategy built in the committed forward guidance that makes monetary policy expansionary at the ZLB. In a June 10, 2020, press conference, Powell (Board of Governors 2020d) noted that in the prepandemic period the unemployment rate was extremely low (3.5 percent in February 2020) and inflation never exceeded 2 percent. The implication was that the FOMC could maintain the funds rate at the ZLB at least until the unemployment rate approached its prepandemic level. Powell (Board of Governors 2020b, 9–10) stated:

> We saw a lot of great things happening in the [prepandemic] labor market, things that we'd love to get back to. We didn't see any problems with price inflation. . . . We'd . . . welcome very low readings . . . on unemployment just based on what we . . . saw . . . in the last expansion. . . . We're not even thinking about thinking about raising rates.

Charles Evans (2021, 7–8), president of the Chicago Fed, explained the strategy:

> The first prong calls for the federal funds rate to remain at the effective lower bound until our employment mandate is met and inflation reaches 2 percent and is on target to overshoot. Then, the second prong involves increasing the federal funds rate slowly enough to maintain the accommodation needed to achieve moderate overshooting for some time, so that inflation actually averages 2 percent. And last month we augmented this with guidance saying we will maintain our current pace of asset purchases until substantial further progress has been made toward our maximum and inclusive employment and price stability goals. For this approach to be successful, economic agents must have strong confidence

that policy will remain sufficiently accommodative to generate these outcomes.

It will take years to get average inflation up to 2 percent, which means that monetary policy will be accommodative for a long time. This translates into low-for-long policy rates, and indicates that the Fed will be continuing our current asset purchase program for a while as well. So economic agents should be prepared for a period of very low interest rates and an expanding Fed balance sheet.

26.2. AN EVOLVING PHILLIPS CURVE SIDELINES INFLATION

The revised strategy announced by Chair Powell came in the context of the deep recession and loss of employment due to the Covid-19 virus. It also reflected the prior recovery from the Great Recession during which for an extended period the funds rate was near the ZLB, and inflation fell short of the FOMC's 2 percent target. The revised strategy comprised two related changes. First, the FOMC abandoned the Volcker-Greenspan policy of preemptive increases in the funds rate intended to forestall the emergence of inflation. Second, the FOMC aimed to raise inflation above the 2 percent target for an indeterminate period. Taken together, they outlined a strategy of pursuing an expansionary policy to produce a sustained decline in the unemployment rate until inflation rose persistently above 2 percent.

FAIT represented a rejection of the earlier interest-rate "normalization" policy pursued after December 2015 and especially after December 2016 of raising the funds rate in response to sustained growth in output above potential (sustained declines in the unemployment rate). The earlier policy carried over the Volcker-Greenspan policy of preemptive tightening in response to labor market tightness to avoid the emergence of inflation (see chaps. 19 and 20; and Hetzel 2008, chap. 21). A rationale for FAIT and for abandonment of the preemptive policy was the constraint placed on monetary policy by a secular decline in the risk-free ("natural") rate of interest.

The argument was that periodically negative aggregate-demand shocks will require lowering the funds rate to the ZLB. (The acronym ELB represents "effective lower bound," which can be negative. However, the FOMC has refused to consider a negative funds rate.) In these periods at the ZLB, because monetary policy is constrained, inflation will decline below the FOMC's 2 percent target. Without the expectation that the FOMC will compensate in the future with inflation above 2 percent, the public will expect inflation less than the 2 percent target. In his NPR interview, Powell (2020e) commented:

When inflation is very, very low, it means lower interest rates. . . . If people expect inflation to be very low, then interest rates will keep going
down. Again, we've seen this around the world, lower and lower interest
rates, lower and lower inflation. When interest rates get very low, the
Fed will have less room to cut interest rates to support the economy. That
means that unemployment will be higher, more of the time.

Evaluation of the likely success of FAIT requires assessment of the
framework it embodies for trade-offs between its dual objectives of price
stability and maximum employment. In the NPR interview, Powell (2020e)
predicted a favorable trade-off. NPR's Steve Inskeep asked him if the following was an accurate summary of Powell's Jackson Hole speech: "You're
going to worry less about the economy overheating. If inflation gets a little
high, if employment gets a little high, you're going to be less quick to stamp
on it. Is that a fair summary?" Powell replied, "Yes, it is. . . . What we've
learned is that unemployment can be even lower than we thought and not
result in troubling levels of inflation. . . . We had 3.5% unemployment . . . and
we didn't see inflation result."

Powell explained inflation within the framework of a Phillips curve,
which summarizes the empirical relationship between slack in the economy
(unemployment) and inflation. A Keynesian Phillips curve endows these
empirical correlations with structural significance. The policy maker can
manipulate the joint behavior of inflation and unemployment with predictable results. In that sense, the Phillips curve is "exploitable." In contrast,
Friedman (1968 [1969]) argued that the empirical correlations summarized
in Phillips curves are a reduced form generated by unpredictable monetary
policy and cannot serve as a reliable basis for policy.

Within the framework of a Keynesian Phillips curve, there is a taxo-
nomic classification of the causes of inflation, which includes two broad
categories: demand-pull and cost-push (Ackley 1961). The first captures real
expenditures by the public in excess of the economy's ability to produce
goods and services. The second measures the extent to which relative prices
(prices determined by supply and demand factors particular to individual
markets) pass through to the price level.

In 2021, the FOMC believed that demand-pull inflation was not a problem
because of the large amount of slack in the economy and because the Phillips
curve is flat reaching down to low levels of unemployment. Cost-push inflation was not a problem because of globalization. Powell (2020e) commented:

If you go back 50 years, inflation would have reacted very strongly to
low levels of unemployment. . . . The economy's ever evolving and the

Fed has to have a framework for reacting to changes in the economy. . . .
So, low and declining inflation has been a phenomenon really around
the world for the last few decades. . . . With globalization, things can be
made anywhere, and that means it's difficult to raise wages or prices. . . .
So those factors are just very important in establishing a mindset where
prices and wages don't go up. . . . So inflation—high inflation—has not
been a problem in the United States. It's a different economy.

Given the assumption that the FOMC is operating on a flat section of
the Phillips curve, there is presumably no way to predict inflation. What
then determines inflation? It is whatever the public expects it to be. Powell
(2020e) commented:

Both wage and price inflation are a bit of a mental phenomenon. If people believe that prices will be pretty stable, then they will be—because
they won't ask for very high wage increases and people who sell things
won't be asking for high price increases. So, once that psychology sets in,
it tends to perpetuate itself.

With FAIT, the FOMC committed to implementing an expansionary
monetary policy to restore unemployment to its prepandemic level. It
would push down the unemployment rate until reaching an upward sloping section of the Phillips curve that raises inflation above 2 percent. Given
the FOMC's forecast of protracted high unemployment, the FOMC could
provide the forward guidance that the funds rate would be near zero for a
long time. Powell (2020e, 4) commented: "The economy's going to need
low interest rates, which support economic activity, for an extended period
of time. . . . It will be measured in years. . . . We're not going to prematurely
withdraw the support that we think the economy needs. . . . There's still
another 10 or 11 [million] who are not back to work."

Powell accepted the Keynesian assumption that raising interest rates
slows the growth of the economy and raises unemployment. In populist
terms, "The Fed controls inflation on the backs of the working man." The
unemployment rate is a target, not simply one indicator of whether through
sustained declines output is growing unsustainably fast. In the 1970s period of stop-go monetary policy, the FOMC acted on this assumption by
raising interest rates only hesitantly in economic recoveries until inflation
emerged and it had a rationale to raise rates. Out of fear that higher inflation
would pass into expected inflation, it then raised rates sufficiently to cause
a recession. Volcker and Greenspan rejected these attempts to manipulate
Phillips curve trade-offs through the policy of preemption. That is, they

raised interest rates vigorously enough in economic recovery to prevent the emergence of inflation in favor of maintenance of price stability.

26.3. THE RETURN OF THE PHILLIPS CURVE

With the onset of the pandemic and the decline in employment, the FOMC decided to pursue an expansionary monetary policy to hasten a return to the low unemployment rate that existed in early 2020. The issue then arose of how to implement the required stimulus in a controlled way, that is, in a way that would also limit an undesirable rise in inflation. The theoretical construct that promises such control is the Phillips curve. A Phillips curve captures a nonmonetary view of inflation in which there exists a predictable relationship between slack in the economy, presumed under the control of the FOMC, and inflation.

However, the issue then arises, what Phillips curve? Chair Powell (2021a) pointed out that no such empirical relationship exists in the data:

> We have a flat Phillips curve, meaning there's still a small connection ["between slack in the labor market and inflation"] but you need a microscope to find it. We've also got low persistence of inflation, so that if inflation were to go up for any reason it [inflation] . . . doesn't stay up. . . . Remember, we're a long way from maximum employment. There's plenty of slack in the labor market.

The FOMC needed such a Phillips curve relationship to ensure its achievement of inclusive maximum employment with only a moderate increase in inflation. If the relationship is needed, it must exist.

However, not only was there no Phillips curve in the empirical data; also there was no historical precedent for successful use of a Phillips curve. In the recovery from the recession with a trough in March 1991, just as in the recovery from the Great Recession, a falling unemployment rate failed to predict an increase in inflation. The Modigliani-Papademos framework failed as the unemployment rate declined from 7.8 percent in June 1992 to 3.8 percent in April 2000 while inflation changed only minimally. Inflation, measured by the core PCE deflator, went from 2.2 percent in 1992Q2 to 1.3 percent in 2000Q2. Measured by the headline PCE deflator, it remained unchanged over this period at 1.8 percent.[1]

1. In a letter published in the *Wall Street* Journal, Daniel Thornton (2018) wrote: "Prof. Blinder suggests nobody knows what the nonaccelerating rate of unemployment (Nairu), the neutral (natural) rate of interest (aka r-star or r^*) and the Phillips curve are today. This is hardly new. Estimates of Nairu and the Phillips curve have changed con-

The Greenspan FOMC, however, did not abandon a policy of preemptive increases in the funds rate. Greenspan (Board of Governors, *FOMC Transcript*, June 27–28, 2000, 25, 24) told the FOMC: "The law of supply and demand says that there is a level of the unemployment rate that must of necessity drive compensation increases beyond the rate of increase in productivity. . . . The gap between the NAIRU, as defined in the model, and the unemployment rate has been very large for a very long period. And, clearly, we have not seen the process that is described in the Greenbook forecast emerge." Nevertheless, in 2020, the FOMC placed its bets on the existence of a structural Phillips curve.

26.4. MONETARY POLICY BECOMES EXPANSIONARY

The open market purchases starting in March 2020 increased monetary stimulus. Between the statement weeks ending March 11, 2020, and June 11, 2020, the amount of securities held outright by the Fed increased by almost $2.1 trillion. Much of the increase was in longer-term Treasury securities and MBS. Treasury securities with maturities of five years or longer increased by $661 billion, while MBS with maturities of five years or longer increased by $463 billion (Board of Governors, Statistical Release H.4.1).[2] One reason that these open market purchases are stimulative is that the FOMC has signaled that they are unlikely to be reversed for a long time. By announcing at its June 2020 meeting that net asset purchases would continue "at least at the current pace" (Board of Governors, FOMC, statement) the FOMC signaled to markets that it would not unwind the prior large expansion in its securities holdings. LHM (2020j) reported that the FOMC wanted "to reassure markets that the premature Fed withdrawal is not likely."

The "dot plot" for the June 10, 2020, Summary of Economic Projections (Board of Governors 2020e, fig. 2) showed that only two FOMC participants believed that the funds rate should increase from its near-zero value before the end of 2022. Selling securities would be inconsistent with main-

stantly over the last 50 years. Alan Greenspan noted this fact at the December 1995 Federal Open Market Committee meeting: 'saying that the Nairu has fallen, which is what we tend to do, is not very helpful. That's because whenever we miss the inflation forecast, we say the Nairu fell.' Other FOMC participants made similar comments at other meetings, e.g., at the February 1999 meeting William Poole, president of the St. Louis Fed, said, 'the Phillips curve is an unreliable policy guide'; Edward Boehne, president of the Philadelphia Fed, said 'Nairu . . . has about zero value in terms of making policy.'"

2. See Board of Governors, Statistical Release H.4.1, sec. 2, "Maturity Distribution of Securities, Loans, and Selected Other Assets and Liabilities."

taining a stimulative policy. This kind of Fed communication to markets effectively committed the FOMC to an expansionary monetary policy. Backing away from such communication would produce a discrete change in market expectations that could cause the yield curve to rise and produce an unpredictable tightening of monetary policy. The "taper tantrum" of May 2013 offers an example of a discrete rise in bond yields when markets interpreted the reduction in the pace of the FOMC's QE purchases as an earlier-than-anticipated liftoff of the funds rate.

The FOMC also used forward guidance to commit to an extended expansionary policy by emphasizing the Fed's commitment to use monetary policy to achieve socially desirable unemployment goals. LHM (2020k, 3–4) reported:

> Powell has repeatedly emphasized that the Fed can contribute to lowering income inequality and narrowing unemployment rate gaps by a monetary policy that lowers the overall unemployment rate to a very low level. And the FOMC had done this during the long expansion, during which the unemployment rate declined from 10% to 3½%. All those gains have been reversed in just a couple of months. As a result, Powell has now seemingly set a 3½% target for the unemployment rate because of the social benefits of such a tight—let's say "hot"—labor market. Of course, there is a caveat that the policy must not undermine the Fed's inflation mandate. But his attitude about the NAIRU [nonaccelerating inflation rate of unemployment] seems to be that "you'll know it when you see it." And the FOMC didn't see it when the unemployment rate was 3½%.

The strong endorsement by Chair Powell of an expansionary fiscal policy also effectively committed the FOMC to maintaining the funds rate at the ZLB for a significant period. In a press release issued on March 17, 2020, Speaker of the House Nancy Pelosi (2020) reported, "I spoke with Federal Reserve chairman Powell. . . . I was encouraged by the Chairman's perspective that with interest rates at nearly zero, Congress is enabled to think big fiscally as we craft a robust response." LHM (2020c) noted:

> The new troika in D.C. is now Mnuchin-Powell-Pelosi. . . . Bernanke gave the most relevant speech of 2020 in 2002. . . . As Bernanke noted, "a pledge by the Fed to keep the Treasury's borrowing costs low . . . might increase the willingness of the fiscal authorities to [provide fiscal stimulus]. . . ." That's exactly what Powell said to Pelosi today.

Chair Powell obviously cares deeply about his role in dealing with the crisis. Powell (2020b) said, "None of us has the luxury of choosing our challenges; fate and history provide them for us. Our job is to meet the tests we are presented." Probably for that reason, he has departed from the prior Fed practice of not commenting on fiscal policy. Implicitly, however, he is jeopardizing Fed independence by communicating that Congress need not worry that a significant deficit will raise the interest costs of financing the government deficit.

[CHAPTER 27]

How Can the Fed Control Inflation?

Summary: Starting in March 2020 as the Covid-19 pandemic affected the United States, money surged at a historically rapid pace.[1] Historical experience, most recently with the Great Inflation lasting from the mid-1960s through the 1970s, suggests that an uncontrolled surge in inflation will result. If left intact, the bulge in money in spring 2020 creates the outcome of inflation from "too much money chasing too few goods."

The bulge in M2 represents a significant increase in purchasing power. That bulge in purchasing power can be reversed in one of two ways, either through a reduction in the nominal quantity of money (M2) or through significant inflation. The increase in M2 occurred through the bookkeeping operations of banks as the public received government transfer payments and as the Fed engaged in quantitative easing (QE) with the purchase of government Treasury securities and of mortgage-backed securities (MBS). To the extent that the QE purchases matched the increase in the bank deposits in M2, the government did not have to issue debt to the public to finance its transfer payments. The Fed monetized the government deficit.

Reversing the increase in the nominal quantity of M2 requires undoing the bookkeeping operations of the banks that created the deposits. For that to happen, the Fed will need to keep short-term real rates of interest (the funds rate) in line with the "natural" rate of interest, the real rate of interest that keeps savings equal to investment. That is, as the public attempts to spend down its M2 balances (dissave), interest rates must be sufficiently high that the public also pays down bank debt (saves) and thus extinguishes bank deposits.

Inflation then will depend on how the purchasing power embodied in the 2020 bulge in money (M2) is unwound. If it is unwound through a reduction in the nominal quantity of bank deposits, then any significant price rise will be a one-time event. However, simply spending funds in a

1. This chapter uses material from the author's working paper "Will the Pandemic Bulge in Money Cause High Inflation?," Studies in Applied Economics 180, May 2021, Johns Hopkins Institute for Applied Economics, Global Health, and the Study of Business Enterprise.

bank deposit does not make the deposit disappear. The deposit is transferred to the recipient of the expenditure. Without a reduction in the aggregate quantity of money, money is a hot potato, and its purchasing power will have to be run down through an inflation rate higher than the inflation predicted by a Phillips curve and the level of unemployment.

Starting in March 2020, money growth surged. For the three months ending in June 2020, the annualized growth in M2 amounted to 56 percent. From February 2020 through May 2021, M2 rose by 31.6 percent. In the past, most recently over the decade and a half starting in 1965, rapid money creation led to high inflation.

As of mid-2021, financial markets were assuming that the bulge in liquid savings built up during the pandemic would result in a surge of spending due to pent-up demand as the service sector reopened. There would be a desirable one-time increase in spending and in the price level. For a one-time increase in spending and the price level to occur, however, the FOMC must eliminate the additional purchasing power represented by the bulge in M2 through reducing its nominal quantity. The alternative is for the additional purchasing power to dissipate through an undesirably large increase in inflation. To reduce the nominal quantity of M2, the FOMC must be ready to implement some combination of asset sales and of increases in interest rates sufficient to cause households to repay bank debt.

In fall 2008, Chairman Bernanke introduced credit policy as a significant component of policy. Because monetary policy understood as control over money creation as opposed to credit policy understood as control over financial intermediation is the central part of policy required for the control of inflation, it is essential to distinguish the two kinds of policy. Section 27.1 asks when government monetization of debt is inflationary. Section 27.2 discusses how to separate monetary control from financial intermediation given the complicating factor of the payment of interest on reserves (IOR) by the Fed. Section 27.3 explains when money is a useful indicator of the future behavior of the economy.

27.1. IS MONETIZING GOVERNMENT DEBT BY THE FED INFLATIONARY?

In response to the Covid-19 epidemic and the initial decline in employment by 22 million, the government initiated broad income support payments. Stanley (2021a and 2021b) summarized:

The first round of rebate checks distributed in April and May of 2020 totaled about $268 billion. . . . In January 2021, Treasury distributed about

$139 billion in the second round of checks. . . . The latest round of rebate checks [March and April 2021] is easily the largest yet. . . . When all is said and done, close to $400 billion may be disbursed.

Households' liquid assets, as defined by the Fed's count of currency, bank deposits, and money market funds, has surged since the end of 2019. . . . For much of the past decade, the gauge [of liquid assets] rose by roughly $500 billion per year. In contrast, in 2020, it surged by $2.7 trillion. Then, in the first quarter of 2021 alone, partly on the back of yet another round of rebate checks (the largest yet) and the reinstatement of supplementary unemployment benefit checks ($300 per week), liquid assets soared by $1 trillion to over $17 trillion. Thus, since the end of 2019, households' holding of liquid assets have risen by nearly $4 trillion in just 5 quarters.

Taken together, these two excerpts demonstrate not only the enormity of the fiscal stimulus but also how the Fed monetized much of the associated debt issuance. Significant debt monetization started in March 2020 with Fed purchases of the Treasury securities and agency MBS disgorged by hedge funds and real estate investment trusts. To preserve "market function," the New York Desk bought huge quantities of these securities (chap. 25). Over the two-month period from the statement week ending March 11, 2020, to the week ending May 13, 2020, securities held outright by the Fed (Treasury securities and MBS) increased by $1,783 billion (from $3,890 billion to $5,673 billion). (The Fed also added $44 billion of corporate securities to its portfolio as of July 23, 2020.) As Hilsenrath and Timiraos (2020) reported, "Between March 16 and April 16 [2020], it [the Fed] bought Treasury and mortgage securities at a pace of nearly $79 billion a day. By comparison, it bought about $85 billion a month between 2012 and 2014, the third QE program (QE3)." At its December 16, 2020, meeting, the FOMC regularized its open market purchases at a monthly pace of $80 billion of Treasury securities and $40 billion of MBS.

In 2021, households were sitting on a massive amount of liquid assets accumulated since the start of the pandemic in March 2020. That accumulation of liquid assets reflected an exceptionally high personal saving rate out of disposable personal income. Opportunity Insights (Chetty et al. 2021) used estimates of spending from the initial CARES stimulus checks showing that higher-income households saved most of their rebate checks.[2] The

2. Coibion, Gorodnichenko, and Weber (2020, Abstract) found that "using a large-scale survey of US consumers, we study how the large one-time transfers to individuals from the CARES Act affected their consumption, saving and labor-supply decisions. Most respondents report that they primarily saved or paid down debts with their transfers, with only about 15 percent reporting that they mostly spent it."

increased saving in the form of bank deposits appeared in a decline in the velocity of money (the ratio of expenditures to money). A similar decline in velocity occurred in World War II. Friedman and Schwartz (1963a, 559) attributed it to the unavailability of consumer durables. Because interest rates were low, money balances were a convenient way to save for purchases when the war ended. It follows that households will spend down the savings accumulated since March 2020 on services not currently available when confidence returns with widespread vaccination.

As of mid-2021, there was a vigorous debate over whether the significant increase in inflation that began with the core CPI in April was transitory or persistent. No doubt, there was a transitory element to price increases related to the reopening of the service sector. However, the expansionary character of monetary policy militated in favor of a persistent increase in underlying inflation. First, even though households saved a significant part of their transfer payments, the liquid character of those savings made monetary policy expansionary. Second, debt monetization that creates money is inflationary if not unwound.[3]

As background, consider how the Fed's open market purchases of Treasury securities and MBS make the asset portfolios of households more liquid and set off a portfolio rebalancing effect. Consider first the counterfactual of a CARES Act payment made in March 2020 financed entirely by issuance of government debt. The household receives an electronic deposit, and its bank receives an equal amount of reserves at the Fed. The payment reduces the Treasury's account at the Fed (the Treasury General Account or TGA). By assumption, the Treasury issues a security to the public to replenish the account. Bank deposits and reserves then decline to their original level while the public holds more Treasury debt. When confidence returns in the postpandemic world, households will attempt to increase their spending by selling the Treasury securities they acquired. Because there must be buyers for those securities, saving accompanies dissaving, which moderates the increased postpandemic spending. However, for such sales to find buyers other than the Fed, interest rates must rise.

As actually happened, however, the Fed replenished the TGA by buying Treasury securities and MBS from the public. Bank deposits and reserves then increased through the bookkeeping operation of the Fed. The exchange of a relatively long-term asset (a Treasury or MBS) for a bank deposit made the asset portfolio of the public more liquid. The attempt to

3. A normal amount of debt monetization occurs in the form of seigniorage. The Fed can buy Treasury securities to accommodate a regular increase in the demand for currency without inflation.

restore the desired degree of liquidity to the asset portfolio set off portfolio rebalancing in which the public attempts to exchange a deposit for an alternative illiquid asset. The first round effect is simply to bid up the price of these alternative illiquid assets.

In the language of the market, the Fed's open market purchases reduced the "duration" of the public's asset portfolio. Removing duration by adding long-term bonds to the Fed's portfolio makes the portfolios of investors more liquid by replacing illiquid, long-term bonds with liquid bank deposits. The counterpart to reducing the maturity of the public's portfolio is the lengthening of the maturity of the Fed's portfolio. That lengthening can be summarized in terms of the addition of ten-year securities. Lorie Logan (2020), executive vice president of the Federal Reserve Bank of New York's Markets Group, reported that "the total duration included in our Treasury purchases so far [through mid-July 2020] represents the equivalent of about $1 trillion in 10-year securities."

Friedman (1961 [1969], 255) explained the portfolio rebalancing that occurs when the central bank undertakes open market purchases (quantitative easing or QE) and how that rebalancing ultimately stimulates expenditure:

> The [public's] new balance sheet [after an open-market purchase] is in one sense still in equilibrium . . . since the open-market transaction was voluntary. . . . An asset was sold for money because the terms were favorable; however . . . from a longer-term view, the new balance sheet is out of equilibrium, with cash being temporarily high relative to other assets. Holders of cash will seek to purchase assets. . . . The key feature of this process is that it tends to raise the prices of sources of both producer and consumer services relative to the prices of the services themselves; for example, to raise the prices of houses relative to the rents of dwelling units, or the cost of purchasing a car relative to the cost of renting one.[4] It therefore encourages the production of such sources (this is the stimulus to "investment" . . .) and, at the same time, the direct acquisition of services rather than the source (this is the stimulus to "consumption" . . .).

The prices of assets like equities must rise to make investors willing to hold a more liquid asset portfolio.[5] The rise in asset prices is expansionary.

4. This phenomenon is also known as "Tobin's Q."
5. The transmission of monetary policy cannot be completely described by the behavior of "the" interest rate relative to the natural rate of interest but must include a complex of real yields, including the exchange rate of the dollar. Brunner and Meltzer (1968) stressed this point in discussing money creation in the context of a liquidity trap. See also Melcangi and Sterk (2020).

The expansionary impact of the Fed's QE purchases is cumulative in that continued purchases make investors' portfolios increasingly liquid and thus make monetary policy increasingly expansionary. Undoing the impact of an expansionary monetary policy is not like turning off a water spigot. Asset prices must come down, and that can take time and be disruptive.

Friedman also pointed out the difficulty of implementing an activist monetary policy to control gaps in macroeconomic variables, that is, a feedback policy of changing the central bank's instrument to eliminate differences between the values of actual and targeted macroeconomic variables. The example used below is for a target for the price level. The important point is that monetary stimulus and contraction work only with "long and variable lags." Friedman (1960, 87–88) wrote:

> The Federal Reserve System does not control the price level. It controls the volume of its own earning assets and, at one remove . . . the stock of money. . . . The link between the stock of money and the price level . . . is not direct and rigid, nor is it fully understood. While the stock of money is systematically related to the price level *on the average*, there is much variation in the relation over short periods of time. . . . There is much evidence that monetary changes have their effect only after a considerable lag and over a long period and that the lag is rather variable. . . . I find it virtually impossible to conceive of an effective procedure [for making the price level "or for that matter any other set of economic indicator . . . an effective guide"] when there is little basis for knowing whether the lag between action and effect will be 4 months or 29 months or somewhere in between. (italics in original)

No doubt there is agreement that the hyperinflation in countries like Zimbabwe and Venezuela arises from the monetization of government debt by the central bank. Is there an analogue with the monetization of the government debt that occurred through the massive QE that began in March 2020? Everything will depend on how the purchasing power embodied in the 2020 bulge in money (M2) is unwound. If it is unwound through a reduction in the nominal quantity of bank deposits, then any price rise associated with the end of the pandemic will be a one-time event. However, simply spending funds in a bank deposit does not make the deposit disappear. The deposit is transferred to the recipient of the expenditure. Money is a hot potato. With no reduction in the nominal quantity money, the purchasing power embodied in the bulge in M2 will have to be run down through inflation.

For the nominal quantity of money to decline, the FOMC must have procedures that cause the real funds rate to track the natural rate of interest. The natural rate of interest is the real rate of interest that eliminates excess demand in the goods market. Alternatively, equality between the real rate of interest and the natural rate of interest implies that savings equals investment. With that equality, there is no excess supply of bonds for the central bank to monetize in the bond market as a consequence of defending its rate peg. Without such debt monetization, there is then no excess supply in the market for the quantity of money requiring an increase in the prevailing price level.[6] When households attempt to run down their excess money balances, they dissave. A sufficiently high real rate of interest causes a corresponding amount of saving in the form of paying down bank debt and extinguishing bank deposits (money). Of course, the process of unwinding the M2 bulge is aided if the Fed sells securities.

27.2. THE CONTROL OF MONEY CREATION AND INFLATION WITH IOR (INTEREST ON RESERVES)

In a regime of fiat money creation, what makes a central bank unique and what gives it its power to determine the behavior of the price level and its power to disrupt the operation of the price system and the economy are its ability to create and destroy the reserves of the banking system. Because bank reserves are the instrument for effecting finality of payment, the central bank exercises power over broader measures of money used to make payments. Because the central bank possesses a monopoly over the bookkeeping operations that create and destroy reserves, only it can control reserves creation. With an interest-rate instrument, this monetary control works through the discipline placed on the demand for money. With a monetary rule that maintains price stability, operating procedures that keep the real rate of interest equal to the natural rate of interest cause real and nominal money demand to grow in line with real and potential output. The banking system accommodates the demand for money, and the central bank accommodates the derivative demand for bank reserves. With nomi-

6. An analogy is price fixing in an individual market in which a below-market fixed price creates excess demand. To extend the analogy to the macroeconomy, consider Patinkin (1965), who exposits the macroeconomy in terms of three markets: a goods market, a bond market, and a market for the quantity of money. If the central bank maintains an interest rate below the natural rate of interest, it raises the price of bonds with an artificially low rate of interest. There is then an excess supply of bonds, which the central bank must monetize to maintain its interest-rate peg. Money creation becomes an independent source of disturbance. The resulting excess supply in the market for the quantity of money spills over into the goods market.

nal money growing in line with real money demand, price stability obtains. Money is a veil.

Money (deposits) is created through the bookkeeping operations of banks when they credit customer accounts by extending loans or when they buy an asset such as a Treasury security. Banks creating deposits are concerned about the loss of reserves when customers draw on their deposits. They need to maintain a ratio of reserves to deposits sufficiently large to allow them to clear interbank transactions. An individual bank can replace lost reserves in numerous ways. Since the 1960s, the federal funds market has been the most important. To control the reserves creation of the banking system, the Fed must set its interest-rate target, which sets the marginal replacement cost of reserves for banks, in a way that controls credit creation by banks. Nothing changes in this respect with the payment by the Fed of interest on bank reserves, IOR. There remains an opportunity cost to the loss of reserves (the IOR).

With the funds rate equal to the natural rate of interest, money is not helicopter money (determined independently of real money demand). Assume, for example, that households desire to reduce their money holdings. They spend the excess money, and it passes to other parties. They also buy Treasury debt, which raises its price and lowers its yield. To preserve its interest-rate target, the Fed sells securities and extinguishes bank deposits. Households pay down bank debt and thus extinguish deposits.[7] However, if the central bank maintains the short-term real interest rate below the natural rate of interest, the resulting money creation is helicopter money. QE adds to the amount of helicopter money.

The payment of IOR complicates the story without altering any basic principles. What changes with IOR is that the Fed can make an open market purchase of, say, an MBS, which increases bank reserves, without reducing the funds rate. IOR effectively sterilizes the additional reserves by paying banks to hold them. IOR can give the central bank the character of a GSE (government-sponsored enterprise like Fannie Mae). To understand this point, assume that the FOMC follows a monetary policy that ensures price stability. The policy not only causes the interest rate to track the natural rate of interest, r^*, but also provides for a stable nominal anchor in the form of nominal expectational stability. Both real and nominal market interest rates are then equal to r^*.

Nominal money demand and the associated reserves demand are then

7. If the natural rate of interest and the yield on Treasury debt are all zero, there will still exist credit card debt, car loans, home equity lines of credit, etc., which pay positive interest. If a household pays down this debt, bank deposits and money are extinguished.

determined by the value of market interest rates and income. When the Fed uses an interest-rate instrument, commercial banks create the demandable deposits desired by the public. The New York Desk supplies the associated amount of reserves demanded by banks, Res*. Res* allows banks to clear the interbank-deposit flows associated with the payments made using bank demand deposits. It measures the reserves creation that the central bank needs to fulfill its responsibility as a central bank charged with price stability. Assuming the Fed creates the reserves demanded only through the purchase of Treasury bills, the Fed is engaged solely in monetary policy.

With IOR, the Fed can create additional reserves beyond Res* without lowering short-term interest rates below its interest-rate target, taken here as the benchmark natural rate, $r*$.[8] The reason is that the Fed sterilizes that additional reserves creation by paying banks interest on the reserves. Beyond the amount of reserves required to support the clearing of deposits associated with the nominal money stock, Res*, the reserves created by the purchase of assets, say, MBS, by the Fed are liabilities associated with financial intermediation. On the Fed's balance sheet, the MBS are assets, and the interest-bearing reserves of banks are liabilities.

To illustrate, consider figure 27.1 which displays the pre-IOR reserves market. With an amount of reserves consistent with the funds-rate target, Res*, the purchase of an MBS by the Fed causes the supply of reserves to exceed the amount of reserves associated with the funds-rate target and the funds rate falls below the target rate. The Fed must sell a Treasury security to restore the initial condition in the reserves market. Consider now the reserves market with IOR shown in figure 27.2. The Fed can buy MBS to provide for an amount of reserves greater than Res* without lowering the funds rate. Now, in contrast to the pre-IOR case, the public exchanges an MBS for additional bank deposits. However, those additional deposits are matched on the bank's balance sheet by additional excess reserves. There is no increase in financial intermediation—the transfer of real resources from households to investors. The increase in reserves from the MBS purchase,

8. The Fed introduced IOR in October 2008. The original purpose was not to turn the Fed into a financial intermediary. The "problem" was that programs established to lend to various segments of the financial system created reserves. The FOMC, still concerned with inflation, did not want markets to misinterpret the reduction in the funds rate due to this reserves creation as an easing of monetary policy (chap. 22).

In actual practice, IOR is an instrument used to control the targeted funds rate set by the FOMC. The reason for targeting the funds rate has to do with the political economy fact that the Board of Governors not the FOMC sets IOR. However, simplifying without any loss of insight, it is convenient to assume that the FOMC uses the IOR rate as its instrument. Based on the current and forecasted value of IOR, markets arbitrage other interest rates and transmit monetary policy.

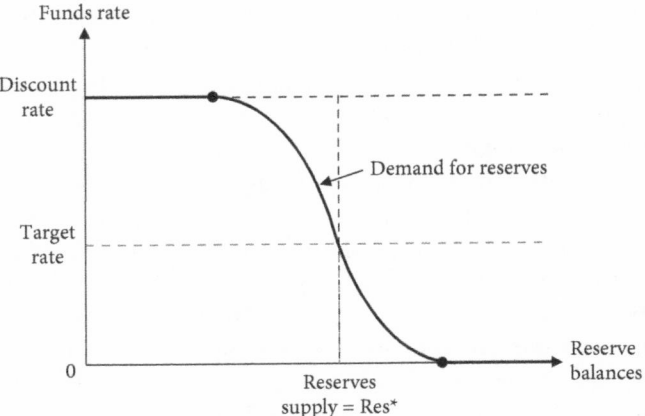

Figure 27.1. Market for Reserves without IOR
Diagram from Keister et al. (2008).

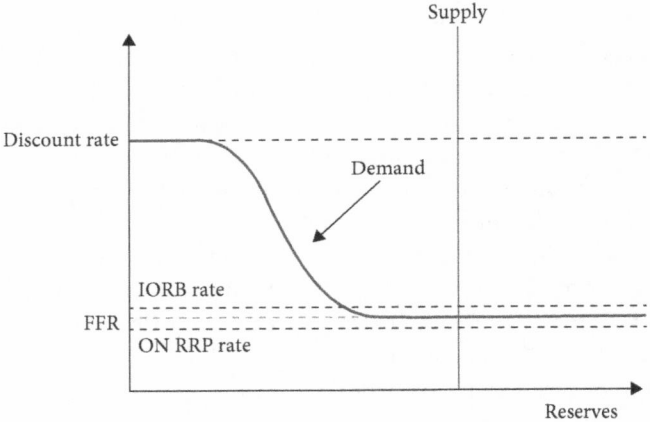

Figure 27.2. Market for Reserves with IOR (or IORB,
Interest Paid on Reserve Balances)
FFR is federal funds rate. ON RRP is overnight reverse repurchase rate. Diagram from Ihrig and Wolla (2020).

however, measures the extent to which IOR allows the Fed to engage in financial intermediation.

27.3. RESTORING MONEY AS AN INDICATOR

To prevent an uncontrolled surge in inflation, as argued here, the FOMC needs to unwind the bulge in M2 that arose starting in March 2020. It needs to follow some combination of raising the funds rate and reducing the size of its asset portfolio by selling Treasury securities and MBS. However, why should the FOMC use M2 as an indicator when it has lacked predictive power since 1980? The answer is that the reasons that money lost predictive power earlier do not hold in the special postpandemic situation. To explain, one must understand why money lost predictive power.

First, as explained in section 14.2, with passage of the Depository Institutions Deregulation and Monetary Control Act in 1980, real money demand became interest sensitive. M1 especially ceased to be useful as an indicator of the stance of monetary policy by moving countercyclically. When the economy weakens, money market interest rates decline. Banks, however, lower the interest rates they pay on deposits only with a lag. Consequently, funds from the money market flow into bank deposits. This reintermediation causes the monetary aggregates to grow. It would of course be a mistake for the Fed to raise the funds rate. (At a deeper level, the demand for liquidity by the public remained a stable function, but the measured monetary aggregates, M1 and M2, became defective measures of the amount of that liquidity.)

Second, especially in fall 2008, with the turmoil in financial markets, an increased demand for liquidity caused inflows into demand deposits that increased money without making monetary policy expansionary. Finally, as explained in section 27.2, when the Fed follows a rule that keeps the real rate of interest equal to the natural rate of interest, money is a veil. It has no independent predictive power.

27.4. CONCLUDING COMMENT

With the Volcker disinflation, with brief exceptions, monetary policy remained focused on restoring and then maintaining price stability. During the recovery from the Great Recession, the funds rate remained at the ZLB for seven years. The unemployment rate fell to 3.5 percent in February 2020 while inflation remained below the FOMC's 2 percent target (chap. 24). Based on these experiences, policy makers and markets forgot that sustained expansionary monetary policy causes inflation. At the onset of the Covid-19 crisis in March 2020, it was important for monetary policy to be expansionary to avoid deflation. Monetary stability, however, required that monetary policy cause the March 2020 bulge in money to unwind. If significant inflation does emerge, the country is unlikely to tolerate another recession to eliminate it. The United States will then be in danger of moving from a monetary environment of price stability to one of endemic inflation and price controls.

CHAPTER 28

Making the Monetary Standard Explicit

Summary: An enduring debate in monetary economics is the desirability of conducting monetary policy based on a rule as opposed to discretion.[1] In the traditional debate, a rule is associated with a formula for setting the central bank's instrument to ensure achievement of desirable long-run goals. Discretion is associated with a lack of discipline over time on the period-by-period choice of the central bank's instrument. The goal here is to formulate a rule based on the consistent (rule-like) behavior of the FOMC in the Volcker-Greenspan era of the Great Moderation.

With this era taken as a template, one can understand FOMC debate as organized around two forecasts: the behavior of inflation and the behavior of real GDP growth. The discipline this exercise imposes is that the FOMC communicates to financial markets a path for the funds rate that will make these forecasts compatible with its dual objective. First, forecasts of inflation should end with price stability (low, stable inflation). Second, forecasts of real GDP should end with a sustained zero output gap, that is, with output growing at potential. The FOMC makes these forecasts based on an implicit model that explains the relationship between inflation and real output.

The assumption here is that there exists considerable stability in the formulation of monetary policy. The proposal is to elucidate this rule-like behavior by requiring that the FOMC move to a committee SEP (Summary of Economic Projections) as opposed to the current collection of individual participant forecasts. This FOMC SEP would start with a Board staff forecast of inflation and output based on a model. The committee would choose the nature of the model and the reaction function used in the model forecast. The result would clarify the character of the monetary standard that the Fed has created. The resulting FOMC SEP would enable the FOMC chairs in their communications to place

---

1. This chapter is based on the author's papers "Rules vs. Discretion Revisited: A Proposal to Make the Strategy of Monetary Policy Transparent," Mercatus Working Paper, Mercatus Center at George Mason University, Arlington, VA, June 2019; and "A Rule to Preserve Monetary Stability," Mercatus Center Working Paper, Mercatus Center at George Mason University, Arlington, VA, October 2020.

FOMC actions in the context of a rule that imposes consistency over time in those actions.

The Federal Reserve System operates under a "dual mandate" from Congress to provide for stability in prices and maximum employment. Because the mandate is so general, it provides no guidance as to the actual monetary standard that policy makers have determined. The failure of policy makers to articulate the monetary standard means that it can evolve in unpredictable and disruptive ways. Moreover, it has been difficult to learn what sort of rule is stabilizing.

28.1. WHY THE FOMC COMMUNICATES THE WAY IT DOES

Proponents of a rule often want a numerical rule for determining monetary policy actions that eliminates all judgment. Such a rule is not feasible. FOMC decision-making is based on forecasts, and those forecasts inevitably involve judgment. The proposal here argues for using the FOMC's SEP forecasts to move toward rule-based decision-making. The change requires moving from an exercise based on forecasts of individuals to an exercise based on an FOMC forecast.

Regardless of the extent to which one can characterize FOMC decision-making as rule-like, the FOMC chair does not characterize it as such. To understand why, it is useful to note that the chair communicates on two channels: one to financial markets and one to Congress and the public. The way in which communication takes place depends on the channel. To markets, the FOMC communicates its view of the most likely path for the funds rate. Because that path is contingent on incoming information on the economy, the FOMC must also communicate an understanding of its strategy. Communication via the financial market channel takes place through the FOMC statement, minutes, and speeches. It requires inference about the systematic part of monetary policy strategy.

To understand FOMC communication to the Congress and the public, it is important to appreciate that the Fed is trapped in a bad political equilibrium. All monetary policy strategies since the Treasury-Fed Accord are based on the lean-against-the-wind (LAW) procedures initiated by FOMC chairman William McChesney Martin. With these procedures, in response to sustained growth in output above potential measured by increased rates of resource utilization (sustained declines in the unemployment rate), the FOMC raises the funds rate above its prevailing value in a measured, persistent way. Explicitness about LAW would limit the ability of the chairman to communicate through the public channel in a way that deflects populist attacks. Populist congressmen would claim that the Fed is controlling inflation "on the backs of the working man" by retarding the growth of the economy and raising unemployment. "Allowing the price system to work in an unfettered way by tracking the natural rate of interest" is hardly a cogent argument to a populist.

The language of discretion, in contrast, allows the chair to communicate policy in terms of the desirability of individual policy actions. An increase in the funds rate can be defended as acting against "inflationary pressures." Criticism of individual policy actions requires maintaining an ongoing knowledge of the economy that is possible only for full-time business economists or Fed staff. Politicians are immediately out of their depth in a debate over the economy. Ultimately, the issue is whether to trust open debate and the American political process.

To avoid communication that could be used to attack the Fed for raising unemployment to control inflation, the FOMC communicates its presumed successful pursuit of the dual mandate. This communication takes the form of long-run forecasts of the economy in which both objectives (price stability and maximum employment) are achieved. Shocks to unemployment and inflation arise externally. The FOMC then packages individual policy actions as optimal in the context of the contemporaneous behavior of the economy. The implicit assumption is that they concatenate to an optimal monetary policy strategy and successful fulfillment of the dual mandate.

The FOMC renders the two channels of communication compatible by lack of explicitness over its strategy. The chair controls the format of FOMC meetings to produce a monetary policy action combined with language in the statement, which, when followed over time, allows markets to infer the monetary policy strategy (reaction function or rule). However, nothing in the format of FOMC meetings or the resulting statement and minutes makes that strategy explicit. The format of FOMC meetings is not organized around a monetary policy strategy. FOMC chairmen impose the continuity required to implement the strategy through the way in which they control over time individual monetary policy actions. As a by-product of this format for FOMC meetings, the chairmen enhance their control over FOMC decision-making.

28.2. RULES VERSUS DISCRETION
AS SEEN BY A FED INSIDER

The summaries offered below of the speeches by Stanley Fischer appear to place him on both sides of the rules versus discretion debate.[2] The resolu-

2. Fischer was vice chair of the Board of Governors from May 2014 to October 2017. He had previously served as governor of the Bank of Israel from January 2005 to June 2013.

tion offered here for the apparent conundrum provides insight into how to place FOMC decision-making along a continuum running from discretion (judgment) to rules.

Fischer (2017b, 1) appeared to come down in favor of rules:

> It has been increasingly acknowledged that monetary policy implementation relies importantly on the management of market expectations. . . . Clarity about the central bank's reaction function . . . helps meet the central bank's policy targets, with the result that the markets are working in alignment with the policymaker's goals. . . . Clear communication of the Federal Open Market Committee's (FOMC's) views on the economic outlook and the likely evolution of policy is essential in managing the market's expectations.

The spirit of Fischer (2017b, 1) is that the FOMC should "avoid unintended surprises in the conduct of policy." That spirit argues for consistency in and explicitness about an FOMC strategy.

Fischer appeared to make the case for implementation of a policy based on rules when he talked about the Board of Governors' staff model, FRB/US. Fischer (2017a, 6–7) said:

> An increase in the federal funds rate affects expectations of future values of that rate, which in turn affect interest rates on longer-term bonds, equity prices, and the exchange value of the US dollar. Households and firms are forward looking. . . . [They] set out a plan—a contingency plan—for consumption, savings, and employment for the future. . . . So the expectations of decisionmakers, be they households, firms, or investors, are at the center of how monetary policy works—both in the real world and in FRB/US.

The FOMC must impose a consistency on its decision-making that causes the public to make forecasts of its future actions based on an explicit FOMC strategy. For financial markets, that consistency is a prerequisite for causing the term structure of interest rates to respond in a stabilizing way to incoming news about the economy.

In contrast, Fischer also discounted the use of models in favor of judgment. Fischer (2017a, 1) recounted how, when he was a student at the London School of Economics in the early 1960s, he believed that economists could construct econometric models that would "accurately predict the future course of the economy." Given their objectives, policy makers could use the model to solve for "the desired values of the target variables." He then added that "it has not yet happened."

In another venue, the Hoover Institution, Fischer (2017c, 1) gave a speech, "Committee Decisions and Monetary Policy Rules," that carried the message that the FOMC, at its meetings,

> should consult the prescriptions of policy rules, but . . . should avoid applying them mechanically. . . . Policymakers might have good reasons for deviating from these rule benchmarks [interest-rate rules]. . . . They could appropriately behave in ways that are not very well characterized by simple monetary policy rules.

Fischer (2017c, 3) cited commentary by Don Kohn (1999) to say that policy makers "do not see their past actions as a very firm guide to current or future policy."[3] Fischer drew the conclusion that "policymakers will from time to time change their assessment of what rule they regard as the appropriate benchmark." The thrust of Fischer's speech was that decision-making by committee is desirable but that it precludes use of a rule. Fischer (2017c, 4) argued that "committee decision-making is, on average, preferable to the use of a rule. . . . Adherence to a simple policy rule is not the most appropriate means of achieving macroeconomic goals."

Fischer (2017a, 3) asked the central question, "How does the FOMC choose its interest rate decision?" In response to his rhetorical question, Fischer (2017a, 4) responded that its members look at the prescriptions of rules and model simulations as inputs. "In reaching its decision, the Committee will examine the prescriptions of different monetary rules and the implications of different model simulations." However, Fischer did not address why such models would be useful in predicting the impact of the FOMC's decision. In the spirit of Lucas (1980 [1981]), to yield reliable forecasts, the FOMC must have articulated the rule embodied in the model and have committed to it so that it knows with certainty that the rule shapes the expectations of the "decisionmakers, be they households, firms, or investors."

Fischer's characterization of FOMC decision-making was that at each meeting members consider a variety of rules and model simulations, but then decide on a monetary policy action based on criteria unrelated to those rules and simulations. Fischer (2017c) left unanswered the question of how the FOMC fulfills the imperative stated in Fischer (2017a) and Lucas (1980 [1981]) of disciplining the expectations of the public. What imposes the required consistency to policy?

3. Donald Kohn was FOMC secretary from 1987 to 2002 and director of the Division of Monetary Affairs from 1987 to 2001. He became a member of the Board of Governors in 2002 and was vice chair from 2006 to 2010, when he retired from the Board.

A reading of FOMC transcripts suggests that policy makers do not make policy using an analytical framework. They make it judgmentally. There is no explicit framework to relate objectives to the instrument (the funds rate). FOMC participants believe they will make the right decision each period provided they have information on the near-term evolution of the economy. Models are useful only if they predict the near-term behavior of the economy. Meltzer's (2009, 82) assessment still holds: "In the 1950s, there was neither a common framework nor a common set of beliefs about monetary policy."

28.3. A CASE STUDY IN FOMC DECISION-MAKING: THE AUGUST 2011 MEETING

Governor Fischer used the August 2011 FOMC meeting as a case study in FOMC decision-making. As with other meetings, FOMC decision-making was not guided by a commonly accepted framework or model. The forecast by the staff of the Board of Governors contained in Tealbook Book A organized FOMC discussion.[4] The forecast is judgmental. The staff imposes consistency in the components of GDP through accounting identities, but the forecast does not come from a model. Tealbook Book B does contain model simulations and estimated policy rules like the Taylor rule that yield funds-rate forecasts. However, in the 162 pages of the FOMC transcript there were almost no references to these simulations or estimated policy rules.

From the June to the August Tealbook, predicted inflation for the year 2011 remained stable, going from 1.7 percent to 1.8 percent (personal consumption expenditures chain-weighted price index excluding food and energy). The key fact for the August 2011 meeting was the decline in forecasted real GDP growth from the June Tealbook. For the year 2011, predicted real GDP went from 2.7 percent to 1.8 percent while annualized real GDP growth predicted for 2011Q3 fell from 3.9 percent to 2.9 percent. As is generally the case, the change from one meeting to the next primarily reflected the incorporation of new data. The FOMC go-around on the economy started with a staff summary of the Tealbook Book A. David Wilcox (Board of Governors, *FOMC Transcript*, August 9, 2011, 17), director of the Division

4. Prior to FOMC meetings, the staff of the Board of Governors distributes briefing materials informally termed the "Tealbook": "Report to the FOMC on Economic Conditions and Monetary Policy." Forecasts of the economy are contained in the Tealbook part A (formerly called the Greenbook): "Book A—Economic and Financial Conditions: Current Situation and Outlook." Policy alternatives and simulations of the economy based on different rules are contained in the Tealbook part B (formerly called the Bluebook): "Book B—Monetary Policy: Strategies and Alternatives." They are available with a lag of five calendar years on the Board of Governors website.

of Research and Statistics, reported on "a seemingly unrelenting stream of negative news about the pace of the recovery that we received during the intermeeting period."

The Board staff estimated a growth gap of −0.3 percent: 1.8 percent minus 2.1 percent. The 1.8 percent figure is the predicted growth in real GDP for 2011, and the 2.1 percent figure is estimated potential growth for 2011 (Board of Governors, Tealbook Book A, 22, table "Decomposition of Potential GDP"). It would have been desirable for that figure to be positive given that the estimated output (GDP) gap was −6.0 percent. The estimated unemployment gap was 3.2 percent: 9.2 percent minus 6.0 percent. The 9.2 percent figure was the estimated unemployment rate for 2011Q3, and the 6.0 percent figure was the estimated NAIRU, or nonaccelerating inflation rate of unemployment, measuring full employment (the latter figures come from Board of Governors, Tealbook Book A, August 3, 2011, 101, table 3, "Other Macroeconomic Indicators").

As an indication of the difficulty of forecasting in real time, the Tealbook (Book A, August 11, 2011, 1) offered only conjectures for the halting recovery:

> The specific identity of the forces imposing greater-than-expected restraint on the expansion is not readily apparent. One possibility is that the shocks that have hit the economy are more severe and more persistent in their effects on aggregate demand than we previously recognized. Another possibility is that the self-equilibrating tendency of the economy has been greatly weakened by the damage resulting from the financial crisis. A third possibility is that the economic weakness reflects structural factors—and a lower path of potential GDP—to a greater degree than we had been assuming.

As illustrated by the decline in the forecasted value of real GDP for 2011 from 2.7 percent in the June 15, 2011, Tealbook to 1.8 percent in the August 3, 2011, Tealbook, forecasting even the near-term evolution of the economy is problematic (see figure 14.9).[5]

FOMC debate at the August 2011 meeting concentrated on the causes of the slowdown in the economy. The hawks argued that potential growth

5. Hetzel (2012b) used forecasts from the Tealbooks (formerly Greenbooks) from January 1980 through December 2005 and showed that, even for forecasts of GDP growth made in the last month of a quarter for the succeeding quarter, the accuracy of the forecasts was only slightly better than a simple extrapolation of past data. Simulations from the publicly available Federal Reserve System DSGE models always show a quick reversion to trend growth.

had also slowed. The growth gap therefore was zero. Jeffrey Lacker (Board of Governors, *FOMC Transcript*, August 9, 2011, 43), president of the Federal Reserve Bank of Richmond, argued that structural change in the labor market due to worker mismatch and a low probability of exiting long-term unemployment had raised the natural rate of unemployment. Charles Plosser (Board of Governors, *FOMC Transcript*, August 9, 2011, 53), president of the Federal Reserve Bank of Philadelphia, argued that recent downward revisions to GDP growth by the Bureau of Economic Analysis reflected a lower rate of growth of potential output. James Bullard (Board of Governors, *FOMC Transcript*, August 9, 2011, 57–58), president of the Federal Reserve Bank of St. Louis, argued that the promise of a low funds rate for a long time would cause markets to expect deflation. That expectation would raise the real rate of interest and make policy tighter. Narayana Kocherlakota (Board of Governors, *FOMC Transcript*, August 9, 2011, 59), president of the Federal Reserve Bank of Minneapolis, talked about an "erosion of skills . . . translating into a corrosive effect on the supply side of the economy."

Thomas Hoenig (Board of Governors, *FOMC Transcript*, August 9, 2011, 61), president of the Federal Reserve Bank of Kansas City, argued that "flooding more liquidity into the market" would not deal with the fundamental problem, which was the need for households to reduce debt burdens. Richard Fisher (Board of Governors, *FOMC Transcript*, August 9, 2011, 44, 116, 127), president of the Federal Reserve Bank of Dallas, contended that the slowdown in spending came from an undermining of confidence due to nonmonetary factors, namely, government negotiations over the debt ceiling. He argued that there was nothing the Fed could do to correct problems created by uncertainty over fiscal policy. Ultimately, presidents Fisher, Kocherlakota, and Plosser dissented. Lacker and Bullard were not voting members.

The doves prevailed. The FOMC consensus was that there existed a cyclically high negative output gap, which called for a positive growth gap. Sandra Pianalto (Board of Governors, *FOMC Transcript*, August 9, 2011, 123), Cleveland Fed president, summarized the supporting consensus forecast of how the economy would evolve with a lower expected funds-rate path. "If the FOMC was currently publishing the fed funds rate path that underlies our current economic projections, then the public would already know that we don't expect to raise the fed funds rate until about mid-2013, that we expect at that time the unemployment rate is going to be at 7½ percent, and that we anticipate having subdued inflation until mid-2013." William Dudley (Board of Governors, *FOMC Transcript*, August 9, 2011, 130), New York Fed president, concurred: "The Committee has a forecast. Now, people may disagree with the forecast, but is it unreasonable for the Committee to have a view, that the Committee, in its totality, today anticipates that this is what is likely?"

What can one conclude from this case study? There is no numerical rule or structural model of the economy that provides the FOMC with the actual-natural benchmarks for the growth gap and the output (unemployment) gap. There is a need for judgment in implementing the lean-against-the-wind procedures, which call for tightening in response to persistent above-trend growth in real output, and conversely for below-trend growth. The need to make decisions contemporaneously renders difficult the identification of persistent as opposed to transitory strength (weakness).

At the same time, the FOMC does arrive at a near-term forecast of the economy based on a consensus understanding of these guideposts. To arrive at a monetary policy action, the FOMC uses LAW rules of thumb, which rely on estimates of the strength of economic activity and the implications for the change in the rate of resource utilization. Although the starting point for discussion is the staff's judgmental forecast in the Tealbook Book A, the FOMC employs a myriad of pieces of information on the economy.

At the August 2011 meeting, the statement read, "The Committee decided today to keep the target range for the federal funds rate at 0 to ¼ percent. The Committee currently anticipates that economic conditions . . . are likely to warrant exceptionally low levels for the federal funds rate at least through mid-2013." The FOMC substituted "at least through mid-2013" for the prior in the June statement "for an extended period" (Board of Governors, *FOMC Transcript*, August 9, 2011). In reference to the language in the first two paragraphs of the statement, Chairman Bernanke (Board of Governors, *FOMC Transcript*, August 9, 2011, 87) stated, "Simply darkening our statement . . . and taking no action [would] have one big . . . disadvantage. The big disadvantage is that I think the markets and the economy would react very poorly to that. It seems as though the Fed is saying that the situation has gotten significantly worse, but we're not willing to do anything about it." Bernanke's recommendation reflected the "lean-against-the-wind" (LAW) tradition of William McChesney Martin.

The communication to financial markets occurs through the postmeeting statement.[6] The first paragraph summarizes the change in economic activity since the last meeting. The second paragraph provides the com-

---

6. The Tealbook Book B contains three alternatives, which span FOMC sentiment from dovish to hawkish as determined informally by the chair and the FOMC presidents before the FOMC meeting. Alternative B is the likely consensus statement in an approximate form. At the FOMC meeting, the chair adjusts the language in an attempt to avoid dissents.

mittee's near-term outlook for the economy. The next paragraph places the decision on the funds rate and its likely path in the context of the character-ization of the economy provided in the first two paragraphs. In August 2011, given the existing ZLB, the FOMC communicated its intention to imple-ment a lower funds-rate path not through a funds-rate reduction but instead through language indicating a longer period before liftoff of the funds rate from the ZLB (see figure 24.6). Markets infer the FOMC's reaction function by observing the consistency in FOMC behavior over time as registered in the statement.

Communication with financial markets requires an FOMC consensus and clarity about that consensus. The FOMC needs to reach a consensus so that the language of the statement and the public commentary of the chairman convey a clear message to financial markets. Using the example of the May 2013 taper tantrum in which bond rates rose when Chairman Bernanke mentioned phasing out the FOMC's policy of quantitative eas-ing, Fischer (2017b, 1–2) stressed how strongly the FOMC works to avoid "market surprises." Avoiding market surprises requires consistency in the FOMC's monetary policy strategy over time. Because the FOMC does not articulate that consistency as a rule, Fed watchers must infer it.

Policy has the spirit of "guess and then correct" as new information ar-rives. It entails a search procedure for the natural rate of interest. Although there is no numerical formula that reveals the natural rate to the FOMC or the associated actual-natural rate benchmarks for growth and the output gap, the search procedure imposes discipline and consistency. The issue then is to discover how to make that consistency and discipline explicit. The answer provided here is to adopt an FOMC Summary of Economic Projec-tions (SEP) based on an explicit reaction function.

28.4. USING THE SEP TO MOVE TOWARD RULE-BASED POLICY

The FOMC also uses the quarterly SEP exercise to communicate to finan-cial markets. It shows median values of the forecasts submitted by FOMC participants.[7] Forecasts comprise the four-quarter growth rate of real GDP ending in the fourth quarter, the fourth-quarter unemployment rate, and headline and core PCE inflation over the four-quarter interval ending in the fourth quarter. The so-called dot plot displays by year the individual

7. "Participants" are all the governors and regional Reserve Bank presidents while "members" are only those voting.

forecasts for the funds rate for the fourth quarter. Forecasts are for the contemporaneous year, for three additional years, and for a "longer run."

The SEP communicates to two different audiences. One audience is financial markets. Markets focus on median values under the assumption that they reflect the consensus view achieved by the FOMC chair. Markets are interested in the FOMC's estimate of the likely funds-rate path. They are also interested in how the path is likely to change in response to incoming information on the economy. The dot plot offers information on the estimate of the likely funds-rate path. Markets also watch how the quarterly changes in the economic forecasts affect this estimated path.

The other audience for the SEP is Congress. The SEP builds in the message that the FOMC is pursuing the dual mandate. As Fischer (2017a, 2) put it:

> [SEP] projections are based on each individual's assessment of appropriate monetary policy. Each FOMC participant writes down what he or she regards as the appropriate path for policy. They do not write down what they expect the Committee to do. . . . "Appropriate monetary policy" is Fedspeak for a policy that delivers on the Committee's interpretation of its legislated mandate. The fact that FOMC participants' forecasts are conditional on each participant's conception of the appropriate monetary policy . . . means that their forecasts will tend to converge over time to the Committee's 2 percent inflation objective and to each individual's interpretation of maximum employment.

As Fischer noted, the SEP records individual participants' forecasts based on an assumption of "appropriate monetary policy." Unfortunately, the term "appropriate monetary policy" is without content. Each participant simply choses a funds-rate path that makes his or her forecasts converge to the FOMC's inflation target and puts unemployment at its full-employment level. What model, if any, that conditions those forecasts is lost.

There is no way to separate the forecasts made by individual FOMC participants much less evaluate them for internal coherence. The individual forecasts are jumbled together as separate forecasts of real GDP, prices, the unemployment rate, and the funds rate. There is no identifiable, common set of conditioning variables (behavior of the exchange rate, stock market, etc.). There is no way to associate participants' funds-rate paths with their forecasts of the economy. Fed watchers cut through the disconnected mass of information presented in the SEP by looking at median values under the assumption that they portray the consensus views of the FOMC achieved by the chair.

Any meaningful reform of FOMC communication should start by making the SEP an FOMC forecast. An FOMC SEP would make explicit what the FOMC must do in any event, namely, reach a consensus on a funds-rate path and a consistent forecast of the near-term evolution of the economy that it can communicate to financial markets. However, at present, that consensus is only implicit. Also implicit is the underlying consistency the chair imposes on how the FOMC changes its projected funds-rate path in response to incoming information on the economy—the FOMC's reaction function.

What would be required to implement an FOMC SEP? At its initial meeting of the year, the FOMC would debate and presumably reaffirm its preferred reaction function. The first-difference rule shown in formula 28.1 is illustrative.[8]

$$(28.1) \ i_t = i_{t-1} + 0.5(\pi_{t+3|t} - \pi^*) + 0.5(y_{t+3|t} - y^*_{t+3|t}) + 0.5og_{t+3|t},$$

Where i_t is the funds rate for quarter t. $\pi_{t+3|t}$ is forecasted quarterly inflation three quarters ahead, and π^* is the inflation target. Quarterly real GDP and potential real GDP (in logarithms) are q_t and q^*_t, respectively. Quarterly annualized real GDP growth is $y_t = (q_t - q_{t-1}) \times 400$, and the potential growth counterpart is $y^*_t = (q^*_t - q^*_{t-1}) \times 400$. (The logarithmic differences are percentage changes.) $(y_{t+3|t} - y^*_{t+3|t})$ is forecasted three-quarters-ahead quarterly real GDP growth relative to potential growth. The output gap is $og_t = (q_t - q^*_t) \times 100$.

Formula 28.1 captures the FOMC's LAW procedures. The FOMC moves the funds rate relative to its current value to counter sustained changes in the economy's rate of resource utilization. That is, it moves the funds rate to maintain $(y_{t+3|t} - y^*_{t+3|t}) = 0$. Output cannot grow indefinitely above trend without raising inflation; conversely, output cannot grow indefinitely below trend without causing disinflation. The FOMC gauges expectations of inflation in bond markets to check that markets do not believe that it is "behind the curve."

Orphanides (2019, 26) estimated a reaction function like formula 28.1:

$$(28.2) \ i_t = i_{t-1} + 0.5(\pi_{t+3|t} - \pi^*) - (u_{t+3|t} - u_{t-1|t}).$$

The forecasted change in the unemployment rate, $(u_{t+3|t} - u_{t-1|t})$, captures whether the economy is growing faster or slower than potential, as mea-

8. It is from "Analysis of Policy Paths and Confidence Intervals" in Tealbook Book B, August 4, 2011, 43. For a discussion of the rule, see Orphanides (2003a). See also Orphanides (2001, 2002, 2003b, 2003c, and 2004a) and, especially for first-difference rules, Orphanides and Williams (2002).

sured by whether the rate of resource utilization in the labor market is declining or rising. As a proxy for the forecasted values, Orphanides used the Survey of Professional Forecasters (SPF) and, when it became available, the quarterly FOMC SEP forecasts. Orphanides (2019, 26) wrote:

> Evidently, even though the FOMC has not clearly articulated a policy strategy, its policy decisions can be broadly characterized with a simple and robust monetary policy rule that is based on participants' economic projections. Simple policy rules based on near-term projections of inflation and economic activity can serve as a useful tool to communicate the Federal Reserve's strategy and provide a rationale for policy decisions.

The terms in the reaction function shown in formula 28.1 are forecasts, not hard data. That fact reflects actual practice, which, in part, reflects lags in the availability of data. Forecasts also possesses the advantage that a forecast removes the idiosyncratic noise of the contemporaneous behavior of the economy. The issue is how to make the FOMC accountable for those forecasts through public scrutiny. The proposal here builds on that concern. At its first meeting of the year, FOMC participants would articulate a reaction function. For the remainder of the year, the Board of Governors staff would prepare their forecasts using that reaction function.[9] As at present, at quarterly meetings, the FOMC would release an SEP, but the SEP would be a consensus FOMC forecast. As essential background, the FOMC would also release the Tealbook Book A, containing the Board of Governors staff forecasts. At present, Tealbooks are released only with a lag of five calendar years.

As captured by formulas 28.1 and 28.2, the FOMC works off forecasts of the economy. There is no feasible way, however, that the nineteen participants sitting around the boardroom table in Washington could by themselves arrive at a consensus forecast of the economy. Necessarily, they start with and then modify the Tealbook forecast. In the case of the regional bank presidents, contacts in the business community furnish additional near-real-time information on the economy. Scrutiny of the consensus FOMC SEP forecast of the economy by outside observers, therefore, would neces-

---

9. Tealbook forecasts are judgmental. As at present, Board staff would base their initial forecast of the economy by starting with a funds-rate path decided on by senior staff. Using the resulting initial forecast of the economy, staff would calculate the funds-rate path based on formula 28.1. If, say, the funds-rate path calculated using the formula were to lie above the initial preliminary path, the staff would repeat the forecasting process imposing a somewhat lower growth rate for GDP and its constituent parts. Through an iterative process, the staff would arrive at a forecast for the economy and a path for the funds rate consistent with formula 28.1.

sarily start with the detailed base forecast in the Tealbook and then examine the plausibility of the FOMC's modification.

At the chair's press conferences with an SEP, both the consensus FOMC SEP and the Tealbook Book A with the staff forecast would be available. The FOMC forecast could be more optimistic or more pessimistic about the economy than the staff's forecast. The chair would explain differences between the FOMC's outlook and the Tealbook's outlook and the corresponding difference in the projected funds-rate path. Because the consensus FOMC SEP forecast presented by the chair would not be constrained by the reaction function in 28.1, the FOMC would not be strictly constrained to follow a rule but would possess room for judgment. However, the chair would discuss the funds-rate decision in the context of a rule.

The proposal for an FOMC SEP would allow the chair to talk about the strategy for monetary policy in terms of a reaction function. It would make available to the public the nature of the consistency already conveyed implicitly to financial markets. At the same time, the chair can treat the reaction function as a guidepost that yields a consistent strategy over time rather than a definitive numerical formula for the funds-rate target. Reasons for deviating from the reaction function could include unusual uncertainty over the international situation or turmoil in financial markets.

28.5. USING A MODEL TO EXPLAIN THE MONETARY STANDARD

When central banks make mistakes, the results are catastrophic. Significantly contractionary monetary policy brings down the world economy. Significantly expansionary monetary policy creates inflation. At the same time, monetary policy is effectively determined by a small number of individuals: the FOMC chair and vice chair, the vice chair of the Board of Governors, and typically a few forceful governors and regional Bank presidents. There is a need for more of a vetting of monetary policy—a vetting that needs to come from a more robust interaction between Fed policy makers and academics versed in monetary economics. The proposal here is that on a quarterly basis the Fed organize an exchange between key policy makers, obviously including the FOMC chair, and academic economists known for their work in monetary economics. For a useful exchange to occur, policy makers must communicate using the language of economics, that is, in terms of a model.[10]

---

10. As background for the academic economists, the FOMC should release transcripts of its meetings with a short lag, say, three months. At present, transcripts are released only with a lag of five calendar years.

At present, the Fed communicates only in general terms its objectives and its near-term forecasts of the economy. It does not communicate how its behavior translates into stabilizing behavior for the economy. Such communication requires a model that explains the relationship between the FOMC's response to the behavior of the economy (its rule) and the resulting behavior of the economy (summarized in the operation of the price system). In short, the Fed needs to communicate its understanding of the monetary standard that it has created. The following attempts to construct the implicit model underlying the monetary standard put in place formally with the Jackson Hole speech of Chair Powell (2020d). The contention here is that the model is Keynesian in spirit. If this characterization is correct, then an academic exchange could focus on why such a model failed in the 1970s and what is different in the pandemic period.

With the onset of the virus, employment (total nonfarm payroll) plummeted by 22.4 million from February 2020 to April 2020. Richard Clarida (Timiraos 2020), Board of Governors vice chair, interpreted the decline in employment as an aggregate-demand shock requiring an expansionary monetary policy: "I always thought if we got hit with a virus spread that it would, in net, be a shock to aggregate demand, and that's what I think it is." The resulting commitment to an expansionary monetary policy to stimulate aggregate demand came at a time of social tension encapsulated in the Black Lives Matter movement. A highly expansionary monetary policy, unseen since the 1970s, then occurred in the context of the establishment of a socially desirable low rate of unemployment as an objective on an equal footing with long-term inflation of 2 percent.

LHM (2021b) summarized remarks of Chair Powell (2021c):

> Powell gave remarks yesterday focused on disparities in economic circumstances across educational levels, racial groups, genders, and income levels. He said that "The Fed can contribute as well" to addressing these disparities through its monetary policy. He tied this objective to the design of the new framework: "We view maximum employment as a broad and inclusive goal. Those who have historically been left behind stand the best chance of prospering in a strong economy with plentiful job opportunities."

Comments by John Williams, president of the New York Fed, illustrate the Keynesian character of policy. The Fed controls inflation through its control over the amount of slack in the economy. With job loss above prepandemic levels, there is sufficient slack in the economy to prevent a sustained, high rate of inflation. Given significant slack, the inflation that does occur must be cost-push, reflecting relative price changes in particular markets, and, as such, must be transitory. Slack is defined by employment relative to a socially desirable low rate of unemployment. Implicitly, monetary policy needs to be expansionary because the price system by itself would work too slowly to restore full employment. Monetary policy works through its influence on financial intermediation.

J. C. Williams (2021) remarked:

> Let's not forget that there are about eight and a half million fewer jobs today [May 3, 2021] than before the pandemic. . . . This means we will need big jobs numbers for some time to fully get the country back to work. . . . The labor market indicator that gets the most media attention is the unemployment rate. But that statistic may not be the best measure of the overall health of the labor market because people who temporarily drop out of the labor force don't get counted as unemployed. . . . One measure that I find useful is the employment-to-population ratio, or "EPOP." . . . Before the pandemic, when the labor market was quite strong, EPOP was about 61 percent. . . . It's still more than three percentage points below pre-pandemic levels.
>
> Once the price reversals and short run imbalances from the economy reopening have played out, inflation will come back down to about 2% next year. . . . The data and conditions we are seeing now are not nearly enough for the FOMC to shift its monetary policy stance. . . .
>
> Maintaining very low interest rates serves two purposes. First, it makes it easier for households and businesses to meet their borrowing needs, for things like opening businesses and buying homes. Second, low interest rates foster broader financial conditions that help promote the rebound in spending and investment needed to return the economy to full strength.

Chair Powell (Board of Governors 2021, 6) commented:

> It seems unlikely frankly that we would see inflation moving up in a persistent way that would move inflation expectations up while there's still significant slack in the labor market. . . . It's much more likely that . . . having achieved maximum employment conditions we would also be seeing 2% inflation.

With a structural Phillips curve used as the construct for FOMC control of inflation, no FOMC participant ever mentions money. Friedman's (1963

[1968], 39) dictum "Inflation is always and everywhere a monetary phenomenon" never appears. Governor Quarles (2021, 8) commented:

> I am not worried about a return to the 1970s. We designed our new mon-
> etary policy framework for the very different world we live in now, which
> involves an equilibrium for the economy with slow workforce growth,
> lower potential growth, lower underlying inflation, and, therefore, lower
> interest rates. One of those differences is that the kinds of "wage-price
> spirals" that characterized inflation dynamics in the 1970s have not been
> present for a long time. It's quite possible that this situation now prevails
> because inflation is never high enough for long enough to enter decision
> making in a material way.

The analytical construct within which the FOMC conducted monetary
policy with the start of the pandemic may turn out to have been optimal.
The point here is that one must infer it. It is then extremely hard to learn
from experience because of the need to infer the monetary standard. The
FOMC should make it explicit and have a regular forum for debating it with
academic economists.

28.6. RULES, INDEPENDENCE, AND ACCOUNTABILITY

Central bankers emphasize the need for independence. Public support for
that independence rests on a sense of legitimacy, which in turns comes from
a belief that policy makers are accountable. For that to happen, there must
exist clarity about their objectives and their strategy for achieving those
objectives.

The Constitution of the United States assigns to Congress the power "to
coin money and regulate the value thereof." Originally, that meant the Congress could establish a mint that would provide dollars in specie in return
for a specified weight in gold or silver. That assignment of powers came out
of the British system of government in which Parliament had control of the
mint. In the United States, this assignment of powers ensures that Congress
retains control over fiscal policy through the control of the seigniorage that
comes from money creation.

Congress, however, lacks the capacity to direct the operation of monetary policy. It has delegated that responsibility to the Federal Reserve. At
the same time, it has also effectively delegated to the Fed the responsibility
for determining the nature of the monetary standard not just the responsibility to run it. This delegation is awesome, and debate over accountability
is natural. One proposal is to limit the regional character of the Fed either

by removing the regional Reserve Bank presidents from the FOMC or by requiring their appointment by the president. Given the short tenures of most governors and the four-year terms of the chair and vice chair of the Board of Governors, the practical result would be to increase the influence over monetary policy of the administration relative to Congress. To date, Congress has not removed the checks and balances of a regional system.

A long-standing proposal for reform is to require the formulation of monetary policy subject to an explicit rule. Fed spokespersons have protested that the rules proposed entail an arithmetical formula for the determination of the funds rate. They are correct in asserting that setting the funds rate involves ongoing judgment about the evolution of the economy. Forecasting the economy entails a process of trial and error with continual feedback from financial markets and incoming news about the economy. However, when successful, that process is disciplined by a fixed north star in terms of maintaining expected inflation equal to target and of maintaining growth of output along its potential path. The proposal here makes that discipline explicit and provides for the formulation of monetary policy in the spirit of a rule.

The proposed FOMC SEP would make monetary policy more transparent and would facilitate communication using the language of economics. The absence of clarity about the strategy of monetary policy obscures the nature of the monetary standard and its evolution over time. As a result, the FOMC possesses no systematic way to learn from historical experience. Bad outcomes can always be rationalized as due to a bad shock. Moreover, the absence of an intellectual consensus over the nature of the monetary standard makes the regime fragile. Given the vagaries of the political appointments process, there is little to ensure institutional continuity. Because Congress delegated responsibility for the design of the monetary standard to the Fed, the Fed has a responsibility to explain the nature of the standard it has created. To do so, it must communicate using the language of rules and economics.

The FOMC "Statement of Longer-Run Goals and Monetary Policy Strategy" includes the language: "The Committee seeks to explain its monetary policy decisions to the public as clearly as possible. Such clarity facilitates well-informed decision-making by households and businesses, reduces economic and financial uncertainty, increases the effectiveness of monetary policy, and enhances transparency and accountability, which are essential in a democratic society."[11] The most important step the FOMC could take

---

11. See Board of Governors, Monetary Policy, About the FOMC, FOMC Longer-Run Goals and Monetary Policy Strategy, https://www.federalreserve.gov/.

toward fulfillment of this statement of intent would be to move toward an explicit FOMC SEP.

The proposal here builds on existing practice. It is radical only in that it moves the FOMC toward greatly increased transparency and accountability. However, the additional explicitness is important. Monetary stability is the ultimate prize.

CHAPTER 29

What Is the Optimal Monetary Standard?

Summary: The New Keynesian (NK) model is the big-tent model used by macroeconomists. It is the starting point for clarifying one's views about how the world works but must be supplemented by empirical generalization. The assumption of rational expectations rules out monetary instability as a cause of real instability. All the agents (households, firms, and the central bank) know the structure of the economy. Because the central bank understands the structure of the economy, it will always implement a stabilizing monetary policy. Monetary policy can never cause a serious recession.

The version of the NK model consistent with the monetarist tradition is the Goodfriend and King (1997) version. In this version, price stickiness is the key friction. A policy of price stability then removes the friction, and the real business cycle core of the economy determines real variables. In this sense, the economy exhibits a "classical dichotomy" in that real variables are determined independently of the price level. A central bank with a target for price stability does not literally have a simple feedback rule with which it moves its instrument (the funds) rate in response to deviations of the price level from a fixed value. The basic NK model needs to be supplemented with the Aoki (2001) version containing a sticky-price sector and a flexible-price sector. Firms in the sticky-price sector are constrained to change prices only infrequently. Firms in the flexible-price sector operate in auction markets in which prices are determined continuously.

To allow the price system to determine relative prices, the central bank should control inflation in the sticky-price sector and allow inflation originating in the flexible-price sector to pass through to headline inflation. It can do so indirectly through a credible rule that conditions the price setting of firms in the sticky-price sector. The central bank then turns the determination of real variables over to the operation of the price system through procedures that cause the real funds rate to track the natural rate of interest, where the latter is the real interest rate (actual and expected) that maintains real aggregate demand equal to potential output (maintains the output gap equal to zero).

This monetary policy characterized the Volcker-Greenspan era. In that era, the discipline required to restore the nominal expectational stability lost in the stop-go era required abandonment of the prior activist aggregate-demand management policy in which the FOMC tried to balance off the two assumed competing goals of price stability and full employment. That discipline required the FOMC to follow a rule to restore nominal expectational stability while allowing the price system an unfettered ability to determine real variables like employment and output. The central bank controls trend inflation through a credible rule that causes firms in the sticky-price sector to coordinate on the same expectation of inflation in setting prices for multiple periods. The control of inflation then does not require that the FOMC exercise control over the real-nominal trade-offs summarized in Phillips curves.

The monetary standard explains how the actions of the central bank translate into the behavior of firms and households. To understand the nature of the monetary standard, one must explain how the central bank varies its instrument in response to incoming information on the economy given its objectives: the reaction function. One must then explain how the reaction function works to produce the desired collective behavior of firms and households given the structure of the economy.

In particular, the monetary standard elucidates the influence of the central bank over the nominal (dollar) expenditure of households and firms. That influence must be indirect rather than one of direct control. There is no wartime rationing or centralized control of production. There are no wartime price controls. The central bank does not directly control the nominal expenditure of agents and the price setting of firms. That is, it must work through the operation of the price system and through expectations of its (the central bank's) future behavior.

A monetary standard that provides for macroeconomic stability incorporates a rule that disciplines the consistency of the behavior of the central bank over time (its reaction function). Implicit in the choice of an optimal rule is an understanding of the structure of the economy. The monetarist-Keynesian debate advanced competing visions.

Monetarists placed monetary control at the center of central bank decision-making. The responsibility of the central bank is to discipline the bookkeeping operations of banks that create bank deposits (money). The implication of controlling something nominal rather than real is giving the price system an unfettered ability to work to control real variables. In contrast, Keynesians placed nominal-real trade-offs at the center of monetary policy. The responsibility of the central bank is to vary nominal expenditure to balance off competing goals between a real variable (unemployment) and a nominal variable (prices). The Phillips curve expresses the relevant trade-offs. Keynesians believed that the central bank should supersede the working of the price system to achieve a desirable balance between inflation and unemployment.

One needs a model to understand the monetary standard both in terms of how the actual standard has evolved over time and in terms of an optimal standard by which to assess the impact of the different actual standards. The big-tent model used by economists is the New Keynesian (NK) model. However, such models are completely general. The issue is how to choose between competing versions under the assumption that formal methods of estimation will fail to distinguish between alternative versions but rather will fit all versions to the same historical time series.

29.1. FROM MONETARISM TO THE "BASIC" NEW KEYNESIAN DSGE MODEL

Friedman (1960) is famous for his advocacy of a rule for steady money growth. What does the rule imply about a monetarist model of the economy? A core principle of monetarism is that the ideal monetary standard implements a "classical dichotomy." The central bank should provide a stable nominal anchor and then turn the determination of real variables over to the unfettered operation of the market economy. The price system works well to stabilize the economy provided the central bank operates with a rule that supplies a stable nominal anchor.

Friedman's steady-money-growth rule would provide a nominal anchor. At the time of its formulation, given the stability and interest insensitivity of real money demand and given steady growth in potential real output, the rule would have ensured steady trend growth in nominal expenditure and in inflation. That is, it would have supplied a stable nominal anchor. The rule would have turned over to the price system the sole determination of relative prices and real variables. The separation of the determination of relative prices from the behavior of the absolute price level has always been the desideratum of quantity theorists. Of course, controversy arose from the challenge by the Keynesian consensus that a free market economy was inherently unstable and left alone would yield long periods of unemployment above full employment.

Friedman proposed his rule as an alternative to Keynesian activist aggregate-demand management. With the latter, the Fed sets an explicit target for a macroeconomic variable and then uses a feedback rule to eliminate deviations of the variable from its targeted value. In the 1970s, although the FOMC never articulated explicit values for targets for unemployment and inflation, it understood policy as targeting the competing goals of price stability and full employment (4 percent unemployment) subject to the trade-offs embodied in the Phillips curve. Friedman illustrated his critique using an explicit value for a stable price level as the target variable. The critique later gained the moniker of "long and variable lags" (see Friedman 1960, 87–88, quoted in sec. 27.1).

The New Keynesian (NK) model as exposited by Goodfriend and King (1997) makes price-level stability optimal. This version embodies the "classical dichotomy" advanced by monetarists. It will, however, be necessary to explain how the FOMC can implement a rule that provides for price-level stability without running afoul of the Friedman long-and-variable-lags critique.

29.2. THE NK MODEL

Understanding the monetary standard requires a model to separate causation from correlation. That is, a model is about identification. A model organizes variables into those that are endogenously determined as part of the working of the price system and those that are exogenously determined outside of it. One of the great intellectual achievements of modern macroeconomics is the DSGE (dynamic, stochastic, general equilibrium model) model. Such models with their forward-looking agents are ideal for studying monetary economics. One reason is that money possesses value in exchange because people expect it to possess value in the future.

At the same time, NK models are completely general. An NK model is not identified in that one can take it to the data and reject it or evaluate it relative to other models. All models fit the data in the sense of explaining the historical time series. The model builder (the econometrician) chooses equations with an eye to the data. For consumption, there is habit persistence, for investment there is time to build, for inflation there are rule-of-thumb price setters, and so on. Most important, each sector of a DSGE model comes with its own shock, and there will always be some constellation of shocks that will make the model explain the historical time series. An illustration used by Chari, Kehoe, and McGrattan (2009) is that the Great Contraction, from 1929 to 1933, can be explained equally well in DSGE models by an increased preference for leisure or by increased monopoly power of wage setters (unions). In the absence of a supportive narrative (increased demand for resorts or increased unionization), they regard neither explanation as credible.

Moreover, the reaction functions chosen for the central bank by the econometricians who construct models are reduced forms not structural equations. The reactions functions assume a knowledge of the structure of the economy not possessed by policy makers. In real time, policy makers do not know the output gap. They do not know the values of any natural variables, that is, the market-determined values of real variables in the absence of nominal price rigidities. By default, in actual practice, a central bank reaction function must constitute a search procedure to discover the natural rate of interest.

One way to choose between versions of the NK model is to determine which one is most useful in organizing a historical narrative explaining when the behavior of the central bank has been stabilizing and when it has been destabilizing. A historical narrative imposes a discipline that shocks cannot be completely ad hoc but must accord with a variety of information contemporaneously available. The version of the NK model exposited by Goodfriend and King (1997) usefully organizes a monetarist narrative. It supports the monetarist hypothesis that the optimal rule is one in which the central bank implements the classical dichotomy by maintaining a stable nominal anchor in the form of the expectation of price stability and then by allowing the price system an unfettered ability to work to determine real variables.

In the Goodfriend-King version of the NK model, there exists only one nominal friction. Namely, firms can reset dollar prices only at infrequent intervals. If the central bank follows a rule that implements price stability, it neutralizes the friction. As shown in equation 29.3 in footnote 1, with actual and expected inflation equal to zero, the output gap, which is the difference between actual and potential output, is zero.[1] Relative prices and real variables then are determined solely by the real business cycle core of the economy. The term "classical dichotomy" refers to this characteristic of the model. The empirical assumption that the price system works well to

---

1. The exposition here uses the notation in Barsky et al. (2014). The real rate of interest, r_t, is $r_t = i_t - E_t\pi_{t+1}$, where i_t is the market rate of interest and $E_t\pi_{t+1}$ is expected inflation. The natural rate of interest, r_t^n, equals equation 29.1,

$$(29.1)\ r_t^n = \rho_t + s^{-1}E_t(\Delta y_{t+1}^n),$$

where y_t^n is the natural rate of output, ρ_t is the subjective rate of time preference, s is the intertemporal elasticity of substitution in consumption, and Δ is a first-difference operator. The output gap equals $\tilde{y}_t \equiv y_t - y_t^n$. y_t is real output with the variables expressed as logarithms. Using equation 29.1 and its counterpart for actual real values and solving forward yields equation 29.2:

$$(29.2)\ \tilde{y}_t = -s\Sigma_{k=0}^{\infty}E_t(r_{t+k} - r_{t+k}^n).$$

That is, the output gap equals the sum of future interest-rate gaps. Finally, equation 29.3 expresses the NK Phillips curve:

$$(29.3)\ \pi_t = \beta E_t[\pi_{t+1}] + k\tilde{y}_t.$$

mitigate the impact of real shocks on the output gap given such a rule makes the model monetarist in spirit.

As shown in equation 29.2 of footnote 1, a rule that maintains the output gap equal to zero through price stability is equivalent to a rule that maintains actual and expected real rates of interest equal to their natural counterparts. As Barsky et al. (2014, 38) noted, "[An] interest rate path in which the actual real rate is always equal to the natural rate achieves both an output gap of zero . . . and zero inflation." Because the Fed does not literally target a constant price level, one must explain when its procedures do and do not work to track the natural rate of interest. Since the 1951 Treasury-Fed Accord, the Fed has followed lean-against-the-wind (LAW) procedures (chap. 14). Giving empirical content to the Barsky et al. statement therefore requires an empirical generalization identifying a baseline LAW procedure that is consistent with economic stability and that flags departures from the baseline that predict instability. When do LAW procedures track the natural rate of interest, and when do they fail? Addressing this question explains how the Fed can pursue the goal of price stability while avoiding Friedman's long-and-variable-lag critique.

29.3. LAW WITH CREDIBILITY AND LAW WITH TRADE-OFFS (CYCLICAL INERTIA)

Formula 29.4, which reproduces formula 28.1 in sec. 28.4, serves as a benchmark for the FOMC's LAW procedures. They can be understood as a search procedure for discovering the natural rate of interest (chap. 14):

$$(29.4)\ i_t = i_{t-1} + 0.5(\pi_{t+3|t} - \pi^*) + 0.5(y_{t+3|t} - y^*_{t+3|t}) + 0.5og_{t+3|t}.$$

As expressed in formula 29.4, with LAW, the FOMC moves the funds rate relative to its current value to counter sustained changes in the economy's rate of resource utilization. It moves the funds rate to maintain $(y_{t+3|t} - y^*_{t+3|t}) = 0$. Sustained changes in rates of resource utilization indicate a real interest rate that differs from the natural rate of interest. Output cannot grow indefinitely above trend without raising inflation; conversely, output cannot grow indefinitely below trend without causing disinflation. Translating that assumption into practice leads to two different versions of LAW: LAW with credibility and LAW with trade-offs (chap. 14). These different versions form the basis for the identification scheme used to determine when FOMC procedures are stabilizing (track the natural rate of interest) and destabilizing (fail to track the natural rate of interest).

Consider how LAW with credibility works in practice starting from the trough of a recession. When the FOMC feels assured that the recovery is sustainable, that is, the second right-hand term in formula 29.4, $(y_{t+3|t} - y^*_{t+3|t})$ > 0 will remain positive despite measured, persistent increases in the funds rate, it begins to raise its funds-rate target. In the background, the FOMC has an estimate of the magnitude of the output gap, og_t, but measured only with great imprecision. As the recovery proceeds and when the FOMC sees signs of stress on rates of resource utilization, especially overheating in the labor market, it forecasts inflation, that is, $(\pi_{t+3|t} - \pi^*)$ > 0. With both terms in formula 29.4 positive, the FOMC raises the funds rate in a decided way to avoid the actual realization of inflation. The intention is to achieve a glide path that causes real output to move to potential without an overshoot and then for output to grow at potential.

In the contrasting monetary standard, the FOMC believes that it can manage inflation-output trade-offs. In practice, LAW with trade-offs is the equivalent of LAW with cyclical inertia in the funds-rate target. In an economic recovery, the FOMC's behavior is different in response to signs of stress on rates of resource utilization. Now, the FOMC acts not based on forecasts of inflation but rather based on actual inflation. During economic recovery, the predominant concern is with raising the funds rate too strongly and slowing the recovery before attaining full employment (the go phases). The FOMC becomes willing to raise the funds rate significantly only with the actual appearance of inflation.

The FOMC then raises the funds rate until recession develops (the stop phases). Out of fear of sending the wrong signal about the inflation rate it would tolerate and thus risking a permanent rise in expected inflation, the FOMC lowers the funds rate only when a serious recession becomes evident. The narrative here associates LAW with credibility with the Volcker-Greenspan era known as the Great Moderation. It associates LAW with trade-offs with the stop-go era when the FOMC attempted to balance off objectives for inflation and an output gap.

Lean-against-the-wind with credibility emerged during the Volcker-Greenspan era. The objective of policy changed to maintaining low, stable expected inflation—that is, to the restoration of the nominal expectational stability lost with the prior stop-go monetary policy. LAW with credibility imposed two kinds of discipline. The first came from the need to eliminate the market's association between cyclical strength in the economy and the later emergence of inflation. To eliminate this association, the FOMC had to remove from its interest-rate target the cyclical inertia that had characterized the earlier period. The second kind of discipline came from the need to eliminate the extrapolation by financial markets of actual inflation to expected inflation. The FOMC moved therefore to a policy of preemptive funds rate increases so that the inflation did not emerge. During economic recoveries, it raised rates in response to cyclically tight labor markets, treating them as a harbinger of inflation and a disappearing negative output gap.

29.4. THE OPTIMAL RULE

The optimal monetarist rule is that the FOMC should provide a stable nominal anchor and allow markets complete freedom to determine real variables like unemployment. To understand why the FOMC can treat the inflation and output terms in formula 29.4 as determined independently, it is useful to supplement the basic NK model as exposited by Goodfriend and King (1997) with the Aoki (2001) version containing a sticky-price sector and a flexible-price sector. Firms in the sticky-price sector are constrained to change prices only infrequently. Firms in the flexible-price sector operate in auction markets in which prices are determined continuously. To allow the price system to determine relative prices, the central bank should focus on inflation in the sticky-price sector and allow inflation originating in the flexible-price sector to pass through to headline inflation.

The central bank does not trade off between inflation and output (unemployment) gaps. In this Goodfriend-King/Aoki world, the optimal rule provides a stable nominal anchor in the form of nominal expectational stability and then allows the price system complete freedom to determine real variables—a classical dichotomy. It turns the determination of real variables over to the unfettered operation of the price system through procedures that cause the real funds rate to track the natural rate of interest, where the latter is the real interest rate (actual and expected) that maintains real aggregate demand equal to potential output (the output gap equal to zero). In this way, LAW with credibility avoids the Friedman long-and-variable-lags critique. Because the rule causes the real funds rate to track the natural rate, it does not introduce monetary policy actions as a distinct source of disruption to the operation of the price system.

In this monetary standard, the FOMC controls trend inflation through its control of the difference between nominal and real expenditure. The price system determines real expenditure. The FOMC controls trend inflation through a credible rule that causes firms in the sticky-price sector to coordinate on the same expectation of inflation in setting prices for multiple periods. Nominal expenditure is determined as the sum of real expenditure and the inflation set by this expectation (plus the noise in the inflation series). The control of inflation does not require that the FOMC exercise control over the real-nominal trade-offs summarized in Phillips curves.

With the classical-dichotomy version of the NK model, monetary stability eliminates the correlations of the Phillips curve. The revision to the FOMC's Statement on Longer-Run Goals and Monetary Policy Strategy announced August 27, 2020 by Chair Powell however, made a flat Phillips curve a key element of FOMC strategy.[2] The FOMC interpreted the decline in unemployment without a corresponding increase in inflation in the recovery from the Great Recession as evidence of a flat Phillips curve with an upward sloping section starting at a historically low unemployment rate. The issue is whether the correlations expressed in such a Phillips curve are structural. That is, do they represent a relationship between unemployment and inflation that the policy maker can use as the basis for a controllable and predictable trade-off between the two variables?

The alternative to a flat Phillips curve as an explanation for the disappearance of a predictable relationship between falling unemployment and rising inflation is that monetary instability produced the correlations formerly observed in the data (Friedman 1968 [1969]). A policy of price stability removed those correlations. Atkeson and Ohanian (2001) made this point when they observed that lagged inflation did a better job of predicting inflation than did Phillips curves, which include resource slack as an explanatory variable. In terms of the Lucas (1976 [1981]) critique, the empirical correlations captured by Phillips curves are a reduced form that depends on the behavior of monetary policy. The disappearance of an upward sloping Phillips curve emerged from the monetary policy pursued in the period known as the Great Moderation.

Robert Lucas (2007, 92) expressed the idea:

> We now understand that there is no tradeoff [between inflation and employment] and periods of price stability are not periods of high unemployment or low growth. There is no systematic connection between these two variables. So when it comes down to the central bank, central bankers can and should be and mostly are focusing on the control of inflation. That is their job. That is their only job.

In terms of the classical-dichotomy New Keynesian model, in the Great Moderation, the nominal expectational stability that stabilized inflation in the sticky-price sector meant that the real sector would operate based on the real business cycle core of the economy. The prior relationship between inflation and unemployment would disappear. That changing relationship did not reflect an evolving economy but rather an evolving monetary policy.

2. See Board of Governors, Monetary Policy, About the FOMC, FOMC Longer-Run Goals and Monetary Policy Strategy, https://www.federalreserve.gov/.

29.5. MONEY AND THE NK MODEL

In the New Keynesian model, money is a veil. With the assumption of rational expectations, households, firms, and the central bank understand the structure of the economy and know the natural values of real variables. With these assumptions, the central bank will follow a rule that causes the real rate of interest to track the natural rate of interest. Excess demand in the goods market will not depart from zero, and consequently excess demands in the bond market and in the market for the quantity of money will be negligible. One can ignore these markets. It follows that the NK model by itself cannot explain serious monetary disturbances. To explain phenomena like the Great Depression and the Great Inflation, it is necessary to resort to the earlier monetarist literature, for example, Friedman and Schwartz (1963a and 1963b) and Poole (1978).

29.6. CONCLUDING COMMENT

The New Keynesian (NK) model is the big-tent model used by macroeconomists today. It is the starting point for clarifying one's views about how the world works but must be supplemented by empirical generalization. The reason is that the assumption of rational expectations rules out monetary instability as a cause of real instability. All the agents (households, firms, and the central bank) know the structure of the economy. The result is built in that money is basically a veil.

A central bank with a target for price stability does not literally have a simple feedback rule with which it moves its instrument (the funds) rate in response to deviations of the price level from a fixed value. The basic NK model needs to be supplemented with the Aoki (2001) version containing a sticky-price sector and a flexible-price sector. To allow the price system to determine relative prices, the central bank should control inflation in the sticky-price sector and allow inflation originating in the flexible-price sector to pass through to headline inflation. It can exercise this control indirectly through a credible rule that conditions the price setting of firms in the sticky-price sector. The central bank then turns the determination of real variables over to the unfettered operation of the price system through procedures that cause the real funds rate to track the natural rate of interest, where the latter is the real interest rate (actual and expected) that maintains real aggregate demand equal to potential output (maintains the output gap equal to zero).

Lean-against-the-wind with credibility characterized the Volcker-

Greenspan era. In that era, the discipline required to restore nominal expectational stability lost in the prior era required abandonment of the policy of activist aggregate-demand management in which the FOMC tried
to balance off the two assumed competing goals of price stability and full
employment. That discipline required the FOMC to follow a rule to restore
nominal expectational stability while allowing the price system complete
freedom to determine real variables like employment and output. The
FOMC controls trend inflation through a credible rule that causes firms in
the sticky-price sector to coordinate on the same expectation of inflation
in setting prices for multiple periods. Trend inflation emerges as the difference between nominal and real expenditure while the price system determines real expenditure. The control of inflation then does not require that
the FOMC exercise control over the real-nominal trade-offs summarized in
Phillips curves.

CHAPTER 30

Why Is Learning So Hard?

Central banks possess no institutional procedures for systematic learning from past experience. Learning requires that central banks admit that they make mistakes and that they can learn from those mistakes. Such an admission would lessen the cost of populist attacks and does not happen. Furthermore, to a significant extent, the academic literature has shifted away from examination of monetary policy. As a result, despite accumulated historical experience, there is no accumulation of accepted knowledge about what constitutes stabilizing (or destabilizing) monetary policy. There is no generally accepted body of tested hypotheses applicable to the design of the optimal monetary standard. What role does the Fed play in the determination of aggregate nominal demand (spending)? What is the optimal monetary policy for controlling inflation? What role, if any, does money play in the transmission of monetary policy? These questions are as contentious in 2021 as they were during the 1960s–70s monetarist-Keynesian debate.

In monetary economics, the main impediment to learning is the absence of the controlled experiments available in much of the sciences. For this reason, it is inherently hard to disentangle causation from correlation. Inevitably, any one episode of economic instability will possess multiple plausible explanations. The approach in this book generalizes the Friedman and Schwartz (1963a) approach. For recessions, they documented the empirical regularity that monetary decelerations preceded business cycle peaks. They then documented information specific to the episodes that provided information about the direction of causation, namely, the motivation behind the behavior of the Fed. A concatenation of episodes of recession should reveal a persistence for a particular candidate for a causal factor not evident in alternative candidates. For example, one can run a horse race between monetary deceleration and fiscal retrenchment as the most persistent feature across recessions.

Because of the instability in real money demand that developed in the 1980s, money no longer serves as a useful measure of the impact of monetary policy on aggregate demand. The approach here expands the work of Friedman and Schwartz beyond money. It treats recessions as a control group and periods of economic stability as a comparison group. The generalization that emerges, entitled the monetary contraction marker (chap. 3), is the cyclical behavior of the short-term interest rate controlled by the Fed. Prior to a business cycle peak, as the economy weakens, the Fed prevents a decline in its policy instrument—a short-term interest rate. The reasons it has done so derive from a concern for a level of expected inflation considered undesirably elevated, concern for presumed speculation, or concern for weakness in the foreign exchange value of the dollar. Finally, a model puts the generalizations into a form that is useful for forecasting, that is, for generating testable hypotheses capable of being refuted by data not available at present.

The Fed has provided striking semicontrolled experiments in the form of different monetary policies. A major example is the contrast between pre–World War II and post–Treasury-Fed Accord policies. Prewar monetary policy derived from the belief that recession and deflation occur because of the collapse of speculative excess. The organizing principle of the Fed was to restrict the extension of credit to "real bills" (short-term commercial paper). Presumably, investment would then be limited to "legitimate" (productive) uses rather than to the speculative uses presumed to cause the boom-bust cycles inherent in a capitalist society. Real bills would tame the "animal spirits" of investors.

In the post-Accord period, lean-against-the-wind replaced real bills. With the latter policy, the Fed moved short-term interest rates in a way that offset sustained weakness or strength in the real economy. In terms of a model, this policy did a better job of allowing the price system to work to stabilize economic activity.

Another major example occurred with the policy of activist aggregate-demand policy in the 1970s. Premised on the need to provide a socially desirable low rate of unemployment taken to be at least as low as 4 percent and premised on the assumption that inflation was due to cost-push pressures, the Fed followed a policy of attempting to trade off between its goals of price stability and low unemployment, subject to the assumed constraint of the Phillips curve. In the post-Volcker disinflation, the Volcker-Greenspan era, the overriding desire to reestablish a stable nominal anchor led to the abandonment of the policy of activist aggregate-demand management. Abandonment of any attempt to exploit a Phillips curve trade-off required a policy of preemptive changes in the funds rate to stabilize inflationary expectations and then to preserve relative price stability. The result was the Great Moderation.

Each recession and each inflation constitutes a semicontrolled experiment within the major experiments just described. Given the accumulation of such episodes over time, why has not monetary economics built up a consensus over what causes real and nominal instability and accordingly a consensus over the optimal monetary standard? The reason is that expositions of models, for example, as in Gali (2008), do not come with a standard, widely accepted list of the semicontrolled experiments delivered by central banks. Through their use of the language of discretion, central banks make such identification difficult and contentious. Knowledge does not accumulate over time. Models then remain general and incapable of discrimination among different hypotheses about the causes of economic instability. Hopefully, this book will help to organize the historical experience that models need to explain.

Acknowledgments

The author benefited from the environment of free debate at the Richmond Fed created by its presidents: Robert Black, Al Broaddus, and Jeffrey Lacker.

Bibliography

Speeches of governors of the Federal Reserve System can be found on the Board of Governors website, federalreserve.gov.

Aastrup, Morten, and Henril Jensen. 2010. "What Drives the European Central Bank's Interest-Rate Changes?" University of Copenhagen. CEPR Discussion Paper 8160.

Acharya, Viral V., and Sascha Steffen. 2020. "The Risk of Being a Fallen Angel and the Corporate Dash for Cash in the Midst of Covid." NBER Working Paper Series WP 27601. July.

Ackley, Gardner. 1961. *Macroeconomic Theory*. New York: Macmillan.

Ahearn, Daniel S. 1963. *Federal Reserve Policy Reappraised, 1951–1959*. New York: Columbia University Press.

Alacevich, Michele, Pier Francesco Asso, and Sebatiano Nerozzi. 2015. "Harvard Meets the Crisis: The Monetary Theory and Policy of Lauchlin B. Currie, Jacob Viner, John H. Williams, and Harry D. White." *Journal of the History of Economic Thought* 37, no. 3 (September): 387–409.

Aldrich, Wilbur. 1903. *Money and Credit*. New York: Grafton.

American Presidency Project. 1837. "Jackson's Farewell Address." University of California, Santa Barbara. https://www.presidency.ucsb.edu/documents/farewell-address-0.

Anderson, Benjamin M., Jr. 1924. "Cheap Money, Gold, and Federal Reserve Policy." *Chase Economic Bulletin* 4 (August 4): 3–26.

———. 1929. "Should Reserve Board Control Speculation? Yes!" *Bankers Magazine*, May, 710–35.

———. 1931. "Equilibrium Creates Purchasing Power." *Chase Economic Bulletin* 11 (June 12): 3–16.

Anderson, Richard G., Robert H. Rasche, and Jeffrey Loesel. 2003. "A Reconstruction of the Federal Reserve Bank of St. Louis Adjusted Monetary Base and Reserves." *Federal Reserve Bank of St. Louis Review*, September/October, 39–69.

Andrews, Edmund L. 2009. "Bank Crisis Deepens." *New York Times*, January 29, https://www.nytimes.com/2008/09/17/business/17insure.html.

Andrews, Edmund L., Michael J. de la Merced, and Mary Williams Walsh. 2008. "Fed's $85 Billion Loan Rescues Insurer." *New York Times*, September 16.

Angell, James W., and Karel F. Ficek. 1933. "The Expansion of Bank Credit: II." *Journal of Political Economy* 41, no. 2 (April): 152–93.

Aoki, Kosuke. 2001. "Optimal Monetary Policy Responses to Relative-Price Changes." *Journal of Monetary Economics* 48:55–80.

AP News. 2020. "Negotiators Close on a Nearly $2 Trillion Virus Aid Package." March 24.

Ashcraft, Adam, Morten L. Bech, and W. Scott Frame. 2010. "The Federal Home Loan Bank System: The Lender of Next to Last Resort." *Journal of Money Credit and Banking* 42, no. 4 (June): 551–83.

Atkeson, Andrew, and Lee E. Ohanian. 2001. "Are Phillips Curves Useful for Forecasting Inflation?" Federal Reserve Bank of Minneapolis *Quarterly Review*, Winter, 2–11.

Axilrod, Stephen H. 1971. "The FOMC Directive as Structured in the Late 1960s: Theory and Appraisal." In Board of Governors of the Federal Reserve System, *Open Market Policies and Operating Procedures—Staff Studies*, July, 3–36.

Baer, Justin. 2020. "The Day Coronavirus Nearly Broke the Financial Markets." *Wall Street Journal*, May 20, https://www.wsj.com/articles/the-day-coronavirus-nearly-broke-the-financial-markets-11589982288.

Bagehot, Walter. 1873. *Lombard Street: A Description of the Money Market*. London: Henry S. King. Reprint: Edited by F. C. Genovese. Homewood, IL: Richard D. Irwin.

Bair, Sheila. 2012. *Bull by the Horns*. New York: Simon and Schuster Paperbacks.

Balke, Nathan S., and Robert J. Gordon. 1986. "Appendix B: Historical Data." In *The American Business Cycle: Continuity and Change*, edited by Robert J. Gordon, 781–810. Chicago: University of Chicago Press.

Ball, Laurence M. 2018. *The Fed and Lehman Brothers: Setting the Record Straight on a Financial Disaster*. New York: Cambridge University Press.

Ball, Laurence, and Sandeep Mazumder. 2015. "A Phillips Curve with Anchored Expectations and Short-Term Unemployment." International Monetary Fund Working Paper WP/15/39. February.

Barrack, Thomas J. 2020. "Preventing Covid-19 from Infecting the Commercial Mortgage Market." *Medium*, March 22, 2020. https://medium.com/@tombarrackjr/preventing-covid-19-from-infecting-the-commercial-mortgage-market-e7444701745e.

Barsky, Robert B., Alejandro Justiniano, and Leonardo Melosi. 2014. "The Natural Rate of Interest and Its Usefulness for Monetary Policy." *American Economic Review*: *Papers and Proceedings* 104 (May): 37–43.

Batchelder, Ronald W., and David Glasner. 1991. "Pre-Keynesian Monetary Theories of the Great Depression: What Ever Happened to Hawtrey and Cassel?" University of California, Los Angeles, Working Paper 626. August.

Bennett, Barbara A. 1982. "'Shift Adjustments' to the Monetary Aggregates." *Federal Reserve Bank of San Francisco Economic Review*, Spring, 6–18.

Bernanke, Ben S. 1983. "Nonmonetary Effects of the Financial Crisis in the Propagation of the Great Depression." *American Economic Review* 73 (June): 257–76.

———. 2002a. "On Milton Friedman's Ninetieth Birthday." Remarks at the Conference to Honor Milton Friedman, University of Chicago, November 8. Federal Reserve Board website.

———. 2002b. "Deflation: Making Sure 'It' Doesn't Happen Here." Remarks before the National Economics Club, Washington, DC, November 21. Federal Reserve Board website.

———. 2003. "An Unwelcome Fall in Inflation?" Remarks before the Economics Roundtable, University of California, San Diego, La Jolla, CA, July 23. Federal Reserve Board website.

————. 2005. "Implementing Monetary Policy." Redefining Investment Strategy Education Symposium, Dayton, OH, March 10. Federal Reserve Board website.

————. 2007. Interview in Randall E. Parker, *The Economics of the Great Depression: A Twenty-First Century Look Back at the Economics of the Interwar Era*, 52–67. Cheltenham, UK: Edward Elgar.

————. 2008a. "Financial Markets, the Economic Outlook, and Monetary Policy." Speech at the Women in Housing and Finance Exchequer Club Joint Luncheon, Washington, DC, January 10. Federal Reserve Board website.

————. 2008b. "Remarks on the Economic Outlook." International Monetary Conference, Barcelona, Spain, June 3. Federal Reserve Board website.

————. 2009a. "The Crisis and the Policy Response." Speech delivered at the Stamp Lecture, London School of Economics, London, January 13. Federal Reserve Board website.

————. 2009b. "On the Outlook for the Economy and Policy." Speech given at the Economic Club of New York, November 16. Federal Reserve Board website.

————. 2015. The *Courage to Act: A Memoir of a Crisis and Its Aftermath*. New York: W. W. Norton.

Bernanke, Ben S., Timothy F. Geithner, and Henry M. Paulson Jr. 2019. *Firefighting: The Financial Crisis and Its Lessons*. New York: Penguin Books.

Biven, W. Carl. 2002. *Jimmy Carter's Economy: Policy in an Age of Limits*. Chapel Hill: University of North Carolina Press, 2002.

Blanchard, Olivier, and Jordi Gali. 2007. "Real Wage Rigidities and the New Keynesian Model." *Journal of Money, Credit, and Banking* 39 (February): 35–65.

Blinder, Alan. 2012. "Fed Offls Dubious Re IOER Cuts but Don't Like MMMF Constraint." Interview. *MNI: Financial Market News Central Banks*, September 5.

————. 2013. *After the Music Stopped: The Financial Crisis, the Response, and the Work Ahead*. New York: Penguin.

Board of Governors of the Federal Reserve System *Annual Report*. Various dates.

————. *The Beige Book*. Summary *of Commentary on Current Economic Conditions by Federal Reserve District*. Various dates.

————. *Federal Reserve Bulletin*. Various dates.

————. *FOMC Minutes*. Various dates starting in 1994.

————. *FOMC Historical Minutes*. Various dates between March 18, 1936, and May 23, 1967. (The transcript of Federal Open Market Committee meetings with attribution to individuals possesses different titles: "Historical Minutes," "Memorandum of Discussion," and "Transcripts." "Minutes" of the Federal Open Market Committee refers to a summary of FOMC discussion without attribution to individuals released shortly after an FOMC meeting.)

————. FOMC Memoranda of Discussion. Various dates between June 20, 1967, and March 16, 1976.

————. *FOMC Transcript*. Various dates from March 29, 1976, to present.

————. *Minutes of the Board of Governors*. Various issues.

————. Statistical Releases. Various dates.

————. Tealbook. "Report to the FOMC on Economic Conditions and Monetary Policy." "Book A—Economic and Financial Conditions: Current Situation and Outlook and Strategy and Alternatives" (formerly called the Greenbook); "Book B—Monetary Policy: Strategy and Alternatives" (formerly called the Bluebook). Various dates.

———. 1943. *Banking and Monetary Statistics: 1914–1941*. Washington, DC: Board of Governors of the Federal Reserve System.

———. 1950. "1950 Survey of Consumer Finances." *Federal Reserve Bulletin* 36 (June): 643–54.

———. 1976. *Banking and Monetary Statistics: 1941–1970*. Washington, DC: Board of Governors of the Federal Reserve System, 1976.

———. 1999. "Memories of William McChesney Martin, Jr., Chairman of the Board of Governors of the Federal Reserve System, April 1951 through January 1970."

———. 2008. Press Release. "Federal Reserve Announces It Will Initiate a Program to Purchase the Direct Obligations of Housing-Related Government-Sponsored Enterprises and Mortgage-Backed Securities Backed by Fannie Mae, Freddie Mac, and Ginnie Mae." November 25.

———. 2009a. Joint Press Release. "The Role of the Federal Reserve in Preserving Financial and Monetary Stability Joint Statement by the Department of the Treasury and the Federal Reserve." March 23.

———. 2009b. "The Supervisory Capital Assessment Program: Overview of Results." May 7.

———. 2020a. Press Release. "Federal Reserve Board Releases Hypothetical Scenarios for Its 2020 Stress Test Exercises." February 6.

———. 2020b. Press Release. "Federal Reserve Actions to Support the Flow of Credit to Households and Businesses." March 15.

———. 2020c. Press Release. "Federal Reserve Takes Additional Actions to Provide Up to $2.3 Trillion in Loans to Support the Economy." April 9.

———. 2020d. Governor Jerome Powell Press Conference. June 10.

———. 2020e. "June 10, 2020: FOMC Projections Materials." June 10.

———. 2020f. "Federal Open Market Committee Announces Approval of Updates to Its Statement on Longer-Run Goals and Monetary Policy Strategy." August 27.

———. 2021. Jerome H. Powell Press Conference. April 28.

Bopp, Karl R., Robert V. Roosa, and Carl E. Parry. 1947. *Federal Reserve Policy*. Postwar Economic Studies 8. Washington, DC: Board of Governors of the Federal Reserve System. November.

Bordo, Michael D. 1993. "The Bretton Woods International Monetary System: A Historical Overview." In *A Retrospective on the Bretton Woods System: Lessons for International Monetary Reform*, edited by Michael D. Bordo and Barry Eichengreen, 3–108. Chicago: University of Chicago Press.

Bordo, Michael D., Michael Edelstein, and Hugh Rockoff. 1999. "Was Adherence to the Gold Standard a Good Housekeeping Seal of Approval during the Interwar Period?" NBER Working Paper 7186.

Bordo, Michael D., Christopher Erceg, and Charles Evans. 2000. "Money, Sticky Wages, and the Great Depression." *American Economic Review* 90 (December):1447–63.

Bordo, Michael D., and David C. Wheelock. 2013. "The Promise and Performance of the Federal Reserve as Lender of Last Resort." In *The Origins, History, and Future of the Federal Reserve: A Return to Jekyll Island*, edited by Michael D. Bordo and William Roberds, 59–98. Cambridge: Cambridge University Press.

Boskin Commission Report. 1996. "Toward a More Accurate Measure of the Cost of Living." Final Report to the Senate Finance Committee from the Advisory Commission to Study the Consumer Price Index." December 4.

Brainard, Lael. 2020. "Navigating Monetary Policy through the Fog of Covid." Speech at the Pandemic Webinar Series, hosted by the National Association for Business Economics, Washington, DC, July 14.

———. 2021. "Full Employment in the New Monetary Policy Framework." Speech at the inaugural Mike McCracken Lecture on Full Employment sponsored by the Canadian Association for Business Economics, January 31.

Bremner, Robert P. 2004. *Chairman of the Fed: William McChesney Martin, Jr. and the Creation of the American Financial System.* New Haven, CT: Yale University Press.

Broaddus, J. Alfred, Jr., and Marvin Goodfriend. 2004. "Sustaining Price Stability." *Federal Reserve Bank of Richmond Economic Quarterly* 90 (Summer): 3–20.

Bruner, Robert F., and Sean D. Carr. 2007. *The Panic of 1907: Lessons Learned from the Market's Perfect Storm.* Hoboken, NJ: John Wiley and Sons.

Brunner, Karl, and Allan H. Meltzer. 1964. *The Federal Reserve's Attachment to the Free Reserve Concept.* House Committee on Banking and Currency, Subcommittee on Domestic Finance. Washington, DC: US Government Printing Office. May.

———. 1968. "Liquidity Traps for Money, Bank Credit and Interest Rates." *Journal of Political Economy* 76 (July): 8–24.

Brunnermeier, Markus K., and Isabel Schnabel. 2016. "Bubbles and Central Banks: Historical Perspectives." In *Central Banks at a Crossroads: What Can We Learn from History?*, edited by Michael D. Bordo, Øyvind Eitrheim, Marc Flandreau, and Jan F. Qvigstad, 493–562. Cambridge: Cambridge University Press.

Bryan, Michael F., and Brent Meyer. 2010. "Are Some Prices in the CPI More Forward Looking Than others? We Think So." *Federal Reserve Bank of Cleveland Economic Commentary* 2010-2 (May 19).

Bryan, William Jennings. 1923. "My Forecast on Next Year's Election." *Hearst's International Magazine*, November, 23.

Burgess, W. Randolph. 1927. *The Reserve Banks and the Money Market.* New York: Harper and Brothers.

———. 1936. *The Reserve Banks and the Money Market.* Rev. ed. New York: Harper and Brothers.

———. 1964. "Reflections on the Early Development of Open Market Policy." *Federal Reserve Bank of New York Monthly Review* 46 (November): 219–26.

Burns, Arthur F. 1946 [1954]. "Economic Research and the Keynesian Thinking of Our Times." In *The Frontiers of Economic Knowledge*, edited by Arthur F. Burns. Princeton, NJ: Princeton University Press.

———. 1947 [1954]. "Keynesian *Economics* Once Again." In *The Frontiers of Economic Knowledge*, edited by Arthur F. Burns. Princeton, NJ: Princeton University Press.

———. 1950 [1954]. "New Facts on Business Cycles." In *The Frontiers of Economic Knowledge*, edited by Arthur F. Burns. Princeton, NJ: Princeton University Press.

———. 1954. "Mitchell on What Happens during Business Cycles." In *The Frontiers of Economic Knowledge*, edited by Arthur F. Burns. Princeton, NJ: Princeton University Press.

———. 1966. *The Management of Prosperity.* New York: Columbia University Press.

———. 1969. "The Nature and Causes of Business Cycles." In *The Business Cycle in a Changing World.* 3–53. New York: NBER.

———. 1970a [1978]. "The Basis for Lasting Prosperity." In *Reflections of an Economic Policy Maker, Speeches and Congressional Statements: 1969–1978.* Washington, DC: American Enterprise Institute.

———. 1970b [1978]. "Inflation: The Fundamental Challenge to Stabilization Policies." In *Reflections of an Economic Policy Maker, Speeches and Congressional Statements: 1969–1978*. Washington, DC: American Enterprise Institute.

———. 1972 [1978]. "The Problem of Inflation." In *Reflections of an Economic Policy Maker, Speeches and Congressional Statements: 1969–1978*. Washington, DC: American Enterprise Institute.

———. 1973 [1978]. "Some Problems of Central Banking." In *Reflections of an Economic Policy Maker, Speeches and Congressional Statements: 1969–1978*. Washington, DC: American Enterprise Institute.

———. 1973. "Money Supply in the Conduct of Monetary Policy." *Federal Reserve Bulletin* 59 (November): 791–98.

———. 1975. Statement before the Subcommittee on Domestic Monetary Policy of the Committee on Banking, Currency and Housing, US House of Representatives, February 6. *Federal Reserve Bulletin* 61 (February): 62–75.

———. 1979 [1987]. "The Anguish of Central Banking." Belgrade, Yugoslavia, Per Jacobsson Foundation. *Federal Reserve Bulletin* 73, no. 9 (September): 687–98.

Burns, Arthur F., and Paul A. Samuelson. 1967. *Full Employment, Guideposts and Economic Stability*. Washington, DC: American Enterprise Institute.

Burns Papers, Nixon File, Ford Library, Ann Arbor, MI.

Butkiewicz, James L. 2008. "Governor Eugene Meyer and the Great Contraction." *Research in Economic History* 26:273–307.

Cahn, Christophe, Julien Matheron, and Jean-Guillaume Sahuc. 2014. "Assessing the Macroeconomic Effects of LTROS." Banque de France Document de Travail No. 528. December.

Calomiris, Charles W. 2017. *Reforming Financial Regulation after Dodd-Frank*. New York: Manhattan Institute for Policy Research.

Calomiris, Charles W., and Joseph R. Mason. 1997. "Contagion and Bank Failures during the Great Depression: The June 1932 Chicago Banking Panic." *American Economic Review* 87 (December): 863–83.

Calomiris, Charles W., and David C. Wheelock. 1998. "Was the Great Depression a Watershed for American Monetary Policy?" In *The Defining Moment: The Great Depression and the American Economy in the Twentieth Century*, edited by Michael D. Bordo, Claudia Goldin, and Eugene N. White, 23–66. Chicago: University of Chicago Press. January.

Cannan, Edwin. 1969. *The Paper Pound of 1797–1821*. New York: Augustus M. Kelley.

Carlson, John A. 1977. "A Study of Price Forecasts." *Annals of Economic and Social Measurement* 6 (Winter): 27–56.

Carlstrom, Charles T., Timothy S. Fuerst, and Matthias Paustian. 2010. "Optimal Monetary Policy in a Model with Agency Costs." *Journal of Money, Credit and Banking* 42, no. 6 (suppl.) (September): 37–70.

Cassel, Gustav. 1928. "The Rate of Interest, the Bank Rate, and the Stabilization of Prices." *Quarterly Journal of Economics* 42 (August): 511–29.

———. 1936 [1966]. *The Downfall of the Gold Standard*. Reprints of Economic Classics. New York: Augustus M. Kelley.

Cecchetti, Stephen G., Michael E. Feroli, Peter Hooper, Anil K. Kashyap, and Kermit L. Schoenholtz. 2017. *Deflating Inflation Expectations: The Implications of Inflation's Simple Dynamics*. Report prepared for the 2017 US Monetary Policy Forum, sponsored by the Initiative on Global Markets at the University of Chicago's Booth School of Business, held in New York, March 3.

Cecchetti, Stephen G., and Kermit L. Schoenholtz. 2020. "The Fed Goes to War: Part 3." *MONeƔ $ BANeING*, April 12.

Chandler, Lester V. 1958. *Benjamin Strong, Central Banker*. Washington, DC: Brookings Institution.

Chappatta, Brian. 2020. "Fed's High-Yield ETF Buying Defies Explanation." *Bloomberg Markets*, April 14.

Chari, V. V., Patrick J. Kehoe, and Ellen R. McGrattan. 2009. "New Keynesian Models: Not Yet Useful for Policy Analysis." *American Economic Journal: Macroeconomics* 1 (January): 242–66.

Chen, Kathryn. 2015. "The Evolving Balance Sheet of the Federal Reserve: From LSAPs to Normalization." Federal Reserve Bank of New York Working Paper.

Chetty, Raj, John Friedman, and Michael Stepner. 2021. "Effects of January 2021 Stimulus Payments on Consumer Spending." Opportunity Insights. *Economic Tracker*, January 28.

Clarida, Richard H. 2020. "US Economic Outlook and Monetary Policy." Remarks at the New York Association for Business Economics, New York, May 21.

———. 2021. "US Economic Outlook and Monetary Policy." Speech at the C. Peter McColough Series on International Economics Council on Foreign Relations, New York, January 8.

Coibion, Olivier, Yuriy Gorodnichenko, and Michael Weber. 2020. "How Did US Consumers Use Their Stimulus Payments?" CESifo Working Paper 8510. August 28.

Cole, Harold L., and Lee E. Ohanian. 2004. "New Deal Policies and the Persistence of the Great Depression: A General Equilibrium Analysis." *Journal of Political Economy* 112 (August): 779–816.

Cook, Timothy. 1989. "Determinants of the Federal Funds Rate: 1979–1982." Federal Reserve Bank of Richmond *Economic Review* 75 (January/February): 3–19.

Coombs, Charles A. 1976. *The Arena of International Finance*. New York: John Wiley and Sons.

Council of Economic Advisers. *Economic Report of the President*. Washington, DC: US Government Printing Office, various issues

Curdia, Vasco, and Michael Woodford. 2009. "Credit Spreads and Monetary Policy." NBER Working Paper 15289. August.

Currie, Lauchlin B. 1933a. "Treatment of Credit in Contemporary Monetary Theory." *Journal of Political Economy* 41 (February): 58–79.

———. 1933b. "Money, Gold, and Income." *Quarterly Journal of Economics* 48 (November): 77–95.

———. 1934a. "The Failure of Monetary Policy to Prevent the Depression of 1929–1932." *Journal of Political Economy* 42 (April): 145–77.

———. 1934b. *The Supply and Control of Money in the United States*. Cambridge, MA: Harvard University Press.

———. 1934c. "Letter to Mr. Eccles." November 17. Box 43, folder 1, item 1, St. Louis FRASER.

———. 1934d. "Memorandum on Confidence." Box 72, folder 2, item 3, Marriner S. Eccles Papers, St. Louis FRASER.

———. 1936a. "Some Monetary Aspects of the Excess Reserve Problem." Notes on meeting of May 18, 1936, led by Mr. Currie. Box 72, folder 4, item 4, Marriner S. Eccles Papers, St. Louis FRASER.

———. 1936b. "Possible Measures to Restrict the Inflow of Foreign Capital." November 23. Box 49, folder 4, item 3, Marriner S. Eccles Papers, St. Louis FRASER.

———. 1936c. "Outline of Present Status and Problems of the Recovery Movement." December 22. Box 72, folder 8, item 1, Marriner S. Eccles Papers, St. Louis FRASER.

———. 1937. "An Appraisal of Current Prospects and a Tentative Program." May 18. Box 72, folder 14, item 2, Marriner S. Eccles Papers, St. Louis FRASER.

———. 1938a. "Causes of the Recession." April 1. Box 63, folder 11, item 9, Marriner S. Eccles Papers, St. Louis FRASER.

———. 1938b. "Memo to Chairman Eccles: Banking Reform." Memo to Chairman Eccles, August 3. Box 73, folder 12, item 1, Marriner S. Eccles Papers. St. Louis FRASER.

———. 1939. "Memorandum on the Question: The Claim Is Made That Private Industry by Itself Cannot Profitably Absorb Current Savings." April 19. Box 73, folder 14, item 4, Marriner S. Eccles Papers, St. Louis FRASER.

Daly, Mary. 2021. "SOMC: Labor Markets and the Fed's Monetary Policy." Manhattan Institute. January 7.

Daniels, Josephus. 1924. *The Life of Woodrow Wilson: 1856–1924*. Chicago: John C. Winston.

Davies, Paul J., Anna Isaac, and Caitlin Ostroff. 2020. "Stress Endures in Market Where Big Companies Turn for Cash." *Wall Street Journal* Markets, April 20, https://www.wsj.com/articles/stress-endures-in-market-where-big-companies-turn-for-cash-11587385996.

De Andoain, Carlos Garcia, Peter Hoffmann, and Simone Manganelli. 2014. "Fragmentation in the Euro Overnight Unsecured Money Market." European Central Bank Working Paper Series 1755. December.

Deutsche Bank Research. 2013. *Focus Europe*. "ECB Reaction Function(s)." September 13.

Donnan, Shawn, and Jenny Leonard. 2019. "How Trump's Trade War Went from Method to Madness." *Bloomberg Businessweek*, November 14.

Douglas, Paul H. 1935. *Controlling Depressions*. New York: W. W. Norton.

Draghi, Mario. 2012. "Introductory Statement to the Press Conference (with Q&A)." European Central Bank. Barcelona. May 3.

Dudley, William. 2020. "Fed's Coronavirus Rescues Invite Bigger Bailouts." Bloomberg Economics. June 5.

Duffie, Darrell. 2020. "Still the World's Safe Haven." Brookings Institution Hutchins Center Working Paper 62. May.

Eccles, Marriner S. 1935. "Summary of Statements by Marriner S. Eccles, Governor of the Federal Reserve Board, on the Banking Bill of 1935." March 4. Box 63, folder 2, item 1, St. Louis FRASER.

Edie, Lionel D. 1931. *The Banks and Prosperity*. New York: Harper and Row.

———. 1932 [1983]. "The Future of the Gold Standard." In *Gold and Monetary Stabilization: Harris Foundation Lectures, 1932*, edited by Quincy Wright, 111–30. New York: Garland.

Edwards, Sebastian. 2018. *American Default: The Untold Story of FDR, the Supreme Court, and the Battle over Gold*. Princeton, NJ: Princeton University Press.

Eggertsson, Gauti B. 2008. "Great Expectations and the End of the Depression." *American Economic Review* 98 (September): 1476–516.

Eggertsson, Gauti B., and Michael Woodford. 2003a. "The Zero Bound on Interest Rates and Optimal Monetary Policy." *Brookings Papers on Economic Activity* 1:139–211.

———. 2003b. "Optimal Monetary Policy in a Liquidity Trap." Working Paper 9968. Cambridge, MA: National Bureau of Economic Research. September.

Eichengreen, Barry. 1986. "The Bank of France and the Sterilization of Gold, 1926–1932." *Explorations in Economic History* 23:56–84.

———. 1995. *Golden Fetters: The Gold Standard and the Great Depression, 1919–1939.* Oxford: Oxford University Press.

Eichengreen, Barry, and Peter Temin. 2000. "The Gold Standard and the Great Depression." *Contemporary European History* 9, no. 2:183–207.

Eisenbeis, Robert. 2020. "The Trade Policies." Cumberland Advisors Market Commentary, January 14.

Engen, Eric M., Thomas Laubach, and David Reifschneider. 2015. "The Macroeconomic Effects of the Federal Reserve's Unconventional Monetary Policies." Finance and Economics Discussion Series 2015-005. Washington, DC: Board of Governors of the Federal Reserve System.

Epstein, Gerald, and Thomas Ferguson. 1984. "Monetary Policy, Loan Liquidation, and Industrial Conflict: The Federal Reserve and the Open Market Operations of 1932." *Journal of Economic History* 44 (December): 957–83.

Eren, Egemen, Andreas Schrimpf, and Vladyslav Sushko. 2020a. "US Dollar Funding during the Covid-19 Crisis—the International Dimension." *BIS Bulletin*, no. 15 (May 12): 1–6.

———. 2020b. "US Dollar Funding Markets during the Covid-19 Crisis—the Money Market Fund Turmoil." *BIS Bulletin*, no. 14 (May 12): 1–6.

European Central Bank. 2008a. "Editorial." *Monthly Bulletin*, July, 5–8.

———. 2008b. The Euro Area Bank Lending Survey. July.

———. 2010a. "Editorial." *Monthly Bulletin*, July, 5–8.

———. 2010b. "Article: The ECB's Response to the Financial Crisis." *Monthly Bulletin*, October, 59–74.

———. 2011. "Editorial." *Monthly Bulletin*, May, 5.

———. 2012. "Editorial." *Monthly Bulletin*, April, 5–6.

Evans, Charles L. 2021. "The New Monetary Policy Framework and Some Implications for Financial Stability." ASSA (Allied Social Science Associations) 2021 Virtual Annual Meeting, January 5.

Evans-Pritchard, Ambrose. 2016. "RBS Cries 'Sell Everything' as Deflationary Crisis Nears." *Daily Telegraph*, January 11, https://www.telegraph.co.uk/business/2016/02/11/rbs-cries-sell-everything-as-deflationary-crisis-nears/.

Federal Reserve Board. 1920. "Reply of the Federal Reserve Board to a Letter from Senator Robert L. Owen Criticizing Certain Policies of the Federal Reserve System." December. St. Louis FRASER.

———. 1921. "Seventh Annual Report of the Federal Reserve Board Covering Operations for the Year 1920." Washington, DC: US Government Printing Office / St. Louis FRASER.

———. 1922. "Eighth Annual Report of the Federal Reserve Board Covering Operations for the Year 1921." Washington, DC: US Government Printing Office / St. Louis FRASER.

———. 1924a. "Tenth Annual Report of the Federal Reserve Board Covering Operations for the Year 1923." Washington, DC: US Government Printing Office / St. Louis FRASER.

———. 1924b. "Meeting of the Open Market Investment Committee for the Federal Reserve System"; "Report of the Open Market Investment Committee." July 16. St. Louis FRASER.

———. 1924c. "Meeting of the Open Market Investment Committee for the Federal Reserve System," "Report of the Open Market Investment Committee." December 19. St. Louis FRASER.

———. 1929. "Fifteenth Annual Report of the Federal Reserve Board Covering Operations for the Year 1928." Washington, DC: US Government Printing Office / St. Louis FRASER.

———. 1931. "Seventeenth Annual Report of the Federal Reserve Board Covering Operations for the year 1930." Washington, DC: US Government Printing Office / St. Louis FRASER.

Ferrell, Robert H. 2013. *Inside the Nixon Administration: The Secret Diary of Arthur Burns, 1969–1974*. Lawrence: University Press of Kansas.

Fettig, David. 2002. "Lender of More Than Last Resort." Federal Reserve Bank of Minneapolis. December 1.

Fève, Patrick, Julien Matheron, Jean-Guillaume Sahuc. 2009. "Inflation Target Shocks and Monetary Policy Inertia in the Euro Area." Document de Travail 243, Banque de France. August.

———. 2010. "Disinflation Shocks in the Eurozone: A DSGE Perspective." *Journal of Money, Credit and Banking* 42 (March–April): 289–323.

Financial Times. 1998. "Camdessus Warns of 'Biggest Crisis' for IMF." May 6, 6.

———. 2013a. "Beijing Returns to Global Metals Market." June 3, 15.

———. 2013b. "ECB's Untimely Change of Mind." June 5, 8.

———. 2016. "Soaring Yen Defies Tokyo's Effort to Spur Growth and Head off Deflation." April 8, 1.

Fischer, Stanley. 2017a. "I'd Rather Have Bob Solow Than an Econometric Model, But . . ." Remarks at the Warwick Economics Summit, Coventry England, February 11.

———. 2017b. "Monetary Policy Expectations and Surprises." Speech at the Columbia University School of International and Public Affairs, New York, April 17.

———. 2017c. "Committee Decisions and Monetary Policy Rules." Speech at "The Structural Foundations of Monetary Policy," a Hoover Institution Monetary Policy Conference, Stanford University, Stanford, CA, May 5.

Fisher, Irving. 1896. *Appreciation and Interest*. New York.

———. 1907. *The Rate of Interest*. New York: Macmillan.

———. 1911 [1963]. *The Purchasing Power of Money* (2nd rev. ed. 1922). New York: A. M. Kelley.

———. 1920. *Stabilizing the Dollar: A Plan to Stabilize the Price Level without Fixing Individual Prices*. New York: Macmillan.

———. 1923. "The Business Cycle Largely a 'Dance of the Dollar.'" *Journal of the American Statistical Society* 18:1024–28.

———. 1925. "Our Unstable Dollar and the So-Called Business Cycle." *Journal of the American Statistical Society* 20 (June): 179–202.

———. 1926. "A Statistical Relation between Unemployment and Price Changes." *International Labour Review* 13:785–92.

———. 1929 [1997]. Address of Professor Irving Fisher delivered at a meeting of the District of Columbia Bankers Association, October 23, 1929. In *The Works of Irving Fisher*, edited by William J. Barber, vol. 10, *Booms and Depressions*. London: Pickering and Chatto.

———. 1933. "The Debt-Deflation Theory of Great Depressions." *Econometrica* 1:337–57.

———. 1934. *Stable Money: A History of the Movement* (assisted by Hans R. L. Cohrssen). New York: Adelphi.

———. 1935. *100% Money*. New York: Adelphi.

Freeman, James. 2009. "Banking on a Rescue." Business Bookshelf. *Wall Street Journal*, August 12, A13.

Freeman, Richard B. 1998. "Spurts in Union Growth: Defining Moments and Social Processes." In *The Defining Moments*, edited by Michael D. Bordo, Claudia Goldin, and Eugene N. White. Chicago: University of Chicago Press.

Friedman, Milton. 1960. *A Program for Monetary Stability*. New York: Fordham University Press.

———. 1963 [1968]. "Inflation: Causes and Consequences." In *Dollars and Deficits*, edited by Milton Friedman, 17–71. Englewood Cliffs, NJ: Prentice-Hall.

———. 1961 [1969]. "The Lag in Effect of Monetary Policy." In *The Optimum Quantity of Money and Other Essays*, ed Milton Friedman, 237–60. Chicago: Aldine.

———. 1968 [1969]. "The Role of Monetary Policy." In *The Optimum Quantity of Money and Other Essays*, edited by Milton Friedman. Chicago: Aldine, 95–110.

———. 1970. *The Counter-revolution in Monetary Theory*. London: Institute of Economic Affairs.

———. 1982. "Monetary Policy: Theory and Practice." *Journal of Money, Credit, and Banking* 14 (February): 98–118.

———. 1984. "Monetary Policy for the 1980s." In *To Promote Prosperity: US Domestic Policy in the Mid-1980s*, edited by John. H. Moore, 23–60. Stanford, CA: Hoover Institution Press.

———. 1988. "The Fed Has No Clothes." *Wall Street Journal*, April 15.

———. 1989. "The Quantity Theory of Money." In *The New Palgrave Money*, edited by John Eatwell, Murray Milgate, and Peter Newman, 1–40. New York: W. W. Norton.

———. 1997. "John Maynard Keynes." Federal Reserve Bank of Richmond *Economic Quarterly* 83 (Spring): 1–23.

Friedman, Milton, and Anna J. Schwartz. 1963a. *A Monetary History of the United States, 1867–1960*. Princeton, NJ: Princeton University Press.

———. 1963b. "Money and Business Cycles." *Review of Economics and Statistics* 45 (February): 32–64.

———. 1970. *Monetary Statistics of the United States*. New York: National Bureau of Economic Research.

Gagnon, Joseph, Matthew Raskin, Julie Remache, and Brian Sack. 2011. "Large-Scale Asset Purchases by the Federal Reserve: Did They Work?" Federal Reserve Bank of New York *Economic Policy Review* 17, no. 1 (May): 41–59.

Gaines, Tilford C. 1956. "Chairman Martin's Memorandum Dated April 17, 1956, to Mr. Sproul." April 27. Allan Sproul Papers, New York Fed Archives.

Gali, Jordi. 2008. *Monetary Policy, Inflation, and the Business Cycle: An Introduction to the New Keynesian Framework*. Princeton, NJ: Princeton University Press.

Garrett, Garet. 1931. "A Story of Banking." *Saturday Evening Post*, August 8.

Giglio, Stefano, Matteo Maggiori, Johannes Stroebel, and Stephen Utkus. 2020. "Inside the Mind of a Stock Market Crash." NBER Working Paper 277272. May.

Glass, Carter. 1927. *An Adventure in Constructive Finance*. Garden City, NY: Doubleday, Page.

Goldberg, Linda S., Craig Kennedy, Jason Miu. 2010. "Central Bank Dollar Swap Lines and Overseas Dollar Funding Costs." NBER Working Paper 15763. February.

Goldenweiser, E. A. 1925. *Federal Reserve System in Operation*. New York: McGraw-Hill.

———. 1937. "Member Bank Reserves." January 14. Board of Governors of the Federal Reserve System. Box 99, folder 9, item 1, St. Louis FRASER.

———. 1945. "Jobs." In *Jobs, Production, and Living Standards*, 1–17. Postwar Economic Studies 1. Washington, DC: Board of Governors of the Federal Reserve System. August.

Goldman Sachs. 2015. "European Economics Analyst: Euro Area Inflation Expectations and QE: Moments of Truth." *Economics Research*, April 2, 3.

———. 2016a. "European Economics Analyst: Explaining Time-Varying Rate Sensitivity to Inflation in the Euro Area." *Economics Research*, May 5.

———. 2016b. "European Economics Analyst: Unconventional Monetary Policy and Financial Stability." *Economics Research*, June 9.

Gonzalez-Páremo, Jose Manuel. 2013. "Innovations in Lender of Last Resort Policy in Europe." In *Handbook of Safeguarding Global Financial Stability: Political, Social, Cultural, and Economic Theories and Models*, edited by Gerard Caprio Jr., 435–42. London: Elsevier.

Goodfriend, Marvin. 1993. "Interest Rate Policy and the Inflation Scare Problem." Federal Reserve Bank of Richmond *Economic Quarterly* 79 (Winter): 1–24.

———. 1994. "Why We Need An 'Accord' for Federal Reserve Credit Policy." *Journal of Money, Credit, and Banking* 26 (August): 572–84.

Goodfriend, Marvin, and Robert G. King. 1988. "Financial Deregulation, Monetary Policy and Central Banking." Federal Reserve Bank of Richmond *Economic Review*, May/June, 3–22.

———. 1997. "The New Neoclassical Synthesis." NBER *Macroeconomics Annual*, edited by Ben S. Bernanke and Julio Rotemberg.

———. 2005. "The Incredible Volcker Disinflation." *Journal of Monetary Economics* 52 (July): 981–1015.

Goodfriend, Marvin, and William Whelpley. 1993. "Federal Funds." In *Instruments of the Money Market*, 7th ed., edited by Timothy Q. Cook and Robert L. LaRoche, 7–33. Federal Reserve Bank of Richmond.

Goodwin, Craufurd D., and R. Stanley Herren. 1975. "The Truman Administration: Problems and Policies Unfold." In *Exhortation and Controls*, edited by Craufurd D. Goodwin, 9–93. Washington, DC: Brookings Institution.

Gordon, Robert J., and James A. Wilcox. 1981. "Monetarist Interpretations of the Great Depression: An Evaluation and Critique." In *The Great Depression Revisited*, edited by Karl Brunner, 49–107. Boston: Kluwer-Nijhoff.

Gorton, Gary. 2010. *Slapped by the Invisible Hand: The Panic of 2007*. Oxford: Oxford University Press.

Grant, James. 1992. *Money of the Mind: Borrowing and Lending in America from the Civil War to Michael Milken.* Farrar Straus Giroux: New York.

Greenspan, Alan. 1993. Remarks before the Economic Club of New York, April.

———. 1997. Statement before the House Committee on the Budget, October 8, 1997. In *Federal Reserve Bulletin* 83 (December): 963–67.

———. 2001. "Economic Developments." Remarks before the Economic Club of New York, May 24.

———. 2005. "Closing Remarks." Symposium sponsored by the Federal Reserve Bank of Kansas City, Jackson Hole, Wyoming, August 27.

Group of 30. 2009. Working Group on Financial Reform: Financial Reform; A Framework for Financial Stability. January 15.

Guvenen, Fatih, Serdar Ozkan, and Jae Song. 2014. "The Nature of Countercyclical Income Risk." *Journal of Political Economy* 122, no. 3 (June): 621–60.

Haberler, Gottfried. 1932 [1983]. "Money and the Business Cycle." In *Gold and Monetary Stabilization: Harris Foundation Lectures, 1932*, edited by Quincy Wright, 43–74. New York: Garland.

Hamilton, James D. 1987. "Monetary Factors in the Great Depression." *Journal of Monetary Economics* 19:145–69.

———. 1988. "The Role of the International Gold Standard in Propagating the Great Depression." *Contemporary Policy Issues* 6, no. 2 (April): 67–89.

———. 1992. "Was the Deflation during the Great Depression Anticipated? Evidence from the Commodity Futures Market." *American Economic Review* 82 (March): 157–78.

Hansen, Alvin H. 1939. "Economic Progress and Declining Population Growth." *American Economic Review* 29, no. 1, Part 1, March, 1–15.

———. 1941. *Fiscal Policy and Business Cycles.* New York: W. W. Norton.

Harding, Robin. 2014. "James Bullard Says Fed Will Need to Alter Guidance." *Financial Times*, August 25, https://www.ft.com/content/9248564e-2c73-11e4-8eda-00144feabdc0.

Harding, W. P. G. 1925. *The Formative Period of the Federal Reserve System.* Cambridge, MA: Houghton Mifflin / Riverside.

Hardy, Charles O. 1932. *Credit Policies of the Federal Reserve System.* Washington, DC: Brookings Institution.

Hargrove, Erwin C., and Samuel A. Morley. 1984. *The President and the Council of Economic Advisers.* London: Westview.

Harris, Seymour E. 1933. *Twenty Years of Federal Reserve Policy.* 2 vols. Cambridge, MA: Harvard University Press.

Harrison Papers. Archives of the Federal Reserve Bank of New York.

Harrod, Roy F. 1964. "Review of *A Monetary History of the United States 1867–1960* by Milton Friedman and Anna Jacobsen Schwartz." *University of Chicago Law Review* 32:188–96.

Hatzius, Jan. 2017. "US: Views; A Bigger Overshoot." *Goldman Sachs Economics Research*, August 6.

Hawtrey, Ralph G. 1919 [1923]. "The Gold Standard." *Economic Journal* 3, no. 4:428–42. Reprinted in Hawtrey, *Monetary Reconstruction*, 48–65. London: Longmans, Green.

———. 1924. "The Tenth Annual Report of the Federal Reserve Board." *Economic Journal* 34 (June): 283–86.

————. 1931. *Trade Depression and the Way Out*. London: Longmans, Green.

————. 1932 [1962]. *The Art of Central Banking*. London: Frank Cass.

————. 1937. "The Credit Deadlock." In *The Lessons of Monetary Experience: Essays in Honor of Irving Fisher*, edited by Arthur D. Gayer. New York: Farrar and Rinehart.

————. 1938 [1962]. *A Century of Bank Rate*. London: Longmans, Green.

Hayek, Friedrich A. 1925 [1999]. "Monetary Policy in the United States after the Recovery from the Crisis of 1920." In *The Collected Works of F. A. Hayek: Good Money, Part I; The New World*, edited by Stephen Kresge, 71–152. Chicago: University of Chicago Press.

————. 1932 [1984]. "The Fate of the Gold Standard." In *Money, Capital and Fluctuations: Early Essays of F. A. Hayek*, edited by R. McCloughy. London: Routledge and Kegan Paul.

Heider, Florian, Marie Hoerova, and Cornelius Holthausen. 2009. "Liquidity Hoarding and Interbank Market Spreads: The Role of Counterparty Risk." Working Paper Series 1126, European Central Bank. December.

Hetzel, Robert L. 1982. "The October 1979 Regime of Monetary Control and the Behavior of the Money Supply in 1980." *Journal of Money, Credit, and Banking* 14 (May): 234–51.

————. 1985. "The Rules versus Discretion Debate over Monetary Policy in the 1920s." Federal Reserve Bank of Richmond *Economic Review* 71 (November/December): 3–14.

————. 1991. "Too-Big-to-Fail: Origins, Consequences, and Outlook." *Economic Review* 77 (November/December): 3–15.

————. 1997. "The Case for a Monetary Rule in a Constitutional Democracy." *Economic Quarterly* 83 (Spring): 45–65

————. 1998. "Arthur Burns and Inflation." Federal Reserve Bank of Richmond *Economic Quarterly* 84 (Winter): 21–44.

————. 1999. "Japanese Monetary Policy: A Quantity Theory Perspective." Federal Reserve Bank of Richmond *Economic Quarterly* 85 (Winter): 1–25.

————. 2002a. "German Monetary History in the First Half of the Twentieth Century." Federal Reserve Bank of Richmond *Economic Quarterly* 88 (Winter): 1–35.

————. 2002b. "German Monetary History in the Second Half of the Twentieth Century: From the Deutsche Mark to the Euro." Federal Reserve Bank of Richmond *Economic Quarterly* 88 (Spring): 29–64.

————. 2003. "Japanese Monetary Policy and Deflation." Federal Reserve Bank of Richmond *Economic Quarterly* 89 (Summer): 21–52.

————. 2004. "Price Stability and Japanese Monetary Policy." Bank of Japan *Monetary and Economic Studies* 22 (October): 1–23.

————. 2008. *The Monetary Policy of the Federal Reserve: A History*. Cambridge: Cambridge University Press.

————. 2012a. *The Great Recession: Market Failure or Policy Failure?* Cambridge: Cambridge University Press.

————. 2012b. "Central Bank Accountability and Independence: Are They Inconsistent?" *Journal of Macroeconomics* 34 (March): 616–25.

————. 2014a. "The Real Bills Views of the Founders of the Fed." Federal Reserve Bank of Richmond *Economic Quarterly* 100 (Second Quarter): 159–81.

————. 2014b. "Should Greece Remain in the Eurozone?" Federal Reserve Bank of Richmond *Economic Quarterly* 100 (Third Quarter): 241–78.

————. 2016. "The Rise and Fall of the Quantity Theory in Nineteenth Century Britain: Implications for Early Fed Thinking." *Federal Reserve Bank of Richmond Economic Quarterly* 102, no. 4 (Fourth Quarter): 281–320.

————. 2019. "What Caused the Great Recession in the Eurozone?" In *Innovative Federal Reserve Policies during the Great Financial Crisis*, edited by Douglas D. Evanoff, George G. Kaufman, and A. G. Malliaris, 257–84. Hackensack, NJ: World Scientific.

————. 2020. "The Evolution of US Monetary Policy." In *Handbook of the History of Money and Currency*, edited by Stefano Battilossi, Youssef Cassis, and Kazuhiko Yago, 883–922. New York: Springer.

Hetzel, Robert L., and Ralph F. Leach. 2001a. "The Treasury-Fed Accord: A New Narrative Account." *Federal Reserve Bank of Richmond Economic Quarterly* 87 (Winter): 33–55.

————. 2001b. "After the Accord: Reminiscences on the Birth of the Modern Fed." *Federal Reserve Bank of Richmond Economic Quarterly* 87 (Winter): 57–64.

Hetzel, Robert L., and Gary Richardson. 2018. "Banking and Monetary Policy in American Economic History from the Formation of the Federal Reserve." In *The Oxford Handbook of American Economic History*, vol. 2, edited by Louis P. Cain, Price V. Fishback, and Paul W. Rhode, 277–301. New York: Oxford University Press.

Hilsenrath, Jon, and Nick Timiraos. 2020. "The Federal Reserve Is Changing What It Means to Be a Central Bank." *Wall Street Journal*, April 27, https://www.wsj.com/articles/fate-and-history-the-fed-tosses-the-rules-to-fight-coronavirus-downturn-11587999986.

Honkapohja, Seppo. 2014. "The Euro Area Crisis: A View from the North." *Journal of Macroeconomics* 39 (March): 260–71.

Hooper, Peter, Brett Ryan, Matthew Luzzetti, and Torsten Sløk. 2017. "Who Is Buying Treasuries, Mortgages, Credit, and Munis?" Deutsche Bank. July.

Hudepohl, Tom, Ryan van Lamoen, and Nander de Vette. 2019. "Quantitative Easing in Stock Markets: Evidence from the Euro Area." De Nederlandsche Bank NV Working Paper 660. December.

Humphrey, Thomas M. 2001a. "The Choice of a Monetary Policy Framework: Lessons from the 1920s." *Cato Journal* 21 (Fall): 285–313.

————. 2001b. "Monetary Policy Frameworks and Indicators for the Federal Reserve in the 1920s." *Federal Reserve Bank of Richmond Economic Quarterly* 87 (Winter): 65–92.

Humphrey, Thomas M., and Richard H. Timberlake. 2019. *The Real Bills Doctrine, the Gold Standard, and the Great Depression*. Washington, DC: Cato Institute.

Ihrig, Jane, and Scott A. Wolla. 2020. "The Fed's New Monetary Policy Tools." *Federal Reserve Bank of St. Louis Page One Economics*, August.

International Monetary Fund. 2016. "Potent Polices for a Successful Normalization." *Global Financial Stability Report*, April.

Irving, Washington. 2008. "A Time of Unexampled Prosperity." In *The Crayon Papers: The Great Mississippi Bubble, 1819–1820*. Reprinted in Richard W. Fisher, *Federal Reserve Bank of Dallas Economic Letter* 3 (April): 1–8.

Irwin, Douglas A. 2012. "The French Gold Sink and the Great Deflation of 1929–32." *Cato Papers on Public Policy* 2:1–41.

Jensen, Michael C., and William H. Meckling. 1976. "Theory of the Firm: Managerial Behavior, Agency Costs and Ownership Structure." *Journal of Financial Economics* 3 (October): 305–60.

Johnson, H. Clark. 1997. *Gold, France, and the Great Depression, 1919–1932*. New Haven, CT: Yale University Press.

Kang, Dae Woong, Nick Ligthart, and Ashoka Mody. 2015. "The European Central Bank: Building a Shelter in a Storm." Griswold Center for Economic Policy Studies Working Paper 248. Princeton University. December 12.

Keister, Todd, Antoine Martin, and James McAndrews. 2008. "Divorcing Money from Monetary Policy." Federal Reserve Bank of New York *Economic Policy Review* 14 (September).

Kemmerer, Edwin. Walter. 1944. *Gold and the Gold Standard*. New York: McGraw-Hill.

Keynes, John Maynard. 1920. *The Economic Consequences of the Peace*. New York: Harcourt, Brace, and Howe.

———. 1930. *A Treatise on Money: The Applied Theory of Money*. Vol 2. New York: Harcourt, Brace.

———. 1936 [1964]. *The General Theory of Employment, Interest and Money*. New York: Harcourt, Brace, and World.

Kiley, M., Thomas Laubach, and Robert Tetlow. 2006. "Optimal-Control Policies." Memo to Members of the Federal Open Market Committee, Board of Governors of the Federal Reserve System. June 20.

Kim, Don H., and Jonathan H. Wright. 2005. "An Arbitrage-Free Three-Factor Term Structure Model and the Recent Behavior of Long-Term Yields and Distant-Horizon Forward Rates." Finance and Economics Discussion Series 2005-33, Federal Reserve Board, Washington, DC.

Kim, Kyungmin, Thomas Laubach, and Min Wei. 2020. "Macroeconomic Effects of Large-Scale Asset Purchases: New Evidence." Finance and Economic Discussion Series 2020-047. Washington, DC: Board of Governors of the Federal Reserve System.

Kohn, Donald L. 1999. "Comment." In *Monetary Policy Rules*, edited by John B. Taylor, 192–99. Chicago: University of Chicago Press.

Kosters, Marvin H. 1975. "Controls and Inflation: The Economic Stabilization Program in Retrospect." American Enterprise Institute for Public Policy Research, Washington, DC.

Kydland, Finn E., and Edward C. Prescott. 1977. "Rules Rather Than Discretion: The Inconsistency of Optimal Plans." *Journal of Political Economy* 85 (June): 473–91.

Lacker, Jeffrey M. 2008. "Financial Stability and Central Banks." European Economics and Financial Centre, London. June 5.

———. 2019. "A Look Back at the Consensus Statement." Cato Institute's 37th Annual Monetary Conference, Washington, DC, November 14.

Laidler, David. 1999. *Fabricating the Keynesian Revolution*. Cambridge: Cambridge University Press.

LHM *Monetary Policy Analytics*. 2020a. "Implementation Note: As Sweet as Saltwater TAF-fy?" March 14.

———. 2020b. "1Tr Commercial Paper FF (Also A-2, Not Just A-1)." March 17.

———. 2020c. "Helicopter Jay: Fiscally Think Big(ly)." March 19.

———. 2020d. "The Devil in the Details." March 23.

———. 2020e. "Recap." March 24.

———. 2020f. "Powell, Candidly." March 27.

———. 2020g. "Deep Dive into New $2.3tn of Fed Lending." April 16.

———. 2020h. "April 2020 FOMC Meeting: Nice Job, Powell!" April 29.

———. 2020i. "Credit to the Fed." May 5.

———. 2020j. "FOMC Minutes: A Grim Outlook, Even under 'Appropriate' Policy!" July 1.

———. 2020k. "Fed Listens: What Did It Contribute to the Review?" August 13.

———. 2020l. "Thanks, Rich." November 20.

———. 2021a. "Q&A Transcript of Fed Chair Powell." February 10.

———. 2021b. "Weekly Update: Still Leaning on 'Some Time.'" May 4.

Lindert, Peter H. 1981. "Comments on Understanding 1929–1933." In *The Great Depression Revisited*, edited by Karl Brunner. Boston: Kluwer-Nijhoff.

Link, Arthur S. 1956. *Wilson: The New Freedom*. Princeton, NJ: Princeton University Press.

Logan, Lorie K. 2020. "The Federal Reserve's Market Functioning Purchases: From Supporting to Sustaining." Remarks at SIFMA Webinar, Federal Reserve Bank of New York, July 15.

Lucas, Robert E., Jr. 1972 [1981]. "Expectations and the Neutrality of Money." In *Studies in Business-Cycle Theory*, by Robert E. Lucas Jr. Cambridge, MA: MIT Press.

———. 1976 [1981]. "Econometric Policy Evaluation: A Critique." In *Studies in Business-Cycle Theory*, by Robert E. Lucas Jr. Cambridge, MA: MIT Press.

———. 1980 [1981]. "Rules, Discretion, and the Role of the Economic Advisor." In *Studies in Business-Cycle Theory*, by Robert E. Lucas Jr. Cambridge, MA: MIT Press.

———. 2007. "Interview." In *The Economics of the Great Depression*, edited by Randall E. Parker, 88–101. Cheltenham, UK: Edgar Elgar.

Lucas, Robert E., Jr., and Thomas J. Sargent. 1978 [1981]. "After Keynesian Macroeconomics." In *Rational Expectations and Econometric Practice*, edited by Robert E. Lucas Jr. and Thomas J. Sargent, 1:295–319. Minneapolis: University of Minnesota Press.

Luzzetti, Matthew, Brett Ryan, and Justin Weidner. 2020. "Minding the Fed's Policy Gap." US Economic Perspectives, Deutsche Bank Research, July 22.

Macaulay, Frederick R. 1938. *Some Theoretical Problems Suggested by the Movements of Interest Rates, Bond Yields and Stock Prices in the United States since 1856*. New York: NBER.

Maisel, Sherman J. 1973. *Managing the Dollar*. New York: W. W. Norton.

Madden, Carl H. 1959. *The Money Side of the "Street."* Federal Reserve Bank of New York.

Mankiw, Gregory N., and Ricardo Reis. 2003. "What Measure of Inflation Should a Central Bank Target?" *Journal of the European Economic Association* 1 (September): 1058–86.

Martin, William McChesney. 1958. Remarks at luncheon meeting of the Executives' Club of Chicago, Grand Ballroom, Hotel Sherman, Chicago, December 12.

———. 1965. Remarks before the 59th Annual Meeting of the Life Insurance Association of America, New York, December 8.

Mayer, Thomas. 1999. *Monetary Policy and the Great Inflation in the United States: The Federal Reserve and the Failure of Macroeconomic Policy, 1965–79*. Northampton, MA: Edward Elgar.

McCracken, Jeffrey, and David Enrich. 2008. "US Firms Gird for Hits and Draw on Credit Now." *Wall Street Journal*, September 25.

Meigs, A. James. 1976. "Campaigning for Monetary Reform: The Federal Reserve Bank of St. Louis in 1959 and 1960." *Journal of Monetary Economics* 2:439–53.

Melcangi, Davide, and Vincent Sterk. 2020. "Stock Market Participation, Inequality, and Monetary Policy." Staff Report 932, Federal Reserve Bank of New York, July.

Meltzer, Allan H. 2003. *A History of the Federal Reserve*. Vol. 1, *1913–1951*. Chicago: University of Chicago Press.

———. 2009. *A History of the Federal Reserve*. Vol. 2, book 1, *1951–1969*. Chicago: University of Chicago Press.

Menand, Lev. 2020. "Unappropriated Dollars: The Fed's Ad Hoc Lending Facilities and the Rules That Govern Them." European Corporate Governance Institute Working Paper Series in Law. May.

Meulendyke, Ann-Marie. 1998. *US Monetary Policy and Financial Markets*. Federal Reserve Bank of New York.

Meyer, Laurence H. 2004. *A Term at the Fed—an Insider's View*. New York: HarperCollins.

Mian, Atif, and Amir Sufi. 2010a. "Household Leverage and the Recession of 2007–09." *IMF Economic Review* 58:74–117.

———. 2010b. "The Great Recession: Lessons from Microeconomic Data." In "Papers and Proceedings of the One Hundred Twenty-Second Annual Meeting of the American Economic Association," *American Economic Review* 100 (May): 51–56.

———. 2011. "House Prices, Home Equity–Based Borrowing, and the US Household Leverage Crisis." *American Economic Review* 101 (August): 2132–56.

Miller, Adolph C. 1935. "Responsibility for Federal Reserve Policies: 1927–1929." *American Economic Review* 25 (September): 442–58.

Mints, Lloyd W. 1945. *A History of Banking Theory*. Chicago: University of Chicago Press.

Mitchell, Wesley Clair, and Arthur F. Burns. 1936. *Production during the American Business Cycle, 1927–1933*. Bulletin 61. New York: National Bureau of Economic Research.

Modigliani, Franco, and Lucas Papademos. 1975. "Targets for Monetary Policy in the Coming Year." *Brookings Papers on Economic Activity* 1:141–63.

———. 1976. "Monetary Policy for the Coming Quarters: The Conflicting Views." Federal Reserve Bank of Boston *New England Economic Review* 76 (March/April): 2–35.

Morgenson, Gretchen, and Joshua Rosner. 2011. *Reckless Endangerment: How Outsized Ambition, Greed, and Corruption Led to Economic Armageddon*. New York: Times Books, 2011.

Mousseau, John. 2020a. "Bond Markets through the Virus." Interview with Oxford University, June 29.

———. 2020b. "The Long Strange Trip of the Muni Market in 2020." Cumberland Advisors Market Commentary, December 28.

National Monetary Commission (NMC). 1912. "Letter from Secretary of the National Monetary Commission Transmitting, Pursuant to Law, the Report of the Commission." January 9. Washington, DC: US Government Printing Office.

NBER Macrohistory Data Base, St. Louis FRED.

Nelson, Edward. 2005. "The Great Inflation of the Seventies: What Really Happened?" *Advances in Macroeconomics* 5, no. 1: article 3.

Nelson, Edward, and Kalin Nikolov. 2004. "Monetary Policy and Stagflation in the UK." *Journal of Money, Credit, and Banking* 36:293–318.

New York Times. 1998a. "Fed Cuts Key Rates Again in 3rd Attack on Global Slump." November 18, A1.

———. 1998b. "Fed Thinks Globally, Acts Locally, to Lukewarm Response." November 18, C1.

Nikkei Weekly. 2008. "BOJ in Need of Some Maneuverability." October 13.

Nurisso, George C., and Edward Simpson Prescott. 2020. "Origins of Too-Big-to-Fail Policy in the United States." *Financial History Review* 2, no. 1:1–15.

Officer, Lawrence H., and Samuel H. Williamson. 2012. "The Annual Consumer Price Index for the United States, 1774–2011." MeasuringWorth.com.

Ohanian, Lee E. 2013. "The Macroeconomic Impact of the New Deal." In *The Handbook of Major Events in Economic History,* edited by Randall Parker and Robert Whaples, 165–78. New York: Routledge.

Orphanides, Athanasios. 2001. "Monetary Policy Rules Based on Real-Time Data." *American Economic Review* 91 (September): 964–85.

———. 2002. "Monetary Policy Rules and the Great Inflation." *American Economic Association Papers and Proceedings* 92, no. 2 (May): 115–20.

———. 2003a. "Monetary Policy Evaluation with Noisy Information." *Journal of Monetary Economics* 50 (April): 605–31.

———. 2003b. "The Quest for Prosperity without Inflation." *Journal of Monetary Economics* 50 (April): 633–63.

———. 2003c. "Historical Monetary Policy Analysis and the Taylor Rule." *Journal of Monetary Economics* 50 (July): 983–1022.

———. 2004a. "Monetary Policy Rules, Macroeconomic Stability and Inflation: A View from the Trenches." *Journal of Money, Credit, and Banking* 36 (April): 151–75.

———. 2004b. "Monetary Policy in Deflation: The Liquidity Trap in History and Practice." *North American Journal of Economics and Finance* 15:101–24.

———. 2019. "Monetary Policy Strategy and Its Communication." Federal Reserve Bank of Kansas City, Jackson Hole Conference, August 23.

Orphanides, Athanasios, and John C. Williams. 2002. "Robust Monetary Policy Rules with Unknown Natural Rates." *Brookings Papers on Economic Activity* 2:63–145.

Owen, Robert L. 1935. "Foreword." In *Money and Its Power,* by F. T. Winslow and B. Broughman, iii–v. Washington, DC: National Home Library Foundation.

Papademos, Lucas. 2013. "The Great Inflation: Lessons for Central Banks." In *The Great Inflation: The Rebirth of Modern Central Banking,* edited by Michael D. Bordo and Athanasios Orphanides, 503–11. Chicago: University of Chicago Press.

Patinkin, Don. 1965. *Money, Interest, and Prices.* New York: Harper and Row.

Paulson, Henry M., Jr. 2013. *On the Brink: Inside the Race to Stop the Collapse of the Global Financial System.* New York: Grand Central.

Pelosi, Nancy. 2020. "Dear Colleague on Latest Progress on Coronavirus Response." Press release, March 17.

Phillips, Chester. 1931. *Bank Credit.* New York: Macmillan.

Phillips, Ronnie J. 1992. "The Chicago Plan and New Deal Banking Reform." Working Paper 76. Jerome Levy Economics Institute of Bard College.

Poole, William. 1978. *Money and the Economy: A Monetarist View.* Reading, MA: Addison-Wesley.

Powell, Jerome H. 2020a. Testimony before the Committee on Financial Services, US House of Representatives, February 11.

————. 2020b. "Covid-19 and the Economy." Speech at the Hutchins Center on Fiscal and Monetary Policy, Brookings Institution, Washington, DC, April 9.

————. 2020c. Interview with Alan Blinder. Benjamin H. Griswold III Center for Economic Policy Studies, Princeton University, May 29.

————. 2020d. "New Economic Challenges and the Fed's Monetary Policy Review." Speech given at "Navigating the Decade Ahead: Implications for Monetary Policy," an economic policy symposium sponsored by the Federal Reserve Bank of Kansas City, Jackson Hole, Wyoming, August 27.

————. 2020e. "Transcript: NPR's Full Interview with Fed Chairman Jerome Powell." National Public Radio, September 4.

————. 2021a. "Transcript: Jerome Powell Interview Hosted by Princeton." WSJPRO Central Banking, January 14.

————. 2021b. Letter from Jerome H. Powell to the Honorable Rick Scott, April 8.

————. 2021c. "2021 Just Economy Conference." Sponsored by the National Community Reinvestment Coalition. Washington, DC, May 3.

Power, Stephen, and Gary Fields. 2008. "How Voter Fury Stopped Bailout." *Wall Street Journal*, September 20.

Prescott, Edward S. 2013. "Too Big to Manage? Two Book Reviews." Federal Reserve Bank of Richmond *Economic Quarterly* 99, no. 2 (Second Quarter): 143–62.

Quarles, Randal K. 2021. "The Economic Outlook and Monetary Policy." Remarks at the Hutchins Center on Fiscal and Monetary Policy, Brookings Institution, Washington, DC, May 26.

Reed, Harold. 1930. *Federal Reserve Policy 1921–1930*. New York: McGraw-Hill.

————. 1935. "The Stabilization Doctrines of Carl Snyder." *Quarterly Journal of Economics* 49, no. 4 (August): 600–620.

Reeve, Joseph E. 1943. *Monetary Reform Movements: A Survey of Recent Plans and Panaceas*. Washington, DC: American Council on Public Affairs.

Riefler, Winfield W. 1930. *Money Rates and Money Markets in the United States*. New York: Harper and Brothers.

————. 1954. "Volume of Borrowing vs. Profitability of Borrowing." Memo to Discount Rate Committee, August 19. Winfield W. Riefler Papers, box 3, 1954–71, St. Louis FRASER.

Rietz, Thomas A. 1988. "The Equity Risk Premium: A Solution." *Journal of Monetary Economics* 22:117–31.

Rivas, Maria Dolores Gadea, and Gabriel Perez-Quiros. 2015. "The Failure to Predict the Great Recession—a View through the Role of Credit." *Journal of the European Economic Association* 13, no. 3 (June): 354–559.

Roberts, Priscilla. 1998. "'Quis Custodiet Ipsos Custodes?': The Federal Reserve's System's Founding Fathers and Allied Finance in the First World War." *Business History Review* 73 (Winter): 585–620.

Robertson, Dennis H. 1929. *Money*. New York: Harcourt Brace.

Romer, Christina D. 1992. "What Ended the Great Depression?" *Journal of Economic History* 52 (December): 757–84.

Romer, Christina D., and David H. Romer. 2002. "A Rehabilitation of Monetary Policy in the 1950's." *American Economic Association Papers and Proceedings* 92 (May): 121–27.

————. 2004. "Choosing the Federal Reserve Chair: Lessons from History." *Journal of Economic Perspectives* 18 (Winter): 129–62.

Roosa, Robert V. 1956. *Federal Reserve Operations in the Money and Government Securities Markets*. Federal Reserve Bank of New York. July.

———. 1960. "The Changes in Money and Credit, 1957–59." *Review of Economics and Statistics* 42 (August): 261–63.

Rosengren, Eric S. 2019. "Lessons from the Experience with Quantitative Easing." In *Innovation Federal Reserve Policies during the Great Financial Crisis*, edited by Douglas D. Evanoff, George G. Kaufman, and A. G. Malliaris, 125–42. Singapore: World Scientific.

Samuelson, Paul, and Robert Solow. 1960 [1966]. "Analytical Aspects of Anti-inflation Policy." In *The Collected Scientific Papers of Paul A. Samuelson*, edited by Joseph Stiglitz, Cambridge, MA: MIT Press, vol. 2, no. 102:1336–53.

Sandilands, Roger J. 1990. *The Life and Political Economy of Lauchlin Currie*. Durham, NC: Duke University Press.

S&P Global. 2020. "Assessing the Potential Credit Effects of Covid-19 on US ABCP." April 9.

Sargent, Thomas J. 1982. "The Ends of Four Big Inflations." In *Inflation: Causes and Effects*, edited by Robert Hall, 41–97. Chicago: University of Chicago Press.

Schreft, Stacey L. 1990. "Credit Controls: 1980." Federal Reserve Bank of Richmond *Economic Review* 76 (November/December): 25–55.

Schrimpf, Andreas, Hyun Song Shin, and Vladyslav Sushko. 2020. "Leverage and Margin Spirals in Fixed Income Markets during the Covid-19 Crisis." *BIS Bulletin*, no. 2 (April 2): 1–6.

Schumpeter, Joseph A. 1934. "Depressions." In *The Economics of the Recovery Program*, edited by Douglass V. Brown, Edward Chamberlain, Seymour E. Harris, Wassily W. Leontief, Edward S. Mason, Joseph A. Schumpeter, and Overton H. Taylor. New York: Whittlesey House McGraw-Hill.

Schwartz, Anna J. 1981. "Understanding 1929–1933." In *The Great Depression Revisited*, edited by Karl Brunner, 5–48. Boston: Kluwer-Nijhoff.

———. 1992. "The Misuse of the Fed's Discount Window." Federal Reserve Bank of St. Louis *Economic Review* (September/October): 58–69.

Selgin, George. 2018. *Floored: How a Misguided Fed Experiment Deepened and Prolonged the Great Recession*. Washington, DC: Cato Institute, 2018.

———. 2020a. *The Menace of Fiscal QE*. Washington, DC: Cato Institute.

———. 2020b. "When the Fed Tried to Save Main Street." *Alt-M*, March 30.

———. "The New Deal and Recovery." Various blog posts on Alt-M, sponsored by the Cato Institute, various dates, https://www.alt-m.org/.

Shapiro, Adam, and Daniel J. Wilson. 2019a. "The Evolution of the FOMC's Explicit Inflation Target." FRBSF *Economic Letter*, April 15, https://www.frbsf.org/economic-research/publications/economic-letter/2019/april/evolution-of-fomc-explicit-inflation-target/.

———. 2019b. "Taking the Fed at Its Word: Direct Estimation of Central Bank Objectives Using Text Analytics." Federal Reserve Bank of San Francisco Working Paper 2019-02.

Shover, John L. 1965. "Populism in the Nineteen-Thirties." *Agricultural History* 39:17–24.

Singh, Daleep. 2020. "Presentation at the Newsday and Long Island Association Webinar." In LHM *Monetary Policy Analytics*, "Summertime Sadness," April 22.

Sløk, Torsten. 2014. "The Fed vs. the Market." Deutsche Bank Research, December 22.

———. 2015. "Mayhem Coming to an End." Deutsche Bank Research, May 29.

———. 2016. "The World Depends on US and China Doing Well." Deutsche Bank Research, May 20.

———. 2017a. "Wall Street Economists Have Been Consistently Wrong in Their Forecasts for the Ten-Year Rate." Deutsche Bank Research, July 6.

———. 2017b. "8trn in Total QE So Far." Deutsche Bank Research, December 5.

———. 2019a. "$12 Trn Bonds Globally Trade at Negative Interest Rates." Deutsche Bank Research, August 13.

———. 2019b. "Fed Balance Sheet Expansion and S&P 500 Performance." Deutsche Bank Research, December 30.

———. 2019c. "QE and Soft QE, Does It Work?" Deutsche Bank Research, November 21.

———. 2020. "Fed Funds: Will the Market Finally Get It Right?" Deutsche Bank Research, July 29.

Snyder, Carl. 1935. "The Problem of Monetary and Economic Stability." *Quarterly Journal of Economics* 49 (February): 173–205.

———. 1940. *Capitalism the Creator*. New York: Macmillan.

Sorkin, Andrew Ross. 2008. "Paulson's Itchy Finger, on the Trigger of a Bazooka." *New York Times*, September 8, https://www.nytimes.com/2008/09/09/business/09sorkin.html.

———. 2018. *Too Big to Fail*. New York: Random House.

Spence, Peter. 2015. "China Leading World towards Global Economic Recession, Warns Citi." *Daily Telegraph*, September 9, https://www.telegraph.co.uk/finance/china-business/11854084/China-leading-world-towards-global-economic-recession-warns-Citi.html.

Sprague, O. M. W. 1929. "Control of Credit Machinery and Stock Speculation." *Trust Companies* 48 (May): 723–26.

Sproul, Allan. 1951. "Changing Concepts of Central Banking." In *Money, Trade and Economic Growth: In Honor of John Henry Williams*, 296–325. New York: Macmillan.

Sproul Papers. Federal Reserve Bank of New York Archives.

Stanley, Stephen. 2020. "Daily Coronavirus Update: Virus, Policy, and the Economy." Amherst Pierpont, April 6.

———. 2021a. "Windfall Economics." Amherst Pierpont, April 19.

———. 2021b. "Burning a Hole in Their Pockets." Amherst Pierpont, June 28.

Stein, Herbert. 1969. *The Fiscal Revolution in America*. Chicago: University of Chicago Press.

———. 1990. *The Fiscal Revolution in America*. Rev. ed. Washington, DC: AEI.

Stein, Jeremy C. 2012. "Dollar Funding and Global Banks." Global Research Forum, International Finance and Macroeconomics, sponsored by the European Central Bank, Frankfurt am Main, Germany, December 17.

Stock, James H., and Mark W. Watson. 2007. "Why Has US Inflation Become Harder to Forecast?" *Journal of Money, Credit and Banking* 39 (February): 3–33.

Sumner, Scott. 2015. *The Midas Paradox*. Oakland, CA: Independent Institute.

———. 2021. *The Money Illusion*. Chicago: University of Chicago Press.

Swanson, Eric T. 2017. "Measuring the Effects of Federal Reserve Forward Guidance and Asset Purchases on Financial Markets." University of California, Irvine, March 23.

Tallman, Ellis W., and Jon R. Moen. 2012. "Liquidity Creation without a Central Bank:

Clearing House Loan Certificates in the Banking Panic of 1907." *Journal of Financial Stability* 8 (December): 277–91.

Taylor, John B. 2009. *Getting Off Track: How Government Actions and Interventions Caused, Prolonged, and Worsened the Financial Crisis.* Stanford, CA: Hoover Institution Press.

Temin, Peter. 1976. Did Monetary Forces Cause the Great Depression? New York: W. W. Norton.

———. 2007. Interview in Randall E. Parker. In *The Economics of the Great Depression*, 44–55. Cheltenham, UK: Edward Elgar.

Temin, Peter, and Barrie A. Wigmore. 1990. "The End of One Big Deflation." *Explorations in Economic History* 27:483–502.

Thornton, Daniel L. 2017. "Effectiveness of QE: An Assessment of Event-Study Evidence." *Journal of Macroeconomics* 52 (March): 56–74.

———. 2018. "Comment on Alan S. Blinder." *Wall Street Journal*, May 4, A15.

Thornton, Henry. 1802 [1939]. "An Enquiry into the Nature and Effects of the Paper Credit of Great Britain." In *An Enquiry into the Nature and Effects of the Paper Credit of Great Britain (1802) and Two Speeches (1811)*, edited with an introduction by F. A. v. Hayek. New York: Rinehart, 1939.

Timberlake, Richard H. 1993. *Monetary Policy in the United States: An Intellectual and Institutional History.* Chicago: University of Chicago Press.

Timiraos, Nick. 2020. "Fed Official Says Lending Programs Will Support Economy, Avoid Deflation." Interview on Bloomberg television. *Wall Street Journal*, April 13.

Tobin, James. 1974. "There Are Three Types of Inflation: We Have Two." *New York Times*, September 6, 33, https://www.wsj.com/articles/fed-official-says-lending -programs-will-support-economy-avoid-deflation-11586778279.

———. 1977 [1980]. "Macroeconomic Models and Policy." Quoted in Raymond Lombra and Michael Moran, "Policy Advice and Policymaking at the Federal Reserve." *Carnegie-Rochester Conference Series on Public Policy: Monetary Institutions and the Policy Process* 13 (Autumn): 9–68.

Todd, Walker F. 1993. "New Discount Window Policy Is Important Element of FDI-CIA." *Banking Policy Report* 12, no. 5 (March 1): 1, 11–17.

———. 1996. "The Federal Reserve Board and the Banking Crisis of the 1930s." In *Research in Financial Services: Private and Public Policy*, edited by George G. Kaufman, 8:97–139. Greenwich, CT: JAI.

———. 2019. "The Constitutionality of the Federal Reserve's Role as Lender of Last Resort." Western Economic Association International Annual Meeting, San Francisco.

Tooze, Adam. 2019. *Crashed: How a Decade of Financial Crises Changed the World.* Penguin Books.

Torres, Craig. 2020. "Treasury Will Have $454 Billion for Fed to Leverage, Says Toomey." Bloomberg Yahoo Finance, March 25.

Torres, Craig, and Matthew Boesler. 2016. "Private Records Show Dudley's Staff Urging Bold Fed Action." Bloomberg, December 7.

Truman, Edwin M. 2017. "The End of the Bretton Woods International Monetary System." Working Paper 17-11. Peterson Institute for International Economics. October.

Tucker, Paul. 2020. "On Central Bank Independence." Finance and Development (International Monetary Fund), May.

Underhill, Hershel E. 1941. *The Kansas City Federal Reserve District: Origins and Developments*. Boston: Spaulding Moss.

US Congress. 1923. *Stabilization of Purchasing Power of Money*. Hearings before the House Committee on Banking and Currency. 67th Cong., 4th sess., on H.R. 11788, December 18, 19, 20, and 21, 1922.

———. 1926. *Stabilization*. Hearings before the House Committee on Banking and Currency, pt. 1. 69th Cong., 1st sess., March and April.

———. 1926–27. *Stabilization*. Hearings before the House Committee on Banking and Currency, pt. 2. 69th Cong., 1st sess., April, May, and June 1926 and February 1927.

———. 1928. *Stabilization*. Hearings before the House Committee on Banking and Currency. 70th Cong., 1st sess., March, April, and May.

———. 1931. *Operation of the National and Federal Reserve Banking Systems*. Hearings before the Subcommittee of the Senate Committee on Banking and Currency. 71st Cong., 3rd sess., Pursuant to S. Res. 71, pt. 1, January 19, 20, 22, 23, 26, 29, 30, and 31; and appendix, pt. 6 ("Federal Reserve Questionnaires").

———. 1932a. *Stabilization of Commodity Prices*. Hearings before the Subcommittee of the House Committee on Banking and Currency (Goldsborough Committee) on H.R. 10517. *For Increasing and Stabilizing the Price Level and for Other Purposes*. 72nd Cong., 1st sess., pts. 1 and 2, March 16–18, 21–22, and 28–29 and April 13–14.

———. 1932b. *Restoring and Maintaining the Average Purchasing Power of the Dollar*. Hearings before the Committee on Banking and Currency. US Senate. 72nd Cong., 1st sess. on H.R. 11499, An Act for Restoring and Maintaining the Purchasing Power of the Dollar, and S. 4429, A Bill to Restore and Maintain the Average Purchasing Power of the Dollar by the Expansion and Contraction of Credits and Currency, and for Other Purposes, May 12, 13, and 18.

———. 1935a. *Banking Act of 1935*, pt. 2. Hearings before the House Committee on Banking and Currency, 74th Cong., 1st sess., March 13, 14, 15, 18, 19, and 20.

———. 1935b. *Banking Act of 1935*. Hearings before a Subcommittee of the Committee on Banking and Currency. Senate. 74th Cong., 1st sess., April 19 to June 3.

———— 1947. *Anti-inflation Program as Recommended in the President's Message of November 17, 1947*. Hearings of the Joint Committee on the Economic Report. 80th Cong., 1st sess., November 25, 133–69.

———. 1951. *Economic Report of the President*, January. Hearings. 82nd Cong., 1st sess., January 22, 24, 25, 29, and 31 and February 2.

———. 1958. *Statement of William McChesney: January 1958 Economic Report of the President*. Hearings before the Joint Economic Committee, 85th Cong., 2nd sess., February 6.

———. 1959. *Statement of Martin, William McChesney: January 1959 Economic Report of the President*. Hearings before the Joint Economic Committee, 86th Cong., 1st sess., February 6.

———. 1969. *The 1969 Economic Report of the President*. Hearing before the Joint Economic Committee. 91st Cong., 1st sess., February 25, 26, and 27 and March 5 and 6.

———. 1971. *The 1971 Midyear Review of the Economy*. Hearings before the Joint Economic Committee. 92nd Cong., 1st. sess., July 7, 8, 20, 21, 22, and 23.

———. 1973a. *The 1973 Economic Report of the President*. Hearings before the Joint Economic Committee" 93rd Cong., 1st sess., pt. 1, February 6, 7, 8, and 12; pt. 2, February 13, 14, 20, 22, and 23.

———. 1973b. *How Well Are Fluctuating Exchange Rates Working?* Hearings before the Subcommittee on International Economics of the Joint Economic Committee. 93rd. Cong., 1st sess., June 20, 21, 26, and 27.

———. 1974a. *Oversight on Economic Stabilization.* Hearings before the Subcommittee on Production and Stabilization of the Committee on Banking, Housing and Urban Affairs. 93rd Cong., 2nd sess., January 30 and 31; February 1 and 6.

———. 1974b. *Statement in "Federal Reserve Policy and Inflation and High Interest Rates."* Hearings before the House Committee on Banking and Currency. 93rd Cong., 2nd sess., July 16, 17, 18, and 30; August 7 and 8.

———. 1974c. *Examination of the Economic Situation and Outlook.* Hearings before the Joint Economic Committee. 93rd Cong., 2nd sess., July 29 and 30; August 1, 2, 6, and 14.

———. 1974d. *The Federal Budget and Inflation.* Hearings before the Committee of the Budget. Senate. 93rd Cong., 2nd sess., August 14, 15, 21, and 22.

———. 1974e. *Review of the Economy and the 1975 Budget.* Hearings before the Committee on the Budget. House of Representatives. 93rd Cong., 2nd sess., September 17, 19, and 25.

———. 1979. *The 1979 Joint Economic Report.* Report of the Joint Economic Committee on the 1979 Economic Report of the President. 96th Cong., 1st sess., March 22.

———. 1989. *Conduct of Monetary Policy.* Hearings before the Subcommittee on Domestic Monetary Policy of the House Committee on Banking, Finance and Urban Affairs. 101th Cong., 1st sess., February 21 and 22 and March 1.

———. 1993a. *Federal Reserve's First Monetary Policy Report for 1993.* Hearing before the Senate Committee on Banking, Housing, and Urban Affairs. 103rd Cong., 1st sess., February 19.

———. 1993b. *Hearing before the House Subcommittee on Economic Growth and Credit Formation of the Committee on Banking, Finance and Urban Affairs.* 103rd Cong., 1st sess., July 20.

———. 1994. *The 1994 Economic Report of the President: The Economic Outlook.* Hearing before the Joint Economic Committee. 103rd Cong., 2nd sess., January 31.

———. 1995a. *The Economic Outlook for the Nation.* Hearing before the Senate Committee on Finance. 104th Cong., 1st sess., January 25.

———. 1995b. *Federal Reserve's First Monetary Policy Report for 1995.* Hearing before the Senate Committee on Banking, Housing, and Urban Affairs. 104th Cong., 1st sess., February 22.

———. 1996. *Conduct of Monetary Policy.* Hearing before the House Subcommittee on Domestic and International Monetary Policy of the Committee on Banking and Financial Services. 104th Cong., 2nd sess., February 20.

———. 1997. *Federal Reserve's First Monetary Policy Report for 1997.* Hearing before the Senate Committee on Banking, Housing, and Urban Affairs. 105th Cong., 1st sess., February 26.

———. 1998a. *Federal Reserve's Second Monetary Policy Report for 1998.* Hearing before the Senate Committee on Banking, Housing, and Urban Affairs. 105th Cong., 2nd sess., July 21.

———. 1998b. *Hedge Fund Operations.* Hearing. House Committee on Banking and Financial Services. 105th Cong., 2nd sess., October 1.

———. 1999a. *Conduct of Monetary Policy.* Hearing before the House Committee on Banking and Financial Services. 106th Cong., 1st sess., February 24.

———. 1999b. *Conduct of Monetary Policy*. Hearing before the House Committee on Banking and Financial Services. 106th Cong., 1st sess., July 22.

———. 1999c. *Federal Reserve's Second Monetary Policy Report for 1999*. Hearing before the Senate Committee on Banking, Housing, and Urban Affairs." 106th Cong., 1st sess., July 28.

———. 2000. *Federal Reserve's First Monetary Policy Report for 2000*. Hearing before the Senate Committee on Banking, Housing, and Urban Affairs. 106th Cong., 2nd sess., February 23.

———. 2001. *Conduct of Monetary Policy*. Hearing before the House Committee on Financial Services. 107th Cong., 1st sess., July 18.

———. 2003. *Federal Reserve's Second Monetary Policy Report for 2003*. Hearing before the Senate Committee on Banking, Housing, and Urban Affairs. 108th Cong., 1st sess., July 16.

———. 2004. *Economic Outlook and Current Fiscal Issues*. Hearing before the House Committee on the Budget. 108th Cong., 2nd sess., February 25.

US Department of the Treasury. 2009. *Financial Regulatory Reform: A New Foundation—Rebuilding Financial Supervision and Regulation*. Washington, DC: US Government Printing Office, June 23.

US Economic Report of the President transmitted to the Congress annually together with the *Annual Report of the Council of Economic Advisers*. Washington, DC: US Government Printing Office, various issues.

US GAO (Government Accountability Office). 2011. *Federal Reserve System*, July 2011.

US Treasury. 1951. *1951 Annual Report*.

Velde, François. 2004. "Poor Hand or Poor Play? The Rise and Fall of Inflation in the US." Federal Reserve Bank of Chicago *Economic Perspectives*, Quarter 1, 34–51.

———. 2020. "Experiments with Paper Money." In *Handbook of the History of Money and Currency*, edited by Stefano Battilossi, Youssef Cassis, and Kazuhiko Yago New York: Springer, 413–29.

Viner, Jacob. 1937. *Studies in the Theory of International Trade*. New York: Harper and Brothers.

Viorst, Milton. 1969. "The Burns Kind of Liberal Conservatism." *New York Times Magazine*, November 9, 30–131.

Vissing-Jorgensen, Annette, and Arvind Krishnamurthy. 2011. "The Effects of Quantitative Easing on Interest Rates: Channels and Implications for Policy." Brookings Papers on Economic Activity 2011, no. 2.

Volcker, Paul A. 1980a. Remarks before the National Press Club, Washington, DC, January 2.

———. 1980b. "A Rare Opportunity." Remarks before the 43rd Annual Dinner of the Tax Foundation, New York, December 3.

———. 1983. "We Can Survive Prosperity." Remarks at the Joint Meeting of the American Economic Association–American Finance Association, San Francisco, December 28.

———. 1994. "Monetary Policy" and "Summary of Discussion." In *American Economic Policy in the 1980s*, edited by Martin Feldstein, 145–51 and 157–64. Chicago: University of Chicago Press.

———. 2001. "An Interview with Paul A. Volcker." Interviewed by Perry Mehrling. *Macroeconomic Dynamics* 5 (June): 434–60.

———. 2008. "Fed 'at Edge of Its Lawful and Implied Power.'" Speech at Economic Club of New York. In *WSJ Blogs*, "Real Time Economics," April 8.

Volcker, Paul A., and Toyoo Gyohten. 1992. *Changing Fortunes: The World's Money and the Threat to American Leadership*. New York: Random House.

Wallison, Peter J. 2016. *Hidden in Plain Sight*. New York: Encounter Books.

Wall Street Journal. 1994. "Dollar Intervention Signals Concerns about Rising Rates, Falling Currency." May 2, A2.

———. 2008a. "Lehman Is Seeking Overseas Capital, as Its Stock Declines: Wall Street Firm Expands Search for Cash, May Tap Korea." June 4, https://www.wsj.com/articles/SB121253687372943195.

———. 2008b. "The Weekend That Wall Street Died." December 29, 1, https://www.wsj.com/articles/SB123051066413538349.

———. 2020a. "Treasury Department Asks Congress to Let It Backstop Money Markets." March 18, https://www.wsj.com/articles/treasury-department-asking-congress-for-permission-to-backstop-money-markets-11584546598.

———. 2020b. "Why the Fed Had to Backstop Money-Market Funds, Again." March 21, https://www.wsj.com/articles/why-the-fed-had-to-backstop-money-market-funds-again-11584788401.

———. 2020c. "Fed Official Says Lending Programs Will Support Economy, Avoid Deflation." April 13.

———. 2020d. "Private-Equity Firms Scramble to Shore Up Coronavirus-Hit Holdings." April 13, https://www.wsj.com/articles/private-equity-firms-scramble-to-shore-up-coronavirus-hit-holdings-11586770202.

———. 2020e. "Private-Equity Firms Offer Cash Lifelines to Public Companies." April 17, https://www.wsj.com/articles/private-equity-firms-offer-cash-lifelines-to-public-companies-11587121203,

———. 2020f. "The Federal Reserve Is Changing What It Means to Be a Central Bank." April 27, https://www.wsj.com/articles/fate-and-history-the-fed-tosses-the-rules-to-fight-coronavirus-downturn-11587999986.

———. 2020g. "Treasury Yields Are Supported by Borrowing Binge." May 2.

———. 2020h. "Aviation Industry Races for Cash with Record Bonds Sales." May 4, https://www.wsj.com/articles/aviation-industry-races-for-cash-with-record-bond-sales-11588607851.

Warburg, Paul M. 1910. "The Discount System in Europe." National Monetary Commission. Washington, DC: US Government Printing Office. Available in Federal Reserve Bank of St. Louis FRASER.

Warburton, Clark. 1946 [1966]. "The Misplaced Emphasis in Contemporary Business-Fluctuation Theory." In *Depression, Inflation, and Monetary Policy: Selected Papers, 1945–1953*, edited by Clark Warburton. Baltimore: Johns Hopkins University Press.

Warburton, Clark. 1952 [1966]. "Monetary Difficulties and the Structure of the Monetary System." In *Depression, Inflation, and Monetary Policy: Selected Papers, 1945–1953*, edited by Clark Warburton. Baltimore: Johns Hopkins University Press.

Washington Post. 2008a. "How Lehman Brothers Veered Off Course." July 3, D1.

———. 2008b. "Parsing the Bailout." November 26, A10.

Weinstein, Michael M. 1981. "Some Macroeconomic Impacts of the National Industrial Recovery Act, 1933–1935." In *The Great Depression Revisited*, edited by Karl Brunner, 262–81. Boston: Kluwer-Nijhoff.

Wessel, David. 2009. *In Fed We Trust: Ben Bernanke's War on the Great Panic*. New York: Crown Business.

Whalen, Christopher. 2013. "Washington and Wall Street: Lehman Brothers and the Failure of Regulation." Breitbart, September 10.

Wheelock, David C. 1991. *The Strategy and Consistency of Federal Reserve Monetary Policy, 1924–1933*. Cambridge: Cambridge University Press.

White, William Allan. 1938. *A Puritan in Babylon: The Story of Calvin Coolidge*. New York: Macmillan.

Wicker, Elmus. 1966. *Federal Reserve Monetary Policy, 1917–1933*. New York: Random House.

———. 2000. *Banking Panics of the Gilded Age*. Cambridge: Cambridge University Press.

———. 2005. *The Great Debate on Banking Reform: Nelson Aldrich and the Origins of the Fed*. Columbus: Ohio State University Press.

Wicksell, Knut. 1898 [1962]. *Interest and Prices*. New York: Augustus M. Kelley.

———. 1935 [1978]. *Lectures on Political Economy, Money*. Vol. 2. Fairfield, NJ: Augustus M. Kelley.

Wikipedia. 2019. "National Industrial Recovery Act 1933." Last edited April 28, 2019.

———. 2020. "Term Asset-Backed Securities Loan Facility." Last edited March 28, 2020.

———. 2021. "Cross of Gold Speech." Last edited January 27, 2021.

———. n.d. "Charles E. Mitchell."

Wilkerson, Chad R. 2013. "Senator Robert Owen of Oklahoma and the Federal Reserve's Formative Years." Federal Reserve Bank of Kansas City *Economic Review*, Third Quarter, 95–117.

Williams, John C. 2013. "Forward Policy Guidance at the Federal Reserve." VOX CEPR's Policy Portal, October 16.

———. "2021. The Economic Recovery: Are We There Yet?" Remarks at Women in Housing and Finance 2021 Annual Symposium, May 3.

Williams, John H. 1931. "The Monetary Doctrines of J. M. Keynes." *Quarterly Journal of Economics* 45:547–87.

———. 1932 [1983]. "Monetary Stability and the Gold Standard." In *Gold and Monetary Stabilization: Harris Foundation Lectures, 1932*, edited by Quincy Wright, 133–58. New York: Garland, 1983.

Willis, H. Parker. 1932 [1983]. "Federal Reserve Policy in Depression." In *Gold and Monetary Stabilization: Harris Foundation Lectures, 1932*, edited by Quincy Wright, 77–108. New York: Garland, 1983.

———. 1933. "The Future in Banking." *Yale Review*, December 1933, 233–47.

Wood, Elmer. 1954. "Recent Monetary Policy." Summary of Remarks before the Midwest Economics Association, Peoria, Illinois, April 22, 1954, in memo from Allan Sproul to Dr. Williams and Mr. Roosa, May 17. Sproul Papers Federal Reserve Bank of New York Archives.

Wood, John H. 2005. *A History of Central Banking in Great Britain and the United States*. New York: Cambridge University Press.

———. 2006. "The Stability of Monetary Policy: The Federal Reserve, 1914–2006." Wake Forest University, December 20.

Woodford, Michael. 2003. *Interest and Prices: Foundations of a Theory of Monetary Policy*. Princeton, NJ: Princeton University Press.

———. 2012. "Inflation Targeting and Financial Stability." NBER Working Paper 17967. April.

Woolley, John, and Gerhard Peters. 1999–2015. The American Presidency Project, "Political Party Platforms." http://www.presidency.ucsb.edu/ws/?pid=29590.

World Health Organization. Various dates. "Novel Coronavirus (2019-nCoV)," Situation Report, various issues.

Wu, Jing Cynthia, and Fan Dora Xia 2016. "Measuring the Macroeconomic Impact of Monetary Policy at the Zero Lower Bound." *Journal of Money, Credit and Banking* 48, nos. 22–23 (March–April): 254–91.

Wyatt, Edward. 1997. "10 Years After, Lessons of an Earlier Market Peak." *New York Times*, August 24.

Yeager, Leland B. 1966. *International Monetary Relations: Theory, History and Policy.* New York: Harper and Row.

Yellen, Janet L. 2005. "Policymaking and the FOMC: Transparency and Continuity." *FRBSF Economic Letter*, September 2.

———. 2015. "The Economic Outlook and Monetary Policy." Remarks at the Economic Club of Washington, December 2, https://www.frbsf.org/economic-research/publications/economic-letter/2005/september/policymaking-on-the-fomc-transparency-and-continuity/.

———. 2017a. "Yellen Says Fed's Focus Has Shifted to Holding Growth Gains." Interview with Susan Collins, Dean of the Ford School, University of Michigan, Ann Arbor, April 10. Bloomberg Markets.

———. 2017b. "Inflation, Uncertainty, and Monetary Policy." Remarks at the 59th Annual Meeting of the National Association for Business Economics." Cleveland, OH, September 26.

Young, Allyn A. 1927. "Position of the New York Bank in the Reserve System." *Annalist*, May 13.

Index

Bank of England, 35n3, 36n4, 40, 72, 85–
87, 101, 109, 113, 140–41, 165, 168, 172,
261, 273, 279, 468n12
Bank of France, 101, 166, 178
Bank of Japan, 468n12
Bank of New England, 501, 502
Bank of United States, 230; failure of,
161, 174
bank panic (1907), 27, 33–34, 85, 182n10
bank panics, 8, 33. *See also* individual
bank panics
bank runs, 8, 40, 82, 132–33, 145, 161–62,
164, 182n10, 195, 201, 237, 247, 252,
470n13
Banque de France, 101, 166, 178
Barclays, 483
Barrack, Thomas, 558
Barsky, Robert B., 629n1, 630
Basel III Accords: liquidity coverage ratio
(LCR), 554–55, 555n6; supplementary
leverage ratio (SLR), 554–55
Bear Stearns, 473, 478–79, 481, 485,
487–88n4, 500, 502; Fed bailout, 480,
484, 496
Berlin (Germany), 309
Bernanke, Ben, 439–40, 443–44, 448n2,
453, 455, 457, 460–62, 464–65,
470–71, 476, 483–87, 489, 490–92,
494, 500–506, 529, 536, 541, 543, 547,
558n11, 582, 596, 614–15; and moral
hazard, 576
bills only policy, 10, 337, 339–40, 361, 503;
debate over, 342–43, 345
bimetallism, 32
Black, Eugene R., 206, 256, 256n8, 257,
392
Black, Robert, 432
BlackRock, 479
Blanchard, Olivier, 517n12
Blinder, Alan, 448n1, 485, 489, 591–92n1
Bluebook, 454
BNP Paribus, 474, 493
Board of Governors: Commercial Paper
Funding Facility (CPFF), 493, 561,
569n21; Keynesian tilt of, 349–50,
362–63, 395; Open Market Investment
Committee (OMIC), 67; sacrifice

ratio, 396. *See also* Federal Reserve
Board
Boehne, Edward, 591–92n1
Bopp, Karl R., 58
Boskin Commission, 544n7
Boston Reserve Bank, 95, 246–47
Brainard, Lael, 586
Brazil, 414, 418, 434, 442, 446, 514, 514n8,
547
Bretton Woods system, 11, 167, 266, 355–
56, 363, 381, 390, 402–3
Brexit, 541
BRIC, 442, 446, 514, 547. *See also* Brazil;
China; India; Russia
Britain: gold standard, abandonment of,
8, 146, 164, 170, 172, 224–25, 238; gold
standard, return to, 86, 101. *See also*
England
Broaddus, Al, 436
Brüning, Heinrich, 169
Brunner, Karl, 43, 59–60, 114, 293, 315,
599n5
Brunnermeier, Markus K., 440–41
Bryan, Malcolm, 345–46, 360–61n3
Bryan, William Jennings, 54; bimetallism,
32; "cross of gold" speech, 33; eastern
establishment, assault on, 93–94;
populist coalition of, 31
Buffett, Warren, 494
Bullard, James, 460, 537, 613
bullion standard, 100–101
Burgess, W. Randolph, 46, 49, 63, 65, 67,
69, 72–73, 108–9, 121–22, 186–87, 206,
227, 227n1, 228, 234–35, 247–48, 251,
254, 256, 315–16
Burns, Arthur, 16–17, 152, 176–77, 333,
350, 354, 366–67, 375, 381, 389–93,
403, 424, 438, 581–82, 584; business
cycle, and psychology, 10–11, 369;
business cycle, managing of, 369,
371; confidence of businessman,
managing of, 369, 372, 378, 394, 425;
"consensus of specific cycles," 370;
Faustian bargain with Nixon, 365,
380; as FOMC chairman, failure of,
373; incomes policy, advocate of, 365,
368, 368n2, 374, 377, 379, 384–85, 394;

tion, blame for, 288n3, 290; Great Depression, responsibility for, 27, 110, 114, 166, 187, 270, 285, 291; helicopter money, 602; as hybrid central bank, 576; hyperinflation, 600; identification, 4; independence, maintaining of, 314–15, 317, 338, 340–41, 405, 576, 594; independent reservoirs of funds, 252; inflation, controlling of, 392–93, 423, 620, 625; inflation, excess aggregate demand, 308–9; inflation, and monetary control, 380–81, 607–8; inflationary expectations, responsibility for, 404, 424–25; inflation scare, 428; inflation targeting, 445; interest on reserves (IOR), 573, 577–78, 602–3, 603n8, 604; interest rates, 302, 318, 325, 338–39, 344, 349; interest rates, pegging of, 193, 304n5, 305–6, 308–9; lean-against-the-wind (LAW), 300, 630; learning from the past, failure of, 506, 636; legislated rules, rejection of, 274; macroeconomic stabilization, 7; maintaining reserves, responsibility of, 76; market confidence, maintaining of, 478–79; mistakes, inability to learn from, 81, 185; model of, 2; money creation, control of, 82–83, 144; monetary policy, and achieving socially desirable unemployment goals, 593; monetary policy, understanding of, 342; money, as veil, 602, 605; money creation, 504; Money Market Investor Funding Facility (MMIFF), 494–95, 558; moral hazard, 556–57, 560, 576; mortgage-backed securities (MBS), 503, 558–59, 564, 569, 572–73, 595, 597–98, 602–4; natural rate of interest, 193, 262, 602; New York City bankruptcy, fear of, 583; nominal anchor, 4, 325, 404–5; oil price shock, 381; Open Market Investment Conference, 68; Operation Twist, 361; opposition to, 31, 34; panic, precipitating of, 562; paper money creation, 263; political arena, dragging into, 578; politics of controls, 391; portfolio rebalancing, 598–99; price level, stabilizing of, 48–50; price stability, 322–23, 325, 425–26, 625; private risk taking, subsidizing of, 500; quantitative easing (QE), 595, 597, 600, 602; reaction function, 298, 525, 509n3, 629; real bills, 7, 39, 43, 46–47, 111, 115, 123, 158, 339, 424, 637; real bills principles, based on, 6; and recessions, 43, 95–96; reserve requirements, 217, 221; reserves creation, control of, 308; Riefler-Burgess doctrine, 140; rules vs. discretion debate, 608; speculation, quashing of, 137–38, 158–59; speculative excess, 44, 86, 116, 186, 215, 299, 316, 322; stability, in prices and employment, 2; stabilizing price levels, 285; stimulating economy, failure to, 153; stop-go policy, 347; stress tests, 498; swap lines, 577; Term Asset-Backed Securities Loan Facility (TALF), 496; toxic assets, buying of, 496; Treasury, control over, 89; Treasury, ill will with, 309, 313–14; Treasury-Fed Accord, as watershed for, 309; Treasury General Account (TGA) at, 598; two-tier market, 569; world recession, role in, 261. *See also* Federal Open Market Committee (FOMC); Federal Reserve Board; *individual Federal Reserve banks*

Federal Savings and Loan Insurance Corporation, 465
Fettig, David, 465n10
Fève, Patrick, 324n1
fiat money creation, 31, 41, 48, 54–55, 272; printing of money, 287
fiat money standard, 60
Ficek, Karel F., 292
financial market volatility, 554, 560
financial panics, 6, 28–29, 31, 162; of 1857, 28; of 1893, 33
financial safety net, 557; dollar carry trade, and no fail culture, 500; risk taking, 473
Financial Services Administration, 483
Financial Services Regulatory Act, 461n8